SACRAMENTO PUBLIC LIBRARY
828 "I" Street
Sacramento, CA 95814
05/16

Fodor's

NOVA SCOTIA & ATLANTIC CANADA

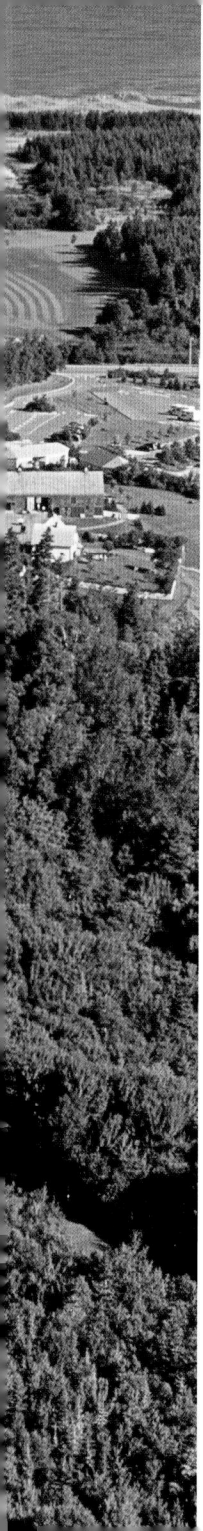

WELCOME TO NOVA SCOTIA & ATLANTIC CANADA

Bordered by the sea, Canada's easternmost provinces share an appealing, low-key vibe as well as striking natural beauty. Nova Scotia's capital, Halifax, is the region's largest city. Elsewhere, coastal towns dot the landscape, adding mellow charm with weathered wharves and lighthouses. You can visit Prince Edward Island's Green Gables sites, hike around New Brunswick's Bay of Fundy, or marvel at Newfoundland's spectacular parks. Wherever you go, lobster suppers and traditional music sessions are signs of the region's unique maritime and cultural history.

TOP REASONS TO GO

★ **Marine marvels:** Whales, seabirds, icebergs, and the planet's highest tides.

★ **Coastal scenery:** Drives such as the Cabot Trail reveal beautiful ocean vistas.

★ **Historic sites:** The Vikings, French, and British all left their mark here.

★ **Beaches:** Sandy strands for swimming, pebble-strewn coves, surfers' favorites.

★ **Succulent seafood:** Lobster, oysters, salmon, and scallops don't come any fresher.

★ **Traditional music:** Listening to Celtic or Acadian tunes is a memorable experience.

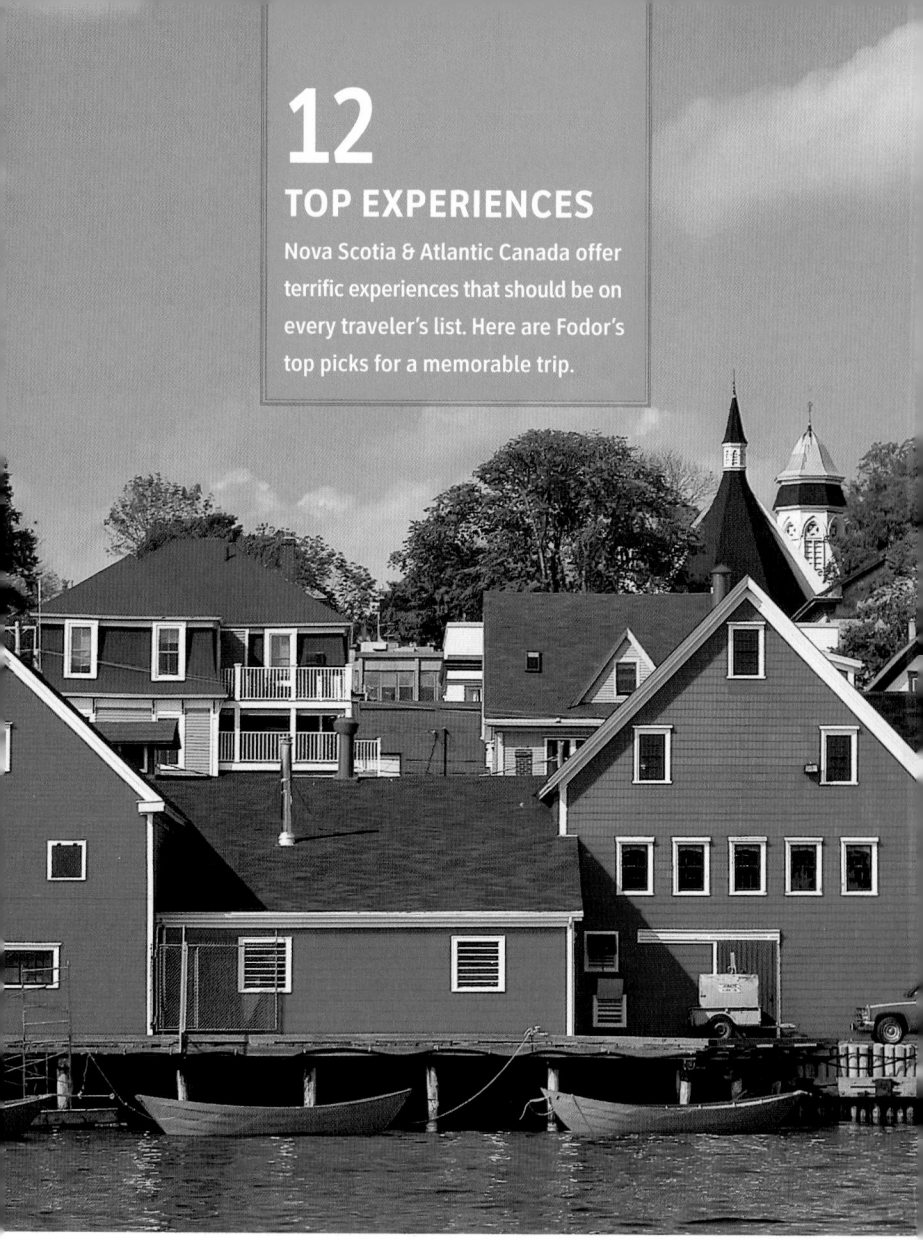

12 TOP EXPERIENCES

Nova Scotia & Atlantic Canada offer terrific experiences that should be on every traveler's list. Here are Fodor's top picks for a memorable trip.

1 Lunenburg, Nova Scotia

"Timeless" is a word that's justifiably applied to the South Shore's signature port town. Hundreds of colorful 18th- and 19th-century buildings line the steep streets of its historic core, a UNESCO World Heritage Site. *(Ch. 2)*

2 Gros Morne National Park, Newfoundland

The stellar scenery encompasses a fjord, glacier-carved Western Brook Pond, and the Tablelands, a rock massif created millions of years ago. *(Ch. 5)*

3 Bay of Fundy, New Brunswick

Fundy's phenomenal tides—the highest in the world—rise and fall twice daily with dramatic results. For proof, you can watch the waters peak and ebb at the Hopewell Rocks. *(Ch. 3)*

4 Anne's Land, Prince Edward Island

On PEI it's hard to avoid a certain redheaded orphan. For fans of the 1908 novel *Anne of Green Gables*, the sites around Cavendish are much-loved ground. *(Ch. 4)*

5 Beaches, Prince Edward Island

Lapped by the warmest waters north of the Carolinas, PEI's pebbly shores and sandy crescents attract swimmers, sun worshippers, and bird-watchers. *(Ch. 4)*

6 Cabot Trail, Nova Scotia

Cape Breton's winding highway by the ocean proves the journey is more important than the destination: it's often called one of the most gorgeous roads on earth. *(Ch. 2)*

7 Seafood Feasts

Lobster, scallops, oysters, salmon, and more: whether you dine at casual waterfront shacks or in fine dining rooms, sublime fresh seafood tops the menu. *(Ch. 2–5)*

8 Halifax, Nova Scotia

The province's capital manages to feel at once traditional and trendy. Atlantic Canada's largest city is built around the world's second-largest natural harbor. *(Ch. 2)*

9 Confederation Trail, Prince Edward Island

Following a former railroad bed, this gently graded bike path crosses the island, winding past green fields, red clay cliffs, sandy beaches, and the blue sea. *(Ch. 4)*

10 Golf Courses, Prince Edward Island

PEI is said to have more golfing options per square mile than anywhere else in Canada, with 30-plus courses, some quite scenic, open from May through October. *(Ch. 4)*

11 Notre Dame Bay, Newfoundland

Spectacular icebergs weighing 100,000 to 200,000 tons serenely float offshore from June through early July. Humpback whales frolic near Twillingate until September. *(Ch. 5)*

12 St. Andrews-by-the-Sea, New Brunswick

Century-old homes and manicured gardens give this resort village a genteel vibe, but proximity to the Bay of Fundy means there are options for outdoor adventure as well. *(Ch. 3)*

CONTENTS

1 EXPERIENCE NOVA SCOTIA AND ATLANTIC CANADA 11
What's Where 12
When to Go 14
Province Picker 15
Nova Scotia and Atlantic Canada Today 16
If You Like. 18
Quintessential Nova Scotia and Atlantic Canada 20
Nova Scotia and Atlantic Canada with Kids 22

2 NOVA SCOTIA 23
Welcome to Nova Scotia 24
Halifax. 33
South Shore and Annapolis Valley. .51
The Eastern Shore and Northern Nova Scotia 82
Cape Breton Island 100

3 NEW BRUNSWICK. 123
Welcome to New Brunswick 124
Saint John 132
The Fundy Coast. 143
The Acadian Coast 167
St. John River Valley 180
Fredericton 188

4 PRINCE EDWARD ISLAND . . . 199
Welcome to Prince Edward Island. 200
Charlottetown 207
Central Coastal Drive. 220
Points East Coastal Drive 233
North Cape Coastal Drive 239

5 NEWFOUNDLAND 247
Welcome to Newfoundland. 248
St. John's, Newfoundland 257
Avalon Peninsula 275
Eastern Newfoundland. 282
Central Newfoundland and Notre Dame Bay. 291
Western Newfoundland 299

UNDERSTANDING NOVA SCOTIA AND ATLANTIC CANADA 313
Books, Movies, and Miniseries . . .314
French Vocabulary 315
Menu Guide 318

TRAVEL SMART NOVA SCOTIA AND ATLANTIC CANADA 321

INDEX. 334

ABOUT OUR WRITERS. 344

MAPS

Halifax. 37
South Shore and Annapolis Valley. .53
The Eastern Shore and Northern Nova Scotia 84
Cape Breton Island 102
Saint John 134
The Fundy Coast. 144
Fundy National Park 156
Moncton. 162
The Acadian Coast and The St. John River Valley 169
Fredericton 190
Charlottetown 210
Central Coastal Drive. 220
Points East Coastal Drive 233
North Cape Coastal Drive 240
St. John's 260
Avalon Peninsula 276
Eastern Newfoundland and Gander. 283
Western Newfoundland 301

ABOUT THIS GUIDE

Fodor's Recommendations

Everything in this guide is worth doing—we don't cover what isn't—but exceptional sights, hotels, and restaurants are recognized with additional accolades. Fodor'sChoice★ indicates our top recommendations. Care to nominate a new place? Visit Fodors.com/contact-us.

Trip Costs

We list prices wherever possible to help you budget well. Hotel and restaurant price categories from **$** to **$$$$** are noted alongside each recommendation. For hotels, we include the lowest cost of a standard double room in high season. For restaurants, we cite the average price of a main course at dinner or, if dinner isn't served, at lunch. For attractions, we always list adult admission fees; discounts are usually available for children, students, and senior citizens.

Hotels

Our local writers vet every hotel to recommend the best overnights in each price category, from budget to expensive. Unless otherwise specified, you can expect private bath, phone, and TV in your room. For expanded hotel reviews, facilities, and deals visit Fodors.com.

Top Picks

★ Fodor'sChoice

Listings

- Address
- Branch address
- Telephone
- Fax
- Website
- E-mail
- Admission fee
- Open/closed times
- Subway
- Directions or Map coordinates

Hotels & Restaurants

- Hotel
- Number of rooms
- Meal plans
- Restaurant
- Reservations
- Dress code
- No credit cards
- Price

Other

- See also
- Take note
- Golf facilities

Restaurants

Unless we state otherwise, restaurants are open for lunch and dinner daily. We mention dress code only when there's a specific requirement and reservations only when they're essential or not accepted. To make restaurant reservations, visit Fodors.com.

Credit Cards

The hotels and restaurants in this guide typically accept credit cards. If not, we'll say so.

EUGENE FODOR

Hungarian-born Eugene Fodor (1905–91) began his travel career as an interpreter on a French cruise ship. The experience inspired him to write *On the Continent* (1936), the first guidebook to receive annual updates and discuss a country's way of life as well as its sights. Fodor later joined the U.S. Army and worked for the OSS in World War II. After the war, he kept up his intelligence work while expanding his guidebook series. During the Cold War, many guides were written by fellow agents who understood the value of insider information. Today's guides continue Fodor's legacy by providing travelers with timely coverage, insider tips, and cultural context.

EXPERIENCE NOVA SCOTIA AND ATLANTIC CANADA

WHAT'S WHERE

1 Nova Scotia. Nova Scotia is the land of lighthouses and lobster traps: throw a dart at the map and you'll likely hit one or the other. But there are inland highlights, too, like sylvan orchards and dramatic highlands. If you're looking for urban amenities, the capital—hip, historic Halifax—is the largest city in Atlantic Canada and has the region's broadest range of dining and nightlife options.

2 New Brunswick. Fronted by the Bay of Fundy, New Brunswick is a fine place to witness the action of the planet's highest tides as they rise and fall a phenomenal 48 feet twice daily. Beyond the bay, the province boasts rivers, mountains, and dense forests—all of which offer abundant adventure opportunities—plus two rich cultures (English and French) and more than four centuries of history.

3 Prince Edward Island. PEI is rightly nicknamed "The Gentle Island" because it's generally prettier and more pastoral than its neighbors. PEI's rich red soil supports thriving farms, while its sandy warm-water beaches and nostalgia-inducing towns are a magnet for vacationers. Being largely flat, Canada's smallest province is also hugely popular with cyclists and golfers.

4 Newfoundland. The province of Newfoundland and Labrador is rugged and remote (Newfoundland sits alone in the North Atlantic; Labrador is tucked into northern Québec). It's also relatively cold, which allows for iceberg-watching in summer, great snow sports in winter, and wildlife-viewing year-round. Nevertheless, a warm welcome is assured: people here have been greeting visitors since the Vikings arrived 1,000 years ago.

Nain
Hopedale
ATLANTIC OCEAN
Smallwood Reservoir
LABRADOR
Cartwright
Happy Valley-Goose Bay
Red Bay
CANADA
4
St. Barbe
Réserve Faunique de Sept-Îles-Port-Cartier
Port au Choix
Natashquan
Sept-Îles
Port-Menier
Île d'Anticosti
Gros Morne N.P.
Lewisporte
Terra Nova N.P.
Gaspésie
Gaspé
1
Corner Brook
Gander
Péninsule de la Gaspésie
Gulf of St. Lawrence
NEWFOUNDLAND
Bay du Nord Wilderness Reserve
1
St. John's
11
Bathurst
8
Miramichi
Îles de la Madeleine
Channel-Port aux Basques
Argentia
PRINCE EDWARD ISLAND
3
Cape Breton Highlands N.P.
NEW BRUNSWICK
Charlottetown
Souris
Sydney
St. Pierre & Miquelon (FRANCE)
Avalon Wilderness Reserve
2
Moncton
Wood Islands
104
New Glasgow
Saint John
Cape Breton Island
Bay of Fundy
101
NOVA SCOTIA
Digby
1
Halifax
103
Yarmouth
CANADA

WHEN TO GO

July and August, when long, warm days let you fully enjoy attractions and activities, are the most popular months to visit Atlantic Canada. Beaches beckon in summer, sites open their doors for extended hours, and outfitters go full tilt, offering both soft and extreme outdoor adventures. As an added bonus, the seafood is freshest during those sunny days (or at least it seems so when you're eating at a waterside café) and the calendar is packed with festivals. Fall brings bountiful harvests, excellent whale-watching, and, of course, brilliant foliage. The trees, which start turning in late September, are at their most dazzling in October, and events like Cape Breton's Celtic Colours International Festival are scheduled to coincide with the vivid display.

Although many outlying inns and eateries close for the coldest months, there is a lot to do in Atlantic Canada during the winter. Snowmobilers and skiers, for example, can chill in northern New Brunswick, which gets as much as 157 inches of snow annually. March and April are the months for maple syrup and north-bound migratory birds, but travelers typically avoid this time as the weather is often frosty and wet. Late spring, though, is delightful. Apple trees bloom, wildflowers reappear, seasonal tourism operations reopen, and the visitor-to-local ratio remains low.

Climate

As a general rule, spring arrives later in coastal regions than inland, and nights are cool by the water even in summer. The balmiest land temperatures are recorded in July and August, while the ocean is at its warmest in August and early September. Autumn can last well into November, with warm, clear days and crisp nights. Most of Atlantic Canada is blanketed by snow in winter.

As far as main cities go, it may be handy to note that St. John's is uncommonly cold and Halifax, due to the Gulf Stream, is relatively moderate in winter.

PROVINCE PICKER

Not sure which of the four Atlantic provinces is right for you? All have hospitable people and stunning scenery, but not every one might offer that unique mix of attributes that makes it ideal for your trip. Use this chart to compare how each province will measure up to your idea of the perfect vacation. Remember, if you're looking for big cosmopolitan cities and TMZ-worthy nightlife, you'd be better off in a different part of the world.

	Nova Scotia	New Brunswick	Prince Edward Island	Newfoundland and Labrador
Cold-water beaches	◐	◐	○	●
Warm-water beaches	◐	●	●	○
Water sports	●	●	●	●
Snow sports	◐	●	○	●
Golfing	●	◐	●	◐
National parks	●	●	●	●
Rugged coastline	●	●	◐	●
Scenic drives	●	●	●	●
Lighthouses	●	●	●	●
Lobster	●	●	●	●
Iceberg-watching	○	○	○	●
Whale-watching	●	●	○	●
Bird-watching	●	●	●	●
Historic sites	●	●	◐	◐
Museums	●	●	◐	◐
Arts and crafts	●	●	●	●
Wineries and distilleries	●	○	◐	○
Spas	◐	◐	◐	◐
Cool capitals	●	◐	◐	◐

● = Noteworthy, ◐ = Some, ○ = Little or none

NOVA SCOTIA AND ATLANTIC CANADA TODAY

Canada's east coast is justifiably famous for its natural beauty—after all, its photogenic headlands, highlands, and harbors provide endless photo opportunities. However, it is the people who live here that really set this place apart. Here's a look at what Atlantic Canadians are focused on now.

The Economy

The economic outlook in Halifax remains bright, as demonstrated by the amount of construction downtown. Being the de facto capital of Atlantic Canada, Halifax is the regional center for health care and education (which gives it a strong white-collar presence); the Canadian navy's Atlantic fleet is also based here (thus adding a lot of "sailor blue"). As a port city, it is further benefiting from a multi-year, C$25-billion shipbuilding contract. Unfortunately, the picture isn't so rosy elsewhere. St. John's, previously reveling in an offshore oil boom, is beginning to feel the impact of dropping oil prices. Rural areas, meanwhile, are struggling throughout the region. Heritage industries still form their economic backbone: farming is one, forestry and its offshoots (like the pulp-and-paper business) is another. Fishing, of course, also counts because seafood here isn't merely a menu staple— along much of the coast, it provides residents' livelihood. Not surprisingly, tourism in such spots is especially important.

Their Roots

In today's fast-changing world locals might not be sure where they're going, but they are very conscious of where they came from. Mi'Kmaq communities continue to honor traditions handed down from the land's original inhabitants, and the legacy of early European settlers is equally apparent. Witness the living culture of Francophone Acadians, who proudly fly their own Stella Maris flag in parts of Nova Scotia, New Brunswick, and PEI. Their *joie de vivre* tinges everything from the instruments they play to the delicacies they devour (think spoons and *rappie* pie respectively). On Cape Breton, conversely, descendants of Scots who arrived centuries ago still nibble oatcakes and step-dance to Celtic fiddle music. African Canadians celebrate their past at the Black Loyalist Heritage Centre in Birchtown, Nova Scotia: unveiled in 2015, it recalls the 3,000 former slaves who, in the aftermath of the American Revolution, made Birchtown the largest free settlement of its kind on the continent. Newer immigrant groups have also staked their claim, showcasing their contributions to the region at events like the annual Nova Scotia Multicultural Festival.

The Great Outdoors

Urban sprawl is virtually unheard of around here, and huge tracts of land—particularly in Newfoundland and Labrador and central New Brunswick—remain undeveloped. Generously sized civic green spaces (picture Halifax's Point Pleasant Park or Saint John's Rockwood Park) are plentiful as well, so it's easy for outdoorsy sorts to find a place to play. Fresh-air fans regularly lace up hiking boots, pick up paddles, hop on bikes, lob golf balls, and grab fishing gear. All their energy isn't expended on exercise, though. Conservation groups are active across the region, and locals work hard to preserve their natural heritage for future generations. This explains why they have successfully lobbied to protect Sable Island (which was threatened by the oil industry) as a national park, and to win UNESCO

Biosphere Reserve status for both the Bay of Fundy and more than 13,770 square km (5,316 square miles) of pristine southwest Nova Scotian terrain.

Their Creative Side

Atlantic Canada is home to a disproportionate number of high-quality artisans and craftspeople: some are native born, others are CFAs ("come from aways") drawn by inspiring vistas and a comparatively low cost of living. The region abounds with potters, painters, and pewter smiths, as well as practitioners of folk disciplines such as quilting, wood carving, and rug hooking—many of whom give traditional motifs an updated twist. These creative types can be found in city centers and quiet rural locales. Notable among the latter is Newfoundland's remote Fogo Island, where an extraordinary, übermodern arts colony featuring studios and residency programs was recently built from scratch by the Shorefast Foundation. But they can also be found in postsecondary institutions because several schools (including a New Brunswick craft college and a Nova Scotia university devoted to art and design) lend the scene academic cred and added prestige.

Fine Food

Long before the Slow Food and Eat Local movements gained momentum, folks here tended to be locavores. Now a matter of preference, it was once a matter of necessity. In cities, "local" was all that you could buy fresh. In the countryside, where people fished, raised, picked, or otherwise procured their own food, it was all that was available. Yet the down-home diet has never presented any great hardship since stellar seafood is prevalent across all four provinces; and, in Newfoundland especially, game gets added to the list (if you have never tried moose burgers or caribou medallions, here's your chance!). Factor in a cornucopia of farm produce, plus a bounty of wild berries, and you have the makings for memorable meals. Visitors can sample these at a range of innovative eateries and old-school restaurants. Want to learn to prepare them yourself? Nova Scotia's award-winning Trout Point Lodge offers gourmet cooking vacations.

Local Libations

Like all Canadians, those on the Atlantic coast are crazy about Tim Hortons coffee. (Forget that mocha-choca latte: the standard order here is Timmie's large double-double—shorthand for a big cup of Joe with two creams and two sugars.) Residents, however, are always ready to imbibe something stronger. And they don't just drink it: they make it, too. Nova Scotian wine is a case in point. Samuel de Champlain and his thirsty French crew planted the former colony's first grapevines back in 1611. Today the wine industry adds more than C$200-million a year to the provincial economy, and Nova Scotia has even been granted its own appellation (Tidal Bay, a crisp white that was introduced in 2012). The number of grape growers and boutique wine producers is also increasing almost annually, the newest of the bunch being Lightfoot & Wolfville Vineyards, which aims to become the first certified biodynamic winery in the province. Thanks to a mild microclimate, most local wineries are concentrated in the lovely Annapolis Valley, and several (including Domaine de Grand Pré, Luckett Vineyards, and Sainte-Famille Wines) organize regular tours and tastings.

IF YOU LIKE

On-the-Water Activities

PEI and Newfoundland are both islands; and Nova Scotia is almost one. New Brunswick, meanwhile, is cut by mighty rivers and boasts three coasts that extend for a collective 2,250 km (1,398 miles). That's good news for beachgoers, as well as for travelers eager to try something more adventurous than sunbathing or sand-castle building.

Beach Bumming. Prince Edward Island tops most beach lovers' lists. It has classic crescents and several variations on the theme, including shores backed by rare parabolic dunes and ones composed of "singing sand" that squeaks when you walk on it (check out Basin Head for that).

Surfing. The water may be frigid, but that doesn't deter the surfers who routinely head to Nova Scotia's Eastern Shore to indulge their passion. Lawrencetown Beach and Martinique Beach have the best breaks, especially in late summer when the tail ends of hurricanes whip up waves.

Salmon Fishing. Grab your rod and hip waders. The Miramichi in New Brunswick, the Margaree in Nova Scotia, and the Humber in Newfoundland are legendary salmon rivers. Pulling a trophy-sized specimen from one is the Alpha and Omega-3 of fishing experiences.

Scuba Diving. Rather be underwater? In Newfoundland, divers can explore WWII wrecks or opt for eco-oriented excursions that offer up-close encounters with marine creatures. If you're not certified, Ocean Quest Adventures will take you out to snorkel with humpback whales.

Scenic Drives

It's no surprise that Atlantic Canada earns an A+ for scenery. Crashing surf, craggy headlands, forest-clad mountains, rolling farmland, meandering rivers: they're all here. Each of the four provinces has designated camera-ready drives (Nova Scotia alone has 11 so-called scenic travelways); and these showcase the best of the best, making auto touring easy.

Cabot Trail, Nova Scotia. This renowned 298-km (185-mile) road ranks among the region's most dramatic. Timid motorists should note that tackling its vertiginous, ocean-hugging turns is no easy task: sound brakes and steady nerves are required. Yet its sheer beauty rewards the effort.

Central Coastal Drive, Prince Edward Island. Compact PEI is a driver's dream. Highlighting the province's midsection, this route loops through top sites (including Cavendish, the island's national park, and Charlottetown), taking in vintage Victoria and other pretty villages.

River Valley Scenic Drive, New Brunswick. Discover a more bucolic side to New Brunswick by veering inland from the wave-lashed Fundy coast and following the St. John River. The route's southern portion, with its covered bridges and little cable ferries, is particularly picturesque.

Road to the Isles, Newfoundland. This 172-km (107-mile) stretch of the Kittiwake Coast focuses on Notre Dame Bay. Stop at Twillingate, where summertime visitors can ogle icebergs and watch for whales—specifically the supersized "Humpbacks of Notre Dame."

National Parks

With the addition of Sable Island in 2013, Atlantic Canada now has nine national parks. Several are hard to miss: for example, Fundy National Park (one of New Brunswick's big draws) sits between Saint John and Moncton, while the famed Cabot Trail runs right through Cape Breton Highlands National Park.

Gros Morne National Park, Newfoundland. Notable for geologic features that date back almost 500,000,000 years, Gros Morne wears its age well. Recreational opportunities in the rugged park include hiking, fishing, and boat tours on glacier-sculpted Western Brook Pond.

Prince Edward Island National Park, Prince Edward Island. More than a playground for the sun-and-sand set, this park—running from Cavendish to Dalvay, with a Greenwich Peninsula adjunct—also appeals to bird-watchers and, since Green Gables sits on its property, Anne fans.

Kejimkujik National Park, Nova Scotia. Both a National Park and a National Historic site, "Keji" combines natural splendor with a rich Aboriginal heritage. Today you can paddle through pristine woodlands using the same canoe routes that the ancient Mi'Kmaq people once followed.

Kouchibouguac National Park, New Brunswick. Washed by the warm Northumberland Strait, the beaches here provide a quiet counterpoint to busy Parlee Beach in nearby Shediac. The park's lagoons shelter sea life and dune grasses protect birds such as the endangered piping plover.

Living History

With all due respect to Columbus, it was actually Viking explorer Leif Eriksson who "discovered" the New World when he landed on Newfoundland's Great Northern Peninsula in AD 1000. By the 1600s, French and English forces were duking it out in the rest of the region; and, in the next century, war in America and poverty in Europe brought waves of immigrants. Hence this area is rife with history, and there are many places where you can step back in time.

L'Anse aux Meadows, Newfoundland. The Viking settlement, unearthed in the 1960s, is now a UNESCO World Heritage Site with excavated and replicated sod huts, plus an artifact-filled visitor center. Activities range from guided walks to weaving lessons.

Fortress of Louisbourg, Nova Scotia. Return to the 1700s, when France fought for control of the continent, at North America's largest historical reconstruction. Costumed interpreters lend an air of authenticity to the 12-acre property.

Highland Village Museum, Nova Scotia. Honor the area's Scottish immigrants (remember, Nova Scotia is Latin for "New Scotland") by learning a thing or two about Celtic culture at this engaging, open-air attraction in Cape Breton.

Kings Landing Historical Settlement, New Brunswick. History buffs can hit the pause button at this sprawling riverfront site, which re-creates life among the United Empire Loyalists (also known as the Tories, depending on which side of the American Revolution you supported).

QUINTESSENTIAL NOVA SCOTIA AND ATLANTIC CANADA

Succulent Seafood

Atlantic salmon, Digby scallops, Malpeque Bay oysters—this part of Canada is nirvana for seafood connoisseurs. Nothing, however, makes true aficionados swoon like fresh local lobster. The King of Crustaceans is served countless ways (anyone for lobster Benedict?) and can be ordered almost anywhere, from haute-cuisine eateries to fast-food outlets (both McDonald's and Subway sell lobster rolls here in peak season). Food Channel devotees can buy lobster right off the wharf and boil it themselves. In some places, curious visitors can even learn how to haul traps before devouring the catch. The communal lobster suppers hosted each summer by rural churches and community centers are a tasty alternative: just look for signs posted in coastal areas. At these unpretentious gatherings, tables are long, prices are low, and the ambience is unforgettable.

Illuminating Lighthouses

Nowhere is the seafaring heritage of Atlantic Canada more evident than in the 400-plus lighthouses that stand sentry on the coast. Each has its own claim to fame. Newfoundland's Cape Spear Light, for example, marks North America's most easterly point, and the one at Peggy's Cove, near Halifax, is one of the continent's most photographed. Amazing views of ferries, fishing boats, and, occasionally, spouting whales set New Brunswick's Swallowtail Light apart. But PEI's Cape Bear beacon has a sadder distinction: it received the first SOS from the *Titanic* as she sank in 1912. Though designed to be seen from afar, many now offer visitors up-close experiences. Some house museums, shops, or restaurants. A few—like Newfoundland's Quirpon, Nova Scotia's Cape d'Or, and PEI's West Point—even offer lodgings in the lighthouse itself or the lighthouse keeper's residence.

If you want to genuinely experience Atlantic Canada, as opposed to merely seeing it, you must first learn what makes Atlantic Canadians tick. Sampling these tried-and-true activities will give you the inside track.

Lively Languages

Canada's multicultural model isn't a melting pot so much as a simmering stew that enables each group to maintain its distinctive character. In this region one result is a unique linguistic mélange. For most folks English is the mother tongue, yet in northern New Brunswick (Canada's only officially bilingual province), French predominates. Ditto for Nova Scotia's Acadian Coast and parts of PEI, so you may want to practice your *bonjour* and *merci* before arriving. Gaelic is added to the mix in Cape Breton, which is home to North America's only Gaelic college: you won't be on the island long before someone wishes you *Céad Míle Fáilte* (a hundred thousand welcomes). Newfoundland famously has a lingo all its own. You best twig to it, too, or you might be a chucklehead and decline if invited out for a scoff and a scuff (dinner and a dance).

A Slower Pace

You might as well ease your foot off that gas pedal because in Atlantic Canada no one's in a hurry to get anywhere. Despite their quick wits, people here choose to move at a slower pace and will happily interrupt almost any activity to chat with a friend, a neighbor—or you, if given a chance. Such behavior can frustrate travelers intent on sticking to a strict itinerary. If you're open to opportunities, though, you'll not only see firsthand how friendly Atlantic Canadians are, you will likely also come away with in-the-know info on hidden back roads, undiscovered eateries, and one-of-a-kind events. Taking time out may mean you have to pare back the destinations you cover or drop some attractions from your sightseeing checklist. Well, so be it. After all, this is a vacation, not *The Amazing Race*. Slow down and savor the experience.

NOVA SCOTIA AND ATLANTIC CANADA WITH KIDS

Traveling with kids? Here's the lowdown on what to do where.

Prince Edward Island

PEI is so compact that you can do it all. Most families, however, home in on the central section. It's a buffet for beach lovers because you can enjoy the unspoiled splendor of **Prince Edward Island National Park** as well as the kitschy seaside amusements around **Cavendish,** including **Shining Waters Family Fun Park** and **Ripley's Believe It or Not!** Of course, this is also L. M. Montgomery's native turf and two *Anne* sites—**Green Gables** plus a replica of **Avonlea Village** appeal to young fans. If your children weren't raised on "Anne with an E," brush up by seeing **"Anne of Green Gables—The Musical"** at the Confederation Centre in **Charlottetown.** The tuneful tearjerker has played to packed houses every summer since 1965. While in the city, also take in **Founders' Hall,** where state-of-the-art technology explains how Canada was created during the Charlottetown Conference of 1864.

Nova Scotia

In Nova Scotia, make **Halifax** your base. Aside from the amenities you'd expect in Atlantic Canada's largest urban center, Nova Scotia's capital has standout attractions, such as the historic Halifax Citadel (where reenactors drill daily in summer) and bustling **Waterfront Boardwalk.** On or near the latter, you can visit a pair of cool, kid-centric museums (the **Maritime Museum of the Atlantic** and the **Canadian Museum of Immigration at Pier 21**), before choosing one of the many boat tours that operate out of **Cable Wharf.** For a taste of traditional coastal life, spend a morning scrambling over the rocks at the **Peggy's Cove Lighthouse;** or a full day exploring time-warped South Shore towns (most notably **Lunenburg**) with a beach break in between.

New Brunswick

Although New Brunswick is relatively large, you can tick off many family-oriented sites if you focus on the Moncton area. The city itself is home to the **Magic Mountain Water Park,** the **Magnetic Hill Zoo,** and **TreeGO Aerial Adventures** (an overhead obstacle course for Tarzan wannabes). Moreover, Moncton puts you in easy shooting distance of both **Fundy and Kouchibouguac National Parks,** as well as the fabled **Hopewell Rocks.** As an added bonus, **Parlee Beach** is about 20 minutes away in **Shediac.** The 3-km (2-mile) expanse of sand—complete with tempting tidal pools—draws big crowds in summer. Shediac also bills itself as "The Lobster Capital of the World," and kids can see how they're caught on a fun Lobster Tales Cruise.

Newfoundland

National parks like **Gros Morne** engage kids through dedicated programs; ditto for National Historic Sites like **L'Anse aux Meadows**—a visit to which can be combined with one to nearby **Norstead,** a recreated Norse village featuring costumed staffers and a full-scale Viking ship. The downside is that vast distances separate many attractions and, frankly, the province's simple charms are often lost on children. **St. John's** is an exception to the rule. Clusters of houses are painted in Crayola colors, and spots like the geology-themed **Johnson GEO CENTRE** will score points with your offspring. Be sure to hike up **Signal Hill** and make the short drive to **Cape Spear:** from either you might spot whales or icebergs. For a different perspective, hop on a harbor tour boat.

NOVA SCOTIA

WELCOME TO NOVA SCOTIA

TOP REASONS TO GO

★ **See the coast:** There are postcard-perfect fishing villages and sprawling sandy beaches. The water is inviting, too, for kayaking, sailing, or whale-watching.

★ **Dine on crustaceans:** This province is shaped liked a lobster claw, a happy coincidence because the lobster here is so delicious. Mussels and oysters are also plentiful, and Digby lays claim to the world's finest scallops.

★ **Shop for crafts:** Nova Scotians—from the quilters at Suttles and Seawinds in Mahone Bay to the students of Halifax's Centre for Craft & Design—create high-quality products.

★ **Experience the culture:** Cape Breton "kitchen parties" combine music and dancing, allowing you to sample the region's rich Celtic culture. For a French-tinged alternative, substitute a rollicking Acadian soirée.

★ **Enjoy the camaraderie:** Bluenosers (the long-standing nickname for Nova Scotians) are famously friendly and very social. So be responsive—with a little encouragement you'll likely be embraced like long-lost kin.

1 Halifax. The Halifax Regional Municipality is Atlantic Canada's biggest city and—as Nova Scotia's capital—has been a military, commercial, political, and cultural powerhouse for more than 250 years. Its downtown showcases the best of old and new through waterfront restaurants, pubs, galleries, heritage properties, and modern office towers.

2 South Shore and Annapolis Valley. The South Shore, on the Atlantic coast, is "classic" Nova Scotia, complete with weathered fishing villages, craggy coves, and white-sand beaches. The Annapolis Valley, on the Bay of Fundy side, is more pastoral and better known for orchards, vineyards, and picturesque farming villages.

GETTING ORIENTED

Nova Scotia is all but surrounded by water, save for the narrow stretch of land that links it to the rest of Canada. Secondary highways hug the coastline and meander through historic small towns, while "100-series" arterial highways offer the fastest travel routes. Halifax, the capital, sits on the eastern coast, roughly in the middle of the province's mainland. Southwest of the city, the South Shore runs all the way to Yarmouth. The Annapolis Valley, beside the Bay of Fundy, is the eastern spine of Nova Scotia. The central and northern areas lie beside Northumberland Strait (on a fine day you can see across to Prince Edward Island); while the northernmost region, Cape Breton Island, is connected to the remainder of the province by a 1.6-km (1-mile) causeway.

3 Eastern Shore and Northern Nova Scotia. The area east and north of Halifax reveals remarkable variety within a relatively short distance. The sparsely populated Eastern Shore has pounding surf, thick forests, and remote cranberry barrens, while Northumberland Strait boasts hiking trails and sandy warm-water beaches.

4 Cape Breton. The Island of Cape Breton is the Celtic heart of Nova Scotia, where music and dancing are a part of daily life. The gritty, industrial past of its towns and cities is a sharp contrast to the unspoiled natural beauty that defines the rural areas. The island is home to the Cabot Trail, a spectacular drive through the Cape Breton Highlands.

Updated by Penny Phenix

For many, Nova Scotia evokes images of seascapes. To the south and east, the Atlantic crashes against rocky outcrops or washes placidly over white sand. To the northwest, Fundy tides—the highest in the world—recede to reveal mudflats, then rush back in, raising the sea level by more than 50 feet. To the north, warm, relatively shallow Northumberland Strait flows between Nova Scotia and Prince Edward Island, providing a livelihood for fishermen on both sides. Nova Scotia is one of the world's largest exporters of seafood, particularly lobsters. But the province is much more than its coastline alone; its coastal capital, Halifax, is a lively and attractive business and tourism hub.

It was Thomas Chandler Haliburton who first said "seeing is believing," and the observation applies to his home province because it's hard to fathom such a variety of cultures and landscapes packed into an area smaller than West Virginia without witnessing it firsthand. Within the perimeter drawn by that convoluted coastline, lie the rolling farmlands of the Annapolis Valley, which yields vintner's grapes, apples, corn, peaches, and plums. In the middle of the province, dense forests are interspersed with blueberry patches, cranberry bogs, and, in spring and summer, open fields of wildflowers—purple and blue lupines, yellow coltsfoot, pink fireweed—that blanket the ground with color. In Cape Breton are highlands that rival Scotland's, rugged rock-rimmed inlets, woodlands that provide spectacular fall foliage, and mountains that plunge dramatically down to meet the waves. Throughout the province there is great biodiversity, including a number of endangered and threatened species that are being actively protected. In the western arm, the Southwest Nova UNESCO Biosphere Reserve, the second largest in Canada, includes the remote Kejimkujik National Park, which protects old-growth transitional woodland and all the wildlife that depends upon it.

The people of Nova Scotia are equally diverse. The original inhabitants, the Mi'Kmaqs, have been here for 10,000 years and remain a major cultural presence. In the early days of European exploration, they were joined by the French and English who settled on the shores and harvested the sea. Later, waves of immigrants came: Germans in Lunenburg County; Highland Scots displaced by their landlords' preference for sheep; New England Loyalists fleeing the American Revolution; freedmen or escaped slaves; then Ukrainians, Poles, West Indians, Italians, and Lebanese drawn to the industrial centers of Halifax and Sydney.

That multicultural mélange accounts for the fact that you'll see Gaelic signs in Mabou and Iona, German sausage and sauerkraut prominently featured on menus in Lunenburg, and Francophones proudly flying their own tricolor flag in Acadian communities along the western Fundy coast and places such as Chéticamp in Cape Breton. It also helps explain why Nova Scotians, who originally hailed from so many different places themselves, are so famously hospitable to "people from away."

PLANNING

WHEN TO GO

Spring comes late in Nova Scotia: trees don't get leafy until mid-May, and it takes until mid-June for temperatures to heat up. As a result, many find July and August to be the ideal months here, but even then, come prepared. Bring a raincoat for morning fog and showers, a sweater to keep the ocean breezes at bay at night, and your bathing suit for the blazing sun in between. Autumn has its own charm: September has warm days, refreshingly cool nights, and hot events like Halifax's Atlantic Film and Atlantic Fringe festivals. Late September through October is peak time for foliage fans. The downside is that wildlife cruises, cycling tours, and kayaking outfitters generally only operate from mid-June through September. Keep in mind, too, that outside major tourist centers, many resorts, inns, and B&Bs close after Canadian Thanksgiving (Columbus Day in the United States) and don't reopen until Victoria Day in late May. Some shops, restaurants, and sites are also seasonal.

FESTIVALS

Nova Scotia hosts hundreds of festivals each year, and at first glance you might think most were devoted to food. Several coastal communities celebrate seafood, including Digby, Pictou, Shelburne, and Yarmouth, and the Annapolis Valley hosts events for apple-blossom time and the pumpkin harvest. Many events, though, highlight the diversity of the Nova Scotian people, from Halifax's multiculturalism to the Scottish heritage of Antigonish and Cape Breton to the North Shore's Acadian culture. Theater festivals range from Shakespeare to fringe, and music lovers will find much to choose from.

Apple Blossom Festival. The beauty of the Annapolis Valley orchards provides reason enough to visit the apple-growing region in late spring, but this six-day, family-friendly festival in late May heightens the experience with tours, a beauty pageant, concerts, art shows, and apple-themed food. ✉ *Kentville* ⊕ *www.appleblossom.com.*

Atlantic Film Festival. The output of Eastern Canada's burgeoning film industry, along with films from around the world, is presented at this eight-day event held in Halifax in mid-September. ☎ *902/422–3456* ⊕ *www.atlanticfilm.com.*

Atlantic Fringe Festival. Various venues in downtown Halifax present alternative dramas, comedy, and other performances as part of this popular festival held in late August, early September, or both. ✉ *Halifax* ⊕ *www.atlanticfringe.ca.*

Fodor's Choice ★ **Celtic Colours International Festival.** For nine days in early October, Cape Breton showcases the very best Celtic musicians and dancers—international artists and homegrown talent—in more than three dozen island communities. Activities celebrating Gaelic language, lore, history, crafts, and culture complement the joyful sounds. ☎ *888/355–7744* ⊕ *www.celtic-colours.com.*

Chester Race Week. The Chester area has some of the Eastern Seaboard's best sailing, and the town hosts this fixed-keel regatta, Canada's largest, in mid-August. Onshore events include barbecues and dancing to live music. ✉ *Chester* ☎ *902/275–3747 Chester Yacht Club* ⊕ *www.chesterraceweek.com.*

FAMILY **Digby Scallop Days.** Digby scallops are widely regarded as the best in the world, and this festival celebrates both the mollusk and the fishing fleet with events including a parade, shucking contests, entertainment, fireworks, and feasts. ☎ *No phone* ⊕ *www.digbyscallopdays.com.*

FAMILY **Festival Acadien de Clare.** The village of Pointe de l'Église hosts the Atlantic provinces' oldest Acadian celebration with parades on land and water, concerts, theater, children's events, and other activities. ✉ *Pointe d'Église* ☎ *902/769–0832* ⊕ *www.festivalacadiendeclare.ca.*

FAMILY Fodor's Choice ★ **Halifax International Busker Festival.** Street performers from many countries are the stars of this six-day event on the Halifax Waterfront in late July and early August. The lineup includes street theater, circus arts, music, magicians, visual arts, and comedy, with acts for audiences of all ages. It's all free, but you're welcome to show your appreciation by tipping the hat. ✉ *Halifax* ☎ *No phone* ⊕ *www.buskers.ca.*

Halifax Pride. In mid- to late July a huge rainbow flag flutters over downtown Halifax, heralding 11 days of Pride activities that include a theater festival, sports events, drag shows, comedy, disco parties, concerts, and the grand parade on the last Saturday of the month. ✉ *Halifax* ⊕ *halifaxpride.com.*

FAMILY **Hants County Exhibition.** Staged annually since 1765, this is the continent's oldest agricultural fair, taking place over six days in mid-September. It is still an old-fashioned affair complete with ox pulls, livestock and horse shows, horticultural exhibits, crafts displays and demonstrations, and entertainment. ✉ *Hants County Exhibition Park, 249 Wentworth Rd., Windsor* ⊕ *www.hantscountyex.com.*

Highland Games. The biggest and oldest Highland Games outside of Scotland is held in Antigonish each July. The energetic weeklong event includes caber tossing and hammer throwing. Pipe-band concerts, Highland dance competitions, and ceilidhs round out the schedule. ✉ *Antigonish* ⊕ *www.antigonishhighlandgames.ca.*

FAMILY **Pictou Lobster Carnival.** This three-day festival in early July, which celebrated its 80th year in 2014, marks the end of its region's fishing season with concerts, parades, lobster-boat racing, and a midway and other attractions. ✉ *Pictou* ⊕ *www.pictoulobstercarnival.ca.*

Royal Nova Scotia International Tattoo. The centerpiece of Nova Scotia's signature festival is a fast-paced, 2½-hour extravaganza of military instruments (brass, bagpipes, and drums), military-inspired music, acrobatics, and traditional and modern music and dance performed by participants from around the world. The event takes place during the first week of July and includes other free concerts, parades, and other activities around town. ✉ *Scotiabank Centre, 1800 Argyle St., Halifax* ☎ *902/420–1114, 800/563–1114* ⊕ *www.nstattoo.ca.*

FAMILY **Seafest.** Yarmouth honors its seafaring roots with 11 days of festivities in mid- to late July. Highlights include a street parade, mackerel tossing, driftwood-art contests, beach parties, concerts, fireworks, and a parade of illuminated boats. ✉ *Yarmouth* ⊕ *www.seafest.ca.*

Shelburne County Lobster Festival. The county celebrates the local lobster industry in early June with four days of events, entertainment, and lobster suppers. ✉ *Shelburne* ⊕ *www.discovershelburnecounty.com/shelburnecountylobsterfestival.*

TD Halifax Jazz Festival. Musicians representing a variety of styles perform at this popular nine-day event held in early July. Some of the concerts are free. ✉ *Halifax* ⊕ *www.jazzeast.com.*

GETTING HERE AND AROUND

AIR TRAVEL

Halifax's Stanfield International Airport is Atlantic Canada's largest airport, with flights from the United States via New York, Boston, Newark, Chicago, and Philadelphia (plus Detroit and Atlanta in season), and from major European cities via London and Glasgow in the United Kingdom, Frankfurt in Germany, and Keflavik in Iceland. Ground transportation into Halifax takes from 30 to 40 minutes. Limousine and taxi services, as well as car rentals, are available on-site. MetroTransit Bus 320 serves the airport every 30 minutes at peak time, otherwise hourly; the fare is C$3.50. Maritime Bus operates a shuttle service from the airport to downtown Halifax, including Dalhousie and St. Mary's universities and hotels in Halifax and Dartmouth (fare C$22 one-way, C$40 round-trip) and from other destinations in Atlantic Canada. Regular taxi fares into Halifax are C$63 each way. If you book ahead with A Sunshine Share-A-Cab, the fare is around C$32, depending on your time of arrival, but you must share your cab with another passenger; call ahead, before 8 pm, to book your appointment.

Visitors proceeding on to other Nova Scotian destinations can take buses to the Annapolis Valley and shuttles to Cape Breton. Cape Breton–bound travelers short on time can also fly into Sydney's airport.

Airports **Halifax Stanfield International Airport.** ✉ *1 Bell Blvd. Extension, Enfield* ☎ *902/873–4422* ⊕ *www.hiaa.ca.* **J.A. Douglas McCurdy Sydney Airport.** ✉ *280 Silver Dart Way, Sydney* ☎ *902/564–7720* ⊕ *www.sydneyairport.ca.*

Transportation **A Sunshine Share-A-Cab.** ✉ *Halifax* ☎ *902/429–5555, 800/565–8669* ⊕ *www.ashareacab.com.*

BUS TRAVEL

Long-distance bus service to Nova Scotia is limited. Maritime Bus runs the length of the Trans-Canada Highway from Rivière-du-Loup, Québec, through New Brunswick to Truro and Halifax, North Sydney, and Kentville. It can also get you to Nova Scotia from Prince Edward

Island. Seats must be reserved in advance. Buses between Halifax and Sydney are also run by Cape Shuttle (C$70) and Scotia Shuttle (C$75).

Contacts **Cape Shuttle.** ☎ *902/539-8585, 800/349-1698* ⊕ *www.capeshuttleservice.com.* **Maritime Bus.** ☎ *800/575-1807* ⊕ *maritimebus.com.* **Scotia Shuttle.** ☎ *902/435-9686, 800/898-5883* ⊕ *www.scotiashuttle.ca.*

CAR TRAVEL

The only overland route to Nova Scotia crosses the Isthmus of Chignecto: a narrow neck of land that joins the province to New Brunswick. The Trans-Canada Highway (Highway 2 in New Brunswick) becomes Highway 104 in Amherst, the first town after the border. From there you can make it to Halifax, connecting to Highway 102 at Truro, in two hours. If you're headed to Cape Breton via New Glasgow and have time to spare, you can opt for a scenic drive along Route 6, which runs along the coast of Northumberland Strait.

FERRY TRAVEL

Car ferries connect Nova Scotia with New Brunswick, Prince Edward Island, and Newfoundland. Bay Ferries cross the Bay of Fundy from Saint John, New Brunswick to Digby; Northumberland Ferries provide service from Wood Islands, on Prince Edward Island to Caribou; Marine Atlantic makes the crossing between Port aux Basques or Argentia, Newfoundland, to North Sydney.

Contacts **Bay Ferries Ltd.** ☎ *888/249-7245 reservations, 506/649-7777 Saint John Terminal, 902/245-2116 Digby Terminal* ⊕ *www.ferries.ca.* **Marine Atlantic.** ☎ *800/341-7981 reservations, 800/897-2797 customer relations* ⊕ *www.marineatlantic.ca.* **Northumberland Ferries.** ☎ *800/565-0201 Caribou and Wood Islands terminals, 877/762-7245 reservations* ⊕ *www.ferries.ca.*

TRAIN TRAVEL

VIA Rail offers overnight service from Montréal to Halifax three times a week. The trip takes about 23 hours and 20 minutes. An economy seat costs C$158.67 including tax and luggage allowance. A sleeper cabin for two with a shower costs C$555.33, including tax and luggage allowance.

Contacts **VIA Rail.** ☎ *888/842-7245* ⊕ *www.viarail.ca.*

DISCOUNTS AND DEALS

The Nova Scotia Museum Pass grants you admission to 28 facilities—including popular picks like Halifax's Maritime Museum of the Atlantic, Lunenburg's Fisheries Museum of the Atlantic, and Cape Breton's Highland Village—as many times as you want for a full year. Priced at C$46.85 for adults and C$92.65 for a family of four, the pass is an excellent value. Call ☎ *800/632-1114*, go to ⊕ *museum.novascotia.ca* or visit any provincial museum for details.

OUTDOOR ACTIVITIES

Hiking, biking, and horseback riding routes make inland exploring a breeze; kayak and canoe routes let you splash out with ease; and there are snowmobile and cross-country skiing options, too. The province's trail site (⊕ *www.trails.gov.ns.ca*) will put you on the right path.

NOVA SCOTIA GREAT ITINERARIES

Don't let the fact that Nova Scotia is Canada's second-smallest province fool you. Driving will likely take longer than you expect.

IF YOU HAVE 3 DAYS

Spend your first full day in **Halifax.** Explore downtown, leaving time to linger on the harbor-front boardwalk, and have a fun evening out in one of the many pubs and clubs. Don't stay out too late, though—you'll need to be up early to beat the crowds to **Peggy's Cove.** From there, head down to the "Holy Trinity" of South Shore towns: Chester, Mahone Bay, and Lunenburg. Take a coffee break in **Chester** before proceeding to lovely **Mahone Bay** for lunch and boutique browsing. In **Lunenburg** visit the Fisheries Museum and sign up for one of the boat tours departing from its dock. Next, drive on to the Liverpool area (an hour away), where you'll stop for the night. Depending on your preferences, you can dedicate the morning of Day 3 to blissful beaches or immediately veer northwest on Highway 8, which connects Liverpool to Annapolis Royal. Hikers can dally en route at **Kejimkujik National Park and Historic Site.** History buffs can drive 90 minutes straight through, thereby allowing more time to visit the heritage sites in and around **Annapolis Royal** and **Wolfville.** Given that Halifax is about 200 km (124 miles) from the former and 90 km (56 miles) from the latter, completing the loop and returning to the capital for your final night is easy.

IF YOU HAVE 5 DAYS

Stick to the above itinerary but, rather than returning to Halifax at the end of Day 3, bed down at a **Wolfville** inn. As you've already seen the Atlantic and Bay of Fundy, it seems unsporting not to add Northumberland Strait to your itinerary. So, on the morning of Day 4, take the pretty three-hour drive cross country to **Pictou.** There you can visit Hector Heritage Quay, where the Scots landed in 1773, and take a dip in the strait's warm, salty water. On the morning of Day 5, explore a bit more of the **Sunrise Trail** by car or kayak, then make the two-hour trek back to **Halifax.**

IF YOU HAVE 7 DAYS

Cape Breton Island is a nice place to spend a week, or a lifetime, but you can cover the basics in two days. Follow the route above, but instead of spending Day 5 on the Sunrise Trail, head east via Antigonish to Port Hawkesbury. From here, follow the 107-km (67-mile) Ceilidh Trail passing through music-loving **Mabou** on the way to Chéticamp. Stop here for lunch, then take the **Cabot Trail** north, looping around **Cape Breton Highlands National Park.** The cliff-hugging trail ranks among the world's most dramatic drives. There should be time for a whale-watching trip or a scenic hike along the way. Spend the night at **Ingonish.** On Day 6, continue on the Cabot Trail to **Baddeck** to explore the Alexander Graham Bell site, the Highland Village, and perhaps get out on the lovely Bras d'Or Lakes. On Day 7, get an early start for the 80-minute drive to **Louisbourg.** Devote the morning to the reconstructed 18th-century French fortress. After lunch, backtrack to Sydney then follow Highway 4 along the southern shore of Bras d'Or Lake to Port Hawkesbury and return to Halifax, about a five-hour drive.

Motorists can sample Nova Scotia's sensational scenery by following any of the province's 11 Scenic Travelways. There are five in Cape Breton and six on the mainland, all clearly identified by roadside signs with icons that correspond to route names. Nova Scotia Tourism's encyclopedic *Doers and Dreamers Guide* has the lowdown (☎ *902/425–5781 or 800/565–0000* ⊕ *www.novascotia.com*). The two best places for whale-watching are on the Bay of Fundy, from Digby down to Digby Neck, or in Cape Breton on Pleasant Bay. There are other spots to go whale-watching (Halifax, for instance) but the chances of sightings aren't as great.

In addition to the commercial outdoor-activities outfitters listed throughout the chapter, the following organizations are also valuable resources: **Bicycle Nova Scotia** (☎ *902/425–5450 Ext. 316* ⊕ *www.bicycle.ns.ca*); **Canoe Kayak Nova Scotia** (☎ *902/425–5454 Ext. 316* ⊕ *www.ckns.ca*); **Golf Nova Scotia** (⊕ *www.golfnovascotia.com*); **Nova Scotia Golf Association** (☎ *902/468–8844* ⊕ *www.nsga.ns.ca*); **Nova Scotia Trails Federation** (☎ *902/425–5450 Ext. 325* ⊕ *www.novascotiatrails.com*); **Sail Nova Scotia** (☎ *902/425–5450 Ext. 312* ⊕ *www.nsya.ns.ca*); and **Surfing Association of Nova Scotia** (⊕ *www.surfns.com*).

RESTAURANTS

The eating has always been good in Nova Scotia. The ocean's bounty lured the first Europeans across the Atlantic, and seafood remains a prime attraction for visitors today. From Halifax's high-end restaurants to the most casual coastal café, seafood is treated with the utmost respect. Many Nova Scotian chefs are committed to sourcing locally—you only have to visit one farmers' market here to appreciate the range and quality of the ingredients available to them. Generally speaking, eating out is not a stuffy affair in Nova Scotia. Even the finest dining destinations tend to be relatively casual, though you'd likely want to change out of your shorts before entering the swankiest places. One of the classic gastronomic experiences, of course, is to simply don a plastic bib and get to work on a fresh-cooked lobster within sight of the boat that delivered it from the sea. You can also follow the Taste of Nova Scotia Chowder Trail ⊕ *tasteofnovascotia.com/the-chowder-trail/*, featuring 61 places to enjoy a nourishing bowl.

HOTELS

Nova Scotia is famous for its picturesque, historic bed-and-breakfast inns, of which there are many spread across the province's cities, towns, harbors, and countryside. Most B&Bs preserve the heritage and style of the building they occupy but come fully equipped with modern requirements such as Wi-Fi, flat-screen TVs, and updated bathrooms. It's worth doing some research, though, if modern conveniences are important to you—there are a few establishments that really do want to transport you back in time. As for hotels, most major chains have a presence, and every town of any size will have an acceptable motel or two on the outskirts. Nova Scotia is also renowned for the friendly welcome it extends to visitors, and this holds true for all types of accommodations. Far from being a cliché, there is a widespread and genuine desire to please that goes well beyond issuing a routine "have a nice day."

Hotel reviews have been shortened. For full information, visit Fodors.com.

	WHAT IT COSTS IN CANADIAN DOLLARS			
	$	$$	$$$	$$$$
Restaurants	under C$12	C$12–C$20	C$21–C$30	over C$30
Hotels	under C$125	C$125–C$174	C$175–C$250	over C$250

Restaurant prices are per person for a main course at dinner. Hotel prices are for two people in a standard double room in high season, excluding harmonized sales tax (HST).

TOURS

Multiday packaged bus tours to and within Nova Scotia are available through Atlantic Tours.

Atlantic Tours. In addition to multiprovince tours in Atlantic Canada, this company has a three-day trip to Cape Breton and a two-day, one-night South Shore Getaway, taking in Peggy's Cove, Lunenburg, and Mahone Bay. ☎ *902/423–7172, 800/565–7173* ⊕ *www.atlantictours.com* ✉ *From C$511.*

VISITOR INFORMATION

Nova Scotia Tourism. ☎ *902/425–5781, 800/565–0000* ⊕ *www.novascotia.com.*

HALIFAX

1,240 km (770 miles) east of Montréal; 1,137 km (705 miles) northeast of Boston; 275 km (171 miles) southeast of Moncton, New Brunswick

Surrounded by natural treasures and glorious seascapes, Halifax is an attractive and vibrant hub with noteworthy historic and modern architecture, great dining and shopping, and a lively nightlife and festival scene. The old city manages to feel both hip and historic. Previous generations had the foresight to preserve the cultural and architectural integrity of the city, yet students from five local universities keep it lively and current. It's a perfect starting point to any tour of the Atlantic provinces, but even if you don't venture beyond its boundaries, you will get a real taste of the region.

It was Halifax's natural harbor—the second largest in the world after Sydney, Australia's—that first drew the British here in 1749, and today most major sites are conveniently located either along it or on the Citadel-crowned hill overlooking it. That's good news for visitors because this city actually covers quite a bit of ground.

There's easy access to the water, and despite being the focal point of a busy commercial port, Halifax Harbour doubles as a playground, with one of the world's longest downtown boardwalks. It's a place where container ships, commuter ferries, cruise ships, and tour boats compete for space, and where workaday tugs and fishing vessels tie up beside glitzy yachts. Like Halifax as a whole, the harbor represents a blend of the traditional and the contemporary.

GETTING HERE AND AROUND

For those not arriving by air into Halifax's Stanfield International Airport, public transportation to the city is somewhat limited. VIA Rail offers "The Ocean" service from Montréal three times a week. The journey takes 23 hours and 20 minutes, and fares range from C$158.67 for an economy seat to C$1,043 for a double-bedroom suite. Maritime Bus offers service to Halifax from New Brunswick and Prince Edward Island, with stops at a number of places along the Trans-Canada Highway and links from certain major towns not along the Trans-Canada. By car, the Trans-Canada Highway heads south across the New Brunswick border, where it changes from Highway 2 to Highway 104. At Truro, Highway 102 branches off for Halifax.

Halifax is an intimate city that's large enough to have the trappings of a capital, yet compact enough to be explored with ease. Because most sites are comparatively close, walking is a good way to get around. The caveat is that streets connecting the waterfront to Citadel Hill are steep. If you're not prepared for a nine-block uphill hike, take a bus or grab a cab. Metro Transit operates comprehensive bus and ferry services. Fares are C$2.50 per ride or C$20 for 10 tickets. MetroLink ($3) and MetroX (C$3.50) buses, which have limited stops, are designed for commuters. You'll need the exact amount because drivers don't carry change. Transfers are valid for up to 90 minutes and may be used on any route. Taxi rates begin at C$3.20 and increase by C$1.69 per kilometer (from 5% to 10% more if traffic is heavy; extra charges are made for additional passengers and bulky luggage; a crosstown trip should cost from C$7 to C$8, depending on traffic). You can usually hail a taxi downtown or pick one up at a hotel stand. Otherwise, call **Casino Taxi** or **Yellow Cab.**

TOURS

BOAT TOURS **Metro Transit Commuter Ferry.** An affordable alternative to a Murphy's tour is to take the ferry from the boardwalk terminal at Lower Water Street across the harbor to downtown Dartmouth. Inaugurated in 1752, it's North America's oldest saltwater ferry service, and offers a 20-minute ride across the harbor to Dartmouth. ☎ *902/490–4000, 311 within Halifax* ⊕ *www.halifax.ca/transit* ✉ *C$2.50 each way.*

FAMILY **Murphy's The Cable Wharf.** Narrated tours include bus tours throughout Halifax, including their parent company's Gray Line hop-on, hop-off service aboard double-decker buses and trips to outlying communities like Peggy's Cove and Lunenburg. Murphy's also runs the broadest selection of boat tours, sailing various vessels from mid-May to late October, among them a 75-foot ketch and a Mississippi-style sternwheeler. Murphy's even has an amphibious Harbour Hopper for those who want to tour by land and water. If you're traveling with kids, try a Big Harbour tour aboard *Theodore Tugboat*, a seafaring version of Thomas the Tank Engine, and even children unfamiliar with the Canadian character will get a kick out of the tugboat's broad grin and bright red cap. Dinner cruises and party boats are also available, and private charters can be arranged. ✉ *1751 Lower Water St.* ☎ *902/420–1015* ⊕ *www.mtcw.ca* ✉ *From C$19.99 plus fuel surcharge.*

ESSENTIALS

Taxi and Bus Contacts **Casino Taxi.** ✉ *Halifax* ☎ *902/429-6666, 902/425-6666* 🌐 *www.casinotaxi.ns.ca.* **Metro Transit.** ☎ *902/490-4000, 311 within Halifax* 🌐 *www.halifax.ca/transit.* **Yellow Cab.** ✉ *Halifax* ☎ *902/420-0000* 🌐 *yellowcabltd.ca.*

Visitor Information **Halifax Tourism.** ✉ *Halifax* ☎ *902/422-9334, 877/422-9334* 🌐 *www.destinationhalifax.com.* **Visitor Information Centre.** ✉ *Sackville Landing, 1655 Lower Water St.* ☎ *902/424-4248.*

EXPLORING

TOP ATTRACTIONS

Art Gallery of Nova Scotia. In an 1867 Italianate-style building that previously served as a post office, bank, and the headquarters of the Royal Canadian Mounted Police, this provincial art gallery has an extensive permanent collection of more than 17,000 works—so many that there are also two floors of gallery space within the neighboring Provincial Building. Some are primarily of historical interest; others are major works by contemporary Canadian painters like Christopher Pratt, Alex Colville, and Tom Forrestall. The gallery also has a major collection of Annie Leibovitz photographs. The gallery's heart, however, is an internationally recognized collection of maritime folk art by artists such as wood-carver Sydney Howard and painter Joe Norris. The Provincial Building annex also contains the actual home of the late painter Maude Lewis (Canada's answer to Grandma Moses), whose bright, cheery paintings cover the tiny structure inside and out. A guided tour of the collection is given Tuesday through Sunday at 2:30, with an extra one added on Thursday at 7. The gallery's gift shop carries an excellent selection of arts and crafts. ✉ *1723 Hollis St.* ☎ *902/424-5280, 902/424-7542* 🌐 *www.artgalleryofnovascotia.ca* 💲 *C$12; free Thurs. 5–9 pm* ⏲ *Mon.–Sat. 10–5 (to 9 Thurs.), Sun. noon–5.*

FAMILY
Fodor's Choice
★

Canadian Museum of Immigration at Pier 21. Affectionately dubbed "Canada's Front Door," Pier 21 served as the entry point for nearly a million immigrants—refugees, evacuees, war brides, and others—between 1928 and 1971, and in a country where the population has still not reached 36 million, it's a significant number. It's now a national museum, and in honor of the huge contribution that these immigrants have made to Canada, it has been expanded and redesigned. The Canadian Immigration Hall showcases the benefits immigrants have brought to Canada's culture and economy, while other areas cover the history of immigration in general terms and the role Pier 21 played during World War II. A highlight of the museum is the personal stories collected from immigrants, offering insight into their quest for a new life. The Scotiabank Family History Centre is often buzzing with new generations of Canadians discovering their genealogy, while temporary exhibitions highlight issues such as asylum seekers, peace through diversity, and the foreign cultures that continue to enrich Canadian life. The museum also offers a work-experience and mentoring program to help ease newly arrived immigrants into the workplace—your guide might have his or her own personal immigration story to tell. ✉ *1055 Marginal Rd.*

A GOOD WALK

Starting your walk at the **Halifax Citadel National Historic Site** is practical because, as the city's highest point, it puts you on a downhill course. More important, visiting the star-shaped fortress—built in the 1800s as an outpost for the then-expanding British Empire—is like taking a crash course in civic history. After exploring the site, descend the stairs (a more direct route for pedestrians than the road) to the **Town Clock,** which has been keeping time for more than two centuries.

From here, cross Brunswick Street and head down Carmichael, passing the Metro Centre (Halifax's main sporting venue) and the World Trade and Convention Centre en route to the Grand Parade. Once used for military drills, the leafy rectangle is now the setting for summertime picnics and free concerts. Anchoring its right end is **St. Paul's Church** (dating from 1750, it's the country's oldest Protestant church); the Second Empire–style stone building on the left end is **Halifax City Hall.** As you exit the park, Carmichael Street becomes George Street. Follow it two blocks down to Hollis, then make a short detour to see the impressive collection of folk art in the **Art Gallery of Nova Scotia. Province House,** Canada's oldest legislative building, is just across the street and is also open for tours. Walking down another two blocks lands you on Water Street, where you'll find the **Historic Properties,** a cluster of restored warehouses linked by cobblestone lanes, that contain shops and eateries.

If you go straight through, you will reach the **Halifax Waterfront Boardwalk,** which runs all the way to Marginal Road. This is where decision making gets difficult. Depending on your tastes (and budget), you might board a sightseeing boat at **Cable Wharf,** hop the **Metro Transit Commuter Ferry** to the Dartmouth side of the harbor, take in the action from a waterfront restaurant, or simply ogle the tugboats and transatlantic yachts that often tie up here. Whatever you choose, be sure to leave time for the **Maritime Museum of the Atlantic,** where you can learn about Nova Scotia's seafaring past. A final stop lies to the south, just off the boardwalk: the Port of Halifax seawall development, which includes the cruise ship terminal, the **Halifax Seaport Farmers' Market,** and **Pier 21,** a former immigration depot that now houses the **Canadian Museum of Immigration.** You could spend several hours at Pier 21 alone, so if you're staying in the city longer, save this for another day. Instead, cap your walking tour with a libation in a local pub. Halifax is said to have more pubs per capita than anywhere else in Canada.

☎ *902/425–7770, 855/526–4721* ⊕ *www.pier21.ca* ✉ *C$10* ⏲ *Early May–end Oct., daily 9:30–5:30; Nov., Tues.–Sat. 9:30–5; Dec.–Mar., Tues.–Sat. 10–5; Apr., Mon.–Sat. 10–5.*

FAMILY Fodor's Choice ★ **Halifax Citadel National Historic Site.** You can't miss the Citadel, literally or figuratively. Erected between 1826 and 1856 on Halifax's highest hill, it still dominates the skyline and, as Canada's most-visited National Historic Site, remains a magnet for tourists. The present Citadel, with its dry moat and stone ramparts, was the fourth defensive structure to be built

Alexander Keith's Nova Scotia Brewery **13**
Anna Leonowens Gallery **10**
Art Gallery of Nova Scotia **7**
Canadian Museum of Immigration at Pier 21 ..... **19**
Deadman's Island **4**
Discovery Centre **16**
Fairview Lawn Cemetery **5**
Government House **14**
Halifax Citadel National Historic Site **3**
Halifax Public Gardens **1**
Halifax Seaport Farmers' Market **17**
Halifax Waterfront Broardwalk **6**
Historic Properties **11**
Maritime Museum of the Atlantic **12**
Mary E. Black Gallery **18**
Nova Scotia Museum of Natural History **2**
Point Pleasant Park **15**
Province House ..**9**
St. Paul's Anglican Church **8**

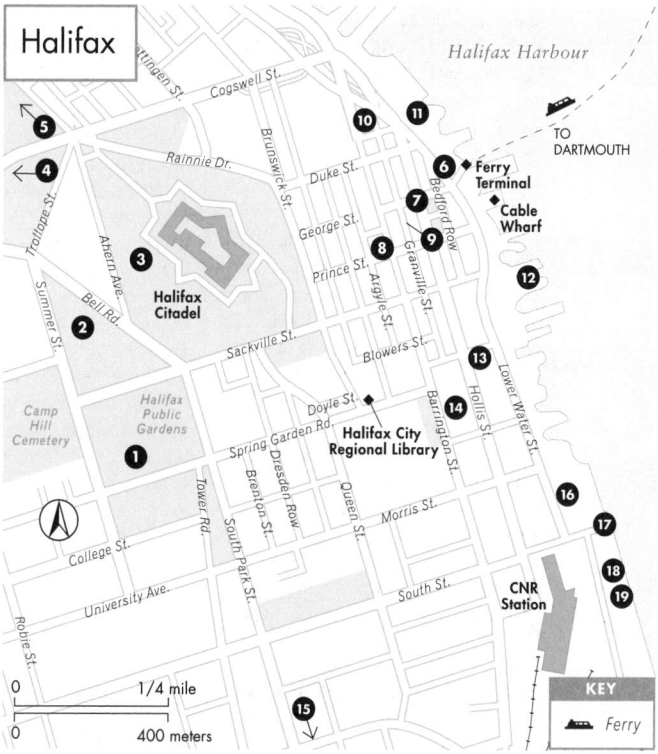

on the site, and formerly was linked to smaller forts and gun emplacements on the harbor islands and the bluffs above the harbor entrance. A multimedia presentation that runs every 15 minutes recounts this story. You can visit the barracks, guardroom, and powder magazine before heading for the parade ground to watch reenactors, sporting kilts and tall feather "bonnets," practice their drills. If you book ahead, you can participate in full uniform in the "Soldier for a Day" program (C$199), which for adults includes learning how to handle and fire a weapon. Tours that help bring the history of both the fort and the city to life take place throughout the day in high season, but the best time to visit is just before noon when the Noon Gun is fired—a tradition since 1857. The Citadel is also home to the **Army Museum**, with excellent exhibits and a War Art Gallery. Before leaving the Citadel, pause to enjoy the view. In front of you are the spiky downtown buildings, crowded between the hilltop and the harbor; the wooded islands at the harbor's mouth; and the naval dockyard. Behind you is the 235-acre Halifax Common with its ball fields, tennis courts, playground, skateboard park, and open green. Worried about losing track of time while touring? Don't be. Simply keep an eye on Citadel Hill's **Town Clock.** Given to Halifax by Prince Edward, Duke of Kent (the military commander here from 1794 to 1800), it has ticked in its octagonal tower for more than 200 years. ✉ *Citadel Hill, 5425 Sackville St.* ☎ *902/426–5080* *www.pc.gc.ca June–mid-Sept. C$11.70; May and mid-Sept.–Oct. C$7.80; rest of year free (grounds only); on-site parking C$3.15 per visit Early May–June, Sept., and Oct., daily 9–5; July and Aug., daily 9–6; Nov.–early May grounds and washrooms daily 9–5.*

FAMILY Fodor's Choice ★ **Halifax Waterfront Boardwalk.** Running from Casino Nova Scotia to Pier 21, this photogenic 3-km (2-mile) footpath offers backdoor access to the Historic Properties and the Marine Museum of the Atlantic. Newer landmarks such as **Purdy's Wharf** (site of Halifax's two grandest skyscrapers) and **Bishop's Landing** (an attractive complex with condos and shops) are on the route; while others, including the Seaport Farmers' Market, Pier 21, and the cruise-ship terminal, are only a few minutes' walk away. The boardwalk has multiple entry points and many tourist-friendly amenities. Shops and restaurants line the section between Sackville Landing and the Historic Properties, and in peak season, bagpipers, ice-cream peddlers, and street performers do, too. The water, however, remains the real attraction. To get out on it, take one of the many boat tours that depart from the boardwalk's Cable Wharf. *Halifax.*

HALIFAX AND THE *TITANIC*

When the *Titanic* sank in 1912, Halifax became, in a sense, the fabled ship's final destination. Being the closest major port, it was the base for rescue and recovery operations, and 150 victims were ultimately buried in city cemeteries. Emergency-response skills honed in the aftermath of the sinking were put to use five years later when tragedy struck again. In December 1917, two ships collided in Halifax Harbour, one of them loaded with explosives. The event sparked the greatest man-made explosion before Hiroshima, leveling 2 square miles of the city and claiming nearly 2,000 lives.

Historic Properties. This series of restored waterfront warehouses dates from the days of yore, when trade and war made Halifax prosperous. They were built by such raffish characters as Enos Collins, a privateer, smuggler, and shipper whose vessels defied Napoléon's blockade to bring American supplies to the Duke of Wellington. The buildings have since been taken over by shops, offices, restaurants, and pubs including those in Privateer's Warehouse. Seven of them, all erected between the late 18th and early 19th century, have been designated as National Historic Sites. *1869 Upper Water St. 902/429–0530 www.historicproperties.ca.*

FAMILY **Maritime Museum of the Atlantic.** The exhibits in this waterfront museum, housed partly in a restored chandlery, include small boats once used around the coast, as well as displays describing Nova Scotia's proud sailing heritage. The most memorable ones, though, are devoted to the *Titanic* and the Halifax Explosion. The former has 20-odd artifacts, including the ship's only surviving deck chair. Also on display are a section of wall paneling, a balustrade molding and part of a newel from the dual curving staircase, a mortuary bag, and the log kept by a wireless operator in Newfoundland on the night the ship sank. In the explosion exhibit, "Halifax Wrecked," newspaper accounts and quotes from survivors are poignantly paired with everyday objects recovered from the rubble, among them a schoolboy's book bag and a broken pocket watch that will forever record the time of impact.

Other exhibits cover the Canadian Navy, sailing ships, small craft, the Age of Steam, and shipwrecks, and the museum has outdoor attractions, too. On the boardwalk right behind it is a ship-shaped children's playground and, steps away at the wharf, you'll see the hydrographic steamer CSS *Acadia*. After a long life of charting the coasts of Labrador and the Arctic, she's now permanently moored and museum-ticket holders can board her for tours from May through September. ✉ *1675 Lower Water St.* ☎ *902/424–7490* 🌐 *maritimemuseum.novascotia.ca* 💲 *May–Oct. C$9.55; Nov.–Apr. C$5.15* ⏲ *May–Oct., daily 9:30–5:30 (to 8 pm Tues.; Sun. 1–5 in May); Nov.–Apr., Tues. 9:30–8, Wed.–Sat. 9:30–5, Sun. 1–5.*

WORTH NOTING

Alexander Keith's Nova Scotia Brewery. Although Alexander Keith served three terms as mayor of Halifax, his political achievements are overshadowed by another accomplishment: he was colonial Nova Scotia's first certified brewmaster. Today, the popular beer is brewed in several modern facilities across Canada, but you can visit the original 1820 brewery building, a local landmark. On hour-long tours you can see how Keith's India Pale Ale was originally made, then sample a pint or two in the Stag's Head Tavern. (Nonalcoholic beverages are also available.) Actors in period outfits provide the explanations as well as old-fashioned maritime entertainment. Tours run every half hour. ✉ *Brewery Market, 1496 Lower Water St.* ☎ *902/455–1474, 877/612–1820* 🌐 *keiths.ca* 💲 *C$24.95* ⏲ *June–Oct., Mon.–Sat. noon–7:30, Sun. noon–5; Nov.–May, Fri. 4–7:30, Sat. noon–7:30, Sun. noon–5.*

Anna Leonowens Gallery. Victorian wunderkind Anna Leonowens is famous for the time she spent as a royal governess in Thailand (then Siam), which inspired Rodgers and Hammerstein's musical *The King and I*. But she also spent two decades in Halifax, where she founded the Nova Scotia College of Art and Design; it later returned the favor by opening the Anna Leonowens Gallery. Its three exhibition spaces, which focus on contemporary studio and media art, serve as a showcase for the college faculty and students. The gallery mounts about 125 exhibitions a year. ✉ *1891 Granville St.* ☎ *902/494–8223* 🌐 *www.nscad.ca* 💲 *Free* ⏲ *Tues.–Fri. 11–5, Sat. noon–4.*

OFF THE BEATEN PATH

Deadman's Island. This tiny spit is the final resting place of almost 200 American prisoners of war who died while imprisoned in Halifax during the War of 1812. The U.S. Department of Veterans Affairs unveiled a memorial in 2005 to honor the men, who died of communicable diseases such as smallpox and were buried in mass graves. Over time, the island has become naturally linked to the mainland, so you can walk to it without getting your feet wet. ✉ *Halifax* ✣ *6 km (4 miles) west of downtown. On Purcells Cove Rd. near Melville Cove, look for the Deadman's Island sign at Pinehaven Dr.* 💲 *Free* ⏲ *Always accessible.*

FAMILY

Discovery Centre. Halifax's interactive science center is an exciting place for children, and keeps many a parent enthralled, too, with exhibits like "Build Your Own Coaster," explaining the laws of physics and engineering, a life-sized suspension bridge with detachable cables, a LEGO Building Centre, The Bubble Room, with all kinds of ways to learn about viscosity, and plenty more. Donations have been pouring in to the center and as a result, its splendid new location on the waterfront is set to open in late 2016, and will include Atlantic Canada's first immersive Dome Theatre. ✉ *1593 Barrington St.* ☎ *902/492–4422* 🌐 *thediscoverycentre.ca* 💲 *C$10* ⏲ *Daily 10–5 (to 8 Wed.).*

OFF THE BEATEN PATH

Fairview Lawn Cemetery. This cemetery is the final resting place of 121 victims of the *Titanic*. The graves are easily found, in a graceful arc of granite tombstones. One—marked J. Dawson—attracts particular attention from visitors. Alas, it's not the fictional artist played by Leonardo DiCaprio in the 1998 film, but James Dawson, a coal trimmer from Ireland. Nineteen other victims are buried in Mount Olivet Catholic Cemetery and 10 in the Baron de Hirsch Jewish Cemetery. The Maritime Museum of the Atlantic has an exhibit about the disaster. Fairview Lawn also includes many graves of victims of the Halifax Explosion. ✉ *3720 Windsor St., 3 km (2 miles) northwest of downtown.*

FAMILY

Halifax Public Gardens. One of the oldest formal Victorian gardens in North America, this city oasis had its start in 1753 as a private garden. Its layout was completed in 1875 by Richard Power, former gardener to the Duke of Devonshire in Ireland. Gravel paths wind among ponds, trees, and flower beds, revealing an astonishing variety of plants from all over the world. The centerpiece is an ornate gazebo-like band shell, erected in 1887 for Queen Victoria's Golden Jubilee, where free Sunday afternoon concerts take place at 2 from mid-June through mid-September. There's a café in the gardens and twice-weekly story time for children. The gardens are closed in winter, but you can still enjoy a pleasant stroll along the perimeter. ✉ *Bounded by Sackville, Summer, and S. Park Sts. and Spring Garden Rd.* 🌐 *www.halifaxpublicgardens.ca* 💲 *Free* ⏲ *Apr.–Nov. (depending on weather), daily 8 am–dusk.*

Halifax Seaport Farmers' Market. Green in more ways than one, this waterfront market that hosts more than 200 local farmers, food producers, and artisans is one of Canada's most eco-friendly buildings. Noteworthy features include wind turbines, solar-energy and water-conservation systems, and a "biowall" that allows natural ventilation. There's a wonderful array of fresh produce and crafts, and the international backgrounds of many vendors make it particularly interesting, with some unique offerings. Sampling and shopping opportunities abound, though aside from Saturday not every vendor is out in force (unless a cruise ship is in). Don't confuse this venue with Brewery Square's Historic Farmers' Market, whose vendors didn't want to move here. Both claim to be the country's oldest farmers' market—and in a way, they both are. ✉ *1209 Marginal Rd.* ☎ *902/492–4043* 🌐 *www.halifaxfarmersmarket.com* ⏲ *Weekdays 10–5, Sat. 7–3, Sun. 9–3.*

Mary E. Black Gallery. Between Pier 21 and the Seaport Farmers' Market, the exhibit space of the Nova Scotia Centre for Craft and Design, home of the Mary E. Black Gallery, presents shows of pottery, jewelry, textiles, metalwork, and other innovative, high-end crafts. The center also holds classes, including one- and two-day workshops, from fall through spring. ✉ *1061 Marginal Rd., Suite 140* ☎ *902/492–2522* 🌐 *www.craftdesign.ns.ca* 💲 *Gallery free; workshops individually priced* ⏲ *Tues.–Fri. 9–5, weekends 11–4.*

FAMILY **Nova Scotia Museum of Natural History.** This is the place to learn about fossils and dinosaurs, as well as the flora and fauna prevalent in Nova Scotia today. The Nature Centre is home to live snakes, frogs, insects, and other creatures. The museum also hosts major traveling exhibits as well as nature talks, walks, and workshops that appeal to all interests and ages. ✉ *1747 Summer St.* ☎ *902/424–7353* 🌐 *naturalhistory.novascotia.ca* 💲 *C$6.30* ⏲ *Mid-May–Oct., daily 9–5 (to 8 Wed.); Nov.–mid-May Tues.–Sun. 9–5 (to 8 Wed.; also Mon. 9–5 during March Break).*

FAMILY **Point Pleasant Park.** Most of the city's former fortifications have been turned into public parks, including this one. The park encompasses 186 wooded acres on a headland south of downtown with walking trails and seafront paths. The major military installation here is a massive round tower dating from the late 18th century, but the greatest threat the park ever faced came from Mother Nature. In September 2003, Hurricane Juan tore through, uprooting or damaging 75,000 trees (about 75% of the park's total) in a matter of hours, in the process leaving present-day parkgoers the same harbor views that must have inspired its use as a military command post in the first place. Having been nurtured since the storm, Point Pleasant is again immensely popular with strollers, joggers, and dog walkers. The perfect vantage point from which to watch ships entering the harbor, in summer it's the site of Shakespeare by the Sea performances. ✉ *5718 Point Pleasant Dr.* ☎ *902/490–4700* 🌐 *www.pointpleasantpark.ca* 💲 *Free* ⏲ *Daily 6 am–midnight (parking lots close earlier).*

Province House. Charles Dickens proclaimed this structure, now a National Historic Site, "a gem of Georgian architecture." Erected in 1819 to house Britain's first overseas self-government, the sandstone building still serves as the meeting place for the provincial legislature. The politicos' proceedings are notoriously dull, but the free tours of the building yield many interesting tidbits. ✉ *1726 Hollis St.* ☎ *902/424–5982* 🌐 *www.nslegislature.ca* 💲 *Free* ⏲ *July and Aug., weekdays 9–5, weekends and holidays 10–4; Sept.–June weekdays 9–4.*

St. Paul's Anglican Church. Opened in 1750, this is Canada's oldest Protestant church and the burial site of many colonial notables. It played a pivotal role during the 1917 Halifax Explosion, as the vestry was used as a makeshift hospital. Evidence of the damage done to the building can be seen in the still-broken Explosion Window and debris embedded above the Memorial Doors. Designated as a National Historic Site, St. Paul's remains an active church. A pew is always reserved for Queen Elizabeth at Sunday morning services, and other out-of-town worshippers are welcome as well. ✉ *1749 Argyle St., on the Grand Parade* ☎ *902/429–2240* 🌐 *www.stpaulshalifax.org* ⏲ *June–Aug., Mon.–Sat. 9–4:30; Sept.–May, weekdays 9–4:30. Guided tours: weekdays 10:30–3. Services: June–Aug., Wed. at 11 and Sun. at 10; Sept.–May, Sun. at 9 and 11.*

BEACHES

FAMILY **Rainbow Haven Beach Provincial Park.** For ocean swimming, this sand and cobble beach is the closest serviced option to Halifax, but avoid the area near the channel when the tide is going out because strong rip currents make this section hazardous. Lifeguards, on duty in July and August, set out markers to indicate the dangerous areas. Elsewhere, Rainbow Haven is safe and great for families. The beach is free for day use, and there is a campground (fee) with its own swimming area. Change houses are available, and boardwalks aid accessibility. The beach's access road closes at 8 pm, so plan your time accordingly. **Amenities:** food and drink; lifeguards; parking (free); showers; toilets. **Best for:** swimming; walking. ✉ *2248 Cow Bay Rd., Cole Harbour* ✣ *Off Bissett Rd., 8 km (5 miles) east of Cow Bay* ⊕ *www.novascotiaparks.ca.*

WHERE TO EAT

$$$ INTERNATIONAL ✕ **The Bicycle Thief.** Chic, casual, and hugely popular (with good reason), this place has a patio right on the waterfront—on the landward side look for the old bicycles parked outside. The lengthy menu slants Italian, incorporating the finest Nova Scotian ingredients. You could start with local mussels or a generous salami board, then shift into "2nd Gear" with authentic minestrone, a lobster and fish chowder, or one of the handmade pasta dishes. "High Gear" choices might include pistachio honey-crusted Atlantic salmon, rack of lamb chops with minted summer pea couscous, or fall-off-the-bone ribs. The lunch menu is equally interesting and more modestly priced. $ *Average main: C$28* ✉ *Bishop's Landing, 1475 Lower Water St.* ☎ *902/425–7993* ⊕ *bicyclethief.ca* ⊘ *Closed Sun.*

$$$ ECLECTIC ✕ **Chives Canadian Bistro.** "Canadian" cuisine is broadly defined here (French, German, and Asian influences are all evident), but there is no mistaking the provenance of chef and cookbook author Craig Flinn's ingredients, which are fresh and local. The menu adapts to whatever is available at the fishmongers' and farmers' markets, but each meal begins with Chives's signature buttermilk biscuits—and each *should* end with maple crème brûlée. In between, enjoy starters such as yellowfin tuna tartar, warm summer kale salad, or Jamo's perogies, then make the difficult choice between dishes like braised beef Wellington, grilled Digby scallops, or the N.S. Heritage Pork cut of the day. Each dish on the menu has wine suggestions, and gluten-free and vegetarian options are available. $ *Average main: C$24* ✉ *1537 Barrington St.* ☎ *902/420–9626* ⊕ *www.chives.ca* ⊘ *No lunch.*

$$$$ ITALIAN ✕ **Da Maurizio.** This Northern Italian restaurant is a classic big-night-out choice. Subdued lighting, elegant furnishings, fresh flowers: all the details have been attended to, and ditto the food, which is impressive and satisfying. Excellent seared foie gras is always on the menu, as is veal scaloppine sautéed with lobster and topped with a creamy garlic-and-cognac sauce. Prices on the specialty wine list go as high as C$600, but there are also fine bottles for under C$50. $ *Average main: C$32* ✉ *1496 Lower Water St.* ☎ *902/423–0859* ⊕ *damaurizio.ca* ⊘ *Closed Sun. No lunch.*

CLOSE UP

Local Flavors

Nova Scotia's verdant landscapes and churning seas provide a feast for the eyes and one for the table as well. Residents contend that the best meals are made using local ingredients—Lunenburg lobster, Digby scallops, Atlantic salmon, Annapolis Valley apples—and generations-old recipes. If you're serious about discovering down-home favorites, seek out dishes with curious names like Hodge Podge (a summer staple of beans, peas, carrots, and baby potatoes, cooked in cream), Solomon Gundy (a pickled-herring pâté), *rappie* pie (a hearty stew, usually of chicken, with dried, shredded potatoes), and blueberry grunt (a steamed pudding made with Nova Scotia's finest berries). For more sophisticated fare, check out the fine-dining establishments in Halifax and the southern part of the province that put their own spins on Nova Scotian classics, preparing time-honored dishes with contemporary flair. The province's annual free *Taste of Nova Scotia: Culinary Adventure Guide* (🌐 *www.tasteofnovascotia.com*) will help you find them. A companion Adventures in Taste app is also available, free, at 🌐 *adventuresintaste.ca*.

For local libations, try a beer (or two) from the growing number of microbreweries. The Craft Brewers Association of Nova Scotia 🌐 *nscraftbeer.ca* currently lists 19, including brewpubs, and six of them are in Halifax: Propeller, Rogue's Roost, Rockbottom, Garrison, North Brewing Company, and Granite. The rest are evenly spaced across the province, and all draw on the history of the region and produce distinctive ales, lagers, stouts, and other brews. Local wines are gaining in popularity and reputation as well. Try Jost from Malagash, Sainte Famille Winery from Falmouth, and Domaine de Grand Pré near Wolfville. The Winery Association of Nova Scotia 🌐 *winesofnovascotia.ca* is a good source of information. And what better way to cap a Nova Scotian dinner than with a dram of the acclaimed Glen Breton 🌐 *www.glenoradistillery.com*, North America's original single-malt whiskey. (Nova Scotia may mean "New Scotland," but you still can't call it "Scotch" unless it's actually produced in Scotland.) In Gaelic, they call single malt *Uisge beatha* ("the water of life"): sip some Glen Breton, and you'll know why.

$$$$ SEAFOOD ✕ **Five Fishermen.** Installed in a heritage building across from the Grand Parade, this restaurant is splurge-worthy. Tables are backlit through a wall of stained glass, and the seafood is so good locals keep coming back. Main courses are pricey but each comes with complimentary salad and mussels. For more modest, less pricey fare, head to the Five Fishermen Grill, downstairs from the main restaurant. Also open for lunch, it has an Oyster Happy Hour from 4 to 6:30 daily. Valet parking is available after 5 pm. $ *Average main: C$32* ✉ *1740 Argyle St.* ☎ *902/422-4421* 🌐 *www.fivefishermen.com* ⏲ *No lunch.*

$$ CANADIAN ✕ **The Foggy Goggle.** They call it "comfort food with attitude" and it's certainly struck a chord with locals and visitors, who flock to this bar to fill up on dishes like lobster mac and cheese, ribs roasted in root beer, and Foggy Spuds (roasted potatoes with chopped bacon, corn, and red onion, sautéed in a rich cream sauce and topped with cheese). There are lighter choices, too: soups, sandwiches, wraps, seafood, and vegetarian options such as "Meet" loaf. Ten beers on tap, innovative cocktails, and a kitchen that's open until 2 am on Friday and Saturday round out the appeal. $ *Average main: C$13* ✉ *1667 Argyle St.* ☎ *902/444–1414* ⊕ *thefoggygoggle.ca.*

$$ BRITISH ✕ **The Henry House.** Haligonian brewers uphold beer-making traditions dating back to 1754, and you can sample the results at this pub in what was once the house of William Alexander Henry, a prominent Canadian politician. The Henry House serves five unpasteurized English-style ales crafted by Halifax's own Granite Brewery, plus special blends like Black Velvet (though cider is mixed with the stout here, rather than the usual champagne). The food is impressive, too—especially the fishcakes and homemade bread pudding. Best of all, the kitchen stays open late (until midnight from Thursday through Saturday, and until 10 on other nights). In winter fireplaces keep the ironstone building toasty, and in summer a tiered patio provides both access to the afternoon sun and shelter from the wind. $ *Average main: C$15* ✉ *1222 Barrington St.* ☎ *902/423–5660* ⊕ *www.henryhouse.ca.*

$$ CANADIAN ✕ **Lower Deck.** History surrounds you in Privateer's Warehouse, where two eateries share old stone walls and hand-hewn beams as well as a few menu items such as chicken-and-ribs or fish-and-chips. The main-floor pub sticks to pub grub, which is served at long trestle tables; the patrons here consider ale an entrée, so order a Keith's and join the fun. Holler "Sociable!" occasionally, and you'll be mistaken for a native in no time. The second-floor Beer Market is less casual and includes more refined dishes on the menu. The Lower Deck has nightly live music, including various festival events. There's another branch in Clayton Park. $ *Average main: C$15* ✉ *Historic Properties, 1869 Upper Water St.* ☎ *902/425–1501* ⊕ *www.lowerdeck.ca.*

$$$$ SEAFOOD ✕ **McKelvie's.** In a handsome 1906 firehouse across from the Maritime Museum of the Atlantic, McKelvie's is that rare find that hits the sweet spot between upmarket and down-home. Though all the menu mainstays are here, from oysters Rockefeller to surf and turf, the best bets are the contemporary twists on seafood classics, among them Caribbean-inspired calamari, lobster pot stickers, and Thai shrimp pasta. Although the restaurant has been in business for more than 25 years, its look is as fresh as the ingredients used here, and the service is always friendly. $ *Average main: C$32* ✉ *1680 Lower Water St.* ☎ *902/421–6161* ⊕ *www.mckelvies.com* ⏲ *No lunch weekends.*

$$ CONTEMPORARY ✕ **Morris East.** Casually cool, yet somehow warm and intimate, Morris East stakes its reputation on locally sourced artisanal ingredients, many of them fresh from the Halifax Seaport Farmers' Market a few blocks away. Gourmet wood-fired pizzas, topped with the region's best veggies, cheeses, and charcuterie and cooked using Annapolis Valley applewood, are the house specialty. Libations have local flavor, too: spirits handcrafted in the province go into the artisanal cocktails made here. There's a short wine list (six whites, seven reds, one rosé), or you can bring your own (corkage C$15 per bottle). There's a second location in New Bedford. $ *Average main: C$17* ✉ *5212 Morris St.* ☎ *902/444–7663* ⊕ *www.morriseast.com* ✍ *Reservations not accepted.*

$$$$ CANADIAN Fodor's Choice ★ **The Press Gang.** Easily one of the city's hippest upscale establishments, the Press Gang prepares fish and meat with equal panache. You can start with crab dumplings or oysters on the half shell, complemented by a glass of Muscadet from the well-stocked cellar, then tuck into pan-seared halibut and prawns with littleneck clam beurre blanc, or grilled beef tenderloin with a beet-and-red-onion confit. Or simply let the chef present his four-course tasting menu (C$160 for two). Thick, cold stone walls testify to the building's era (1759), but comfy seating and intimate lighting soften the effect. A trio plays classic rock, Motown, and New Orleans jazz on Friday and Saturday nights. *Average main: C$36 5218 Prince St. 902/423–8816 thepressgang.net No lunch.*

$$$ SEAFOOD **Salty's.** Overlooking Privateer's Wharf and the rest of the harbor, this restaurant wins the prize for best location in Halifax. Steaming bowls of shellfish stew and curried scallops crown a menu that is sure to satisfy any seafood lover, though there are also meat and pasta options. Request a table with a window view and save room for the house dessert, Cadix (chocolate mousse over a praline crust). There is a less expensive Bar & Grill on the ground level. Salty's serves meals outside on the wharf in summer, but be warned: it can be very windy. *Average main: C$29 Historic Properties, 1869 Upper Water St. 902/423–6818 www.saltys.ca No upstairs lunch on weekday holidays, but Bar & Grill is open.*

$$$$ CANADIAN Fodor's Choice ★ **Stories.** In the elegant dining room of the historic Haliburton Hotel, exquisitely set tables set the scene for a sophisticated meal, which might start with carpaccio of bison tenderloin with pickled winter vegetables, or scallops with ginger sesame vinaigrette. Main courses might feature grilled harpoon swordfish with saffron tomato fennel butter or roast duck magret with bourbon-mashed sweet potato, black cherry, and ancho. Needless to say, desserts are divine—try the raspberry, blackberry, and brown-butter tart with cassis ice cream. It's a perfect place for a special-occasion dinner, or just to make an ordinary day special. *Average main: C$33 Haliburton Hotel, 5184 Morris St. 902/444–4400 www.storiesdining.com No lunch.*

$$$ ECLECTIC **The Wooden Monkey.** This fun, funky spot attracts health-conscious diners with its macrobiotic and organic food, locally brewed beer and wines, and fair-trade coffee. Aside from being good for you, though, the food here is also just plain good. Menu mainstays (the vegan dumplings, lentil-based veggie burger, free-range ginger beef, and chocolate tofu pie) are bound to win over skeptics. The menu includes coding for those who may need to know about vegan and gluten-free options, dairy, raw items, and nuts, and there are a few dishes for kids. There's a second location on the Dartmouth waterfront. *Average main: C$25 1707 Grafton St. 902/444–3844 www.thewoodenmonkey.ca.*

WHERE TO STAY

$$ HOTEL FAMILY **Cambridge Suites Halifax.** Homey comforts are a big selling point at this property, and the location—five blocks from the waterfront and one from the Spring Garden Road shopping district—is convenient. **Pros:** Continental breakfast included; harbor views from some suites and the rooftop deck. **Cons:** hard walk uphill from waterfront *steep*;

some rooms billed as suites don't have separate sleeping areas. $ *Rooms from: C$159* ✉ *1583 Brunswick St.* ☎ *902/420–0555, 800/565–1263* 🌐 *www.cambridgesuiteshalifax.com* ▭ *No credit cards* 🛏 *115 rooms, 85 suites* 🍴 *Breakfast.*

$$ HOTEL FAMILY **Chocolate Lake Hotel.** A lakeside location, superfriendly staff, and range of room types make this Best Western Plus hotel a good alternative to downtown lodgings, and it's less than 5 km (3 miles) from the heart of the city. **Pros:** right on Chocolate Lake, with water access; some drive-up rooms. **Cons:** far from downtown; breakfast buffet area is a bit cramped. $ *Rooms from: C$159* ✉ *250 St. Margaret's Bay Rd.* ☎ *902/477–5611, 800/780–7234 reservations* 🌐 *chocolatelakehotel.com* 🛏 *133 rooms, 9 suites.*

$$ HOTEL FAMILY **Delta Halifax.** Though the Delta Halifax is a business-class hotel with spacious, attractive rooms, many vacationers choose it specifically for the water views: 126 rooms offer "premium" views and 80 have balconies. **Pros:** pleasant pool area; good setting for walkers; kids six and under eat free. **Cons:** awkward location for drivers; add-ons for phone calls, parking, and other amenities add up. $ *Rooms from: C$159* ✉ *1990 Barrington St.* ☎ *902/425–6700, 888/890–3222* 🌐 *www.deltahotels.com* 🛏 *281 rooms, 15 suites* 🍴 *No meals.*

$$$ HOTEL **Halifax Marriott Harbourfront.** Built low to match the neighboring ironstone buildings, this waterfront hotel is convenient to the Historic Properties and the boardwalk. **Pros:** only hotel right on the harbor; deals and value-added packages available. **Cons:** parking is pricey; some rooms could use upgrading. $ *Rooms from: C$195* ✉ *1919 Upper Water St.* ☎ *902/421–1700, 800/943–6760* 🌐 *www.marriott.com* 🛏 *333 rooms, 19 suites* 🍴 *No meals.*

$$ HOTEL **The Halliburton.** Three early-19th-century town houses were cleverly combined to create Halifax's original boutique hotel, a couple of blocks from the waterfront and Spring Garden Road shopping. **Pros:** location means there's no climb uphill at the end of the day; quality linens; Continental breakfast included. **Cons:** some parking is a block away; some rooms far from reception; no elevator. $ *Rooms from: C$159* ✉ *5184 Morris St.* ☎ *902/420–0658, 888/512–3344* 🌐 *www.thehalliburton.com* 🛏 *25 rooms, 4 suites* 🍴 *Breakfast.*

$$$ HOTEL **Prince George Hotel.** A complete renovation has brought this fine hotel bang up to date, with a huge gleaming lobby and open-aspect sitting areas with some fun features, like a giant chair and modern art. **Pros:** good-value packages often available; upgraded bathrooms; lots of restaurants and bars in surrounding streets. **Cons:** parking garage can be confusing; breakfast and parking not always included (and pricey); steep climb up from the waterfront. $ *Rooms from: C$229* ✉ *1725 Market St.* ☎ *902/425–1986, 800/565–1567* 🌐 *www.princegeorgehotel.com* 🛏 *186 rooms, 15 suites* 🍴 *No meals.*

$$ B&B/INN **Waverley Inn.** Like Oscar Wilde and P. T. Barnum, two of its former guests, the Waverley is best described as theatrical. **Pros:** an urban-inn experience; has loads of character; on-site parking. **Cons:** "traditional" category rooms are small; front rooms get street noise. $ *Rooms from: C$135* ✉ *1266 Barrington St.* ☎ *902/423–9346, 800/565–9346* 🌐 *www.waverleyinn.com* 🛏 *34 rooms* 🍴 *Breakfast.*

$$ HOTEL FAMILY **Westin Nova Scotian.** This imposing 1930s hotel sits beside the train station, with the cruise ship harbor behind and Cornwallis Park in front, and though it provides top-notch business services, it also has a resort-y feel. **Pros:** half the rooms have harbor views; free downtown shuttle on weekdays; front and back parking lots. **Cons:** on southern edge of the action; some bathrooms are cramped. *Rooms from: C$159 ✉ 1181 Hollis St. ☎ 902/421–1000, 888/679–3784 🌐 www.thewestinnovascotian.com 310 rooms No meals.*

NIGHTLIFE AND PERFORMING ARTS

There are up-to-date entertainment listings in the *Coast* (Halifax's free alternative newspaper); you can also log on to 🌐 *www.thecoast.ca.*

NIGHTLIFE

BARS AND MUSIC CLUBS

Bearly's House of Blues and Ribs. This dimly lit tavern's name gives music and food equal billing, but the outstanding blues artists the place books makes clear where its loyalty lies. You can catch an act every day, with bands on Tuesday and Thursday to Saturday; a country jam on Monday, stand-up comedy followed by killer karaoke on Wednesday, and a Sunday matinee from 4 to 7:30, followed by a blues jam. Cover charge, when there is one, is usually C$4 or C$5. ✉ *1269 Barrington St.* ☎ *902/423–2526* 🌐 *www.bearlys.ca.*

Old Triangle. A traditional Irish alehouse, the Old Triangle reels in patrons with better-than-average pub food and pints of Guinness, then keeps them fixated with live Celtic music on most nights. Traditional open sessions take place on Sunday afternoons and Tuesday evenings. ✉ *5136 Prince St.* ☎ *902/492–4900* 🌐 *www.oldtriangle.com.*

Seahorse Tavern. Now in a great new location, with the Marquee Ballroom upstairs, the Seahorse continues to draw an eclectic indie crowd for late-night music. The two spaces showcase the very best in local, national, and international music. Cover charge is usually around C$7 to C$10, but some nights are free. ✉ *2037 Gottingen St.* ☎ *902/423–7200* 🌐 *www.theseahorsetavern.ca.*

The Split Crow. Halifax's oldest watering hole (its earliest incarnation opened in 1749) has an old-time ambience and a full menu heavy on finger foods and deep-fried seafood. Nevertheless, it's the beer/band combination—mostly classic rockers, nightly and on Saturday afternoons—that accounts for the bar's enduring popularity. ✉ *1855 Granville St.* ☎ *902/422–4366* 🌐 *www.splitcrow.com.*

CASINOS

Casino Nova Scotia. Right on the waterfront, the casino has a full range of gaming tables and hundreds of slots, and is open around the clock in summer. There's entertainment, too, mostly provided by tribute bands and C-listers on their way up—or down. Patrons must be 19 or older. ✉ *1983 Upper Water St.* ☎ *902/425–7777, 888/642–6376* 🌐 *www.casinonovascotia.com.*

DANCE CLUBS

Reflections Cabaret. Consider this an *alternative* alternative. Though it started out as a gay hangout, Reflections is better described as a "no labels, everyone welcome" bar. Drag queens mingle with throngs of university students who hit the strobe-lit dance floor, and there are live acts, comedy, and drag shows, too. ✉ *5187 Sackville St.* ☎ *902/422–2957* ⏲ *Mon. 10 pm–2:30 am, Thurs.–Sat. 10 pm–4 am, with special events some Sun., Tues., and Wed.*

PERFORMING ARTS

CONCERTS

Dalhousie Arts Centre. The Rebecca Cohn Auditorium at Dalhousie University's Arts Centre hosts a full program of performances, including touring national and international entertainers—recent shows have ranged from Dweezil Zappa to Loreena McKennit to Billy Connolly—and opera and classical concerts featuring Symphony Nova Scotia. ✉ *6101 University Ave.* ☎ *902/494–3820, 800/874–1669.*

THEATER

FAMILY **Grafton Street Dinner Theatre.** Performances are staged here from two to six times weekly, depending on the season, and the lighthearted fun begins when you arrive in the lounge. ✉ *1741 Grafton St.* ☎ *902/425–1961* 🌐 *www.graftonstdinnertheatre.com.*

Neptune Theatre. The country's oldest professional repertory playhouse—it opened in 1915—is also the largest in Atlantic Canada, with a main stage and studio theater under one roof. It presents year-round performances ranging from classics to comedy and contemporary Canadian drama, plus occasional concerts. ✉ *1593 Argyle St.* ☎ *902/429–7070, 800/565–7345* 🌐 *www.neptunetheatre.com.*

Shakespeare by the Sea. From July through early September, actors perform works by the Bard and others in Point Pleasant Park, at the southern end of the Halifax peninsula. The natural setting—dark woods, rocky shore, and ruins of fortifications—provides a dramatic backdrop. Performances take place from Tuesday through Friday at 7 pm, and on weekends at 1 pm (weather permitting) and you can arrive up to two hours before to secure a good spot. ✉ *Cambridge Battery, Point Pleasant Park, Point Pleasant Dr.* ☎ *902/422–0295* 🌐 *www.shakespearebythesea.ca* 💵 *C$20 donation suggested; reserved seating C$25, chair rental C$2, blanket rental C$1.*

SPORTS AND THE OUTDOORS

CANOEING

St. Mary's Boat Club. Beautiful century-old homes dot the placid Northwest Arm, and the bench of a canoe is definitely the best seat from which to view them. On weekends from June through September, St. Mary's loans canoes for a maximum of one hour to adults 18 years and older and to younger certified canoeists. There's no charge, and the boat house is open from 11 am, with the last canoe pick up at 6 pm. Safety equipment is provided. ✉ *1641 Fairfield Rd.* ✣ *Off Jubilee Rd., below Connaught* ☎ *902/490–4538.*

GOLF

Glen Arbour Golf Course. Natural features, including elevation changes and mature woodlands, lakes, and streams, make the 18-hole championship course here a scenic and memorable experience, culminating in the featured hole (the 18th), a 565-yard downhill par 5 with a dazzling view. The club also has a nine-hole, par-three course designed for novices. ✉ *40 Clubhouse La., Hammonds Plains* ☎ *902/835–4653* 🌐 *www.glenarbour.com* 💲 *Championship Course, C$55–C$105; Executive Course, C$9–C$14 for 9 holes, C$13–C$22 for 18 holes* ⛳ *Championship Course: 18 holes, 6800 yards, par 72; Executive Course: 9 holes, 1688 yards, par 27* ⏲ *Closed early Oct.–Apr.*

Granite Springs Golf Club. This lush, semiprivate course, an easy drive west of downtown Halifax, overlooks Shad Bay. It progresses across rolling hillsides with granite outcroppings, water features, and sand traps. Fairways are narrow, calling for accurate shots, but four sets of tees cater to different levels of golfing ability. ✉ *4441 Prospect Rd., Bayside* ☎ *902/852–3419* 🌐 *www.granitespringsgolf.com* 💲 *C$30–C$60* ⛳ *18 holes, 6401 yards, par 72* ⏲ *Closed mid-Oct.–Mar.*

HIKING

McNab's Island Provincial Park. At the mouth of Halifax Harbour, this island appeals to adventuresome spirits. Accessible only by boat, it has 14 km (9 miles) of wooded trails and birding sites, plus a 19th-century fort. Several companies provide water taxis or tours from different Halifax locations. The trip takes 25 minutes from the Halifax boardwalk and costs C$15–C$20 for the round-trip. There is no drinking water available on the island, so you must bring your own. ✉ *Halifax* 🌐 *mcnabsisland.ca.*

Point Pleasant Park. Free, easy to reach, and threaded with woodland and waterside trails, this park is popular with locals and visitors alike. If you overstay and the parking lot is locked, call 311 to be let out. ✉ *Point Pleasant Dr. and Tower Rd.* ☎ *902/490–4700* 🌐 *www.pointpleasantpark.ca.*

Sir Sandford Fleming Park. This park, free and very accessible, has a 2.8-km (1¾-mile) trail, with views across the Northwest Arm to Point Pleasant Park on the opposite shore. Marked by an impressive stone tower called the Dingle (open in summer), it's named for the inventor of standard time zones, who summered on the property and donated it to the city. ✉ *260 Dingle Rd.* ✣ *Follow signs off Purcell's Cove Rd.*

HORSEBACK RIDING

FAMILY **Hatfield Farm Adventures.** Horseback-riding experiences are available for all levels and all shapes and sizes, including trail rides, lessons, summer camps, and pony rides. ✉ *1840 Hammonds Plains Rd., Hammonds Plains* ☎ *902/835–5676, 877/835–5676* 🌐 *www.hatfieldfarm.com* 💲 *C$42 for regular trail ride, C$62 for private trail ride; kids' pony rides start at C$8.70.*

SEA KAYAKING

East Coast Outfitters. This outfitter rents kayaking equipment and offers instruction and guided excursions from May through September. Half-day, full-day, and shorter midday and sunset tours are available, and there's the option to have a customized tour or just rent a kayak. ✉ *2017 Lower Prospect Rd., Lower Prospect* ✣ *Follow Rte. 333 toward Peggy's Cove, turn left on Terence Bay Rd. and continue for 9 km (5½ miles)* ☎ *902/852–2567, 877/852–2567* 🌐 *www.eastcoastoutfitters.com* 💲 *Tours C$50–C$135; rentals from C$20.*

Mountain Equipment Co-op. Part of a small nationwide chain, this downtown sports store rents kayaks and other outdoors equipment. ✉ *1550 Granville St.* ☎ *902/421–2667* 🌐 *www.mec.ca* 💲 *Kayak rental: C$30 a day, C$20 per additional day, C$140 per wk.*

CRAFTY RESOURCES

If you're looking specifically for fine arts and crafts, pick up a free copy of the Halifax Art Map or view it online at 🌐 *www.halifaxartmap.com.* Updated annually, it lists more than 70 artists' shops and galleries around the city and 40 art-related advertisers. For elsewhere in the province, try the Nova Scotia Centre for Craft and Design's annual guide (🌐 *www.craftdesign.ns.ca/guide*) or Studio Rally's independently prepared Fine Art & Craft Studio Map (🌐 *www.studiorally.ca*).

SWIMMING

FAMILY **Chocolate Lake.** In summer, lifeguards supervise this lake, just off the Northwest Arm, that's popular for swimming. The name doesn't mean that the water is delicious, but rather comes from a former chocolate factory on the site. Although it's in a residential area, the lake is surrounded by trees, giving it a secluded feel, and there's a nice beach. Water quality is tested weekly (locals avoid swimming in Halifax Harbour or the Northwest Arm itself because of the dubious water quality there). ✉ *2 Melwood Ave.* ☎ *902/490–5458.*

SHOPPING

BOOKS

Bookmark. This friendly independent bookstore has been serving the reading public for more than 25 years, with an excellent range of fiction, nonfiction, and local-interest books. ✉ *5686 Spring Garden Rd* ☎ *902/423–0419* 🌐 *www.bookmarkreads.ca.*

FAMILY **Woozles.** The country's oldest children's bookshop is packed with books, many of them by Canadian and local authors. The store somehow manages to shoehorn a slew of toys amid the tomes. ✉ *1533 Birmingham St.* ☎ *902/423–7626, 800/966–0537* 🌐 *www.woozles.com.*

CRAFTS AND GIFTS

Jennifer's of Nova Scotia. Tempting Jennifer's sells pottery, glass, handmade soaps, hooked mats, ceramics, pewter, and other craft items made in Nova Scotia by nearly 30 artisans. ✉ *5635 Spring Garden Rd.* ☎ *902/425–3119* 🌐 *www.jennifers.ns.ca.*

NovaScotian Crystal. The boardwalk is *the* place to watch master craftsmen blowing glass into graceful decanters and bowls, which can be purchased in this shop's showroom. ✉ *5080 George St.* ☎ *902/492–0416, 888/977–2797* 🌐 *www.novascotiancrystal.com.*

FOOD

Fodor's Choice ★ **Halifax Seaport Farmers' Market.** Steps from the boardwalk's southern terminus, this eco-conscious venue is bright, airy, and contemporary. It's open daily, giving you ample opportunity to stock up on edibles and quality crafts from its more than 250 vendors—or to just indulge in the city's best people-watching. Saturday is the best day; vendors don't all show up on other days unless a cruise ship has docked. ✉ *1209 Marginal Rd.* ☎ *902/492–4043* ⊕ *www.halifaxfarmersmarket.com.*

SHOPPING COMPLEXES AND MALLS

Historic Properties. A pleasant place to stroll through some of the city's oldest buildings, this delightful complex also houses interesting shops and restaurants. ✉ *1869 Upper Water St.* ⊕ *www.historicproperties.ca.*

OFF THE BEATEN PATH

Hydrostone Market. This block-long building, a Parks Canada Federal Heritage Site and recipient of a Nova Scotia Built Heritage Award, lures shoppers to the city's North End with all sorts of one-of-a-kind items. Flattened by the Halifax Explosion in 1917, the market site and surrounding area were rebuilt in a charming English-garden style using hydrostone—aka concrete. Shops of note include **The Bogside Gallery** for fine crafts, **Lady Luck** for jewelry and accessories, and **L.K. Yarns** for yarns and needlecraft accessories. After browsing, break for lunch at **Epicurious Morsels.** ✉ *5515–5547 Young St., between Isleville and Gottigen Sts., North End* ⊕ *www.hydrostonemarket.ca.*

Park Lane. The shops at this specialty mall near the Halifax Public Gardens sell home furnishings, clothing, jewelry, gifts, and accessories. ✉ *5657 Spring Garden Rd.* ☎ *902/420–0660* ⊕ *www.shopparklane.ca.*

The Piazza at Bishop's Landing. An attractive complex of shops, condos, and a marina, Bishop's Landing's Piazza contains worth-a-peek jewelry, fashion, handmade candies and rum cakes, and other boutiques. ✉ *1475 Lower Water St.* ⊕ *bishopslanding.com.*

Spring Garden Place. Accessories for you and your home are the focus of this boutique-like downtown mall, with retailers, restaurants, and a spa. ✉ *5640 Spring Garden Rd.* ☎ *902/420–0675* ⊕ *www.springgardenplace.ca.*

SOUTH SHORE AND ANNAPOLIS VALLEY

The South Shore is on the Atlantic side of the narrow Nova Scotia peninsula; the Annapolis Valley is on the Bay of Fundy side. Although they're less than an hour apart by car, the two seem like different worlds. The former, with its rocky coast, island-dotted bays, and historic fishing villages, has launched 1,000 ships—and 1,000 postcards. The latter is most notable for its fertile farmlands, vineyards, and orchards. Highway 103, Highway 3, and various secondary roads form the province's designated Lighthouse Route, which leads southwest from Halifax down the South Shore. It ends in Yarmouth, where the Evangeline Trail begins. This trail winds along St. Mary's Bay through a succession of Francophone communities collectively known as the Acadian Shore. The villages blend into one another for about 50 km (35 miles), each one, it seems, with its own wharf, fish plant, and Catholic church.

The verdant Annapolis Valley runs northeast, sheltered on both sides by the North and South mountains. Occasional roads over the South Mountain lead to the South Shore; short roads over the North Mountain lead to the Fundy Shore. Like the South Shore, the valley has numerous historic sites—some of Canada's oldest among them—and is punctuated by pleasant small towns with a generous supply of Victorian architecture.

PEGGY'S COVE

48 km (30 miles) southwest of Halifax.

Peggy's Cove is the home of Canada's most photographed lighthouse. As you wind along the edge of St. Margaret's Bay, woodlands eventually give way to rugged outcroppings that were deposited when the last glaciers swept through. On one side, massive granite boulders stand semi-erect in scrubby fields; on the other, they lie prone, creating the granite shelf on which Peggy's Cove is perched. The hamlet itself consists of little more than a Lilliputian harbor with a tiny wooden church, a cluster of shingled houses, and some salt-bleached jetties. What distinguishes Peggy's Cove, though, is the solitary lighthouse towering over a slab of wave-blasted rock. Just don't be tempted to venture too close to the edge—many an unwary visitor has been swept out to sea by the mighty surf that sometimes breaks here. (Repeat this mantra: dark rocks are wet rocks, and must be avoided.) In addition to navigating the rugged terrain, you'll have to contend with the crowds in summer—750,000 tourists descend annually. To avoid them in July and August, plan to arrive early or late in the day.

THE ACADIANS

The Acadians are descendants of French colonists who settled here in the 1600s. In 1755, they were expelled by the British for refusing to pledge allegiance to the Crown. Some eluded capture and slowly crept back, many making new homes in New Brunswick and along this shore of Nova Scotia. Others, however, migrated south to another region held by France at the time: Louisiana, where their name was shortened to Cajun. (Say "Acadian" five times fast and the reason will be apparent!)

GETTING HERE AND AROUND

There is no public transportation to Peggy's Cove. Travelers based in Halifax can drive here by taking either Exit 2 or Exit 5 from Highway 103 onto Highway 333. The former is mostly inland while the latter runs along St. Margaret's Bay. The ideal scenario, though, is to go via one and return via the other. At Peggy's Cove you can drive almost to the base of the lighthouse, but you'd do better to park in the spacious public lot below and make the three-minute walk up to this Canadian icon. Bus tours from Halifax are another option.

ESSENTIALS

Visitor Information **Peggy's Cove Visitor Information Centre.** ✉ *109 Peggy's Point Rd.* ☎ *902/823-5501* ⊕ *www.peggyscoveregion.com.*

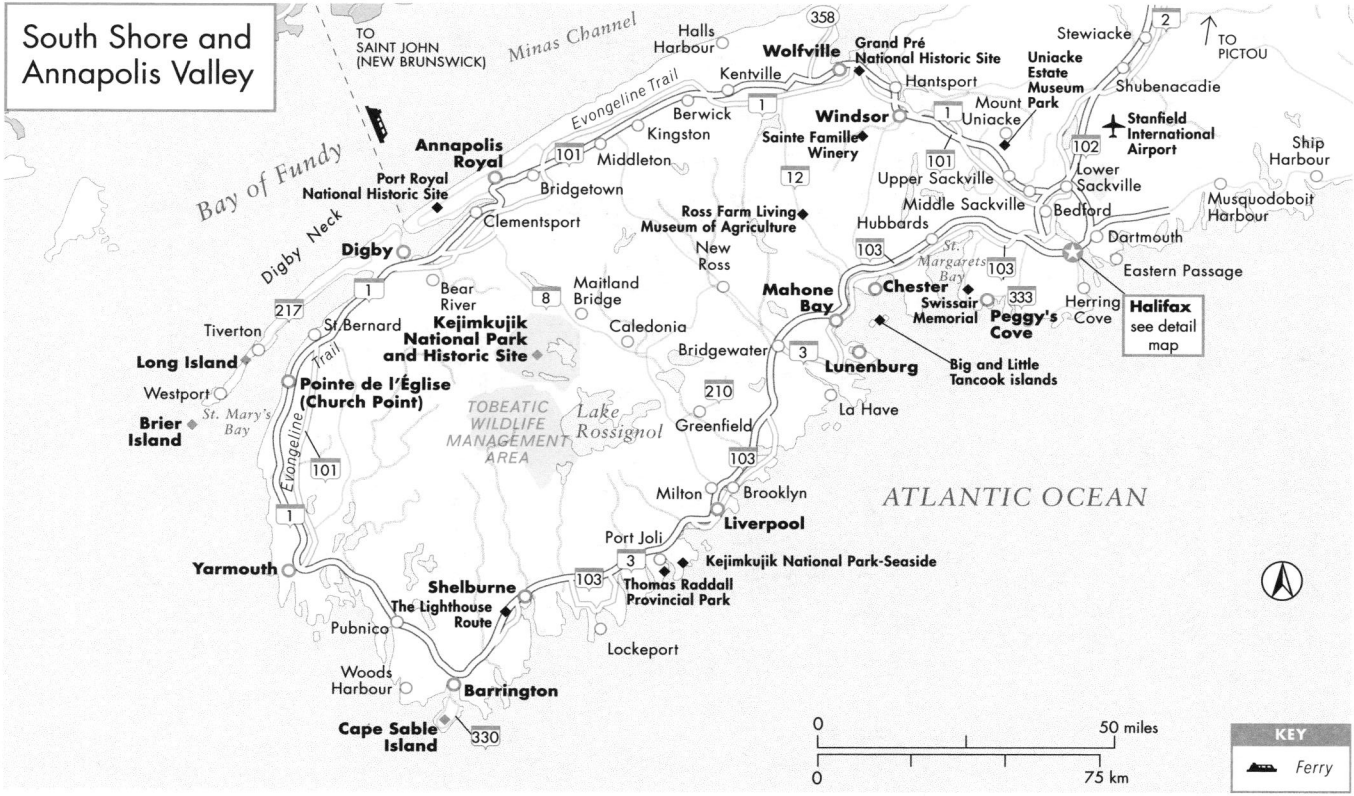
South Shore and Annapolis Valley
TO SAINT JOHN (NEW BRUNSWICK)
Minas Channel
Halls Harbour
358
Wolfville
Grand Pré National Historic Site
Kentville
Hantsport
Stewiacke
2
TO PICTOU
Uniacke Estate Museum Park
Shubenacadie
Evangeline Trail
Berwick
1
Windsor
Mount Uniacke
Stanfield International Airport
Kingston
Sainte Famille Winery
101
102
Ship Harbour
Annapolis Royal
Middleton
12
Upper Sackville
Lower Sackville
Bay of Fundy
Port Royal National Historic Site
Bridgetown
Middle Sackville
Bedford
Musquodoboit Harbour
Digby Neck
Clementsport
Ross Farm Living Museum of Agriculture
Hubbards
Dartmouth
Digby
New Ross
103
St. Margarets Bay
Eastern Passage
Bear River
Maitland Bridge
Mahone Bay
Chester
Swissair Memorial
333
Herring Cove
Halifax see detail map
217
8
Kejimkujik National Park and Historic Site
Caledonia
Peggy's Cove
Tiverton
St Bernard
Trail
Bridgewater
3
Lunenburg
Big and Little Tancook islands
Long Island
Westport
Pointe de l'Église (Church Point)
210
La Have
Brier Island
St. Mary's Bay
TOBEATIC WILDLIFE MANAGEMENT AREA
Lake Rossignol
Greenfield
Evangeline
ATLANTIC OCEAN
Milton
Brooklyn
Liverpool
Port Joli
Kejimkujik National Park-Seaside
Yarmouth
Shelburne
Thomas Raddall Provincial Park
The Lighthouse Route
Pubnico
Lockeport
Woods Harbour
Barrington
Cape Sable Island
330
0
50 miles
0
75 km
KEY
Ferry

EXPLORING

deGarthe Memorial. A local artist carved the striking 100-foot deGarthe Memorial, a bas-relief carved from local granite. The memorial commemorates fishermen who lost their lives here. ✉ *109 Peggy's Point Rd.* ✣ *Off Hwy. 333.*

Swissair Memorial. A tribute to Swissair Flight 111, which crashed into the waters off Peggy's Cove in 1998, this memorial commemorates the 229 casualties and honors the courageous local fisherfolk involved in recovery efforts and in comforting the grieving families. ✉ *Hwy. 333* ✣ *1½ km (1 mile) north of the village.*

WHERE TO EAT AND STAY

$$$ SEAFOOD ✕ **Sou'wester Restaurant.** Poised on the rocks near the base of Peggy's Cove lighthouse, this sprawling 180-seat dining room serves a variety of seafood, including orange brandy shrimp and scallops, lobster dinners, and Down East specialties such as salt-fish hash and beans. There are also chicken, steak, and vegetarian options, and breakfast is served from 8:30 to 11 am. Sou'wester is a pleasant spot to linger over coffee and warm homemade gingerbread, provided the tour buses that regularly park out back haven't just disgorged hordes of hungry passengers. A large—generally kitschy—souvenir shop is on-site. $ *Average main: C$24* ✉ *178 Peggy's Point Rd.* ✣ *Off Hwy. 333* ☎ *902/823–2561* ⊕ *www.peggys-cove.com.*

$$ B&B/INN FAMILY **Oceanstone Seaside Resort.** Resembling a traditional seaside hamlet, Oceanstone's cluster of buildings sits picturesquely on the shore of St. Margaret's Bay, a short and peaceful distance from Peggy's Cove. **Pros:** most options have water views; eco-conscious owners. **Cons:** café only serves light fare and is closed on Monday from December through April; one cottage stands alone by the road. $ *Rooms from: C$135* ✉ *8650 Peggy's Cove Rd., Indian Harbour* ✣ *3½ km (2 miles) north of Peggy's Cove* ☎ *902/823–2160, 866/823–2160* ⊕ *www.oceanstoneresort.com* ⇨ *12 rooms, 2 suites, 8 cottages* ⊘ *No meals.*

SPORTS AND THE OUTDOORS

Boat excursions are available around Peggy's Cove from spring through fall.

Four Winds Boat Charters. Based at Shining Waters Marine, about a 20-minute drive from Peggy's Corner, this company runs tours, weather permitting, in July and August aboard a Cape Islander. There's a 90-minute scenic cruise, a three-hour nature cruise, and four-hour fishing trips, with prices starting at C$35. ✉ *148 Nautical Way, Tantallon* ☎ *902/492–0022, 877/274–8421* ⊕ *www.fourwindscharters.com.*

SHOPPING

Beales' Bailiwick. Maritime-designed clothing, pewter, and jewelry are among the crafts sold here. The adjoining coffee shop affords one of the best photo ops in Peggy's Cove, and the renovated red schoolhouse next door is a venue for summertime theater and concerts. ✉ *124 Peggy's Point Rd.* ☎ *902/823–2099, 877/823–2099* ⊕ *www.beales.ns.ca* ⏲ *Closed early Nov.–Apr.*

CHESTER

64 km (40 miles) west of Peggy's Cove.

Although Chester is a short drive west of Peggy's Cove, you'll be forgiven for thinking you've taken a wrong turn and ended up in Maine or Massachusetts. New England planters settled the site in 1759, and their numbers were later bolstered by Loyalists escaping the American Revolution and Boston Brahmins who simply wanted to escape the city in summer. Thanks to the clapboard saltboxes and Cape Cod–style homes they left behind, Chester still calls to mind a classic New England community. Most visitors are content to explore its tree-shaded lanes or make forays into the surrounding countryside. Yachtsmen invariably stick close to the water.

GETTING HERE AND AROUND

There is no public transportation to Chester. From Halifax it's a 68-km (42-mile) drive via NS–103 and NS Trunk 3 W, or a slightly longer, much slower, meandering drive along St. Margaret's Bay Road, NS–213, and NS Trunk 3 W.

ESSENTIALS

Visitor Information **Chester Visitor Information Centre.** ✉ *Old Train Station, 20 Smith Rd., Hwy. 3* ☎ *902/275–4616, 902/275–4709* 🌐 *vic.chesterchamber.ca.*

EXPLORING

Big and Little Tancook islands. Out in Mahone Bay, 8 km (5 miles) out from Chester, these scenic islands have trails for hiking and biking, and provide great bird-watching and photography opportunities. There are sandy beaches, too, one of which is great for fossil hunting. Reflecting its part-German heritage, Big Tancook claims to have the best sauerkraut in Nova Scotia. The boat from Chester runs four times daily on weekdays and twice daily on weekends. The 50-minute ride costs C$7 per adult for the round-trip (cash only). ✉ *Chester* ☎ *902/228–2927 Rec Centre, summer only, 902/275–7885 ferry information* ⏲ *Ferry departs Chester weekdays at 7, 10:20, 3:40, and 5:30, Sat. at 1 and 7, Sun. and holidays at 10 and 6. From Tancook it departs weekdays at 6, 8, 1:30, and 4:30, Sat. at 9 and 6, Sun. and holidays at 9 and 5, but always check in advance.*

FAMILY **Ross Farm Living Museum of Agriculture.** A restored 19th-century farm illustrates the evolution of agriculture from 1600 to 1925. The animals are those found on an 1800s farm—draft horses, oxen, and other heritage breeds—and traditional activities such as blacksmithing or spinning are demonstrated. Hands-on programs are regularly scheduled for kids who'd like to help out with the chores. The Peddler's Shop here sells items made in the community. ✉ *4568 Rte. 12, New Ross* ✢ *30 km (18 miles) northwest of Chester via NS Trunk 3 E* ☎ *902/689–2210, 877/689–2210* 🌐 *rossfarm.novascotia.ca* 💵 *C$6, free Sun. 9:30–11 am* ⏲ *Daily 9:30–5:30.*

WHERE TO EAT AND STAY

$$ CANADIAN ✕ **Fo'c'sle Tavern.** This rustic midtown spot—a former store, stable, and Nova Scotia's oldest rural inn, dating to 1764—is full of natural pine and local art, and its staff and clientele treat regulars and newcomers

like kin. In the windowed front section, a woodstove keeps things warm on chilly nights, and year-round you can order from a menu that's strong on seafood and comfort food—haddock stuffed with shrimp, scallops, tomato, and Parmesan, for instance, or liver, bacon, and onions with mashed potatoes. Lighter fare is also served, along with plenty of craft beers. Musicians perform on some nights, and there are pool tables and TVs. $ *Average main: C$14* ✉ *42 Queen St.* ☎ *902/275–1408* 🌐 *www.focslechester.com.*

$$$ CANADIAN ✕ **Nicki's Inn.** The pleasant dining room has white tablecloths and fresh flowers and is flooded with light from its huge windows. The menu is chalked on a big blackboard behind the bar and changes seasonally. Expect accomplished treatment of local seafood, including maple and citrus–marinated planked salmon, and satisfying meat dishes such as lamb shank braised in Cabernet Sauvignon with celeriac mash and vegetables. On Sundays there's always a traditional roast. The three suites of the inn are very nice, too. $ *Average main: C$26* ✉ *28 Pleasant St.* ☎ *902/275–4342* 🌐 *www.nickisinn.com* ⏲ *Closed Mon.–Wed. No lunch.*

$$ B&B/INN **Mecklenburgh Inn.** Nautical touches abound in this heritage B&B at the top of one of Chester's main streets. **Pros:** complimentary gourmet breakfast; claw-foot tubs in three rooms. **Cons:** two blocks from the water; books up a year ahead for Race Week; one bathroom, while private, is not en suite. $ *Rooms from: C$135* ✉ *78 Queen St.* ☎ *902/275–4638, 866/838–4638* 🌐 *www.mecklenburghinn.ca* ⏲ *Closed Jan.–Apr.* 🛏 *4 rooms* 🍽 *Breakfast.*

NIGHTLIFE AND PERFORMING ARTS

Chester Playhouse. A summer theater season, spring and fall music seasons, movie screenings, community theater, and other events keep this venue hopping. ✉ *22 Pleasant St.* ☎ *902/275–3933, 800/363–7529* 🌐 *www.chesterplayhouse.ca.*

SHOPPING

Amicus Gallery. Jewelry, stained glass, and other crafts by local artisans can be found here, along with the owner's own pottery. ✉ *20 Pleasant St.* ☎ *902/275–2496* 🌐 *www.amicusgallery.ca.*

Jim Smith Fine Studio Pottery. The earthenware pottery at this studio is as cheerful as the bright yellow-and-green building on the front harbor in which it's housed. ✉ *Corner of Duke and Water Sts.* ☎ *902/275–3272* 🌐 *www.jimsmithstudio.ca* ⏲ *June–Sept., Mon.–Sat. 10–6, Sun. noon–6; Oct.–May by chance or appointment.*

MAHONE BAY

24 km (15 miles) west of Chester.

Three vintage churches along a grass-fringed shoreline set a tranquil tone for this pastoral town that wraps around a sweeping curve of water. Of course, life here wasn't always so serene. Mahone Bay was once a thriving shipbuilding center. Before that, it was popular with pirates and privateers. In fact, Mahone Bay was named for the type of low-lying ship they used: it's a corruption of the French word *mahonne* (a low-lying bargelike boat).

Mahone Bay's outdoor pleasures include kayaking into secret coves or around the many islands, including Oak Island, reputedly a favorite haunt of the notorious Captain Kidd. Modern-day treasure hunters are better off onshore, perusing the galleries and studios along Main Street and environs. Although Mahone Bay has a population of just 1,100, it supports an enviable assortment of craftspeople.

GETTING HERE AND AROUND

There is no public transportation to Mahone Bay. To drive here, leave Highway 103 at Exit 10, turning onto NS–3.

ESSENTIALS

Visitor Information **Mahone Bay Visitor Information Centre.** ✉ *165 Edgewater St.* ☎ *902/624–6151, 888/624–6151* 🌐 *www.mahonebay.com.*

EXPLORING

Mahone Bay Museum. Housed in one of the delightful old buildings in this pretty little town, the museum contains interesting displays about the long history of Mahone Bay and some of the people who shaped its future. The collection includes boatbuilding items and models, ceramics, household antiques, and a display relating the story of the first settlers who arrived in the 1750s. Museum volunteers can also arrange tours by appointment. ✉ *578 Main St.* ☎ *902/624–6263* 🌐 *mahonebaymuseum.com* 🎟 *Free (donations welcome)* ⏲ *May–Sept., daily 10–4.*

WHERE TO EAT AND STAY

$$$ CANADIAN ✕ **Kedy's Inlet Restaurant.** Diners at this chronically cute restaurant at Kedy's Landing—you'll see it just as you approach town off Exit 10—are treated to a fine view of Mahone Bay and the city's three charming churches. The Canadian-style menu emphasizes chowders and seafood, but there are meat and vegetarian options as well. The delicious Heavenly Chicken (in a mushroom, white-wine, and cream sauce) has been a mainstay for years, and the apple strudel, made in-house by the Bavarian-born chef, is alone worth a visit. $ *Average main: C$22* ✉ *249 Edgewater St.* ☎ *902/531–3030* 🌐 *kedysinlet.com* ⏲ *Closed Jan.–mid-Mar.*

$$ CANADIAN FAMILY ✕ **Mug & Anchor Pub.** Take in a view of the bay from inside this old, British-style alehouse, or enjoy waterside dining on the back deck. The menu includes basic pub fare, such as fish-and-chips and steak and ale pie, but you can also order fish cakes and other Lunenburg County favorites. Lunenburg scallops are a specialty, as is the Mug & Anchor meat pie, and there's a "tykes" menu that will please even the fussiest young diner. The pub swells with the sounds of live jazz, blues, and folk music on Saturday evenings; in the off-season, Wednesday is Trivia Night. $ *Average main: C$15* ✉ *643 Main St.* ☎ *902/624–6378* 🌐 *www.themugandanchorpubltd.com.*

$$ CANADIAN ✕ **Rebecca's Restaurant.** Head to Rebecca's for freshly prepared, flavorful, and beautifully presented dishes. Creamy seafood chowder, topped with a smoked-salmon-wrapped scallop, is a popular starter, while hearty and interesting mains might include scallop burger topped with arugula, sprouts, and a lime aioli, or a satisfying stew of free-range local lamb in tomato and roasted red pepper sauce. There's always a vegetarian option (vegan on request) and several items can be made gluten free. On alternate Wednesdays "Songspeak" will entertain you with songs and stories from local artists, and there are monthly jazz nights. $ *Average main: C$20* ✉ *619 Main St.* ☎ *902/531–3313* 🌐 *www.rebeccas-restaurant.ca* ⏲ *Closed Mon.*

$$ B&B/INN **Amber Rose Inn & Gallery.** The building dates from 1875 and is furnished with antiques, but you'll also find up-to-date creature comforts such as mini-refrigerators, coffeemakers, and whirlpool tubs. **Pros:** leafy grounds with a brook in back; quiet location. **Cons:** not on the water; off the main commercial stretch; two-night minimum on weekends June to Thanksgiving. $ *Rooms from: C$135* ✉ *319 Main St.* ☎ *902/624–1060* 🌐 *www.amberroseinn.com* 🛏 *3 suites* 🍽 *Breakfast.*

SPORTS AND THE OUTDOORS

FAMILY **South Shore Boat Tours.** Ninety-minute narrated nature cruises around Mahone Bay depart three times a day, from June through October. You'll see the seal colony, perhaps a porpoise or two, and a range of birdlife such as bald eagles, osprey, terns, and loons, and also cruise past picturesque villages and islands. A four-hour puffin-viewing trip to Pearl Island and fishing charters are also available. ✉ *Mahone Bay Civic Marina, 683 Main St.* ☎ *902/527–8544* 🌐 *www.southshoreboattours.com* 🎟 *C$40.*

FAMILY **Sweet Ride Cycling.** Before setting out on your ride, you can buy old-fashioned treats at this bicycle-slash-candy shop. Half-day rentals (up to four hours) cost C$20, full-day ones C$30, with C$20 for additional days and C$100 for a week; child trailers and bikes run C$15 per day. Electric-assist bikes (C$30 half day, C$50 full day) are also available. Organized rides (May–September) include a Wednesday night road ride, Thursday night mountain biking (intermediate level), and a Saturday morning, women-only ride on rail trails and quiet roads. ✉ *523 Main St.* ☎ *902/531–3026* 🌐 *sweetridecycling.com* ⏲ *Closed Sun. and Mon. in winter.*

SHOPPING

Amos Pewter. Inside a former boatbuilding shop that dates to 1888, the artisans at Amos Pewter design and create pewter items using traditional methods. Jewelry, sculptures, tableware, and pewter renditions of shells and other natural objects are among the items for sale, along with a new original-design Christmas ornament each year. Interpretive displays explain the history of pewter and Amos Pewter's involvement with the "Economuseum Network," which emphasizes traditional skills. If watching the artisans at work gets your creative juices flowing, you can participate in the Hands-On Experience (C$5), and take home what you make. ✉ *589 Main St.* ☎ *902/624–9547, 800/565–3369* 🌐 *www.amospewter.com* ⏲ *Closed Sun. in Jan. and Feb.*

Suttles and Seawinds. Renowned worldwide for its distinctively designed, high-quality quilts and clothing, the company displays its colorful goods on two floors of a heritage building. ✉ *466 Main St.* ☎ *902/624–8375* 🌐 *www.suttles.ca.*

LUNENBURG

14 km (9 miles) south of Mahone Bay.

Fodor's Choice ★ This remarkably preserved town has a colorful past and some *very* colorful buildings, a combo that earned it a UNESCO World Heritage Site designation. The British probably had something more staid in mind when they founded Lunenburg in 1753, but the German, Swiss, and French Protestants recruited to settle here put their own stamp on it. The result? Rainbow-hued houses characterized by the "Lunenburg Bump": a detailed dormer over the front door. Naturally, locals didn't spend *all* their time on home improvements. By the 1850s they'd transformed the town into a world-class fishing and shipbuilding center. Today, blacksmiths and dory builders continue to work on the waterfront and, appropriately, the Fisheries Museum of the Atlantic is the top attraction. An in-the-middle-of-it-all location, plus a growing supply of fine lodging, dining, shopping, and touring options, makes Lunenburg one of the best bases for a Nova Scotia vacation.

GETTING HERE AND AROUND

When the Beatles sang about "the long and winding road," they might have had the Lighthouse Route in mind. The curvy back roads that make up most of it hug the South Shore from Halifax to Yarmouth and are undeniably scenic, but a shorter option is to get to Lunenburg via Highway 103, using Exit 10 or Exit 11; either exit will take about the same amount of time, but Exit 11 has nice views around Mahone Bay. Once you're in town, walking is the way to go, provided you're not daunted by the steep hill.

TOURS

Lunenburg Town Walking Tours. Landlubbers can get their exercise on one of the guided strolls conducted by this company, with a lively narrative of local history, folklore, and personal stories from the guides. The Essential Lunenburg tour is each day at 10 am and 2 pm and the Haunted Lunenburg tour is each evening at 8:30 pm. You can also arrange for a tour of the Lunenburg Academy building. The outfit's website has a link to an online waterfront tour. ✉ *Lunenburg* ☎ *902/521–6867* 🌐 *www.lunenburgwalkingtours.com* 💵 *C$20* ⏲ *Closed mid-Oct.–early Apr.*

ESSENTIALS

Visitor Information **Lunenburg Visitor Information Centre.** ✉ *11 Blockhouse Hill Rd.* ☎ *902/634–8100, 902/634–3656, 888/615–8305* 🌐 *www.lunenburgns.com.*

EXPLORING

FAMILY Fodor's Choice ★ **Fisheries Museum of the Atlantic.** Flanked by sailing ships and painted a brilliant red, this museum on the Lunenburg waterfront strikes a dazzling pose, and the exhibits and activities experienced here more than live up to the initial impression. With an aquarium featuring 14 tanks devoted to native species, tidal touch tanks, themed films, daily activities, and displays about shipbuilding, whaling, and other maritime endeavors, there's plenty to keep the whole gang happy. Demonstrations on topics such as sailmaking, boatbuilding, and dory launching are also given, and dockside you can visit a restored saltbank schooner and a steel-hulled trawler and hear a few fish tales. If you think you might want to visit more than once, a season pass costs less than two separate visits.

As if the comprehensive overview of Nova Scotia's fishing industry weren't enough, the *Bluenose II* (☎ *902/634–4794 or 866/579–4909* ⊕ *www.bluenose.novascotia.ca*), the province's sailing ambassador, calls the museum home. Built in 1963, she's a faithful replica of the original *Bluenose,* the Lunenburg-built schooner that gained prominence during the 1920s and 1930s as the North Atlantic fleet's fastest vessel, which sank in 1946 after striking a reef. If the *Bluenose II* isn't sitting pretty in port when you arrive (the ship has an extensive sailing schedule), you can still get a glimpse of the famed ship by digging a Canadian dime out of your pocket—it's pictured on the back. ✉ *68 Bluenose Dr.* ☎ *902/634–4794, 866/579–4909* ⊕ *fisheriesmuseum.novascotia.ca* 💵 *C$10* ⏲ *Mid-June–mid-Oct., daily 9:30–5:30; mid Oct.–mid-June, weekdays 9:30–5.*

WHERE TO EAT

$$$$ EUROPEAN Fodor's Choice ★ ✕ **Fleur de Sel.** In-the-know foodies flock to this classy Continental alternative to the South Shore's dime-a-dozen fish joints. Tucked into a heritage home on Montague Street, the restaurant has an elegant, airy interior, and the food is superb, from the house-smoked salmon through the Lunenburg scallops, or perhaps the smoked beef brisket, to the final bite of *fromage*. To try the chef's tasting menu—five courses for C$70, plus C$45 to add wine pairings, or seven courses for C$90, plus C$58 to add wine pairings—you need to notify the restaurant ahead of your visit. If you can't score one of the 35-odd seats at dinner, come for Sunday brunch, when stellar dishes such as lobster eggs Benedict and brioche French toast are served. [$] *Average main: C$34* ✉ *53 Montague St.* ☎ *902/640–2121, 877/723–7258* ⊕ *fleurdesel.net* ⏲ *Closed Mon. and Tues. No lunch* ✍ *Reservations essential.*

$$$ ECLECTIC ✕ **Magnolia's Grill.** Exuberant and unabashedly eccentric, this place is the Auntie Mame of Lunenburg restaurants. The booths are close together and the walls cluttered with pictures, yet somehow it all works, and so does the menu, featuring items such as haddock fish cakes with house-made rhubarb chutney, Moroccan chicken, and the lobster linguine featured on The Food Network's "You Gotta Eat Here." Once you see the key lime pie, you might want to skip straight to dessert. The small space fills fast, so make a reservation or be prepared to wait. [$] *Average main: C$22* ✉ *128 Montague St.* ☎ *902/634–3287* ✍ *Reservations essential.*

$$$ SEAFOOD FAMILY ✕ **Old Fish Factory Restaurant & Ice House Bar.** Lunenburg is riddled with seafood restaurants, but this one stands out for its location inside a former fish-processing plant at the Fisheries Museum of the Atlantic. The eatery overlooks Lunenburg Harbour and offers wharf-side dining in warm months. Seafood is the specialty, of course—try Grandmother's Lobster Pie, cooked in a Pernod cream sauce under buttery cracker topping—but you can also opt for chicken, steak, or vegetarian pasta. In summer the adjacent bar has a live jam on Friday nights. [$] *Average main: C$23* ✉ *68 Bluenose Dr.* ☎ *902/634–3333, 800/533–9336* ⊕ *www.oldfishfactory.com* ⏲ *Closed Nov.–Apr.*

$$$ SEAFOOD ✕ **Rum Runner Restaurant.** A wall of windows makes the most of this restaurant's Lunenburg Harbour location, creating an appropriately nautical setting for savoring the expertly prepared seafood the kitchen turns out. Thanks to its owners' German heritage, the Rum Runner has an attractive European-style dining room, where patrons enjoy jumbo shrimp Martini, seafood chowder, and mains that might include lemon-crusted local haddock or steamed Nova Scotia lobster. Ribs, steaks, and chicken are also on the menu, and there's always a vegetarian option. Though its main entrance is on a parallel street, this casual eatery can also be accessed on Bluenose Drive, opposite the Fisheries Museum. $ *Average main: C$25* ✉ *66 Montague St.* ☎ *902/634–8778* 🌐 *www.rumrunnerinn.com* ⏲ *Closed Tues. and Nov.–mid-May.*

WHERE TO STAY

$$ HOTEL **Lunenburg Arms Hotel & Spa.** It's rare to find hotel-style amenities in small-town heritage properties, but this place has them, including an on-site restaurant—the cool, contemporary Tin Fish—and a full-service Aveda spa. **Pros:** mid-hill location; complimentary use of spa's steam shower and hot tub. **Cons:** dining deck faces the street; free breakfast in the off-season only. $ *Rooms from: C$149* ✉ *94 Pelham St.* ☎ *902/640–4040, 800/679–4950* 🌐 *www.eden.travel/lunenburg* 🛏 *22 rooms, 2 suites* 🍴 *No meals.*

$$ B&B/INN **Lunenburg Inn.** This luxurious lodging has rooms that are spacious and furnished with antiques. **Pros:** free phone calls within Nova Scotia; fresh-baked cookies in high season; guest take-one, leave-one book exchange. **Cons:** street can be noisy; a bit outside the main tourist area. $ *Rooms from: C$149* ✉ *26 Dufferin St.* ☎ *902/634–3963, 800/565–3963* 🌐 *www.lunenburginn.com* ⏲ *Closed late Nov.–Mar.* 🛏 *5 rooms, 2 suites* 🍴 *Breakfast.*

$ B&B/INN FAMILY **Pelham House Bed & Breakfast.** Close to downtown, with a veranda overlooking Lunenburg Harbour, this circa-1906 sea captain's home is decorated in homey, country style. **Pros:** a sustaining breakfast is included; discounts for multiple nights; suite works well for families. **Cons:** no grounds to speak of; Harry, the cute resident dog, means this may not be for people with pet allergies. $ *Rooms from: C$100* ✉ *224 Pelham St.* ☎ *902/634–7113, 800/508–0446* 🌐 *www.pelhamhouse.ca* 🛏 *3 rooms, 1 suite* 🍴 *Breakfast.*

SPORTS AND THE OUTDOORS

Lunenburg Bike Barn. Rentals, which include helmet, bike rack, lock, and repair kit, start at C$18 for up to four hours at this friendly shop 2 km (1 mile) east of the town center. Panniers are also available from C$4 per day. ✉ *579 Blue Rocks Rd.* ☎ *902/634–3426* 🌐 *bikelunenburg.com* ⏲ *Closed Sun., except by chance or appointment.*

Lunenburg Ocean Adventures. The thrill-seeker activities this outfitter makes possible include deep-sea and shark fishing and diving to explore various wrecks and East Point Reef. Boats depart from the Fisheries Museum of the Atlantic. ✉ *68 Bluenose Dr.* ☎ *902/634–4833* 🌐 *www.lunenburgoceanadventures.com* 🎟 *Fishing C$55; shark fishing C$1,200 per day for up to 6 people; call for diving prices* ⏲ *Closed Oct.–mid-May.*

Lunenburg Whale-Watching Tours. Whales, seals, and other marine life are the star attractions of these tours. The three-hour trips depart four times daily, from May through October, from the Fisheries Museum Wharf. You can arrange for bird-watching excursions and tours of Lunenburg Harbour, too. ✉ *Lunenburg* ☎ *902/527–7175* ⊕ *www.novascotiawhalewatching.com* 💲 *C$52.*

FAMILY **Pleasant Paddling.** Guided excursions include a four-hour trip to view a seal colony (C$75), paddling to a secluded beach on one of the islands (C$65), or coastal tours lasting two hours to a full day (C$50–C$125), Kayak rentals are priced from C$30 for a single kayak for two hours to C$90 per day for a double. ✉ *245 The Point Rd., Blue Rocks* ☎ *902/541–9233* ⊕ *www.pleasantpaddling.com.*

FAMILY **Star Charters.** From June through October, 90-minute daytime and sunset sailing trips take place aboard a 48-foot wooden ketch; you may even get the chance to take the helm or help raise the sails. ✉ *Fisheries Museum Wharf, Bluenose Dr.* ☎ *902/634–3535 June–Oct., 877/386–3535, 902/634–3537 Nov.–May* ⊕ *www.novascotiasailing.com* 💲 *C$35* ⏲ *Closed Nov.–May.*

SHOPPING

Bluenose II Company Store. Official merchandise from the ship *Bluenose II* is sold here, along with other quality crafts. You can pick up all kinds of nautical memorabilia, from a splendid model of the *Bluenose* to a jaunty cap, and there's art, clothing, pewter crafts, and much more. ✉ *121 Bluenose Dr.* ☎ *902/640–3177, 855/640–3177* ⊕ *www.bluenose2store.ca* ⏲ *Closed Jan.–Apr.*

EN ROUTE

DesBrisay Museum. Artifacts dating back to the mid-19th century, including rare photographs of local shops, factories, and shipyards, are among the holdings of this museum of Lunenburg County history. There's also a folk-art gallery. Walking trails wind from behind the museum building through nearby parkland. ✉ *130 Jubilee Rd., Bridgewater* ☎ *902/543–4033* ⊕ *www.desbrisaymuseum.ca* 💲 *C$3.50, free on Sat.* ⏲ *June–Aug., Tues.–Sat. 9–5, Sun. 1–5; Sept.–May, Wed.–Sun. 1–5.*

Ironworks Distillery. Load up on liquid souvenirs here. Named for the old marine-blacksmith's shop it occupies, Ironworks produces hand-distilled vodka from Annapolis Valley apples and luscious liqueurs from local berries. Tours (C$10) are offered daily mid-May–early September at 12:30, 2:30, and 4:30. ✉ *The Blacksmith's Shop, 2 Kempt St.* ☎ *902/640–2424* ⊕ *www.ironworksdistillery.com* ⏲ *Closed Sun.–Wed. Jan.–mid-May.*

FAMILY **Lexicon Books.** Run by authors and book enthusiasts, this independent bookstore has a hand-picked selection with a focus on fiction, poetry, small press, graphic novels, young adult, and children's books. They run writing workshops in addition to a monthly book club, and a teen book club, and also host author readings. ✉ *125 Montague St.* ☎ *902/634–4015* ⊕ *www.lexiconbooks.ca.*

LIVERPOOL

69 km (43 miles) southwest of Lunenburg.

In recent years, a paper mill has been Liverpool's economic mainstay, but between the American Revolution and the War of 1812, privateering was the most profitable pursuit. New Englanders who had turned on their former neighbors with a vengeance founded the town in 1759. Armed with a "Letter of Marque" from the British Crown, they made a booming business out of seizing American ships and the valuable cargo they carried. Depending on which side you were on, such activity was interpreted as political expediency or legalized piracy. Each July, the town celebrates its notorious past with its Privateer Days festival.

GETTING HERE AND AROUND

There is no public transportation to Liverpool. By road, it's off Highway 103 at the White Point Connector, then a left turn onto White Point Road. The town is small and easily walkable.

ESSENTIALS

Visitor Information **Liverpool Visitor Information Centre.** ✉ *28 Henry Hensey Dr.* ☎ *902/354-5421* 🌐 *www.regionofqueens.com/visit.*

EXPLORING

TOP ATTRACTIONS

Fort Point Lighthouse Park. The Port of the Privateers exhibit inside this structure—one of Canada's oldest surviving lighthouses—recounts its decades of stalwart service, from its completion in 1855 until 1989, when operations ceased. Even if the lighthouse isn't open when you arrive, there are interpretive signs outside, and the views of Liverpool Harbour from the park are splendid. ✉ *21 Fort Point La., off Main St.* ☎ *902/354-5741* 💲 *Free* ⏲ *Daily.*

Kejimkujik National Park-Seaside. One of the last untouched tracts of coastline in Atlantic Canada, this park has isolated coves, broad white beaches, and imposing headlands, all of which are managed by Kejimkujik National Park and Historic Site (just plain "Keji" to locals or the linguistically challenged). A hike along a 6-km (4-mile) trail reveals a pristine coast that's home to harbor seals, eider ducks, and many other species. To protect nesting areas of the endangered piping plover, parts of St. Catherine's River beach (the main beach) are closed to the public from late April to early August. ✉ *Off Hwy. 103, 25 km (16 miles) southwest of Liverpool, Port Joli* ☎ *902/682-2772* 🌐 *www.pc.gc.ca* 💲 *C$3.90* ⏲ *Park daily, visitor center mid-May–late June and early Sept.–mid-Oct., daily 8:30–6; late June–early Sept., daily 8:30–8.*

FAMILY **Rossignol Cultural Centre.** A refurbished high school is now home to this eclectic center that contains three art galleries and six museums—including one devoted entirely to outhouses. Among the varied offerings are a trapper's cabin, an early-20th-century drugstore, 50 stuffed-wildlife exhibits, and a complete wood-paneled drawing room brought over from an English manor house. ✉ *205 Church St.* ☎ *902/354-3067* 🌐 *www.rossignolculturalcentre.com* 💲 *C$5* ⏲ *Mid-May–mid-Oct., Tues.–Sun. 10–5.*

WORTH NOTING

FAMILY **Thomas Raddall Provincial Park.** With four migratory seabird sanctuaries nearby, this 1,600-acre park is a great spot for birding, and it has some good hiking trails. Or you could just stretch out on one of the white-sand beaches. Occasional organized activities include family fun days, a sand sculpture contest in September, and stargazing. ✉ *529 Raddall*

Park Rd., East Port l'Hebert ☎ 902/683–2664 🌐 www.novascotiaparks.ca 💲 Free ⏲ Mid-May–mid-Oct.

BEACHES

FAMILY **Summerville Beach Provincial Park.** The Liverpool area has easy access to some of the South Shore's best beaches, and this one has more than a kilometer of fine, pale-colored sand. Backing the beach is a dune system that shelters nesting sites for piping plovers—a clue to the location's uncrowded tranquility—and beyond this are salt marshes. Make sure to stick to the designated paths here. The shallow water makes Summerville ideal for families, and near the beach is a picnic area with tables that have sunshades. **Amenities:** parking (free); toilets. **Best for:** solitude; sunset; swimming; walking. ✉ *7533 Hwy. 3, Summerville Centre ✢ 14½ km (9 miles) southwest of Liverpool 🌐 www.novascotiaparks.ca 💲 Free ⏲ Mid-May–mid-Oct.*

WHERE TO EAT AND STAY

$$ B&B/INN **Lane's Privateer Inn.** Downtown Liverpool, though long on history, is short on accommodations, so this 200-year-old inn, once occupied by famed privateer Captain Joseph Barss, is a fortunate find, and most of its comfortable rooms have a river or harbor view. **Pros:** convenient location; pet-friendly; rate includes hot breakfast; some ground-floor rooms. **Cons:** room sizes vary; room renovation work in progress. 💲 *Rooms from: C$125 ✉ 27 Bristol Ave. ☎ 902/354–3456, 800/794–3332 🌐 lanesprivateerinn.wordpress.com 🛏 27 rooms 🍽 Breakfast.*

$$$$ RENTAL FAMILY **Quarterdeck Beachside Villas & Grill.** Built just above the high-water mark, on the edge of the Summerville Beach Provincial Park, these quality villas make you feel as if you're staying on a houseboat. **Pros:** terrific beach; babysitting service; restaurant offers room service and takeout; all units have whirlpool tubs. **Cons:** restaurant is closed from mid-October to mid-May. 💲 *Rooms from: C$349 ✉ 7499 Hwy. 3, Port Mouton ✢ 15 km (10 miles) west of Liverpool ☎ 902/683–2998, 800/565–1119 🌐 www.quarterdeck.ca 🛏 13 villas, 1 cottage 🍽 No meals.*

SPORTS AND THE OUTDOORS

Rossignol Surf Shop. The shop rents boards and wet suits and conducts two-hour surfing lessons for adults and one-hour lessons for children ages 9–12 (reservations recommended). If you're not staying at White Point Beach Resort, you'll need to pick up a day pass from the front desk. ✉ *White Point Beach Resort, 75 White Point Beach Resort Rd., White Point ✢ 10 km (6 miles) south of Liverpool ☎ 902/354–7100 🌐 www.surfnovascotia.com 💲 Board rentals from C$20; wet-suit rentals from C$15; adult lessons C$75.*

KEJIMKUJIK NATIONAL PARK AND HISTORIC SITE

67 km (42 miles) northwest of Liverpool; 45 km (28 miles) southeast of Annapolis Royal.

This inland woodsy area, within the UNESCO Southwest Nova Biosphere Reserve, attracts campers, canoeists, hikers, bird-watchers, and cyclists.

GETTING HERE AND AROUND

You'll need a car to get to the park, which is off Highway 8 between Liverpool and Annapolis Royal. Just south of Maitland Bridge, the Kejimkujik Main Parkway heads east into the park from the highway.

EXPLORING

FAMILY **Kejimkujik National Park.** You'll have to veer inland to see this 381-square-km (147-square-mile) national park, which is about halfway between the Atlantic and Fundy coasts. The Mi'Kmaq used these gentle waterways for thousands of years, a fact made plain by the ancient petroglyphs carved into rocks along the shore. You can explore "Keji" on your own or take a guided interpretive hike—perhaps spying beavers, owls, loons, white-tailed deer, and other wildlife along the way. Guided paddles and children's programs are also available in summer, and leaf peepers can see the deciduous forests blaze with color in autumn. Designated a Dark Sky Preserve by the Royal Astronomical Society of Canada, the park conducts nighttime programs for stargazers. ✉ *Kejimkujik Main Pkwy., Maitland Bridge* ✣ *Off Hwy. 8* ☎ *902/682–2772* 🌐 *www.pc.gc.ca* 💲 *C$5.80* ⏲ *Park: accessible year-round; Visitor Reception Centre: late June–early Sept., daily 8:30–8; mid-May–late June and early-Sept.–mid-Oct., Mon.–Thurs. 8:30–4:30, Fri. 8:30–7 or 8, Sat. 8:30–6.*

WHERE TO STAY

$ RESORT **Mersey River Chalets and Nature Retreat.** Swimming, paddling, hiking, and bedtime bonfires fill the agenda at this 375-acre wilderness resort 5 km (3 miles) north of Kejimkujik National Park. **Pros:** pets welcome; snowshoeing and cross-country skiing offered in winter; excellent accessibility for wheelchair-bound guests. **Cons:** on-site restaurant only offers Continental breakfast and snacks, and closes from October through April (though lodge guests have use of shared kitchen). 💲 *Rooms from: C$115* ✉ *322 Mersey River Chalets Rd. E, Caledonia* ✣ *Off Hwy. 8, 44 km (27 miles) south of Annapolis Royal, 75 km (47 miles) north of Liverpool* ☎ *902/682–2443, 877/667–2583* 🌐 *www.merseyriverchalets.ns.ca* 🛏 *9 chalets, 4 lodge rooms, 1 log house, 5 tipis* 🍽 *Breakfast.*

$ B&B/INN **Whitman Inn.** Proximity to the Kejimkujik National Park is the big draw here, and the cozy lodgings at this friendly inn ensure that you can go wild without sacrificing creature comforts. **Pros:** nice grounds; bed-and-breakfast intimacy with extra amenities. **Cons:** breakfast only included in a package; no air-conditioning; dinner orders must be made by 5 pm. 💲 *Rooms from: C$79* ✉ *12389 Hwy. 8, Kempt* ☎ *902/682–2226, 800/830–3855* 🌐 *www.whitmaninn.com* ⏲ *Closed mid-Oct–Mar.* 🛏 *8 rooms, 1 apartment* 🍽 *No meals.*

SPORTS AND THE OUTDOORS

Whynot Adventure Outfitters. Also known as Keji Outfitters, this company inside Kejimkujik National Park rents bicycles, rowboats, kayaks, canoes, and camping gear from mid-May through mid-October. Guided trips and shuttle services are also available. ✉ *Kejimkujic National Park, Kejimkujik Main Pkwy., Jakes Landing* ☎ *902/682–2282* 🌐 *www.whynotadventure.ca* 💲 *Rentals from C$10 per hr, C$26 per day, C$140 per wk.*

SHELBURNE

67 km (42 miles) southwest of Liverpool.

Shelburne, about two-thirds of the way down the Lighthouse Route, has a frozen-in-time appearance that many travelers love. It was settled after the American Revolution, when 10,000 Loyalists briefly made it one of the largest locales in North America—bigger than either Halifax or Montréal at the time. A smaller, temporary influx of Americans changed the face of Shelburne again in 1994, when film director Roland Joffe and crew arrived to shoot his version of *The Scarlet Letter.* The movie, starring Demi Moore, was an unequivocal mess, but the producers helped tidy up the town and raise awareness about its rich architectural heritage. Today's waterfront district looks much as it did when it was laid out in the 1780s, and many of the existing structures date from that period.

GETTING HERE AND AROUND

There is no public transportation to Shelburne. If you're driving from the Halifax direction, turn off Highway 103 at Exit 25 and follow Woodlawn Drive and then King Street. From the Yarmouth direction, you can take Exit 27 or Exit 26. Once in Shelburne, you'll find it pleasant to stroll around.

ESSENTIALS

Visitor Information **Shelburne Visitor Information Centre.** ✉ *43 Dock St.* ☎ *902/875-4547.*

EXPLORING

Black Loyalist Heritage Site. When Shelburne's population exploded after the Revolutionary War, Black Loyalists were relegated to land 7 km (4½ miles) northwest of town. The community they created—Birchtown, named for the British general who oversaw their evacuation from New York—became the biggest free settlement of African Americans in the world. Birchtown's virtually forgotten story was told in Lawrence Hill's award-winning novel *The Book of Negroes*, adapted for a CBC TV miniseries in 2015 and filmed locally, and its founders are now honored at this site, which includes a national historic monument, a 1½-km (1-mile) interpretive trail, and a small museum.

In June 2015 a new Heritage Centre opened here, replacing its predecessor that was destroyed in a fire. ✉ *98 Old Birchtown Rd., Birchtown* ✣ *Off Hwy. 103* ☎ *902/875-1310, 888/354-0772* ⊕ *www.blackloyalist.com* ₹ *Monument and trail: free; museum: C$8* ⏲ *Monument and trail: daily year-round; museum: May–Sept., daily 11–5; Oct.–Apr., by appointment.*

Shelburne Museum Complex. Shelburne's big-ticket attraction includes three properties operated by the Shelburne Historical Society. The **Ross-Thomson House and Store** is reputedly the oldest surviving (and from the looks of it, best stocked) general store in North America, restored to its 1820s appearance. Shelburne once had a thriving boatbuilding industry, turning out the traditional dories that were the mainstay of the fishing fleet. At the former waterfront workshop that houses the **J.C. Williams Dory Shop,** you can watch artisans craft new ones using old-fashioned techniques. Rounding out the trio, the **Shelburne County Museum** provides an overview of area history. ✉ *20 Dock St.* ☎ *902/875–3219* 🌐 *www.shelburnemuseums.com* 💲 *C$4 per museum, C$10 for the whole complex* ⏲ *June–mid-Oct., daily 9:30–5:30. Shelburne County Museum also open mid-Oct.–May, weekdays 9:30–noon and 1:30–4:30. Off-season hrs may vary.*

WHERE TO EAT AND STAY

$$$ EUROPEAN Fodor's Choice ★ ✕ **Charlotte Lane Café.** Chef-owner Roland Glauser whips up creative seafood, meat, and pasta dishes in a restored building that started out as a butcher shop in the mid-1800s. The chowder is great for lunch, and the rack of lamb with port-wine orange sauce and sun-dried berries is ideal at dinner, especially when capped with a refreshing lemon panna cotta. The café has a pleasant garden patio (a big plus, as there are only about 25 seats inside), plus a shop selling quality crafts. Reservations aren't accepted at lunch but are requested for dinner. 💲 *Average main: C$26* ✉ *13 Charlotte La.* ☎ *902/875–3314* 🌐 *www.charlottelane.ca* ⏲ *Closed Sun. and Mon. and mid-Dec.–early May.*

$ B&B/INN FAMILY **Cooper's Inn.** Shelburne's historic waterfront was the site of a major Loyalist landing in 1783, and a year later the structure that now houses this inn went up. **Pros:** lovely location with water-view garden; some rooms have massage chairs. **Cons:** only breakfast is served on-site; no air-conditioning. 💲 *Rooms from: C$110* ✉ *36 Dock St.* ☎ *902/875–4656, 800/688–2011* 🌐 *www.thecoopersinn.com* ⏲ *Closed mid-Dec.–Apr.* 🛏 *7 rooms, 1 suite* 🍴 *Breakfast.*

SPORTS AND THE OUTDOORS

Shelburne Harbour Boat Tours. You can explore Shelburne's beautiful natural harbor aboard the MV *Brown Eyed Girl,* a 44-foot trawler. Daily tours depart at 9 am for 3 hours, at 2 pm for 3½ hours, and the 2½-hour evening tour sets out at 6 pm. The eight-hour McNutt's Island Adventure includes the harbor tour and time on the island, where you can hike up to the Cape Roseway Lighthouse. Every Thursday June–August there's also a two-hour 6 pm Kitchen Party Cruise, with live Nova Scotia music and finger food. ✉ *107 Water St.* ☎ *902/875–6521* 🌐 *www.shelburneharbourboattours.com* 💲 *Kitchen Party Cruise C$30, evening tour C$25, all other tours C$35* ⏲ *June–Sept.*

BARRINGTON AND CAPE SABLE ISLAND

48 km (35 miles) south of Shelburne.

Cape Sable Island—not to be confused with Sable Island, way out in the Atlantic—is a sleepy spot just off the beaten path, known for its contribution to the province's seafood harvest. You'll find colorful fishing boats afloat in Clark's Harbour. There are fine sandy beaches as well, one of which, Hawk Beach, offers excellent bird-watching and views of the 1861 Cape Sable Island Lighthouse.

GETTING HERE AND AROUND

Cape Sable Island is Nova Scotia's most southern point, located south of Shelburne and acessed via the short Cape Sable Island Causeway (NS–330 South). Barrington is on the mainland side of the causeway along Highway 3.

EXPLORING

Archelaus Smith Museum. This museum, named for an early New England settler, is worth a visit. It recaptures late-1700s life with household items such as quilts and toys, plus fishing gear and information about shipwrecks and sea captains. ✉ *915 Hwy. 330, Cape Sable Island* ☎ *902/745–2642* 💲 *Free* ⏲ *Late June–late Aug., Mon.–Sat. 10–4:30, Sun. 1:30–4:30.*

Barrington museums. The town of Barrington, on the mainland side of the Cape Sable Island Causeway, has several old buildings along Highway 3 that are worth visiting. These include the **Woolen Mill Museum,** at No. 2368; the **Old Meeting House,** at No. 2408, where gatherings, elections, and religious services were held; the **Seal Island Light Museum,** at No. 2410, which occupies a replica lighthouse; and the **Western Counties Military Museum,** at No. 2401. They are all administered by the Cape Sable Historical Society, based in the Old Courthouse at No. 2401. ✉ *Hwy. 3, Barrington* ☎ *902/637–2185 Cape Sable Historical Society* 🌐 *capesablehistoricalsociety.com* 💲 *C$5 each museum (ask about discount if visiting 3 or more)* ⏲ *June–Sept., Mon.–Sat. 9:30–5:30, Sun., 1–5:30.*

YARMOUTH

98 km (61 miles) west of Shelburne.

Yarmouth's status as a large port and its proximity to New England accounted for its early prosperity, and today the town's shipping heritage is still reflected in its fine harbor, marinas, and museums. The ferry service from Maine makes this an obvious destination for U.S. travelers, and the handsome Victorian architecture and a pleasantly old-fashioned main street make it worth a visit. Since the Evangeline Trail and Lighthouse Trail converge here, Yarmouth also allows easy access to the Acadian villages to the north or the Loyalist communities to the south.

GETTING HERE AND AROUND

If you're coming from or via Maine, the Portland–Yarmouth ferry service operated by Nova Star Cruises, daily from June to mid-October, offers an overnight sailing, departing Portland's Ocean Gateway Terminal at 8 pm (final boarding 7:15) and arriving in Yarmouth at 8 am. One-way passenger fares, excluding port fees and fuel surcharges, start at US$95, or US$179.20 round-trip, and vehicles cost from US$94 one-way. For a family of two adults and two children under 14, the round-trip, including a vehicle and cabin, will cost around US$750. Within Nova Scotia, Bernie's Shuttle Service links Halifax to Yarmouth once a day (C$75 one-way), leaving Halifax (including pickups at and Stanfield International Airport) each afternoon between 2 and 4 pm for the 3½-hour journey. The trip back departs Yarmouth at 8 am. If you're driving, Yarmouth is at the eastern end of Highway 103 along the South Shore and Highway 101 along the Fundy coast. For getting around, a new bus service follows a circular route around the town for a flat rate of C$3 per day or C$15 per week.

ESSENTIALS

Visitor Information **Yarmouth Visitor Information Centre.** ✉ *228 Main St.* ☎ *902/742-5033* 🌐 *www.yarmouthandacadianshores.com.*

EXPLORING

Art Gallery of Nova Scotia (Western Branch). This is the gallery's satellite location. As with the flagship in Halifax, this one is housed in a heritage building and has a broad mandate, yet it's at its best when showcasing the works of regional artists. The branch exhibits art from the main gallery's permanent collection and mounts temporary shows of folk art and other disciplines. Family Sundays and children's workshops occasionally take place. If you plan to visit both branches, keep your receipt—it will give you a reduction on the second admission fee. ✉ *341 Main St.* ☎ *902/749-2248* 🌐 *www.artgalleryofnovascotia.ca* 💲 *C$6* ⏲ *Weekdays 8:30–4:30, weekends 11–5.*

Cape Forchu Lighthouse. It isn't the South Shore's most photogenic lighthouse—the one at Peggy's Cove wins that award—but this one finishes a close second, scoring points for its dramatic vistas and the dearth of other camera-clutching tourists. Erected in 1962 on the site of an earlier lighthouse, the concrete structure rises 75 feet above the entrance to Yarmouth Harbour. The adjacent keeper's quarters houses a small museum, a tearoom serving local treats, and a gift shop. ✉ *1856 Cape Forchu Rd., off Hwy. 304, Cape Forchu* ☎ *902/742-4522* 🌐 *www.capeforchulight.com* 💲 *Donations accepted* ⏲ *June–late Sept., daily 11–7.*

Yarmouth County Museum & Archives. One of the largest collections of ship paintings in Canada resides here, along with exhibits of household items, musical instruments (including rare mechanical pianos and music boxes), and other items that richly evoke centuries past. There's even a Norse runic stone dating back to Viking transatlantic explorations around AD 1000. The museum has a preservation wing and an archival research area, where local history and genealogy are documented. Next door is the **Pelton-Fuller House,** summer home of the original Fuller Brush Man, which is maintained and furnished much as the family left it. The museum offers guided tours of a third building in high season: the **Killam Brothers Shipping Office.** Located at 90 Water Street, it recalls a long-standing family business that was established here in 1788. ✉ *22 Collins St.* ☎ *902/742-5539* 🌐 *yarmouthcountymuseum.ca* 💲 *Museum C$3, Pelton-Fuller House C$3, combined ticket C$5. Killam Brothers Shipping Office, call for details* ⏲ *Museum: June–Sept., daily 9–5; Oct.–May, Tues.–Sat. 2–5. Pelton-Fuller House: June–Sept. or by appointment; Killam Brothers Shipping Office: July and Aug. only.*

WHERE TO EAT AND STAY

$ CANADIAN

✕ **JoAnne's Quick 'n Tasty.** Laminated tables, vinyl banquettes, and bright lights greet you at this retro diner that still looks much as it did circa 1960. Options include fresh seafood and no-nonsense standbys like turkey burgers and club sandwiches. Devotees, however, swear by the hot lobster sandwich. Indeed, Haligonians have been known to make the three-hour trek just to dine on the creamed crustacean concoction that was supposedly invented here. $ *Average main: C$11* ✉ *490 Hwy. 1, 4 km (2½ miles) northeast of Yarmouth, Dayton* ☎ *902/742–6606* ⏲ *Closed Dec.–Feb.*

$$ SEAFOOD ✕ **Rudder's Seafood Restaurant and Brew Pub.** As its name implies, this hopping waterfront spot serves the expected fish dishes along with pub grub like steak with seafood and fries and Acadian rappie pie, all of which can be washed down with ales handcrafted on-site. Seating is inside a converted warehouse supported by 18th-century beams or, in fine weather, at picnic tables on the wraparound deck. Since Rudder's doubles as a microbrewery, you can also buy beer to go. Live entertainment on Wednesday, Friday, and Saturday evenings is good reason to linger, and if you're sailing in, they have their own floating-dock marina. $ *Average main: C$18* ✉ *96 Water St.* ☎ *902/742–7311* 🌐 *www.ruddersbrewpub.com.*

$$ B&B/INN **Harbour's Edge Bed & Breakfast.** If you're looking for waterside gardens, appealing rooms, and welcoming hosts, you'll find them all at this 1864 home. **Pros:** the only Yarmouth lodging that's on the water; exemplary hosts; terrific French toast at breakfast. **Cons:** road outside can be busy; private bath for the "Clara Caie" room's bathroom, while private, is down the hall. $ *Rooms from: C$145* ✉ *12 Vancouver St.* ☎ *902/742–2387* 🌐 *www.harboursedge.ns.ca* 🛏 *4 rooms* 🍽 *Breakfast.*

$$$ RESORT Fodor's Choice ★ **Trout Point Lodge.** Guests at this wilderness eco-resort can get away from it all without sacrificing luxury, excellent food, and top-notch amenities. **Pros:** Relais & Chateaux property; hot tub, sauna, and in-room massages available. **Cons:** can be too secluded for some; no children under 14; no cell phone coverage. $ *Rooms from: C$249* ✉ *189 Trout Point Rd., East Kemptville* ✣ *Off East Branch Rd. and Hwy. 203, 40 km (25 miles) northeast of Yarmouth* ☎ *902/761–2142* 🌐 *www.troutpoint.com* 🛏 *11 rooms, 1 suite, 2 cottages* 🍽 *Some meals.*

SHOPPING

Hands On Crafts. Local artisans make all the cool jewelry, knitwear, birch-bark soap, and other items sold at this downtown co-op. ✉ *314 Main St.* ☎ *902/742–3515* 🌐 *www.handsoncrafts.ca.*

The Yarmouth Wool Shoppe. Whether you're looking for a gift or something to keep you warm on chilly Nova Scotian evenings, this local institution, open since 1883, has got you covered. Much of the inventory consists of high-end imported items from England, Ireland, and Scotland, including duffel coats, mohair throws, cashmere shawls and sweaters, Guernsey fisherman-knit sweaters, and tartan robes. If you'd rather create your own garment, they also have knitting yarns. ✉ *352 Main St.* ☎ *902/742–2255.*

POINTE DE L'ÉGLISE (CHURCH POINT)

70 km (43 miles) north of Yarmouth.

As small as they are, you still can't miss the communities that collectively make up the Acadian Shore. Each one on this stretch, beginning roughly in Beaver River and ending in St. Bernard, seems to have a surplus of Stella Maris flags, a disproportionately large Catholic church, and a French-speaking populace with an abiding passion for *rappie* pie, a hearty chicken stew with shredded potatoes. Church Point, called Pointe de l'Église by Francophones, tops the rest on all three counts.

GETTING HERE AND AROUND

There is no public transportation to Pointe de l'Église. By car, it's on Highway 1, the Evangeline Trail, which follows the coast parallel to Highway 101. Coming from the west, take Exit 29 onto Little Brook Road, then go north on the Evangeline; from the east, take Exit 28 onto the Evangeline at St. Bernard.

EXPLORING

Rendez-vous de la Baie. An arts and cultural complex that tries to be all things to all people—and succeeds—the Rendez-vous de la Baie serves locals, tourists, and students. Housed in a contemporary structure on the Université Sainte-Anne campus, the center has as its highlight the **Acadian Interpretive Centre and Museum,** whose exhibits provide an evocative overview of Acadian culture and history. The Rendez-vous complex also includes an art gallery that shows contemporary works, a theater for live and media presentations, an Internet café that hosts events, and a visitor information center. The gift shop at the interpretive center carries an excellent selection of Acadian music. ✉ *Université Sainte-Anne, 23 Lighthouse Rd, Unit 1, Pointe d'Église* ☎ *902/769–2345* ⊕ *rendezvousdelabaie.ca* ⏲ *Sept.–mid-June, daily 7–4:30; mid-June–Aug., weekdays 8–6, weekends 9–5 (café and boutique close at 3).*

St. Mary's Church (Église Ste-Marie). The *église* for which this village is named stands proudly on the main road overshadowing everything around it. That's hardly surprising given that it is the largest wooden church in North America. Completed in 1905, St. Mary's is 190 feet long by 185 feet high, and the steeple, which requires 40 tons of rock ballast to keep it steady when ocean winds blow, can be seen for miles. The church is a registered museum with a stunning interior, two exhibit rooms housing a collection of vestments, and a souvenir shop that sells religious articles. Bilingual guides give tours regularly in summer and off-season by appointment. ✉ *1713 Hwy.1, Pointe d'Église* ☎ *902/769–2832* ⊕ *www.museeeglisesaintemariemuseum.ca* 💵 *C$2 recommended donation* ⏲ *Mid-May–mid-Oct., daily 9–5; mid-Oct.–mid-May by appointment.*

WHERE TO EAT AND STAY

$$$ SEAFOOD Fodor's Choice ★

✕ **La Cuisine Robicheau.** Firmly established as *the* place to eat along this stretch of the coast, this restaurant specializes in seafood and Acadian cuisine. The excellent *pâté à la râpure* (rappie pie)—a traditional Acadian dish in this case containing grated potatoes and chicken or clams, all baked until brown—is usually the first thing to sell out. Come early if you'd like to sample it—or come early anyway, since they close at 8 pm. Other good choices include the *fricot aux poutines râpées à la poule* (chicken soup with potato dumplings) and the haddock topped with lobster. The restaurant, which overlooks the ocean, occupies a restored and extended house, and its five individually styled seating areas make for an intimate dining experience. If you want wine with your meal, you'll need to bring your own. $ *Average main: C$21* ✉ *9651 Hwy. 1, Saulnierville* ☎ *902/769-2121* 🌐 *www.lacuisinerobicheau.com* ⏲ *Closed Mon.* ✍ *Reservations essential.*

$ B&B/INN **Château d'la Baie.** Beautifully restored, this grand Victorian mansion sits on the ocean side of the Evangeline Trail and offers large and sunny rooms furnished with antiques. **Pros:** exceptionally large rooms; convenient for the Université Sainte-Anne and Pointe de l'Église. **Cons:** some rooms don't have a sea view; not everyone cares for the communal breakfast-table concept. $ *Rooms from: C$95* ✉ *959 Hwy. 1, Little Brook, Baie Sainte-Marie* ☎ *902/769-3113* 🌐 *www.havreducapitaine.ca/chateau* 💳 *No credit cards* ⏲ *Closed Nov.–Apr.* 🛏 *7 rooms* 🍽 *Breakfast.*

$ HOTEL **Havre du Capitaine.** Within easy reach of both Pointe de l'Église and Yarmouth, this low-rise lodging along the Evangeline Trail has sea views and modern, good-size rooms. **Pros:** friendly service; convenient location. **Cons:** breakfast a little disappointing. $ *Rooms from: C$87* ✉ *9118 Hwy. 1, Meteghan* ☎ *902/769-2001* 🌐 *www.havreducapitaine.ca* 🛏 *18 rooms* 🍽 *Breakfast.*

THAT SOUNDS HEAVENLY!

Musique Saint-Bernard. The neo-Gothic St. Bernard Church, a stone structure famous for its acoustics, hosts classical concerts on some summer Sundays at 4 pm. Acclaimed artists from Canada and beyond perform here under the Musique Saint-Bernard banner. The church, a few miles north of Church Point, seats 1,000. Tickets are available at the door. ✉ ***Evangeline Trail, St. Bernard*** ☎ ***902/837-5687*** 💵 ***C$15 (cash only).***

DIGBY

35 km (22 miles) northeast of Pointe de l'Église/Church Point.

Digby is underappreciated: people tend to race to or from the ferry connecting it with Saint John, New Brunswick. Yet there is quite a bit to the town, including a rich history that dates to the 1783 arrival of Loyalists, and an appealing waterfront. Then, of course, there are the legendary Digby scallops. The world's largest in-shore scallop fleet docks in the harbor, and the plump, sweet "fruits of the sea" unloaded here are deemed to be delicacies everywhere. Come, if you can, for the Digby Scallop Days festival in early August. There *are* other fish in the sea, though, and while walking along the waterfront, you can buy ultrafresh halibut, cod, and lobster—some merchants will even cook your purchase for you right on the spot. You can also sample Digby chicks (aka salty smoked herring) in local pubs or buy them from fish markets.

GETTING HERE AND AROUND

Bay Ferries Ltd. sails the *Fundy Rose* between Saint John, New Brunswick, and Digby year-round. There is at least one round-trip per day—two per day mid-May to mid-October and in December—and the crossing takes about two hours 15 minutes. If you are already in Nova Scotia, you'll need to drive here on Highway 1, the Evangeline Trail, or Highway 101 (which are the same road as you approach Digby). Take Exit 26. The town itself is easily explored on foot.

ESSENTIALS

Visitor Information **Digby Tourist Bureau.** ✉ *110 Montague Row* ☎ *888/463-4429, 902/245-5714.*

EXPLORING

Admiral Digby Museum. The town, county, and this museum are named for Britain's Rear Admiral Robert Digby, who during the American Revolution helped evacuate Loyalists to Nova Scotia following the British surrender of New York City. You can learn a little bit about the admiral and a fair amount about Digby County history viewing the artifacts, paintings, and maps displayed here. ✉ *95 Montague Row* ☎ *902/245-6322* 🌐 *admiraldigbymuseum.ca* 💲 *By donation* ⏲ *July and Aug., Mon.–Sat. 9–noon and 1–5; Sept., Mon. 1–4:30, Tues.–Fri. 9–noon and 1–4:30; Oct., Nov., Mar., and Apr., Tues.–Fri. 1–4:30; May, weekdays 1–4:30; June, Mon.–Wed. 1–4:30.*

WHERE TO EAT AND STAY

$$$ SEAFOOD FAMILY ✕ **Fundy Restaurant.** A waterfront location with stunning harbor views and great seafood make this a prime spot in Digby to sample the world-famous local scallops as well as lobster, salmon, Bay of Fundy halibut, and a few non-seafood dishes for good measure. The lunch menu is lighter and includes chowder, sandwiches, fish-and-chips, and a crispy "seaburger," plus a kids' menu with plenty of choices. On the same premises, the Dockside Restaurant and Bar has a waterfront deck. 💲 *Average main: C$28* ✉ *34 Water St.* ☎ *902/245-4950* 🌐 *www.fundyrestaurant.com.*

$$ RESORT FAMILY **Digby Pines Golf Resort and Spa.** Complete with walking trails, lavish gardens, and Annapolis Basin views, this casually elegant 300-acre property offers myriad comforts. **Pros:** kids under seven eat free; no charge for Digby shuttle service. **Cons:** nearest beach is small, rocky, and across the road. 💲 *Rooms from: C$163* ✉ *103 Shore Rd.* ☎ *902/245-2511, 800/667-4637* 🌐 *www.digbypines.ca* ⏲ *Closed mid-Oct.–May* 🛏 *84 rooms, 6 suites, 31 cottages* 🍴 *No meals.*

SPORTS AND THE OUTDOORS

FAMILY **Fundy Adventures.** Based in Gulliver's Cove, about 18 km (11 miles) from Digby, this company organizes clam digging, periwinkle picking, dulse harvesting, lobster hauling, and other tasty activities from April through September. ✉ *685 Gulliver's Cove Rd.* ✣ *Off Hwy. 217* ☎ *902/245-4388* 🌐 *www.fundyadventures.com* 💲 *C$66–C$111.*

FAMILY **Fundy Complex.** If you want to get out on the water, drop by the complex to rent a kayak. Singles, doubles, and stand-up paddleboards are available from June through September. ✉ *34 Water St.* ☎ *902/245-4950, 866/445-4950* 🌐 *www.fundyrestaurant.com* 💲 *Rentals from C$39, including all equipment.*

LONG ISLAND AND BRIER ISLAND

About 46 km (40 miles) southwest of Digby.

You don't just stumble across these islands—reaching them requires a commitment. It's well worth the effort because Long Island and Brier Island are surrounded by water rich in plankton, which attracts a variety of whales along with harbor porpoises, seals, and abundant seabirds. Bring your binoculars.

GETTING HERE AND AROUND

First, follow Highway 217 down to the end of Digby Neck, a narrow peninsula separating St. Mary's Bay and the Bay of Fundy, to the hamlet of East Ferry. From there hop a five-minute ferry for Tiverton, Long Island. If you're going on to Brier Island, take a second, eight-minute ferry ride onward from Freeport, Long Island, to Westport. Brier Island Ferry links the two islands. Ferries must scuttle sideways to fight the ferocious Fundy tidal streams coursing through the narrow gaps. They operate hourly, year-round, at a cost of C$7 for each ferry (cash only) for the round-trip for car and passengers.

ESSENTIALS

Ferry Contact **Brier Island Ferry.** ✉ *Westport* ☎ *902/839–2302.*

WHERE TO EAT AND STAY

$ HOTEL **Brier Island Lodge and Restaurant.** Atop a bluff at Nova Scotia's most westerly point, this three-building complex commands a panoramic view of the Bay of Fundy. **Pros:** whale-watching tours; on-site gift shop. **Cons:** motel-quality rooms; main lodge rooms lack ocean views; breakfast not included in off-season. $ *Rooms from: C$99* ✉ *557 Water St., Westport* ☎ *902/839–2300, 800/662–8355* 🌐 *www.brierisland.com* ⏲ *Closed Nov.–Apr.* 🛏 *38 rooms* 🍴 *Some meals.*

SPORTS AND THE OUTDOORS

FAMILY Fodor's Choice ★ **Brier Island Whale and Seabird Cruises.** Of several operators of seasonal boat tours, this is best. On thrice-daily trips, from early June until mid-October, you travel out of Westport on the MV *Mega Nova*, with researchers who collect data for international organizations. A portion of the fare funds further research. The same company also offers adrenaline-fueled Zodiac excursions five times daily from mid-May through mid-October. ✉ *223 Water St., Westport* ☎ *902/839–2995* 🌐 *www.brierislandwhalewatch.com* 💲 *Mega Nova C$50, Zodiac C$62.*

FAMILY **Mariner Cruises Whale & Seabird Tours.** Narration by an onboard naturalist makes this operator's cruises (from 2½ to 4½ hours) a solid choice. Boats depart Westport daily from early June to mid-October. ✉ *325 Water St., Westport* ☎ *902/839–2346, 800/239–2189* 🌐 *www.novascotiawhalewatching.ca* 💲 *C$49.*

FAMILY **Ocean Explorations Whale Cruises.** Tom Goodwin, a marine and wildlife biologist, conducts well-regarded trips in fast-paced, open-top Zodiacs to view whales and other marine life. ✉ *Hwy. 217, opposite old ferry wharf, Tiverton* ☎ *902/839–2417, 877/654–2341* 🌐 *www.oceanexplorations.ca* 💲 *C$65.*

ANNAPOLIS ROYAL

37 km (23 miles) northeast of Digby.

Fodor's Choice ★ Annapolis Royal's history spans nearly four centuries, and the town's bucolic appearance today belies its turbulent past. One of Canada's oldest settlements, it was founded by the French in 1605, destroyed by the British in 1613, rebuilt by the French as the main town of Acadia, and then fought over for the better part of a century. Finally, in 1710, New England colonists claimed the town and renamed it in honor of Queen Anne. There are approximately 150 historic sites and heritage buildings here, including the privately owned DeGannes-Cosby House, the oldest wooden house in Canada (built in 1708), which happens to sit on St. George, Canada's oldest street.

As if it didn't have enough history on its own, Annapolis Royal is also the ideal starting point for excursions to Port Royal, the place where European settlement of Canada began.

GETTING HERE AND AROUND

There is no public transportation to Annapolis Royal. To drive here, take the Evangeline Trail or Highway 101 to Exit 22. If you are traveling from the east, Highway 201 is also an option.

ESSENTIALS

Visitor Information **Annapolis Royal Visitor Information Centre.** ✉ *204 Prince Albert Rd.* ☎ *902/532-5454* ⊕ *www.annapolisroyal.com.*

EXPLORING

TOP ATTRACTIONS

Historical Association of Annapolis Royal. Because Annapolis Royal flip-flopped between the French and English so many times, the past here is a complicated affair, but the members of the historical association are happy to walk you through it. They've developed a series of high-season strolls led by guides dressed in typical 18th-century fashion. This is an entertaining way to learn more about the historic significance and cultural heritage of the region. Options include daytime tours of the National Historic District and sites associated with the Acadian Experience, and in July and August there's an Acadian Candlelight tour on Monday nights. Reservations for tours aren't necessary, but call or check the website for times. The wildly popular Candlelight Graveyard Tour of Canada's oldest English cemetery (at Fort Anne) takes place at 9:30 pm several times a week from early June through mid-October. The association has put together a self-guided walk pamphlet for visitors who'd rather wander independently. ✉ *Annapolis Royal* ☎ *902/532-3035* ⊕ *www.tourannapolisroyal.com* ₵ *From C$9.*

FAMILY
Fodor's Choice
★

Port Royal National Historic Site. Downriver from Annapolis Royal is this reconstruction of Sieur de Monts and Samuel de Champlain's fur-trading post. The French set up shop here in 1605—two years before the English established Jamestown—making this the first permanent European settlement north of Florida. Port Royal also set other New World records, claiming the first tended crops, the first staged play, the first social club, and the first water mill. Unfortunately, it didn't have the first fire department: the original fortress burned down within a decade. At this suitably weathered replica, which is ringed by a log palisade, you're free to poke around the forge, inspect the trading post, pull up a chair at the dining table, or simply watch costumed interpreters perform traditional tasks in the courtyard. Children can play dress-up, too, donning period outfits and wooden sabot shoes. ✉ *Annapolis Royal* ✣ *Hwy. 1 to Granville Ferry, then left 10½ km (6½ miles), following* *signs for Port Royal ☎ 902/532–2898, 902/532–2321 🌐 www.pc.gc.ca 💲 C$3.90 ⏲ Late June–early Sept., daily 9–5:30; mid-May–late June and early Sept.–mid-Oct., Tues.–Sat. 9–5:30; grounds open year-round.*

WORTH NOTING

Annapolis Royal Farmers' and Traders' Market. On Saturday mornings from 8 to 1 mid-May through mid-October and on Wednesdays from 10 to 2 in July and August, the best place in Annapolis Royal to stock up on picnic supplies is the farmers' market, which sets up on lower St. George Street next to Ye Olde Towne Pub. Expect artisanal bread, cured meats, homemade sweets, and preserves, plus fresh Annapolis Valley produce. Local craftsmen attend, too, and there's live entertainment. Most vendors only accept cash. *✉ 178 St. George St. ☎ 902/245–4824 🌐 www.annapolisroyalfarmersmarket.com.*

Annapolis Royal Historic Gardens. Like everything else in this town, the plants here are a blast from the past—17 heritage-themed acres represent different eras and include a glorious Victorian garden, a knot garden, a typical Acadian house garden, and a 2,000-bush rose collection with about 250 varieties. *✉ 441 St. George St. ☎ 902/532–7018 🌐 www.historicgardens.com 💲 C$11.75 ⏲ Mid-May–June and Sept.–mid-Oct., daily 9–5; July and Aug., daily 9–8.*

Fort Anne National Historic Site. Gazing over the grassy knolls, it's hard to believe that this fort qualifies as the "most attacked spot in Canadian history" or that those knolls are actually nearly 400-year-old earthwork ramparts built up, in part, with rubble and blood. First fortified in 1629, the site preserves what is left of the fourth military edifice to be erected here, an early-18th-century gunpowder magazine and officers' quarters. The latter now houses a small museum, and anyone who believes a picture is worth 1,000 words should be sure to see the massive Heritage Tapestry displayed inside. Its four meticulously detailed panels depict four centuries of local history and as many local cultures. Special events at the fort include reenactments and Mi'Kmaq cultural presentations. You can download the Explora GPS app or rent a device on-site. *✉ 323 St. George St. ☎ 902/532–2397 June–Sept., 902/532–2321 Oct.–May 🌐 www.pc.gc.ca 💲 Grounds free, museum C$3.90 ⏲ Grounds: daily dawn–dusk; museum: late June–early Sept., daily 9–5:30, early–late June and early–late Sept., Tues.–Sat. 9–5:30.*

FAMILY **Upper Clements Parks.** A theme park with rides and an adventure park where you can test your skills and stamina clambering through the treetops are the stars here, all in a setting of apple orchards and lawns. The theme park has more than 30 rides and attractions, many of which are kiddy classics such as mini planes and trains and an old-fashioned carousel. More action-oriented guests can brave the wooden Tree Topper Roller Coaster, free-fall from The Tower, or zoom above the property on a 300-foot zip line, then splash out on the 230-foot waterslide. There's also horseback-riding and a BMX course. *✉ 2931 Hwy. 1 ✣ On the Evangeline Trail, 5 km (3 miles) southwest of Annapolis Royal ☎ 902/532–7557, 888/248–4567 🌐 www.upperclementsparks.com 💲 Theme Park C$29.50 including unlimited rides, Adventure Park C$29.50, zip line from C$20 ⏲ Mid-June–early Sept., daily 11–7.*

WHERE TO EAT

$$ CANADIAN **Ye Olde Towne Pub.** The substantial lunches and dinners served at this merry, low-key pub are a hit with locals who appreciate the good homemade fare, including the always excellent apple crisp. Diners sometimes spill out of the 1884 brick building and onto the patio, which is adjacent to a square where the farmers' market takes place. In a town short on nightlife, it's also a good place for post-dinner lounging. $ *Average main: C$15* ✉ *9–11 Church St.* ☎ *902/532–2244.*

WHERE TO STAY

$$ B&B/INN Fodor's Choice ★ **The Bailey House.** This blissful B&B, in an immaculately restored Georgian home on North America's oldest streetscape, does everything right—and it's on the waterfront. **Pros:** only B&B in town on the water; comfy feather-topped beds; lovely garden. **Cons:** no air-conditioning. $ *Rooms from: C$140* ✉ *150 St. George St.* ☎ *902/532–1285, 877/532–1285* ⊕ *www.baileyhouse.ca* *4 rooms, 1 suite* *Breakfast.*

$ B&B/INN **Bread and Roses Inn.** This historic Queen Anne–style mansion in the heart of town retains many original architectural details, such as soaring windows and mahogany and black-walnut moldings. **Pros:** stunning public areas; some rooms are überromantic; two rooms have river views. **Cons:** room sizes vary; third floor has only 8-foot ceilings. $ *Rooms from: C$124* ✉ *82 Victoria St.* ☎ *902/532–5727, 888/899–0551 reservations only* ⊕ *www.breadandroses.ns.ca* *Closed Nov.–Mar.* *8 rooms* *Breakfast.*

$ B&B/INN **Hillsdale House Inn.** Princes, kings, and prime ministers have all visited this historic 1859 property, which is convenient to the town's attractions and restaurants yet shielded from the downtown bustle. **Pros:** pet-friendly; impeccably clean. **Cons:** some bathrooms have a shower but no tub; air-conditioning in third-floor and some second-floor rooms only. $ *Rooms from: C$119* ✉ *519 George St.* ☎ *902/532–2345, 877/839–2821* ⊕ *www.hillsdalehouseinn.ca* *13 rooms* *Breakfast.*

$$ B&B/INN **Queen Anne Inn.** A beautiful Victorian building that's rimmed with gardens may not be out of the ordinary in Annapolis Royal, but what really distinguishes this inn is the consistent quality of the guest rooms, all generously proportioned and handsomely decorated. **Pros:** family-friendly; in-room extras include fluffy bathrobes. **Cons:** dinner served Wednesday to Sunday only; inn closed off-season. $ *Rooms from: C$129* ✉ *494 St. George St.* ☎ *902/532–7850, 877/536–0403* ⊕ *www.queenanneinn.ns.ca* *Closed late Oct.–early May* *10 rooms, 2 suites* *Breakfast.*

NIGHTLIFE AND PERFORMING ARTS

King's Theatre. Drama, concerts, comedy, and independent films are among the offerings at this intimate but up-to-date venue that opened in 1921 as a movie house. ✉ *209 St. George St.* ☎ *902/532–7704* ⊕ *www.kingstheatre.ca.*

SHOPPING

Catfish Moon Studio. Whimsical earthenware made on-site is sold here, as well as fun local crafts and folk art. ✉ *170 St. George St.* ☎ *902/532–3055* ⊕ *www.catfishmoon.com.*

Lucky Rabbit Pottery. Classic porcelain pieces decorated with contemporary designs are the specialty here. ✉ *15 Church St.* ☎ *902/532–0928* 🌐 *www.luckyrabbitpottery.ca* ⏲ *July and Aug., daily; otherwise Sat. 8–1 or by appointment.*

WOLFVILLE

114 km (71 miles) east of Annapolis Royal.

Settled in the 1760s by New Englanders, Wolfville is a fetching college town with ornate Victorian homes (some of which have been converted into B&Bs), a lively arts scene, and several fine restaurants. Established in 1838, Acadia University and its handsomely groomed hillside campus dominate the town, and the student population rivals that of the residents. The natural setting is impressive, too: after all, the fields here are fertile enough to support a thriving wine industry. That's due partly to a mild microclimate and partly to an elaborate system of dikes built by the Acadians in the early 1700s to reclaim arable land from the unusually high tides. They can still be viewed along many of the area's back roads. The original Acadians didn't get to enjoy the fruits of their labor, but their legacy lives on at nearby Grand-Pré.

GETTING HERE AND AROUND

Maritime Bus offers daily service on its Halifax–Kentville route, with bus stops at Acadia University (Horton Avenue) and the Mud Creek Mini Mart (Skyway Avenue). If you're driving, the Evangeline Trail runs right through town, and Highway 101 runs along the southern edge—take Exit 10 or Exit 11.

ESSENTIALS

Visitor Information **Wolfville Visitor Information Centre.** ✉ *11 Willow Ave.* ☎ *902/542–7000, 877/999–7117* 🌐 *www.wolfville.ca.*

EXPLORING

TOP ATTRACTIONS

Fodor's Choice ★ **Domaine de Grand Pré.** With award-winning vintages and sigh-inducing Fundy views, a stop at Domaine de Grand Pré is doubly pleasing. Vineyard tours and tastings are offered three times daily. They take about 45 minutes, but you'll likely want to linger on this picturesque 10-acre property, so plan to have a meal at Le Caveau Restaurant or sip a glass of wine under the pergola. ✉ *11611 Hwy. 1* ✣ *3 km (2 miles) east of Wolfville* ☎ *902/542–1753, 866/479–4637* 🌐 *grandprewines.ns.ca* 💲 *Tour and tasting C$7* ⏲ *Wineshop: Mon.–Wed. 10–6, Thurs.–Sat. 10–7, Sun. 11–6; tours: May–mid-Oct., daily at 11, 3, and 5.*

Grand Pré National Historic Site. Added to UNESCO's list of World Heritage Sites in 2012, this site commemorates the expulsion of the Acadians by the British in 1755. The tragic story is retold at the visitor center through artifacts and an innovative multimedia presentation that depicts *Le Grand Dérangement* from both a civilian and military perspective. The latter is shown in a wraparound theater that's modeled on a ship's interior. A bronze statue of Evangeline, the title character of Longfellow's tear-jerking epic poem, stands outside a memorial stone church that contains Acadian genealogical records. The manicured grounds have a garden, a duck pond, and, appropriately enough, French weeping willows. ✉ *Grand Pré Rd., Grand Pré* ✣ *Off Hwy. 1 (Evangeline Trail), 5 km (3 miles) east of Wolfville* ☎ *902/542–3631, 866/542–3631* ⊕ *www.grand-pre.com* 💲 *C$7.80* ⏲ *Mid-May–mid-Oct, daily 9–5; grounds open year-round.*

OFF THE BEATEN PATH

Hall's Harbour. You'll see one of the best natural harbors on the upper Bay of Fundy and some of the highest tides *anywhere* in Hall's Harbour, a small community about 30 km (18 miles) northwest of Wolfville via Kentville and Highway 359. Go for a walk on a gravel beach bordered by cliffs, try sea kayaking, or seek out the artisans whose studios open here during summer months. The small Red Fishhouse Museum, with local artifacts, is open in summer. ☎ *902/678–7001* ⊕ *www.hallsharbour.org.*

Hall's Harbour Lobster Pound & Restaurant. If you're in the neighborhood during lobster season, this site is well worth a visit. It's one of the largest lobster holding facilities in Canada, storing live lobsters in temperature-controlled pounds until they can be packed and shipped to international destinations. You can pick out a lobster and have it prepared in the "cook shack" and delivered to you in the waterfront dining room. Or buy a live one to go. ✉ *1157 W. Halls Harbour Rd., Hall's Harbour* ☎ *902/679–5299* ⊕ *www.hallsharbourlobster.com* ⏲ *Mid-May–June and Sept.–mid-Oct., daily noon–7; July and Aug., daily 11:30–9.*

WORTH NOTING

Acadia University Art Gallery. Temporary exhibitions here are devoted to established and up-and-coming artists, and there's a permanent collection strong on maritime and Inuit art, works on paper, and works by women artists. It amounts to more than 1,700 works, though not all are on display. ✉ *Beveridge Arts Centre, 10 Highland Ave. at Main St.* ☎ *902/585–1373* ⊕ *gallery.acadiau.ca* 💲 *Free* ⏲ *Tues.–Sun. noon–4.*

Harriet Irving Botanical Gardens. These 6-acre gardens are devoted mainly to indigenous plants from the Acadian Forest Region. Nine native habitats are displayed, and there's also a medicinal and food garden, a beautiful walled garden, and a conservatory. ✉ *32 University Ave.* ✣ *Entry through the K.C. Irving Environmental Science Centre* ☎ *902/585–5242* ⊕ *botanicalgardens.acadiau.ca* 💲 *Free* ⏲ *Daily dawn–dusk, weather permitting; conservatory 8 am–10 pm.*

Robie Tufts Nature Centre. Many Wolfvillians will tell you that the best show in town is watching swifts—aerobatic birds that fly in spectacular formation—descend on the Tuft Centre's oversized chimney at dusk on summer evenings. The venue is named in honor of the late ornithologist, author, and longtime resident who published *Birds of Nova Scotia* in 1961. The illustrated tome is still considered the bible for birders in the province, and he had lots of material to work with because Nova Scotia, being located on the Atlantic flyway, is an important staging point for migratory species. Birders can tick several off their "must-see" list without straying too far from Wolfville. Each summer as many as half a million sandpipers and plovers flock to Evangeline Beach near Grand Pré to gorge on the Minas Basin's nutrient-rich mudflats before continuing nonstop to South America. Winter, meanwhile, brings hundreds of regal bald eagles to Sheffield Mills, northeast of Kentville. The Nova Scotia

Bird Society (☎ *902/852–2077,* ⊕ *nsbs.chebucto.org*) has information about birding here and elsewhere in the province. ✉ *117 Front St.*

WHERE TO EAT AND STAY

$$$$ ✕ **Le Caveau.** The restaurant at the Domaine de Grand Pré vineyard
ECLECTIC has been showered with accolades, including being named "one of the world's 20 best winery restaurants" by *Wine Access Magazine.* Clearly, there is much more on offer here than "lining" for the wine sampling. For dinner you might start with cream of white onion and cumin soup, or milk-poached Acadian smoked sturgeon, then choose Southern slow-roasted lamb shoulder, rabbit torchon, or pan-seared sustainable blue rainbow trout with Moroccan stewed lentils, labneh, and harissa. Desserts are equally delicious and inventive (candied beets with the chocolate cake, for instance). Wines produced right here are joined on the list by a good international selection. $ *Average main: C$32* ✉ *11611 Hwy. 1, Grand Pré* ☎ *902/542–7177* ⊕ *grandprewines.ns.ca/restaurant/.*

$$ **Blomidon Inn.** Teak and mahogany furnishings, marble fireplaces,
B&B/INN Victorian-style wallpaper, and a painted ceiling mural all add to the ambience at this 1887 sea captain's mansion. **Pros:** complimentary afternoon tea; 14 rooms have Jacuzzis and propane fireplaces; the standalone Perth Cottage offers maximum privacy. **Cons:** dinner reservations recommended even for guests; room sizes vary; only a cold breakfast buffet. $ *Rooms from: C$139* ✉ *195 Main St.* ☎ *902/542–2291, 800/565–2291* ⊕ *www.blomidon.ns.ca* ⇨ *26 rooms, 2 suites, 1 cottage, 4 apartments* ⊡ *Breakfast.*

$$ **Farmhouse Inn Bed and Breakfast.** In a pleasant shipbuilding village
B&B/INN amid lovely countryside, this 1860 B&B is perfect for outdoor enthusiasts. **Pros:** surrounded by good hiking country; open year-round. **Cons:** you have to pay in advance; removed from Wolfville's restaurants; two-night minimum on certain dates. $ *Rooms from: C$139* ✉ *9757 Main St., Canning* ✣ *15 km (10 miles) north of Wolfville* ☎ *902/582–7900, 800/928–4346* ⊕ *www.farmhouseinn.ca* ⇨ *2 rooms, 4 suites* ⊡ *Breakfast.*

$$ **Tattingstone Inn.** Set back from the street amid more than an acre
B&B/INN of gardens, this inn has an interesting history and many exceptional features including the pool and the delightful conservatory, where delicious breakfasts are served. **Pros:** Jacuzzi tubs in some rooms; pleasant atmosphere; peaceful. **Cons:** a bit of a walk to downtown. $ *Rooms from: C$128* ✉ *620 Main St.* ☎ *902/542–7696, 800/565–7696* ⊕ *www.tattingstone.ns.ca* ▭ *No credit cards* ⇨ *9 rooms* ⊡ *Breakfast.*

$$ **Victoria's Historic Inn & Carriage House.** An 8-foot stained-glass win-
B&B/INN dow imported from Britain more than a century ago sets the decorative mood at this elegant 1893 mansion. **Pros:** some rooms have fireplaces, balconies, or both; friendly, efficient staff. **Cons:** a few rooms are overdecorated. $ *Rooms from: C$139* ✉ *600 Main St.* ☎ *902/542–5744, 800/556–5744* ⊕ *www.victoriashistoricinn.com* ⇨ *15 rooms, 1 suite* ⊡ *Breakfast.*

SPORTS AND THE OUTDOORS

FAMILY **Blomidon Provincial Park.** This park on the shores of the Minas Basin has four main trails that collectively cover 14 km (9 miles). The beach is accessible at low tide, but be sure to check the tide tables; the water comes back in quite rapidly. The 1.6-km (1-mile) Lookoff Trail yields especially fine cliff-top vistas. ✉ *3138 Pereau Rd., Cape Blomidon* ✣ *Off Hwy. 101, 31 km (19 miles) north of Wolfville* ☎ *902/582-7319* ⊕ *www.novascotiaparks.ca* ₤ *No charge for day use* ⏲ *Mid-May–early Sept.*

WINDSOR

25 km (16 miles) southeast of Wolfville.

Windsor has much in common with Bridgewater on the South Shore in that both are historic towns that have evolved into regional service centers. One marker of Windsor's history is King's-Edgehill School. Founded in 1788, it is the oldest independent school in the British Commonwealth. The countryside around Windsor is pretty, particularly in autumn, and Haligonians often make the 66-km (41-mile) drive to the "Gateway of the Annapolis Valley" for its Pumpkin Festival.

GETTING HERE AND AROUND

When driving from east or west, take Exit 6 off Highway 101.

ESSENTIALS

Visitor Information **Windsor Visitor Information Centre.** ✉ *Colonial Rd., north off Hwy. 101, Exit 6* ☎ *902/798-2690.*

EXPLORING

Haliburton House Museum. This was once home to Judge Thomas Chandler Haliburton (1796–1865), a lawyer, politician, historian, and, above all, humorist. Hugely popular in his own day, Haliburton inspired Mark Twain and put Nova Scotia on the literary map with *The Clockmaker,* a book that used a fictional Yankee clock peddler named Sam Slick to poke fun at provincial foibles. Although you may not be familiar with Haliburton's name, you surely know some of the phrases he coined. The Windsor wordsmith gave us expressions like "quick as a wink," "it's raining cats and dogs," and "the early bird gets the worm." Themed programs and events are offered throughout the summer.

Thomas Haliburton is also remembered for making the first recorded reference to hockey—the sport that was "born" here in the early 1800s. Fittingly, the **Windsor Hockey Heritage Centre** (☎ *902/798-1800,* ⊕ *www.birthplaceofhockey.com/museum*) resides at Haliburton House, and several rooms contain items from the collection. These include antique skates, hand-carved sticks, wooden pucks, trophies, team uniforms, and photographs. ✉ *414 Clifton Ave.* ☎ *902/798-2915* ⊕ *www.haliburtonhouse.novascotia.ca* ₤ *C$4, includes Windsor Hockey Heritage Centre* ⏲ *June–early Oct., Mon.–Sat. 10–5, Sun. 1–5.*

FAMILY **Mermaid Theatre of Nova Scotia.** Puppets and performers retell classic and contemporary children's stories here. The troupe's home base is the 400-seat MIPAC (Mermaid Imperial Performing Arts Centre) adjacent to its Gerrish Street headquarters, but catching a show can be tricky because of the hectic worldwide touring schedule. If you can't time your trip to coincide with a play date, you can still marvel at Mermaid's props and puppets, as several floors filled with them are open for public viewing. ✉ *132 Gerrish St.* ☎ *902/798–5841* 🌐 *www.mermaidtheatre.ns.ca* 💲 *By donation* ⏲ *Year-round, weekdays 9–4.*

Sainte Famille Winery. Visits to the family-owned Sainte Famille Winery in Falmouth, 5 km (3 miles) west of Windsor, combine ecological history with the intricacies of growing grapes and aging wine. Tasting is done in the gift shop, where bottles are sold at bargain prices. The best time to come is at the end of the season when Sainte Famille hosts its annual Harvest Wine Fest. The one-day event features food, entertainment, and a competitive Grape Stomp. Even the kids' category is hotly contested. ✉ *11 Dudley Park La.* ☎ *902/798–8311, 800/565–0993* 🌐 *www.st-famille.com* 💲 *Tours C$5, tastings C$5* ⏲ *Tours: June–Sept., daily at 10 and 2. Shop: Year-round Mon.–Sat. 9–5 (also Sun. 11–5 Apr.–Dec.).*

OFF THE BEATEN PATH

Uniacke Estate Museum Park. This country mansion was built in about 1815 for Richard John Uniacke, attorney general and advocate general to the admiralty court during the War of 1812. Now a provincial museum, the Georgian-style house is preserved in its original condition, right down to the antique furnishings. Seven walking trails wend through the large lakeside property. There are picnic tables and a small tearoom on-site. The access road is gated, and the gates are locked at dusk. ✉ *758 Hwy. 1, Mount Uniacke* ✣ *30 km (19 miles) east of Windsor* ☎ *902/866–0032* 🌐 *uniacke.novascotia.ca* 💲 *Museum C$3.90* ⏲ *June–early Oct., Mon.–Sat. 9:30–5, Sun. 11–5.*

WHERE TO EAT AND STAY

$$ ✕ **Cocoa Pesto Bistro.** A warm welcome and elegant surroundings provide
ECLECTIC a great first impression here, but it's the delicious, fresh, *and* health-conscious cuisine that lingers in memory. The menu changes seasonally, but might include pecan-crusted salmon or sweet- and dry-rub pork ribs straight from an apple-wood smoker. The bistro's rooms have a minimalist look that nicely balances the heritage building's original architectural features, and a patio provides outside dining in summer. 💲 *Average main: C$19* ✉ *494 King St.* ☎ *902/472–3300* 🌐 *www.cocoapesto.com* ⏲ *No lunch.*

$ **Clockmakers Inn.** A distinctive 1894 building houses this appealing
B&B/INN inn on the Evangeline Trail, just outside downtown, that provides a range of services and room styles. **Pros:** family-friendly; garden playground; two bicycles available for guest use. **Cons:** no elevator, though staff will help with luggage. 💲 *Rooms from: C$119* ✉ *1399 King St.* ☎ *902/792–2573, 866/778–3600* 🌐 *www.theclockmakersinn.com* 🛏 *8 rooms* 🍽 *Breakfast.*

THE EASTERN SHORE AND NORTHERN NOVA SCOTIA

From the rugged Atlantic coastline to the wave-ravaged rim of the Bay of Fundy and the gentle shores of Northumberland Strait, the area east and north of Halifax is characterized by contrasts. The road toward Cape Breton meanders past thinly populated fishing villages and thick forests, whereas attractive towns and sandy beaches border Northumberland Strait. The Fundy Shore, meanwhile, scores points for dramatic scenery—expect steep cliffs harboring prehistoric fossils and intense tides that draw back to reveal the muddy sea floor.

This region has three excellent driving routes. The 316-km (196-mile) Sunrise Trail wends its way along Northumberland Strait, from the wild Tantramar Marsh in Amherst (on the New Brunswick border) to the thriving college town of Antigonish. The 315-km (195-mile) Marine Drive travels through romantic seaside villages and the living-history museum in Sherbrooke. Highlights on the 365-km (226-mile) Glooscap Trail include a majestic lighthouse at Cape d'Or and the notable fossil finds in Joggins. Any one leg could be done comfortably in two days from Halifax with a single overnight along the way.

SHERBROOKE AND SHERBROOKE VILLAGE

187 km (122 miles) northeast of Halifax.

Established by the French in the middle of the 17th century, this little town prospered briefly on the back of a gold rush in the late 19th century, and it's something of a thrill to know that 80% of Sherbrooke's gold is still buried underfoot. Today, however, it's better known for the Atlantic salmon that rush up St. Mary's River (though you can't fish for them) and for the excellent Sherbrooke Village open-air museum. The town makes a good base for exploring the rugged coastline.

GETTING HERE AND AROUND

There's no public transportation to Sherbrooke. From Halifax, drive east on Highway 107, then Trunk 7 E, via Musquodoboit Harbour and Sheet Harbour. If you're coming from the Northumberland Shore, head for New Glasgow and take Highway 347 south, turning onto Trunk 7 W for the last 20 km (12 miles) or so.

EXPLORING

FAMILY
Fodor's Choice
★

Sherbrooke Village. Most visitors come to Sherbrooke to see this living-history museum, set within the contemporary town. It contains more than two dozen restored buildings (including an operating water-powered sawmill) that re-create life during the town's heyday. Between 1860 and 1914, this was a prime shipbuilding, lumbering, and gold-rush center. These days, costumed interpreters and artisans recapture the bustle by demonstrating blacksmithing, weaving, wood turning, soap making, and similar skills. Special events, such as old-fashioned Christmas and courthouse concerts, are held throughout the year. ✉ *42 Main St., Hwy. 7, Sherbrooke* ☎ *902/522–2400, 888/743–7845* ⊕ *sherbrookevillage.novascotia.ca* ₤ *C$12.75* ⏲ *June–late Sept., daily 9:30–5; Christmas celebrations the last weekend in Nov.*

BEACHES

OFF THE BEATEN PATH

Port Bickerton Lighthouse Beach Park. Hiking trails and a boardwalk lead to a sandy beach here, but the park's main attraction is its two lighthouses, which share the lofty bluff above. One is still working; the other, built in the early 1920s, houses the Nova Scotia Lighthouse Interpretive Centre, which recounts the history, lore, and vital importance of

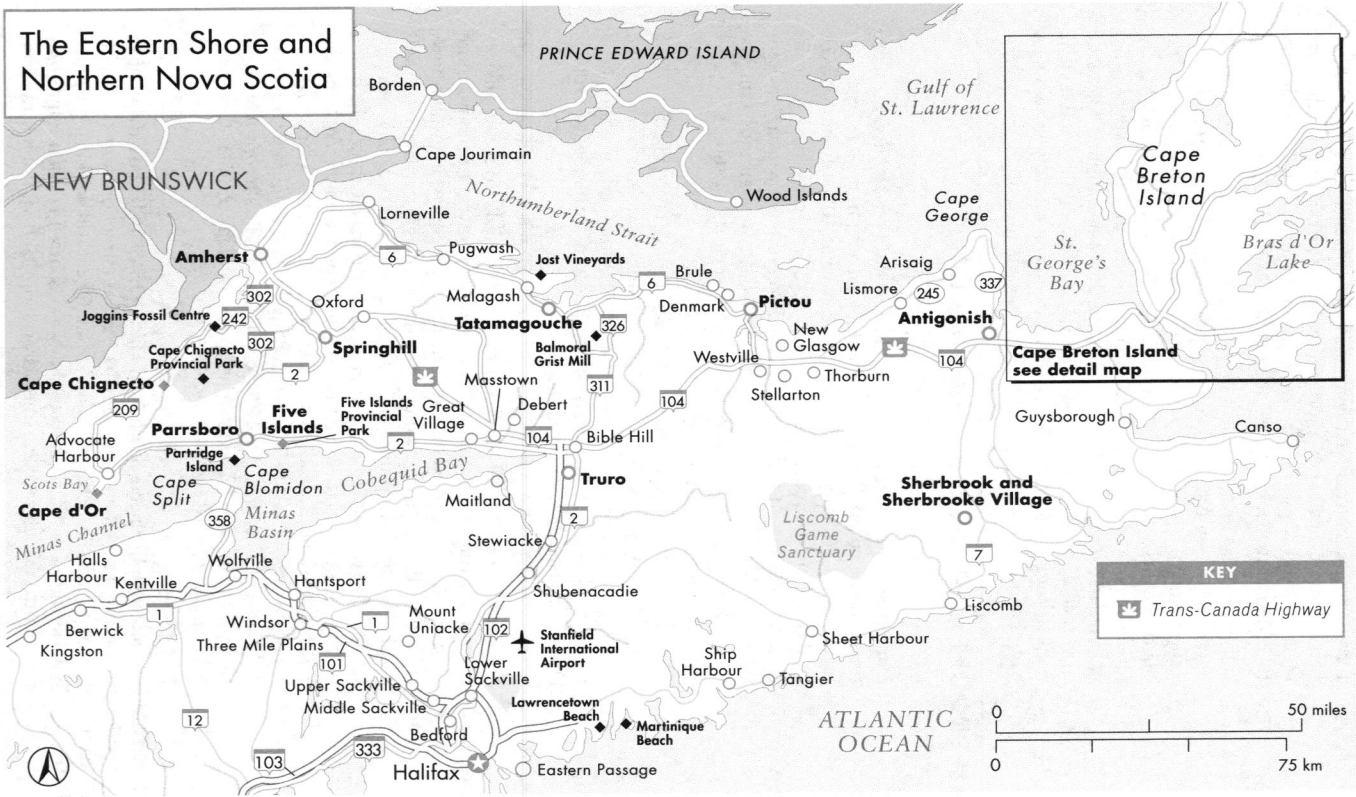
The Eastern Shore and Northern Nova Scotia
PRINCE EDWARD ISLAND
Gulf of St. Lawrence
NEW BRUNSWICK
Northumberland Strait
Borden
Cape Jourimain
Wood Islands
Cape George
Lorneville
Pugwash
Jost Vineyards
Brule
Arisaig
Amherst
Oxford
Malagash
Denmark
Pictou
Lismore
Antigonish
Joggins Fossil Centre
Tatamagouche
Balmoral Grist Mill
New Glasgow
Cape Chignecto Provincial Park
Springhill
Westville
Thorburn
Cape Chignecto
Masstown
Stellarton
Five Islands Provincial Park
Great Village
Debert
Five Islands
Parrsboro
Bible Hill
Guysborough
Canso
Advocate Harbour
Partridge Island
Scots Bay
Cape Split
Cape Blomidon
Cobequid Bay
Truro
Cape d'Or
Maitland
Sherbrook and Sherbrooke Village
Minas Channel
Minas Basin
Liscomb Game Sanctuary
Stewiacke
Halls Harbour
Wolfville
Kentville
Hantsport
Shubenacadie
Liscomb
Berwick
Kingston
Windsor
Mount Uniacke
Stanfield International Airport
Sheet Harbour
Three Mile Plains
Lower Sackville
Ship Harbour
Tangier
Upper Sackville
Middle Sackville
Lawrencetown Beach
Martinique Beach
Bedford
Halifax
Eastern Passage
ATLANTIC OCEAN
Cape Breton Island
St. George's Bay
Bras d'Or Lake
Cape Breton Island see detail map
KEY
Trans-Canada Highway
0
50 miles
0
75 km

CLOSE UP

Surf's Up Down East

Being sparsely developed, the Eastern Shore—which starts on the fringes of Halifax and covers more than 200 km (125 miles) of coast—has few residents and even fewer tourist attractions. But, oh boy, does it have beaches! Two of the best are Lawrencetown and Martinique. About 27 km (17 miles) and 57 km (35 miles), respectively, from downtown Halifax, both strands are designated provincial parks and have lifeguards on duty in season to supervise swimming. Yet it's not so much swimmers as surfers that these beautiful, wave-blasted beaches attract.

Summer is prime time here, especially when northward-tracking hurricanes churn up the Atlantic, so if you've already got surf gear all you have to do before hitting the water is check the local surf forecast at *magicseaweed.com*. Otherwise, there are several outfitters who rent or sell boards and wet suits (you'll want a suit because the water is cold).

Happy Dudes Surf Emporium (*902/827-4962* *happydudes.wordpress.com*) has two locations—one at Martinique (*2137 E. Petpeswick Rd., East Petpeswick*) and the other 3 km (2 miles) east of Lawrencetown Beach (*4891 Hwy. 207, Three Fathom Harbour*). In addition, a mobile outlet is typically parked right at Lawrencetown when the surf is up. Groups of three or more can get 3½ hours of lessons for C$50 per person, plus equipment rental; private lessons cost C$120 per person, or C$60 each for two people.

Also close to Lawrencetown Beach is the **Kannon Beach Surf Shop** (*4144 Lawrencetown Rd., East Lawrencetown* *902/471-0025* *www.kannonbeach.com*). The shop, in the basement of MacDonald House, also offers lessons, with equipment included, starting at C$95—and you get to keep the equipment for the rest of the day. Rentals cost C$40 per day for a board and a wet suit, including boots and gloves.

At the same location as Kannon, **One Life Surf School** (*902/880-7873* *www.onelifesurf.com*) is run by—but not exclusively for—women. Lessons start at C$70 per person for groups or C$100 for an individual. Equipment is included.

For more information and event listings, visit the website for the Surfing Association of Nova Scotia (*www.surfns.com*).

the province's lights. **Amenities:** parking (free); toilets. **Best for:** walking. *640 Lighthouse Rd., Port Bickerton* *Off Hwy. 211, about 32 km (20 miles) east of Sherbrooke* *www.portbickertonlighthouse.ca* *Beach free, lighthouse site C$3* *Beach daily, lighthouse site mid-June–mid-Sept., daily 9–5.*

WHERE TO STAY

$$ RESORT FAMILY **Liscombe Lodge Resort.** In a superb natural setting, with a choice of lodge rooms or secluded chalets and cottages, this place pairs an away-from-it-all location with a wide range of activities. **Pros:** fun packages and free experiential programs; Camp Adventure and other activities for kids; complimentary use of boats. **Cons:** rooms could use a redo;

better suited to families than singles; large wedding parties can sometimes affect the atmosphere. *Rooms from: C$165 2884 Hwy. 7, Liscomb Mills 27 km (17 miles) southwest of Sherbrooke on Hwy. 7 902/779-2301, 800/665-6343 www.liscombelodge.ca No credit cards Closed mid-Oct.–Apr. 329 rooms, 1 suite, 17 chalets, 5 cottages Some meals.*

ANTIGONISH

61 km (38 miles) north of Sherbrooke; 115 km (71 miles) east of Truro; 55 km (34 miles) west of the Canso Causeway.

Pretty Antigonish, on the main route to Cape Breton Island, is home to St. Francis Xavier University, a center for Gaelic studies and the first coeducational Catholic institution to graduate women. The campus also has several cultural attractions.

GETTING HERE AND AROUND

Maritime Bus offers a daily service from Halifax, connecting at Truro with buses from New Brunswick and Prince Edward Island. Driving couldn't be easier—the town is right on the Trans-Canada Highway (Highway 104). Coming up from Sherbrooke, you'd need Nova Scotia Trunk 7 E.

ESSENTIALS

Visitor Information **Antigonish Visitor Information Centre.** *Antigonish Mall Complex, Church St., off Hwy. 104, Exit 33 N 902/863-4921 www.antigonishcounty.ns.ca/vic.htm.*

EXPLORING

Bauer Theatre. During the school year, the Bauer is home to Theatre Antigonish, a nonprofit community company that presents classic and contemporary works. *St. Francis Xavier University, West St., off Hwy. 104 902/867-3333 www.sites.stfx.ca/theatreantigonish C$16.*

StFX Art Gallery. St. Francis Xavier University's campus art gallery mounts a dozen exhibits of mostly contemporary works each year and hosts talks with regional and other artists. *Bloomfield Centre 103, West St., off Hwy. 104 902/867-2303 www.sites.stfx.ca/artgallery Free May–Aug. weekdays noon–5; Sept.–Apr., Tues.–Fri. noon–6, weekends 1–4.*

WHERE TO EAT AND STAY

$$$ ECLECTIC FAMILY **Gabrieau's Bistro.** Gabrieau's has earned a place in Antigonish hearts with its pleasant interior and an epicurean yet affordable menu that includes seafood, meat dishes such as braised lamb shank marinated in red wine, garlic, rosemary and thyme, pasta, tapas, and various vegetarian dishes. There are luscious desserts, and the wine list impresses, too. If the weather is nice, take a seat on the sunny patio and watch the town go by. To learn how to duplicate your favorite dish, you can take one of the public cooking classes conducted in the separate, open-kitchen Hawthorne Room. *Average main: C$24 350 Main St. 902/863-1925 www.gabrieaus.com Closed Sun. No lunch Sat.*

$$ B&B/INN **Antigonish Victorian Inn.** Turn-of-the-20th-century Victorian style—but with modern amenities—reigns at this beautifully restored turreted mansion. **Pros:** just a short walk from the town center; open year-round; delicious hot breakfast. **Cons:** not all options have en suite bathrooms; room size varies widely. *Rooms from: C$130 149 Main St. 902/863–1103, 800/706–5558 www.antigonishvictorianinn.ca 11 rooms, 2 apartments Breakfast.*

SPORTS AND THE OUTDOORS

Antigonish Landing Trail. A 4.8-km (3-mile) walking trail along the shoreline of Antigonish Harbour borders a large tidal marsh and wildlife sanctuary teeming with ospreys, bald eagles, and other birds. To find the trailhead, park at the Antigonish Heritage Museum, on East Main Street, then cross the railroad tracks and bear right on Adam Street. Bring drinking water and watch out for poison ivy. *Trailhead at end of Adam St. Free.*

SHOPPING

Lyghtesome Gallery. The gallery sells paintings, sculptures, prints, drawings, and other works by Nova Scotian artists, at reasonable prices. *166 Main St. 902/863–5804 www.lyghtesome.com Weekdays 10–5 and Fri. evening by appointment.*

The Made in Nova Scotia Store. For the town's most comprehensive selection of crafts, natural products, and incredible edibles, drop by this store, which represents more than 200 regional artisans. *324 Main St. 902/867–2642 www.themadeinnovascotiastore.com.*

PICTOU

74 km (46 miles) northwest of Antigonish; 66 km (41 miles) northeast of Truro.

Many people come to Pictou for the sole purpose of catching the ferry onward to Prince Edward Island (it departs from Caribou, just minutes away), but the town itself is lovely, with a revitalized waterfront centered on a very different vessel. In 1773 an aging cargo ship named the *Hector* arrived here carrying the initial load of Scottish Highlanders, making Pictou "The Birthplace of New Scotland." Each year in mid-August, the quay is the focal point for the weekend-long **Hector Festival**, which celebrates the Scots' arrival. Held in early July to mark the close of this region's fishing season, the raucous **Pictou Lobster Carnival** features lobster-boat races, trap-hauling contests, and, of course, a chance to eat the tasty crustaceans.

GETTING HERE AND AROUND

The Wood Islands Ferry from Prince Edward Island will land you in Pictou, but that's the only public transportation there is. The ferry runs from May through late December, with a minimum of three sailings a day, and up to nine in peak season. The fare for a vehicle, including passengers, is C$67.50; walk-on passengers pay C$17. Driving to Pictou is via the Trans-Canada Highway (Highway 104), branching onto Highway 106 for the last stretch.

TOURS

Pictou Island Charters. The charter company operates ferry service between Caribou and Pictou Island and conducts three-hour, tip-to-tip vehicle tours of the island, which has some lovely beaches, on Thursday and Friday in July and August. ✉ *Pictou* ☎ *902/921–1033, 902/497–5974 tour reservations* ⊕ *www.pictouislandcharters.ca* ₹ *Ferry C$5, tours C$50.*

EXPLORING

Hector Heritage Quay. A 110-foot fully rigged replica of the *Hector* is moored here, and you can sometimes see maintenance work in progress. The handsome post-and-beam interpretive center recounts the story of the first hardy pioneers (33 families plus 25 unmarried men) who arrived aboard the original vessel in 1773, and the flood of Scots who followed them. The site also has working blacksmith, rigger, and carpentry shops. ✉ *33 Caladh Ave.* ☎ *902/485–4371* ⊕ *shiphector.com* ₹ *C$7* ⏲ *Mid-May–mid-Oct., daily 10–5.*

BEACHES

FAMILY **Melmerby Beach Provincial Park.** One of Nova Scotia's most popular beaches, Melmerby has a boardwalk, picnic tables, and some of the warmest water north of the Carolinas. Beaches straddle both the inner and outer edges of this horseshoe of land, the inner portion a glorious stretch of white sand. Swimming is safe here unless winds are high, when strong currents develop. The supervised area (in July and August) is clearly marked. Beware of poison ivy in the sand dunes and, between mid-July and early August, jellyfish in the water. **Amenities:** food and drink; lifeguards; parking (free); showers; toilets. **Best for:** swimming. ✉ *6380 Little Harbour Rd.* ✣ *About 30 km (18 miles) east of Pictou* ⊕ *www.parks.gov.ns.ca.*

WHERE TO STAY

$ B&B/INN FAMILY **Auberge Walker Inn.** A registered Heritage Property built in the 1860s, this centrally located inn is a block from the waterfront. **Pros:** some rooms have water views; suite has kitchenette and private entry. **Cons:** lots of stairs but no elevator; only a cold breakfast buffet included. $ *Rooms from: C$89* ✉ *78 Coleraine St.* ☎ *902/485–1433, 800/370–5553* ⊕ *www.walkerinn.com* ⏲ *Closed mid-Nov.–mid-May* ⇨ *10 rooms, 1 suite* ⊞ *Breakfast.*

NIGHTLIFE AND PERFORMING ARTS

DeCoste Entertainment Centre. The center presents a summer-long program of concerts, pipe bands, Highland dancing, and ceilidhs with Gaelic music and dance. Past headliners have included acts ranging from k.d. lang to the Scottish Symphony Orchestra. ✉ *99 Water St.* ☎ *902/485–8848, 800/353–5338* ⊕ *decostecentre.ca.*

SPORTS AND THE OUTDOORS

Jitney Trail. The Jitney is a 5-km (3-mile) paved water's-edge route around Pictou Harbour to Brown's Point that puts you in sight of marine life, birdlife, and working wharves. Hikers and bikers frequent it, and there are benches and picnic tables along the way. ✉ *Pictou* ⊕ *www.trails.gov.ns.ca.*

SHOPPING

Grohmann Knives. You can see handcrafted Grohmann knives displayed at the Museum of Modern Art in New York—but you can buy them at the factory outlet store here. Prices are discounted and free factory tours usually take place on weekdays from 9 to 11:30 and 1:30 to 3:30. ✉ *116 Water St.* ☎ *902/485–4224, 888/756–4837* ⊕ *www.grohmannknives.com.*

Pictou County Weekend Market. Craftspeople sell quality goods at this lively waterfront market that takes place on weekends between 10 and 5 from mid-June through mid-September. ✉ *Caledonian Curling Club, 66 Caladh Ave.* ☎ *902/695–5836* ⊕ *www.pictouweekendmarket.com.*

Water Street Studios. This artisans' co-op sells a wide range of crafts, many of which are handcrafted in the Maritimes. Items include hand-dyed and natural yarns, felted woolen items and knits, weaving, blankets, pottery, stained glass, jewelry, and woodwork. ✉ *110 Water St.* ☎ *902/485–8398* ⊕ *waterstreetstudio.weebly.com.*

TATAMAGOUCHE

54 km (33½ miles) west of Pictou.

Though it only has about a thousand residents, tiny Tatamagouche is a force to be reckoned with. Canada's second-largest Oktoberfest (☎ *800/895–1177* ⊕ *www.nsoktoberfest.ca*)—a boisterous event complete with sausages, schnitzel, and frothy steins of beer—takes place here each fall. Summer brings strawberry and blueberry festivals, lobster, and chowder suppers. On the waterfront, Creamery Square is the hub of the town with a museum complex, a farmers' market, and a center for the arts with a small theater, which opened in 2015. Within a 10-minute drive of Tatamagouche you have the opportunity to visit two historic mills.

GETTING HERE AND AROUND

There is no public transportation to Tatamagouche. If you're driving on the Trans-Canada Highway (Highway 104), go north at Truro via Highway 311; heading west from Pictou or east from Amherst, Highway 6 along the coast is the way to go.

EXPLORING

Balmoral Grist Mill. Built in 1874, this is one of the few water-powered mills still operating in Nova Scotia, now serving as the centerpiece of a small museum. You can observe flour-milling demonstrations and walk the site's 1-km (½-mile) trail. ✉ *660 Matheson Brook Rd., Balmoral Mills* ✣ *14 km (8½ miles) southeast of Tatamagouche via Hwy. 311* ☎ *902/657–3016, 902/424–7398* ⊕ *balmoralgristmill.novascotia.ca* 💵 *C$3.90* ⏲ *June–early Oct., Tues.–Sat. 10–5, Sun. 1–5.*

Jost Vineyards. The Jost winery produces wines from an astonishing number of varietals, consistently winning awards for its ice wine, a sweet affair made from grapes left on the vines until frost has "iced" them. You can taste wines year-round at the store here, and take winery tours from mid-June to mid-September. ✉ *48 Vintage La., Malagash* ✣ *17 km (11 miles) northwest of Tatamagouche via Hwy. 311*

☎ 902/257–2636, 800/565–4567 🌐 devoniancoast.ca/our-vineyards/jost-vineyards/ 💵 Tours: C$5 (can be applied toward wine purchases of C$20 or more) ⏲ Store: mid-June–mid-Sept., daily 10–6; mid-Sept.–mid-June, daily 10–5. Tours: mid-June–mid-Sept., daily at noon and 3.

Margaret Fawcett Norrie Heritage Centre. Creamery Square is the hub of activity in Tatamagouche, and this waterfront heritage center on the square has gathered together several museums that were previously dotted around town. Located in a former dairy facility, the center appropriately includes the **Creamery Museum,** with butter-making equipment and related displays. The **Sunrise Trail Museum** traces Tatamagouche's Mi'Kmaq, Acadian, French, and Scottish roots through interactive displays. The **Anna Swan Museum** relates the story of local giantess Anna Swan (1846–88), who grew to the height of 7 feet 11½ inches. Finally, the **Brule Fossil Centre** preserves 290-million-year-old fossil tracks that were discovered nearby in 1994. Demonstrations on boatbuilding and butter making are regularly staged. This is also the site of a Saturday-morning farmers' market from February through December. *✉ 39 Creamery Rd. ☎ 902/657–3449 🌐 www.creamerysquare.ca 💵 C$5, free Sat. 9–10 am ⏲ Mid-May–mid-Oct., Sun.–Fri. 10–6, Sat. 9–6.*

THE GIANT ANNA SWAN

Anna Swan, born near Tatamagouche in 1846, weighed 18 pounds and was 27 inches long at birth, was 4 feet 6 inches when she was four years old, and 6 feet 2 inches by the time she was 10. The supersized Swan joined P. T. Barnum's museum when she was 7 feet 2 inches, but continued to grow for several more years until she reached her full height of 7 feet 11½ inches. She married another famously tall person: Martin Van Buren Bates, who is believed to have been at least 7 feet 9 inches tall.

The Sutherland Steam Mill Museum. Dating from 1894, this mill participated in the transition from water to steam power. Steam engines allowed greater flexibility about location—mills no longer *had* to be near a river or other water source—and provided more raw power to run factory machinery. Workers at the Sutherland mill manufactured useful items ranging from carriages and sleds to wooden bathtubs, and you'll see hundreds of examples displayed inside, along with tools of the trade. Interesting demonstrations and hands-on activities sometimes take place in July and August. *✉ 3169 Denmark Station Rd., Denmark ✣ Off Hwy. 326 ☎ 902/657–3365 🌐 sutherlandsteammill.novascotia.ca 💵 C$4 ⏲ June–early Oct., Tues.–Sat. 10–5, Sun. 1–5.*

WHERE TO STAY

$$ B&B/INN **Train Station Inn.** Guests at this ingeniously restored inn can sleep in an 1887 train station or one of eight beautifully converted cabooses parked on the tracks outside. **Pros:** the Trans Canada Trail runs alongside the property; close to the water; memorable gift shop. **Cons:** air-conditioning in railcars only; often booked well in advance. *$ Rooms from: C$130 ✉ 21 Station Rd. ☎ 902/657–3222, 888/724–5233 🌐 www.trainstation.ca ⏲ Closed Nov.–May 🛏 8 rooms, 1 suite 🍽 No meals.*

SPORTS AND THE OUTDOORS

The Butter Trail. Named for the creamery it backs onto, this is part of the Trans-Canada Trail system. The 26-km (16-mile) multiuse path follows the reclaimed rail bed that the Train Station Inn's cabooses once traversed. ✉ *Tatamagouche* ⊕ *www.trails.gov.ns.ca.*

SHOPPING

Sara Bonnyman Pottery. Here you can watch the shop's namesake potter herself at work, producing mostly tableware and also hooked rugs. In July and August informal tours are given. Visitors are also welcome to explore the large gardens. ✉ *326 Maple Ave. (Hwy. 246)* ✣ *1½ km (1 mile) uphill from post office* ☎ *902/657-3215* ⊕ *www.sarabonnymanpottery.com* ⏲ *July and Aug., Mon.–Sat. 10–4; Sept.–June, by chance or appointment.*

SPRINGHILL

75 km (46½ miles) west of Tatamagouche.

If you're not going to be visiting Cape Breton, Springhill (on Highway 2) is worth a stop because it gives you a second chance to sample Nova Scotia's music-and-mining combo. This town was both the birthplace of acclaimed songstress Anne Murray and, before that, home to the ill-fated coal mine immortalized in "The Ballad of Springhill" (aka "Springhill Mining Disaster") by Peggy Seeger and Ewen McColl. The mines closed in 1962, but Springhill is still using them—as a source of geothermal energy.

GETTING HERE AND AROUND

There is no public transportation to Springhill. By road, it's just west of the Trans-Canada Highway (Highway 104) between Oxford and Amherst; take Exit 5 onto Highway 142.

EXPLORING

Anne Murray Centre. The likable Springhill-born, part-Acadian pop singer spread her tiny wings and flew away to worldwide fame and fortune, but she still celebrates her roots—and her hometown pays tribute to her illustrious career—at this repository of costumes, gold records, photographs, and other artifacts. Diehard fans can record a (virtual) duet with Murray, providing instant bragging rights to having performed with a partner who has sold more than 50 million records to date. ✉ *36 Main St.* ☎ *902/597-8614* ⊕ *www.annemurraycentre.com* 💵 *C$7* ⏲ *Mid-May–mid-Oct., daily 9–4:30.*

Springhill Miners Museum. The site of several tragedies, the Springhill coalfield gained international attention in 1958 when an earthquake created a "bump" that trapped mine workers underground (75 of them died), but today at this museum you can descend into a mine under safer circumstances. Some of the guides are retired miners who provide firsthand accounts of their working days. Children under five are not admitted. ✉ *145 Black River Rd.* ✣ *Off Hwy. 2* ☎ *902/597-3449* 💵 *C$7* ⏲ *Mid-May–mid-Oct., daily 9–5.*

AMHERST

33 km (21 miles) northwest of Springhill.

Amherst is a quaint, quiet town with a central location, but from the mid-1800s to the early 1900s, it was a bustling center of industry and influence. Four of Canada's Fathers of Confederation hailed from Amherst, including Sir Charles Tupper, who later became prime minister. From Amherst, Nova Scotia's Sunrise Trail heads toward Northumberland Strait, and the Glooscap Trail runs west through fossil country. Amherst is a mere 7 km (4 miles) from New Brunswick and 55 km (34 miles) from the Confederation Bridge, which connects the Maritimes mainland to Prince Edward Island.

GETTING HERE AND AROUND

Maritime Bus provides daily service from Halifax to Amherst, where the bus stop is at the Circle K on South Albion Street. It takes a little over three hours and the fare is C$46.84 one way. Maritime also operates bus service from Fredericton (C$54.22; four hours) and Moncton (C$18.34; one hour). Although the train station is closed, you can disembark here from trains on the Montréal–Halifax route, but, with only three trains per week, it's not a very useful option. Amherst is on the Trans-Canada Highway (Highway 104), just south of the Nova Scotia–New Brunswick border; take Exit 3 or Exit 4. The town itself has no public transit system.

ESSENTIALS

Visitor Information **Amherst Visitor Information Centre.** ✉ *90 Cumberland Loop* ☎ *902/667-0787* ⊕ *www.amherst.ca/visitors.*

EXPLORING

Joggins Fossil Centre. On the Glooscap Trail, 35 km (22 miles) southwest of Amherst and 70 km (43 miles) northeast of Cape Chignecto, Joggins is famous for Coal Age fossils that were embedded in sandstone, then uncovered through erosion caused by Fundy's surging tides. You can spy them outside, in the sea cliffs, or inside the center. Opened in 2008—the same year Joggins was named a UNESCO World Heritage Site—this striking museum has a large, well-curated collection of specimens dating back some 300 million years, along with interesting displays outlining the region's geological and archaeological history. The admission fee includes a half-hour guided beach tour; two-hour guided cliffs tours take place daily in peak months; and an in-depth four-hour tour occurs monthly. Bear in mind that the beach is reached by a steep slope and staircase, over boulders and watercourses. ✉ *100 Main St., Joggins* ☎ *902/251-2727, 888/932-9766* ⊕ *www.jogginsfossilcliffs.net* 💲 *C$10.50, includes a 30-min tour of the beach; C$25, includes 1½–2-hr tour (reservations essential); C$75, includes 4-hr guided tour and lunch (reservations essential)* ⏲ *Late Apr.–May, Sept., and Oct., daily 10–4; June–Aug., daily 9:30–5:30; rest of yr by appointment 5 days in advance for 4 or more visitors.*

Tantramar Marshes. Spanning the Nova Scotia–New Brunswick border and covering more than 20,000 acres, the Tantramar Marshes stretch from Amherst up to Sackville and are alive with incredible birdlife and other wildlife. The name comes from the French *tintamarre* (meaning din or hubbub) because of the racket made by vast flocks of wildfowl. Said to be the world's largest marsh, the Tantramar is a migratory route for hundreds of thousands of birds and a breeding ground for more than 100 species. ✉ *Amherst.*

WHERE TO STAY

$$ B&B/INN **Amherst Shore Country Inn.** With a 600-foot private beach and 20 acres of lawns and gardens overlooking Northumberland Strait, this inn on the Sunrise Trail Coastal Route has an interesting range of lodging options. **Pros:** tranquil location; outstanding dining; friendly hosts. **Cons:** most accommodations are away from the inn; breakfast is not included. $ *Rooms from: C$129* ✉ *Hwy. 366 (Tyndal Rd.), Lorneville* ✢ *32 km (20 miles) northeast of Amherst* ☎ *902/661–4800, 800/661–2724* 🌐 *www.ascinn.ns.ca* ⏲ *Closed weekdays Nov.–May* 🛏 *4 rooms, 4 chalet, 3 cottages* 🍴 *No meals.*

$$ B&B/INN **The Regent Bed & Breakfast.** Set peacefully back from the street, this picturesque 1898 Georgian house stands out for its grandeur, and the hosts are extremely welcoming and helpful. **Pros:** open year-round; luxurious linens; innkeepers will take guests sightseeing upon request. **Cons:** there's not that much to see in Amherst. $ *Rooms from: C$125* ✉ *175 East Victoria St.* ☎ *902/667–7676, 866/661–2861* 🌐 *www.theregent.ca* 🛏 *4 rooms* 🍴 *Breakfast.*

CAPE CHIGNECTO AND CAPE D'OR

105 km (65 miles) southwest of Amherst.

Two imposing promontories—Cape Chignecto and Cape d'Or—reach into the Bay of Fundy near Chignecto Bay.

GETTING HERE AND AROUND

There is no public transportation to the capes. From the Trans-Canada Highway (Highway 104) at Amherst, you need to head southwest via Highways 302, 242, and 209. Highway 209 loops around a peninsula, with turnoffs for both capes.

EXPLORING

Advocate Harbour. This little fishing community is set on a Bay of Fundy natural harbor that loses all its water at low tide. A delightful coastal walk here follows the top of an Acadian dike that was built by settlers in the 1700s to reclaim farmland from the sea. Nearby is rocky Advocate Beach, noted for its monumental supply of tide-cast driftwood, which stretches for about 5 km (3 miles) east from Cape Chignecto.

Age of Sail Heritage Museum. Exhibits spread out over six buildings trace the history of the Fundy region's shipbuilding and lumbering industries, and the museum has an archive and genealogical-research area. The Wind and Wave Building is shaped to resemble an inverted half-model of a ship. You can also view a restored Methodist church, a blacksmith shop, a boathouse, and a lighthouse. A cute café serves light meals—chowder, lobster rolls, sandwiches, and the like. ✉ *8334 Hwy. 209, Port Greville* ☎ *902/348–2030* 🌐 *www.ageofsailmuseum.ca* 💵 *C$5* ⏲ *Mid-May–mid-Oct., daily 10–6.*

Cape Chignecto Provincial Park. Miles of untouched coastline, more than 10,000 acres of old-growth forest harboring deer, moose, and eagles, and a variety of unique geological features are preserved in Nova Scotia's largest provincial park. It's circumnavigated by a 51-km (31-mile) hiking trail along rugged cliffs that rise 600 feet above the bay. Wilderness cabins and campsites are available. ✉ *1108 W. Advocate Rd., Point de l'Eglise* ✣ *Off Hwy. 209* ☎ *902/392–2085, 902/254–3241 off-season* ⊕ *www.novascotiaparks.ca* ₹ *Free* ⊙ *May–Oct., daily 8–8.*

Fodor's Choice ★ **Cape d'Or** (*Cape of Gold*). The explorer Samuel de Champlain poetically, but inaccurately, named Cape d'Or—there's copper in these hills, not gold. The region was actively mined a century ago, and at nearby Horseshoe Cove you may still find nuggets of almost pure copper on the beach, along with amethysts and other semiprecious stones. Cape d'Or's hiking trails border the cliff edge above the Dory Rips, a turbulent meeting of currents from the Minas Basin and the Bay of Fundy punctuated by a fine lighthouse. ✉ *Cape d'Or.*

WHERE TO EAT AND STAY

$$$ CANADIAN ✕ **Wild Caraway Restaurant & Café.** The young proprietors of this eatery are enthusiastic about using local products in their cuisine. Casual but quality options like lobster rolls, fish cakes, quiche, and a daily pasta are served at lunch. Dinners are more sophisticated and might include panfried halibut, local scallops, and a 10-ounce rib eye. Brunch is served on Sundays only, starting at 9 am. The 1860s building housing the restaurant has windows that overlook the wharf. There are also two basic guest rooms (C$90, breakfast included) on the top floor, with a shared bathroom, for overnight stays. $ *Average main: C$22* ✉ *3721 Hwy. 209, Point de l'Eglise* ☎ *902/392–2889* ⊕ *wildcaraway.com* ⊙ *Closed Tues. and Wed. Call for off-season hrs.*

$$ RENTAL **Driftwood Park Retreat.** Five modern chalets are steps from the Fundy shore at this eco-friendly property. **Pros:** private balconies with a great view and a barbecue; free laundry room. **Cons:** there's not much else around; Wi-Fi only available in the office; TVs are available but must be requested. $ *Rooms from: C$165* ✉ *47 Driftwood La., Advocate Harbour* ☎ *902/392–2008, 866/810–0110* ⊕ *www.driftwoodparkretreat.com* ⊙ *Closed late Oct.–Apr.* ⇄ *5 cottages, 1 studio* ⊘ *No meals.*

$ B&B/INN **The Lighthouse on Cape d'Or.** Before automation, two lighthouse keepers manned the light on rocky Cape d'Or, and their cottages have been transformed into a small inn with unparalleled views of the Minas Basin. **Pros:** cool concept; warm hosts. **Cons:** difficult access; breakfast not included; no credit cards accepted. $ *Rooms from: C$90* ✉ *Cape d'Or* ✣ *Off Hwy. 209, 6 km (4 miles) from Advocate Harbour* ☎ *902/670–8314* ⊕ *www.capedor.ca* ⊙ *Closed Nov.–Apr.* ⇄ *4 rooms* ⊘ *No meals.*

$ B&B/INN FAMILY **Reid's Century Farm Tourist Home.** Nestled between Cape d'Or and Cape Chignecto, this is a working cattle farm where you can enjoy the bucolic pleasures of country life or take a short drive to the Fundy shore. **Pros:** rooms have coffeemakers; cottages have propane barbecues. **Cons:** remote location; bathrooms have shower but no tub; no breakfast served. $ *Rooms from: C$75* ✉ *1391 W. Advocate Rd., West Advocate*

☎ 902/392–2592 ⊕ www.reidstouristhome.ca ⏲ Closed Oct.–May ☐ 3 rooms, 2 cottages ⊠ No meals.

SPORTS AND THE OUTDOORS

FAMILY **NovaShores Adventures.** These kayak tours explore the unspoiled coast of Cape Chignecto on the Bay of Fundy daily from mid-May through September. Prices for a day tour are C$99, or C$125 including a lobster dinner on the beach; two- and three-day options are also available. *✉ 37 School La., Advocate Harbour ☎ 902/392–2222, 866/638–4118 ⊕ www.novashores.com.*

PARRSBORO

55 km (34 miles) east of Cape d'Or.

Parrsboro, the main town on the north shore of the Minas Basin, is a hot spot for rock hounds and fossil hunters.

GETTING HERE AND AROUND

There is no public transportation to Parrsboro. By road, it's on Highway 2, which can be accessed from the Trans-Canada Highway (Highway 104) near Amherst, Springhill, or Truro.

EXPLORING

TOP ATTRACTIONS

FAMILY **Fundy Geological Museum.** Not far from the Minas Basin, where some of the oldest dinosaur fossils in Canada have been found, this museum showcases 200-million-year-old specimens alongside other mineral, plant, and animal relics. The opportunity to peer into a working geology lab and to see bright new interactive exhibits (like the Bay of Fundy Time Machine) give this museum real kid appeal. On Fridays and Saturdays in July and August, the curator leads fascinating two- to four-hour field trips through the surrounding area, but you need your own transportation because most don't start at the museum. *✉ 162 Two Island Rd. ☎ 902/254–3814 ⊕ fundygeological.novascotia.ca ☐ C$8.25, C$25 including admission and curatorial field trip ⏲ June–mid-Oct., daily 9:30–5:30; mid-Oct.–May, weekdays 8:30–4:30.*

WORTH NOTING

Minas Basin. The cliffs that rim the Minas Basin are washed by the world's highest tides twice daily: the result is a wealth of plant and animal fossils revealed in the rocks or carried down to the shore. *✉ Parrsboro.*

Nova Scotia Gem and Mineral Show. The combination of fossils and semi-precious stones makes Parrsboro a natural place to hold this long-established show (it celebrated 50 years in 2015) during the third weekend of

THE MYSTERY OF THE *MARY CELESTE*

The *Mary Celeste*, originally christened the *Amazon*, was built on Spencer's Island in 1861. Its first captain died on the ship's maiden voyage and the boat was renamed. In 1872 the ship set sail for Europe carrying a cargo of wine and liquor. Less than a month later it was discovered abandoned at sea, all sails set and undamaged but without a trace of the crew and passengers. A cairn at Spencer's Island Beach (across from the Beach House Restaurant on Highway 209) commemorates the vessel.

August. In addition to dozens of exhibitors, the event includes themed demonstrations and geological field trips. Experts are on hand to identify any treasures you turn up. ✉ *Lions Arena, King St. and Western Ave.* ☎ *902/254–3814 Fundy Geological Museum.*

Ottawa House-by-the-Sea Museum. Although fossils have become Parrsboro's claim to fame, this harbor town was also a major shipping and shipbuilding port, and its history is chronicled here. The house, which overlooks the Bay of Fundy, is the only surviving building from a 1700s settlement. It was later the summer home of Sir Charles Tupper (1821–1915), a former premier of Nova Scotia and briefly the prime minister of Canada. Those with roots in Nova Scotia can research their ancestors in the genealogical archives. ✉ *1155 Whitehall Rd., 3 km (2 miles) south of downtown* ☎ *902/254–2376* 🌐 *www.ottawahousemuseum.ca* 💲 *C$2* ⏲ *Late May–mid-Sept. or early Oct., daily 10–6.*

FAMILY **Parrsboro Rock and Mineral Shop and Museum.** The world's smallest dinosaur footprints, along with rare minerals, rocks, and fossils, are displayed at Eldon George's shop and museum. George, a goldsmith, lapidary, and wood-carver, sells his work in his shop and hosts tours for fossil and mineral collectors. ✉ *349 Whitehall Rd.* ☎ *902/254–2981* 💲 *Donations accepted* ⏲ *May–Oct., daily 10–6.*

Partridge Island. Semiprecious stones such as amethyst, quartz, and stilbite can be found at Partridge Island, 1 km (½ mile) offshore and connected to the mainland by an isthmus. The Partridge Island Trail can be followed from the beach up to a lookout on the high point. ✉ *Parrsboro.*

WHERE TO STAY

$ B&B/INN **Gillespie House Inn.** Colorful gardens border the driveway leading up to this 1890 home that is convenient to Parrsboro but also a great choice for active visitors—the hosts can organize golfing, kayaking, and hiking experiences for you. **Pros:** impeccable rooms; customized packages available; eco-friendly, including some solar power. **Cons:** complimentary Continental breakfast is the only meal served; no elevator. 💲 *Rooms from: C$119* ✉ *358 Main St.* ☎ *902/254–3196, 877/901–3196* 🌐 *www.gillespiehouseinn.com* ⏲ *Closed Nov.–Apr.* 🛏 *7 rooms* 🍽 *Breakfast.*

$ B&B/INN **Maple Inn, Parrsboro.** Two Italianate homes built in 1893 have been combined to form this charming inn within walking distance of downtown Parrsboro and the waterfront. **Pros:** full breakfast included. **Cons:** no elevator; potential floral-wallpaper overload. 💲 *Rooms from: C$99* ✉ *2358 Western Ave.* ☎ *902/254–3735, 877/627–5346* 🌐 *www.mapleinn.ca* ⏲ *Closed Nov.–Apr.* 🛏 *6 rooms, 2 suites* 🍽 *Breakfast.*

$$ B&B/INN **Parrsboro Mansion Inn.** Although this 1880 home, set far back on a 4-acre lawn, presents an imposing face, it's bright and modern inside. **Pros:** German breakfast buffet; host is a certified massage therapist with an on-site treatment room; heated pool. **Cons:** old-style small-screen TVs; one-week minimum stay from mid-October to mid-June. 💲 *Rooms from: C$129* ✉ *3916 Eastern Ave.* ☎ *902/254–2585, 866/354–2585* 🌐 *www.parrsboromansion.com* 🛏 *3 rooms, 1 suite* 🍽 *Breakfast.*

NIGHTLIFE AND PERFORMING ARTS

Ship's Company Theatre. Top-notch plays, comedy, and a concert series are presented from July through September at this three-stage facility. At its heart is the *Kipawo,* a former Minas Basin ferry that was transformed into the original floating theater in the 1980s. Evening shows start at 8, Sunday matinees at 2. ✉ *18 Lower Main St.* ☎ *902/254–2003, 800/565–7469* 🌐 *www.shipscompanytheatre.com* 💲 *C$28 for shows, C$24 for Mon.-night concerts, C$40 for Second Stage; pay-what-you-can for preview nights.*

SPORTS AND THE OUTDOORS

FAMILY **Spirit Reins Ranch.** Both experienced horseback riders and complete novices will find trail riding to suit their abilities, with scenic rides through countryside or along the beach and packages that include fossil tours and picnics. Lessons and summer horse camps for children are also available. Trail rides range from 1 to 4½ hours. ✉ *432 Prospect Rd, RR1* ☎ *902/254–3138, 902/254–4262* 🌐 *www.spiritreinsranch.com* 💲 *C$50–C$110.*

FIVE ISLANDS

25 km (15½ miles) east of Parrsboro.

Located between Parrsboro and Truro, Five Islands is one of the most scenic areas along Highway 2, with spectacular views of the Bay of Fundy. According to Mi'Kmaq legend, these islands were created when the god Glooscap threw handfuls of sod at Beaver, who had mocked and betrayed him.

GETTING HERE AND AROUND

There is no public transportation to Five Islands. Highway 2 can be accessed off the Trans-Canadian Highway (Highway 104).

EXPLORING

Cobequid Interpretation Centre. The geology, history, and culture of the Five Islands area are interpreted here with pictures, videos, and panels, and you can get a sweeping view of the countryside and the impressive tides from the World War II observation tower. Cobequid is home base for the **Kenomee Hiking and Walking Trails,** where hikers traverse varied landscapes ranging from forested valleys to coast and cliffs. ✉ *3246 Hwy. 2, Economy* ☎ *902/647–2600* 🌐 *www.cobequidinterpretivecentre.com* 💲 *By donation* ⏲ *Mid-to-late June and Sept.–mid-Oct., daily 9–5; July and Aug., daily 9–6.*

BEACHES

Five Islands Provincial Park. On the shore of Minas Basin, the park has a beach for combing, trails for hiking, and mudflats for clam digging. Interpretive displays reveal the area's intriguing geology—semiprecious stones, Jurassic-period dinosaur bones, and fossils can all be found within the park's 1,500 acres. You can learn about geology and other topics, among them astronomy, rockhounding, and tidal-pool exploration, during complimentary programs offered during high season (check the website). Because the water recedes nearly a mile at ebb tide, you can walk on the ocean floor, though you'll have to run back mighty fast when the tide turns. That's precisely the goal of 2,000 or so participants in the **Not Since Moses 10K Race** (*www.notsincemoses.com*), an early-August event of (almost) biblical proportions. **Amenities:** parking (free); showers; toilets. **Best for:** swimming; walking. *618 Bentley Rd., Hwy. 2 902/254–2980 www.novascotiaparks.ca Free Park accessible year-round; services open mid-June–mid-Oct., daily dawn–dusk.*

TRURO

91 km (57 miles) east of Parrsboro.

Truro's central location places it on many travelers' routes: this is rightly called "The Hub of Nova Scotia" because if you're driving down the Trans-Canada Highway, you'll have to pass by. Within Truro itself, watch for the Tree Sculptures, a creative tribute to trees killed by the dreaded Dutch elm disease. Artists have been transforming the dead trees into handsome sculptures of historical figures, wildlife, and cultural icons. There's a large farmers' market every Saturday from mid-May to the end of October.

GETTING HERE AND AROUND

Truro is on the Trans-Canada Highway (Highway 104). Maritime Bus can get you here from Halifax in just under 2 hours (C$25.56), with several buses daily, or from various points in New Brunswick (Fredericton, 5½ hrs, C$68.06) and Prince Edward Island (Charlottetown, about 3½ hrs C$56.98; requires one transfer).

EXPLORING

FAMILY **River Breeze Farm.** For up-close appreciation of local produce, this farm has pick-your-own strawberry and raspberry fields in summer and Atlantic Canada's largest corn maze in the fall. The place turns decidedly scary for Halloween, when "Fear Farm" is haunted by gruesome characters (real live actors) in the maze and a haunted house. *660 Onslow Rd. Upper Onslow, off Hwy. 102, Exit 14A 902/895–6541 www.riverbreeze.info Berry-picking price varies. Corn Maze: C$10. Fear Farm: C$25 Berry picking: July–early Sept., 8:30–4 (days vary, check website or call). Corn Maze: mid-Sept.–mid-Oct., weekends noon–5 (last entry 3:30). Fear Farm: every Fri. and Sat. in Oct. 6:30–9:30.*

FAMILY **Victoria Park.** At 400 acres, this park on the edge of downtown is Truro's biggest asset, with wooded hiking trails, a winding stream, two waterfalls, public tennis courts, and an outdoor (heated) pool that becomes a skating rink in the winter. Even if you're not staying in Truro, this park can be a good pit stop for car-weary travelers: kids especially will enjoy the pool, picnic pavilion, and playground. Free open-air family movies are screened on certain Friday nights in July and August, and a Sunday afternoon concert series runs from mid-June through early September at the Bandshell. *Park Rd., off Brunswick St. 902/893–6078 off-season, 902/895–7078 during season www.truro.ca/vic-park.html Park free, pool C$6.50 Daily dawn–dusk.*

WHERE TO EAT AND STAY

$$ CONTEMPORARY Fodor's Choice ★ **Bistro 22.** Rich farmland fringes Truro, and the menu makes the most of the fabulous produce grown around here. The 32-seat eatery has an upscale-casual feel and a small but mighty menu. Salads, sandwiches, and whole-grain pizzas topped with fresh ingredients dominate at lunch, while dinner includes meatier options such as pork stuffed with locally made Gouda, or chicken breast marinated with herbs, lemon, and garlic, all served with seasonal vegetables. Prime rib is on offer every Thursday. Desserts, always made in-house, come generously portioned. [$] *Average main: C$16* ✉ *16 Inglis Pl.* ☎ *902/843–4123* ⊕ *www.bistro22.ca* ⏲ *Closed Sun. and Mon. No dinner Tues. and Wed.*

$$ B&B/INN **Suncatcher Bed and Breakfast.** Rooms at this modest B&B are cheerful and bright: ditto for owner Ruth Mailloux, who knows the province from stem to stern and will happily advise you about itineraries and attractions. **Pros:** knowledgeable host; two-day stained-glass workshops available by reservation. **Cons:** 6½ km (4 miles) from Truro; can be difficult to find. [$] *Rooms from: C$132* ✉ *25 Wile Crest Ave., North River* ☎ *902/893–7169, 877/203–6032* ⊕ *www.suncatcherbnb.com* ⇨ *2 rooms* |O| *Breakfast.*

SPORTS AND THE OUTDOORS

FAMILY **Shubenacadie River Adventure Tours.** On these adrenaline-inducing three-hour Zodiac inflatable-boat trips, you ride the waves created by the famous Fundy tides as the waters surge upstream. The intensity of the tides determines the intensity of your ride; call or check the company's website to find out when your trip will be (relatively) mellow or fierce. ✉ *10061 Hwy. 215, South Maitland* ☎ *902/261–2222, 888/878–8687* ⊕ *www.shubie.com* ⇨ *From C$85.*

Fodor's Choice ★ **Shubenacadie River Runners.** Riding the white water churned up as the Fundy tidal bore rushes into Nova Scotia's largest river is an adventure you won't soon forget. With Shubenacadie River Runners you can confront the waves head-on in a self-bailing Zodiac. Tide conditions and time of day let you choose mildly turbulent or ultrawild rides. ✉ *8681 Hwy. 215, Maitland* ☎ *902/261–2770, 800/856–5061* ⊕ *tidalborerafting.com* ⇨ *Full day, high-tide "Super Wild" ride C$103.50, including steak barbecue; other full-day rides C$80–C$92; half-day C$60–C$70, including hot drinks and snacks.*

SHOPPING

FAMILY Fodor's Choice ★ **Sugar Moon Farm Maple Products & Pancake House.** This sugar camp, store, and pancake house in the Cobequid Mountains, about 30 km (19 miles) north of Truro off Highway 311, is Nova Scotia's only year-round maple destination. Daily in the summer and on weekends the rest of the year you can tour the working facility and hike the sugar woods. In spring, when the sap is running, you can also watch demonstrations. Afterward, tuck into whole-grain buttermilk pancakes and waffles with maple syrup, local sausage, fresh biscuits, maple baked beans, and organic coffee at the lodge. Multiple times per year, a guest chef prepares a gourmet dinner (C$75) that cleverly incorporates maple products. At the store, you can buy your own sweet souvenirs, among them maple syrup, maple cream, maple candy, and maple butter. ✉ *221 Alex MacDonald Rd., Earltown* ☎ *902/657–3348, 866/816–2753* ⊕ *www.sugarmoon.ca.*

Thrown Together Pottery and Art. The owner's clay creations are created in the studio here and sold in the on-site shop alongside works by more than 20 other local artisans. ✉ *37 King St.* ☎ *902/895–9309* ⊕ *www.throwntogetherpottery.com* ⏲ *Closed Sun. and Mon. year-round; only open by chance Tues. and Wed. Jan.–Mar.*

CAPE BRETON ISLAND

Fodor's Choice ★ There isn't much new in the northeastern corner of Nova Scotia and that's precisely the point; Cape Breton Island's reputation rests on simple pleasures and heartfelt hospitality. Spectacular scenery doesn't hurt either, and the very best of it is found on the Cabot Trail, a scenic 298-km (185-mile) stretch of road, winding along ocean-side cliffs. This rugged terrain made the Highland Scots, who settled here in the 18th century, feel right at home and their influence remains obvious: North America's first single-malt whiskey distillery is on Cape Breton, as is its only college devoted to Gaelic language, arts, and culture. Elsewhere on the coast you'll find Francophone villages full of Acadian joie de vivre, plus historic attractions like the mighty Fortress at Louisbourg, which bear witness to the area's long-standing French presence. Bras d'Or Lake—a vast, almost landlocked inlet of the sea occupying the entire center of Cape Breton—is still home to ancient Mi'Kmaq communities, yet it appeals equally to an international contingent of boaters who come to cruise the lake's unspoiled coves and islands. And golfers are very excited about the new Cabot Cliffs course, already being hailed as one of the best in the world.

GETTING HERE AND AROUND

To reach Cape Breton Island, you can drive from mainland Nova Scotia via the Canso Causeway; take a Marine Atlantic ferry from Newfoundland; or fly into Sydney's J.A. Douglas McCurdy Airport. Maritime Bus has service from the mainland, with stops at Port Hawkesbury, Whycocomagh, Baddeck, and North Sydney. The bus ride from Halifax takes about 6½ hours and costs C$81.05 one-way. The island itself has five convenient, camera-ready driving routes—and since these collectively cover about 710 km (440 miles), you should allow five days to explore. Enter by way of the causeway on Highway 104. Turning left at the rotary, take Highway 19 (the Ceilidh Trail), which winds along the hillside through fields and glens for 107 km (67 miles) before meeting the west end of the fabled Cabot Trail. Alternately, from the causeway you could follow the Bras d'Or Lakes Scenic Drive, which loops along lesser-known roads of central Cape Breton and around the massive lake that lent the route its name; or veer east on the linked Fleur-de-Lis/Marconi Trail, which takes you to the must-see Fortress of Louisbourg and then onward to Sydney (Cape Breton's main city). Note that driving in this direction also puts your vehicle on the waterside for most of the trail, making it easier to pull over for photo ops.

ESSENTIALS

Visitor Information **Port Hastings Visitor Information Centre.** ✉ *96 Hwy. 4, Port Hastings* ☎ *902/625-4201* 🌐 *dcba-info.com.* **Tourism Cape Breton.** ☎ *902/563-4636, 888/562-9848* 🌐 *www.cbisland.com.*

JUDIQUE

30 km (18 miles) north of the Canso Causeway; 75 km (47 miles) northeast of Antigonish.

Like so many Cape Breton communities, Judique is only a little clutch of buildings with Highway 19 running straight through as the main street. Nevertheless, the presence of **the Celtic Music Interpretive Centre** makes Judique an essential destination for anyone interested in the island music scene. Need some fresh air before getting back in the car and continuing up the Ceilidh Trail? The coastal area around Judique is good for hiking (a portion of the Trans-Canada Trail threads through) as well as swimming. For an offshore experience, consider taking a tour out of Little Judique Harbour.

GETTING HERE AND AROUND

There is no public transportation to Judique. By road, it's on the Ceilidh Trail (Highway 19)—a left turn at the traffic circle over the Canso Causeway.

EXPLORING

Celtic Music Interpretive Centre. Packed with exhibits detailing the fine points of fiddling, the center also has an archive with classic recordings and oral history interviews. Visitors eager to pick up a bow can play along to a video tutorial. If you'd rather just get an earful, that's no problem. In summer, daily except Sunday, musical demonstrations (C$12, admission to exhibits included) take place about a dozen times, and the center's dining room hosts lunchtime ceilidhs (free for the entertainment but not the lunch) from 11:30 to 3 and on Sunday afternoons starting at 3 (C$8). Wednesday-evening ceilidhs (C$6) run from July through mid-October. The adjacent Buddy McMaster School of Fiddling offers weeklong courses during October's Celtic Colours International Festival. ✉ *5471 Hwy. 19* ☎ *902/787-2708* 🌐 *www.celticmusiccentre.com* 💵 *C$7* ⏲ *Mid-June–mid-Oct., Mon.–Sat. 9–5, Sun. 11–6:30.*

MABOU

28 km (17 miles) northeast of Judique.

The village of Mabou is very Scottish (Gaelic-language signs attest to it), and the residents' respect for tradition is apparent in everything from the down-home meals they serve to the music they so exuberantly play; arguably the best place to sample both is at the Red Shoe.

GETTING HERE AND AROUND

There is no public transportation to Mabou. It's on the Ceilidh Trail.

EXPLORING

The best touring in the Mabou area is along the hiking trails that riddle the hills here.

BEACHES

FAMILY **West Mabou Beach Provincial Park.** A wide sweep of sandy beach backed by a dune system is the standout feature of this 530-acre park on Mabou Harbour. The only public-access beach in the area, it also has a fishpond, a picnic area, and change rooms, but its status as a protected natural environment prevents any further development and preserves its peaceful quality. Behind the beach are 12 km (7½ miles) of hiking trails, through agricultural land and marshes, that have fine views. **Amenities:** parking (free); toilets. **Best for:** swimming; walking. ✉ *1757 Little Mabou Rd.* ✣ *Off Hwy. 19* ⊕ *www.novascotiaparks.ca* ₵ *Free.*

WHERE TO EAT AND STAY

$$ CANADIAN FAMILY ✕ **Mull Café & Deli.** It's doubtful you'll drive by this informal restaurant on Mabou's main thoroughfare without seeing a parking lot full of cars. Owned by the proprietors of the Duncreigan Country Inn, it's a popular hangout for Cape Bretoners but also draws "come from away" diners thanks to its long lunchtime menu of hearty salads, creamy chowders, deep-fried seafood plates, and homemade desserts. After 5 (all day on Sunday) the dinner menu goes more upscale with dishes like scallops in white-wine and cream sauce, and lemon-chicken supreme. At peak times, reservations are recommended. The café displays local artwork, making this a pleasant place to linger, but for those in a rush

CLOSE UP

The Music of Cape Breton

Weaned on old-time Scottish tunes, Cape Breton Island's traditional musicians are among the world's finest—and there's a widely held belief (in Scotland, too) that here the music has been preserved in a purer form than in the old country itself. In summer you can hear these musicians play at festivals, concerts, and, of course, ceilidhs (pronounced KAY-lees). The word, Gaelic for "visit," derives from the days when folks would gather in a neighbor's kitchen for music, stories, and step dancing. Today ceilidhs have evolved into public events that visitors are welcome to join. Bulletin boards, newspapers, and visitor information centers are a good source for listings. Inverness County, which encompasses the Ceilidh Trail and is the epicenter of activity, has its own ceilidh lineup online at *www.inverness-ns.ca*. Any night of the week in peak season, you'll also be able to attend a square dance somewhere in Inverness County. Propelled by virtuoso fiddling, locals of every age whirl through taxing "square sets," shaking the floor and rattling the rafters in the process. The highlight of the musical calendar is undoubtedly the Celtic Colours International Festival, held every October at the height of the island's spectacular fall-colors season. It gathers together Celtic musicians, singers, and dancers from around the corner and around the world for concerts and ceilidhs across the region.

there's a take-out deli counter. $ *Average main: C$17* ✉ *11630 Hwy. 19* ☎ *902/945–2244* ⊕ *www.mullcafe.com.*

$$ CANADIAN FAMILY Fodor's Choice ★ ✕ **Red Shoe.** More than a mere pub, this Cape Breton institution has evolved into an attraction in its own right, in part because it is owned by four of the Rankins, Canada's most celebrated singing siblings. There's music here just about every night, and sometimes during the day (some free, some with a cover charge of C$8–C$10), and the "Shoe" is a magnet for the finest fiddlers and step dancers. As for the food, expect the usual pub favorites: fish-and-chips, pulled-pork sandwiches, grilled salmon, stuffed chicken, and mussels steamed in ale, garlic, and bacon. $ *Average main: C$19* ✉ *11533 Hwy. 19* ☎ *902/945–2996* ⊕ *www.redshoepub.com* ⏲ *Closed mid-Oct.–late May.*

$$ B&B/INN **Duncreigan Country Inn.** With its harborside deck and peaceful location, the inn provides a great place to unwind after a day spent exploring Cape Breton. **Pros:** full buffet breakfast included; open year-round. **Cons:** no restaurant on-site; trees block some harbor views. $ *Rooms from: C$145* ✉ *11409 Hwy. 19* ☎ *902/945–2207, 800/840–2207 reservations* ⊕ *www.duncreigan.ca* 🛏 *7 rooms, 1 suite* 🍴 *Breakfast.*

$$ B&B/INN **Glenora Inn & Distillery.** North America's first single-malt whiskey distillery adjoins this whitewashed inn north of Mabou, so if you stay here it'll be easy to sample a wee dram of Glenora's own Glen Breton Rare. **Pros:** unique atmosphere; sylvan property bisected by a brook. **Cons:** rooms could use a refresh; road to chalets is steep and tricky to negotiate at night. $ *Rooms from: C$169* ✉ *13727 Hwy. 19,*

Glenville ☎ 902/258–2262, 800/839–0491 🌐 www.glenoradistillery.com ⏲ Closed Nov.–mid-May 🛏 9 rooms, 6 chalets 🍴 No meals.

NIGHTLIFE

Strathespey Place. Concerts, plays, and musicals are presented at this arts center that is also one of the many venues for the annual Celtic Colours Festival. ✉ *11156 Hwy. 19 ☎ 902/945–5300 🌐 www.strathspeyplace.com.*

SPORTS AND THE OUTDOORS

Cabot Cliffs Golf Course. Along with Cabot Links, this course is turning Cape Breton into an international golf destination. Cabot Cliffs, perched atop 80-foot cliffs with a stunning view, was designed by the impressive team of Bill Coore and Ben Crenshaw, and promises superlative golf in classic links style. ✉ *20 Beach Rd., Inverness ☎ 902/258–4653, 855/652–2268 🌐 www.cabotlinks.com/golf/cabot-cliffs 💲 C$110–C$150 ⛳ 18 holes, 6851 yards, par 72.*

Fodor's Choice ★ **Cabot Links.** As Canada's only true links course, designed by Rod Whitman and opened in 2012, Cabot Links has caused much excitement among players and golf media alike, and with good reason. Set along the rugged Cape Breton seashore near Inverness, it is both challenging and stunningly scenic, and comes with superb lodging and dining options as well. This is a walking-only course, so no buggy rentals. ✉ *15933 Central Ave., Inverness ✣ 22 km (14 miles) north of Mabou on the Cabot Trail ☎ 902/258–4653, 855/652–2268 🌐 www.cabotlinks.com 💲 C$165–C$195 ⛳ 18 holes, 6942 yards, par 72 ⏲ Mid-May–mid-Nov.*

Mabou Highlands. The Cape Mabou Trail Club, a volunteer organization, maintains 30 km (18 miles) of nature trails, 17 in total, on this mountain range. Gaelic-speaking immigrants from Scotland settled this region of plunging cliffs, isolated beaches, rising mountains, and glens, meadows, and hardwood forests, and some of the trails follow tracks made by carts traveling to and from the pioneer settlements. Today the area is so hauntingly quiet that you might halfway expect to meet the *sidhe*, the Scottish fairies, capering on the hillsides. Trail maps can be purchased from local retailers or viewed online. ✉ *Mabou 🌐 www.capemabouhiking.com.*

MARGAREE HARBOUR

53 km (33 miles) north of Mabou.

Aside from pleasant pastimes like hillside hiking and saltwater swimming (Whale Cove and Chimney Corner are the local's top picks for the latter), the Margaree area promises world-class fly-fishing. Margaree Harbour not only marks the point where the Ceilidh Trail joins the Cabot Trail, it also sits at the mouth of the Margaree River: a designated Canadian Heritage River known for legendary salmon runs.

GETTING HERE AND AROUND

There is no public transportation to Margaree Harbour. It's just north of where the Ceilidh Trail meets the Cabot Trail, so is accessible cross-country from Baddeck as well as up the coast.

EXPLORING

Margaree Salmon Museum. Exhibits at this unassuming and yet widely renowned museum are proudly old-school, which seems fitting because they're housed in a former one-room schoolhouse. On display are all manner of fishing tackle, photographs, hand-tied flies, and other memorabilia related to salmon angling on the Margaree—check out the rod that once belonged to a wartime British spy who shared fly-fishing tips with Hermann Goering. Visitors can watch videos, study models of the river, and peek into the fish tank. ✉ *60 E. Big Intervale Rd., Northeast Margaree* ☎ *902/248–2848* 🌐 *www.margareens.com/margaree_salmon.html* 💲 *C$2* ⏲ *Mid-June–mid-Oct., daily 9–5.*

WHERE TO STAY

$$ B&B/INN **Normaway Inn and Cabins.** Set on 500 acres in the Margaree Valley, this inn has rooms full of country character, hiking trails on the doorstep, and it rings with the sound of live traditional music from top Cape Breton fiddlers. **Pros:** bucolic site; central to island touring loops; own landing strip. **Cons:** isn't luxurious, and doesn't aspire to be. 💲 *Rooms from: C$129* ✉ *691 Egypt Rd.* ☎ *902/248–2987, 800/565–9463* 🌐 *www.thenormawayinn.com* ⏲ *Closed Nov.–May; cabins available off-season by arrangement* 🛏 *9 rooms, 3 suites, 15 cabins* 🍽 *No meals.*

SPORTS AND THE OUTDOORS

The Margaree has two fishing seasons: the early-summer run, which opens annually on June 1, and the fall run, from mid-September through October, which coincides with the peak foliage period. Salmon-fishing licenses cost about C$62 per week for anglers who don't live in Nova Scotia. In Margaree, they're available from LeBlanc's Store, Ingraham's Irving & Convenience Store, and the Big Intervale Fishing Lodge. Before planning a fishing trip, check the latest catch-and-release regulations, imposed in 2015 amid concerns about declining stocks in Margaree and other rivers.

Margaree Salmon Association. The association is heavily involved in salmon conservation and habitat restoration, and has put together a pamphlet, available on its website, outlining Margaree River fishing etiquette. In addition to the fishing advice, the pamphlet lists the names and contact information of guides who know the river well and can help you catch that trophy-size salmon. The guides typically charge C$175–C$200 per day. ✉ *Margaree Harbour* ☎ *902/248–2059 general information, 902/248–2578 for fishing guides* 🌐 *www.margareesalmon.org.*

CHÉTICAMP

25 km (16 miles) north of Margaree Harbour.

In Chéticamp, an Acadian enclave for more than 200 years, Francophone culture and traditions are still very much alive. That's why the Gaelic-inflected lilt in locals' voices is replaced by a distinct French accent. (You might be greeted in French but can respond in English—most residents are bilingual.) Size is another distinguishing factor because, with population of about 4,000, Chéticamp feels like a major metropolis compared to other Western Shore communities. The landscape is different, too. Poised between mountains and sea, Chéticamp stands exposed on a wide lip of flat land below a range of bald green hills, behind which lies the high plateau of the Cape Breton Highlands. Commercial fishing is the town's raison d'être, but rug hooking is its main claim to fame, a fact reflected in local attractions and shops. So pause to peruse them before racing into the adjacent national park.

GETTING HERE AND AROUND

There is no public transportation to Chéticamp. By road, it's on the Cabot Trail just south of the Cape Breton Highlands National Park.

ESSENTIALS

Visitor Information **Chéticamp Visitor Information Centre.** ✉ *Les Trois Pignons, 15584 Cabot Trail* ☎ *902/224-2642* ⊕ *www.cheticamp.ca.*

EXPLORING

Les Trois Pignons Cultural Center. The center, which contains the Elizabeth LeFort Gallery, displays samples of the rugs, tapestries, and related artifacts that helped make Chéticamp the World Rug Hooking Capital. Born in 1914, Elizabeth LeFort created more than 300 tapestries, some of which have hung in the Vatican, the White House, and Buckingham Palace. (One standout depicting U.S. presidents is made from 11 km (7 miles) of yarn!) Les Trois Pignons is also an Acadian cultural and genealogical information center. ✉ *15584 Cabot Trail Rd.* ☎ *902/224-2642* ⊕ *www.lestroispignons.com* 💲 *C$5* ⏲ *July and Aug., daily 9–7; mid-May–June and Sept.–mid Oct., daily 9–5; mid-Oct.–mid-May by appointment.*

WHERE TO EAT AND STAY

$$ CANADIAN ✕ **Le Gabriel Restaurant and Lounge.** Casual Le Gabriel's—you can't miss its large lighthouse entranceway—offers simple but substantial fare that includes North American standards and traditional Acadian favorites. The latter include *tourtière* (meat pie with a crispy crust) and *fricot* (a hearty stew with potatoes, pork bits, chives, and beef or chicken). Fresh fish dishes are popular, too, with snow crab and lobster available in season. Lighter fare includes hot and cold sandwiches, wraps, soups, and fish-and-chips. The menu and opening hours are more limited in the off-season. The lounge has billiard tables, and there's live music on most Saturday nights. 💲 *Average main: C$19* ✉ *15424 Cabot Trail Rd.* ☎ *902/224-3685* ⊕ *www.legabriel.com.*

$$ RENTAL FAMILY **Cabot Trail Sea & Golf Chalets.** Linked to Le Portage Golf Club by a private pathway, these ocean-side chalets work well for golfers and anyone wanting more than a mere hotel room. **Pros:** discounted weekly rates; great golfing. **Cons:** books quickly; no meals available. 💲 *Rooms from: C$159* ✉ *71 Fraser Doucet La.* ☎ *902/224-1777, 877/224-1777* ⊕ *www.seagolfchalets.com* ⏲ *Closed mid-Oct.–mid-May* 🛏 *12 chalets, 1 suite* 🍽 *No meals.*

$ B&B/INN **Chéticamp Outfitters' Inn Bed & Breakfast.** Clean, cozy rooms overlook the ocean, mountains, and valley at this hilltop inn, and there's a top-floor patio along the length of the cedar house that takes full advantage of the view. **Pros:** walking distance to beach; breakfast includes memorable blueberry muffins. **Cons:** outside Chéticamp.

Rooms from: C$95 13938 Cabot Trail Rd. 902/224-2776 cheticampns.com/category/accommodations/ Closed Dec.–mid-Apr. 6 rooms, 1 chalet Breakfast.

SPORTS AND THE OUTDOORS

On whale-watch cruises departing from Chéticamp's government wharf, you can see minkes, humpbacks, and finbacks in their natural environment.

FAMILY **Captain Zodiac Whale Cruise.** The operators of these cruises aboard Zodiac vessels are so confident you'll spot a whale—finbacks, humpbacks, minkes, and pilots are the ones most sighted—that they'll refund your money if you don't. They also offer "soft-in-water" snorkeling with the whales—where you enter the water quietly and calmly float on the surface so as not to disturb or alarm the whales. If you're lucky, they'll swim up to take a look at you. Trips take place daily from early July through late August. *Chéticamp 877/232-2522 www.novascotiawhales.com Whale-watching C$59; snorkeling with whales C$95, includes wet suit and snorkeling equipment.*

Le Portage Golf Club. The beautiful but formidable holes at Le Portage overlook the Gulf of St. Lawrence. Course designers Robert and David Moote incorporated 60 sand bunkers, which together with the area's heavy winds provide no end to challenges no matter what your skill level. *15580 Cabot Trail Rd. 902/224-3338, 888/618-5558 www.leportagegolfclub.com C$45–C$80 Course: 18 holes, 6777 yards, par 72 Mid-Apr.–Oct.*

SHOPPING

Cape Breton Photography Gallery. This gallery has more than 60 framed photographs ranging from seascapes to wild creatures and is a great place to pick up a souvenir. *15403 Cabot Trail 902/224-3768 www.capebretonphotos.com Closed weekends.*

Sunset Art Gallery. This folk-art-wood-carving gallery features irresistibly colorful and fun creatures. You can't miss the brightly painted group of buildings, one of which houses the Frog Pond Café, serving French pastries and organic fair-trade coffee. *15856 Cabot Trail 902/224-1831 sunsetartgallery.ca Closed mid-Oct.–mid-May.*

CAPE BRETON HIGHLANDS NATIONAL PARK

5 km (3 miles) north of Chéticamp; 108 km (67 miles) north of Ingonish.

Encircled by one of the world's most scenic driving routes—the glorious, partly coast-hugging, switchback Cabot Trail—this beautiful national park rises from sea level to forested mountaintops, with stunning views, wilderness hiking, and a wealth of wildlife and plants. Fall colors here are nothing short of breathtaking.

GETTING HERE AND AROUND

There is no public transportation to the park. The Cabot Trail loops around it, past the western entrance, at Chéticamp, and the eastern one, at Ingonish.

EXPLORING

Fodor's Choice ★ **Cape Breton Highlands National Park.** A 950-square-km (366-square-mile) wilderness of wooded valleys, barren plateaus, and steep cliffs, Cape Breton Highlands National Park stretches across northern Cape Breton from the gulf shore to the Atlantic.

High-altitude bogs here are home to wild orchids and other unique flora. For animal lovers there's much to see as well, including moose, eagles, deer, bears, foxes, bobcats, and coyotes. Your chances of spotting wildlife naturally improve if you venture off the main road and hike one of the trails at dusk or dawn. Be advised, though, that it's illegal to feed or approach any animal in the park, and all should be observed from a safe distance.

Within the park, there are 26 hiking trails, ranging from a few yards to a lookout point to 12-km (7½-mile) treks to salmon pools or to a remote cove. Guided hikes are among various activities on offer in the park. For your safety, never hike isolated trails alone. Even motorists must remain alert, particularly when driving in moose zones, which are marked by highway signs. Moose sometimes claim the road as their own, and things won't end well if you hit an animal weighing 1,200 pounds.

A permit or pass is required for entering sections of the Cabot Trail within the national park and for use of the facilities such as exhibits, hiking trails, and picnic areas; there are additional fees for camping, fishing, and golf. Full details are available at the gateway information centers. ✉ *Entrances on Cabot Trail near Chéticamp and Ingonish, 37639 Cabot Trail, Ingonish* ☎ *902/224–2306, 902/224–3814 bookstore* 🌐 *www.parkscanada.ca* 💲 *C$7.80* ⏲ *Park: year-round. Visitor centers: mid-May–mid-Oct., daily 9–5 (8:30–7 in peak season).*

PLEASANT BAY

41 km (26 miles) north of Chéticamp.

Because it's about halfway around the Cabot Trail, Pleasant Bay is a convenient place to stop. Local fishermen catch lobster in spring and snow crab in summer. The water yields much bigger creatures, too, and it could be said that whales here outnumber people. Of course, that isn't hard considering the population is just about 350.

GETTING HERE AND AROUND

There is no public transportation to Pleasant Bay. By road, it's on the Cabot Trail just as it briefly emerges from the northwest boundary of the Cape Breton Highlands National Park.

EXPLORING

OFF THE BEATEN PATH

Gampo Abbey. Nova Scotia is a center of Shambhala Buddhism, and though Shambala International is headquartered in Halifax, this abbey is its monastic heart. Finding the site high above the sea, however, requires more than soul searching. From Pleasant Bay, a spur road creeps along the cliffs to Red River; beyond that, a gravel road twists and turns for some 3 km (2 miles) before reaching the broad, flat bench of land upon which the monastery sits. You can tour the abbey and wander through some of its 230 acres to visit a small shrine and grotto.

If the abbey is closed for a retreat or other event, continue down the road for about ½ km (¼ mile) to see the Stupa of Enlightenment, a large and elaborate shrine dedicated to world peace. ✉ *1533 Pleasant Bay Rd., Chéticamp* ☎ *902/224–2752* 🌐 *www.gampoabbey.org* ⏲ *Tours early July–late Aug., weekdays 1:30 and 2:30.*

FAMILY **Whale Interpretive Centre.** Visitors who like to stay on dry land while observing sea life should stop by the center. Using zoom scopes on the whale-spotting deck, you may catch a close-up glimpse of the many different species that often frolic just off-shore. Exhibits and models inside the center's modern structure explain the unique world of whales. ✉ *104 Harbour Rd.* ☎ *902/224–1411* 💲 *C$5* ⏲ *June–mid-Oct., daily 9–5.*

SPORTS AND THE OUTDOORS

FAMILY **Captain Mark's Whale & Seal Cruise.** Sightings are guaranteed on tours, from June through mid-September, aboard inflatable boats (C$44) or a 42-foot research vessel (C$35). Well-trained guides and researchers from Dalhousie University narrate the tours on the research vessel. ✉ *Harbour Rd., off Cabot Trail* ☎ *902/224–1316, 888/754–5112* 🌐 *www.whaleandsealcruise.com* 💲 *Zodiac tours C$49, research vessel C$39* ⏲ *Closed mid-Oct.–May.*

CAPE NORTH

30 km (19 miles) east of Pleasant Bay.

This is where explorer Giovanni Caboto (aka John Cabot) made land in 1497. Not only does Cape North still feel like a new discovery, it also provides access to locales that are even more remote, like Bay St. Lawrence and Meat Cove.

GETTING HERE AND AROUND

There is no public transportation to Cape North. By road, it's at the northernmost point on the Cabot Trail.

BEACHES

Cabots Landing Provincial Park. This long, sandy beach remains untouched by modern development, other than the picnic tables on the adjoining grassland. It's a great place for beachcombing and pondering the journeys of First Nations boatmen who once set out from here to paddle to Newfoundland. A cairn in the park, commemorating the purported arrival of John Cabot from England in 1497, offers further historical insights, but the jaw-dropping views of Aspy Bay and the surrounding wilderness area provide the best reasons to come here. **Amenities:** parking (free). **Best for:** solitude; walking. ✉ *1904 Bay St. Lawrence Rd., Bay St. Lawrence* ✣ *2 km (1 mile) north of Four Mile Beach Inn* 🌐 *parks.gov.ns.ca* 💲 *Free.*

WHERE TO STAY

$ B&B/INN **Four Mile Beach Inn.** Views of Aspy Bay and the ridge of the highland mountains are fantastic from this large 19th-century house near Cabot's Landing. **Pros:** breakfast buffet included; knowledgeable hosts. **Cons:** smallish rooms; two rooms have shared bathrooms, and one has a bathroom across the corridor. 💲 *Rooms from: C$99* ✉ *1528 Bay St.*

Lawrence Rd., Sugarloaf ☎ 902/718–7366 ⊕ www.fourmilebeachinn.com ⊙ Closed mid-Oct.–mid-May (season varies) ⇨ 7 rooms, 1 apartment ⊞ Breakfast.

SPORTS AND THE OUTDOORS

FAMILY **Cabot Trail Adventures.** Based in Dingwall, which neighbors Cape North, this outfitter offers kayak tours as well as boat and bike rentals, from May through October. ✉ *299 Shore Rd., South Harbour, Dingwall ☎ 902/383–2552, 888/616–1689 ⊕ www.kayakingcapebreton.ca ⊞ Tours C$45; bike rentals from C$10 per hr; boat rentals from C$15 per hr.*

Captain Cox's Whale Watch. Several tours in a speedy Zodiac set out daily from July to mid-September from Bay St. Lawrence Wharf. Tours last between 2 and 2½ hours, and if you don't see a whale, you get another trip for free. ✉ *Bay St. Lawrence Rd., off Cabot Trail, Bay St. Lawrence ☎ 902/383–2981, 888/346–5556 ⊕ www.whalewatching-novascotia.com ⊞ C$45 ⊙ Closed Nov.–mid June.*

FAMILY **Oshan Whale Watch.** The C$30 charge for a 2½-hour trip on a working lobster boat is a bargain, and if you don't sight a whale, you get another trip free. ✉ *3384 Bay St. Lawrence Rd., Bay St. Lawrence ☎ 902/383–2883, 877/383–2883 ⊕ www.oshan.ca.*

INGONISH

35 km (22 miles) southeast of Cape North.

The western gateway to the Cabot Trail, Ingonish is one of the leading vacation destinations on Cape Breton, largely because it's home to the much-touted Keltic Lodge Resort and adjacent Highland Links golf course. The spot is actually comprised of five villages—Ingonish proper, Ingonish Centre, Ingonish Beach, Ingonish Harbour, and Ingonish Ferry. Poised on two bays and divided by a long narrow peninsula, all together they cover about 16 km (10 miles).

GETTING HERE AND AROUND

There is no public transportation to Ingonish. By road, it lies on the eastern section of the Cabot Trail.

EXPLORING

Cape Smokey Provincial Park. The park that caps the 984-foot Cape Smokey Peak has a challenging 5-km (3-mile) coastal trail that is breathtaking in more ways than one. Hiking it takes about four hours. There are also picnic tables and lookout points—and great skiing if you come in winter. ✉ *40301 Cabot Trail Rd., Ingonish Ferry ⊕ parks.gov.ns.ca ⊞ Free ⊙ Mid-May–early Oct., daily.*

WHERE TO STAY

$$$$ RESORT FAMILY **Keltic Lodge Resort and Spa.** Spread across the sea cliffs, this resort has glorious views of Cape Smokey and the surrounding highlands. **Pros:** breakfast is included; lots to do. **Cons:** rooms vary in size; some rooms could use a makeover. ⊞ *Rooms from: C$267 ✉ 383 Keltic Inn Rd., Middle Head Peninsula, Ingonish Beach ☎ 902/285–2880, 800/565–0444 ⊕ www.kelticlodge.ca ⊙ Closed mid-Oct–mid-May ⇨ 72 rooms, 2 suites, 10 cottages ⊞ No meals.*

$$ B&B/INN FAMILY **Lantern Hill & Hollow.** Hearing the surf is no problem at this intimate property because the six cottages are just steps from a private 3-km (2-mile) beach that is ideal for quick dips and nightly bonfires; firewood and beach toys are supplied. **Pros:** gorgeous property; convenient location. **Cons:** no meals provided; self-catering; has only light housekeeping. *Rooms from: C$170 36845 Cabot Trail, Ingonish Beach 902/285–2010, 888/663–0225 www.lanternhillandhollow.com Closed Mid-Oct.–late May 3 suites, 6 cottages No meals.*

SPORTS AND THE OUTDOORS

Highlands Links. Perennially ranked as one of Canada's top courses, Highlands was designed by Stanley Thompson, who dubbed it "the mountains and ocean" course. It's a delight to play, with many challenges presented in the land or prevailing winds—even if you think a shot looks easy, it's unlikely that it will be, so be prepared. Over the past few years work has been done to open up the views, so you can now see the ocean from 11 holes. *Cape Breton Highlands National Park, 247 Keltic Inn Rd., Ingonish Beach 902/285–2600, 800/441–1118 www.highlandslinksgolf.com C$53.95–C$102.65 18 holes, 6592 yards, par 72 Mid-May–late Oct.*

ST. ANN'S BAY AND AROUND

Extends for 65 km (40 miles) from Ingonish south to St. Ann's.

Continuing down the Cabot Trail from Ingonish, you'll skirt St. Ann's Bay where communities are of the blink-and-you'll-miss-it variety. Other than North America's only Gaelic college, there are few actual attractions, but there are fun outdoor opportunities and some of Atlantic Canada's most distinctive shops.

GETTING HERE AND AROUND

There is no public transportation to the St. Ann's Bay area. By road, approach from the north on the Cabot Trail; from the south take the Trans-Canada Highway (Highway 105, aka "Mabel and Alexander Graham Bell Way") north from Baddeck, then turn onto Highway 312, and continue through Englishtown.

EXPLORING

Gaelic College of Celtic Arts and Crafts. Being home to direct descendants of the Gaelic pioneers, St. Ann's Bay is a logical site for this college, established in 1938 with a mission to promote and preserve the settlers' heritage. And mission accomplished, because today the campus provides a crash course in Gaelic culture. For instance, after learning about Scottish history in the **Great Hall of Clans** (particularly the Highland Clearances which sparked a mass exodus of Scots to the New World during the 18th century), you can view a short Gaelic-language film, then discover traditional disciplines like weaving and dancing at interactive stations. Not surprisingly, music at the college is especially noteworthy. Weeklong summer-school courses—as well as occasional weekend workshops—focus on topics such as bagpiping and fiddling. The college hosts a Wednesday-evening ceilidh in summer and in fall is a key site for the Celtic Colours Festival. *51779 Cabot Trail Rd.,*

St. Ann's, South Gut St. Ann's ☎ 902/295–3411 🌐 www.gaeliccollege.edu 💲 Great Hall of the Clans C$8, ceilidhs C$10–C$15 ⏲ June–Oct., weekdays 9–5.

OFF THE BEATEN PATH

When you reach the Barachois River Bridge, you can stay on the Cabot Trail as it turns inland or choose a coastal route (the 312) that goes onward to Jersey Cove. From there you can take a ferry across St. Ann's Bay to Englishtown; then follow Highway 105 into Baddeck. Weather permitting, the ferry operates 24/7 year-round. Although you save minimal driving time (about 15 minutes), the 2-minute trip is pretty and the one-way fare a mere C$5 per car.

WHERE TO STAY

$$ B&B/INN

English Country Garden Bed & Breakfast. Well positioned for those wishing to explore the bay area, this 37-acre lakefront property is ideal for strolling, though at the end of the day there's a lot to draw you indoors. **Pros:** no stairs; reduced rates for extended stays; romance packages. **Cons:** a long drive to other restaurant options; very rural. 💲 *Rooms from: C$145 ✉ 45478 Cabot Trail Rd., Indian Brook ☎ 866/929–2721, 902/929–2721 🌐 englishcountrygardenbb.ca ▭ No credit cards 🛏 5 suites, 1 cottage 🍽 Breakfast.*

SPORTS AND THE OUTDOORS

North River Kayak Tours. Guided excursions are conducted by this outfitter. A light lunch is included in the former, and full-day tours include a hot lunch cooked on the beach. Basic rentals are also available. Aspiring songwriters—no experience required—can take the Songwriting Kayaker Tour, including a full day of kayaking, a night's stay at a B&B, a songwriting lesson from an East Coast Music Award–nominated musician, and a copy of the tune you create. ✉ *644 Murray Rd., North River Bridge ✢ 40 km (25 miles) northeast of Baddeck via Cabot Trail ☎ 902/929–2628, 888/865–2925 🌐 www.northriverkayak.com 💲 Half-day C$64, full-day C$109, Songwriting Kayaker Tour C$249 ⏲ Closed mid-Oct.–mid-May.*

SHOPPING

Gaelic College of Celtic Arts and Crafts Gift Shop. Filled with Celtic and clan-related items—crafts, books, clothing, and music—this shop has a custom-kilt maker on-site. ✉ *51779 Cabot Trail Rd., St. Ann's ☎ 902/295–3411 🌐 www.gaeliccollege.edu/craft-shop.*

Glass Artisans Studio & Gallery. Gorgeous glassware—be it stained, painted, blown, or fused—is sold here. ✉ *45054 Cabot Trail, North Shore ☎ 902/929–2585, 888/262–6435 🌐 www.glassartisans.ca.*

Iron Art & Photographs. In addition to the metal sculptures with engaging and elegant forms, this gallery features photographic art and craft items. ✉ *48084 Cabot Trail Rd., Tarbot, St. Ann's ☎ 902/929–2821 🌐 www.ironart.ca.*

Leatherworks. Purses, pet collars, wallets, and bags are the specialties here, all crafted in the adjoining workshop. ✉ *45808 Cabot Trail Rd., Indian Brook, South Gut St. Ann's ☎ 902/929–2414 🌐 www.leather-works.ca.*

Piper Pewter. Much of the lead-free pewter giftware created here is inspired by Celtic designs. ✉ *46112 Cabot Trail, Indian Brook, South Gut St. Ann's* ☎ *902/929–2227* 🌐 *www.piperpewter.com.*

Sew Inclined. Need a new outfit, or something to top off the one you're wearing? Fashions and theatrical, handmade hats in almost every imaginable style and fabric, crafted by milliner and costume designer Barbara Longva, are sold here from May through November. ✉ *41819 Cabot Trail, Wreck Cove* ☎ *902/929–2259, 902/929–2050* 🌐 *www.sewinclined.ca.*

Wildfire Pottery. Cool clay creations, many of them in the shape of area animals, are the specialty here. ✉ *44429 Cabot Trail, North Shore* ☎ *902/929–2315* 🌐 *www.wildfirepottery.ca* ⏲ *Closed Nov.–May.*

Woodsmiths Studio. Wooden bowls, boxes, toys, and trinkets are made on-site here. ✉ *44556 Cabot Trail Rd., Englishtown* ☎ *902/929–2111* 🌐 *www.woodsmithstudio.com* ⏲ *Closed weekends and mid-Oct.–mid-May.*

BADDECK

20 km (12 miles) southwest of St. Ann's.

Baddeck has enough down-to-earth amenities (like a grocery store) to make it a service center, and enough charm to make it a tourist destination. The population is only about 1,000 residents but the town's larger-than-usual concentration of lodgings, restaurants, and shops attracts motorists who are ending (or starting) a Cabot Trail trek. Boaters also come to explore Bras d'Or Lake. The most competitive among them raise anchor during Regatta Week, Baddeck's main event, which begins the first Sunday in August at the Bras d'Or Yacht Club (☎ *902/295–2107* 🌐 *www.brasdoryachtclub.ca*).

GETTING HERE AND AROUND

Maritime Bus serves Baddeck with one bus daily. The journey from Halifax takes about 5½ hours and costs C$75.30 one-way; the time from Truro is about 3½ hours and the fare is C$58.63. Call for other routes *(see Planning for contact information)*. Baddeck is on the Trans-Canada Highway (Highway 105).

BOAT TOURS

FAMILY **Amoeba Sailing Tours.** Take a tour aboard a sleek schooner, lasting from 90 minutes to two hours, which views bald eagles and the Bell Estate. Trips depart daily at 11, 2, and 4:30 from June to mid-October, with an extra sailing at 6:30 pm in July and August. ✉ *Baddeck Wharf* ☎ *902/295–7780* 🌐 *www.amoebasailingtours.com* 💵 *C$25.*

FAMILY **Donelda's Puffin Boat Tours.** The Bird Islands, 2 km (1 mile) from the entrance to Bras d'Or Lake, are the breeding grounds for Atlantic puffins, as well as other seabirds and gray seals. To see them, sign up for one of these narrated nature cruises. Boats depart daily from Englishtown, about 28 km (17 miles) northeast of Baddeck. ✉ *1099 Hwy. 312, Englishtown* ✣ *Just before the Englishtown Ferry* ☎ *902/929–2563, 877/278–3346* 🌐 *www.puffinboattours.ca* 💵 *C$42* ⏲ *Closed late Sept.–mid-May.*

Paddle Dog. Easy 90-minute to two-hour guided kayak tours on Bras d'Or Lake are offered three times daily in July and August. ✉ *22 Water St.* ☎ *902/929–2628* 🌐 *www.paddledog.ca* 💲 *C$49.*

ESSENTIALS

Visitor Information **Baddeck Visitor Information Centre.** ✉ *454 Chebucto St.* ☎ *902/295–1911* 🌐 *www.visitbaddeck.com.*

EXPLORING

FAMILY **Alexander Graham Bell National Historic Site.** This site pays homage to Bell's many inventions and humanitarian work. Inside the main building, films, photos, artifacts, and models provide a window into his ideas for creating telephones, man-carrying kites, airplanes, and a record-setting hydrofoil boat (a full-scale replica of which dominates one exhibit hall). A kid's corner hosts demos and hands-on activities for aspiring young inventors. Bell spent large blocks of time, from 1886 until his death in 1922, at his Baddeck estate—Beinn Bhreagh, Gaelic for "beautiful mountain." In fact, Bell so loved the region, he once wrote "I have travelled the globe. I have seen the Canadian and American Rockies, the Andes and the Alps and the highlands of Scotland, but for simple beauty, Cape Breton outrivals them all." His home (which is still owned by the family) and some of that scenery can be seen from the roof of the National Historic Site that bears his name. ✉ *559 Chebucto St.* ☎ *902/295–2069* 🌐 *www.pc.gc.ca* 💲 *C$7.80* ⏲ *Mid-May–late Oct., daily 9–5; Nov.–mid-May, by appointment.*

Usige Bàn Falls Provincial Park. The focal point of this park, 14½ km (9 miles) north of Baddeck, is a forested 1½-km (1-mile) round-trip trail to a much-photographed 50-foot-high waterfall (*uisge* is Gaelic for "water"). ✉ *715 N. Branch Rd., Baddeck Forks* ☎ *902/662–3030 Parks & Recreation Division* 🌐 *www.novascotiaparks.ca* 💲 *Free* ⏲ *Daily mid-May–mid-Oct.*

Wagmatcook Culture & Heritage Centre. The center spotlights the ancient history and rich traditions of the native Mi'Kmaq people, with aboriginal guides providing interpretations and cultural entertainment, including drumming and song performances on Mondays, Wednesdays, and Fridays in July and early August. The restaurant here serves traditional foods (such as moose and eel), as well as more contemporary fare, and a crafts shop sells items made by members of this First Nations community. ✉ *10765 Hwy. 105, 16 km (10 miles) west of Baddeck* ☎ *902/295–1542, 866/295–2999* 🌐 *www.wagmatcookcentre.com* 💲 *Free (fees for some services); donations are welcome* ⏲ *May–Oct., daily 11–4; Nov.–Apr., weekdays 9–4 (hrs are flexible, so check first).*

WHERE TO EAT AND STAY

$$$ SEAFOOD ✕ **Baddeck Lobster Suppers.** For superfresh seafood overlooking Bras d'Or Lake, head for this former legion hall. It can seat 100 diners inside, and more on the deck, but it gets busy, particularly when a tour bus unloads (though these are by reservation only so you can call to check whether one is expected). There are just four options on the main-course menu—lobster, planked salmon, snow crab, and grilled steak—each of which can also come as a fixed-price feast with unlimited mussels, seafood chowder, homemade rolls and biscuits, desserts, and nonalcoholic

beverages (yes, all of these items are unlimited) for C$36. Unlike some similar spots, this one is fully licensed so you can wash all that down with a cold brew. Dinner service starts at 4 pm. $ *Average main: C$24* ✉ *17 Ross St.* ☎ *902/295–3307* 🌐 *www.baddecklobstersuppers.ca* ⏲ *Closed Nov.–May. No lunch.*

$ B&B/INN **Baddeck Heritage House.** Since town sites are within walking distance, this 1860s B&B serves as a good base for touring, but just relaxing on the sunny deck, with views of the Bras d'Or Lakes, is a pleasant pastime, too. **Pros:** attentive, eco-conscious owners; substantial breakfasts. **Cons:** smallish rooms; the friendly family cat may make allergies flare. $ *Rooms from: C$115* ✉ *121 Twining St.* ☎ *902/295–3219, 877/223–1112* 🌐 *www.baddeckheritagehouse.ca* ⏲ *Closed late Oct.–early May* 🛏 *4 rooms* 🍽 *Breakfast.*

$$$ B&B/INN **Castle Moffett.** Though not a historic property (it was erected in 1992), this "castle" is enticingly regal and sits on 200 acres of grounds overlooking Bras d'Or Lake. **Pros:** the property is stunning in fall; the suite is spacious. **Cons:** very pricey; some multinight minimum-stay requirements; dining room has only one seating at 7 pm. $ *Rooms from: C$199* ✉ *11980 Hwy. 105, 19 km (12 miles) from Baddeck, Bucklaw* ☎ *902/756–9070, 888/756–9070* 🌐 *castlemoffett.com* ⏲ *Closed Nov.–Apr.* 🛏 *3 rooms, 1 suite* 🍽 *Breakfast.*

$$ RESORT FAMILY **Inverary Resort.** This 11-acre lakeside resort has idyllic views, lots of sporting opportunities, and a range of options, including cottages, suites, efficiency units, and rooms in an 1850 lodge or a modern building. **Pros:** very family-friendly; walking distance to town. **Cons:** breakfast not included; though open year-round, there are reduced services November through May. $ *Rooms from: C$159* ✉ *368 Shore Rd.* ☎ *902/295–3500, 800/565–5660* 🌐 *capebretonresorts.com* 🛏 *129 rooms, 5 cottages* 🍽 *No meals.*

NIGHTLIFE AND PERFORMING ARTS

The Baddeck Gathering Ceilidhs. Featuring traditional music and dancing, ceilidhs (pronounced *kay-lees*) are held at St. Michael's Parish Hall every evening in July and August, starting at 7:30. The hall opens at 5 for ticket sales, or you can be sure to get in by phoning ahead for a reservation. ✉ *6 Margaree Rd.* ☎ *902/295–0971* 🌐 *www.baddeckgathering.com* 🎟 *C$10.*

SPORTS AND THE OUTDOORS

Bell Bay Golf Club. In addition to panoramic views from nearly all its holes, the club has a highly regarded golf school and one of the largest practice facilities in Eastern Canada. Thomas McBroom, responsible for several-dozen courses in Canada, along with some in Europe and the Caribbean, designed Bell Bay, and its wide fairways and large greens are well kept. It's suitable for novices, but also has some challenges for more experienced players. ✉ *761 Hwy. 205* ☎ *902/295–1333, 800/565–3077* 🌐 *www.bellbaygolfclub.com* 🎟 *C$70–$90* ⛳ *18 holes, 7037 yards, par 72* ⏲ *Mid-May–Oct., depending on weather.*

OFF THE BEATEN PATH

Highland Village Museum. The 40-acre "village" is set high on a mountainside with a spectacular view of Bras d'Or Lake and narrow Barra Strait. Its 11 historical buildings (among them a forge, a school, a church, and a barn filled with heritage breeds of livestock) were assembled from all over the province to depict the Highland Scots' way of life, from their origins in the Hebrides to the present day. Costumed animators who tackle daily chores lend the village a further touch of authenticity and are always on the ready to give an impromptu Gaelic lesson. Interactive programs include games and activities for children. There's a gift shop on-site as well as a Genealogy and Family History Center (open by appointment) that may be of interest to anyone with Cape Breton blood in their veins. ✉ *4119 Hwy. 223* ☎ *902/725–2272, 866/442–3542* 🌐 *highlandvillage.novascotia.ca* 💲 *C$11* ⏲ *June–mid-Oct., daily 10–5; gift shop year-round, weekdays 10–5.*

SYDNEY

62 km (39 miles) northeast of Iona; 77 km (48 miles) east of Baddeck.

If you come directly to Cape Breton via plane, ferry, or cruise ship, Sydney is where you'll land. If you're seeking anything resembling an urban experience, it's also where you'll want to stay: after all, this is the island's sole city. Admittedly, it is not the booming center it was a century ago when the continent's largest steel plant was located here (that era is evoked in *Fall on Your Knees,* an Oprah Book Club pick penned by Cape Bretoner Anne-Marie MacDonald). However, Sydney has a revitalized waterfront and smattering of Loyalist-era buildings that appeal to visitors. Moreover, it offers convenient access to popular attractions in the region—like the Miner's Museum in nearby Glace Bay (named for the *glace,* or ice, that filled its harbor in winter), the Fortress at Louisbourg, and beautiful Bras d'Or Lake.

GETTING HERE AND AROUND

Sydney is on the Marconi Trail, one of the province's main driving routes, and it has Cape Breton's only real airport. There are year-round air connections via Halifax on Air Canada/Jazz and seasonal ones (from May through October) via Toronto on WestJet. Scheduled flights to the French-held islands of St-Pierre and Miquelon also run. Marine Atlantic operates ferries between Newfoundland and North Sydney, about 20 km (12 miles) north, year-round. Maritime Bus can get you here from many places in Nova Scotia, New Brunswick, and Prince Edward Island, though connections will need to be made for some routes. From Halifax it's straight through, takes nearly seven hours, and the one-way fare is C$81.05.

TOURS

Old Sydney Society. The Old Sydney Society, which operates Cossit House and a trio of other restored buildings and museums (Jost House, St. Patrick's Church, and the Cape Breton Centre for Heritage and Science), organizes 90-minute Ghost Walks through the historic North End on Thursday evenings in July and August, starting at 7 pm. ✉ *The Lyceum, 225 George St.* ☎ *902/539–1572* 🌐 *www.oldsydney.com* 💲 *C$13.*

ESSENTIALS

Visitor Information **Sydney Visitor Information Centre.** ✉ *20 Keltic Dr.* ☎ *902/539-9876* 🌐 *www.sydney.capebretonisland.com.*

EXPLORING

Cape Breton Miners' Museum. Here you can learn about the difficult lives of the local men whose job it was to extract coal from undersea collieries. After perusing the exhibits, you can don a hard hat and descend into the damp, claustrophobic recesses of a shaft beneath the museum with a retired miner who'll recount his own experiences toiling in the bowels of the earth. The 15-acre property also includes a replica village that gives you a sense of workers' home life, and it has a theater where the Men of the Deeps choir, a world-renowned group of working and retired miners, performs in summer. ✉ *17 Museum St., Glace Bay* ✣ *Quarry Point, 20 km (13 miles) east of Sydney* ☎ *902/849-4522* 🌐 *www.minersmuseum.com* 💲 *Museum C$6, museum and mine tour C$12* ⏲ *July and Aug., daily 10–6 (until 7 on concert nights); Sept. and Oct., daily 10–6; Nov.–May, weekdays 9–4 by appointment.*

Cossit House. Built in 1787, this unpretentious wooden building was originally home to Reverend Ranna Cossit—Cape Breton's first protestant minister—his wife Thankful, and their 10 children. Now faithfully restored and occupied by costumed interpreters, the North End residence is furnished with period pieces based on Cossit's own inventory. ✉ *75 Charlotte St.* ☎ *902/539-7973* 🌐 *cossithouse.novascotia.ca* 💲 *C$2* ⏲ *June–mid-Oct., Tues.–Sat. 9–5.*

Marconi National Historic Site. On a spectacular headland, this site commemorates the spot at Table Head where, in 1902, Guglielmo Marconi built four tall wooden towers and beamed the first official wireless messages across the Atlantic Ocean. An interpretive trail leads to the foundations of the original towers and transmitter buildings. The visitor center has large models of the towers as well as artifacts and photographs chronicling the radio pioneer's life and work. ✉ *15 Timmerman St., Glace Bay* ✣ *23 km (14 miles) northeast of Sydney; follow signs from Hwy. 255* ☎ *902/295-2069, 902/842-2530 summer* 🌐 *www.pc.gc.ca* 💲 *Free (C$2.50 donation suggested)* ⏲ *July–early Sept., daily 10–6.*

Sydney Mines Heritage Museum and Cape Breton Fossil Centre. Two affiliated facilities across the harbor from Sydney proper chronicle the area's prehistoric and more recent pasts. The mines museum, which occupies a small converted train station, surveys area history but focuses on Sydney's coal-mining connection. Displays at the fossil center include 300-million-year-old specimens from the Sydney Coal Fields. The fossil center's curator leads two-hour fossil-hunting field trips, by reservation, on Tuesdays and Thursdays at 10 am; you'll need your own transportation to the trip's starting point. ✉ *159 Legatto St., Sydney Mines* ☎ *902/544-0992* 🌐 *www.cbfossil.org* 💲 *Museum C$7, field trip C$12* ⏲ *June–mid-Oct., Tues.–Sat. 9–5.*

WHERE TO EAT AND STAY

$$$ ✕ **Flavor Downtown.** In a city where deep fryers reign supreme, this
CONTEMPORARY small bistro-style eatery is a welcome find. The haddock is poached, the scallops seared, the prawns tossed in pesto sauce—and the absence

of greasy batter means Flavor's flavors shine through. The menu is a broad one: homemade pastas are popular, as are the inventive sandwiches and all-day breakfast items. There are several gluten-free, vegan, and vegetarian options, too (a rarity in these parts), plus a Paleo Menu, providing low-carb, low-sugar, zero-gluten, high-protein meals (a rarity anywhere). Brunch is served on Saturday, and you can eat outside on the patio in summer. Another two branches are Flavor 19, at the Lingan Golf Course, and Flavor on the Water, in the cruise ship pavilion on the harbor. *Average main: C$23 16 Pitt St. 902/562–6611 www.cbflavor.com Closed Sun.*

$$$ CONTEMPORARY **Governor's Pub and Eatery.** Sydney's first mayor, Walter Crowe, once lived in this Victorian home, built in the late 1800s. The restaurant, with hardwood floors, a fireplace, and high ceilings, is known for fresh seafood and hand-cut steaks, though there are lighter options such as salads, wraps, and burgers. Both the restaurant and the pub upstairs have large patios that overlook Sydney Harbour. On most nights the atmosphere is bustling and lively, with locals and travelers mixing over a pint, and there's regular live entertainment. The desserts are all homemade. *Average main: C$25 233 Esplanade 902/562–7646 governorseatery.com.*

$$ HOTEL FAMILY **Cambridge Suites Hotel.** You can put yourself in the center of Sydney's waterfront action by staying at this comfortable all-suites hotel. **Pros:** free Continental breakfast buffet; pet-friendly. **Cons:** other people's pets are sometimes audible; conventional room style. *Rooms from: C$139 380 Esplanade 902/562–6500, 800/565–9466 www.cambridgesuitessydney.com 147 suites Breakfast.*

NIGHTLIFE AND PERFORMING ARTS

BARS

Governors Pub and Eatery. In addition to some of the best seafood in town, this historic bar has some great summer entertainment, including a traditional Irish session every Wednesday (8 pm–2 am), guest bands and songwriter sessions on weekends (10 pm–2 am), and the "openest mike in Sydney" every Tuesday. *233 Esplanade St. 902/562–7646 www.governorseatery.com.*

CASINOS

Casino Nova Scotia. At the casino you can try your luck at slot machines, test your skill at gaming tables, or simply settle in to enjoy the live entertainment—assuming you're at least 19 years old, the legal gambling (and drinking) age in Nova Scotia. *525 George St. 902/563–7777, 866/334–1114 www.casinonovascotia.com.*

THEATER AND CONCERTS

Cape Breton University. The area's leading cultural institution, the university includes the 337-seat Boardmore Playhouse and the CBU Art Gallery (the only public gallery on the island). *1250 Grand Lake Rd. 902/539–5300, 888/959–9995, 902/563–1652 box office www.cbu.ca.*

Joan Harriss Cruise Pavilion. More than just a port for the many cruise ships that dock here each year, the pavilion is a popular entertainment venue, too. Its main stage and lighthouse stage host many musical acts, especially during events like Sydney's nine-day midsummer

Action Week (🌐 *www.actionweek.com*) and the 10-day Celtic Colours International Festival (*www.celtic-colours.com*). Even if you're not arriving by ship, the pavilion is easy enough to find: just look for the 60-foot fiddle that towers outside it. ✉ *74 Esplanade* ☎ *902/564–9775* 🌐 *www.sydneyport.ca.*

SPORTS AND THE OUTDOORS

Peterfield Provincial Park. Take a hike through history at this park on the south arm of Sydney Harbour. Initially developed as the private domain of David Matthews, a onetime mayor of New York City who remained loyal to the crown during the War of Independence, its 56 acres are laced with trails. ✉ *1126 Westmount Rd., Westmount* ✣ *Off Hwy. 239* ☎ *902/662–3030 Nova Scotia Provincial Parks* 🌐 *www.novascotiaparks.ca* 💲 *Free* ⏲ *Mid-May–mid-Oct.*

SHOPPING

Fodor's Choice ★ **The Cape Breton Centre for Craft and Design.** Showcasing the work of traditional and cutting-edge Cape Breton artisans in its airy second-floor gallery, the center, which houses on-site studios for pottery, weaving, and glass- and jewelry-making, also hosts hands-on workshops that are open to craft aficionados. Pick up a copy of the Artisan Trail Map here to find studios elsewhere. ✉ *322 Charlotte St.* ☎ *902/270–7491* 🌐 *www.capebretoncraft.com* ⏲ *Closed Sun.*

Harbourside Boutiques. Top island retailers—among them Hattie's Heirlooms, the Cape Breton Curiosity Shop, Man of War Gallery, and Tastes of Cape Breton—are represented at Harbourside Boutiques in the Joan Harriss Cruise Pavilion. They're only open seasonally, though, sometimes daily in high season, sometimes just when cruise ships are in port. ✉ *74 Esplanade* ☎ *902/564–9775* 🌐 *www.sydneyport.ca.*

LOUISBOURG

53 km (33 miles) south of Glace Bay.

Though best known as the home of the largest historical reconstruction in North America, Louisbourg is also an important fishing community with a lovely harbor front. There are a number of good places to stay here, too.

GETTING HERE AND AROUND

There is no public transportation to Louisbourg. By road it's about a two-hour drive from the Canso Causeway, via Highway 125 then (at Exit 8) Route 22.

ESSENTIALS

Visitor Information **Louisbourg Visitor Information Centre.** ✉ *7495 Main St.* ☎ *902/733–2321* 🌐 *www.louisbourgtourism.com.*

EXPLORING

FAMILY Fodor's Choice ★ **Fortress of Louisbourg National Historic Site.** This may be Cape Breton's most remarkable attraction. After the French were forced out of mainland Nova Scotia in 1713, they established their headquarters here in a walled, fortified town on a low point of land at the mouth of Louisbourg Harbour. The fortress was captured twice (once by New Englanders in

1745, once by the British in 1758), and after the second attack the formidable military complex was razed. Its demise was critical in ending France's dream of a North American empire, but in the 1960s, archaeologists took up where the imperialists left off, rebuilding a fifth of the fortress to look just as it did before the initial siege. From June through mid-October, costumed interpreters convincingly re-create the activities of the original inhabitants, so you can watch a military drill, see nails and lace being made, or dine in the town's three inns on food prepared from 18th-century recipes. Free guided tours are given in high season and events available at extra cost—including themed dinner theaters and archaeological programs—make a visit here even more memorable. On the other hand, an off-season visit, without all these activities, can paint a more compelling picture of life in the fort 300 years ago. Plan on spending most or all of a day here, and bring a warm sweater or jacket—Louisbourg tends to be chilly at any time of year. ✉ *265 Parks Service Rd.* ☎ *902/733–2280* 🌐 *www.fortressoflouisbourg.ca* 💲 *C$17.60 late June–mid-Oct, C$7.30 mid-Oct–late June; guided tour C$3.90* ⏲ *Mid-May–mid-Oct., daily 9:30–5; mid-Oct.–mid-May weekdays 9:30–4.*

WHERE TO EAT AND STAY

$$ CANADIAN FAMILY ✕ **Grubstake Restaurant.** *Coquilles St. Jacques* (scallops with mushrooms in a white wine–cream sauce), seafood pasta, and shrimp-and-scallop flambé are popular dishes at this 120-seat restaurant. Although seafood is the specialty, the baked Chicken Royale with mushrooms and the country-style barbecue pork are also excellent. The cocktail lounge is a great place to relax with a drink and meet some locals. Service is friendly and laid-back—though this sometimes translates into *slow*. Desserts are made on-site. $ *Average main: C$18* ✉ *7499 Main St.* ☎ *902/733–2308* 🌐 *www.grubstake.ca* 💳 *No credit cards* ⏲ *Closed mid-Oct.–mid-June.*

$ B&B/INN **Cranberry Cove Inn.** This cozy cranberry-hued house, built in 1904, overlooks the harbor and is just a short drive from the Fortress of Louisbourg. **Pros:** cooked breakfast included; impeccable rooms. **Cons:** no elevator for three-story building; Wi-Fi is spotty in some rooms. $ *Rooms from: C$105* ✉ *12 Wolfe St.* ☎ *902/733–2171, 800/929–0222* 🌐 *www.cranberrycoveinn.com* 💳 *No credit cards* ⏲ *Closed mid-Oct.–mid-May* 🛏 *7 rooms* 🍽 *Breakfast.*

$$ B&B/INN **Louisbourg Harbour Inn Bed & Breakfast.** The central location of this grand, former sea captain's residence means it's just a few minutes' walk to the Louisbourg Playhouse, Main Street, and the harbor. **Pros:** cooked breakfast included; lovely views. **Cons:** no elevator for three-story building; several rooms are small; two-night minimum for the best room; children not accommodated. $ *Rooms from: C$125* ✉ *9 Lower Warren St.* ☎ *902/733–3222, 888/888–8466* 🌐 *www.louisbourgharbourinn.com* ⏲ *Closed early Oct.–early June* 🛏 *7 rooms* 🍽 *Breakfast.*

$$ HOTEL **Point of View Suites.** This modern hotel, built to resemble an oversize beach house, is the closest property to the Fortress of Louisbourg and the only one in town that is on the water. **Pros:** private pebble beach; knowledgeable owners who grew up in the area. **Cons:** non-ocean-view units overlook an RV lot; limited restaurant menu off-season. $ *Rooms from: C$125* ✉ *15 Commercial St. Extension* ☎ *902/733–2080, 888/374–8439* 🌐 *www.louisbourgpointofview.com* ⏲ *Closed mid-Oct.–mid-May* 🛏 *19 rooms* 🍽 *No meals.*

NIGHTLIFE AND PERFORMING ARTS

Louisbourg Playhouse. You can take in traditional Cape Breton music and other entertainments nightly at the Louisbourg Playhouse, a 17th-century-style theater that was modeled after Shakespeare's Globe. Originally constructed as part of the Disney movie set for *Squanto: A Warrior's Tale,* the venue was donated to the community in 1994 after filming wrapped. ✉ *11 Aberdeen St.* ☎ *902/733–2996, 888/733–2787* ⊕ *louisbourgplayhouse.ca* ⏲ *Mid-June–mid-Oct., nightly at 8.*

SPORTS AND THE OUTDOORS

Fortress of Louisbourg property. The sprawling property has a series of free hiking trails, some with historical and First Nations relevance, that lead to a lighthouse, redoubts, and a swimmable beach at Kennington Cove where the conquering New Englanders and Brits both came ashore. ✉ *259 Parks Service Rd.* ☎ *902/733–2280* ⊕ *www.pc.gc.ca.*

BIG POND

50 km (31 miles) west of Louisbourg.

This tiny community consists of a few houses dotted along the highway, and a famous tearoom.

GETTING HERE AND AROUND

There is no public transportation to Big Pond, which is off Route 4.

EXPLORING

Rita's Tea Room. The tiny community of Big Pond consists of a few houses dotted along the highway, but most people come to see one in particular: the former home of the late singer-songwriter Rita MacNeil, who died in 2013. Rita lived with her children in this former one-room schoolhouse and opened the tearoom in 1986. The building has been expanded to accommodate the multitude of visitors who arrive to sample Rita's Tea Room Blend Tea, which is served along with light meals and tasty baked goods. You can visit a display room of Rita's awards and photographs and browse the gift shop. ✉ *8077 Hwy. 4* ☎ *902/828–2667* ⊕ *www.ritamacneil.com/tearoom.html* ⏲ *Late June–mid-Oct., daily 10–5 (gift shop open June 1).*

ARICHAT

62 km (38 miles) southwest of Big Pond.

Arichat is the principal village on Isle Madame: the largest island in a 44-square-km (17-square-mile) archipelago of the same name, which sits at Cape Breton's southernmost tip. Known for its friendly Acadian culture and many secluded coves and inlets, Arichat has a deep harbor that made it an important fishing, shipbuilding, and trading center during the 19th century. Some fine old buildings from that period still remain. The two cannons overlooking the harbor were installed after John Paul Jones sacked the village during the American Revolution.

GETTING HERE AND AROUND

To get here from Big Pond, take Route 4 to Highway 320, which leads through Poulamon and D'Escousse before bridging Lennox Passage. Highway 206 meanders through the low hills to a maze of land and water at West Arichat. Together, the two routes encircle the island, meeting at Arichat.

One of the best ways to experience Isle Madame is on foot. Try Cape Auguet Eco-Trail, an 8½-km (5-mile) hiking trail that extends from Boudreauville to Mackerel Cove and follows the rocky coastline overlooking Chedabucto Bay. Another good half-day hike leads to Gros Nez, the "large nose" that juts into the sea. The island also lends itself to biking, as most roads glide gently along the shore.

EXPLORING

LeNoir Forge Museum. This restored 18th-century French blacksmith shop occupies a handsome stone structure on the waterfront. In its 19th-century heyday, it supplied parts to local shipbuilders. ✉ *712 Veterans Memorial Dr.* ✣ *Off Hwy. 206* ☎ *902/226–9364* 💲 *Free, donations welcome* ⏲ *June, weekdays 10–5; July and Aug., daily 10–5; Sept.–May by appointment.*

NEW BRUNSWICK

WELCOME TO NEW BRUNSWICK

TOP REASONS TO GO

★ **Go whale-watching:** Double the fun of the Bay of Fundy by getting out onto the water to view several types of whales, plus seals, porpoises, and seabirds.

★ **Experience Acadian culture:** Attractions such as Le Pays de la Sagouine or Acadian Historical Village on the Acadian Coastal Drive portray the French heritage of the region. Hear the distinctive accent at Dieppe Farmers' Market.

★ **Eat and drink well:** Enjoy freshly caught salmon, scallops, and lobster, organic produce and meat (including buffalo) from local farms, and some highly regarded local wines and craft beers.

★ **Take a hike:** New Brunswick's provincial and national parks have amazing hiking trails and plenty of great spots to contemplate the gorgeous scenery or watch birds from an ocean cliff.

★ **Go for a swim:** New Brunswick is blessed with beaches, rivers, and lakes; you can choose from water that's cold or warm, fresh or salty, on long sandy shores or in intimate coves.

1 Saint John. The port city of Saint John has become a vibrant urban destination, with a revitalized waterfront, an eclectic restaurant scene, a lively nightlife and festivals, fun street art, and one of Canada's loveliest city parks. There's plenty of history, too, from first-class museums and historic sites to streets lined with 19th-century homes.

2 The Fundy Coast. With the highest tides in the world, the Bay of Fundy is a diverse region with dramatic coastlines, tiny fishing villages, charming islands, and rocky beaches perfect for treasure hunting. Stretching inland is the first Global Geopark in North America—the Stonehammer—with fascinating sites portraying the geological history of the planet. The city of Moncton, billed as the "crossroads of the Maritimes" or "Hub City," is a great place to visit, with a new heritage museum and fun attractions for the kids. With its very close neighbor, Dieppe, it is a stronghold of Acadian culture and is paired with its Cajun cousin, Lafayette, Louisiana, as a "sister city."

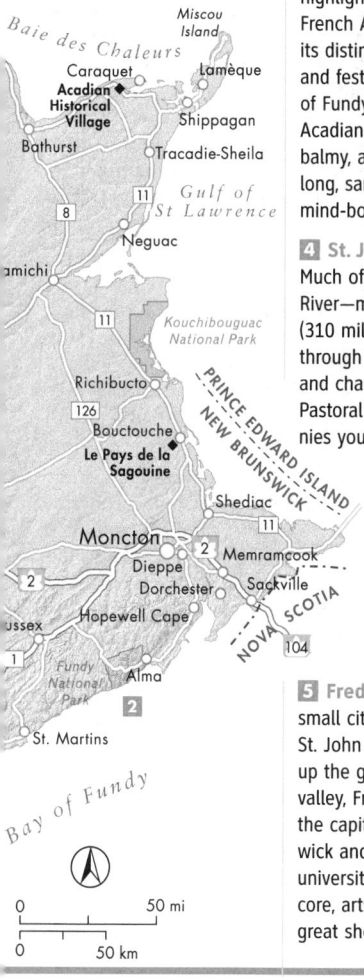

3 The Acadian Coast. A highlight of this region is French Acadian culture with its distinct foods, music, and festivals. Unlike the Bay of Fundy, the water on the Acadian Coast is downright balmy, and the selection of long, sandy beaches can be mind-boggling.

4 St. John River Valley. Much of the wide St. John River—more than 500 km (310 miles) of it—meanders through cities, townships, and charming villages. Pastoral farmland accompanies you most of the way.

5 Fredericton. A gracious, small city bisected by the St. John River and spreading up the gentle slopes of its valley, Fredericton is the capital of New Brunswick and home to two universities. It has a historic core, arts and culture, and great shopping.

GETTING ORIENTED

Snug up against the U.S. border (Maine) to the west, New Brunswick is roughly square in shape, with the St. Lawrence River and Québec to the north, the Bay of Fundy and Nova Scotia to the south, and the Northumberland Strait and Prince Edward Island to the east. All its main towns and cities lie either on or near one of the coastlines or on a major river—notably the St. John and the Miramichi. Elsewhere, there are agricultural areas and a handful of vineyards, but mostly trees, trees, and more trees. The highest point is Mt. Carleton, at 2,690 feet. It's the highest mountain in the Maritimes, which lies in the northern reaches of the New Brunswick section of the International Appalachian Trail.

Updated by Penny Phenix

Stunning scenery, vast forests, and world-class attractions characterize New Brunswick. Topping the list is the Bay of Fundy, with the higest tides in the world, marine life that includes several species of whales, stretches of wilderness coastline, and charming harbor villages.

Add to this national and international historic sites, national parks teeming with wildlife, great beaches, vibrant towns and cities, and a thriving diversity of cultures, and you might wonder how the population can remain so utterly laid-back, but that's just another facet of New Brunswick's charm. The province is an old place in New World terms, and the remains of a turbulent past are still evident in some of its quiet nooks. Near Moncton, for instance, wild strawberries perfume the air of the grassy slopes of Fort Beauséjour, where, in 1755, one of the last battles for possession of Acadia took place, with the English finally overcoming the French. Other areas of the province were settled by the British; by Loyalists, American colonists who chose to live under British rule after the American Revolution; and by Irish immigrants, many seeking to avoid the famine in their home country. If you stay in both Acadian and Loyalist regions, a trip to New Brunswick can seem like two vacations in one.

For every gesture in the provincial landscape as grand as the giant rock formations carved by the Bay of Fundy tides at Hopewell Cape, there is one as subtle as the gifted touch of a sculptor in a studio. For every experience as colorful as the mountains of lobster served at Shediac's annual Lobster Festival, there is another as low-key as the gentle waves of the Baie des Chaleurs. New Brunswick is the luxury of an inn with five stars and the tranquillity of camping under a million.

At the heart of New Brunswick is the forest, which covers 85% of the province—nearly all its interior. The forest contributes to the economy, defines the landscape, and delights hikers, anglers, campers, and bird-watchers, but New Brunswick's soul is the sea. The biggest of Canada's three Maritime provinces, New Brunswick is largely surrounded by coastline. The warm waters of the Baie des Chaleurs, Gulf of St. Lawrence, and Northumberland Strait lure swimmers to their sandy beaches, and the chilly Bay of Fundy, with its monumental tides, draws breaching whales, whale-watchers, and kayakers.

PLANNING

WHEN TO GO

Each season brings unique reasons to travel to New Brunswick. Winter means skiing, snowmobiling, skating on public rinks, and cozy dinners. Spring is the time for canoeing the inland rivers, fishing, picking fiddleheads, and watching the province come alive.

Summer is peak tourist season, and Parlee Beach attracts thousands of sun worshippers. The resort towns of Fundy, including Alma, St.

Andrews, and St. George, get busy, too. It's a good time to trek up to the lighthouse at Cape Enrage. Summer festivals abound, and the province's two national parks, Fundy and Kouchibouguac, are filled with nature lovers.

Fall means country fairs, harvest suppers, and incredibly beautiful scenic drives to enjoy autumn foliage. Fall colors are at their peak from late September through mid- to late October. The Autumn Foliage Colours Line (☎ *800/268–3255*) provides daily updates on which drives are best.

FESTIVALS

FAMILY **Buskers on the Bay.** For four days in mid-July an international array of acrobats, musicians, street theater, and comedy troupes provide high-energy entertainment by the waterfront in Saint John. ✉ *1 Market Sq., Saint John* ☎ *506/658–3600* ⊕ *www.marketsquaresj.com.*

FAMILY **Chocolate Fest.** Chocaholics flock to "Canada's Chocolate Town," home town of the Ganong Bros. chocolate company, for the first week of August, for the full program of events, entertainment, and, of course, tastings. ✉ *St. Stephen* ☎ *506/465–5616* ⊕ *chocolate-fest.ca.*

Fodor's Choice ★ **Foire Brayonne.** The annual Foire Brayonne, held in Edmundston over the long weekend surrounding New Brunswick Day (beginning on the Wednesday before the first Monday in August), is one of the largest Francophone festivals outside of Québec. It's also one of the liveliest and most vibrant cultural events in New Brunswick, with concerts by acclaimed artists as well as local musicians and entertainers. ✉ *Edmundston* ☎ *506/739–6608* ⊕ *www.foirebrayonne.com.*

Fodor's Choice ★ **Harvest Jazz and Blues Festival.** Hundreds (literally) of world-class musicians perform at around 30 venues in downtown Fredericton over six days in mid-September, encompassing many genres of jazz, blues, rock, and more. 2015 marked the festival's 25th anniversary. ✉ *81 Regent St., Fredericton* ☎ *506/455-4523, 888/622–5837* ⊕ *www.harvestjazzandblues.com.*

New Brunswick Highland Games and Scottish Festival. The grounds of the riverside Government House is the venue for this long-established late-July festival, one of the best of its kind in North America. In addition to the competitive games, pipe bands, traditional music, and dancing, it features a 5-km (3-mile) kilted run. ✉ *51 Woodstock Rd., Fredericton* ☎ *506/452–9244, 888/368–4444* ⊕ *www.highlandgames.ca.*

New Brunswick Summer Music Festival. For about 10 days in August, Fredericton hosts some of Canada's finest classical musicians, mostly at Memorial Hall at the University of New Brunswick, with some free concerts in the cathedral and on Officer's Square. ✉ *University of New Brunswick, Bailey Dr., Fredericton* ☎ *506/458–7836* ⊕ *nbsummermusicfestival.ca.*

FAMILY **Shediac Lobster Festival.** The "lobster capital of the world" has been celebrating the crustacean since 1949 with a five-day festival in early July. Events and entertainment include concerts, a parade, a midway, and a lobster-eating contest. ✉ *Belliveau Ave., Shediac* ☎ *506/532–1122* ⊕ *www.shediaclobsterfestival.ca.*

PLANNING YOUR TIME

A good way to tour New Brunswick is to follow one of the five scenic drives into which the province is divided: The River Valley Scenic Drive follows more than 500 km (310 miles) of road along the St. John River; the Fundy Coastal Drive has potential views of whales and wildlife in the region of the Bay of Fundy; the Acadian Coastal Drive offers sandy beaches, picturesque villages, and vibrant culture; the Miramichi River Route is home to salmon fishing and folk festivals; and the Appalachian Range Route has serene mountain vistas and beautiful bays. The Fundy Coast is perhaps the most popular area, and many prefer to spend most of their time there. Overnight in lively, historic Saint John, the only city on the Bay of Fundy; Alma, the little coastal town that services Fundy National Park; or in Moncton, which, while not on the coast, is in easy reach and has some good restaurants, shopping, and fun amusements for children.

GETTING HERE AND AROUND

AIR TRAVEL

New Brunswick has three major airports: Saint John Airport, about 15 minutes east of downtown Saint John; Greater Moncton International Airport, about 10 minutes east of downtown Moncton; and Fredericton Airport, 10 minutes east of downtown Fredericton.

BOAT AND FERRY TRAVEL

Bay Ferries Ltd. runs from Saint John, New Brunswick, to Digby, Nova Scotia, and back once or twice a day, depending on the season. Passenger fares are C$43 per adult, C$86 for a car, and C$161–C$672 for a motorhome or car with trailer (depending on length), plus a C$20 fuel surcharge for the three-hour, one-way trip July through September. Off-season rates are cheaper.

The year-round 20-minute ferry crossing from L'Etete, on mainland New Brunswick, to Deer Island is a free service operated by Coastal Transport for the government of New Brunswick. From Deer Island, East Coast Ferries Ltd. runs services to Campobello, New Brunswick, and Eastport, Maine, from late June to mid-September. On the Campobello route, the fares are C$16 for a car and driver, C$4 for each adult passenger. The crossing takes about 30 minutes. On the Eastport route, the fares are C$13 for a car and driver and C$4 for each adult passenger. On both routes a fuel surcharge of C$4 is also applied, and credit cards are not accepted.

Coastal Transport has up to seven crossings per day from Blacks Harbour to Grand Manan late June through mid-September and four crossings per day the rest of the year. Round-trip fares, payable on the Grand Manan side, are C$35.80 for a car and C$12 for an adult. A one-way crossing takes about 1½ hours.

Contacts **Bay Ferries Ltd.** ✉ *170 Digby Ferry Rd., off Lancaster St., Saint John* ☎ *506/694-7777 Saint John Terminal, 888/249-7245 reservations* ⊕ *www.ferries.ca.* **Coastal Transport.** ☎ *506/662-3724, 855/882-1978* ⊕ *www.coastaltransport.ca.* **East Coast Ferries Ltd.** ☎ *506/747-2159, 877/747-2159* ⊕ *www.eastcoastferriesltd.com.*

NEW BRUNSWICK ITINERARIES

IF YOU HAVE 4 DAYS

Start in **Saint John,** steeped in English and Irish traditions and rich in history and art. The resort town of **St. Andrews by-the-Sea** is an hour's drive west and has plenty of art, crafts, history, nature, and seafood. Whale-watching tours leave from the wharf, and the outstanding **Kingsbrae Garden** invites lingering. Spend a day and a night, then backtrack through Saint John, taking Route 1 then Route 111 to St. Martins and the **Fundy Trail Parkway.** Loop north then, via Route 111, rejoin Route 1 just east of Sussex, and take Route 114 to **Fundy National Park,** perhaps spending the night in Alma. Route 915, east of the park, hugs the coast. At **Cape Enrage** you can visit a working lighthouse, enjoy a cup of seafood chowder, and try out zip-lining or rock climbing. There are lots of things to do around **Hopewell Cape,** where the Fundy tides have sculpted gigantic rocks into flowerpot formations that turn into islands at high tide. Finish the trip with **Moncton,** a microcosm of New Brunswick culture and just an hour's drive from Fundy National Park.

IF YOU HAVE 7 DAYS

Add an Acadian Coast experience to the four-day tour above. Head north from **Moncton** and explore the area around **Shediac,** famous for its lobsters and Parlee Beach. Just beyond is **Bouctouche,** where visitors can walk for miles on a boardwalk over the dunes, and the make-believe land of Le Pays de la Sagouine, which pays tribute to Acadian author Antonine Maillet and La Sagouine, the washerwoman character she created. Another 50 km (31 miles) north is **Kouchibouguac National Park,** with protected beaches, forests, and peat bogs. The coastal drive from the park to **Miramichi,** about 75 km (47 miles), passes through several bustling fishing villages. Most of the communities are Acadian, but as you approach Miramichi, English dominates again. A stopover here positions you perfectly to begin your exploration of the Acadian Peninsula. It's only about 120 km (74 miles) from Miramichi City to **Caraquet,** where the Acadian Historical Village is a careful re-creation of traditional Acadian way of life.

IF YOU HAVE 10 DAYS

Follow the seven-day itinerary above. From **Caraquet,** plan at least half a day to drive across the top of New Brunswick (Route 134 along the coast and Route 17 inland through the forest) to the St. John River valley. Begin your explorations among the flowers and the music of the New Brunswick Botanical Gardens in St-Jacques, outside **Edmundston.** The drive from here to Fredericton is about 275 km (171 miles) of panoramic pastoral and river scenery, including a dramatic gorge and waterfall at **Grand Falls,** the longest covered bridge in the world at Hartland, and historic Woodstock, New Brunswick's first town. **Kings Landing Historical Settlement,** near Fredericton, is a faithful depiction of life on the river in the 19th century. With its Gothic cathedral, Victorian architecture, museums, and riverfront pathways, **Fredericton** is a great stopping place and the seat of the province's government. The drive from Fredericton back to Saint John on Route 102 is just over 100 km (62 miles).

BUS TRAVEL

Maritime Bus runs buses within the province and to destinations in Nova Scotia, Prince Edward Island, and Québec. Routes include the length of the Trans-Canada Highway from Québec to the Nova Scotia border and beyond, branching off to Prince Edward Island just south of Sackville. Another route heads up the Acadian Coast from Shediac to Campbelton, and there's a loop south from Oromocto, near Fredericton, to Saint John and Sussex. Tickets must be reserved. Be aware, though, that some stops are on the edge of town and might be inconvenient for passengers trying to get downtown.

Contacts Maritime Bus. ☎ *800/575-1807* ⊕ *www.maritimebus.com.*

CAR TRAVEL

New Brunswick is the largest of the Atlantic provinces, covering nearly 78,000 square km (30,000 square miles): around 320 km (200 miles) north to south and 240 km (150 miles) east to west. Unless you plan to fly into one of the hubs and stay there for your visit, you'd be wise to have a car. There's a good selection of car-rental agencies, but book early for July and August (and be aware that debit cards may not be accepted and you'll need a credit card); call or visit the websites to search for pickup and drop-off locations throughout the province (bear in mind that rentals from airports carry a surcharge).

From Québec, the Trans-Canada Highway (Route 2, marked by a maple leaf) enters New Brunswick at St-Jacques and follows the St. John River through Fredericton and on to Moncton and the Nova Scotia border. From Maine, Interstate 95 crosses at Houlton to Woodstock, New Brunswick, where it connects with the Trans-Canada Highway. Those traveling up the coast of Maine on Route 1 cross at Calais to St. Stephen, New Brunswick, or via the Fundy Islands car ferries. New Brunswick's Route 1 extends through Saint John and Sussex to join the Trans-Canada Highway near Moncton.

Route 7 joins Saint John and Fredericton. Fredericton is connected to Miramichi City by Route 8. Route 15 links Moncton to the eastern coast and to Route 11, which follows the coast north to Miramichi, around the Acadian Peninsula, and up to Campbellton.

DRIVING TIPS Watch out for moose, deer, black bears, porcupines, and raccoons, especially at night. Although major highways mostly have moose and deer fences—the Trans-Canada Highway is not yet fenced everywhere—many of the secondary roads do not, and twilight is an especially dangerous time for wildlife entering the roads. Reduce speed at night.

TRAIN TRAVEL

Train travel options in New Brunswick are limited: VIA Rail offers a thrice-weekly passenger service from Montréal to Halifax, stopping in New Brunswick at Campbellton, Bathurst, Miramichi, Moncton, and Sackville, with request stops at a number of smaller towns along the route. The Montréal to Moncton economy fare is C$125.32 each way. There is no train service to the cities of Saint John or Fredericton.

Train contact VIA Rail. ☎ *888/842-7245 toll-free in North America, 506/857-9830 Moncton* ⊕ *www.viarail.ca.*

RESTAURANTS

You can eat extremely well in New Brunswick, with many restaurants sourcing top-quality ingredients from local farmers, fishermen, and artisan producers. At the top end are some of Canada's finest restaurants, such as the outstanding Windjammer in Moncton's Delta Beauséjour Hotel, Little Louis', also in Moncton, and the Saint John Ale House in Saint John. St. Andrews by-the-Sea has long been a culinary hot spot, notably Savour in the Garden and the Rossmount, while gastropubs like Moncton's Tide and Boar are gaining ground throughout the province. At the other end of the scale, if you want to try some authentic Acadian food, there's a little paper-plate diner in Shediac, Le Menu Acadien, that cooks *poutine rappé* (boiled potato dumpling with meat filling), *fricôt* (chicken stew), and other delicacies according to Grandma's recipes.

HOTELS

Just about every kind of lodging experience is available in New Brunswick, including a plethora of high-end bed-and-breakfasts, rental properties, a smattering of boutique hotels, and, lording it over them all, the superbly renovated historic Algonquin Resort in St. Andrews by-the-Sea—part of the Marriott Autograph Collection. When it comes to chain hotels, all the North American names have a good presence in or around the major cities, but the Delta group is the cream of the crop, offering high standards of accommodations, superb restaurants, well-trained staff, and attractive room rates. In peak season rooms are snapped up quickly, particularly in the best bed-and-breakfasts, so it's wise to book as far in advance as possible.

Outside peak season many of the bed-and-breakfasts and rental properties are closed, although those in the cities tend to stay open year-round.

Hotel reviews have been shortened. For full information, visit Fodors.com.

	WHAT IT COSTS IN CANADIAN DOLLARS			
	$	$$	$$$	$$$$
Restaurants	under C$12	C$12–C$20	C$21–C$30	over C$30
Hotels	under C$125	C$125–C$174	C$175–C$250	over C$250

Restaurant prices are per person for a main course at dinner. Hotel prices are for two people in a standard double room in high season, excluding harmonized sales tax (HST).

TOURS AND VISITOR INFORMATION

Whale-watching, sea kayaking, bird-watching, scuba diving, garden touring, vineyard and winery tours, city culinary tours, river cruising, golfing, fishing, skiing, and snowmobiling are just a few of New Brunswick's alluring experiences. Bicycling in particular is a great way to tour New Brunswick. Two favorite biking areas in the province are the 33 km (20 miles) of country roads on Grand Manan Island (you can rent bikes from Adventure High; *See the Grand Manan listings*) and the Quoddy Loop, which goes around Passamaquoddy Bay and the western mouth of the Bay of Fundy.

Baymount Outdoor Adventures operates bicycle tours for large groups along the Fundy shore near Hopewell Cape, and Off-Kilter Bike Tours organize fixed and customized excursions around St. Andrews by-the-Sea. B&Bs frequently have bicycles for rent.

FAMILY **Baymount Outdoor Adventures.** This outfitter leads sea-kayaking tours at Hopwell Rocks, and hiking and mountain-biking tours in the Bay of Fundy biosphere reserve and Caledonia Highlands. ✉ *Hopewell Rocks Park, Rocks Rd., Hopewell Cape* ☎ *506/734–2660, 877/601–2660* ⊕ *www.baymountadventures.com* ₮ *From $59.*

Golf New Brunswick. A resource for nearly 50 golf courses in the province, all with carts and clubs to rent. ✉ *500 Beaverbrook Ct., Suite 440, Fredericton* ☎ *877/833–4662* ⊕ *www.golfnb.ca* ⏲ *Closed weekends.*

Uncorked Tours. Hugely popular escorted tours to New Brunswick wineries and breweries (with tastings) follow scenic routes and some include cheese sampling, lunch or dinner, or visits to artisan studios. Tours, with departures from Saint John, Moncton, Fredericton, and St. Andrews, are usually half- or full-days, but can be customized, and include transportation and pick-up from area hotels. Walking tours of Saint John combine wine, beer, and food sampling with historic sights. ✉ *Saint John* ☎ *506/324–4644* ⊕ *www.UncorkedNB.com* ₮ *From $49.*

Visitor Information **New Brunswick Trails Council.** ☎ *506/459–1931, 800/526–7070* ⊕ *www.sentiernbtrail.com.* **Tourism New Brunswick.** ☎ *800/561–0123* ⊕ *www.tourismnewbrunswick.ca.*

SAINT JOHN

Like any seaport worth its salt, Saint John is a welcoming place but, more than that, it is fast transforming into a sophisticated urban destination worthy of the increasing number of cruise ships that dock at its revitalized waterfront. Such is the demand that a second cruise terminal opened in 2012, just two years after the first one, and 2014 saw the arrival of the 1,000th cruise ship. All the comings and goings over the centuries have exposed Saint Johners to a wide variety of cultures and ideas, creating a characterful Maritime city with a vibrant artistic community. Visitors will discover rich and diverse cultural products in its urban core, including a plethora of art galleries and antiques shops uptown. In the summer of 2016, eight artists from seven countries are taking part in an international sculpture symposium in the city. You can watch them create sculptures in New Brunswick granite on the waterfront between early August and mid-September, then their works will be moved to locations on the International Sculpture Trail that runs between Maine and the town of Sussex, New Brunswick, joining the 14 sculptures created during two previous symposia. This is the third of a planned five-biennial symposia, which will eventually place more than 35 large-scale granite art works along the trail (⊕ *www.sculpturesaintjohn.com*).

Industry and salt air have combined to give parts of Saint John a weather-beaten quality, but you'll also find lovingly restored 19th-century wooden and redbrick homes as well as modern office buildings, hotels, and shops.

The St. John River, its Reversing Rapids, and St. John Harbour divide the city into eastern and western districts. The historic downtown area (locally known as "uptown") is on the east side, where an ambitious urban-renewal program started in the early 1980s, has transformed the downtown waterfront. Older properties have been converted into trendy restaurants and shops, while glittering new apartment buildings and condos will take full advantage of the spectacular view across the bay. Harbour Passage, a redbrick walking and cycling path with benches and interpretive information, begins downtown at Market Square and winds along the waterfront all the way to the Reversing Rapids. A shuttle boat between Market Square and the falls means you have to walk only one way. On the lower west side, painted-wood homes with flat roofs—characteristic of Atlantic Canadian seaports—slope to the harbor. Industrial activity is prominent on the west side, which has stately older homes on huge lots.

Regardless of the weather, Saint John is a delightful city to explore, as so many of its key downtown attractions are linked by enclosed overhead pedways known as the "Inside Connection."

GETTING HERE AND AROUND

Saint John airport receives flights from Halifax, Montréal, and Toronto, all of which provide connections to international flights; Saint John Transit Bus No. 32 will get you into the city on weekdays, otherwise you'll need to take a taxi. There is no rail service to Saint John, but Maritime Bus provides long-distance bus service to the city from Montréal, Québec City, Halifax, and Charlottetown, and numerous towns and cities within Atlantic Canada. If you arrive in the downtown area by car, park and proceed on foot for full enjoyment. If it's just a day trip, you might consider using Saint John Transit's Parcobus park-and-ride service, which has three parking lots on the outskirts. The city bus network is quite extensive, with fares of C$2.50–C$3.50, but bear in mind that some city sights, such as Rockwood Park and the Cherry Brook Zoo or Irving Nature Park, are beyond the downtown area, and you might need your car. Additionally, Saint John Transit offers two-hour sightseeing bus tours of historic areas from June to October on days when a cruise ship is in port, with two departures daily at 10 am and 12:30 pm. Times may be adjusted to suit cruise ship arrival times, but the tours are not restricted to cruise passengers. The pickup and drop-off point is just up the street from the cruise ship terminal. Tickets, which can be purchased from the driver (cash only), cost C$20 for adults.

ESSENTIALS

Bus Contacts **Maritime Bus.** ☎ *506/672-2055, 800/575-1807* ⊕ *maritimebus.com.* **Saint John Transit.** ✉ *55 McDonald St.* ☎ *506/658-4700* ⊕ *www.saintjohntransit.com.*

Visitor Information **Visitor Information Centre.** ✉ *Shoppes of City Hall, 15 Market Sq.* ☎ *506/658-2855, 866/463-8639* ⊕ *discoversaintjohn.com.*

Carleton Martello Tower 14
Cherry Brook Zoo 7
Handworks Gallery 11
Irving Nature Park 15
King's Square and King Street 10
Loyalist Burial Ground 9
Loyalist House 5
Market Square ... 3
New Brunswick Museum 2
Peter Buckland Gallery 12
Prince William Street 13
Reversing Rapids 1
Rockwood Park 8
Saint John City Market 4
Stone Church 6

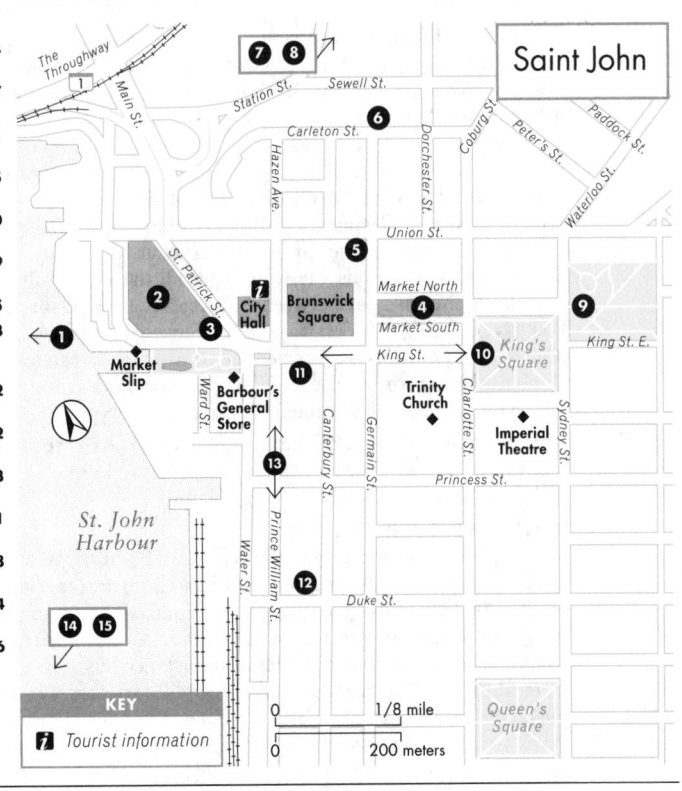

EXPLORING

TOP ATTRACTIONS

FAMILY **Cherry Brook Zoo.** Big cats and other exotic species are highlights of this charming 35-acre zoo, run as a nonprofit organization by its dedicated team. There are pleasant woodland trails, a waterfowl habitat with a boardwalk and floating gazebo, and an Aboriginal Medicine Wheel and Garden. The Discovery Center has touchable displays to engage and educate children. The zoo also has a monkey house, a miniature golf course, and the Vanished Kingdom Park, a display that focuses on extinct animals. ✉ *Rockwood Park, 901 Foster Thurston Dr.* ☎ *506/634–1440* ⊕ *www.cherrybrookzoo.com* ₹ *C$10.50; mini-golf C$5.50* ⏲ *Daily: June–early Sept. 10–8; late Sept.–May 10–5 (last admission one hour before closing).*

Irving Nature Park. The ecosystems of the southern New Brunswick coast are preserved in this lovely 600-acre park on a peninsula close to downtown. Roads, a salt-marsh boardwalk, eight walking trails, a seal observation deck, and a lookout tower make bird- and nature-watching easy. Many shorebirds breed here, and it's a staging site on the flight path of shorebirds migrating between the Arctic and South America—a wildlife tracking system here feeds data to Bird Studies Canada as part of an important research and conservation project. Motor vehicles are

CLOSE UP

Walking Tour of Downtown Saint John

Saint John is a city on hills, and **King Street,** its main street, the shortest, steepest main street in Canada, slopes down to the harbor. A system of escalators, elevators, and skywalks inside buildings allows you to climb to the top and take in some of the more memorable spots without effort, though you can also walk outside. A year-round information center is located about halfway in the Shoppes of City Hall.

Start at the foot of King, at **Market Slip.** This is where the Loyalists landed in 1783 and is the site of **Barbour's General Store** and the Little Red Schoolhouse. At Market Square, restored waterfront buildings house historical exhibits, shops, restaurants, and cafés. Also here are the Saint John Regional Library, a year-round visitor information center, a replica of the *Marco Polo* ship, and the fine **New Brunswick Museum.**

From the second level of Market Square, a skywalk crosses St. Patrick Street and an escalator takes you up into the city hall shopping concourse. Here, you can branch off to Harbour Station, with its busy schedule of concerts, sporting events, and trade shows. Once you're through city hall, another skywalk takes you across Chipman Hill and into the Brunswick Square complex of shops and offices, adjoining the city's largest hotel, the Delta Brunswick. To visit historic **Loyalist House,** exit onto Germain Street and turn left; it's on the corner at the top of the hill. Continue on for a block to see the venerable **Stone Church.** In the **Saint John City Market,** across from Brunswick Square, make sure to look up at the ceiling, which resembles the inverted hull of a ship. The oldest continuing farmers' market in Canada, constructed in 1875–76, it's also a great place to stop for lunch. When you leave by the door at the top of the market, you're near the head of King Street and right across Charlotte Street from **King's Square.** Take a walk through the square, past the statues and bandstand, to Sydney Street. Notice the walkways in the shape of the Union Jack Flag. Cross Sydney and you're in the **Loyalist Burial Ground.** Make your way back to Sydney Street and head south, turning right on King's Square South, where you can catch a glimpse of the handsome Imperial Theatre. Follow King's Square South and cross Charlotte Street to reach the back door of historic **Trinity Church.**

Finally, make your way back to King Street and walk down the hill toward the water. **Prince William Street** is at the foot of the hill, just steps from where you began at Market Slip. Turn left for antiques shops, galleries, restaurants, and historic architecture.

TIMING: Allow the better part of a day for this walk if you include a few hours for the New Brunswick Museum and some time for shopping. On Sunday the indoor walkways are open but the City Market is closed.

excluded on Saturday before noon. ✉ *Sand Cove Rd.* ✣ *From downtown take Rte. 1 west to Exit 119A (Catherwood Rd.) south; follow Sand Cove Rd. 4½ km (3 miles)* ☎ *506/653–7367* ⊕ *www.jdirving.com/jd-irving-sustainability-nature-parks-irving-nature-park.aspx* 💲 *Free* ⏲ *May–mid-Sept., daily 8–8; mid-Sept.–mid-Oct., daily 8–6.*

Loyalist Burial Ground. Established soon after the United Empire Loyalists arrived in 1783, the cemetery closed in 1848 and was sadly neglected until 1995, when the Irving family restored it as a gift to the people of Saint John. Now, brick and granite walkways lead from the memorial gates through the restored gravestones—the oldest is that of Coonradt Hendricks, dated 1784—and crypts amid shady trees and flowers. A highlight of the grounds is a magnificent beaver-pond fountain created to depict the hard work and tenacious spirit of the city's founders and those who followed them. ✉ *Sydney St., between King and E. Union Sts.* 💲 *Free* ⏲ *Daily 24 hrs.*

Market Square. The waterfront area at the foot of King Street is where the Loyalists landed in 1783. Today it's a lively and appealing area—the site of restaurants, pubs, and a venue for festivals and street performers—but it still conveys a sense of the city's maritime heritage. There's access to the Harbour Passage Trail; a floating wharf accommodates boating visitors to the city and those waiting for the tides to sail up the St. John River; and there's a beach area with imported sand and volleyball nets. ✉ *Saint John.*

FAMILY
Fodor's Choice
★

New Brunswick Museum. Imaginative and engaging in its approach, the provincial museum has fascinating displays covering the history, geology, and culture of New Brunswick. The popular whale exhibit includes Delilah, a full-size young right whale skeleton, suspended from the ceiling. You can also watch the phenomenal Bay of Fundy tides rise and fall in a glass tidal tube connected to the harbor and find out why the nearby Stonehammer Geopark has global importance. There is a large and outstanding collection of artwork in the galleries, and the Family Discovery Gallery has fun and educational games for all ages. ✉ *1 Market Sq.* ☎ *506/643–2300, 888/268–9595* ⊕ *www.nbm-mnb.ca* 💲 *C$8, C$7 Nov.–mid-May; free Thurs. and Sun. in Feb. and on certain holidays and notable days (website has details)* ⏲ *Mid-May–Oct., weekdays 9–5 (to 9 pm Thurs.), Sat. 10–5, Sun. noon–5; Nov.–mid-May closed Mon.*

Reversing Rapids. The strong Fundy tides rise higher than the water level of the river, so twice daily, at the Reversing Rapids, the tidewater pushes the river water back upstream and the rapids appear to reverse themselves. When the tide ebbs, the river once again flows downstream over the rock ledges and on into the bay. You can get an overhead view from a zip-line tour. A pulp mill on the bank is not so scenic, but multimillion-dollar upgrades to pollution controls have eliminated any unpleasant odors. It takes time to appreciate the Reversing Rapids fully; you need to visit at high, slack, and low tides—any visitor information office has tide times. ✉ *Fallsview Av.* ☎ *506/658–2937* 💲 *Free; charge for zip line* ⏲ *Daily dawn–dusk; jet-boat tours and zip line early June–early Oct., daily 10–5 (weather permitting).*

CLOSE UP

The Secrets of the Stonehammer

In 2010, a great swathe of southern New Brunswick became North America's first designated, UNESCO-supported Global Geopark, where the rocks have given up secrets of the planet's development over a billion years. The 2,500-square-km (964-square-mile) park stretches roughly from Lepreau to Norton and from the Fundy Trail to the Kingston Peninsula.

Of its more than 60 significant sites, a dozen can be visited, and are interpreted either by information panels or through outfitters who can guide you on foot or by kayak. Even if you're not among the geologists and paleontologists who would find a lifetime's fascination within what to the rest of us are just rocks, there's much to excite the imagination—the birthplace of the Atlantic Ocean, land that was once joined to what is now Africa, and terrain where some of the planet's earliest creatures have left evidence of their existence.

Saint John itself holds many of these sites, and a good place to start is the **New Brunswick Museum**, for some background information and to pick up free pamphlets. Then head out to see the **Reversing Rapids**, where two continents collided; **Irving Nature Park**, with its Ice-Age stories to tell; **Rockwood Park** and **Dominion Park**, with their geology on show—or even the many uptown buildings constructed using ancient stones.

For more information, visit *www.stonehammergeopark.com.*

FAMILY **Rockwood Park.** Encompassing 2,200 acres, this is one of the largest urban parks in Canada and is also one of the dozen or so highlighted elements of the Stonehammer Geopark, designated as such by UNESCO for its global geological importance. There are 55 hiking trails through the forest, 13 lakes, several sandy beaches, a campground, a golf course with an aquatic driving range, the Cherry Brook Zoo, events, concerts, and a unique play park for people of all ages. The Interpretation Centre organizes guided nature walks and has trail maps and information on events. ✉ *142 Lake Dr. S, off Mt. Pleasant Ave.* ☎ *506/658–2883* ⊕ *www.rockwoodpark.ca* 💲 *Free* ⏲ *Daily 8 am–dusk.*

Fodor's Choice ★ **Saint John City Market.** The inverted ship's hull ceiling of this handsome market—the oldest continuously operating farmers' market in Canada (1876)—occupies a city block between Germain and Charlotte streets. Inside, its temptations include both live and fresh-cooked lobsters, great cheeses, dulse, fresh produce, and tasty, inexpensive snacks, along with plenty of souvenir and crafts items made by resident artists. ✉ *47 Charlotte St.* ☎ *506/658–2820* ⊕ *www.sjcitymarket.ca* ⏲ *Weekdays 7:30–6, Sat. 7:30–5.*

WORTH NOTING

FAMILY **Carleton Martello Tower.** The four-level tower, a great place from which to survey the harbor and Partridge Island, was built during the War of 1812 as a precaution against an American attack. Guides portray the spartan life of a soldier living in the stone fort, and an audiovisual presentation in the visitor center outlines the tower's role in the defense of Saint John during World War II. The Sunday afternoon "Saint John Privateers" program in July and August, included in admission fee and available in English and French, brings the era to life for families with children ages 6 to 11 (call to reserve space). ✉ *454 Whipple St.* ☎ *506/636–4011* 🌐 *www.pc.gc.ca* 💵 *C$3.90* ⏲ *Late June–early Sept., daily 10–5:30.*

Handworks Gallery. Some of the best professional crafts and fine art created in New Brunswick are carried by this lively gallery, which represents more than 80 Saint John artists and artisans. Special events sometimes enable you to meet the artists in-store. The historic building was the home of 19th-century painter, J.C. Miles. ✉ *12 King St.* ☎ *506/631–7626* 🌐 *www.handworks.ca* ⏲ *Closed Sun.*

King's Square and King Street. Laid out in a Union Jack pattern, this green refuge has a two-story bandstand that hosts summer concerts and a number of monuments. The mass of metal on the ground in the northeast corner is actually a great lump of melted tools from a neighboring hardware store that burned down in Saint John's Great Fire of 1877, in which hundreds of buildings were destroyed. It's a great place to picnic on food bought at the City Market across the street. From the west side of the square, King Street, the steepest, shortest main street in Canada, heads down toward the waterfront, with a variety of shops and restaurants along the way. ✉ *Between Charlotte and Sydney Sts.*

Loyalist House. The former home of the Merritt family, wealthy Loyalist merchants, this imposing Georgian structure with eight fireplaces was built in 1817 and is furnished with authentic period pieces, including a working piano organ and kitchen equipment. Visitors can explore on their own or join a guided tour. ✉ *120 Union St.* ☎ *506/652–3590* 🌐 *www.loyalisthouse.com* 💵 *C$5* ⏲ *Loyalist Day (May 18)–June 30, weekdays 10–5; July–mid-Sept., daily 10–5 (last admission 4:45); off-season by appointment.*

Fodor's Choice ★ **Peter Buckland Gallery.** Art expert Peter Buckland carries contemporary paintings, drawings, and sculpture by Canadian artists in his exceptional gallery—one of the finest private galleries in the province. In 2012, Peter received the Queen's Diamond Jubilee Medal for his contribution to the arts. ✉ *35 Duke St.* ☎ *506/693–9721* ⏲ *Thurs. and Fri. 10–5, Sat. 10–4, or by appointment.*

Prince William Street. Off King Street one block back from the waterfront, this street is full of historic bank and business buildings that now hold shops, galleries, and restaurants so good and plentiful that it has become a dining destination. The triple-bulb lamp known as the Three Sisters, at the far end of Prince William Street, was erected in 1848 to guide ships into the harbor. Next to it is a replica of the Celtic cross on nearby Partridge Island, where many immigrants landed and were quarantined. ✉ *Saint John.*

Stone Church (*St John's Church*). The first stone church in the city was built in the 1820s for the garrison posted at nearby Fort Howe, using stone brought from England as ships' ballast. ✉ *87 Carleton St.* ☎ *506/634–1474* 🌐 *www.stjohnsstonechurch.org* 💵 *By donation* ⏲ *July and Aug., Tues., Wed., and Fri. 8:30–3:30.*

WHERE TO EAT

$$$ SEAFOOD ✕ **Billy's Seafood Company.** It's a restaurant, it's an oyster bar, it's a fish market, and it's lots of fun, too, with jazzy background music and amusing fish paintings on the walls. The fresh fish selection is impressive, and everything is cooked to perfection. The scallops in warm citrus vinaigrette with sweet peas and beer-candied bacon are always a hit, as is the halibut poached in spicy lobster broth, with lobster cake and greens. Local lore says that this is where cedar-planked salmon originated, and it's delicious. Dining outside is a treat on a nice day, and you can get live and cooked lobsters packed to go. Breakfast is served on Saturday (until noon). $ *Average main: C$26* ✉ *Saint John City Market, 49–51 Charlotte St., Downtown* ☎ *506/672–3474, 888/933–3474* ⊕ *www.billysseafood.com.*

$$$ BISTRO Fodor's Choice ★ ✕ **East Coast Bistro.** Take a good look at the surroundings when you arrive—exposed brick walls, artworks, hardwood floors— because once the food appears, it will have your full attention. Artfully plated dishes like local goat cheese terrine and house-smoked salmon, lead into main courses that might include yogurt-and-coriander-roasted chicken breast or pan-seared sustainable blue trout with chorizo, caramelized onion roesti, and sautéed greens. Everything is made in-house from locally sourced ingredients. $ *Average main: C$22* ✉ *60 Prince William St.* ☎ *506/696–3278* ⊕ *eastcoastbistro.com* ⊘ *Closed Sun. No dinner Mon.*

$$ THAI ✕ **Lemongrass Thai Fare.** If you shy away from Thai food because of its reputation for spicy hotness, do not hesitate to try this stylish restaurant within Saint John's culinary hot spot of Market Square. Lemongrass caters to all tastes, and will prepare your pad thai to match your preference for heat, or lack of. Thai stir-fries, noodle dishes, and curries, many featuring ginger and coconut, share the menu with both mild and fiery Indian dishes, to be enjoyed indoors or on the patio. The lunch menu is a great value and there's a pub here, too. $ *Average main: C$20* ✉ *1 Market Sq., Downtown* ☎ *506/657–8424* ⊕ *lemongrasssaintjohn.com.*

$$$ CANADIAN Fodor's Choice ★ ✕ **Saint John Ale House.** This gastropub is one of the best places to eat in the city—and it couldn't have a better location, with a great patio overlooking the downtown waterfront. Drawing on supplies from local farmers, fishermen, and food producers, the menu presents "progressive pub food." This might include seared halibut with dandelion and ramp kimchi, sweet peas and beet vinegar butter sauce, hand-stuffed pork sausages with house-fermented cabbage and mustard jus, or a tender, 30-day dry-aged steak with bordelaise sauce; even the fish-and-chips and cheeseburgers have a gourmet touch. The beer menu includes 32 beers on tap and 56 bottled options from local and international breweries. There's live entertainment Wednesday through Saturday. $ *Average main: C$28* ✉ *1 Market Sq., Downtown* ☎ *506/657–2337* ⊕ *www.saintjohnalehouse.com.*

$$ LATIN AMERICAN ✕ **Taco Pica.** This modest restaurant is a slice of home for the former Guatemalan refugees, now proud Canadian citizens, who run it as a worker's co-op. The atmosphere is colorful—ornamental parrots rule in the dining room—and the Guatemalan, Mexican, and Spanish recipes are authentically seasoned with garlic, mint, coriander, and cilantro. The *pepian* (beef stew) and the garlic shrimp are standout options on a menu that ranges from vegetarian quesadillas to Tequila Cactus Pork to Paella. There's regular live entertainment, including salsa every Friday night. [$] *Average main: C$17* ✉ *96 Germain St., Downtown* ☎ *506/633–8492* 🌐 *www.tacopica.ca* ⏲ *Closed Sun.*

$$$ DELI ✕ **Urban Deli.** Cool yet pleasingly unpretentious, this downtown eatery gets rave reviews from an eclectic mix of businesspeople, shoppers, students, and city visitors. The daytime menu features classic deli fare, including sandwiches piled high with meat smoked on the premises, hearty soups, imaginative salads, and comfort food such as mac and cheese and ribs. Wednesday through Saturday, from 5 pm, Italian classics are on the menu, including vegetarian options and gluten-free pasta. If you have to stand in line for lunch, be assured it's worth the wait. [$] *Average main: C$24* ✉ *68 King St., Downtown* ☎ *506/652–3354* 🌐 *www.urbandeli.ca* ⏲ *Closed Sun. No dinner Mon. and Tues.*

WHERE TO STAY

$$ HOTEL FAMILY **Delta Brunswick Hotel.** Right in the heart of the city, this hotel is within the Brunswick Square complex of shops and services and linked to other shopping and entertainment venues (and parking) by an indoor walkway, making it perfect for a winter visit. **Pros:** friendly and helpful staff; near all downtown attractions. **Cons:** most rooms only have a street view. [$] *Rooms from: C$129* ✉ *39 King St.* ☎ *506/648–1981* 🌐 *www.deltahotels.ca* 🛏 *254 rooms* 🍽 *Breakfast.*

$$ HOTEL FAMILY Fodor's Choice ★ **Hilton Saint John.** This stunningly renovated hotel is sleek and very stylish, with open-aspect public areas flooded with natural light, spacious rooms, and an unbeatable city-center waterfront location. **Pros:** in the hub of the city's restaurants, shopping, and summertime action; wonderful views; great amenities for families, including adjoining rooms; very pleasant and helpful staff. **Cons:** atmosphere can be affected by conventioneers. [$] *Rooms from: C$159* ✉ *1 Market Sq.* ☎ *506/693–8484, 800/561–8282 in Canada* 🌐 *www.hilton.com* 🛏 *196 rooms, 1 suite* 🍽 *No meals.*

$ B&B/INN **Homeport Historic Bed & Breakfast Inn.** Graceful arches, fine antiques, Italian marble fireplaces, Oriental carpets, and a maritime theme distinguish this pair of mansions overlooking the harbor. **Pros:** hospitable, well-versed owners; great sense of history; close to downtown and the Reversing Rapids. **Cons:** the amazing view is sometimes obscured by fog; not a pretty walk to downtown. [$] *Rooms from: C$109* ✉ *80 Douglas Ave.* ☎ *506/672–7255, 888/678–7678* 🌐 *www.homeport.nb.ca* 🛏 *7 rooms, 3 suites* 🍽 *Breakfast.*

$ B&B/INN **Shadow Lawn Inn.** In an affluent suburb with tree-lined streets, palatial homes, tennis, golf, and a yacht club, this inn fits right in, with its clapboards, columns, antiques, and original artwork. **Pros:** great food; hospitable service. **Cons:** the location means a ride into town if you want to go out at night; dinner not available on Sunday. [$] *Rooms from: C$120* ✉ *3180 Rothesay Rd., 12 km (7 miles) northeast of Saint John, Rothesay* ☎ *506/847–7539, 800/561–4166* 🌐 *www.shadowlawninn.com* 🛏 *9 rooms, 2 apartments* 🍽 *Breakfast.*

TASTES OF NEW BRUNSWICK

Seafood is plentiful all year (lobsters, oysters, crabs, mussels, clams, scallops, and salmon) and prepared in as many ways as there are chefs, and just about anywhere in New Brunswick you'll find some kind of fish-and-chips. Try snacking on dulse, a dried purple seaweed as salty as potato chips and as compelling as peanuts.

A spring delicacy is fiddleheads—emerging ferns that look like the curl at the end of a violin head. These emerald gems are picked along riverbanks, then boiled and sprinkled with lemon juice, butter, salt, and pepper.

The beers of choice are Moosehead, brewed in Saint John, Alexander Keith's (originally a Nova Scotia brewery, now owned by Labatt, a subsidiary of Anheuser-Busch) and, of course, the various Molson brews. A number of local breweries—notably the Northampton Brewing Company, makers of Picaroons Traditional Ales, based in Fredericton, and Moncton's Pump House Brewery—are also popular. New Brunswick also has 14 wineries so ask what's available in stores and restaurants. A good introduction would be to take one of the Uncorked Tours out of Saint John, Fredericton, Moncton, or St. Andrews, which specialize in local wineries and artisan breweries.

New Brunswick's maple products are sought the world over, and chocolates made by Ganong Bros. Limited of St. Stephen, who have been in the candy business for a century and a quarter, are a popular treat.

NIGHTLIFE AND PERFORMING ARTS

NIGHTLIFE

Canterbury Lounge. Come to this cool spot for early-evening cocktails, inside or on the patio, or make it your late-night destination for high-energy dancing to DJ spins until 2 am. It's open Thursday to Saturday. ✉ *47 Canterbury St.* ☎ *506/646–1811* ⊕ *www.thecanterburylounge.com.*

O'Leary's Pub. In the downtown historic district, this pub specializes in old-time Irish fun complete with Celtic performers on off-season Tuesdays; on Wednesdays, Brent Mason, a well-known neofolk artist, starts the evening and then turns the mike over to the audience, and Fridays and Saturdays (and some Thursdays) it's mostly live cover bands, starting at 10 pm. ✉ *46 Princess St.* ☎ *506/634–7135* ⊕ *www.olearyspub.com.*

PERFORMING ARTS

Fodor's Choice ★ **Imperial Theatre.** Saint John's theater, opera, ballet, and symphony productions, along with touring bands and comedians, take place at this beautifully restored theater—and the 1913 vaudeville venue offers the most comprehensive programming in Atlantic Canada. Tours (C$2) are available from May through August during regular business hours, or by appointment September through April. ✉ *24 King's Sq. S* ☎ *506/674–4100, 800/232–7469, 506/674–4111 for tours* ⊕ *www.imperialtheatre.nb.ca.*

Saint John Arts Centre. Several galleries here display the work of local artists and artisans and occasional musical events range from string quartets to singer-songwriters. ✉ *20 Peel Plaza* ☎ *506/633–4870* 🌐 *www.saintjohnartscentre.com* ⏲ *Tues.–Sat. 9–5.*

SPORTS AND THE OUTDOORS

FAMILY **DayTripping.** Based in Rockwood Park, this outfitter offers a variety of outdoor experiences, from rock-climbing on Stonehammer Geopark's 500-million-year-old cliffs to guided hikes. You can also rent kayaks, canoes, stand-up paddleboards, pedal boats, mountain bikes, tandems, and geocaching GPS units. It's open daily 10–6 in summer; otherwise Saturday 10–5 and Sunday noon–5, and may close for a period in winter. ✉ *Lily Lake Pavilion, 55 Lake Dr. S* ☎ *506/657–2102* 🌐 *www.daytrippingnb.com* 💲 *Rock climbing C$50; guided walks C$40 per hr; geocaching C$15; rentals from C$20 per hr.*

Osprey Adventures. Northeast of Saint John, the beautiful Kennebacasis River is a calm and peaceful haven of wildlife, and Osprey's experts lead informative guided kayaking trips. Also available are excursions in their superb Voyageur canoe, built by the local Oromocto Indian Band, which will accommodate up to 10 paddlers (a minimum of 5 is required). Or you can rent a kayak, canoe, or stand-up paddleboard to explore on your own. It's also advisable to reserve tours and rentals. ✉ *Lighthouse Park River Centre, 1075 Main St.* ☎ *506/832–6025, 506/721–4356* 🌐 *www.ospreyadventures.net* 💲 *Tours from C$23; rentals from C$25.*

SHOPPING

Brunswick Square. This large mall is connected to the city's "Inside Connection" covered walkway and contains more than 60 top-quality boutiques on three floors. The complex also includes a parking garage, offices, and the Delta Brunswick Hotel. ✉ *King and Germain Sts.* ☎ *506/658–1000* 🌐 *www.brunswicksquare.ca.*

Exchange on Germain. A classy, mid- to high-end consignment store, Exchange on Germain has fun and classic designer clothes, footwear, and accessories at tempting prices—and the shop is in the market for your old Prada and Dior cast-offs, too. You'll also find active clothing and menswear on the racks. ✉ *117 Germain St.* ☎ *506/642–9803* 🌐 *www.exchangeongermain.com* ⏲ *Closed Sun.*

EN ROUTE

Lepreau Falls Provincial Park. It may not be Niagara, but these beautiful falls tumble over rocks that are around 325 million years old, and are a featured site within the Stonehammer Geopark. Though fossils are few, an important and rare tetrapod trackway was discovered here in 1974, made by one of the earliest reptiles on the planet. There are tantalizing views of the falls from the boardwalk in the wooded surroundings, one of which has an explanatory panel detailing the geological and historic significance of the site. Picnic tables are available and, at the right time of year, you can pick wild strawberries. ✉ *Lepreau Falls Rd., Lepreau* ✣ *40 km (25 miles) west of Saint John via Hwy. 1 and Hwy. 175* ☎ *506/643–2300* *www.stonehammergeopark.com/lepreau-falls-provincial-park.html Free Always accessible.*

EN ROUTE

New River Beach. Unlike most Bay of Fundy beaches, this one is sandy and great for swimming, especially if you wait until the tide is coming in. The sun warms the sand at low tide, and the sand warms the water as it comes in. There are quite a lot of steps down to the beach, and the toilets, canteen, and picnic tables are at the top. It's part of the New River Beach Provincial Park that also has a boardwalk through a bog, a playground, interpretive programs, hiking trails, kayak rentals, and campsites. The annual Sand Sculpture Competition in late July is a popular event. **Amenities:** food and drink; parking; toilets; water sports. **Best for:** swimming; walking. *78 New River Beach Rd., Lepreau Lepreau, off Hwy. 1, 50 km (30 miles) west of Saint John 506/755-4078 parcsnbparks.ca C$8 vehicle entrance to park (May–Oct.).*

3

THE FUNDY COAST

Bordering the chilly and powerful tidal Bay of Fundy, where the world's most extreme tides rise and fall twice daily, is some of New Brunswick's most dramatic coastline. This area extends from the border town of St. Stephen and the lovely coastal resort village of St. Andrews, past tiny fishing villages and rocky coves, through Saint John, and on through Fundy National Park and beyond. A vast area, encompassing inland areas and the coastline, is now designated the Stonehammer Geopark, North America's only Global Geopark, with a dozen specific sites illustrating remarkable geological features formed over billions of years. The Fundy Islands—Grand Manan Island, Deer Island, and Campobello—are havens of peace that have lured harried mainlanders for generations. Some of the impressive 50-km (31-mile) stretch of coastline between St. Martins and Fundy National Park can be viewed from the Fundy Trail Parkway.

ST. ANDREWS BY-THE-SEA

31 km (19 miles) southeast of St. Stephen.

Fodor's Choice ★

A designated National Historic District on Passamaquoddy Bay, St. Andrews by-the-Sea is one of North America's prettiest resort towns. It has long been a summer retreat of the affluent, and mansions ring the town. Of the town's 550 buildings, 280 were erected before 1880, and 14 of those have survived from the 1700s. Some Loyalists even brought their homes with them piece by piece from Castine, Maine, across the bay, when the American Revolution didn't go their way. Pick up a walking-tour map at the visitor information center and follow it through the pleasant streets. Water Street, by the harbor, has eateries, gift and craft shops, and artists' studios. The harbor has a cluster of whale-watching boats and outfitters for other activities.

GETTING HERE AND AROUND

There is no public transportation to St. Andrews by-the-Sea. By road, it's about 100 km (60 miles) west of Saint John via Highway 1 then Route 127. If you're crossing the border from Calais, Maine, it's about

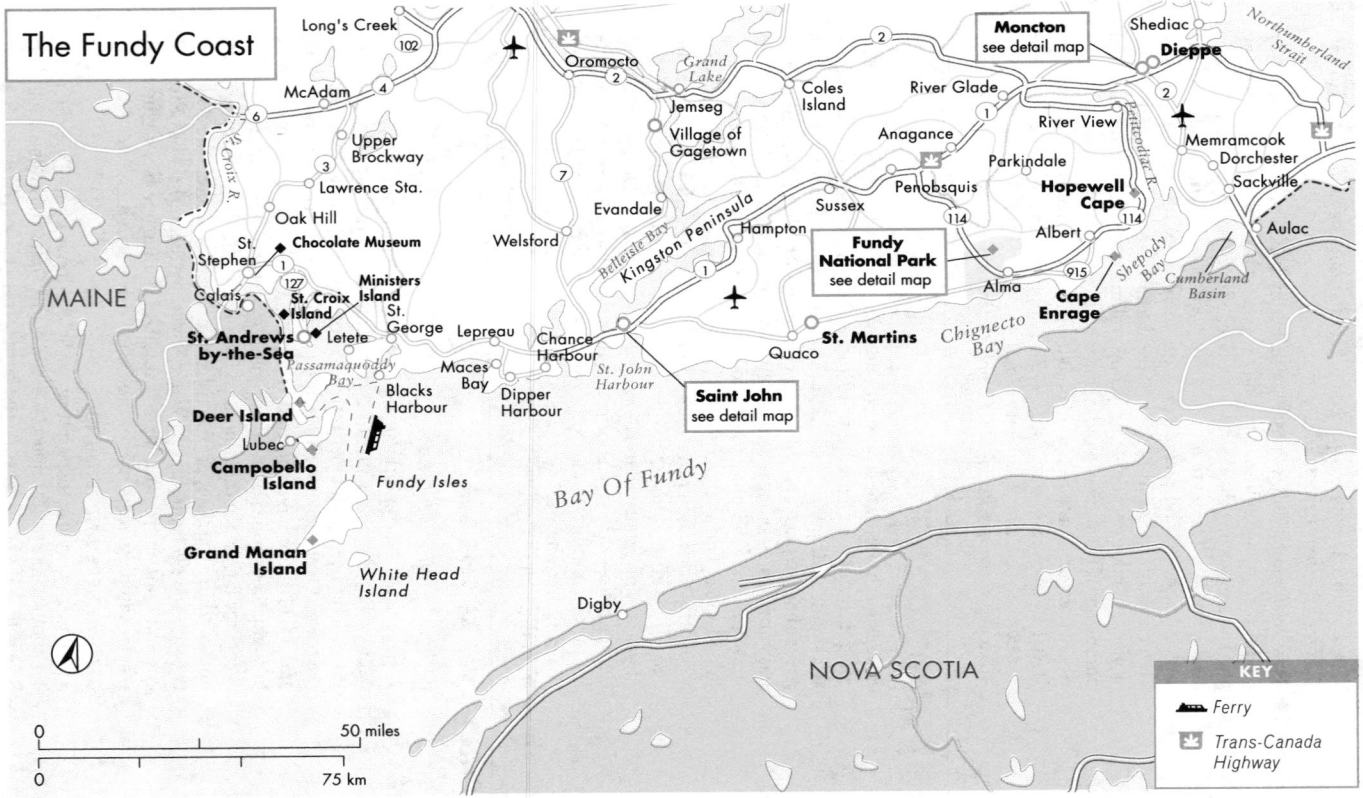
The Fundy Coast
Long's Creek
102
McAdam
4
6
St. Croix R.
Upper Brockway
3
Lawrence Sta.
Oak Hill
St. Stephen
Chocolate Museum
1
127
Calais
St. Croix Island
Ministers Island
St. George
MAINE
St. Andrews by-the-Sea
Letete
Passamaquoddy Bay
Deer Island
Lubec
Campobello Island
Fundy Isles
Grand Manan Island
White Head Island
Blacks Harbour
Maces Bay
Dipper Harbour
Lepreau
Chance Harbour
St. John Harbour
Saint John
see detail map
Welsford
Evandale
Oromocto
7
Grand Lake
Jemseg
Village of Gagetown
Belleisle Bay
Kingston Peninsula
Hampton
Coles Island
Sussex
Quaco
St. Martins
Fundy National Park
see detail map
Bay Of Fundy
Digby
NOVA SCOTIA
Moncton
see detail map
River Glade
Anagance
Penobsquis
114
Alma
Chignecto Bay
Parkindale
River View
Petitcodiac R.
Hopewell Cape
Albert
915
Cape Enrage
Shepody Bay
Shediac
Dieppe
Northumberland Strait
Memramcook
Dorchester
Sackville
Aulac
Cumberland Basin
0
50 miles
0
75 km
KEY
Ferry
Trans-Canada Highway

a half-hour drive via Route 127 north, then Route 170 west. Once there, the Water Street and harbor area is delightfully walkable, but a car would be needed to get to some of the attractions.

ESSENTIALS

Visitor Information **St. Andrews.** ✉ *24 Reed Ave., St. Andrews* ☎ *506/529-3556* 🌐 *www.townofstandrews.ca.*

EXPLORING

TOP ATTRACTIONS

OFF THE BEATEN PATH

Chocolate Museum. Ganong have been making chocolates in St. Stephen since 1873 and their original candy factory now houses this museum. It explores the sweet history of candy making with hand-dipping videos, a collection of antique chocolate boxes, and hands-on exhibits. A Heritage Chocolate Walking Tour includes a guided tour of the museum and a stroll around town, pointing out buildings associated with the chocolate industry here. There are occasional activities for children, and a chocolate festival in early August. Happily, after all those tempting displays, there's a year-round retail outlet on-site in which to buy a few treats. ✉ *73 Milltown Blvd., St. Stephen* ☎ *506/466-7848* 🌐 *www.chocolatemuseum.ca* 💲 *C$10, Heritage Chocolate Walk C$15* ⏲ *July and Aug., Mon.–Sat. 9–6, Sun. 11–3; June, Mon.–Sat. 10–4, Sun. 11–3; May and Sept., weekdays 10–4, Sat. 11–3; Mar., Apr., and Oct.–late Nov., weekdays 10–4. Heritage Walk June–Aug., Mon.–Sat. at 10 and 2.*

FAMILY

Huntsman Fundy Discovery Aquarium. This small but interesting aquarium, established in 1969, is at the Huntsman Marine Science Centre, a private not-for-profit research and education institution. Marine exhibits include a huge two-story tank with indicators showing the varying levels of the Fundy tides, teeming touch tanks that delight children (and adults), rare wolffish, sea horses, squid, salmon, and a pair of very entertaining harbor seals (fed at 11 and 4 daily), as well as free movies and slide shows. Check the website or call for driving directions—it's not easy to find. ✉ *1 Lower Campus Rd.* ☎ *506/529-1200* 🌐 *www.huntsmanmarine.ca* 💲 *C$14* ⏲ *May–Sept., daily 10–5.*

FAMILY
Fodor's Choice ★

Kingsbrae Garden. Horticulture and art combine in this spectacular public garden. Nearly 2,500 varieties of trees, shrubs, and plants cover the 27 acres, with woodland trails and many theme gardens, including one specially designed for touch and smell, a rose garden, a bird and butterfly garden, and a gravel garden. A children's fantasy garden offers child-centered activities, and there are daily programs for kids under 12 (1:30 in July and August). One of the oldest and rarest trees in the world, a Wollemi pine, named Pericles, is a big attraction, as is the opportunity to participate in a ladybug release program every morning at 10:30. The Sculpture Garden features works by Don Pell, exhibits on loan from the Beaverbrook collection, and many other established and emerging artists, including winners of the annual Kingsbrae Garden Canadian Sculpture Competition. Kingsbrae also has an art gallery, a café, and the superb Savour in the Garden restaurant. ✉ *220 King St.* ☎ *506/529-3335, 866/566-8687* 🌐 *www.kingsbraegarden.com* 💲 *C$16; 7-day pass C$24.50; guided tours C$3; free for plant center, café, and folk art display only* ⏲ *Mid-May–mid-Oct., daily 9–sunset.*

WORTH NOTING

Charlotte County Courthouse and Old Gaol. Active since 1840 and a National Historic Site since 1983, the courthouse is an exceptionally fine example of 19th-century Greek Revival architecture—one of the finest in Canada. The adjacent Old Gaol, on the other hand, is a grim reminder of the conditions that awaited local wrongdoers. The courthouse is also the home of Charlotte County Archives, whose volunteers offer free tours of the courthouse and the Old Gaol (June to September). Ask about their Ghost Walks, too. ✉ *123 Frederick St.* ☎ *506/529–4248* 🌐 *www.ccarchives.ca* 💲 *Donations* ⏲ *Apr., May, and Oct., Tues.–Fri. 1–4; June and Sept., weekdays 10–4:30; July and Aug., Mon.–Sat. 10–4:30; Nov.–Mar. by appointment.*

Greenock Church. After a remark was made at an 1822 dinner party about the "poor" Presbyterians not having a church of their own, Captain Christopher Scott took exception to the insult and spared no expense on this building. The church is decorated with a carving of a green oak tree in honor of Scott's birthplace, Greenock in Scotland. ✉ *146 Montague St.*

OFF THE BEATEN PATH

Ministers Island. This huge island estate, once completely self-sufficient, was the summer home of Sir William Van Horne, chairman of the Canadian Pacific Railway from 1899 to 1915. Tours of the property include Covenhoven, Sir William's 50-room summer home; a tidal swimming pool; a livestock barn; a cottage; an old windmill; and the 1790 Minister's House from which the island takes its name. To get to the island you drive, walk, or bike at low tide; be sure to leave the island before the tide comes in or you will be stuck for another six hours. The website gives details of accessible hours for each open day. ✉ *Via Bar Rd., off Rte. 127, 5 km (3 miles) north of St. Andrews* ☎ *506/529–5081* 🌐 *www.ministersisland.net* 💲 *C$10 (cash only), includes guided tour* ⏲ *Mid-May–mid-Oct., daily; times vary according to tides.*

WHERE TO EAT

$$ SEAFOOD

✕ **The Gables.** A relaxing meal on the outdoor deck of this friendly harborside eatery is the perfect way to end a day of whale-watching or craft shopping. The lobster club sandwich is a favorite, and in addition to seafood, there are steaks and other non–fish dishes on the menu. The hearty seafood chowder will warm the heart and soul on a foggy Fundy night, and homemade desserts top off the experience. The outdoor patio and deck offer breathtaking views of the harbor, and if the winds come up, there are warm fleece blankets available. 💲 *Average main: C$20* ✉ *143 Water St.* ☎ *506/529–3440* ⏲ *Closed Nov.–mid-Apr.*

$$$ SEAFOOD FAMILY

✕ **Harbour Front.** This is a great spot for a casual meal and the large covered deck, right on the water's edge near the harbor, is deservedly popular when the weather's right. Inside, the beautifully restored building's long history is apparent, with massive old beams and accoutrements from its past. The long menu majors on seafood, such as lobster, sole almandine, and seafood casserole in a creamy sauce, but there are steaks, chicken dishes, salads, and sandwiches, along with a children's menu. 💲 *Average main: C$22* ✉ *225 Water St.* ☎ *506/529–4887* ⏲ *Closed late Oct–mid-May.*

$$ CANADIAN **Niger Reef Tea House.** Overlooking the bay with seating inside or out on a rustic deck, this 1926 former meetinghouse now houses a fine restaurant. Everything is top quality, from the simple but expertly produced lunchtime options—seafood chowder, sandwiches, frittata—to more substantial dinner selections. These might include traditional cedar-planked salmon with a ginger glaze, or lamb shanks braised in tomato-and-red-wine sauce. The splendid mural was painted by American artist Lucille Douglass. Arrive early for dinner; the Tea House closes at 8 pm, and reservations are recommended. *Average main: C$20 1 Joes Point Rd. 506/529–8005 www.nigerreefteahouse.com Closed Nov.–Apr. No dinner May and Oct.*

$$$$ CANADIAN Fodor's Choice ★ **Savour in the Garden.** Within the lovely Kingsbrae Garden, this restaurant is open to all for dinner on Thursday, Friday, and Saturday evenings. Creative tasting menus—consisting of three or six courses—are based on available fresh local ingredients. One recent dish, Six Wings to Fly, featured duck ragout, seared quail breast and braised leg, partridge terrine, roasted potato shell, mushroom demiglace, sautéed carrots, sugar snap peas, chanterelles, and beet ketchup—yes, that's just one dish. During the day, light healthy meals are served to garden visitors. Reservations are recommended for dinner. *Average main: C$72 Kingsbrae Garden, 220 King St. 506/529–3335, 866/566–8687 www.kingsbraegarden.com No dinner Sun.–Wed.*

WHERE TO STAY

$$$ RESORT Fodor's Choice ★ **The Algonquin Resort.** One of Canada's iconic resorts, the Algonquin has been meticulously restored to perfectly recapture the historic elegance that made it legendary. **Pros:** personal service; luxurious surroundings; includes a top-class golf course; indoor pool has a three-story waterslide. **Cons:** a bit of a walk from the waterfront hub (but there's a free shuttle). *Rooms from: C$199 184 Adolphus St. 506/529–8823, 855/529–8693 algonquinresort.com 220 rooms, 13 suites No meals.*

$$$$ HOTEL Fodor's Choice ★ **Kingsbrae Arms.** Expect excellent service from the hosts and staff at this restored 1897 estate, where eclectic antiques fill the rooms, and pampering touches include plush robes and daily afternoon tea. **Pros:** lovely grounds; close to Kingsbrae Garden; delicious local food prepared by creative chef; kid- and pet-friendly. **Cons:** in winter the only meal offered is breakfast. *Rooms from: C$329 219 King St. 506/529–1897 www.kingsbrae.com 8 suites, 2 rooms Breakfast.*

$ B&B/INN **Montague Rose B&B.** Two blocks back from the harbor, this lovely French empire–style home offers a warm welcome and individually styled, comfortable bedrooms. **Pros:** friendly hosts; good location close to all downtown attractions. **Cons:** bathrooms have either a tub or shower; fixed time for breakfast, at 8:30 am. *Rooms from: C$110 258 Montague St. 506/529–8963, 888/529–8963 www.themontaguerose.com 4 rooms Breakfast.*

$$ HOTEL **Rossmount Inn Hotel Restaurant & Bar.** Surrounded by 87 acres at the base of Chamcook Mountain, this inn is renowned for hospitality and outstanding food and is particularly convenient for visiting Ministers Island. **Pros:** impeccable surroundings and details; amazing dinners.

Cons: some rooms are very small; stairways are steep. *Rooms from: C$125 4599 Rte. 127 506/529-3351 www.rossmountinn.com Closed Jan.–Easter 18 rooms No meals.*

SPORTS AND THE OUTDOORS

BIKING

Off-Kilter Bike Tours. Two-hour, full-day, and multiday bike tours include the loan of a helmet . . . and a kilt—yes, the Scottish garment. Owner Kurt Gumushel's father, a tailor, originally made the lightweight custom kilts for a particular group of mountain bikers, and the idea caught on. The price of the full-day tour also includes water, lunch, and snacks. *18 King St. 506/466-8388 www.offkilterbike.com From C$60.*

DIVING

Navy Island Dive. In addition to equipment rentals, this company runs dive trips to view the wonderful marine life of the Bay of Fundy. Navy Island Dive also teaches beginners. *15 William St. 506/529-4555 www.navyislanddive.nb.ca From C$30.*

GOLF

Algonquin Golf Club. On the shores of Passamaquoddy Bay, this is a beautifully landscaped historic signature course, redesigned in 2000 by Thomas McBroom. The holes on the back 9—especially the 12th—have beautiful sea views, as does the Clubhouse Grill, within Canada's oldest clubhouse. Part of the Algonquin resort, it's also open to nonguests and has a "traditional golf" dress code. *465 Brandy Cove Rd., off Rte. 127 506/529-8165 algonquinresort.com/golf C$35–C$85 18-holes, 7000 yards, par 72.*

KAYAKING

Eastern Outdoors. Single and double kayaks and mountain bikes are available for rent, as well as lessons, and tours around Navy Island, Deer Island, and Passamaquody Bay. *165 Water St. 506/529-4662, 800/565-2925 www.easternoutdoors.com Kayak full-day tours C$125; kayak rentals from C$55 for half day.*

WHALE-WATCHING

Whale-watching season is from June or July through late October. Whale and nature cruises all begin at the town wharf, heading out into the Bay of Fundy for sightings of several species of whale, plus dolphins, porpoises, seals, and other marine life. Birdlife includes bald eagles, ospreys, puffins, and sheerwaters. Sightings can't be guaranteed, but the success rate averages between 95% and 100%. All outfitters supply flotation devices, and some provide drinks and snacks while others suggest you bring your own. All recommend warm clothing, regardless of the onshore temperature. You should arrive at the wharf up to 45 minutes before sailing time, and be aware that tours depend on weather conditions.

FAMILY **Fundy Tide Runners.** A 24-foot Zodiac will zip you out into the bay on a two-hour trip. *16 King St. 506/529-4481 www.fundytiderunners.com C$60 (a fuel surcharge may apply).*

FAMILY **Quoddy Link Marine.** Whale- and wildlife-watching tours lasting 2½–3 hours are on a powered catamaran that takes up to 47 passengers. *20 King St. 506/529-2600, 877/688-2600 www.quoddylinkmarine.com C$58.*

FAMILY **Tall Ship Whale Adventures.** The *Jolly Breeze* is an elegant (and quiet) sailing vessel for whale-watching, and particularly good for families. In addition to watching the whales, children can dress in pirate costumes, have their faces painted, steer the ship, hoist sails, learn a sea shanty, and dabble in the marine touch tank. Breakfast is included on morning sailings, hot soup is served on later sailings, and there's a bar on board. Tours, which last 3½ hours, run daily from late June through mid-October. ✉ *4 King St.* ☎ *506/529–8116, 866/529–8116* 💵 *C$58.*

SHOPPING

Crocker Hill Store/Steven Smith Designs. Owner-artist Stephen Smith is inspired by nature, and his art—on framed prints, T-shirts, tote bags, and note cards—focuses on local birdlife. The shop is in an 1837 heritage building within a garden, with some interesting features inside. Call to check off-season opening hours. ✉ *45 King St.* ☎ *506/529–4303, 888/255–4251* 🌐 *www.crockerhill.com.*

Garden by the Sea. This aromatic shop specializes in all-natural body products made in New Brunswick, including Bay of Fundy sea salts and ecoflowers (made from various recycled materials including wood, paper, and fabric), as well as fresh flowers and 130 varieties of ethical, fair trade, and organic teas. ✉ *217 Water St.* ☎ *506/529–8905* 🌐 *gardenbytheseanb.com.*

Oven Head Salmon Smokers. Regulations no longer allow tours of the smokehouse, but the friendly owners will explain the process of producing some of New Brunswick's best cold-smoked salmon and salmon jerky, and you can buy the finished product. You'll also see it for sale in local grocery stores and on the menu at many regional restaurants. ✉ *101 Oven Head Rd., Bethel* ✣ *Off Hwy. 1, toward Saint John; take Exit 45* ☎ *506/755–2507, 877/955–2507* 🌐 *www.ovenheadsmokers.com.*

Serendipin' Art. Fine art, handblown glass, hand-painted silks, jewelry, and other crafts by more than 100 New Brunswick artists are sold here, and the second gallery next door has works produced elsewhere in the Maritimes. ✉ *168–170 Water St.* ☎ *506/529–3327, 866/470–5500* 🌐 *www.serendipinart.ca* ⏲ *May–Oct., daily; Nov.–Apr. call to check hrs.*

Fodor's Choice ★ **Toose's Bijoux.** Owner Pam Vincent's sense of style is reflected in the artsy and quirky range of gifts, jewelry, greetings cards, homewares, and irresistible chocolate truffles in this upscale boutique. ✉ *147 Water St.* ☎ *506/529–4040.*

GRAND MANAN ISLAND

48 km (30 miles) east of St. Andrews by-the-Sea to Blacks Harbour, then 1½ hrs by car ferry.

Grand Manan, the largest of the three Fundy Islands, is also the farthest from the mainland. You might see whales, seals, or the occasional puffin on the way over. Circular herring weirs dot the island's coastal waters, and fish sheds and smokehouses lie beside long wharfs that reach out to bobbing fishing boats. Place-names are evocative: Swallowtail, Southern Head, Seven Days Work, and Dark Harbour. It's easy to get around; only about 32 km (20 miles) of road lead from the lighthouse at Southern Head to the one at North Head. John James Audubon, that human encyclopedia of birds, visited the island in 1831, attracted by the more than 240 species of seabirds that nest here. The puffin may be the island's symbol, but whales are the stars. Giant finbacks, right whales, minkes, and humpbacks feed in the rich waters. With only 2,700 residents, it may seem remote and quiet, but there is plenty to do including birding, kayaking, whale-watching, and beachcombing. You can visit lighthouses, hike a heritage trail, or just hang around the busy wharves and chat with the fishermen. A day trip is possible, but you'll wish you had planned to stay at least one night.

GETTING HERE AND AROUND

Ferry service to Grand Manan is provided by **Coastal Transport,** which leaves the mainland from Blacks Harbour, off Route 1, and docks at North Head on Grand Manan Island. If you haven't made a reservation online, plan to be at the ferry early for the best chance of getting on. There are four crossings daily year-round, and seven daily between late June and mid-September. Rates are C$35.80 for a car, excluding the driver, and C$12 for adults, payable on return passage from Grand Manan. If you pay on the ferry, you'll need cash or a debit card; online and phone reservations accept credit cards.

Contact **Coastal Transport.** *506/662-3724, 855/882-1978 www.coastaltransport.ca.*

TOURS

Adventure High. Kayaking tours on the Bay of Fundy range from two hours to weeklong trips, and some include a lobster dinner on the beach. You can rent bicycles here, too. *83 Rte. 776, Grand Manan 800/732-5492, 506/662-3563 www.adventurehigh.com From $30.*

WHERE TO STAY

$$ B&B/INN **Inn at Whale Cove Cottages.** The main inn building here dates back to 1816 and has a shared living room with a fireplace and library and traditional, country-style rooms. **Pros:** great rustic feel; lovely property for wandering. **Cons:** restaurant not open all year; only one bathroom has both tub and shower. *Rooms from: C$150 26 Whale Cottage Rd., off Whistle Rd., Grand Manan 506/662-3181 www.whalecovecottages.ca 3 rooms, 5 cottages, 1 apartment Breakfast.*

$ B&B/INN FAMILY **Marathon Inn.** This mansion on 10 acres of grounds has been an inn since 1871; built by a sea captain, it sits on a hill with lovely views over the harbor. **Pros:** good food; family rooms have bunks in separate area; discounts available on kayaking and whale-watching trips; free Wi-Fi and long-distance calls within North America. **Cons:** rooms vary in size. *Rooms from: C$89 19 Marathon La., North Head, Grand Manan 506/662-8488, 888/660-8488 www.marathoninn.com 23 rooms No meals.*

SPORTS AND THE OUTDOORS

WHALE-WATCHING

A whale-watching cruise from Grand Manan takes you well out into the bay. Dress warmly, but some boats have winter jackets, hats, and mittens on board for those who don't heed this advice.

FAMILY **Sea Watch Tours.** Interpreters on these tours are very knowledgeable about the birds, whales, and other marine life you might encounter on your cruise. They also offer trips to Machias Seal Island to view Atlantic puffins, either on land or from the skiff. Trips are four to five hours, late June through late September. ✉ *2476 Rte. 776, Grand Manan* ☎ *877/662–8552, 506/662–8552* 🌐 *www.seawatchtours.com* 💲 *From C$55.*

FAMILY **Whales-n-Sails Adventures.** Board a 60-foot sailboat to visit the whales, with narration by a marine biologist. The trips are great for bird-watching, too, and an alternative trip, on Thursday mornings in July, visits the "dark side" of Grand Manan—the spectacular west side, which has limited land access but stunning views from the water (plus whales and birds). Trips (including hot drinks) are four to five hours long and set out twice daily, at 11:30 and 4, late June through mid-September. Bird-watching charters are also available. ✉ *Grand Manan* ☎ *506/662–1999, 888/994–4044* 🌐 *www.whales-n-sails.com* 💲 *From C$70.*

DEER ISLAND

52 km (32 miles) east of St. Andrews by-the-Sea to Letete, 30 minutes by free ferry from Letete.

One of the pleasures of Deer Island is walking around the fishing wharves like those at Chocolate Cove. Exploring the island takes only a few hours; it's a mere 12 km (7 miles) long, varying in width from almost 5 km (3 miles) to a few hundred feet at some points.

GETTING HERE AND AROUND

From Saint John travel west on Highway 1 and take the St. George exit, then take Route 172 south, a total distance of about 85 km (53 miles). The ferry is free, and runs every 30 minutes from 6:30 am to 5 pm, then hourly, with the last one back to the mainland leaving at 10 pm. There is no public transportation or bike rental on the island, so all but avid hikers will need a car.

EXPLORING

Deer Point. A walk through this small nature park is always pleasant, and a great way to pass the time while waiting for the ferry to Campobello Island. Just a few feet offshore in the Western Passage, the **Old Sow,** the second-largest whirlpool in the world, is visible, but its intensity depends on the state of the tide. The water is always highly active, though, and porpoises can often be seen. ✉ *Deer Island Point Rd.* 🌐 *www.deerislandpointpark.com* 💲 *Free* ⏲ *Always accessible.*

WHERE TO EAT

$$$ SEAFOOD ✕ **45th Parallel Restaurant.** Seafood is an integral part of the home cooking at this casual and friendly motel restaurant. The lobster roll is renowned but you can't go wrong with other country-diner options

like fresh panfried haddock or scallops. Old-fashioned chicken dinners—baked chicken, stuffing, real gravy, mashed potatoes, veggies, and cranberry sauce—are served here, too. Soup, sides, and tea or coffee are included in the price. If you want to have a picnic, the obliging folks here will pack a light lunch for you. Flowers surround the restaurant, and its dining terrace overlooks Passamaquoddy Bay. [$] *Average main: C$21* ✉ *941 Hwy. 772, Fairhaven* ☎ *506/747–2222 year-round, 506/747–2231 May–Oct., 877/747–2231* ⊕ *www.45thparallel.ca* ⏲ *Closed Nov.–Mar. and weekdays Apr., May, and Oct.*

SPORTS AND THE OUTDOORS

Seascape Kayak Tours. Quality sea-kayaking experiences and responsible adventure tourism are provided May to October by this outfitter, which has received international recognition for its sustainable tourism practices and was among *Outside Magazine*'s "30 Most Incredible Trips to Take in 2015." Half-day and full-day tours, and two-hour sunset paddles usually include sightings of wildlife, including seals, porpoises, whales, and bald eagles. ✉ *40 N.W. Harbour Branch Rd., Richardson* ☎ *506/747–1884, 866/747–1884* ⊕ *www.seascapekayaktours.com* 💲 *Sunset paddle C$65, half day C$85, full day C$150.*

CAMPOBELLO ISLAND

40 minutes by ferry (June to September) from Deer Island; 90 km (56 miles) southeast of St. Stephen via bridge from Lubec, Maine.

Fodor's Choice ★ Neatly manicured, preening itself in the bay, Campobello Island has always had a special appeal for the wealthy and the famous.

GETTING HERE AND AROUND

From Saint John, follow the directions for Deer Island. Once on Deer Island, drive 12 km (7 miles) to its southern tip for the East Coast Ferries service to Campobello (C$16 for car and driver, C$3 for each adult passenger, and C$4 fuel surcharge), a journey of around 30 minutes. Ferries from Deer Island run hourly from 8:30 am to 6:30 pm. The company also runs a ferry from Eastport, Maine, to Campobello (C$13 for car and driver, C$3 for each adult passenger, and a C$4 fuel surcharge). Once there, a car is essential.

The ferry from Campobello to Deer Island departs on the hour, every hour, until 7 pm.

Contacts **East Coast Ferries Ltd.** ☎ *506/747–2159, 877/747–2159* ⊕ *www.eastcoastferriesltd.com.*

EXPLORING

Herring Cove Provincial Park. The 425-hectare (1,049-acre) park has camping, a restaurant, playgrounds, a 9-hole, par-36 Geoffrey Cornish golf course, a 1.6-km (1-mile) -long sandy beach, and six hiking trails, one of which follows a logging trail once used by the Roosevelts. ✉ *136 Herring Cove Rd., Welshpool, Campobello* ☎ *506/752–7010, 800/561–0123* 💲 *Free.*

Roosevelt Campobello International Park. The 34-room rustic summer cottage of the family of President Franklin Delano Roosevelt is now part of a nature preserve, Roosevelt Campobello International Park, a joint project of the Canadian and U.S. governments. The miles of trails here make for pleasant strolling. Roosevelt's boyhood summer home was also the setting for the 1960 movie *Sunrise at Campobello*. Twice-daily Tea with Eleanor events include a talk about her life on the island. As an alternative to the ferry from Deer Island, drive across the border into Maine from St. Stephen, go down Route 1, and take Route 189 to Lubec, Maine, then cross the bridge to the island. ✉ *459 Rte. 774, Welshpool, Campobello* ☎ *506/752–2922, 877/851–6663* 🌐 *fdr.net* 💲 *Free* ⏲ *House: mid-May–mid-Oct., daily 10–6 ADT (9–5 EDT). Visitor center: mid-May–mid-Oct., daily 10–6 ADT (9–5 EDT); mid-Oct–Oct. 31, daily 10–5 ADT (9–4 EDT). Grounds: year-round, daily half hr before dawn–half hr after dusk.*

WHERE TO STAY

$$ RENTAL **An Island Chalet.** With stunning coastal views from their windows and front porches, and beds for four people, these log cottages (in spite of the singular name, there are five of them) offer great value. **Pros:** close to the FDR Bridge and Roosevelt-Campobello International Park; plenty of space for the price; a real bargain for a party of four. **Cons:** cell phone reception can be unreliable; beach rather difficult to reach. 💲 *Rooms from: C$125* ✉ *115 Narrows Rd., Welshpool, Campobello* ☎ *506/752–2971* 🌐 *www.anislandchalet.com* 🛏 *5 cottages* 🍴 *No meals.*

$ B&B/INN **The Owen House.** With glorious sea views, this 1835 house is full of antiques and original artwork by the owner, Joyce Morrell. **Pros:** a really peaceful haven, free of everyday distractions; many original features; the library next door has Wi-Fi. **Cons:** two rooms share a bathroom; the only TV is set up for video; not everyone likes a communal breakfast table. 💲 *Rooms from: C$115* ✉ *11 Welshpool St., Welshpool, Campobello* ☎ *506/752–2977* 🌐 *www.owenhouse.ca* 🛏 *9 rooms* 🍴 *Breakfast.*

ST. MARTINS

54 km (34 miles) east of Saint John.

The fishing village of St. Martins has a rich shipbuilding heritage, whispering caves, miles of lovely beaches, spectacular tides, and a cluster of covered bridges, as well as several heritage inns and a couple of restaurants right on the beach. It's also the gateway to the spectacular Fundy Trail Parkway.

GETTING HERE AND AROUND

There is no public transportation to St. Martins. From Saint John drive north on Route 1, then head east on Route 111, past the airport, following signs for St. Martins. Coming from the Trans-Canada Highway (Route 2), exit onto Route 1 or Route 10; both will get you to Route 111, signposted St. Martins.

ESSENTIALS

Visitor Information **Visitor Information Center.** ✉ *Lighthouse, 424 Main St.* ☎ *506/833–2006* 🌐 *www.stmartinscanada.com.*

EXPLORING

Fundy Trail Parkway. The scenic drive portion of the Fundy Trail Parkway extends for 16 km (10 miles) along the clifftops through previously inaccessible wilderness with stunning views, and you can stop along the way at the Interpretive Centre at Big Salmon River. If all goes according to plan, the parkway will go all the way to the Fundy National Park by 2018. Various Stonehammer Geopark activities are offered, including walks with an interpreter. The road closely parallels the cycling/walking Fundy Trail along the shore. There are lots of places to park and many accessible scenic lookouts. The 41-km (24-mile) Fundy Footpath, for expert hikers, already continues through to the national park. The parkway portion operates mid-May through mid-October. ✉ *St. Martins* ☎ *506/833–2019, 866/386–3987* 🌐 *www.fundytrailparkway.com* 💲 *C$5.50* ⏲ *Mid-June–mid-Aug., daily 8–8; mid-Aug–early Sept., daily 9–7; mid-May–mid-June and early Sept.–mid-Oct, daily 9–5.*

WHERE TO STAY

$ B&B/INN **St. Martins Country Inn.** High on a hill overlooking the Bay of Fundy, the appeal of this restored sea captain's home comes from both its Victorian interiors and the accomplished cuisine. **Pros:** breakfast available until 11; good food; restaurant open for breakfast, lunch, and dinner. **Cons:** some rooms are small; decoration may seem a little too "busy" to some. 💲 *Rooms from: C$119* ✉ *303 Main St.* ☎ *506/833–4534, 800/565–5257* 🌐 *www.stmartinscountryinn.ca* 🛏 *16 rooms* 🍽 *Breakfast.*

$ B&B/INN **Tidal Watch Inn.** This luxurious property is situated just where the highest tides in the world sweep in and out each day, a mere 150 feet away! **Pros:** comfortable style and atmosphere; good food. **Cons:** some rooms are in newer additions; not all rooms have good views; Wi-Fi not reliable in some rooms. 💲 *Rooms from: C$110* ✉ *16 Beach St.* ☎ *888/833–4772* 🌐 *www.tidalwatchinn.ca* 🛏 *15 rooms* 🍽 *Breakfast.*

FUNDY NATIONAL PARK

135 km (84 miles) northeast of Saint John.

Fodor's Choice ★ Preserving a unique wilderness on the shores of the Bay of Fundy, this national park is the province's top attraction, with areas of true wilderness, beaches, rocky headlands, sea caves and inlets, wildlife, and stunning vistas. In June 2015 the federal government announced a multimillion dollar investment in the park to improve access roads, the trails network, and visitor amenities.

GETTING HERE AND AROUND

Fundy National Park is bisected by Route 114, which loops down from just east of Sussex, leaves the park at Alma, and follows the coast, via Riverview, to Moncton. From the Trans-Canada Highway (Route 2), exit onto Route 10 to Sussex, take Route 1 east for a short distance (signposted Moncton) before exiting onto Route 114 south. There are a number of parking places within the park.

EXPLORING

Alma. The small seaside village of Alma services Fundy National Park with motels, restaurants that serve good lobster, and a bakery that sells sublime sticky buns. There's plenty to do around here—from bird-watching and kayaking to horseback riding. ✉ *Alma* ⊕ *www.villageofalma.ca.*

Fodor's Choice ★ **Fundy National Park.** This incredible 206-square-km (80-square-mile) park is a microcosm of New Brunswick's inland and coastal climates, and has been designated a Dark Sky Preserve by the Royal Astronomical Society of Canada, in recognition of its superb night skies free of light pollution. Park naturalists offer several programs each day, including beach walks and hikes to explore the park's unique climatic conditions and the fascinating evolution evident in the forests. The park has 100 km (60 miles) of varied hiking and mountain-biking trails, camping, golf, tennis, a heated Bay of Fundy saltwater pool, and a playground. Among the most scenic of the trails is Laverty Falls, a 2½-km (1½-mile) trail that takes you on an ascent through hardwood forests to the beautiful Laverty waterfall and arrives at the old Shepody Road. At Third Vault Falls, a 3.7-km (2.3-mile) trail starting from the Laverty Auto Trail Parking Lot, hikers emerge at the falls and can take a refreshing dip in the pool. On the way to the Coppermine Trail, a hike to an abandoned mine at Point Wolfe, visitors wind around a steep curve and through a bright-red covered bridge, a favorite spot for photographers. In the evening there are interactive programs in the amphitheater and campfires. The more than 600 campsites range from full-service to wilderness, and yurts and "oTENTik" accommodations—a combination of tent and cabin—are also available. ✉ *Rte. 114, Alma* ☎ *506/887–6000* ⊕ *www.pc.gc.ca* 🎟 *C$7.80* ⏲ *Accessible year-round; full services July and Aug.; limited services May, June, Sept., and Oct.* ⏲ *Visitor Reception Centre and campgrounds closed mid-Oct.–mid-May.*

WHERE TO STAY

$$ B&B/INN **Falcon Ridge Inn.** Perched high above the village and the ocean, every window (and there are many) in this modern property affords a spectacular view and eliminates any need for air-conditioning. **Pros:** amazing view of the fishing boats of Alma and shale cliffs of Fundy; full breakfast served at individual tables; good-value packages available. **Cons:** Fundy fog can unexpectedly block the vista; you can walk to the village, but it's a steep slope back up. 💲 *Rooms from: C$135* ✉ *24 Falcon Ridge Dr., Alma* ☎ *506/887–1110, 888/321–9090* ⊕ *www.falconridgeinn.nb.ca* 🛏 *4 rooms* 🍴 *Breakfast.*

$ B&B/INN **Parkland Village Inn.** Right on the water, next to the fishermen's wharf in the heart of the bustling village, this long-established inn also has a very good restaurant. **Pros:** view of the Bay of Fundy is extraordinary; nine of the guest rooms overlook the bay. **Cons:** can be hard to get a room or table in peak season; breakfast not included in July and August rates. 💲 *Rooms from: C$120* ✉ *8601 Main St., Alma* ☎ *506/887–2313, 866/668–4337* ⊕ *www.parklandvillageinn.com* ⏲ *Closed Nov.–Apr.* 🛏 *10 rooms, 5 suites* 🍴 *No meals.*

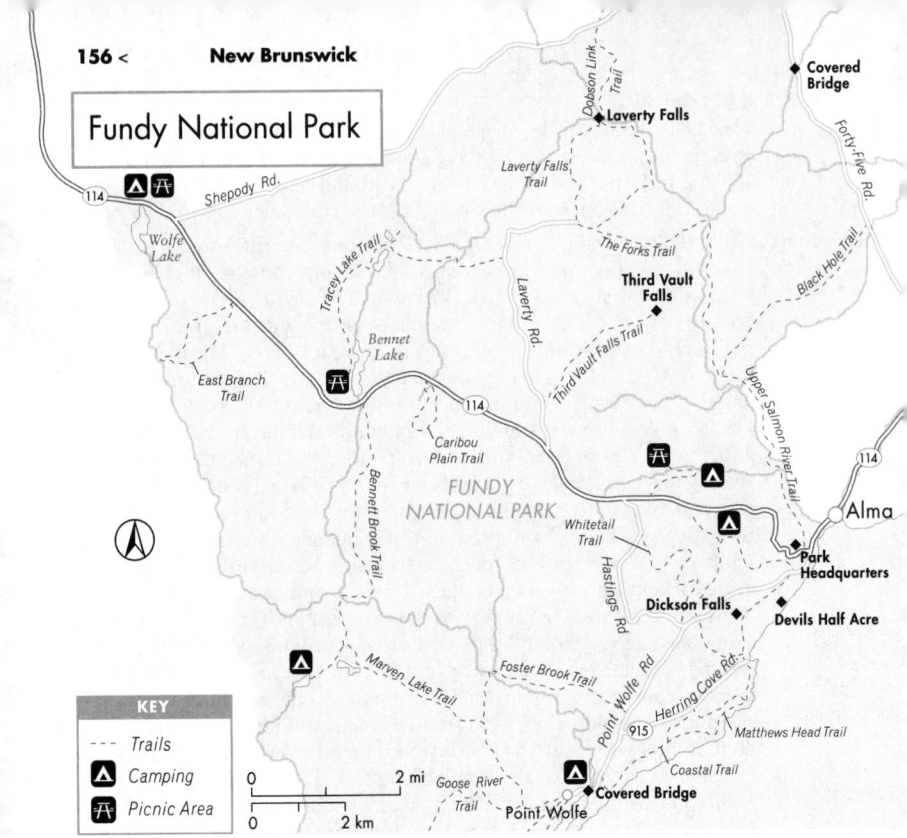

SPORTS AND THE OUTDOORS

GOLF

Fundy National Park Golf Club. This is one of the province's most beautiful and challenging 9-hole courses, near cliffs overlooking the restless Bay of Fundy. Designed by course architect Stanley Thompson, it has some interesting hazards—the 6th green is particularly tricky—and quite taxing elevations (but carts are available), not to mention the distraction of the wonderful views. ✉ *Fundy National Park, near the Alma entrance, Alma* ☎ *506/887–2970* 🌐 *www.pc.gc.ca/eng/pn-np/fundy/activ/ete-summer/golf.aspx* 💲 *C$15.70–C$18.60 for 9 holes; daily rate C$27.40–C$33.30* ⛳ *9 holes, 3083 yards, par 70* ⏲ *Closed early Oct.–mid-May.*

SEA KAYAKING

FreshAir Adventure. Bay of Fundy sea-kayaking excursions last from a half day to three days. Guides, instruction, park fees, and equipment are provided, including camping gear and meals for multiday trips. ✉ *16 Fundy View Dr., Alma* ☎ *506/887–2249, 800/545–0020* 🌐 *www.freshairadventure.com* 💲 *C$69 for half day, C$117 for full day, C$398 for 2 days, C$498 for 3 days* ⏲ *Closed mid-Sept.–early May.*

CAPE ENRAGE, HOPEWELL CAPE, AND NEARBY

15 km (9 miles) east of Alma to Cape Enrage; 40 km (25 miles) from Alma to Hopewell Cape.

Rocky Cape Enrage juts more than 7 km (4½ miles) out into the bay, with a 6-km (4-mile) driftwood-cluttered beach, a lighthouse, and spectacular views, as well as an adventure center with a restaurant. Farther east along the coast, Hopewell Cape has the remarkable phenomenon of the Hopewell Rocks—tiny islands at high tide that reveal themselves as lofty columns rising from the beach at low tide. Between the two capes there are internationally significant nature reserves, an enclave of artists and artisans with studios and galleries to visit, and opportunities for outdoor activities.

GETTING HERE AND AROUND

From Alma, Route 114 follows a scenic route through Riverside-Albert, around Hopewell Cape and all the way to Moncton. There is no public transportation and the only option is to drive. For Cape Enrage, branch off via Route 915.

ESSENTIALS

Visitor Information **Cape Enrage Interpretive Center.** ✉ *650 Cape Enrage Rd., Waterside* ☎ *506/887-2273, 888/423-5454* ⊕ *www.capeenrage.ca.*

EXPLORING

Cape Enrage. If the name of the cape isn't enough of a hint, the 140-year-old (still-working) lighthouse perched on the end of its rocky promontory says much about the nature of the waters here. Add tides that rise as much as 53 vertical feet and this becomes a must-see. If the zip-lining, rappeling, and rock-climbing opportunities represent too much excitement, you can walk the boardwalk to a viewing platform below the lighthouse, and from there head down to the long, "wilderness" beach below (check tide times and leave at least two hours before high tide; staff can advise). ✉ *Cape Enrage Rd., Waterside* ☎ *506/887-2273, 888/423-5454* ⊕ *www.capeenrage.ca* 💲 *C$5 mid-May–mid-Oct.*

FAMILY
Fodor's Choice
★

Hopewell Rocks. These famous "giant flowerpots" have been carved by the Bay of Fundy tides. They're topped with vegetation and form tiny islands at high tide, while low tide reveals the entire columns and you can descend to the exposed seabed for closer study. There are also trails, an interactive visitor center, a café-restaurant, a gift shop, and a children's play area. Guided tours are available. It's about a 15-minute walk from the visitor center to the rocks, but there's also a shuttle service (C$2 each way). The tide comes in very quickly, so check tide tables, keep an eye on your watch, and exit the beach with time to spare. ✉ *131 Discovery Rd., Hopewell Cape* ☎ *877/734-3429* ⊕ *www.thehopewellrocks.ca* 💲 *C$9 (valid for 2 consecutive days)* ⏲ *Mid-June–mid-Aug., daily 8–8; mid-Aug.–early Sept., daily 9–7; mid-May–mid-June and early Sept.–mid-Oct., daily 9–5. Visitors may enter the park on foot in the off-season, but no facilities are open.*

Shepody National Wildlife Area. The three main areas of this freshwater preserve—Germantown Marsh, Mary's Point, and New Horton—comprise an important habitat for species including the American bittern, sora, and pied-billed grebe, and are also a staging point for tens of thousands of migrating shorebirds, such as American black duck, green- and blue-winged teal, and ring-necked duck. The mammal population includes moose, bobcats, white-tailed deer, coyotes, otters, and mink. The shoreline at Mary's Point—a Ramsar-designated conservation site—offers spectacular sightings during the peak season from July 20 through mid-August, and also has an interpretation center. Shepody is a great place for hiking, and at Mary's Point you can follow the shoreline and stroll through forests for land-bird sightings, which include bald eagles and peregrine falcons. The area, now a bird sanctuary and interpretive center, is near Riverside-Albert. ✉ *Riverside-Albert* ✣ *Germantown Marsh is on Hwy. 114; Mary's Point and New Horton are off Rte. 915 near Riverside-Albert* ☎ *800/668–6767* 🌐 *www.naturenb.ca/programs/marys-point/* 💲 *Free.*

WHERE TO STAY

$$ B&B/INN **Florentine Manor Heritage Inn.** With beautiful antique furniture and handmade quilts on the beds, this restored shipbuilder's house is a haven for honeymooners and romantics, and the Fundy Coast is close by. **Pros:** comfortably decorated, but not overstuffed rooms; abundant birdlife; good breakfasts. **Cons:** minimum two-night stay. 💲 *Rooms from: C$125* ✉ *356 Rte. 915, Harvey on the Bay* ☎ *506/882–2271, 800/665–2271* 🌐 *www.florentinemanor.com* 🛏 *8 rooms* 🍽 *Breakfast.*

$ B&B/INN **Innisfree Bed and Breakfast.** An 1847 farmhouse just minutes from Hopewell Rocks now provides stylish and comfortable accommodations in rooms furnished with antiques and quilts. **Pros:** closest bed-and-breakfast to Hopewell Rocks; friendly, helpful hosts; mountain bikes for rent. **Cons:** may be too quiet for some. 💲 *Rooms from: C$120* ✉ *4270 Hwy. 114, Hopewell Cape* ☎ *506/734–3510* 🌐 *www.innisfreebandb.com* 🛏 *5 rooms, 1 suite* 🍽 *Breakfast.*

SPORTS AND THE OUTDOORS

HORSEBACK RIDING

FAMILY **Broadleaf Guest Ranch.** Horseback trail rides go through lowland marshes or along the beach, and options include a six-hour excursion with lunch. Various combinations of riding, cycling, canoeing, and indoor rock-wall climbing are also offered, and in winter there's also cross-country skiing, snowshoeing, sleigh rides, and other pursuits. Packages, including accommodations at the ranch, are also available. ✉ *5526 Rte. 114, Hopewell Hill* ☎ *506/882–2349, 800/226–5405* 🌐 *www.broadleafranch.com* 💲 *C$30 for half-hr ride; C$175 for 6-hr ride including lunch.*

SEA KAYAKING

Baymount Outdoor Adventures. This company provides guided sea kayaking tours at Hopewell Rocks Provincial Park and also offers hiking and biking tours on the Bay of Fundy. ✉ *Hopewell Cape* ☎ *506/734–2660, 877/601–2660* 🌐 *www.baymountadventures.com* 💲 *From C$59.*

ZIP-LINING

Cape Enrage Adventures. Activities includes rappelling, rock-climbing, and zip-lining, and prices, which start at C$45 for 3 zip-line runs and C$90 for rappelling, include admission to the cape. The zip line is usually open daily in the season, but reservations are required for other activities. Weight restrictions for the zip line are 75–275 pounds, which may be adjusted due to weather conditions. A restaurant and a gift shop are on-site. ✉ *650 Cape Enrage Rd., off Rte. 915* ☎ *506/887–2273, 888/423–5454* 🌐 *www.capeenrage.ca* ⏲ *Closed mid-Sept.–June.*

SHOPPING

Albert County Clay Company. In a large converted community hall, Judy Tait makes beautiful and stylish pottery from local clay, imprinted with the forms of leaves and wildflowers. ✉ *900 Albert Mines Rd., Curryville* ✣ *Off Rte. 114 near Hopewell* ☎ *506/734–2851* 🌐 *www.albertcountyclayco.com* ⏲ *Closed late Sept.–Apr.*

Farm Life Studio. Normand Brandford's paintings and prints reflect his affinity with farm animals—some living examples of the subject matter look on from the surrounding pastures—as well as local wildlife, landscapes, and nostalgic scenes. ✉ *474 Albert Mines Rd., Albert Mines, Hopewell Cape* ☎ *506/734–3493* ⏲ *Closed Nov.–Mar.*

Studio on the Marsh. In a perfect setting for wildlife art, this studio sells prints by the late Lars Larsen. His New Brunswick scenes in particular make excellent souvenirs. ✉ *255 Marys Point Rd., off Rte. 915, Harvey-Albert* ☎ *506/882–2917* 🌐 *www.studioonthemarsh.com.*

Wendy Johnston's Pottery and Art Effects Fine Craft Gallery. Contemporary, functional, brightly colored pieces with abstract designs are produced here and the gallery represents more than 50 Maritimes artists and artisans. Call to check opening hours in the off-season. ✉ *3923 Rte. 114, Hopewell Cape* ☎ *506/734–2046* 🌐 *www.wendyjohnstonpottery.com.*

MONCTON AND DIEPPE

80 km (50 miles) northeast of Alma.

Metro Moncton—the second-largest city in Atlantic Canada (after Halifax, Nova Scotia)—is an attractive, welcoming city, with several family-friendly attractions, some world-class restaurants, a splendid new museum, and an ongoing calendar of festivals throughout the year.

Two natural attractions are the main draws here: the Tidal Bore and the Magnetic Hill. The latter is often derided, but the optical illusion does create a very strange sensation and it's worth experiencing. The Tidal Bore, once justifiably described as the other kind of bore, has been restored to its former glory now that riverbank erosion has been addressed, and the bore can be several feet high, depending on the tides. As a result, the city is now making the most of its downtown riverside, with a park and boardwalk and an amphitheater overlooking the best place to view the tidal bore sweep around a bend in the river. In summer, buskers often take advantage of this "stage."

Moncton is an agreeable, lively place, home to two universities and a center for information technology and communications. It is often called the Gateway to Acadia because of its equal mix of English and French and its proximity to the Acadian shore, though it also has a large Irish population and a growing Korean community. The renovated downtown has unique shops and restaurants and such beautiful flower displays that it has won national "Communities in Bloom" awards.

With its twin city of Dieppe—the join is almost imperceptible—Moncton is considered the shopping mecca of Atlantic Canada. Moncton's big chain stores are mostly strung out along Mountain Road and the Trinity Power Centre, while Dieppe is home to Champlain Place, the province's biggest shopping mall. Both cities have good Saturday farmers' markets, and other retail opportunities.

GETTING HERE AND AROUND

Moncton is one of the few places in the province accessible by rail, on VIA Rail's Montréal—Halifax route known as "The Ocean," which runs three times a week. Dieppe is home to Greater Moncton International Airport, one of the province's major airports. Maritime Bus provides long-distance bus service from points all along the Trans-Canada Highway between Québec and Nova Scotia, from Saint John, and down the Acadian Coast from Campbellton. By road, the Trans-Canada Highway (Route 2) loops around the city, with several exit points.

Moncton and Dieppe have an excellent bus system, operated by Codiac Transit; the fare is C$2.25, or you can buy a 10-trip pass for C$19 or a 20-day pass for C$37, available from the bus station at 140 Millennium Boulevard or Shoppers Drug Marts (535 Edinburgh Dr. or 860 Mountain Rd.). Free transfers are available from the driver if you need to change buses to get to a single destination. Buses are equipped with bike racks.

ESSENTIALS

Bus Information **Codiac Transit.** ✉ *140 Millennium Blvd., Moncton* ☎ *506/857-2008* ⊕ *www.codiactranspo.ca.*

Visitor Information **Moncton Visitor Information Centre.** ✉ *Resurgo Place, 20 Mountain Rd., Moncton* ☎ *800/363-4558* ⊕ *www.tourism.moncton.ca.*

TOURS

Roads to Sea. Guided tours run May through October, leaving Moncton for a full-day jaunt along the Bay of Fundy, including the Hopewell Rocks, Cape Enrage, the Fundy National Park, covered bridges, and more. In the off-season, two-hour tours of Moncton are offered for a minimum of four people. ☎ *506/850-7623, 877/850-7623* ⊕ *www.roadstosea.com* 💲 *Moncton tour C$55; coast tour C$167.26.*

Taste This! Moncton has some great restaurants and food producers, and these walking tours, led by enthusiastic and knowledgeable guides, will enable you to sample some of the highlights, including local, traditional, and international flavors, the people behind them, and their inspirational stories. Tours run year-round Tuesday–Saturday, 1–4 and 5–7:30 pm. ✉ *Moncton* ☎ *888/647-9919* ⊕ *www.eastcoast-taste-this.com* 💲 *From C$49.*

EXPLORING

TOP ATTRACTIONS

FAMILY **Magic Mountain Water Park.** This is an excellent water theme park, adjacent to Magnetic Hill. It includes a huge wave pool, thrill-ride body slides, tube and matting rides, and gentler fun including a Splashpad and

Puddle Jumpers Pond. ✉ *2875 Mountain Rd., Moncton ✣ Off Trans-Canada Hwy. Exit 450 (Mountain Rd.) on the outskirts of Moncton* ☎ *506/857–9283* ⊕ *www.magicmountain.ca* 💲 *C$28.50 full-day pass; C$20 afternoon pass* ⏲ *Mid-June–end June and late Aug.–early Sept., daily 10–6; July–late Aug., daily 10–7 (mini-golf until 10 pm all season).*

FAMILY Fodor's Choice ★ **Magnetic Hill.** A bizarre optical illusion has been attracting visitors since the days of horse-drawn wagons. If you park your car in neutral at the designated spot, you seem to be coasting uphill without power. Don't be tempted to turn the vehicle around; the effect is most pronounced when you are going backwards. Get out and try it on foot and it seems harder to walk downhill than up. There are shops and a restaurant within the attached Wharf Village. ✉ *Moncton ✣ North of Moncton off Trans-Canada Hwy. Exit 450 (Mountain Rd.); watch for signs* ☎ *506/384–9527* ⊕ *www.magnetichill.com* 💲 *C$5 per car* ⏲ *July and Aug., daily 8–7; mid-May–June and Sept.–mid-Oct., daily 8–5.*

FAMILY **Magnetic Hill Zoo.** This is the largest zoo in Atlantic Canada, covering 40 acres and housing 575 animals, including a Big Cat exhibit housing two Amur tigers and a leopard in a replication of a Siberian landscape (the New Brunswick climate is also similar to that of Siberia). In addition to imaginative viewing areas, the cats are fed from a zip line, which encourages them to chase and jump. There's no shortage of other exotic species, including lemurs, lions and other big cats, zebras, and ostriches, and around 80 bird species are represented, both indigenous and exotic. A tropical house has reptiles, amphibians, birds, and primates, and at Old MacDonald's Barnyard, children can pet domestic animals or ride a pony in summer. Check feeding times on the way in. ✉ *125 Magic Mountain Rd., Moncton ✣ Off Trans-Canada Hwy. Exit 450 (Mountain Rd.), on the outskirts of Moncton* ☎ *506/877–7718* ⊕ *www.moncton.ca/zoo* 💲 *C$14.99 late June–early Sept.; C$11.99 mid-May–late June and early Sept.–Dec.; C$8.99 mid-Apr.–mid-May* ⏲ *Mid-Apr.–mid-May, daily 10–4; mid-May–early Sept., daily 9–7; early Sept.–late Oct., weekdays 10–6; weekends 9–6; Nov.–early Dec., daily 10–3; early Dec.–Dec. 30, weekdays 5–9, weekends 3–9.*

FAMILY **Resurgo Place.** In a bright new building, this imaginative and highly engaging museum relates the history of Moncton from its earliest settlement, through its various ups and downs (*Resurgo* means "I rise again"), to the present day. Rather than just a collection of old stuff in glass cases, the museum seeks to conjure up a feeling of the age, and technology is used to involve visitors in their discoveries—in one transportation gallery push-carts fitted with iPads connect with various points on the floor, allowing you to explore each subject on the screen before rolling along to the next. The museum also has a great area for kids, where learning through fun activities is taken to a new level to help develop their thought processes. Before you leave, ask if you can try the "Backward Brain Bicycle." ✉ *20 Mountain Rd., Moncton* ☎ *506/856–4383* ⊕ *resurgo.ca* 💲 *C$10 (C$5 Thurs. 5–8 pm)* ⏲ *Mon.–Sat. 10–5, Thurs. 10–8, Sun. noon–5.*

Aberdeen Cultural Centre 2
Acadian Museum 1
Lutz Mountain Heritage Museum 5
Magic Moutain Water Park..... 8
Magnetic Hill ... 6
Magnetic Hill Zoo 7
Resurgo Place.....3
Tidal Bore and Riverfront Park 4

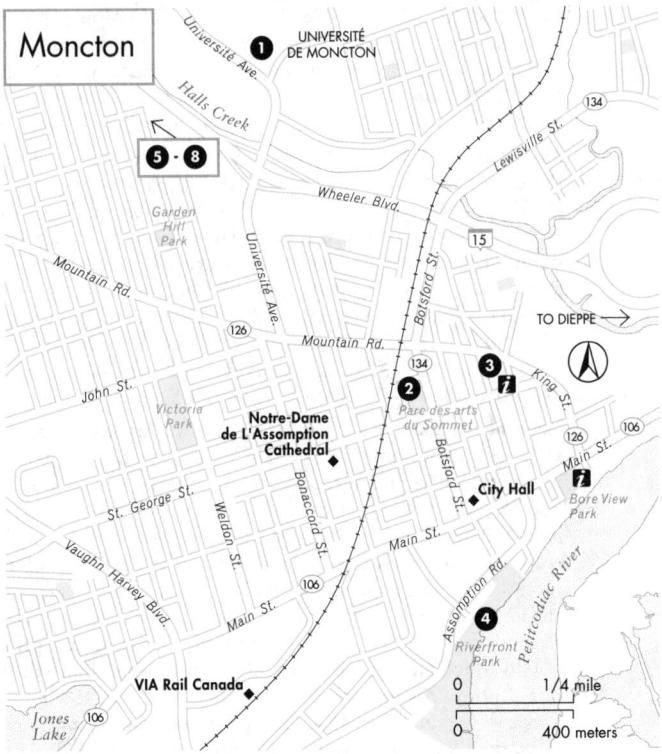

Fodor's Choice ★ **Tidal Bore and Riverfront Park.** When the world's highest tides come in on the Bay of Fundy, the surge of water pushes far upstream on the Petitcodiac River, reversing the flow with a wall of water that raises the level by up to roughly 25 feet and fills the river to its banks. It is an incredible sight, particularly when tides are at their highest. Bore Park on Main Street is the best vantage point, with terraced seating and, in summer, an introductory talk; viewing times are posted. The park is part of the larger **Riverfront Park**, with 5 km (3 miles) of multiuse trails along the banks of the river. Warning: entering the water is extremely dangerous because of the deep, soft mud that lines the river. ✉ *Main St., Moncton.*

WORTH NOTING

Aberdeen Cultural Centre. The halls of the Aberdeen Cultural Centre, a converted schoolhouse home to theater and dance companies, a framing shop, artists' ateliers, and several galleries, ring with music and chatter. **Galerie 12** represents leading contemporary Acadian artists. **Galerie Sans Nom** is an artist-run co-op supporting avant-garde artists from throughout Canada. The artist-run **IMAGO Inc.** is the only print-production shop in the province. Guided tours are available by appointment. ✉ *140 Botsford St., Moncton* ☎ *506/857–9597* ⊕ *www.centreculturelaberdeen.ca* ✉ *Free* ⏲ *Weekdays 10–4.*

Acadian Museum. On the campus of the University of Moncton, this museum has a remarkable collection of artifacts reflecting 300 years of Acadian life in the Maritimes. There's also a fine art gallery showcasing contemporary works by local and national artists. The university is also home to several pieces of public art, so look out for these as you drive through. ✉ *Clement-Cormier Bldg., 405 University Ave., Moncton* ☎ *506/858–4088* ⊕ *www.umoncton.ca/umcm-maum* 💲 *C$4* ⏲ *June–Sept., weekdays 10–5, weekends 1–5; Oct.–May, Tues.–Fri. 1–4:30, weekends 1–4.*

Lutz Mountain Heritage Museum. If you love antiques and would thrill at the notion of discovering an old barn or attic crammed with centuries-old artifacts, it's worth the short trip out from downtown Moncton. Within a restored 1883 meetinghouse, you'll find authentic household, work-related, schoolroom, and even military items of the area's non-Acadian pioneer settlers, including the Lutz family, from as far back as 1766. Ignore your first impression—there's more than immediately meets the eye when you enter, with more than 3,000 artifacts crammed into the upper floor and basement areas as well as the main level and guided tours tell fascinating stories of ordinary people. ✉ *3143 Mountain Rd., Moncton* ☎ *506/384–7719* ⊕ *www.lutzmtnheritage.ca* 💲 *C$2 suggested donation* ⏲ *Mid-June–mid-Sept., Mon.–Sat. 9–5; rest of year by appointment.*

WHERE TO EAT

$ ECLECTIC ✕ **Café Archibald.** This is a great little place for a quick bite or bistro meal in pleasant surroundings at any time of the day—breakfast is served from 7 am and it's open until 11 pm (midnight on Friday and Saturday). Fresh pastries are baked every morning and the open kitchen serves very good crepes, pizzas, salads, sandwiches, and desserts. There's a huge range of coffees and teas as well as wine and beer. There's another branch in Dieppe at 216 Chemin Gauvin. $ *Average main: C$10* ✉ *221 Mountain Rd., Moncton* ☎ *506/853–8819* ⊕ *www.cafearchibald.com.*

$$ VEGETARIAN FAMILY ✕ **Calactacus Vegetarian Restaurant.** It looks inviting from the outside, and you'll be glad you ventured inside as soon as you are engulfed by the tempting aromas emanating from the world of flavors offered on the menu. Specialties include Oaxaca Deep Dish (black beans, grilled veggies, and spicy tomato sauce, baked with cheese), a classic vegetarian lasagna, the Big Marc vegetarian burger, and the highly recommended Taj Mahal Thali, with curried lentils, mixed vegetables, and spiced chickpea sauce, served with pakoras, prune chutney, and chapati. Salads, flutes, melts, pizzas, and vegan desserts are also on the menu, and the kids' menu has a remarkable choice of interesting healthy choices. Fair-trade coffees, craft beers, and organic wines complete the experience. $ *Average main: C$14* ✉ *125 Church St., Moncton* ☎ *506/388–4833* ⊕ *calactacus.ca.*

$$$$ MODERN FRENCH Fodor's Choice ★ ✕ **Little Louis'.** One of the finest restaurants in Atlantic Canada, Little Louis' is well worth seeking out in its unlikely location on a predominantly industrial street. The modern French menu offers complex but perfectly balanced creations based on local seafood, beef, lamb, and poultry, and the daily tasting menu, which comes with or without wine pairings, is a delicious and artistic culinary adventure. Desserts to leave

you speechless include crème brûlée with a basket of fruit and ice-wine pearls, and a much heralded mini-meringue pie with maple. Elegant surroundings, a first-rate wine list, and impeccable service complete the experience. [$] *Average main: C$45* ✉ *245 Collishaw St., Moncton* ☎ *506/855–2022* 🌐 *www.littlelouis.ca* ⏲ *No lunch.*

$$ ✕ **Pastalli Italian Cucina.** Seafood, steaks, lamb, and veal share the menu
ITALIAN with pasta and pizzas at this upbeat Italian restaurant where Old World flavors are showcased in a friendly setting. The large portions and the bread bar are almost as popular as the World Wine Cellar. Reservations are advisable. [$] *Average main: C$18* ✉ *611 Main St., Moncton* ☎ *506/383–1050* 🌐 *www.pastalli.com.*

$$$ ✕ **St James' Gate.** Named after the Guinness brewery in Dublin, this is by
ECLECTIC no means your standard Irish-theme pub. It is as authentic a re-creation of an ancient vaulted stone cellar as you will find, providing an atmospheric location to enjoy the accomplished cooking. The menu is strong on local seafood, such as Atlantic salmon with a hazelnut crust and apple butter, and meat dishes such as Angus beef tenderloin with blue cheese tarragon butter and red wine au jus are equally delicious. There are also snacks, lighter meals, and pub favorites. There's a central, dark-wood bar, a street-side patio, and live music five nights a week. [$] *Average main: C$27* ✉ *14 Church St., Moncton* ☎ *506/388–4283, 888/782–1414 reservations* 🌐 *www.stjamesmoncton.com* ⏲ *No dinner Sun.*

$$ ✕ **Tide and Boar.** The name is a fun play on words, referencing the prox-
ECLECTIC imity of Moncton's tidal bore (and the seafood and boar on the menu), but this classy gastropub is very serious about food, earning it a place on *Maclean's Magazine*'s list of Canada's Top 50 restaurants and a very loyal local following. The well-constructed menu includes upscale pub favorites and inventive combinations, as in the cumin-crusted lamb shank and Cornish hen with arugula pesto, wild grains, and portobello mushrooms. The drinks menu is long, focusing mainly on draught and bottled craft beers. [$] *Average main: C$18* ✉ *700 Main St., Moncton* ☎ *506/857–9118* 🌐 *www.tideandboar.com.*

$$$$ ✕ **Windjammer.** Lists of Canada's top restaurants all include the Wind-
INTERNATIONAL jammer, the richly elegant dining room of the Delta Beauséjour Hotel,
Fodor's Choice where a memorable, pampering dining experience is assured. It's mod-
★ eled after the opulent luxury liners of the early 1900s, with lots of dark wood and brass, and creates an equally rarified atmosphere without being stuffy. The staff is attentive, knowledgeable, and friendly. Executive chef Stefan Mueller's menus feature seasonal ingredients from land and sea and some vegetables, herbs, and edible flowers come from the hotel's roof garden, which also supplies honey from its working beehives. An exceptional choice of seafood includes oysters and caviar appetizers, and a sumptuous specialty steak-house menu features PEI Blue Dot, Australian Wagyu, and Kobe beef. The Chef's Tasting Menu, featuring ingredients sourced within 160 km (100 miles), is worth every cent of the C$78 price tag. [$] *Average main: C$50* ✉ *Delta Beauséjour Hotel, 750 Main St., Moncton* ☎ *506/877–7137* 🌐 *www.deltahotels.com* ⏲ *Closed Sun. and Mon.* ✍ *Reservations essential.*

WHERE TO STAY

$$ HOTEL FAMILY **Crowne Plaza.** This upscale, modern hotel has a wide range of amenities and it's in a great downtown location, with terrific views from the upper levels. **Pros:** great range of amenities; very friendly and helpful staff; views extend across downtown and the river. **Cons:** limited parking; room renovation work planned. *$ Rooms from: C$129 ✉ 1005 Main St., Moncton ☎ 506/854–5340, 866/854–4656 reservations 🌐 www.cpmoncton.com 🛏 181 rooms, 10 suites 🍽 No meals.*

$$ HOTEL FAMILY Fodor's Choice ★ **Delta Beauséjour.** In a great downtown location, this is one of Moncton's finest and friendliest hotels, catering equally to business travelers vacationers, and families, who particularly enjoy the 125-foot indoor waterslide at the indoor pool. **Pros:** right in the hub of downtown; some rooms overlook the river, with good tidal bore viewing. **Cons:** upcoming renovation work. *$ Rooms from: C$159 ✉ 750 Main St., Moncton ☎ 506/854–4344, 888/351–7666 🌐 www.deltahotels.com 🛏 298 rooms, 6 suites 🍽 No meals.*

$ B&B/INN **Magnetic Hill Winery and B&B.** On Lutz Mountain, with a panoramic view over Moncton, this delightful bed-and-breakfast offers warm and friendly personal service from a wine-making family. **Pros:** price includes wine tastings; near Magnetic Hill attractions. **Cons:** Some distance out of town. *$ Rooms from: C$99 ✉ 860 Front Mountain Rd., Moncton ✣ North of Hwy. 2, Exit 450. After turning off Mountain Rd. onto Front Mountain Rd., ignore the Magnetic Hill B&B on the left; the Winery B&B is a little farther on the right ☎ 506/384–9463 🌐 www.magnetichillwinery.com 🛏 2 rooms 🍽 Breakfast.*

$$ HOTEL FAMILY **Rodd Moncton.** In an ideal location right next to Bore Park, the riverfront trail, and many downtown restaurants, this is a gem of a hotel that's run by the friendliest staff you could wish to meet. **Pros:** great river views from some rooms; free Wi-Fi and local calls; free on-site parking. **Cons:** soundproofing could be better; no on-site restaurant (but many great options in walking distance); outdoor pool is nice but quite small. *$ Rooms from: C$150 ✉ 434 Main St., Moncton ☎ 506/382–1664 🌐 www.roddvacations.com/rodd-moncton 🛏 96 rooms, 1 suite 🍽 Breakfast.*

NIGHTLIFE AND PERFORMING ARTS

NIGHTLIFE

Casino New Brunswick. Along with its gaming tables and slots, the casino has a large, state-of-the-art concert hall with a mixed lineup ranging from Charley Pride to Boston to Weird Al Yankovic to Whoopi Goldberg. Lesser-known local acts entertain for free in the pub on weekends. The casino is open from 7 am to 3 am (24 hours on weekends), with table games from noon. *✉ 21 Casino Dr., Moncton ☎ 506/859–7770, 877/859–7775 🌐 www.casinonb.ca.*

Navigators Pub. An antidote to the trendy Rouge next door, Navigators Pub is a no-frills downtown watering hole offering live music, including Acadian reggae on Monday and rock Tuesday through Thursday and Sunday. It has a particularly nice (and sheltered) patio. It's open until 2 am, and music starts at 10. *✉ 191 Robinson Crt., Moncton ☎ 506/854–8427 bar, 506/871–5370 office 🌐 www.navspub.ca.*

The Old Triangle Irish Alehouse. A good re-creation of the quintessential Dublin pub, this place has a buzzing atmosphere, good food, and live music Wednesday through Saturday—some Irish, some easy listening. On weekend afternoons, local Celtic musicians get together here for an informal *seisun* (jam). ✉ *751 Main St., Moncton* ☎ *506/384–7474* 🌐 *www.oldtrianglemoncton.com.*

Pump House Brewery. In addition to the house brews, you can enjoy live music Saturday nights. The pub is also a venue for the HubCap Comedy Festival in February. ✉ *5 Orange La., Moncton* ☎ *506/855–2337* 🌐 *www.pumphousebrewery.ca.*

PERFORMING ARTS

Capitol Theatre. A restored 1920s vaudeville stage, the opulent Capitol Theatre is a beautiful attraction in itself as well as a venue for plays, musicals, ballets, and concerts. Free tours are given when guides are available; call ahead. ✉ *811 Main St., Moncton* ☎ *506/856–4379, 800/567–1922 toll-free in Canada* 🌐 *www.capitol.nb.ca.*

SPORTS AND THE OUTDOORS

GOLF

The Moncton area is home to two of New Brunswick's four signature golf courses.

Fox Creek Golf Club. This is an exceptional course, fast becoming famous for its architectural and natural beauty. Play begins with an uphill shot to the 1st and ends with a long par five at the 18th, with some unique challenges in between—watch out for some high hills, sloped greens, and water and front guard bunkers on the par 3 4th hole. ✉ *200 Golf St., Dieppe* ☎ *506/859–4653* 🌐 *www.foxcreekgolfclub.ca* 💲 *C$99* ⛳ *18 holes, 6065 yards, par 62.*

Royal Oaks Golf Club. This PGA Championship course was the first Canadian course designed by the U.S. golf course architect Rees Jones. ' Its bent grass fairways, strategic bunkering, and plenty of water hazards present a rewarding challenge, and you'll need to be aware of prevailing winds in some areas. There' a dress code and only soft-spiked shoes are permitted. ✉ *401 Royal Oaks Blvd., Moncton* ✢ *5 km (3 miles) north of the Trans-Canada Hwy. off Elmwood Dr.* ☎ *506/388–6257* 🌐 *www.royaloaks.ca* 💲 *C$85; twilight C$59.99* ⛳ *18 holes, 7103 yards, par 72.*

ZIP-LINING

FAMILY **TreeGO Moncton.** Children and adults can clamber through the treetops of Centennial Park, negotiating swinging rope-suspended logs, rope ladders, and zip lines, all while safely harnessed. Parents can watch their kids' progress from the ground. Adults embark on four courses, each more challenging than the last. Check the website for tips on suitable clothing and footwear. ✉ *Centennial Park, 45 Centennial Beach La., Moncton* ☎ *506/388–4646, 877/707–4646* 🌐 *www.treegomoncton.com* 💲 *C$32.75* ⏲ *Early May–mid-Oct., daily 9:30–5 (reservations required).*

SHOPPING

Dieppe's Champlain Place shopping mall and Moncton's downtown boutiques and big-box stores on Mountain Road and the Trinity/Mapleton area make the twin cities one of New Brunswick's major shopping destinations—a lot of people come over from Prince Edward Island to shop here, too. There's also quite a network of secondhand clothing stores, including classy Second Edition with some amazing designer bargains. Farmers' markets in both cities focus on quality foods, arts, and crafts from local producers.

Champlain Place. This huge mall, the largest in New Brunswick, has more than 150 stores. ✉ *477 Paul St., Dieppe* ☎ *506/855–6255* 🌐 *www.champlainplace.com.*

Dieppe Market. Every Saturday, from 7 am to 1:30 pm, this market brims with fresh produce, baked goods, ethnic cuisine, crafts, and live music. ✉ *232 Gauvin Rd., off Acadie Ave., Dieppe* ☎ *506/382–5755* 🌐 *www.marchedieppemarket.com.*

Marché Moncton Market. The market buzzes on Saturday from 7 to 2, with more than 130 vendors selling fresh produce, meat and deli foods, baked goods, and crafts. Vendors serve delicious ethnic lunches here Monday through Saturday. ✉ *120 Westmorland St., Moncton* ☎ *506/389–5969* 🌐 *www.marchemonctonmarket.ca.*

Second Edition. This resale boutique has gently worn designer and brand-name clothing, footwear, and accessories for women at a fraction of the new price. ✉ *215 Park St., Moncton* ☎ *506/855–6300* 🌐 *secondedition.ca* ⏲ *Closed Sun.*

THE ACADIAN COAST

History and nature meet on the Tantramar salt marshes east of Moncton. Bounded by the upper reaches of the Bay of Fundy, the province of Nova Scotia, and the Northumberland Strait, the region is rich in history and culture. The inspiration for Canadian artists such as Alex Colville and of poets from Sir Charles G. D. Roberts to Douglas Lochhead, the marshes provide a highly productive wetland habitat, and the region is among North America's major migratory bird routes.

The white sands and gentle tides of the Northumberland Strait and Baie des Chaleurs are in stunning contrast to the rocky cliffs and powerful tides of the Bay of Fundy. Along the Acadian Coast the water is warm, the sand is fine, and the food delicious. Many people here find their livelihood in the forests, in the mines, and on the sea, and along the Acadian Peninsula working wharves are an attraction within themselves.

DORCHESTER AND MEMRAMCOOK

Memramcook is 24 km (15 miles) southeast of Moncton. Dorchester is 14 km (9 miles) south of Memramcook.

Memramcook and Dorchester are on opposite sides of a marsh, each surrounded by gentle, rolling landscape filled with colorful native grasses. Acadian roots run deep in Memramcook, while Dorchester was a center of British culture and industry long before the Loyalists landed and is home to some of the province's oldest buildings.

GETTING HERE AND AROUND

There is no public transportation to Memramcook and Dorchester, which are 24 km (15 miles) and 38 km (24 miles) southeast of Moncton via Route 106 through Dieppe. From the Trans-Canada Highway (Route 2), take Exit 488 for Memramcook and Exit 482 (Renaissance Street) for Dorchester. Route 106 (Royal Road) links the two towns.

ESSENTIALS

Visitor Information **Visitor Information Center.** ✉ *Keillor House Museum, 4974 Main St., Dorchester* ☎ *506/379-6633* ⊕ *www.dorchester.ca.* **Visitor Information Center.** ✉ *480 Centrale St., Memramcook* ☎ *506/758-9808* ⊕ *www.memramcook.com.*

EXPLORING

Keillor House Museum. An early Regency stone house built in 1813, Keillor House contains thousands of artifacts relating to mid-19th-century life, and docents are in costume. Its Coach House contains a fascinating collection of artifacts from the Dorchester Penitentiary. Just a minute away on foot is the St. James Museum. This former church building now contains the Beachkirk Collection of equipment used in the manufacturing of textiles, including antique looms. You can sometimes see demonstrations of carding, spinning, and weaving, and there are also blacksmiths' and carpenters' tools. ✉ *4974 Main St., Dorchester* ☎ *506/379-6633 mid-June–mid-Sept.* ⊕ *www.keillorhousemuseum.com* 💲 *C$3* ⏲ *June–mid-Sept., Tues.–Sat. 10–5, Sun. noon–5.*

Monument Lefebvre National Historic Site. Commemorating the survival of the Acadians and celebrating the renaissance of Acadian culture, this monument is in the original home of St. Joseph's College, the first degree-granting French-language institution in Atlantic Canada, founded by Father Camille Lefebvre in 1864. A permanent interactive exhibit,"Reflections of a Journey—the Odyssey of the Acadian People," provides an excellent overview, and guided tours are available. ✉ *480 Central St., Memramcook* ☎ *506/758-9808* ⊕ *www.pc.gc.ca* 💲 *C$3.90* ⏲ *June–mid-Oct., daily 9–5; mid-Oct.–mid-Dec. and early Jan.–May, Mon.–Sat. 9–5.*

WHERE TO EAT AND STAY

If you're visiting Dorchester and Memramcook, the closest lodging options would be the Marshlands Inn in Sackville, just 15 km (9 miles) southeast. Otherwise, it's just 35 km (22 miles), via Route 106, to downtown Moncton, where there are plenty of hotels.

$$ CANADIAN FAMILY ✕ **Bell Inn Restaurant.** This restaurant on the village square in Dorchester was built in 1811 as a stagecoach stop and is reputed to be the oldest stone structure in New Brunswick. Wander through the three dining rooms while you wait for an old-fashioned, delicious roast turkey dinner or one of the other comfort-food selections. Soups, salads, sandwiches, brunch items, and light meals are also available, and there's a children's menu. The inn is not licensed for alcohol. 💲 *Average main: C$15* ✉ *3515 Cape Rd., off Rte. 106, Dorchester* ☎ *506/379-2580* ⊕ *www.bellinnrestaurant.com* ⏲ *Closed Mon. and Tues. and Dec.–Feb.*

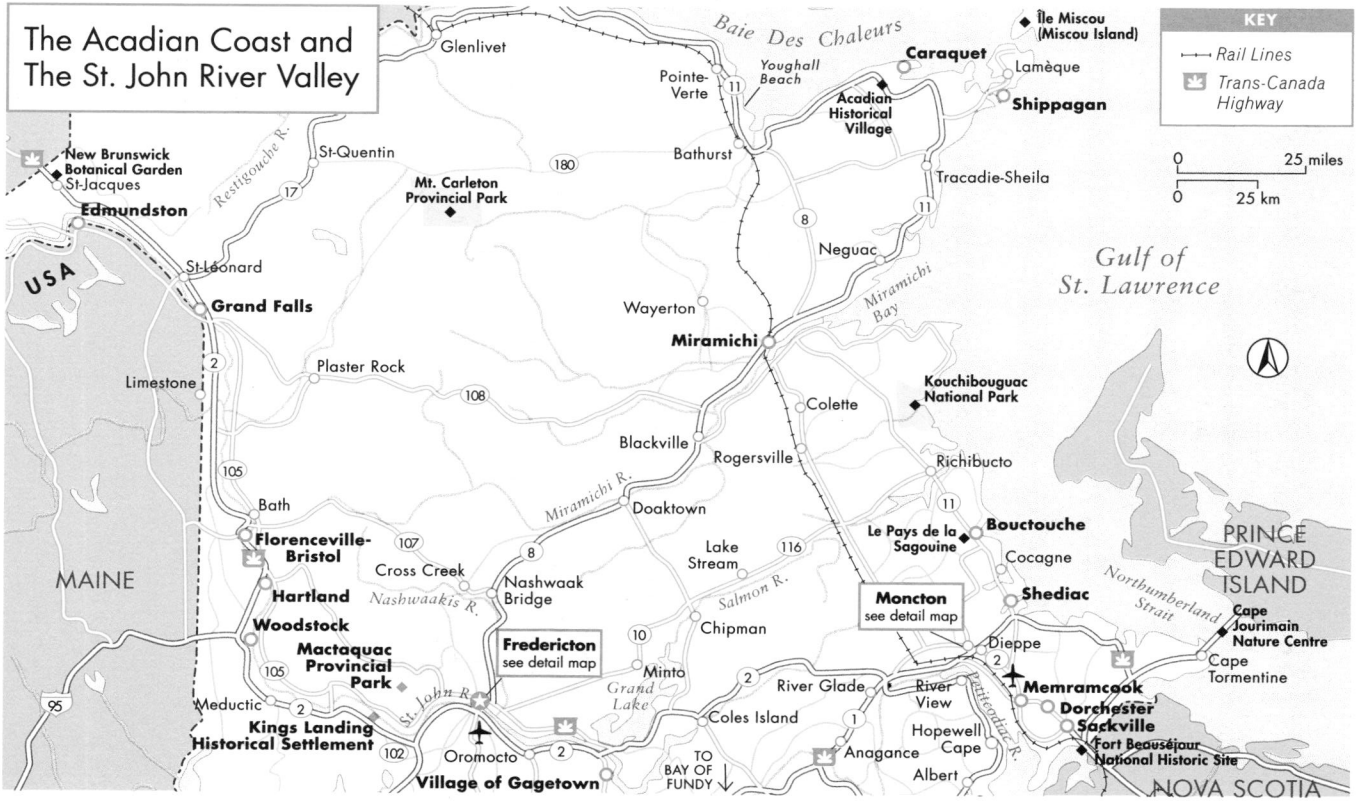
The Acadian Coast and The St. John River Valley
KEY
Rail Lines
Trans-Canada Highway
0 25 miles
0 25 km
Baie Des Chaleurs
Île Miscou (Miscou Island)
Caraquet
Lamèque
Shippagan
Youghall Beach
Acadian Historical Village
Pointe-Verte
Glenlivet
Bathurst
Tracadie-Sheila
Neguac
Gulf of St. Lawrence
Miramichi Bay
Wayerton
Miramichi
Colette
Kouchibouguac National Park
Richibucto
Blackville
Rogersville
Doaktown
Miramichi R.
Le Pays de la Sagouine
Bouctouche
Cocagne
Shediac
Moncton
see detail map
Dieppe
Memramcook
Dorchester
Sackville
Fort Beauséjour National Historic Site
Hopewell Cape
Albert
Anagance
River View
River Glade
Coles Island
Chipman
Lake Stream
Salmon R.
Nashwaak Bridge
Cross Creek
Nashwaakis R.
Fredericton
see detail map
Minto
Grand Lake
St. John R.
Oromocto
Village of Gagetown
TO BAY OF FUNDY
Kennebecasis R.
Northumberland Strait
PRINCE EDWARD ISLAND
Cape Jourimain Nature Centre
Cape Tormentine
NOVA SCOTIA
St-Quentin
Restigouche R.
Mt. Carleton Provincial Park
New Brunswick Botanical Garden
St-Jacques
Edmundston
USA
St-Léonard
Grand Falls
Limestone
Plaster Rock
Bath
Florenceville-Bristol
Hartland
Woodstock
Mactaquac Provincial Park
Meductic
Kings Landing Historical Settlement
MAINE
17
180
11
8
2
108
105
107
116
10
95
102

SPORTS AND THE OUTDOORS

Johnson's Mills Shorebird Reserve. The beaches here, on the Ramsar list of Wetlands of International Importance, are a staging area for migratory shorebirds such as semipalmated sandpipers, of which 80% of the world population stops here. Their numbers are most impressive in July and August, when a Nature Conservancy interpretive center is open to coincide with high tides, and tide times are posted on the website. *✉ Rte. 935, Dorchester ✢ About 8 km (5 miles) south ☎ 506/379–6347 July and Aug. only ⊕ www.natureconservancy.ca.*

SACKVILLE

22 km (14 miles) southeast of Dorchester and Memramcook.

Sackville is an idyllic university town complete with a swan-filled pond. Its stately homes and ivy-clad university buildings are shaded by venerable trees, and there's a waterfowl park right in town. With a program of high-profile festivals and events, it all makes for a rich blend of history, culture, and nature.

GETTING HERE AND AROUND

Sackville is on the Maritime Bus route, with three departures a day from Moncton at 9:20, 2, and 6. The journey time is 40 minutes and the fare is C$18.58. If you're driving, Sackville has two exits (504 and 506) off the Trans-Canada Highway (Route 2), about 50 km (31 miles) south of Moncton and 17 km (10½ miles) north of Amherst, Nova Scotia.

ESSENTIALS

Visitor Information **Visitor Information Center.** *✉ 34 Mallard Dr. ☎ 506/364–4967.*

EXPLORING

Fort Beauséjour National Historic Site. Near the Nova Scotia border in Aulac and 12 km (7 miles) east of Sackville, the site holds the ruins of a star-shaped fort that played a part in the 18th-century struggle between the French and British. The Deportation of the Acadians began here. The fort has fine views of the marshes at the head of the Bay of Fundy, and the visitor center has a fascinating collection of artifacts and interpretive exhibits. *✉ 111 Fort Beauséjour Rd., Aulac ☎ 506/364–5080 late June–early Sept., 506/876–2443 early Sept.–late June ⊕ www.pc.gc.ca/beausejour ₹ C$3.90 ⏲ Late June–early Sept., daily 9–5.*

Owens Art Gallery. The oldest art gallery in Canada, first opened to the public in 1895, is on the Mount Allison University campus. It houses 3,200 works of 19th- and 20th-century European, American, and Canadian artwork in its permanent collection, and there are usually rotating exhibits as well. *✉ 61 York St. ☎ 506/364–2574 ⊕ www.mta.ca/owens ₹ Free ⏲ Weekdays 10–5, weekends 1–5; hrs extended for exhibition openings and special events.*

Sackville Waterfowl Park. In the heart of the town, the park has more than 3 km (2 miles) of boardwalk and trails through 55 acres of wetlands that are home to some 160 species of birds and 200 species of plants. Throughout the marsh, viewing areas and interpretive signs reveal the rare waterfowl species that nest here. There's an interpretive center, and guided tours (C$6, including info kit and a snack at the end) are available in French and English mid-May through late August. A self-guided tour is also available at the visitor center and some stores in downtown Sackville. ✉ *34 Mallard Dr.* ☎ *506/364–4967 May–Aug.* 🌐 *www.sackville.com/visit/attractions/waterfowl* 💲 *Free* ⏲ *May–Aug., daily 9–5.*

WHERE TO STAY

$ B&B/INN Fodor's Choice ★

Marshlands Inn. A list of celebrity guests is displayed in the entrance hall of this grand and elegant inn, including Queen Elizabeth II, who stopped in for afternoon tea and left the signed portrait that now hangs on the upstairs landing. **Pros:** good food; friendly owners. **Cons:** one room has a nice claw-foot bath, but the encircling shower curtain tends to cling. 💲 *Rooms from: C$119* ✉ *55 Bridge St.* ☎ *506/536–0170, 800/561–1266* 🌐 *www.marshlands.nb.ca* 🛏 *17 rooms, 1 suite* 🍽 *No meals.*

SPORTS AND THE OUTDOORS

Canadian Wildlife Service. Without a doubt, bird-watching is the pastime of choice in this region, and these are the people to call for information. ✉ *17 Waterfowl La.* ☎ *506/364–5044.*

OFF THE BEATEN PATH

Cape Jourimain Nature Centre. The National Wildlife Area here covers 1,800 acres of salt and brackish marshes and large numbers of waterfowl, shorebirds, and other species can be seen. The outstanding interpretive center includes a museum and exhibit hall with displays on natural and human history, a restaurant specializing in local fare, and a boutique with nature art and fine crafts. You will also find a viewing tower, 13 km (8 miles) of trails, and daily programs. This is the best location to photograph the striking architecture of the 13-km (8-mile) Confederation Bridge that links New Brunswick to Prince Edward Island. ✉ *5039 Rte. 16, at Exit 51, Bayfield* ☎ *866/538–2220, 506/538–2220* 🌐 *www.capejourimain.ca* 💲 *Free* ⏲ *Late June–early Sept., daily: museum and tours 9–5, restaurant 11–7 (to 9 Thurs.), gift shop 8–7; late May–late June and early Sept.–early Oct. call for hrs.*

SHOPPING

Fog Forest Gallery. Small, friendly, and reputable, this commercial gallery represents nearly 50 Atlantic Canadian artists, with works including fine art, prints, sculpture, crafts, and photography,. ✉ *14 Bridge St.* ☎ *506/536–9000* 🌐 *www.fogforestgallery.ca* ⏲ *Tues.–Sat. 10–5 or by appointment.*

Sackville Harness Shop. Established in 1919, in what is said to be Sackville's oldest building, this is the only shop in North America that makes horse collars by hand, and it has a full range of tack and other equestrian products. If you don't have a horse, check out the Western boots, fine leather belts, wallets, bags, and outdoors wear. They also do shoe repairs. ✉ *39 Main St.* ☎ *506/536–0642, 800/386–4888* 🌐 *www.sackvilleharness.com* ⏲ *Weekdays 8–5, except 1 wk late June/early July; also open Sat. 8–noon Oct.–June.*

SHEDIAC

25 km (16 miles) northeast of Moncton.

Shediac is the self-proclaimed Lobster Capital of the World, and it has a giant lobster sculpture to prove it. Beautiful Parlee Beach also draws people to this fishing village/resort town.

GETTING HERE AND AROUND

From Moncton, take Route 15 east to Exit 31B onto Route 11, then almost immediately exit onto Route 133 and follow signs into the town. The town is great for strolling, but a car is necessary to get to the beaches.

ESSENTIALS

Visitor Information **Visitor Information Center.** ✉ *229 Main St.* ☎ *506/532-7788, 506/532-7000 ext 236 off-season* ⊕ *www.shediac.ca.*

BEACHES

FAMILY Fodor's Choice ★ **Parlee Beach Provincial Park.** The warmest salt water in Canada and a 3-km (2-mile) stretch of glistening sand has earned Parlee Beach the title of the best beach in Canada by several surveys. It is a popular vacation spot for families and plays host to beach-volleyball and touch-football tournaments; an annual sand-sculpture contest and a triathlon are among a schedule of summer events. **Amenities:** food and drink; lifeguards; parking (fee 9 am–5 pm); showers; toilets. **Best for:** sunrise; swimming; walking. ✉ *Exit 37 off Rte. 133* ☎ *506/533-3363* ⏲ *Services open mid-May–Aug. 30, daily 8 am–10 pm.*

FAMILY **Plage de l'Aboiteau.** On the western end of Cap-Pelé, this fine, sandy beach slopes gently into the warm waters of the Northumberland Strait, so it's very popular with families. A boardwalk runs through the adjacent salt marshes where waterfowl nest. The beach complex includes a restaurant and lounge with live music in the evening, and cottages are available for rent year-round. **Amenities:** food and drink; parking (fee); showers; toilets. **Best for:** sunrise; swimming; walking. ✉ *1083 De l'Aboiteau Rd., Cap-Pelé* ✣ *Exit 53 off Rte. 15* ☎ *506/577-2080* ⊕ *www.cap-pele.com/aboiteau* ⏲ *Amenities open early June–early Sept., daily 8–8.*

WHERE TO EAT

$ CANADIAN ✕ **Le Menu Acadien.** Don't expect any frills here—it's a paper-plate diner and take-out, far removed from the touristy center of town—but if you want to taste some authentic Acadian dishes, try the *fricôt* (a hearty chicken soup), *poutine rappé* (a potato dumpling stuffed with ground pork), fish cakes, or traditional baked beans. All are expertly and freshly cooked to the owner's grandmother's recipes. You can also get fried clams, scallops, lobster rolls, and various other fast foods, all made from scratch with fresh ingredients. ⓢ *Average main: C$10* ✉ *55 Ohio Rd.* ✣ *From downtown Shediac drive east on Main St. and turn right at lights by Ultramar gas station* ☎ *506/532-6366* ⊕ *www.menuacadien.ca* ⏲ *Closed Jan.–May.*

$$$ FRENCH ✕ **Le Petit Paris.** This little restaurant serves authentic French cuisine—the chef is from France—on a well-balanced menu based on organic and natural ingredients. The menu changes with the season, but might

CLOSE UP

Acadian Culture

HISTORY

French settlers arrived in the early 1600s and brought with them an efficient system of dikes called *aboiteaux* that allowed them to farm the salt marshes around the head of the Bay of Fundy. In the 1700s they were joined by Jesuit missionaries who brought the music of Bach, Vivaldi, and Scarlatti, along with their zeal. In 1713, England took possession of the region, and authorities demanded that Acadians swear an oath to the English crown. Only those who fled into the forests escaped Le Grand Dérangement—the Expulsion of the Acadians, mostly during the Seven Years' War—which dispersed them to Québec, the eastern seaboard, Louisiana (where they became known as Cajuns), France, and even as far as the Falkland Islands. It was a devastating event that profoundly affected Acadian expression—mobility remains a pervasive theme in the art, literature, and music of Acadian people.

Whether they were hiding deep in Maritime forests or living in exile, Acadians clung tenaciously to their language and traditions. Within 10 years of their deportation, they began to return, building new communities along coasts and waterways in the northeastern part of the province, remote from English settlement. In the 1850s Acadians began to think "nationally." By 1884 there was an Acadian national anthem and a flag, essentially the French tricolor with a bright yellow star on the blue section.

ACADIANS TODAY

The Acadian national holiday, on August 15, provides an official reason to celebrate Acadian culture. Le Festival Acadien de Caraquet stretches the celebration out for the two preceding weeks, with music and cultural events. Caraquet is also home to Théâtre Populaire d'Acadie, which mounts original productions for French communities throughout the Maritimes and encourages contemporary Acadian playwrights. Books by Acadian authors, including internationally renowned Antonine Maillet, circulate in Québec, France, and Belgium.

Modern Acadian artisans create pottery and baskets. Handmade wooden spoons are doubly beautiful—in pairs they keep time for the music at kitchen parties, where Acadian families have traditionally sung their history around the kitchen fire. But it isn't necessary to have a party to enjoy "music de cuisine." Clearly, the love of music endures: it rings clear in churches; the cotillion and quadrille are danced at soirees; and Acadian sopranos and jazz artists enjoy international renown.

3

include a classic *escargots à la Bourguignonne* (snails in garlic butter) or Magdalen Islands charcuterie platter to start, followed, perhaps, by St-Jacques au gratin (scallops broiled with cheese), lamb with mint sauce, or a filet mignon with green peppercorn sauce, then crème brûlée or a dessert of the day. Good French wines are well chosen. Space is a little tight inside (there's a terrace, too), but the atmosphere and service are delightful. $ *Average main: C$28* ✉ *562 Main St.* ☎ *506/533-8805* 🌐 *www.lepetitparis.ca* ⏲ *Closed Sun.–Wed. off-season. No lunch.*

WHERE TO STAY

$ B&B/INN **La Louisianne.** Owned and run by two sisters from Alberta who fell in love with the Maritimes, this 1914 home has been lovingly converted to feature individually styled bedrooms, some with antique furnishings and original features. **Pros:** generous four-course breakfasts, included in the price, feature seasonal specialties. **Cons:** two rooms share a bathroom; about a half-mile walk from downtown. *$ Rooms from: C$110 ✉ 427 Main St. ☎ 506/351-0505 🌐 www.lalouisianne.ca 5 rooms 🍴 Breakfast.*

$$ HOTEL Fodor's Choice ★ **Tait House.** Set back from Shediac's main thoroughfare, this elegant and stately historic mansion is now an upscale boutique hotel with a fine restaurant. **Pros:** good food; pleasing combination of modern amenities and antiques; reduction on room rate for evening diners. **Cons:** only a Continental breakfast is included in the price. *$ Rooms from: C$129 ✉ 293 Main St. ☎ 506/532-4233, 888/532-4233 🌐 www.maisontaithouse.com 9 rooms 🍴 Breakfast.*

BOUCTOUCHE

35 km (22 miles) north of Shediac.

This idyllic, bustling town on the sandy shores of Bouctouche Bay is famous for pristine beauty and for Le Pays de la Sagouine, a theme park based on an Acadian novel. The 12-km (7½-mile) dune of Bouctouche is one of the few remaining on the east coast of North America and is bordered by a 2-km (1¼-mile) boardwalk along the Irving Eco-Centre.

GETTING HERE AND AROUND

Bouctouche is 58 km (36 miles) northeast of Moncton via Route 15 east. From Route 15 take Exit 31B onto Route 11 north, then take Exit 32B for Bouctouche. A car is essential to reach all of the attractions.

ESSENTIALS

Visitor Information **Visitor Information Center.** *✉ 14 Acadie St. ☎ 506/743-8811.*

EXPLORING

FAMILY **Irving Eco-Centre: La Dune de Bouctouche.** The center preserves a superb example of a coastal ecosystem that protects the exceptionally fertile oyster beds in Bouctouche Bay. Hiking trails and boardwalks to the beach make it possible to explore sensitive areas without disrupting the environment of one of the few remaining great dunes on the northwest coast of the Atlantic Ocean. An outstanding interpretive center puts the ecosystem in perspective with nature exhibits, a film presentation, and a saltwater aquarium. The staff regularly conducts guided walks. Swimming is allowed. *✉ 1932 Rte. 475 ☎ 888/640-3300, 506/743-2600 🌐 www.irvingecocentre.com Free ⏲ Hiking trails and boardwalk daily dawn–dusk. Visitor center early June–late Sept., daily 10–5 (to 6 pm July–early Sept.).*

FAMILY **Le Pays de la Sagouine.** La Sagouine is an old charwoman-philosopher created by celebrated Acadian author Antonine Maillet, and this Acadian culture theme park re-creates her world. It's a make-believe island community that comes to life (in French) in daylong musical and theatrical performances, with dinner theater/musical evenings July through September. There's also an English version on Sunday, mid-July through August. Tours are available in English and French, and the Friday-night jam sessions are accessible to English-speaking visitors, too. ✉ *57 rue Acadie, Exit 32 A or B off Hwy. 11* ☎ *506/743–1400, 800/561–9188* 🌐 *www.sagouine.com* 💲 *C$20; evening shows C$30 each* ⏲ *July–early Sept., daily 10–5:30.*

FAMILY **The Olivier Soapery.** A working artisan soapery, Olivier includes a museum with a fascinating array of bath-time memorabilia, from old bars of soap and soap-making equipment to tubs and basins. There's a skin-care art gallery, featuring paintings commissioned for soap labels throughout the years, and, naturally, plenty of soap and other skin-care products are for sale. By far the best attraction, however, is the soap-making demonstration, at 10, 11:30, 2, and 4. ✉ *851 Rte. 505, 10 km (6 miles) north of Bouctouche, Ste.-Anne-de-Kent* ☎ *506/743–8938, 800/775–5550* 🌐 *www.oliviersoaps.com* 💲 *Free* ⏲ *Late June–early Sept., daily 10–7; early Sept.–mid-Oct., weekdays 8:30–4:30, weekends noon–5.*

WHERE TO STAY

$$ B&B/INN **Auberge le Vieux Presbytère de Bouctouche.** Near the water, this lovely inn was formerly a rectory and then a retreat house complete with chapel (now a conference room). **Pros:** friendly staff; lovely grounds. **Cons:** rooms are rather old-fashioned; the inn is sometimes busy with weddings and conferences. 💲 *Rooms from: C$128* ✉ *157 chemin du Couvent* ☎ *506/743–5568, 866/743–1880* 🌐 *www.vieuxpresbytere.nb.ca* ⏲ *Closed Oct.–May* 🛏 *5 rooms, 5 suites, 3 apartments* 🍽 *Breakfast.*

KOUCHIBOUGUAC NATIONAL PARK

40 km (25 miles) north of Bouctouche; 100 km (62 miles) north of Moncton.

On the warm east coast, you'll enter through old-growth forest laced with trails before emerging on glorious golden sands, with dunes and lagoons sheltered by barrier islands and a boardwalk that extends through the salt marshes to the sands.

GETTING HERE AND AROUND

Kouchibouguac National Park is off Route 11. Take Exit 75 onto Route 117 and follow the signs. An alternative route is on the scenic Acadian Coastal Drive, following the starfish road signs.

EXPLORING

FAMILY Fodor's Choice ★ **Kouchibouguac National Park.** The word Kouchibouguac (Kou-she-boo-gwack) means "river of the long tides" in the Mi'Kmaq language, and this natural wilderness park consists of sandy beaches, dunes, bogs, salt marshes, lagoons, and freshwater, and is home to an abundance of birds. The visitor center (open mid-May–mid-Oct) features information and interpretive exhibits. Kellys Beach is supervised and has facilities. There are more than 60 km (37 miles) of trails for biking and hiking in summer and for cross-country skiing, snowshoeing, snow walking, and kick sledding in winter. The forests and peat bogs can be explored along 10 nature trails, each of which has a parking lot. There are lots of nature-interpretation programs, and you can canoe, kayak, and picnic or rent bikes and boats. Reserve ahead for one of the 311 campsites. ✉ *Rte. 117 ✣ 60 km (37 miles) north of Bouctouche, off Hwy. 11* ☎ *506/876–2443* ⊕ *www.pc.gc.ca/kouchibouguac* 💲 *C$7.80 mid-June–early Sept.; C$3.90 Apr.–mid-June and early Sept.–Nov.*

MIRAMICHI

40 km (25 miles) north of Kouchibouguac; 150 km (93 miles) north of Moncton.

Celebrated for salmon rivers that reach into some of the province's richest forests, and the ebullient nature of its residents (Scottish, English, Irish, and a smattering of First Nations and French), this is a land of lumber kings, ghost stories, folklore, and festivals—celebrating the Irish in July, and folk songs and the Scottish in August. Sturdy wood homes dot the banks of Miramichi Bay. The city of Miramichi incorporates the former towns of Chatham and Newcastle and several small villages and is where the politician and British media mogul Lord Beaverbrook grew up and is buried.

GETTING HERE AND AROUND

Miramichi is 175 km (109 miles) northeast of Fredericton via Route 8 (also designated the scenic "Miramichi River Route"). From Moncton take Route 15 east then Route 11 north. A car is necessary to see all the attractions.

ESSENTIALS

Visitor Information **Visitor Information Center.** ✉ *21 Cove Rd., Miramichi City* ☎ *506/778–8444* ⊕ *www.discovermiramichi.com.*

EXPLORING

FAMILY **Beaubears Island.** Formerly a thriving shipbuilding center, this is one of Miramichi's most interesting outdoor spots. Start at the museum-style interpretive center, with interactive audio-visual displays. A short boat trip will then take you to the island to see two historic sites, staffed by characters who love to share their colorful island stories and adventures. There are also guided tours and trips around the island in a 26-foot traditional canoe, and regular special events are another attraction. ✉ *35 St. Patrick's Dr., Nelson* ☎ *506/622–8526* ⊕ *www.beaubearsisland.ca* 💲 *Interpretive center C$5; tours C$10–C$23; canoe trip C$25* ⏲ *Mid-May–mid-June and late Aug.–mid-Oct., Mon.–Sat. 10–4, Sun. noon–4; mid-June–late Aug., Mon.–Sat. 10–6, Sun. noon–8.*

Metepenagiag Heritage Park. Two important First Nations archaeological sites, the Augustine Mound and Oxbow national historic sites, are at the heart of this park, "Where Spirits Live"—where the Mi'Kmaq have lived for more than 3,000 years. In the museum, enthusiastic and knowledgeable staff are on hand to answer questions about the exhibits and there's a good film about the history of the site. Outside, there are a number of walking trails to explore, and events include drumming circles, traditional dancing, and the annual Pow Wow in June. ✉ *2156 Micmac Rd., Red Bank ✣ 36 km (22 miles) west of Miramichi* ☎ *506/836–6118, 888/380–3555* ⊕ *www.metpark.ca* 💲 *C$8* ⏲ *May–Oct., daily 10–5.*

FAMILY **Ritchie Wharf Park.** This waterside public park recalls the area's former shipbuilding industry. It has a nautical-theme playground complete with a "Splash Pad" that sprays water from below and dumps it from buckets above. Shops sell local crafts, and there are several restaurants and docking facilities. An amphitheater showcases local entertainers on Sunday afternoons in summer. ✉ *Norton's La., Newcastle* ☎ *Free* ⏲ *Park daily dawn–dusk. Shops mid-May–early Sept., daily 11–10.*

WHERE TO EAT AND STAY

$$ CHINESE ✕ **Cunard Restaurant.** With its Irish accent and lumberjack history, Miramichi might seem an unlikely place to find a great Chinese restaurant. The Cunard, however, has what it takes to make it anywhere, and has been pleasing locals and visitors since 1980. It is renowned for its Szechuan chicken and orange-glazed beef stir fry, and Canadian dishes also feature on the six-page menu. A small buffet is offered for Friday lunch and early evening on Sunday, but this is principally a table-service restaurant. Monday through Thursday lunch specials are a good value. Take-out is also available. $ *Average main: C$15* ✉ *32 Cunard St., Miramichi City* ☎ *506/773–7107* 🌐 *www.cunardrestaurant.com.*

$ B&B/INN **King George B&B.** In a listed historic building in the former town of Newcastle, a stylish blend of antique and modern furnishings provides upscale accommodations. **Pros:** within walking distance of the Ritchie Wharf boardwalk; evening meal can be arranged for late arrivals; multi-night discounts available. **Cons:** rooms vary in size, the Princess Room, with twin beds, being quite compact. $ *Rooms from: C$115* ✉ *561 King George Hwy., Miramichi City* ☎ *506/352–0557* 🌐 *kinggeorgebandb.com* 🛏 *3 rooms, 1 suite* 🍴 *Some meals.*

$ HOTEL **Metepenagiag Lodge.** Overlooking the Little Southwest Miramichi River in unspoiled countryside, this lovely cedar lodge is run by members of the local Mi'Kmaq First Nations and is close to the Metepenagiag Heritage Park. **Pros:** friendly service; provides a chance to immerse yourself in aboriginal culture. **Cons:** no cell-phone service; sometimes overrun by business conference excursions. $ *Rooms from: C$99* ✉ *2202 Micmac Rd., Red Bank* ☎ *506/836–6128, 800/570–1344* 🌐 *www.met-lodge.com* 🛏 *10 rooms* 🍴 *Breakfast.*

$$ HOTEL **Rodd Miramichi River.** A complete renovation has substantially upgraded this riverside hotel in the downtown Chatham area, and, coupled with its great location, this is a good choice for both business travelers and vacationers. **Pros:** good fishing opportunities; next to a small riverside park; well-equipped meeting and conference spaces. **Cons:** sometimes taken over by business conventions and wedding parties. $ *Rooms from: C$125* ✉ *1809 Water St., Miramichi City* ☎ *506/773–3111* 🌐 *www.roddvacations.com* 🛏 *76 rooms, 4 suites* 🍴 *No meals.*

SHIPPAGAN

37 km (23 miles) north of Tracadie-Sheila.

Shippagan is an important fishing and marine education center as well as a bustling town with lots of amenities and the gateway to the idyllic islands of Lamèque and Miscou.

GETTING HERE AND AROUND

Shippagan is about 110 km (68 miles) northeast of Miramichi via Route 11, taking Exit 217 onto Route 113 for the final 12 km (7½ miles). The town is very walkable, but a car is necessary to get to the islands.

ESSENTIALS

Visitor Information **Visitor Information Center.** ✉ *200 Hôtel-de-ville Ave.* ☎ *506/336-3900* 🌐 *www.shippagan.ca.*

EXPLORING

FAMILY **Aquarium and Marine Centre.** This wonderful aquarium has a serious side and a fun side, with labs that are the backbone of marine research in the province and more than 3,000 specimens to see in 31 indoor tanks, outdoor touch tanks, and the Harbour Seal pool. Feeding time for the seals (at 11 and 4) is always popular, as are the touch tanks, containing such species as sea stars, clams, sea cucumbers, and rare blue lobsters. Another exhibit illustrates the underwater world of the Acadian Peninsula and how fishing is carried out there. ✉ *100 rue de l'Aquarium* ☎ *506/336-3013* 🌐 *www.aquariumnb.ca* 💲 *C$9* ⏲ *May 31–late Sept., daily 10–6.*

Île Miscou (Miscou Island). Accessible by bridge from Île Lamèque, Miscou has white sandy beaches, and the dunes and lagoons are good places to see migrating bird species. ✉ *Shippagan* 🌐 *ilemiscouisland.webs.com.*

Ste-Cécile Church. Across a causeway from Shippagan is Île Lamèque and Ste-Cécile Church. Although the church is plain on the outside, every inch of it is decorated on the inside. Each July, the International Festival of Baroque Music takes place here. ✉ *Rte. 113 at Petite-Rivière-de-l'Île.*

CARAQUET

40 km (25 miles) west of Shippagan.

Perched on Caraquet Bay, along the beautiful Baie des Chaleurs, with Québec's Gaspé Peninsula beckoning across the inlet, Caraquet is rich in French flavor and is the acknowledged Acadian cultural capital. Its beaches are also a draw, and it has begun to attract the attention of the cruise lines that ply the waters of the Atlantic Provinces.

GETTING HERE AND AROUND

Caraquet is 113 km (70 miles) north of Miramichi on Route 11. A car is necessary to get around its scattered attractions.

ESSENTIALS

Visitor Information **Visitor Information Center.** ✉ *39 St.-Pierre Blvd. W* ☎ *506/726-2676* 🌐 *www.caraquet.ca.*

EXPLORING

Fodor's Choice ★ **Acadian Festival.** This two-week celebration of Acadian culture is held here in the first two weeks of August. In the Tintamarre, costumed participants parade noisily through the streets; the Blessing of the Fleet, a colorful and moving ceremony that's usually held on the first Sunday of the festival, eloquently expresses the importance of fishing to the Acadian economy and way of life. Alongside these events is a schedule of concerts, theater, storytelling, poetry, and visual arts. ✉ *Caraquet* ☎ *506/727–2787* ⊕ *www.festivalacadien.ca.*

FAMILY **Acadian Historical Village.** A highlight of the Acadian Peninsula, the more than 40 restored buildings here re-create Acadian communities between 1770 and 1949. There are modest homes, a church, a school, and a village shop, as well as an industrial area that includes a lobster hatchery, a cooper, and a tinsmith shop. The bilingual staff tells fascinating stories and the demonstrations are great fun; visitors are invited to take part. For the full experience, you can enjoy dinner and entertainment during the evening and stay overnight in the grand Hôtel Château Albert, an authentic re-creation of a 1907 hotel—a chauffeured 1925 vehicle transports you and your luggage from the parking lot. ✉ *14311 Rte. 11, 10 km (6 miles) west of Caraquet, Rivière-du-Nord* ☎ *506/726–2600, 877/721–2200* ⊕ *www.villagehistoriqueacadien.com* 💲 *C$17.50 (valid for any 2 days within a 7-day period); C$9 mid–late Sept.; C$12 guided tour late Sept.–early Oct.* ⏲ *Early June–late Sept., daily 10–6; late Sept.–early Oct. by reservation for guided tour only.*

3

WHERE TO EAT AND STAY

$ BISTRO ✕ **Grains de Folie.** This artisan bakery-café is a great place to drop in for a quick bite, with an inviting aroma of fresh-baked bread and freshly brewed coffee to greet you. There's quick counter service for delicious soups, sandwiches, omelets, panini, pizzas, salads, and tempting pastries, with table-service breakfasts until 1 pm on weekends. There's also a deli counter with a great range of cheeses. Huge murals by a local artist cover the walls on both levels, a terrace is open in summer, and there's regular live entertainment. [$] *Average main: C$12* ✉ *171 Blvd. Saint-Pierre W* ☎ *506/727–4001* ⊕ *www.grainsdefolie.ca* ⏲ *Closed Mon. and Tues. Sept.–May. No dinner.*

$$$ FRENCH Fodor's Choice ★ ✕ **La Fine Grobe Sur Mer.** This is one of New Brunswick's finest restaurants, where you can savour chef Georges Frachon's creations while gazing out over the sea through the wall of windows. Drawing on the culinary arts of his French homeland, Georges imparts an expert touch to such dishes as sautéed scallops with garlic and parsley, beef tenderloin, or Poulet à la Provençale, and his wine list is equally outstanding. Herbs and greens are home-grown and baguettes are baked in an outdoor oven. The dining room is casual and bright, with some interesting art and artifacts. Reservations are recommended. There are two bedrooms on the second floor for overnight stays. [$] *Average main: C$25* ✉ *289 rue Principal, Nigadoo* ✣ *16 km (10 miles) north of Bathurst on Rte. 134* ☎ *506/783–3138* ⊕ *www.finegrobe.com* ⏲ *No lunch.*

$$$ HOTEL Fodor's Choice ★ **Hotel Paulin.** A classic Victorian built in 1891, the famous Hotel Paulin is a historic boutique-style hotel on the Baie des Chaleurs. **Pros:** personal service; excellent food. **Cons:** atmosphere can feel a bit stuffy. [$] *Rooms from: C$195* ✉ *143 Blvd. St-Pierre W* ☎ *506/727–9981, 866/727–9981* ⊕ *www.hotelpaulin.com* 🛏 *6 rooms, 6 suites* 🍴 *Some meals.*

SPORTS AND THE OUTDOORS

FAMILY **Sugarloaf Provincial Park.** Eight trails on the 507-foot drop at Sugarloaf Provincial Park accommodate skiers and snowboarders of all levels in winter and mountain bikers in summer; a chairlift operates in both seasons. There are also more than 25 km (16 miles) of bike trails, cross-country ski trails, hiking trails, a summer alpine slide, and other recreational amenities. Instruction and equipment rentals are available, including GPS for geocaching, there's a summer welcome center, and the lodge operates a lounge and restaurant year-round. ✉ *596 Val d'Amour Rd., 180 km (112 miles) northwest of Caraquet, Atholville* ☎ *506/789–2366, 506/753–6825 for ski/snowboard rentals, 800/561–0123 for campsite reservations* ⊕ *parcsugarloafpark.ca* ₹ *Bike park C$5 per ride, C$17 per half day, or C$25 full day. Alpine skiing/snowboarding C$14 evening, C$22–C$29 per day; cross-country skiing/snowshoeing season pass C$30–C$60* ⊙ *Park gates daily 8–dusk. Bike Park mid-June–Aug., Thurs.–Sat. 10–7:30, Sun. 10–5; Sept., weekends 10–5. Winter sports mid-Dec–Mar. (call for hrs).*

ST. JOHN RIVER VALLEY

The St. John River valley scenery is panoramic—gently rolling hills and sweeping forests, with just enough rocky gorges to keep it interesting. The native peoples (First Nations, French, English, Scots, and Danes) who live along the river ensure that its culture is equally intriguing. The St. John River forms 120 km (74 miles) of the border with Maine, then swings inland, eventually cutting through the heart of Fredericton and rolling down to the city of Saint John. Gentle hills of rich farmland and the blue sweep of the water make this a lovely area for driving. In the early 1800s the narrow wedge of land at the northern end of the valley was coveted by Québec, New Brunswick, and the United States. To settle the issue, New Brunswick governor Sir Thomas Carleton rolled dice with the governor of British North America in Québec City. Sir Thomas won—by one point. Settling the border with the Americans was more difficult; even the lumberjacks engaged in combat. Finally, in 1842, the British flag was hoisted over Madawaska County. One old-timer, tired of being asked to which country he belonged, replied, "I am a citizen of the Republic of Madawaska." So began the mythical republic, which exists today with its own flag (an eagle on a field of white) and a coat of arms.

EDMUNDSTON

275 km (171 miles) northwest of Fredericton.

Edmundston, the unofficial capital of Madawaska County, has always depended on the wealth of the deep forest around it—the legend of Paul Bunyan was born in these woods. Even today the town looks to the pulp mills of the Twin Rivers Paper Company as the major source of employment.

GETTING HERE AND AROUND

Edmundston is on the Trans-Canada Highway (Route 2) about 16 km (10 miles) southeast of the Québec border—Exit 18 is best for downtown—and just across the river from Madawaska, Maine. Maritime Bus operates long-distance service via the Trans-Canada Highway from many towns and cities in New Brunswick, Nova Scotia and Prince

Edward Island. A car is necessary to visit the Botanical Garden, on the northern edge of the city.

ESSENTIALS

Visitor Information **Edmundston-Madawaska Tourism.** ✉ *121 Victoria St.* ☎ *506/737-1850, 866/737-6766* 🌐 *tourismedmundston.com.*

EXPLORING

FAMILY **New Brunswick Botanical Garden.** In the Edmunston suburb of St-Jacques, roses, rhododendrons, alpine flowers, and dozens of other annuals and perennials bloom in 10 gardens. Khronos: The Celestial Garden has an astronomical theme, complete with a contemporary stone circle. The music of Mozart, Handel, Bach, and Vivaldi often plays in the background. Two arboretums have coniferous and deciduous trees and shrubs. Mosaiculture plantings on metal frames placed throughout the gardens illustrate legends and cultural themes. Children (and adults) enjoy the living butterfly exhibit. ✉ *15 Main St., St.-Jacques* ☎ *506/737-4444* 🌐 *www.jardinnbgarden.com* 💲 *C$14, C$6 for butterfly exhibit only* ⏲ *May, June, and Sept., daily 9–5; July and Aug., daily 9–8; also for special events for Halloween and Christmas.*

WHERE TO EAT AND STAY

$$$ STEAKHOUSE ✕ **Chantal's Steak House.** You'll need directions to this out-of-the-way spot, but it's well worth seeking out. The interior is chic and stylish, the mother-and-daughter team who run it are friendly and efficient, and the steak, seafood, and ribs are succulent. The strong French influence adds an interesting element to the food, which utilizes imported spices and fresh, locally sourced ingredients. It's a good place to try fiddleheads, too, particularly when paired with shrimp in a cassoulet. Round the meal off with a helping of the traditional *tarte au sucre* (sugar pie), which, in spite of the name, is not too sweet. If you want wine with the meal you'll need to bring your own. 💲 *Average main: C$23* ✉ *721C Victoria St.* ☎ *506/735-8882* 🌐 *chantalsteakhouse.webnode.fr* ⏲ *No lunch Sat.–Wed.*

$ B&B/INN **Auberge les Jardins Inn and Motel Brayon & Chalets.** Fine French cuisine is the major attraction at this inn, although the guest rooms, decorated with woodland themes, are lovely. **Pros:** good food; peaceful despite the highway. **Cons:** not much else to do here; some distance from downtown. 💲 *Rooms from: C$115* ✉ *60 rue Principal, St-Jacques* ☎ *506/739-5514, 800/630-8011* 🌐 *www.lesjardinsinn.com* 🛏 *30 rooms, 7 cottages* 🍽 *Some meals.*

$$ HOTEL **Four Points by Sheraton.** Linked to both the convention center and the shopping mall in downtown Edmundston, this is a superstylish hotel, with the clever use of natural stone, old barn boards, and industrial relics in public areas imparting a sleek and modern look. **Pros:** very comfortable and well equipped; friendly and helpful staff. **Cons:** no nice views; needs more luggage carts. 💲 *Rooms from: C$169* ✉ *100 Rice St.* ☎ *506/739-7321, 800/576-4656* 🌐 *www.fourpoints.com/edmundston* 🛏 *95 rooms, 8 suites* 🍽 *No meals.*

GRAND FALLS

65 km (40 miles) southeast of Edmundston.

The St. John River rushes over a high cliff, squeezes through a narrow rocky gorge, and emerges as a wider river at the town of Grand Falls. The result is a magnificent cascade whose force has worn strange round wells in the rocky bed, some as large as 16 feet in circumference and 30 feet deep.

GETTING HERE AND AROUND

Grand Falls is just off the Trans-Canada Highway (Route 2), at Exit 77 or 79 and is served by Maritime Bus from points along the TCH north and south. From Edmundston an alternative (and about the same distance) is on Route 144, the River Valley Scenic Drive. There's not much to see in town, other than the falls and gorge, but it's an easy walk across the bridge along Broadway Boulevard to cafés and restaurants.

ESSENTIALS

Visitor Information **La Rochelle Tourist Information Centre.** ✉ *1 Chapel St.* ☎ *506/475-7766, 877/475-7769* 🌐 *www.grandfallsnb.com.* **Malabeam Tourist Information Center.** ✉ *25 Madawaska Rd.* ☎ *506/475-7788, 877/475-7769* 🌐 *www.grandfalls.com.*

EXPLORING

Gorge Walk. Starting at the Malabeam Tourist Information Center, the walk covers the full length of the gorge and is dotted with interpretive panels and monuments. Nearby, you can descend the nearly 250 steps to the wells, holes worn in the rocks by the swirling water. Guided walking tours are also available. According to native legend, a young woman named Malabeam led her Mohawk captors to their deaths over the foaming cataract rather than guide them to her village. The bodies of the Mohawks were found the following day, but Malabeam was not found. The view over the gorge from the center is breathtaking, particularly at snowmelt time or after heavy rain. ✉ *25 Madawaska Rd.* ☎ *506/475-7788 information center* 💲 *Walk free; steps to wells C$5; guided walks C$4 or C$8, depending on length* ⏲ *Gorge walk daily dawn–dusk; steps to wells and guided tours daily 10–6.*

Grand Falls Museum. Pioneer and early Victorian artifacts are the basis of a collection that includes memorabilia of Ron Turcotte, the jockey who rode Secretariat to Triple Crown victory in 1973, and the balance beam used by daredevil Van Morrell, who crossed the falls on a tightrope in 1904. ✉ *68 Madawaska Rd., Suite 100* ☎ *506/473-5265* 💲 *Free; donations accepted* ⏲ *June–Aug., weekdays 10–5.*

OFF THE BEATEN PATH

Mount Carleton Provincial Park. This vast area of unspoilt wilderness is centered on Mount Carleton, at 2,690 feet the highest point in all of the Maritimes. Rich in wildlife, including moose, white-tailed deer, lynx, marten, and porcupines, the park is also a Dark Sky Preserve, so an overnight camping trip on a clear night would be well rewarded. Most people come to hike the trails or mountain-bike on old logging roads, and there's canoeing on several lakes. Check out guided hikes and other park events ☎ *800/561-0123* 🌐 *parcsnbparks.ca* 💲 *C$5 per vehicle.*

SPORTS AND THE OUTDOORS

Open Sky Adventures. This outfitter operates a pontoon boat at the lower end of the gorge, offering a fascinating perspective of the cliffs and wells, from May through October; rides are C$25. Zip-lining, rapelling, deepelling (like rapelling only you are facing downward), and kayaking are also offered. ✉ *16087 Rte. 105* ☎ *506/473–4803, 506/477–9799* ⊕ *www.openskyadventures.com.*

Zip-Zag. Two zip lines cross the gorge, one from the Ron Turcotte Bridge and the second crossing the falls to the Malabeam Tourist Center, the latter following the course of Van Morell's historic tightrope walk in 1904. To add even more excitement, you'll be racing against the person on the other zip line. There's a weight limit of 275 pounds, but other than that—racers take note—the heavier you are the faster you'll zip. ✉ *25 Madawaska Rd.* ☎ *888/494–7924* ⊕ *www.zipzag.ca* ₤ *C$40, includes 2 crossings.*

FLORENCEVILLE-BRISTOL

81 km (50 miles) south of Grand Falls.

The title "French Fry Capitol of the World" does nothing to convey how pretty Florenceville is, with its Main Street running right along the riverside, but there's no getting away from the fact that it's also the home of McCain's, the frozen food giant, which, along with other products, produces one-third of all the frozen french fries sold worldwide. The main factory is north of town, various ancillary buildings are dotted around, and vast potato fields spread out in all directions. Upstream, the incorporated twin-town of Bristol has a railroad heritage and one of the best restaurants in the province.

GETTING HERE AND AROUND

Both towns are right on the River Valley Scenic Route (Route 105), with the Trans-Canada Highway running parallel at a discreet distance. Maritime Bus stops on Main Street, Florenceville, but you'll need a car to reach Bristol or Potato World and the Visitor Information Centre.

ESSENTIALS

Visitor Information **Florenceville-Bristol Visitor Information Centre.** ✉ *Potato World, 385 Centreville Rd.* ☎ *506/392–1955* ⊕ *www.florencevillebristol.ca.*

EXPLORING

Andrew and Laura McCain Art Gallery. This lively gallery hosts an eclectic series of exhibitions each year, showcasing Atlantic Canadian artists working in traditional and experimental media, as well as art and craft workshops, seasonal festivals, and children's events. ✉ *8 McCain St., Unit 1* ☎ *506/392–6769* ⊕ *www.mccainartgallery.com* ₤ *Free* ⊙ *Tues.–Sat. 10:30–5 (to 8 pm Thurs.).*

Potato World. In the "French Fry Capital of the World" (aka the location of McCain's HQ) it's hardly surprising that this humble vegetable, which keeps many folks employed hereabouts, is celebrated—but you may be surprised by how interesting it is. Run by the community as a nonprofit enterprise, Potato World has some fascinating displays related to the history, industry, and science of the potato, plus hands-on exhibits; and, when the café is open, you'll have the chance to munch on some hot fries. ✉ *385 Centreville Rd.* ☎ *506/392-1955* 🌐 *www.potatoworld.ca* 💵 *C$5* ⏲ *June–Aug., weekdays 9–6, weekends 9–5; Sept.–mid-Oct., weekdays 9–5.*

WHERE TO EAT AND STAY

$$$$ CANADIAN Fodor's Choice ★ ✕ **Fresh Fine Dining.** Gourmet restaurants rarely show up in such unlikely locations as this—a restored 1930s Canadian Pacific railcar in a small New Brunswick town—and even if you're not traveling the St. John River route, it's well worth a detour (reservations advised). The menu is well balanced, with dishes such as an appetizer of seared salmon in coconut-sesame broth or a main course of Cornish hen stuffed with garlic, tomatoes, green olives, white wine, and sun-dried tomato puree. Most exciting, though, is to opt for the "Chef's Choice"—just say what you *don't* like and something will be created specially for you (and, we are told, even if every diner in the place takes this option, no two will get the same dish). Railroad buffs will also enjoy the displays at the adjacent Shogomoc Railway site. 💲 *Average main: C$32* ✉ *9189 Main St.* ☎ *506/392-6000* 🌐 *www.freshfinedining.com* ⏲ *Closed Sun. No lunch.*

$ B&B/INN 🏨 **Shamrock Suites.** In a converted 19th-century home, the elegant suites have been designed to suit business and leisure travelers for short or long stays, with access to a fully equipped kitchen and guest laundry. **Pros:** lovely setting, on 6 acres of heritage gardens; high levels of comfort and good amenities; full breakfast included; well placed for those with business at McCain's. **Cons:** rooms vary in size. 💲 *Rooms from: C$115* ✉ *8 Curtis Rd.* ☎ *506/392-8801, 506/391-5274 cell* 🌐 *www.shamrocksuites.ca* 🛏 *5 rooms* 🍽 *Breakfast.*

HARTLAND

19 km (12 miles) south of Florenceville-Bristol.

Hartland is best known for having the longest covered bridge in the world, still carrying traffic across the wide St. John River. A sleepy little town for much of the year, it is deluged with busloads of camera-toting tourists in summer. You can also visit the Covered Bridge Potato Chip company, just across the highway, for a tour and tasting of the still warm chips straight off the production line.

GETTING HERE AND AROUND

The town is on Route 105 (the River Valley Scenic Route), and has an exit off the Trans-Canada Highway, which runs a short distance to the east. There's no public transportation.

ESSENTIALS

Visitor Information **Hartland Visitor Information Centre.** ✉ *365 Main St., beside the bridge* ☎ *506/375-4075* 🌐 *www.town.hartland.nb.ca.*

EXPLORING

Longest Covered Bridge. New Brunswick has its fair share of superlatives, but this may be the most surprising. In what is otherwise a rather sleepy little town, the St. John River is spanned by the longest covered bridge in the world—1,282 feet long. A national and provincial historic site, it opened in 1901. It's still used by traffic crossing the river between

Routes 103 and 105, and you can walk across on the safely separated pedestrian walkway that was added in 1945. If you want to drive across (maximum height is 13 feet 9 inches; maximum weight 10 tons), there's only room for traffic going one way at a time, and there are no traffic lights, so stop to check whether anything's coming the other way and wait your turn if necessary, and turn your headlights on; local drivers display a great sense of fairness. ✉ *Hartland Bridge Rd.*

WHERE TO EAT AND STAY

$$$ INTERNATIONAL Fodor's Choice ★ ✕ **Jeremiah's.** Just across the road from the world's longest covered bridge, this fine restaurant occupies a stunning renovation of an 1892 church. Original features have been matched with chic modern fittings and color schemes, and there's an excellent private room downstairs for meetings or parties. Lunchtime offerings (served 11 am to 5 pm) include freshly made soups, salads, sandwiches, and light meals, while the evening menu features such dishes as seafood risotto with fennel, lemon-and-tomato beurre blanc, Portuguese Steak-on-a-Stone, or pork tenderloin painted with lavender honey. Reservations are required for dinner. The lunch menu runs all day on Sunday. $ *Average main: C$30* ✉ *362 Main St.* ☎ *506/375–8200* 🌐 *jeremiahs.ca* 💳 *No credit cards* ⏲ *Closed Mon. No dinner Tues. Off-season opening limited; call to check.*

$ B&B/INN **Covered Bridge B&B.** High above the St. John River, near the world's longest covered bridge and the River Valley Scenic Drive, this superior bed-and-breakfast has exceptionally spacious rooms and top-notch modern bathrooms, some with whirlpool tubs. **Pros:** friendly and helpful owners; children welcome; special rates for longer off-season stays. **Cons:** air-conditioning only in three rooms, but the others have fans; one bathroom, though private, is not en suite. $ *Rooms from: C$105* ✉ *2651 Rte. 103, Somerville* ☎ *506/324–0939* 🌐 *www.coveredbridgebandb.ca* 🛏 *5 rooms* 🍽 *Breakfast.*

WOODSTOCK

93 km (58 miles) northwest of Fredericton.

New Brunswick's first incorporated town (in 1856), Woodstock still preserves many fine old buildings on its leafy streets. A focal point of the town is the meeting of its two rivers, the St. John and the Meduxnekeag, with riverside walks, a nature reserve, a floating dock in summer, and a small marina. The big (for Woodstock) celebrations are Old Home Week and the Dooryard Arts Festival, both in August. Other than that, it's a laid-back town with understated charm.

GETTING HERE AND AROUND

Woodstock is off the Trans-Canada Highway (Route 2) at Exits 188 and 185. Coming from the United States, Interstate 95 becomes Route 95 as it crosses the U.S. border near Houlton, Maine, and continues the short distance to Woodstock. The town is on the Maritime Bus route along the Trans-Canada, but the set-down/pickup point is near the box stores, quite a walk from the center (and a steep climb back up). Downtown is easily explored on foot, though it's quite an uphill trudge to some of the finest old residential streets and main shopping area, and a car is necessary to visit the Old County Court House in Upper Woodstock.

ESSENTIALS

Visitor Information **Provincial Visitor Information Centre.** ✉ *109 Tourist Bureau Rd., Richmond Corner* ☎ *506/325-4427.*

EXPLORING

Connell House. A fine example of Greek Revival architecture, this is the former home of Honorable Charles Connell (1810–73), a politician active in many areas of public life, but perhaps best remembered for putting his own image on the five-cent stamp instead of that of the Queen when he was Postmaster General. The largely restored house, home to the Carleton County Historical Society, contains fine furniture, artifacts, musical instruments, and the Tappan Adney Room, honoring the man who is credited with saving the birch-bark canoe. His grave is in the Upper Woodstock Cemetery. Temporary exhibitions and occasional concerts are added attractions. ✉ *128 Connell St.* ☎ *506/328-9706* ⊕ *www.cchs-nb.ca* ✉ *C$5* ⏲ *July and Aug., Tues.–Sat. 10–6; Sept.–June, Tues.–Fri. 9–4:30. Other times by appointment.*

Old County Court House. Dating from 1833, this splendid galleried former court house was restored after years of neglect and misuse and was opened to the public by H.R.H. Princess Anne in 1986. Guided tours are available in summer, and occasional special events include an annual Christmas concert. ✉ *19 Court St., Upper Woodstock* ☎ *506/328-9706* ⊕ *www.cchs-nb.ca* ✉ *C$2 donation requested* ⏲ *Tues.–Fri. 9–4:30, also Sat. 9–6 July and Aug., Sun. and Mon. by appointment.*

WHERE TO EAT

$$ BISTRO ✕ **Creek Village Gallery and Café.** Organic, vegetarian, and gluten-free food is the specialty of this café-art gallery just off Main Street in the downtown area. You might lunch on ginger carrot soup with organic Red Fife bread, or choose from a range of paninis, wraps, and sandwiches. Dinner features such dishes as wild sockeye salmon, and drinks include wine, cocktails, and local brews. The gallery represents about 30 local artists, and there are periodical artist-reception events. [$] *Average main: C$12* ✉ *119 Connell St.* ☎ *506/328-3232* ⏲ *No dinner Sat.–Wed.*

KINGS LANDING HISTORICAL SETTLEMENT

72 km (45 miles) east of Woodstock; 30 km (19 miles) west of Fredericton.

New Brunswick became home to many Loyalists who headed north across the border after the American Revolution, and this living-history site charmingly replicates their lifestyle beside the St. John River. Buildings from that era have been relocated here to form a complete settlement, including agricultural, industrial, and social exhibits.

GETTING HERE AND AROUND

There's no public transportation to King's Landing. By car, it's just off the Trans-Canada Highway (Route 2), but the River Valley Scenic Drive is a more pleasant option; it's well signposted from both.

EXPLORING

FAMILY
Fodor's Choice
★

Kings Landing Historical Settlement. When the Mactaquac Dam was created in the 1960s, a number of historically important buildings were saved and moved to a new shore, later to be joined by more rescued buildings from elsewhere in New Brunswick. Restored and furnished, they created a living-history museum in the form of a typical Loyalist settlement of 1790 to 1900. The winding country lanes and meticulously restored homes are populated with costumed docents who accurately portray the society and lifestyles of the era. It's interesting to compare the life of the wealthy owner of the sawmill to that of an immigrant farmer. Various "Heritage Workshops" allow visitors to try 19th-century trades, including processing wool and preparing herbal remedies from the plants in the lanes and gardens, and summer camps encourage children to dress in period costume, attend a one-room schoolhouse, and learn the chores, games, and mannerisms of 19th-century youth. There are daily productions in the theater, barn dances, and strolling musicians. Hearty meals and heritage ales are served at the Kings Head Inn. ✉ *5804 Rte. 102, Exit 253 off Trans-Canada (Hwy. 2), Prince William* ☎ *506/363–4999* 🌐 *kingslanding.nb.ca* 💲 *C$16.81* ⏲ *Mid-June–mid-Oct., daily 10–5.*

3

MACTAQUAC PROVINCIAL PARK

25 km (16 miles) west of Fredericton.

Just a short drive from the provincial capital, this 525-hectare (1,300-acre) park alongside the St. John River is geared up for all kinds of summer and winter outdoor pursuits. Highlights include the sandy beaches (with volleyball nets) and the viewpoint and information panel overlooking the natural beaver ponds.

GETTING HERE AND AROUND

The park is on Route 105, west of Fredericton and off the Trans-Canada Highway (Route 2) at Exit 258, via Routes 102 then 105. There are two main entrances: on the northern edge opposite the intersection of Routes 105 and 615, and midway down the western side off Route 105 near the golf course. A third, southern entrance only leads to Walinaik Cove marina.

EXPLORING

Mactaquac Provincial Park. Surrounding the giant pond created by the Mactaquac Hydroelectric Dam on the St. John River is Mactaquac Provincial Park. Its facilities include an 18-hole championship golf course, two beaches, two marinas (one for powerboats and one for sailboats), supervised crafts activities, myriad nature and hiking trails, and a restaurant. There are also guided walks on summer Wednesdays through a nature reserve to beaver ponds. Reservations are advised for the 300 campsites in summer, but winter is fun, too; there are lots of trails for cross-country skiing and snowshoeing, and sleigh rides are available by appointment. The toboggan hills and skating/ice hockey ponds are even lighted in the evening. There's a TreeGO attraction (☎ *506/363–4440,* 🌐 *www.treegomactaquac.ca*) in the adjacent Centennial Park. ✉ *1265 Rte. 105, Mactaquac*

506/363–4747 C$8 per vehicle, mid-May–mid-Oct.; no entrance fee in winter Daily 8 am–dusk; overnight camping mid-May–mid-Oct.

FREDERICTON

The small inland city of Fredericton, on a broad point of land jutting into the St. John River, is a gracious and beautiful place that feels more like a large village. It's especially interesting to visit if history is your passion.

Fredericton's predecessor, the early French settlement of Pointe-Sainte-Anne (Ste. Anne's Point), was established in 1642 during the reign of the French governor Joseph Robineau de Villebon, who made his headquarters at the junction of the Nashwaak and St. John rivers. Settled by Loyalists and named for Frederick, second son of George III, the city serves as the seat of government for New Brunswick's 754,000 residents. Wealthy and scholarly Loyalists set out to create a gracious and beautiful place, and even before the establishment of the University of New Brunswick, in 1785, the town served as a center for liberal arts and sciences.

Fredericton was the first city in Canada to offer free Wi-Fi throughout downtown. To learn more check out *www.fred-ezone.ca.*

GETTING HERE AND AROUND

Fredericton is a little way north of the Trans-Canada Highway (Route 2), with four exits to choose from. Coming from the west, Exit 280 onto Route 8 is best; from the east take Exit 294 onto Route 7. Fredericton has an excellent bus service, operating Monday to Saturday 6:15 am to 11 pm; fares are C$2.25 or 10 trips for C$20, and exact change is required.

Downtown Queen Street runs parallel to the river and has several historic sights and attractions. Most major sights are within walking distance of one another. Bike rentals are available from Savage's on King Street and Radical Edge on Westmorland, and the city has a network of trails through parks and along the river. Dressed in 18th-century costumes, actors from the Calithumpians Theatre Company conduct free historical walks three times a day, from Canada Day (July 1) to Labor Day. The tours start at city hall at 10 am, 2:30 pm, and 5 pm and last about an hour. After dark, actors lead a Haunted Hike (C$14) through historic neighborhoods and ghostly graveyards. Check at the City Hall Visitor Information Centre for details.

ESSENTIALS

Bike Rentals **Radical Edge.** *129 Westmorland St. 506/459–3478 radicaledge.ca.* **Savage's.** *441 King St. 506/457–7452 www.sbcoutlet.com.*

Visitor Information **City Hall Visitor Information Centre.** *397 Queen St. 506/460–2129 May–Oct., 506/460–2041 Nov.–late Apr. www.tourismfredericton.ca.* **Fredericton Tourism.** *11 Carleton St. 506/460–2041, 888/888–4768 www.tourismfredericton.ca.*

TOURS

FAMILY **Calithumpians Theatre Company.** Haunted Hikes (*C$14*) are conducted from July to early September, Monday through Saturday, departing from the Coach House (*796a Queen St.*) at 9 pm. ☎ *506/457–1975* ⊕ *www.calithumpians.com.*

Wolastoq Boat Tours. Hop aboard, right in the heart of downtown Fredericton (just behind the lighthouse), for a sightseeing cruise on the St. John River that offers a unique perspective on city sights. Tours depart Tuesday through Sunday at 2, 4, 6 and 8 pm, and last around 90 to 100 minutes. ✉ *Regent St. Wharf* ☎ *506/471–8680* ₵ *C$19.*

EXPLORING

TOP ATTRACTIONS

Fodor's Choice ★ **Beaverbrook Art Gallery.** A lasting gift of the late Lord Beaverbrook, born and raised in New Brunswick before building his U.K. media empire, this gallery could hold its head high in the company of some of the smaller European galleries. It contains a significant collection of Canadian, American, and British masterworks that rivals many major Canadian galleries. Salvador Dalí's gigantic painting *Santiago el Grande* has always been the star, but a rotation of avant-garde Canadian paintings now shares pride of place. The McCain "gallery-within-a-gallery" is devoted to the finest Atlantic Canadian artists. ✉ *703 Queen St.* ☎ *506/458–8545, 506/458–2028* ⊕ *beaverbrookartgallery.org* ₵ *C$10* ⏲ *May–Sept., Mon.–Sat. 10–5 (to 9 Thurs.), Sun. noon–5; Oct.–Apr., Tues.–Sat. 10–5 (to 9 Thurs.), Sun. noon–5.*

FAMILY Fodor's Choice ★ **Historic Garrison District.** The restored buildings of this British and Canadian post, which extends two blocks along Queen Street, include soldiers' barracks, a guardhouse, and a cell block. This is a National Historic Site and one of New Brunswick's top attractions. Local artisans operate studios in the casemates below the soldiers' barracks in Barracks Square. In July and August free guided tours run throughout the day, and there are regular outdoor concerts in **Officers' Square.** Redcoat soldiers have long stood guard in Officers' Square, and a formal changing-of-the-guard ceremony takes place July and August at 11 am and 4 pm daily, with an additional ceremony at 7 pm on Tuesday and Thursday. It's even possible for children (ages 4 to 12) to live a soldier's life for a while: each summer at 1:15 (or 11:15 for the French version) at the Guardhouse, would-be Redcoats get their own uniforms, practice drilling, and take part in a "mission" (C$9 per child). The square hosts a number of festivals, there's nightly entertainment in summer, and on Sunday evenings in July and August, free classic movies are shown under the stars in Barracks Square at approximately 9 pm. ✉ *Queen St. at Carleton St.* ☎ *506/460–2129* ₵ *Free* ⏲ *Daily 24 hrs.*

Provincial Legislature. The interior chamber of the legislature, where the premier and elected members govern the province, reflects the taste of the late Victorians. The chandeliers are brass, and some of the prisms are Waterford. Replicas of portraits by Sir Joshua Reynolds of King George III and Queen Charlotte hang here. There's a freestanding

Beaverbrook Art Gallery 3
Christ Church Cathedral 5
Fredericton Boyce Farmers' Market 7
Fredericton Region Museum 2
Gallery 78 4
Government House 8
Historic Garrison District 1
Marysville 9
Provincial Legislature 6

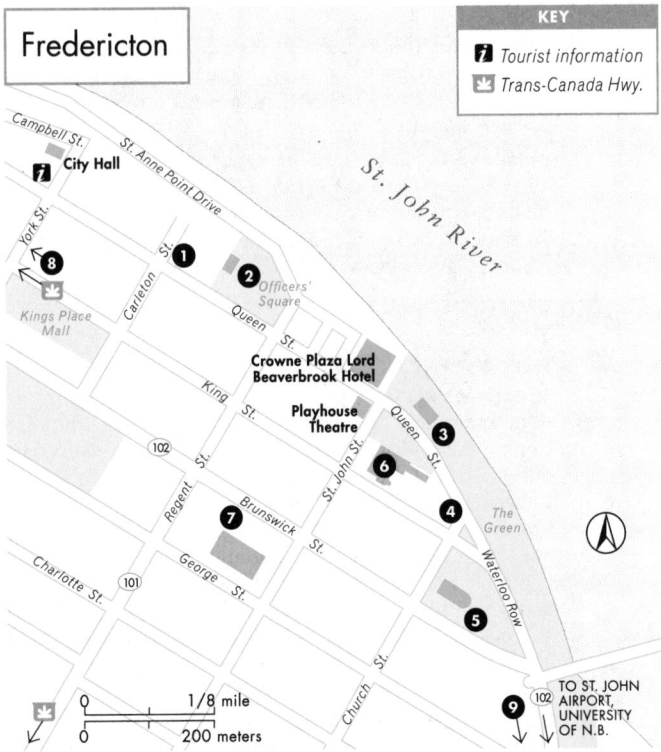

circular staircase, and the library *(☎ 506/453–2338)* owns a complete four-volume set of hand-colored copper engravings of Audubon's *Birds of America,* one of only five sets in Canada. Call in for a look around, or call ahead to arrange a tour. ✉ *706 Queen St.* ☎ *506/453–2527* 🌐 *www.gnb.ca* 💲 *Free* ⏲ *Late June–late Aug., daily 9–5; late Aug.–late June, weekdays 8:30–4.*

WORTH NOTING

Christ Church Cathedral. This gray-stone building, completed in 1853, is an excellent example of decorated neo-Gothic architecture. The cathedral's design was based on an English medieval architectural style, and the cathedral became a model for many American churches. Inside is some fine carved marble and a clock known as "Big Ben's little brother"—it was the prototype for London's famous timepiece, designed by Lord Grimthorpe. ✉ *168 Church St.* ☎ *506/450–8500* 💲 *Free* ⏲ *Self-guided tours: weekdays 9–6, Sat. 10–6, Sun. between services. Guided tours: July and Aug., weekdays 9–6, Sat. 10–6, Sun. 1–5.*

Fredericton Boyce Farmers' Market. It's hard to miss this Saturday-morning market because of the crowds. It's one of the finest markets in Canada, operating since 1951, with the building and surrounding space housing more than 250 local suppliers. Local and organic meat and produce, cheeses, baked goods, maple syrup, crafts, and seasonal items such as wreaths and garden furniture are on offer. Good ready-to-eat food is available as well, from German sausages to tasty samosas. Good luck finding a parking spot, here or on surrounding streets! ✉ *665 George St.* ☎ *506/451-1815* 🌐 *frederictonfarmersmarket.ca* ⏲ *Sat. 6 am–1 pm.*

FAMILY **Fredericton Region Museum.** The Officers' Quarters in the Historic Garrison District house a museum that presents a living picture of the community from the time when only First Nations peoples inhabited the area through the Acadian and Loyalist days to the immediate past. Its World War I trench puts you in the thick of battle, and the shellacked remains of the giant Coleman Frog, a Fredericton legend, still inspire controversy. There is also an artists' co-op store featuring locally produced art and crafts. If you're visiting outside the summer months, wear warm clothing—the historic site has no heating or insulation. ✉ *Officers' Sq., 571 Queen St.* ☎ *506/455-6041* 🌐 *www.frederictonregionmuseum.com* 💲 *C$5* ⏲ *July–early Sept., daily. 10–5; Apr.–June and early Sept.–Nov., Tues.–Sat. 1–4 or by appt; Dec.–Mar. by appt.*

Gallery 78. In a distinctive historic house, the oldest private gallery in New Brunswick has original works by nearly 80 Atlantic Canadian artists. ✉ *796 Queen St.* ☎ *506/454-5192, 888/883-8322* 🌐 *www.gallery78.com.*

Government House. This imposing 1828 Palladian mansion on the south bank of the St. John River has been restored as the official residence and office for New Brunswick's lieutenant governor. A hands-on interpretive center spans 12,000 years of history. Guided tours take in elegantly restored state rooms and art galleries. The 11-acre grounds, once a 17th-century Acadian settlement, borders an early Maliseet burial ground. It's also the venue for a number of festivals and other events every year. ✉ *51 Woodstock Rd.* ☎ *506/453-2505* 🌐 *www.gnb.ca/lg* 💲 *Free* ⏲ *Mid-May–Aug. 31, Mon.–Sat 10–4, Sun noon–4.*

OFF THE BEATEN PATH

Marysville. A National Historic District, Marysville is one of Canada's best-preserved examples of a 19th-century mill town. Its architecture and social history are amazing and can be appreciated with the help of a self-guided walking-tour booklet available at the Fredericton Regional Museum. Marysville itself is on the north side of the St. John River, about 10 km (6 miles) from downtown Fredericton via Route 8. ✉ *Fredericton.*

FREDERICTON ARTS

The **Downtown Fredericton Culture Crawl** takes place the first Thursday of every month, from June to September. During the festival, you can visit around 15 of the art galleries, craft studios, and shops in the downtown area, all within walking distance of each other (all stay open until 8 pm). It's free, and maps are available at City Hall Visitor Information Centre.

WHERE TO EAT

$$$ ✕ **Brewbakers.** Popular with the business community and with a loyal
ECLECTIC local following, this casual upstairs lunch and dinner spot has a cool urban interior, highlighted by stained-glass windows from an old church. The rooftop garden patio is so popular that they've added another enclosed one, a boon in inclement weather. The menu is upscale, with dishes such as porcini-crusted flat-iron steak or citrus-cured salmon with fried egg and orange gastrique, and vegetarian choices such as tofu maple curry penne. Some of the optional add-ons can ramp up the price. [$] *Average main: C$26* ✉ *546 King St.* ☎ *506/459–0067* ⊕ *brewbakers.ca* ⏲ *No lunch weekends.*

$$$ ✕ **[catch] Urban Grill.** The restaurant in the Delta Hotel is a friendly and
SEAFOOD stylish place, with views across the poolside patio to the St. John River. Specializing in seafood (hence the name), the kitchen turns out delicious, expertly constructed dishes like herb-crusted catfish with rice and arugula pineapple salad or sesame seed teriyaki salmon. Meat dishes are succulent and tasty, and the lunchtime pasta buffet is deservedly popular. Date Night Saturdays offer dinner for two and a movie for C$69.99. The staff is friendly, knowledgeable, and enthusiastic. If you're staying in the hotel, the buffet breakfast is exceptionally good. [$] *Average main: C$22* ✉ *225 Woodstock Rd.* ☎ *506/478–4251* ⊕ *www.deltahotels.com/Hotels/Delta-Fredericton.*

$$ ✕ **Isaac's Way.** Not only is the food here delicious, you can almost feel
CANADIAN yourself being nourished by the top-quality ingredients, most of which
FAMILY are sourced locally. On the varied dinner menu, you might find coconut
Fodor's Choice Digby scallops, beef braised in the local Picaroon's beer, herb-roasted
★ lamb, and vegetarian dishes, and lunchtime options include gourmet sandwiches and burgers and some of the dinner dishes, plus salads, house-made soups, and a kids' menu. Housed in the old courthouse in the heart of downtown, the restaurant displays works by local artists, which can be purchased at list price or you can enter into one of the regular silent auctions, when artists donate at least 50% to a local children's art project charity. Isaac's is also a popular place to hang out in the evening. [$] *Average main: C$20* ✉ *649 Queen St.* ☎ *506/474–7222* ⊕ *isaacsway.ca* ⏲ *No breakfast weekdays.*

$$$ ✕ **The Palate Restaurant & Café.** Artwork by local artists enhances the
MEDITERRANEAN colorful, spacious interior, and the open kitchen gives a view of the enthusiastic chefs in action. The menu leans toward Mediterranean and Western European, adding a few exotic touches and interesting combinations of flavors, as in the tequila-and-lime jumbo shrimp starter, a richly flavored pork tenderloin with smoked maple syrup and roasted-garlic mashed potatoes, and lemon meringue salmon, with lemon, Parmesan, and chive aioli. The vegetarian option might be a skillet vegetable-and-bean medley. The lunch menu focuses on creative sandwiches, paninis, stir-fries, and naan pizzas, and brunch is served on Saturday from 10. [$] *Average main: C$22* ✉ *462 Queen St.* ☎ *506/450–7911* ⊕ *www.thepalate.com* ⏲ *Closed Sun. No brunch weekdays.*

WHERE TO STAY

$$ B&B/INN Fodor's Choice ★ **Carriage House Inn.** Originally the 1875 home of Fredericton's mayor, this beautiful pre-Victorian mansion—a Provincial Historic Site—is as authentic as they come, and the welcome couldn't be warmer. **Pros:** excellent location near everything, but on a quiet and stately street; fabulous breakfast; accommodating and friendly hosts. **Cons:** perhaps not for those who favor a more modern style. [$] *Rooms from: C$129* ✉ *230 University Ave.* ☎ *506/452–9924, 800/267–6068* 🌐 *www.carriagehouse-inn.net* 🛏 *10 rooms, 1 suite* 🍴 *Breakfast.*

$$ HOTEL **Crowne Plaza Fredericton–Lord Beaverbrook.** This historic hotel has a great location, overlooking the river at the back, fronting some of the city's most important landmarks, and an easy walk to downtown attractions. **Pros:** has the comfort and amenities you'd expect from a large chain hotel; convenient location; own parking lot. **Cons:** some rooms are small; corridors to some areas are a bit of a warren; some restaurant menu items are overpriced. [$] *Rooms from: C$159* ✉ *659 Queen St.* ☎ *506/455–3371, 866/444–1946* 🌐 *www.cpfredericton.com* 🛏 *155 rooms, 13 suites* 🍴 *No meals.*

$$ RESORT FAMILY Fodor's Choice ★ **Delta Fredericton Hotel.** The Delta group's Atlantic flagship is a chic urban resort where the superfriendly staff create a lively modern atmosphere. **Pros:** high levels of comfort; lots of amenities; enthusiastic staff; wonderful riverside location. **Cons:** outside the downtown area. [$] *Rooms from: C$139* ✉ *225 Woodstock Rd.* ☎ *506/457–7000* 🌐 *www.deltahotels.com* 🛏 *202 rooms, 20 suites* 🍴 *No meals.*

$ B&B/INN **Quatermain House B&B.** An extraordinarily pretty Gothic Revival heritage home, Quartermain House offers an exceptional bed-and-breakfast experience in leafy surroundings just a 10-minute walk alongside the river from downtown. **Pros:** warm hospitality; discount for business travelers; coffeemakers and home-baked cookies provided. **Cons:** no children or pets; all bathrooms are private and large, but only one is en suite. [$] *Rooms from: C$110* ✉ *92 Waterloo Row* ☎ *506/206–5255, 855/758–5255* 🌐 *www.quartermainhouse.com* 🛏 *3 rooms* 🍴 *Breakfast.*

NIGHTLIFE AND PERFORMING ARTS

NIGHTLIFE

Fredericton does not have a particularly lively nightlife scene, although there is some live music in downtown pubs, especially on weekends. King Street and Piper's Lane, off the 300 block of King Street, have a number of spots.

The Capital Complex. An eclectic collection of live bands, covering all genres, plays at the Capital Bar (Thurs.–Sat. 9 pm–2 am); Wilser's Room pub (Tues.–Fri. 4 pm–2 am, Sat. 6 pm–2 am) has live entertainment, open-mike night on Tuesdays, and a monthly comedy club; and the complex also includes The Phoenix Nightclub, with DJs Thurs. 8 pm–2 am, Fri. and Sat. 10 pm–2 am). ✉ *362 Queen St.* ☎ *506/459–3558* 🌐 *www.thecapitalcomplex.com.*

Dolan's Pub. This is a great place to see live rock and blues bands from all over Eastern Canada on Thursday, Friday, and Saturday nights from about 10:30 pm. St. Patrick's Day here is a wild daylong party. ✉ *349 King St.* ☎ *506/454–7474* 🌐 *www.dolanspub.ca* ⏲ *Closed Sun.*

PERFORMING ARTS

Calithumpians Theatre Company. For 35 years, Calithumpians has continued to delight family audiences with their shows about local history, folklore, and legend as well as modern social and environmental issues, always tinged with humor. Their free outdoor performances run daily in summer (12:15 pm weekdays, 2 pm weekends) in Officers' Square, and a 90-minute evening Haunted Hike (C$14; early July–early September, Mon.–Sat. 9 pm) ambles through a historic neighborhood and ghostly graveyards. It sets out from the Coach House (behind Gallery 78) at 796a Queen Street. ✉ *Fredericton* ☎ *506/457–1975.*

Fodor's Choice ★ **Playhouse.** A wide range of entertainment is staged at this fine theater next door to the provincial legislature, from comedy and concerts to cultural performances by Symphony New Brunswick, Theatre New Brunswick, and traveling ballet and dance companies. ✉ *686 Queen St.* ☎ *506/458–8344, 866/884–5800* 🌐 *www.theplayhouse.ca.*

SPORTS AND THE OUTDOORS

CANOEING AND KAYAKING

FAMILY **Second Nature Outdoors.** Canoes, kayaks, and stand-up paddleboards can be rented by the hour (C$15–C$20), and the center also runs a shuttle service (C$5) to Hartt Island, from where you can paddle back downstream with the current to help you. Tours in a 14-person Voyager Canoe (C$35 per person) and three-day family canoe and camping trips (C$375 per person) are also offered. The center is open daily from noon, mid-June through early September. ✉ *Small Craft Aquatic Center, 63 Brunswick St.* ☎ *506/460–2260.*

GOLF

Kingswood Park. The 18-hole championship Signature Course and 9-hole Executive Course, designed by Cooke-Huxham International, offer a rewarding game amid beautiful scenery. The Signature course includes a 30-foot waterfall on the 14th hole and a tricky long par 4 on the 18th. Marshes, rocks, and well-placed bunkers and water hazards add to the challenge of a course that was *Golf Digest's* "Best New Course" when it opened. (Non–golfing members of the family will appreciate the Kingswood Entertainment Centre, with indoor play facilities, a bowling alley, skating rink, and arcade games.) ✉ *31 Kingswood Park* ☎ *506/443–3334, 800/423–5969* 🌐 *www.kingswoodpark.ca* 💲 *Signature Course, C$39–C$89; Executive Course, C$15–C$25* ⛳ *Signature Course: 18 holes, 6601 yards, par 72; Executive Course: 9 holes, 2060 yards, par 27.*

SKIING

Many of Fredericton's 70 km (44 miles) of walking trails, especially those along the river and in Odell and Wilmot parks, are groomed for cross-country skiing.

Ski Crabbe Mountain. The 18 downhill trails here have a vertical drop of 853 feet, and there are good terrain parks, plus trails for Nordic skiing, snowshoeing, and snowmobiling. Other amenities include snowboard and ski rentals, a ski shop, instruction, a skating pond, cross-country skiing, babysitting, and a lounge and restaurant. Check the website for details of half-price offers and special events. ✉ *50 Crabbe Mountain Rd., Central Hainesville* ✣ *55 km (34 miles) west of Fredericton, off Trans-Canada Hwy. at Exit 231, via Nackawic* ☎ *506/463–8311 select 300 for Snow Phone, 902/896–1205* ⊕ *www.crabbemountain.com* 💲 *Lift tickets: C$30 night, C$35 half day, C$40 full day; lift ticket plus equipment rental: C$55 full day* ⏲ *Sept.–mid-Apr., Mon.–Wed. 9–4:30 (to 9 during school holidays), Thurs.–Sun. 9–9; call Snow Phone to check as hrs are subject to weather conditions.*

WALKING

Fredericton has a fine network of walking trails totaling more than 80 km (50 miles), one of which follows the river from the Delta Hotel, passing behind Government House and the Beaverbrook Art Gallery, and in front of the Victorian mansions on Waterloo Row. This also forms part of the Fredericton section of the Trans-Canada Trail, which will cross the whole country when finished (planned for 2017 to mark Canada's 150th birthday). Other trails include Odell Park and the University of New Brunswick campus. The Visitor Information Centre can provide details.

Visitor Information Centre. Get your trail maps here. ✉ *City Hall, 397 Queen St. at York St.* ☎ *506/460–2129* ⊕ *www.tourismfredericton.ca.*

SHOPPING

Downtown shopping is focused on Queen, King, and York streets west of Regent, the latter having an interesting range of fashion and specialty stores. At the top of Regent Street, south of downtown, you'll find the Regent Mall, and the big-box stores of the Corbett Centre and Prospect Street ("Uptown Fredericton"). Shopping north of the river is more workaday, but the relatively new Northside Market on St. Mary's Street (weekends only) gets good reviews. Mammoth indoor crafts markets are held in the fall and run up to Christmas, and a Labor Day–weekend outdoor crafts fair (the New Brunswick Fine Crafts Festival) is held in Officers' Square. You can find pottery, blown glass, pressed flowers, turned wood, leather, and other items, all made by members of the New Brunswick Craft Council.

Aitkens Pewter. The owners of this shop design, produce, and sell pewter jewelry and belt buckles, goblets, candlesticks, and other home decor pieces. They also have stores in Saint John and Halifax. ✉ *408 Queen St.* ☎ *506/453–9474, 800/567–4416* ⊕ *www.aitkenspewter.com.*

Art Jewel Designs by Gallagher and Tremblay. Sparkling wearable works of art are produced here, and you can often see the jewelers at work. ✉ *Isaac's Way Restaurant, 649 Queen St.* ☎ *506/799–1398* ⊕ *www.artjeweldesigns.ca.*

The Barracks Fine Craft Shops. Pottery, jewelry, paintings, and other crafts are made and sold in this shop in the converted soldiers' barracks of the Historic Garrison District, and there's a schedule of art and craft demonstrations. ✉ *Barracks Sq., 485 Queen St., corner of Carleton St.* ☎ *506/460–2837* ⏲ *Closed early Sept.–May.*

Botinicals. Crafts and paintings by more than 50 artists—mostly residents of New Brunswick—are sold here. ✉ *610 Queen St.* ☎ *506/454–6101, 877/450–6101* 🌐 *www.botinicalsgiftshop.com* ⏲ *Closed Sun.*

Eloise. This women's fashion boutique specializes in Canadian clothing lines and footwear. ✉ *69 York St.* ☎ *506/453–7715* 🌐 *eloiseltd.com.*

Endeavours and ThinkPlay. Artistic endeavours are catered to here, with all kinds of art and craft supplies and stationery, funky toys, and games that appeal to all ages. ✉ *412 Queen St.* ☎ *506/455–4278, 800/565–0422* 🌐 *www.artstuff.ca* ⏲ *Closed Sun.*

Urban Almanac General Store. An eclectic collection of household gifts, furniture, loose-leaf teas, gadgets, and gizmos of exemplary design will keep you browsing here. ✉ *75 York St.* ☎ *506/450–4334* 🌐 *www.urbanalmanac.com.*

EN ROUTE

CFB Gagetown Military Museum. Oromocto, off Highway 2, east of Fredericton, is the site of the Canadian Armed Forces base Camp Gagetown, the largest military base in Canada (not to be confused with the pretty Village of Gagetown farther downriver), which has an interesting military museum. Prince Charles completed his helicopter training here. The museum traces Canada's military history back to the 18th century and includes regimental, naval, and air force exhibits. ✉ *Bldg. A5, off Walnut St., Camp Gagetown* ☎ *506/422–1304* 🌐 *www.museumgagetown.ca/EngRNBR.htm* 💲 *Free* ⏲ *Weekdays 8–4.*

VILLAGE OF GAGETOWN

50 km (31 miles) southeast of Fredericton.

Fodor's Choice ★ The historic riverside Village of Gagetown—not to be confused with the Gagetown military base at Oromocto—bustles in summer, when artists welcome visitors, many of whom arrive by boat and tie up at the marina, to their studios and galleries. It also has several small restaurants with interesting menus.

GETTING HERE AND AROUND

If you're driving from Fredericton, the Trans-Canada Highway (Route 2) is fast and direct, leaving at Exit 330, signposted "Village of/de Gagetown" (do not follow the earlier signs for "Gagetown," which lead to the military base). Route 102 from Fredericton is the scenic option. Once there, the village is great for strolling.

ESSENTIALS

Visitor Information Centre. ✉ *Tilley House, 69 Front St.* ☎ *506/488–2966* ⏲ *Closed early Sept.–May.*

EXPLORING

Queens County Museum. Expanding by leaps and bounds, the museum's original building, **Tilley House** (a National Historic Site), was the birthplace of Sir Leonard Tilley, one of the Fathers of Confederation. It displays Loyalist and First Nations artifacts, early-20th-century medical equipment, Victorian glassware, and more. The nearby **Queens County Courthouse** (✉ *16 Courthouse Rd.*) is part of the museum and has archival material and courthouse furniture as well as changing exhibits. The third site is **Flower House** in Cambridge Narrow (✉ *2270 Lower Cambridge Rd.*), built in 1818 by artist Anthony Flower. It relates his family history and contains a collection of his art, alongside works by other New Brunswick artists. ✉ *69 Front St.* ☎ *506/488–2483 seasonal* 🌐 *www.queenscountyheritage.com* 💲 *C$3, C$5 for 2 buildings, C$7 for all 3 buildings* ⏲ *Mid-June–mid-Sept., daily 10–5; May, Oct., and Nov. by appointment.*

WHERE TO EAT AND STAY

$$ INTERNATIONAL ✕ **Creek View Restaurant.** On a corner just one block back from Front Street, this charming little restaurant serves country cuisine in a pleasant atmosphere, with outdoor seating in summer. The wide-ranging menu—the same at lunch and dinner—is strong on seafood and comfort food, and caters well to kids and gluten-averse diners. There's entertainment about twice a month, with cover charges. When there's no entertainment, the restaurant closes at 8 pm (7 pm early in the week); call to check opening hours outside the summer season. 💲 *Average main: C$15* ✉ *38 Tilley Rd., Gagetown* ☎ *506/488–9806* 🌐 *www.thecreekviewrestaurant.com* ⏲ *No breakfast Mon. and Tues.*

$$ B&B/INN **Step-Aside B&B.** In the heart of the village, this waterfront heritage B&B overlooking the marina is renowned for its hospitality. **Pros:** delicious full breakfast and taxes included in the price; friendly and knowledgeable owners. **Cons:** bathrooms in the original house are private but not en suite. 💲 *Rooms from: C$125* ✉ *58 Front St., Gagetown* ☎ *506/488–1808* ⏲ *Closed Jan.–Apr.* 🛏 *4 rooms* 🍽 *Breakfast.*

SHOPPING

Grieg Pottery. Grieg's Pottery carries superior pottery made on the premises. Budding potters can attend off-season weekend workshops (call for details). ✉ *36 Front St., Gagetown* ☎ *506/488–2074* ⏲ *Closed weekends Jan.–Apr. (except by appointment).*

Grimross Crafts. This lovely art-and-crafts store represents 25 local craftspeople. It's open daily in summer and in the last week in November during the village's "Christmas in the Village" event. ✉ *64 Front St., Gagetown* ☎ *506/488–2832* ⏲ *Closed mid-Oct–mid-June.*

Juggler's Cove. This studio-gallery features pottery and paintings. ✉ *27 Front St., Gagetown* ☎ *506/488–2574.*

PRINCE EDWARD ISLAND

WELCOME TO PRINCE EDWARD ISLAND

TOP REASONS TO GO

★ **Experience the Anne phenomenon:** The orphan nobody wanted has been adopted by the world. She's everywhere on the Island, but Cavendish's Green Gables farmhouse is ground zero.

★ **Get beached:** Been there? Dune this. The most jaded, jet-setting beach bum will still be dazzled by the parabolic dunes at Prince Edward Island National Park in Greenwich.

★ **Go golfing:** A concentration of championship courses—among them the Links at Crowbush Cove, Dundarave, and Brudenell River—make PEI a top choice for golfers.

★ **Cycle the Confederation Trail:** Even "I haven't ridden a bike in ages" types can cover the stunning 10-km (6-mile) waterside stretch between Morell and St. Peter's Bay.

★ **Enjoy fresh seafood:** Forget the frozen fish sticks of your childhood. The local seafood here—whether served in a classy restaurant or community hall—is sensational.

1 Charlottetown. PEI's historic capital city has urban amenities and a small-town vibe. Centrally located, it makes an excellent base for exploring the Island.

2 Central Coastal Drive. This 198-km (123-mile) circuit encompasses Green Gables, Prince Edward Island National Park, and the less-touristed Red Sands Shore.

GETTING ORIENTED

Erosion and time have gnawed Prince Edward Island into a ragged crescent, with deep inlets and tidal streams that divide the province into three nearly equal parts, known locally by their county names (from east to west) of Kings, Queens, and Prince. The Island is 195 km (121 miles) long and ranges in width from 6 km (4 miles) to 61¼ km (38 miles). Despite the gentle hills in the eastern and central regions of Prince Edward Island, the land never rises to a height of more than 500 feet above sea level. To the west, from Summerside to North Cape, the terrain is flatter.

3 Points East Coastal Drive. Lovely lighthouses and great golf courses plus fishing ports, hidden coves, singing sands, and fun festivals are all highlights here.

4 North Cape Coastal Drive. Anchored by Summerside (the Island's second-largest city), this region includes a distinctive coastline and a farm-filled interior.

Updated by Penny Phenix

Prince Edward Island is a camera-ready landmass marked by verdant patchwork fields that stretch out beneath an endless cobalt sky to meet white-sand beaches and the surrounding sea. But it's so much more than just another pretty place. Like the water temperature in summer, people here are remarkably warm. Their heartfelt hospitality and slow-paced lifestyle entice visitors to return year after year.

Colonized by France in 1603, Prince Edward Island (or Île Saint-Jean, as it was then called) was handed over to Britain under the Treaty of Paris in 1763. Tensions steadily increased as absentee British governors and proprietors failed to take an active interest in the area's growth; nevertheless, the development of fisheries and agriculture in the early 19th century strengthened the local economy. Soon settlement increased, and those willing to take a chance on the Island prospered.

As relations between emboldened tenants and their distant landlords continued to worsen, heated talk about uniting with other colonies in British North America began. (The Civil War, then raging in the United States, made the idea of forging a peaceable alliance all the more appealing.) So in 1864, the Island's capital city hosted the Charlottetown Conference, a milestone in this nation's history, which ultimately led to the creation of the Dominion of Canada in 1867.

Despite this political alliance, it took another 130 years—and almost 13 km (8 miles) of concrete—for Prince Edward Island to be *physically* linked with the rest of the country. When the Confederation Bridge opened between Borden-Carleton and Cape Jourimain, New Brunswick, in 1997, traditionalists feared it would destroy PEI's tranquillity. (As you explore the villages and fishing ports, it's easy to see why they cherish it so.) Yet outside the tourist hub of Cavendish, the Island still seems like an oasis of peace in an increasingly busy world.

In summer, thanks to the relatively shallow Gulf of St. Lawrence and circulating Gulf Stream, Prince Edward Island beaches have the warmest saltwater north of the Carolinas. (Temperatures can reach 70°F in July and August.) Factor in sandy strands and the result is fine swimming conditions. Best of all, the Island's 1,760-km (1,100-mile) coast means a beach is always close by. Basin Head Beach, near Souris, has miles of singing sands. Often less populated, and with fine ocean sunsets, is West Point. At Greenwich, near St. Peter's Bay, a boardwalk stroll brings you to an endless empty beach.

PLANNING

WHEN TO GO

PEI is generally considered a summer destination—in July and August the beaches have the warmest water north of the Carolinas—but don't overlook the shoulder seasons. May, June, September, and October usually have fine weather and few visitors. In late spring, those famous farm fields look especially green, and bright wildflowers blanket the roadsides. Autumn, too, is multihued thanks to the changing fall foliage. If white is your color, come in winter for cross-country skiing, snowmobiling, and ice-skating. Bear in mind that many sights and services close in mid-October; however, you won't have any problem finding food, lodging, and fun things to do year-round in Charlottetown.

FESTIVALS AND EVENTS

June through mid-October, the calendar is crowded with events—many of them arts-oriented. Summerside, Georgetown, and Victoria-by-the-Sea also host their own summer theater festivals. Different musical genres are represented, too, and sporting events are prevalent. Witness eating as an extreme sport at numerous over-the-top seafood festivals.

Cavendish Beach Music Festival. Cavendish goes a little bit country during July's three-day Beach Music Festival—make that a lot country: Brad Paisley, Keith Urban, and Reba McEntire are past headliners. ✉ *8779 Rte. 6, Cavendish* ☎ *855/929–6336* ⊕ *cavendishbeachmusic.com.*

Charlottetown Festival. PEI's marquee theatrical event is the Charlottetown Festival, where *Anne of Green Gables—The Musical* takes center stage among around a dozen shows in five venues. ✉ *Charlottetown* ☎ *902/628–1864 admin, 800/565–0278 box office* ⊕ *www.charlottetownfestival.com.*

Gran Fondo PEI. Cyclists mount up for rides and races during the three-day Gran Fondo PEI event in late August. ✉ *Charlottetown* ☎ *902/368–4985* ⊕ *granfondo-pei.ca.*

Old Home Week. A favorite among locals, Old Home Week centers on harness racing, with other events including agricultural shows, concerts, and entertainment for kids. It's held in Charlottetown each August. ✉ *Eastlink Centre, 46 Kensington Rd., Charlottetown* ☎ *902/629–6623* ⊕ *oldhomeweekpei.com.*

PEI International Shellfish Festival. Democratic as always, Charlottetown plays no favorites with seafood during the four-day PEI International Shellfish Festival in mid-September. It promises all kinds of seafood galore (some of it prepared by celebrity guest chefs) along with fishing excursions, cooking demos, and other themed events. ✉ *Charlottetown Event Grounds, corner of Grafton and Water Sts., Charlottetown* ☎ *866/955–2003* ⊕ *peishellfish.com.*

PEI Jazz & Blues Festival. The capital gets jazzed up in August for the PEI Jazz and Blues Festival. ✉ *Charlottetown* ☎ *902/894–7131* ⊕ *www.jazzandblues.ca.*

Prince Edward Island Marathon. Runners from across Canada race for the finish line during the Prince Edward Island Marathon in October. It starts out from Brackley Beach in the Prince Edward Island National

Park, follows part of the Confederation Trail, and the finish line is at the south end of University Avenue in Charlottetown. ✉ *Charlottetown* ☎ *902/566–5841* ⊕ *www.peimarathon.ca.*

Summerside Lobster Carnival. Summerside holds a weeklong Lobster Festival every July, with a parade, concerts, triathlon, crafts, sand-castle building, and all kinds of other family fun—and, of course, lobsters. The hub of the action is at Green's Shore. ✉ *Summerside* ☎ *902/724–4925* ⊕ *www.summersidelobsterfest.com.*

Tyne Valley Oyster Festival. Tyne Valley, an attractive Prince County community, hosts an Oyster Festival in late July/early August, complete with fried oyster suppers, oyster chowder competitions, and the Canadian Oyster Shucking Championship. Concerts and food vendors complete the five-day lineup. ✉ *Tyne Valley* ☎ *902/439–1716* ⊕ *www.peioysterfest.com.*

PLANNING YOUR TIME

Covering 5,656 square km (2,184 square miles), PEI is roughly the size of Delaware; and the fact that its area is small is a big advantage for visitors. First timers will want to concentrate on the central section, which includes not only the capital city (Charlottetown), but also the province's most popular beaches, key portions of the Confederation Trail, plus must-see Anne sites. *(To learn more about the irrepressible character L.M. Montgomery introduced in 1908, see the "Who Is Anne, Anyway?" box.)* If you've already covered those bases, travel west or east to enjoy the quiet charms of the adjoining regions.

GETTING HERE AND AROUND

AIR TRAVEL

Scheduled air service operates in and out of Charlottetown Airport (YYG), 5 km (3 miles) north of the capital. Air Canada runs direct service year-round from Halifax, Montréal, and Toronto, with seasonal service from Ottawa from June to September. Connections from 190 destinations worldwide can be made via Toronto and Montréal. WestJet provides year-round service from Toronto. At the airport you can rent a car or grab a cab for the C$14 drive into town.

Contacts **Air Canada.** ☎ *888/247–2262* ⊕ *www.aircanada.ca.* **Charlottetown Airport.** ✉ *250 Maple Hills Av., Charlottetown* ☎ *902/566–7997* ⊕ *www.flypei.com.* **WestJet.** ☎ *888/937–8538* ⊕ *www.westjet.com.*

BUS TRAVEL

Maritime Bus offers daily scheduled service from many towns and cities in Nova Scotia and New Brunswick, via Confederation Bridge. On the Island, service runs between Summerside, Borden-Carleton, Crapaud, Cornwall, and Charlottetown. Mini-bus service to Borden-Carleton, Charlottetown, Summerside, and select destinations is available from Halifax through PEI Express Shuttle or Advanced Shuttle Service.

Contacts **Advanced Shuttle Service.** ☎ *902/888–3353, 877/886–3322* ⊕ *www.advancedshuttle.ca.* **Maritime Bus.** ☎ *800/575–1807* ⊕ *www.maritimebus.com.* **PEI Express Shuttle.** ☎ *902/462–8177, 877/877–1771* ⊕ *www.peishuttle.com.*

CAR OR MOTORCYCLE TRAVEL

Due to limited public transport, having your own wheels is almost a necessity on the Island. Motorists can come via the 13-km (8-mile) Confederation Bridge, which connects Cape Jourimain, New Brunswick, with Borden-Carleton, PEI. The crossing takes about 10 minutes, and the toll is C$18.25 for motorcycles, C$45.50 for cars and, for larger vehicles, C$7.50 per each additional axle. On the Island, there are more than 3,700 km (2,300 miles) of paved roads, including three scenic drives: North Cape Coastal Drive, Central Coastal Drive, and Points East Coastal Drive. Designated Heritage Roads offer an old-fashioned alternative. Surfaced with red clay (the local soil base) and often arched with a canopy of trees, they meander through rural, undeveloped areas where you're likely to see lots of wildflowers and birds. A four-wheel-drive vehicle isn't necessary, but in spring and inclement weather the mud can get quite deep, making narrow, unpaved roads impassable. A highway map of the province is available from Tourism PEI and at visitor centers on the Island.

TIP→ Don't get too excited about crossing over to the Island without purchasing a ferry ticket or paying the bridge toll. Fares are only collected when you leave PEI—giving you further incentive to stay.

Contacts Confederation Bridge. ☎ *902/437–7300, 888/437–6565* ⊕ *www.confederationbridge.com.*

FERRY TRAVEL

Weather permitting, Northumberland Ferries sails between Wood Islands, PEI, and Caribou, Nova Scotia, from May to late December. The crossing takes about 75 minutes, and there are three to nine per day depending on the season. Round-trip rates vary with the length of vehicle; those up to 20 feet long cost C$70 and those up to 50 feet long cost C$113. Foot passengers are charged C$18, cyclists C$20, and motorcyclists C$40. Fuel surcharges (around C$5 for passenger vehicles) must also be added in.

Contacts Northumberland Ferries. ☎ *877/762–7245* ⊕ *www.ferries.ca.*

RESTAURANTS

An island that's world famous for its mussels and renowned for its rich soil is certainly not going to disappoint when it comes to eating out. From humble mom-and-pop spots and creative cafés that give classic dishes a contemporary twist, to splurge-worthy bastions of gourmet dining, there is no shortage of places to eat on Prince Edward Island. In Charlottetown especially (where innovative options like Terre Rouge Bistro Marche are being added to the mix) the restaurant scene is booming. The ambience tends to be casual across the board, and reservations are seldom necessary—though at popular waterfront fish shacks, you may be in for a lengthy lineup.

At every price point, the best eateries offer seasonally inspired menus that emphasize local ingredients. So when you see lobster, mussels, and oysters listed, they're likely from the neighborhood. Ditto for fresh produce: after all, those bucolic fields you drive by aren't just for show. If dining is your true raison d'être, be sure to investigate the PEI

Flavours Culinary Trail (🌐 *www.peiflavours.ca*). It pinpoints locally owned restaurants that take advantage of the area's edible bounty; plus it shows you where to find farmers' markets, fishmongers, flavorful festivals, and fun "culinary adventures" like clambakes and lobster-dinner cruises. Culinary experiences await, in which you can work with chefs, fishermen, and food producers to find out exactly how those delicious ingredients make it onto your plate.

AUTHENTIC EXPERIENCES

Eager to haul a lobster trap or tour a potato farm? Prefer to paint a watercolor or turn PEI's signature red clay into a piece of pottery? How about trying your hand at fiddling or deep-sea fishing? Click 🌐 *www.tourismpei.com/pei-experiences* for complete listings.

HOTELS

Full-service resorts, boutique hotels, vintage motels, and waterside vacation rentals are just some of your lodging options on PEI. Beyond the capital, inns and B&Bs—sometimes with cottage colonies attached—dominate and, design-wise, almost all of them favor the historic and traditional over the hip and trendy. Rodd Hotels & Resorts are a local and reliable small chain, headquartered in Charlottetown, with five locations on the Island. Whatever you choose, it's wise to book three to six months in advance—either directly or through the province's online reservation system (🌐 *www.tourismpei.com/pei-online-reservations*)—if you are planning to arrive in July or August. Note that all accommodations here are nonsmoking and precious few have elevators.

Hotel reviews have been shortened. For full information, visit Fodors.com.

WHAT IT COSTS IN CANADIAN DOLLARS

	$	$$	$$$	$$$$
Restaurants	under C$12	C$12–C$20	C$21–C$30	over C$30
Hotels	under C$125	C$125–C$174	C$175–C$250	over C$250

Restaurant prices are per person for a main course at dinner. Hotel prices are for two people in a standard double room in high season, excluding 13% harmonized sales tax (HST).

TOURS

Coach tour companies offer PEI itineraries, but since exploring quiet nooks and crannies is one of the chief delights here, traveling aboard a big bus can defeat the purpose. One popular alternative is to sign on for a bike tour of the 357-km (222-mile) Confederation Trail, which extends almost the complete length of the Island, from Tignish to Elmira. The trail's gentle grade makes pedaling comparatively easy; moreover, outfits like Eastwind Cycle and Freewheeling Adventures help you cover it in style by providing multiday inn-to-inn trips complete with luggage transfers and van support. If you're more interested in day tours, biking, boating, and fishing excursions are readily available, as are culture-oriented outings. *For other unique options, see our "Authentic Experiences" box.*

Eastwind Cycle. This company organizes bicycle tours on the Island, customized to where you want to go. ☎ *902/471–4424, 866/447–7468* ⊕ *www.eastwindcycle.com* ✉ *From $1,500.*

Freewheeling Adventures. Bicycle tours include the Confederation Trail or a side-roads route through the national park. Sea kayaking and family multisport tours are also offered. All tours last for six days. Self-guided tours include accommodations, breakfasts, luggage transfers, and maps; guided tours also include lunches and dinners. ☎ *902/857–3600, 800/672–0775* ⊕ *www.freewheeling.ca* ✉ *From C$1,995, plus bicycle rental, from C$145.*

Prince Edward Tours. This company offers various scheduled sightseeing tours by bus, including City Highlights in Charlottetown, a four-hour Island Drive & Anne of Green Gables tour, and a full day of "Island's Finest" sights. A portion of the tour fees goes to the Children's Wish Foundation. ☎ *902/566–5466, 877/286–6532* ⊕ *princeedwardtours.com* ✉ *From $19.*

VISITOR INFORMATION

Well-staffed, well-stocked visitor information centers are strategically positioned throughout Prince Edward Island. Provincially operated ones can be found at the Island's main points of entry (Borden-Carleton, near the Confederation Bridge; Wood Islands, at the ferry terminal; and Charlottetown, at the airport) as well as in Cavendish, Souris, and West Prince: ⊕ *www.tourismpei.com/pei-visitor-information* has complete details. Municipally run centers are located in Charlottetown, Summerside, Cavendish, and St. Peter's. For help with advance planning, click PEI's official tourism website (⊕ *www.tourismpei.com*) or call the office (☎ *800/463–4734*) to order a free printed copy of the comprehensive Island Visitor's Guide.

CHARLOTTETOWN

Designated as the Island capital in 1765, Charlottetown is both PEI's oldest and largest urban center. However, since the whole "metropolitan" area only has a population of about 65,000, a pleasing small-town atmosphere remains. The city is a winner appearance-wise as well. Peppered with gingerbread-clad homes, converted warehouses, striking churches, and monumental government buildings, Charlottetown's core seems relatively unchanged from its 19th-century heyday when it hosted the conference that led to the formation of Canada. The city is understandably proud of its role as the "Birthplace of Confederation" and, in summer, downtown streets are dotted with people dressed as personages from the past who'll regale you with tales about the Confederation debate.

GETTING HERE AND AROUND

The city center is compact, so walking is the way to go. If you drive in for a day of sightseeing, you can park at an on-street meter or in garages like those on Pownal, Queen, and Fitzroy streets. Alternately, you can

PRINCE EDWARD ISLAND ITINERARIES

IF YOU HAVE 3 DAYS

Begin your Island escape by crossing the Confederation Bridge from the mainland to Borden-Carleton. The PEI section of the Trans-Canada Highway begins here and continues through Charlottetown to the Wood Islands Ferry Terminal. Following it, make your first stop 22 km (14 miles) east in **Victoria,** one of the Island's quaintest little communities. Proceeding on to **Charlottetown**, you'll have time to see key city sights and catch a performance of *Anne of Green Gables—The Musical* at the Confederation Centre before bedtime. On Day 2 make the 39-km (24-mile) cross-Island drive to the **Green Gables Shore**—aka northern Queens County—for the quintessential PEI sun-and-sand experience. Landing in **Cavendish**, you can lounge on the beach (or take advantage of the educational programming) in Prince Edward Island National Park; make a pilgrimage to the Green Gables farmhouse (Anne's fictional home); then indulge in some cheesy but fun amusements along the Route 6 strip, otherwise known as Cavendish Road. On Day 3, veer 91 km (57 miles) east to **Georgetown** in Kings County. Take a stroll through this classic waterside town, then sign on for one of the up-close seafood encounters run locally by Tranquility Cove Adventures. From Georgetown, it's a 41-km (26-mile) drive south to **Wood Islands,** where you can catch a ferry back to the mainland. Just keep in mind that from May to early November, the last one leaves at 8 pm. Note that this route can essentially be done in reverse if you're entering the Island by way of the Northumberland Strait boat.

IF YOU HAVE 5 DAYS

Stick to the above itinerary but leave an extra day to pursue your passion in both Queens County and Kings County. In the former that might mean investigating more Anne-related sites or sussing out PEI's other famous export—oysters. In the latter, it might mean looking at lighthouses or cycling an especially nice section of the Confederation Trail. Beach-bumming and golfing opportunities also abound in each.

IF YOU HAVE 7 DAYS

Since PEI is so small, you can see it all. Travelers who want comprehensive coverage can spend their additional two days exploring Prince County to the west: **Summerside** (the Island's second city) and windy **North Cape** are well worth a look, as is the rich, agricultural area inland. An alternative, though, is to stop driving and just drink it all in. Prince Edward Island is an ideal place to decompress. So simply park yourself somewhere—anywhere—and give yourself permission to genuinely relax.

rent a bike at **Outer Limit Sports, Go Wheelin Bike Rentals,** or **MacQueen's Bike Shop.** Rentals start around C$25 per day. **Trius Transit** also operates trolley-style buses as part of a public-private partnership (some cover the surrounding communities of Cornwall and Stratford, too). Most have their hub downtown at the Confederation Centre of the Arts, and the fare is C$2.25 in exact change. Prefer a guided tour?

CLOSE UP

A Good Walk

Start your walk at the **Confederation Centre of the Arts** on Richmond Street, in the heart of downtown. Housing the provincial art gallery and a public library, it's also home to the **Charlottetown Festival.** Next door, the **Province House National Historic Site** is where the first meeting to discuss federal union took place. Turn onto Great George Street, dipping into **St. Dunstan's Basilica,** a Roman Catholic church notable for its twin Gothic spires. Then continue down Great George to the water, where you can enjoy lunch at a wharf-side restaurant or a picnic in **Confederation Landing Park.** Next, follow the boardwalk to **Founders' Hall.** After going inside for a crash course in Canadian history, head back to Province House and explore the shops of **Victoria Row** before investigating what Queen Street has to offer in the way of pubs and restaurants. Many visitors will be happy to call it a day there. But if you have the time (and attention span) for one further sight, venture west to visit one of the finest 19th-century residential buildings in the city: **Beaconsfield Historic House.**

TIMING: The downtown area can be explored on foot in a few hours, but the wealth of sights and harbor views warrants a full day.

Options include the **Confederation Players** tours, the **Harbour Hippo** and its dry-land alternative, the Hippopotabus, and **Prince Edward Tours** (a Gray Line affiliate).

ESSENTIALS

Bicycle Rentals **Go Wheelin Bike Rentals.** ✉ *6 Prince St.* ☎ *902/566-5259, 877/286-6532* 🌐 *www.gowheelinpei.com.* **MacQueen's Bike Shop.** ✉ *430 Queen St.* ☎ *902/368-2453, 800/969-2822* 🌐 *www.macqueens.com.* **Outer Limit Sports.** ✉ *330 University Ave.* ☎ *902/569-5690* 🌐 *ols.ca.*

Bus Contacts **Trius Transit.** ☎ *902/566-9962* 🌐 *www.triustransit.ca.*

Visitor Information **Charlottetown Visitor Information.** ✉ *Founders Hall, 6 Prince St.* ☎ *902/368-4444* 🌐 *www.tourismpei.com.*

TOURS

Confederation Players Walking Tours. Costumed guides from the Confederation Players troupe lead history-themed walks in July and August as part of the Charlottetown Festival. English-language tours depart Founders' Hall at 11 and 3, Monday to Saturday. A ghostly evening version is also available at 8, Tuesday to Saturday. Tours last 60 to 90 minutes. ✉ *Charlottetown* ☎ *800/565-0278* 🌐 *www.charlottetownfestival.com* 💲 *C$15.*

Harbour Hippo. Tour the sights by land and sea in an amphibious vehicle, departing from in front of the Confederation Centre of the Arts. The tours run daily June through September. If you'd rather stay on dry land, the Hippopotabus, an open-top double-decker, offers an hour-long tour. ✉ *Lower Prince St. Wharf* ☎ *902/628-8687* 🌐 *www.harbourhippo.com* 💲 *C$26.*

Beaconsfield Historic House 9
Boardwalk 4
Confederation Centre of the Arts 1
Confederation Landing Park 5
Founders' Hall–Canada's Birthplace Pavilion 6
Red Shores Racetrack and Casino 7
St. Dunstan's Basilica 3
Victoria Park 8
Victoria Row 2

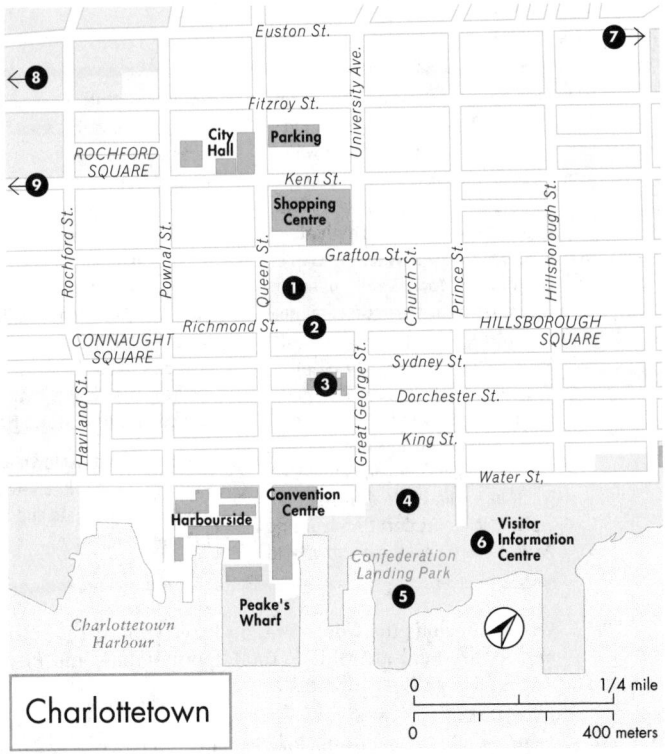

FAMILY **Peake's Wharf Boat Tours.** Departing from Peake's Wharf, this company operates assorted cruises aboard a 45-foot vessel, including 70-minute-long sunset cruises from June to September and 2½-hour seal-watching trips in July and August. ✉ *1 Great George St., Peake's Wharf* ☎ *902/566–4458* 🌐 *www.peakeswharfboattours.com* 💲 *Sunset cruise C$30, seal-watching C$44.*

Prince Edward Tours. The City Highlights double-decker bus tour lasts about 75 minutes and departs from Founders Hall daily at 10, 11:30, and 1. Local guides provide an entertaining and informative commentary. ✉ *Charlottetown* ☎ *902/566–5466, 877/286–6532* 🌐 *princeedwardtours.com* 💲 *C$19.*

EXPLORING

TOP ATTRACTIONS

FAMILY **Beaconsfield Historic House.** Designed by W.C. Harris in 1877 for shipbuilder James Peake Jr., this gracious mansion- *cum*-museum near the entrance to Victoria Park is one of the Island's finest historic homes. The 11 furnished rooms have rich architectural details and accents (imagine ornate plaster moldings and imported chandeliers)—little wonder the once-wealthy Peake went bankrupt soon after his house was completed. Having taken a tour of the first and second floors, pause to enjoy a view of Charlottetown Harbour from the veranda. An on-site bookstore has a variety of Island publications, and special events (such as musical performances and history-themed lectures) are held year-round. A carriage house on the grounds also hosts a children's festival on weekday mornings, mid-July through late-August. ✉ *2 Kent St.* ☎ *902/368–6603* 🌐 *www.peimuseum.com* 💲 *C$5* ⏲ *July and Aug., daily 10–4:30; Sept.–June, call for hrs.*

Boardwalk. Charlottetown's boardwalk extends from Confederation Landing to Victoria Park, wending its way along the water past historic sites and leafy picnic spots, providing views of sailboats and cruise ships en route. As an added bonus, it's lit at night for romantic strolls. ✉ *Charlottetown.*

FAMILY Fodor's Choice ★ **Confederation Centre of the Arts.** With a 1,100-seat main stage theater, a 1,000-seat outdoor amphitheater, and several studio stages, this block-long building—opened in 1964 to mark the centennial of the Charlottetown Conference—is the Island's leading cultural venue. Each year, from late-June through September, it hosts the famous **Charlottetown Festival** (☎ *902/628–1864 or 800/565–0278,* 🌐 *www.charlottetownfestival.com*), which includes *Anne of Green Gables—The Musical,* plus concerts, comedy acts, and other theatrical productions. Weather permitting, the festival offers free lunchtime performances in the amphitheater and on the plaza every day except Sunday. Off-season, a dynamic mix of touring and local productions, choral concerts, and special events is also scheduled. Visitors planning to take advantage of any of these will find that the center's bar and bistro, Mavor's, makes a convenient spot for preshow dining. Also on-site: a provincial art gallery and public library. The former (which has more than 15,000 works in its collection) holds year-round exhibits showcasing Canadian art. The latter, being cool and quiet, offers a welcome break from vacation craziness. ✉ *145 Richmond St.* ☎ *902/566–1267, 800/565–0278* 🌐 *www.confederationcentre.com* ⏲ *Gallery: mid-May–June, daily 9–5; July and Aug., Mon.–Sat., 9–8, Sun, 9–5; Sept.–mid-Oct., daily 9–5; mid-Oct.–mid-May, Wed.–Sat. 11–5, Sun. 1–5. Library: Mon., Fri., and Sat. 10–5, Tues.–Thurs. 10–9 (10–8 in summer), Sun. 1–5.*

FAMILY **Founders' Hall–Canada's Birthplace Pavilion.** The state-of-the-art exhibits and multimedia displays at this 21,000-square-foot interpretive center on the Historic Charlottetown Waterfront merge high tech with history. A case in point: the "Time Travel Tunnel," which transports visitors back to the Charlottetown Conference of 1864, eventually returning them to the present day with a greater understanding of how Canada came together as a country. In addition to its own gift shop, Founders' Hall has a civic visitor information center where you can get maps, brochures, and advice, as well as a kiosk where you can book tours and purchase theater tickets. ✉ *6 Prince St.* ☎ *902/368–1864, 800/955–1864* 🌐 *www.foundershall.ca* 💲 *C$9.50* ⏲ *May, daily 9–5; June, daily 8:30–6; July and Aug., daily 8:30–7; Sept., daily 8:30–5; Oct., daily 9–4; last admission 1 hr before closing.*

Fodor's Choice ★ **Victoria Row.** The section of Richmond Street between Queen and Great George streets is home to a variety of shops (Island crafts, art, hand-knitted sweaters, chocolates, antiques, and glassware are just some of what's inside), together with eateries, cafés, and a dance club. This vibrant, compact stretch of road really comes alive in summer, when traffic is blocked off and you'll frequently see musicians perform at lunchtime or in the evenings. For more shopping, head around the corner to Queen Street or Water Street. ✉ *Charlottetown.*

WORTH NOTING

FAMILY **Confederation Landing Park.** This waterfront recreation area at the bottom of Great George Street occupies the site where the Fathers of Confederation famously landed in 1864. Walkways and park benches offer plenty of opportunities to survey the activity of the harbor, with the added attraction of banks and banks of wild rosebushes behind. During summer, performers in period costume stroll about the area re-creating the events that led up to the Canadian Confederation. Occasionally, the park also doubles as a venue for Canadian acts like Nickelback or Cirque du Soleil. **Peake's Wharf,** right next to it, has casual restaurants and bars, souvenir and crafts shops, and a marina where boat tours can be arranged. It hosts its own outdoor concert series in peak months. Featuring local talent, the free shows start at 2:30 and 6:30 daily. ✉ *Water St. between Queen and Hillsborough Sts.* 💲 *Free* ⏲ *Daily dawn–dusk.*

Red Shores Racetrack and Casino. Since 1880 this track at the eastern end of the city has been the home of a sport dear to islanders—harness racing. An on-site theater simulcasts racing from other tracks, while slot machines and Texas Hold'em provide further gambling options. If you'd rather save your dollars for dinner, there is excellent dining at the Top of the Park Dining Room, too. In August, during **Old Home Week** (☎ *902/629–6623,* 🌐 *www.oldhomeweekpei.com*), Eastern Canada's best harness horses converge here for 10 days of races. Old Home Week also brings the provincial agricultural exhibition and a family-friendly midway to Red Shores. ✉ *21 Exhibition Dr.* ☎ *902/620–4222, 877/620–4222* 🌐 *redshores.ca* 💲 *Free* ⏲ *Mon.–Thurs. 11 am–midnight; Fri. and Sat. 11 am–2 am; Sun. noon–midnight; races Apr.–Jan., schedule varies.*

St. Dunstan's Basilica. One of Canada's largest churches, St. Dunstan's, is the seat of the Roman Catholic diocese on the Island. The church is known for its fine Italian carvings and twin Gothic spires. ✉ *45 Great George St.* ☎ *902/894–3486* 🌐 *www.stdunstans.pe.ca* ⏲ *Weekdays 9–5. Services: weekdays at noon, Sat. at 9 and 5, Sun. at 10:30 and 5.*

FAMILY **Victoria Park.** At the southern tip of the city, overlooking Charlottetown Harbour, sit 40 serene acres that provide the perfect place to stroll, picnic, or cool off on a hot day. Next to the park, on a hill between groves of white birches, is the white Georgian-style **Government House.** Built in 1834 as the official residence for lieutenant governors (the Queen's provincial representatives), it's open weekdays in July and August from 10 to 4 for free guided tours. The collection of antique cannons that still "guard" the city's waterfront is a play area for children, though there is also an actual playground, a pool open daily in summer from

11 to 8, and a water-play area at the northwest entrance to the park. Runners and walkers can take advantage of woodland trails and a boardwalk that edges the harbor. ✉ *Lower Kent St.* ☎ *902/368–1025* ₤ *Free* ⏲ *Daily sunrise–sunset.*

WHERE TO EAT

$ CAFÉ ✕ **Beanz Espresso Bar.** This hip-with-a-heart café is an excellent spot for hearty sandwiches, plus soups, salads, and, of course, coffee. Just remember to save room for the sweets: Beanz's inexpensive squares, bars, and cakes taste as if they came right out of an *Anne of Green Gables* church social. (Bakers who can prepare these old-school recipes are a dying breed!) There's local art on the walls inside and an outside deck, but this is not an evening hangout spot—it closes at 6 Monday–Saturday, at 4 on Sunday. $ *Average main: C$8* ✉ *38 University Ave.* ☎ *902/892–8797* 🌐 *www.beanzespressobar.com.*

$$ ECLECTIC ✕ **The Brickhouse Kitchen & Bar.** In a converted warehouse downtown, this is the sort of place that could pull in a trendy crowd based solely on its exposed brick and wood-beam interior, but the open kitchen also delivers. Local ingredients are used to create dishes with international appeal (think trout with a ginger chili glaze, New York strip with mustard-and-pepper crust or coconut chicken curry). The restaurant has a solid wine list, and classic desserts like berry cobbler and crème brûlée for sweet-toothed diners. Dietary purists will be pleased by the number of vegan, vegetarian, and gluten-free offerings. $ *Average main: C$18* ✉ *125 Sydney St.* ☎ *902/566–4620* 🌐 *brickhousepei.com* ⏲ *Closed Sun. Oct.–Apr. No lunch Sun. May–Sept.*

$$$ SEAFOOD ✕ **Claddagh Oyster House.** Urban style meets rural delicacies at this upscale restaurant, which occupies a handsome brick building downtown. Not surprisingly, given the name and location, seafood is a specialty here—the local oysters, mussels, and lobsters are all memorable. But there are alternatives for vegetarian and meat-loving locavores (think risotto made with market veggies or grilled PEI strip loin served with roasted PEI potatoes). It's a popular spot for tourists and residents alike, and the service is friendly. Upstairs, the Olde Dublin Pub has pub grub, ample ale, and live music on the Guinness Stage seven nights a week from mid-June to mid-September. $ *Average main: C$30* ✉ *131 Sydney St.* ☎ *902/892–9661* 🌐 *www.claddaghoysterhouse.com* ⏲ *No lunch.*

$$ SEAFOOD ✕ **Fishbones Oyster Bar & Seafood Grill.** Fishbones, on pedestrianized Victoria Row right behind the Confederation Centre of the Arts, is a good choice for pre- or post-theater dining. Although focused on fish, the menu is broad enough to include quality options for non–seafood fans, and the service is at once efficient and friendly. Prices are reasonable, too. But the setting—whether under the giant faux tree inside, on the patio outside, where diners are often serenaded by live jazz music, or up on the new rooftop patio—will still make you feel that you're having a proper night out. $ *Average main: C$12* ✉ *136 Richmond St.* ☎ *902/628–6569* 🌐 *www.fishbones.ca* ▭ *No credit cards* ⏲ *Closed late Sept.–late May.*

$$ SEAFOOD **The Gahan House Pub & Brewery.** PEI's original microbrewery, housed in an 1880 brick building downtown, clearly takes pride in its products. Seven handcrafted ales (and one wickedly good root beer) are prominently displayed on the upstairs menu, and tours of the downstairs brewing operation (C$9, samples included) are given in summer. Beer reappears in several dishes as well, including the signature brown-bag fish-and-chips with honey wheat ale–battered haddock and pulled-pork sandwiches accented with IPA barbecue sauce. But even teetotalers will appreciate that the food here is always tasty, affordable, and well presented. *Average main: C$13 126 Sydney St. 902/626–2337 www.gahan.ca.*

$$ CAFÉ **Leonhard's.** Alexandra and Axel Leonhard have gone from humble beginnings selling homemade bread at a local farmers' market to running a full-fledged café where food is made from scratch without additives, preservatives, or artificial flavorings. The room is bright and cheerful, and the devoted clientele keeps coming back for breakfast, casseroles, hearty gluten-free soups, sandwiches, and delicious desserts. Organic teas and freshly roasted coffee are served as well. Renovations have increased the original 6 tables inside to 15 (and a couple more on the street in summer), so waiting time for a seat is not usually an issue—but you can always grab something to go. In any case, come early: Leonhard's closes at 5. *Average main: C$13 142 Great George St. 902/367–3621 www.leonhards.ca No dinner.*

$$$ CONTEMPORARY **The Lucy Maud Dining Room.** Chefs at this restaurant, part of the acclaimed Culinary Institute of Canada, are second-year students working under the supervision of master-chef instructors; service is provided by hospitality students. It's an opportunity to enjoy ambitious dishes that combine local ingredients with international influences, like grilled leg of lamb with Israeli couscous, sun-dried tomatoes, capers, yogurt, and cucumber or a traditional cedar-plank Atlantic salmon with pickled fiddleheads. The institute's dining room could use some freshening up, but nothing can detract from the view of the water out its large windows. *Average main: C$26 4 Sydney St. 902/894–6868 www.hollandcollege.com/culinary-institute-of-canada/lucy-maud-dining-room Closed mid-May–early June, Sept.–mid-Oct., and Sun., Mon., and holidays. No lunch mid-May–mid-Oct. Reservations essential.*

$$$ CANADIAN **The Pilot House.** In the 19th-century Roger's Hardware building, this restaurant has both fine dining and casual fare. Old wooden beams, brick columns, and a unique bar top made of black granite inlaid with bird's-eye maple make the place cozy. A pub menu concentrates largely on classic sandwiches and creative pizzas, while quality PEI-raised beef and fresh seafood dominate the dinner menu. *Average main: C$23 70 Grafton St. 902/894–4800 thepilothouse.ca Closed Sun.*

$$$$ STEAKHOUSE **Sims Corner Steakhouse and Oyster Bar.** The farm-to-plate focus helped earn accolades from the Prince Edward Island Restaurant Association, while the custom-cut, Island-raised beef (it's aged 45 days for richer taste) has earned kudos from patrons. Seafood selections start with a wide range of oysters at the raw bar, and divine desserts are made in-house. All can be washed down with an award-winning selection of Old and New World wines. Earthy colors, brick walls, exposed beams,

ENJOYING SHELLFISH

Prince Edward Island shellfish has a reputation for being among the world's best. Mollusks and crustaceans are harvested all along the coast, so you can spot fishermen in shallow boats scooping up oysters with what look like giant salad servers. Moreover, you can see rows of buoys in bays and estuaries holding up lines covered with mussels, plus solo buoys securing the lobster traps that wait to be hauled offshore. Obviously, you'll see shellfish on almost every Island menu, too, as well as on many activity rosters: tour operators are taking increasing numbers of visitors out to trap, haul, tong, and shuck. Shellfish also pops up on festival calendars.

and plush booths encourage you to linger indoors, but there is also a pleasant patio for warm-weather dining. $ *Average main: C$40* ✉ *86 Queen St.* ☎ *902/894–7467* 🌐 *www.simscorner.ca.*

$$$ ITALIAN ✕ **Sirenella Ristorante.** Northern Italian cuisine and unfailingly good service make Sirenella one of Charlotteville's top restaurant choices. The menu, which changes twice a year, has something for everyone. Owner Italo Marzari handpicks the Italian wines on the list, and noteworthy mains—like the excellent *vitello pizzaiola* (veal in a sauce of white wine, capers, garlic, and oregano, topped with *bocconcini* cheese and tomato sauce)—are complemented by a range of handmade pastas. $ *Average main: C$27* ✉ *83 Water St.* ☎ *902/628–2271* 🌐 *www.sirenella.ca* ⏲ *Closed Sun. No lunch Sat.*

$ VEGETARIAN ✕ **Splendid Essence.** Sharing a pretty house with a Buddhist prayer hall, this little eatery serves vegetarian and vegan fare with Asian flair. Aside from the expected noodles, dumplings, and stir-fries, Splendid Essence has a fine selection of hot and cold teas, which you can enjoy outdoors on the porch in fine weather. $ *Average main: C$9* ✉ *186 Prince St.* ☎ *902/566–4991* 🌐 *www.splendidessence.com* ⏲ *Closed Sun.*

$$$ BISTRO ✕ **Terre Rouge Bistro Marche.** Occupying a heritage brick-and-stone structure, this bistro gives Charlottetown's dining scene a French twist. The menu changes frequently, but the farm-to-table focus never wavers. Expect house-cured charcuterie, artisanal cheeses, plus favorite French dishes (including foie gras, steak frites, duck confit, and roasted marrow bones—all beautifully plated). And for dessert? *Mais oui*, macarons! There's also an on-site "marché" with goodies to go. $ *Average main: C$27* ✉ *72 Queen St.* ☎ *902/892–4032* 🌐 *terrerougepei.com* ⏲ *Closed Sun. and Mon. in winter.*

WHERE TO STAY

$$$ HOTEL **Delta Prince Edward.** Right on the waterfront boardwalk next to Peake's Wharf, and ideal for exploring downtown on foot, this beautifully renovated high-rise hotel has wonderful views and good amenities for leisure and business travelers. **Pros:** modern and fresh lobby area; upper category rooms have Jacuzzis; adjoins the convention center; free Wi-Fi. **Cons:** parking costs C$17 per day. $ *Rooms from: C$209*

✉18 Queen St. ☎902/566–2222, 888/890–3222 reservations ⊕www.deltahotels.com ⇐187 rooms, 24 suites ⓘNo meals.

$$$ B&B/INN **Dundee Arms Inn.** A 1903 Queen Anne mansion and modern annex make up this attractive inn just minutes from downtown. **Pros:** relaxed setting; free Wi-Fi; in-room perks include fluffy robes and Paya Organic bath products. **Cons:** rooms vary widely in size and quality; breakfast not included in high season. $ *Rooms from: C$195 ✉200 Pownal St. ☎902/892–2496, 877/638–6333 ⊕www.eden.travel/dundee ⇐18 rooms, 4 suites.*

$$ B&B/INN **Elmwood Heritage Inn.** Tranquil and retaining its historic elegance, this 1889 inn sits at the end of a tree-lined lane in a residential neighborhood. **Pros:** an acre of grounds; in-room mod cons like iPod docks and flat-screen TVs; free Wi-Fi. **Cons:** rather flowery for some tastes; a 15-minute walk to downtown. $ *Rooms from: C$165 ✉121 N. River Rd. ☎902/368–3310, 877/933–3310 ⊕www.elmwoodinn.pe.ca ⇐5 rooms, 3 suites ⓘBreakfast.*

$$$ B&B/INN Fodor's Choice ★ **Fairholm National Historic Inn and Carriage House.** The Fairholm, a designated National Historic Site, is a prime Maritime example of the architectural Picturesque movement. **Pros:** lovely gardens; superb breakfast coffee, made from Ethiopian beans roasted on the Island; free parking and Wi-Fi. **Cons:** lots of wallpaper; not for those seeking big-hotel amenities; breakfast not included in the room rate. $ *Rooms from: C$180 ✉230 Prince St. ☎902/892–5022, 888/573–5022 ⊕www.fairholminn.com ⇐7 rooms, 6 suites ⓘNo meals.*

$$$ HOTEL Fodor's Choice ★ **The Great George.** This centrally located boutique hotel is fashioned from 15 heritage buildings, and history is clearly in the air (some Fathers of Confederation stayed in them during the Charlottetown Conference), but it's nicely balanced by the contemporary style and 21st-century touches. **Pros:** excellent staff; comfy beds topped with duvets and premium linens; free Wi-Fi and access to hotel gym. **Cons:** street noise is sometimes audible on the Great George side. $ *Rooms from: C$229 ✉58 Great George St. ☎902/892–0606, 800/361–1118 ⊕www.thegreatgeorge.com ⇐34 rooms, 22 suites, 4 condos ⓘBreakfast.*

$$ B&B/INN **Hillhurst Inn.** In the heart of downtown, this grand, renovated 1897 Georgian Revival mansion has tasteful guest rooms. **Pros:** the Confederation Trail is close by; C$10 voucher valid at 13 local restaurants for each day that you forego housekeeping service. **Cons:** small bathrooms; operates seasonally. $ *Rooms from: C$149 ✉181 Fitzroy St. ☎902/894–8004, 877/994–8004 ⊕www.hillhurst.com ⊙Closed Nov.–May ⇐8 rooms ⓘBreakfast.*

$$$$ HOTEL **The Holman Grand Hotel.** Sitting atop the Confederation Court Mall, the 10-story structure's upper floors provide sensational views; lower ones, connected to both the mall and Confederation Centre of the Arts,

CROSSROADS

The intersection of Richmond Street and Great George Street is frequently—although you can never predict when—the place to see all manner of old and new conveyances: modern buses, elegant horse-drawn carriages, open-top double-decker buses, traditional trolleys, and even amphibious vehicles are all used to get around this historic city.

offer indoor access to city amenities. **Pros:** elevator; some suites have kitchenettes; all rooms have mini-refrigerators and Keurig coffeemakers; free Wi-Fi. **Cons:** standard rooms have spa-worthy showers but no tubs; comparatively pricey. [$] *Rooms from: C$260* ✉ *123 Grafton Street.* ☎ *902/367–7777, 877/455–4726* 🌐 *www.theholmangrand.com* 🛏 *62 rooms, 18 suites.*

$$$ HOTEL **The Hotel on Pownal.** This is a contemporary lodging option with high-end atmosphere and high standards of service. **Pros:** on-site gym; free Wi-Fi and buffet breakfast; free coffee, tea, and home-baked treats available 24/7. **Cons:** no elevator; no on-site restaurant; no views. [$] *Rooms from: C$184* ✉ *146 Pownal St.* ☎ *902/892–1217, 800/268–6261* 🌐 *thehotelonpownal.com* 🛏 *40 rooms, 5 suites* 🍽 *Breakfast.*

$$ B&B/INN **Shipwright Inn B&B.** The name of this cottage-y 1860s inn is a nod to the first owner's occupation, and its charming accommodations further attest to his seafaring ways (the Captain's Quarters, the Navigator's Retreat. **Pros:** downtown location with pretty garden; some rooms have balconies and fireplaces. **Cons:** minimalists may find the number of knickknacks disconcerting; five rooms are in a 1996 addition. [$] *Rooms from: C$149* ✉ *51 Fitzroy St.* ☎ *902/368–1905, 888/306–9966* 🌐 *www.shipwrightinn.com* 🛏 *8 rooms, 1 apartment* 🍽 *Breakfast.*

NIGHTLIFE AND PERFORMING ARTS

For complete and current listings of entertainment events check *The Buzz*; you can pick up a free copy at most hotels, restaurants, and newsstands or view it online at 🌐 *www.buzzon.com.*

NIGHTLIFE

The Factory Cookhouse and Dancehall. When dinner is over—and that's worth going for, too, for meats smoked on the premises—the dance floor heats up, with DJs playing a mix of classic rock and country on some nights and live bands from on other nights. There's karaoke several nights a week before the DJ or band. ✉ *189 Kent St.* ☎ *902/370–3663* 🌐 *thefactorycookhouse.com.*

Olde Dublin Pub. This pub has been a top spot for entertainment for more than 30 years, with something going on most days, mostly in the form of live traditional Maritimes music or rock. It draws a mixed crowd of all ages and is open until 2 am. ✉ *131 Sydney St.* ☎ *902/892–6992* 🌐 *www.oldedublinpub.com.*

PERFORMING ARTS

Benevolent Irish Society Hall. Friday night ceilidhs with Celtic dancing, fiddling, and a few stories thrown in for good measure, run weekly mid-May through October. It's worth checking out the winter concert series, too. ✉ *582 N. River Rd.* ☎ *902/892–2367* 🌐 *benevolentirishsocietyofpei.com* 🎟 *C$10.*

Feast Dinner Theatre. Atlantic Canada's longest-running dinner theater specializes in fun, fluffy musicals. Watch lively shows while chowing down on a buffet meal from late-June through August. ✉ *Rodd Charlottetown Hotel, 75 Kent St.* ☎ *902/629–2321* 🌐 *www.roddvacations.com/feast* 🎟 *C$41.99.*

The Guild. The Guild, one of Charlottetown's major cultural centers, hosts plays, musicals, comedy and other performances, and a variety of exhibits throughout the year. ✉ *111 Queen St.* ☎ *902/620–3333, 866/774–0717* 🌐 *www.theguildpei.com.*

The Homburg Theatre. This is the city's main theater, with more than a thousand seats on two levels, hosting the famous *Anne of Green Gables—The Musical* for more than 50 seasons. ✉ *130 Queen St.* ☎ *902/566–1267, 800/565–0278* 🌐 *www.charlottetownfestival.com.*

The Mack. An intimate little theater, The Mack has just 200 seats, arranged cabaret style around tables. Some evening performances have liquor service (so no under-19s are admitted). ✉ *128 Great George St.* ☎ *800/565–0278* 🌐 *www.charlottetownfestival.com/en/theatres-themack.php.*

SPORTS AND THE OUTDOORS

GOLF

Clyde River Golf and Country Club. About 10 minutes west of Charlottetown, this beautiful course on the Clyde River has stunning water views on most holes. The 18-hole parkland course is linked to the 9-hole links course, making for a varied and interesting game. The natural land provides some tricky elements. ✉ *384 Clyde River Rd., Rte. 247, RR No. 2, Clyde River* ☎ *902/675–2585* 🌐 *www.clyderivergolf.ca* 💲 *C$22.80–C$32.46 for 18 holes, C$17.54–C$20.18 for 9 holes* ⛳ *18 holes, 5900 yards, par 71; 9 holes, 3160 yards, par 36* ⏲ *Closed Nov.–Apr.*

Fox Meadow Golf and Country Club. This club is a mere five minutes southeast of the city and is a challenging championship course, designed by Rob Heaslip. In a delightful rural landscape, it overlooks Charlottetown Harbour and the community of Stratford, and, apparently, it lives up to its name—resident foxes have been known to steal golf balls in play (which can be replaced without penalty). ✉ *167 Kinlock Rd., Stratford* ☎ *902/569–4653, 877/569–8337* 🌐 *www.foxmeadow.pe.ca* 💲 *C$60–C$80, or C$80–C$95 to play all day* ⛳ *18 holes, 6836 yards, par 72.*

WATER SPORTS

Saga Sailing Adventures. June to October, you can sail away on a 36-foot sloop and get the chance to take the helm or help with adjusting the sails. You can also do some diving, snorkeling, or swimming—or just relax and enjoy the ride. The trips last 2½-hours and depart daily at 10 am, 1 pm, and 5 pm June–October. Charter tours are also available. ✉ *Charlottetown Yacht Club, 1 Pownal St.* ☎ *902/672–1222* 🌐 *www.sagasailing.com* 💲 *C$60 (food and drink is extra).*

FAMILY **Top Notch Lobster Tours.** For an authentic lobster-fishing experience that's fun and informative, hop aboard the 45-foot *Top Notch* for a 1½- or 2½-hour trip with Captain Mark Jenkins. The tour includes taking a turn at the wheel, learning about on-board technology, hearing about Mark's own lobster-fishing experiences—and a lobster dinner. ✉ *2 Prince St.* ☎ *902/626–6689* 🌐 *www.markscharters.com* 💲 *From C$45.*

SHOPPING

The most interesting shops in Charlottetown are on Peake's Wharf, in Confederation Court Mall (off Queen Street), along Victoria Row (the section of Richmond Street between Queen and Great George streets), and on Water Street. There are also factory outlet stores along the Trans-Canada Highway at North River Causeway near the western entrance to the city, next to Cows Creamery, and the Charlottetown Mall, on the outskirts just north of the university.

SILLY-HAT SYNDROME

A curious affliction seems to strike vacationers in certain locales. In Disney destinations it compels them to don mouse ears; in Caribbean resorts, it manifests itself through the wearing of colorful knit caps with dangling faux dreadlocks. In PEI, you will know you're in the midst of an outbreak when you see otherwise sane people sporting beribboned straw boaters with red *à la Anne* braids attached.

FAMILY **Anne of Green Gables Chocolates.** This local chocolatier sells old-fashioned chocolates, peanut brittle, and assorted candy—all made on the premises. (For a double dose of local flavor, try chocolate-coated PEI potato chips.) Sweet treats for those who can't get enough of the Island's sweetest fictional orphan are available at this location year-round. Other outlets in Avonlea Village, Gateway Village, and on the Cavendish Boardwalk open seasonally. ✉ *100 Queen St.* ☎ *902/368–3131* 🌐 *www.annechocolates.com.*

Charlottetown Farmers' Market. Along with the expected array of local produce, artisanal cheeses, organic meats, and tasty baked goods, you'll find a fine array of Island-made crafts. The market runs from 9 until 2 on Saturday year-round as well as on Wednesday, July through early October. ✉ *100 Belvedere Ave.* ☎ *902/626–3373* 🌐 *charlottetownfarmersmarket.weebly.com.*

Lorimer Gallery. This gallery has earned a name for quality Maritimes, Canadian, Inuit, and international art, including works by the owner, Brian Lorimer. ✉ *82 Great George St.* ☎ *902/892–1953* 🌐 *www.lorimergallery.com.*

Moonsnail Soapworks and Aromatherapy. The vegetable-based soaps sold here are handcrafted and scented with essential oils, and the production area is open to view. The expanding inventory also includes sublime bath and body-care products, and a pet-care line, and the store also features local crafts. ✉ *85 Water St.* ☎ *902/892–7627, 888/771–7627* 🌐 *www.ilovemoonsnail.com.*

Northern Watters Knitwear. This shop carries its own line of chill-chasing knitted sweaters and a wide range of other Island-made products. ✉ *150 Richmond St.* ☎ *902/566–5850, 800/565–9665* 🌐 *www.nwknitwear.com.*

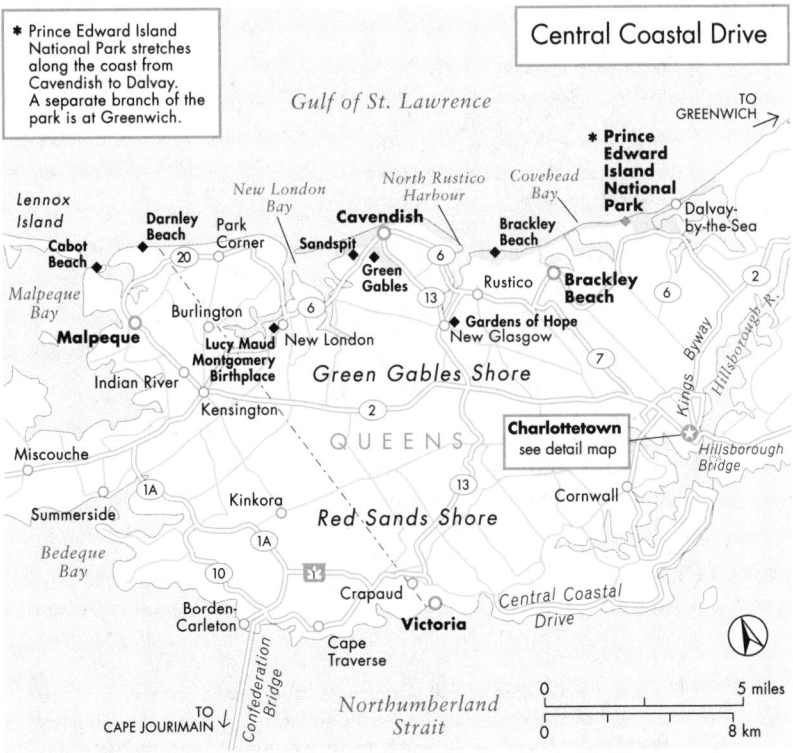

CENTRAL COASTAL DRIVE

The 198-km (123-mile) Central Coastal Drive heads northeast on Route 2 out of Charlottetown and continues, with a left turn onto Route 6, to the north shore. Route 6 takes you by classic fishing communities and the striking strands of Prince Edward Island National Park before depositing you in *Anne of Green Gables* country. (The section around Cavendish is cluttered with commercial tourist traps. If you look beyond the fast-food outlets and tacky gift shops, however, you can still find unspoiled beauty.) This beach-blessed section alone—newly christened the Green Gables Shore—has enough in the way of attractions, amusements, and outdoor opportunities to satisfy many vacationers. Yet it's worth traveling south, too, following the coast to the quieter Red Sands Shore on the other side of the Island, passing rolling farmland and oyster-filled Malpeque Bay en route. Considering that visitors who come to the Island via the Confederation Bridge land smack in the middle of this shore, it seems ironic that its red headlands remain relatively undiscovered. Historic sites, villages harking back to Victorian days, and a distinctive sandstone coastline are here to explore.

PRINCE EDWARD ISLAND NATIONAL PARK

GETTING HERE AND AROUND

There are several entrances to the park system off Routes 6, 13, and 313, but the best place to start your visit is at Cavendish Grove, off Route 6, at the park's Cavendish Destination Centre (open mid-June–early September). If you're not on a guided tour, you'll need a car to visit the park.

EXPLORING

FAMILY Fodor's Choice ★ **Prince Edward Island National Park.** Touched with nature's boldest brushstrokes, here sky and sea meet red sandstone cliffs, woodlands, wetlands, rolling dunes, and long stretches of sand. The original portion of the park, a narrow strip of protected coast, extends for 40 km (25 miles) along the north shore of the Island from Cavendish to Dalvay. A separate adjunct sits about 24 km (15 miles) farther east on the Greenwich Peninsula. Diverse habitats are home to a variety of plants and animals, including more than 300 species of birds and the marram grass that's vital to the survival of the dunes. Boardwalks and carpeted footpaths are the only places where human feet should venture, opening up spectacular vistas.

Numerous beaches can be enjoyed between Cavendish and Greenwich, but boardwalks and stairs to reach them are only in place from mid-May to the end of September. Pet owners should be aware that all beaches within the national park are pet-free areas from April to mid-October every year. A relaxing alternative is to picnic in the titular grove, accompanied by a sound track of songbirds and honking Canada geese that call the nearby pond home. A full slate of cultural and ecological interpretive programs aimed at all ages is also available. More active types can bike or hike on the park's scenic trails. If you'd rather be out on the water, kayaking and canoeing opportunities abound. ✉ *Cavendish* ☎ *902/672–6350* 🌐 *www.pc.gc.ca* 💲 *C$7.80 July and Aug.; C$3.90 other times* ⏲ *Accessible year-round; most services mid-May–mid-Oct, daily dawn–dusk; full services July and Aug. only.*

BEACHES

FAMILY **Brackley Beach.** Less crowded than Cavendish, Brackley Beach stretches for miles along the north shore, so it's easy to find a secluded spot to enjoy the fine sands and clear water. It's a great place for beach walks, and there's also a cycle track a little way back from the shore. It can get very windy here, which is good news for windsurfers. A boardwalk leads from the parking lot to the beach, and there's access to the Gulf Shore Way East trail, with four-wheel pedal-powered Coastal Cruisers for rent from the Stanhope campground. In summer, a Discovery Dome tent has interactive activities and you can learn sand-sculpting techniques on Sunday afternoons. To access the beach you have to pay the entrance fee to the national park. Pets are not allowed on the beach from April through mid-October. **Amenities:** food and drink; lifeguards; parking (free); showers; toilets. **Best for:** swimming; walking; windsurfing. ✉ *Gulfshore Pkwy., Brackley Beach* ☎ *902/672–6350 weekdays 8:30–4:30* 🌐 *www.pc.gc.ca/eng/pn-np/pe/pei-ipe/index.aspx* 💲 *C$7.80, mid-May–Sept. Coastal Cruiser rentals C$40 per half day.*

FAMILY
Fodor's Choice
★

Cavendish Beach. Close to—but far enough from—the tourist hot spots of Cavendish, and protected within the Prince Edward Island National Park, this wonderful beach has a long stretch of clean, soft sand backed by dunes, low cliffs, a boardwalk, and a bike trail. Various access points (with boardwalks and stairs in place mid-May through September 30) add to its popularity, but it's big enough to provide plenty of space for all. Organized activities include lessons in sand sculpting and interactive activities and nature exhibits in the Discovery Dome tent, and there are trails through the dunes with interpretive panels along the way. The admission charge to enter the national park during high season is a small price to pay. Don't head for home when the sun starts to set—the glow of its final rays on the rich red cliffs is an unforgettable sight. Pets are not allowed on the beach from April through mid-October. **Amenities:** food and drink; lifeguards; parking (free); showers; toilets. **Best for:** sunrise; sunset; swimming; walking. ✉ *Graham's La., Cavendish* ☎ *902/672–6350 weekdays 8:30–4:30* 🌐 *www.pc.gc.ca/eng/pn-np/pe/pei-ipe/index.aspx* 💲 *Park entrance fee C$7.80.*

Fodor's Choice
★

Greenwich Beach. Seclusion and stunning scenery is your reward for taking the walk to the beach here, and there are various access points involving varying amounts of walking (the shortest is from the parking lot at the end of Wild Rose Road). But take a longer hike along one of the Greenwich Dune Trail loops and along the way you'll enjoy wonderful views across the dune system and ponds, including sightings of the rich birdlife. Once there, the beach is an unspoiled expanse of fine pink sand that makes a curious sound beneath your feet. It's well worth stopping in at the Interpretation Centre at the entrance, too. Note: the dunes are extremely fragile, so keep to the beach, boardwalks, and marked trails. Pets are not permitted at any time. To access the beach, you need to pay a fee to enter the park. **Amenities:** lifeguards; parking (free); showers; toilets. **Best for:** solitude; walking. ✉ *Wild Rose Rd., Greenwich* ✣ *Via Rte. 313, 6 km (4 miles) west of St. Peters Bay* ☎ *902/672–6350* 🌐 *www.pc.gc.ca* 💲 *C$7.80 July and Aug; C$3.90 other times* ⏲ *Mid-May–mid-Oct., daily dawn–dusk; full services July and Aug. only. Interpretive Centre: early June–mid-Sept.*

WHERE TO EAT AND STAY

$$
SEAFOOD
Fodor's Choice
★

✕ **Richard's Fresh Seafood.** This down-home dockside eatery serves common fare in an uncommonly good way. Befitting its location, the seafood is *very* fresh. Expect lobster rolls, scallop sandwiches, steamed clams, and such served with fries that are twice-cooked for added crispness, plus homemade sauces and slaws. If you'd rather cook up your own fishy feast, the adjacent fish market sells everything you'll need. If you're coming here to eat, you don't need to pay the park entrance fee—just tell the person at the gate. 💲 *Average main: C$12* ✉ *9 Wharf Rd., Covehead Bay* ☎ *902/672–3030* 🌐 *www.richardsfreshseafood.com* ⏲ *Closed Oct.–May.*

$$$
B&B/INN

Dalvay-by-the-Sea. Built in 1895 as the summer retreat for a U.S. oil tycoon, this sprawling Queen Anne Revival "cottage" on the east edge of Prince Edward Island National Park is filled with antique furnishings, giving guest rooms a lovely period look. **Pros:** vintage vibe; 328 feet from the beach; free Wi-Fi. **Cons:** no air-conditioning; no TVs in guest rooms; no kitchens in cottages. $ *Rooms from: C$229* ✉ *16 Cottage Cres., just off Rte. 6, near Dalvay Beach, Stanhope* ☎ *902/672–2048, 888/366–2955* 🌐 *www.dalvaybythesea.com* ⏲ *Closed mid-Oct.–May* 🛏 *26 rooms, 8 cottages.*

SPORTS AND THE OUTDOORS

BIKING

Dalvay Bike Rentals. The resort Dalvay-by-the-Sea rents bikes suitable for all members of the family to guests and nonguests alike. ✉ *Rte. 6, near Dalvay Beach, Stanhope* ☎ *902/672–2048* 🌐 *www.dalvaybythesea.com* 💲 *C$20 per half-day (4 hrs), C$32 per day (8 hrs).*

FISHING

Richard's Deep-Sea Fishing. Captain Pat Gaudet takes eager anglers out on his 45-foot boat three times per day in summer, at 8 am, 1 pm, and 6 pm. Fishing gear is supplied and whatever you catch will be cleaned and filleted. ✉ *5 Wharf Rd., Covehead Bay* ☎ *902/672–2376.*

GOLF

Stanhope Golf and Country Club. The links-style course at Stanhope Golf and Country Club is among the most challenging and scenic on the Island, with greens that can be hard to read. Ocean breezes can help or hinder, and there are great sea views from most holes, particularly on the back nine. The course is a couple of miles west of Dalvay, along Covehead Bay. ✉ *Off Rte. 6, 2961 Bay Shore Rd., Stanhope* ☎ *902/672–2842, 888/672–2842* 🌐 *www.stanhopegolfclub.com* 💲 *C$35–C$99.95 for 18 holes, C$20–C$35 for 9 holes* ⛳ *18 holes, 6600 yards, par 72.*

BRACKLEY BEACH

15 km (9 miles) north of Charlottetown.

Brackley Beach abuts Prince Edward Island National Park, so park access is easy and sand is in ample supply. Because this is more a chunk of coastline than an actual community, Brackley Beach offers considerably fewer amenities than neighboring Cavendish. Activities here are refreshingly simple. Water sports, for example, tend to be the nonmotorized kind, and gentle pursuits like bird-watching are popular (area waterways attract many migratory species). Nevertheless, lodgings such as Shaw's have been in business for generations, so clearly there is enough here to warrant guests' return.

GETTING HERE AND AROUND

Lying along Route 15, just north of Route 6, Brackley Beach is meant for motorists.

WHERE TO STAY

$$ B&B/INN **Barachois Inn.** Rustico, just below Brackley Beach, is one of the oldest communities on the Island—and this 1880 inn's Victorian elegance blends right in with the historic surroundings. **Pros:** themed packages available; thoughtful hosts; free Wi-Fi; on-site gym. **Cons:** pretty far from civilization; gable ceilings not great for tall guests. $ *Rooms from: C$160* ✉ *2193 Church Rd., Rte. 243, Rustico* ✣ *Off Rte. 6, 8 km (5 miles) west of Brackley Beach* ☎ *902/963–2194, 800/963–2194* 🌐 *www.barachoisinn.com* 🛏 *4 rooms, 4 suites* 🍽 *Breakfast.*

$$ RESORT FAMILY **Shaw's Hotel and Cottages.** Canada's oldest family-operated inn has been winning a faithful following since opening in 1860. **Pros:** next to the national park; free use of kayaks and canoes; laundry facilities. **Cons:** there may be mosquitoes in the air or jellyfish in the water; air-conditioning in deluxe inn rooms only. *Rooms from: C$145 99 Apple Tree Rd., Rte. 15 902/672–2022 www.shawshotel.ca Closed early Oct.–May; some cottages open in shoulder months 15 rooms, 3 suites, 25 cottages Breakfast.*

WHAT'S IN A NAME?

Prince Edward Island was named for the fourth son of King George III (the monarch who lost America in the War of Independence). A rather run-of-the-mill royal, Edward seemed destined to be little more than a historical footnote until he was saved from obscurity by Britain's convoluted rules of succession. Because none of Edward's older siblings had living heirs (at least not legitimate ones), his daughter took the throne by default when she was just 18 years old. Her name? Victoria.

NIGHTLIFE AND PERFORMING ARTS

FAMILY **Brackley Drive-In Theatre.** Brackley Drive-In Theatre gives visitors in this neck of the woods a reason to stay up past dark. It shows a pair of first-run flicks nightly from mid-May to mid-September; gates open at 8 pm. Onion rings and other classic snacks from the canteen complement the experience. There's limited RV parking (arrive by 8:30 pm). *3164 Brackley Point Rd., Rte. 15 902/672–3333 drivein.ca C$10 per person, cash only; additional C$30 for RV parking.*

SPORTS AND THE OUTDOORS

Northshore Rentals. Run by Shaw's Hotel, this shop can equip you with kayaks, canoes, and bicycles. Per hour rates are C$12, C$11, and C$6.50 respectively. *Rte. 15 at Shaw's Hotel 902/672–2022.*

SHOPPING

The Dunes Studio Gallery and Café. This gallery sells an array of cool Canadian-made goods. Choose between pottery (you can watch it being crafted on-site), Island art, clothing with an unmistakable Indonesian influence, funky furniture, fine jewelry, contemporary glassware, and other one-of-a-kind items. The café serves lunch and dinner, and there are tables out in the beautiful gardens. *3622 Brackley Point Rd., Rte. 15 902/672–2586 www.dunesgallery.com Closed Nov.–Apr.; café also closed May–early June.*

The Great Canadian Soap Co. Time to come clean! The Great Canadian Soap Co. produces dozens of types of goat's milk soap at its home base near Brackley Beach. (That explains the gamboling goats you'll encounter near the shop). Other all-natural bath and beauty products are available as well. *4224 Portage Rd., Rte. 6 902/672–2242, 800/793–1644 www.greatcanadiansoap.com.*

CAVENDISH

21 km (13 miles) west of Brackley Beach.

Cavendish is the most visited Island community after Charlottetown. The proximity of Prince Edward Island National Park, with its promise of summertime sun and sand, is one reason for the heavy influx of vacationers. The crop of amusement park–style attractions that has sprung up on Route 6 as a counterpoint to the pristine park is another. However, it all began with *Anne of Green Gables*. Thousands of Anneites flock to the Cavendish area every year to visit the homes associated with Lucy Maud Montgomery, who was born and buried in the area, and to explore the places so lovingly described in her books.

GETTING HERE AND AROUND

Most visitors drive themselves to Cavendish, either via Highway 13, which branches north from the two cross-island Highways 1 (the Trans-Canada) and 2, or via Highway 6 that loops along the north coast. Once you're in Cavendish, the main attractions are within easy walking distance, and it's only a 1-km (½-mile) stroll to the beach in the national park.

Visitor Information **Cavendish Visitor Information Centre.** ✉ *7591 Cawnpore Lane, intersection of Rtes. 13 and 6* ☎ *902/963–7830, 800/463–4734* 🌐 *www.cavendishbeachpei.com.*

TOURS

Prince Edward Tours. The four-hour "Island Drive and Anne of Green Gables" tour from Charlottetown includes brief stops along the way and a tour of Green Gables House. The bus departs from Founders Hall Visitor Information Centre at 11:30 am on Tuesday, Wednesday, Friday, Sunday, and on cruise ship days, ✉ *Charlottetown* ☎ *902/566–5466, 877/286–6532* 🌐 *princeedwardtours.com* 💲 *C$59.*

EXPLORING

Gardens of Hope. Need a break from those Cavendish crowds? Gardens of Hope, part of the PEI Preserve Company property, is located about 8 km (5 miles) south of town beside the Island's most beautiful river valley. The garden itself covers more than 12 acres and includes a butterfly house. With 2 km (1 mile) of walking trails that thread past fountains and groomed flower beds, then through natural woodland, it provides ample opportunity for quiet contemplation. ✉ *2841 New Glasgow Rd., New Glasgow* ✣ *Off Rte. 13 south of Cavendish, at intersection of Rtes. 224 and 258* ☎ *902/964–4300, 800/565–5267* 🌐 *preservecompany.com/gardens-of-hope* 💲 *By donation* ⏲ *Daily dawn–dusk.*

FAMILY
Fodor's Choice
★

Green Gables. Green Gables, ½ km (¼ mile) west of Lucy Maud Montgomery's Cavendish Home, is the green-and-white 19th-century farmhouse that served as the inspiration for the Cuthbert place in *Anne of Green Gables*. The house, outbuildings, and grounds, all of which belonged to cousins of the author's grandfather, re-create some of the settings found in the book. The same goes for short walking trails dubbed the Haunted Wood and Lovers Lane/Balsam Hollow. If you're well acquainted with the novel, you'll spy lots of evocative details on-site (say, a broken slate or amethyst brooch). If not, watching an

CLOSE UP

Who is Anne, Anyway?

In Lucy Maud Montgomery's 1908 novel, Marilla Cuthbert and her brother Matthew live on a PEI farm. Getting on in years, the pair decides to adopt an orphan boy to help out with the chores. It's with some surprise, then, that Matthew comes back from the train station with a feisty, 11-year-old, redheaded *girl*. But it's not long before Anne—and her adventures and mishaps and friends—becomes an essential part of Marilla and Matthew's lives. An immediate hit, the book made Anne an essential part of readers' lives as well. Even Mark Twain, who called her "the dearest and most lovable child in fiction since the immortal Alice [in Wonderland]," was smitten.

Montgomery went on to write a total of eight volumes in the series. In 1985, the original was made into a two-part TV movie, which was a huge success, airing first on the CBC in Canada and then on PBS in the United States. That was followed by a series that ran from 1990 to 1996. Anne has also become a stage staple thanks to theatrical productions like *Anne of Green Gables—The Musical* (a must-see at the Confederation Centre in Charlottetown) and *Anne and Gilbert* (a melodious sequel that debuted in 2005). Of course, for the millions of modern-day Anne fans, Cavendish is hallowed ground because the top Green Gables sites and experiences are all in the area. These include **Green Gables**, the **Site of Lucy Maud Montgomery's Cavendish Home**, the **Lucy Maud Montgomery Birthplace**, and the **Anne of Green Gables Museum at Silver Bush.**

introductory film in the visitor center will help you get up to speed. An audiovisual presentation on Montgomery's life shares space with a café in the barn nearby. This National Historic Site has been part of Prince Edward Island National Park since 1937 and hosts daily events throughout July and August such as guided tours, puppet shows, and old-fashioned games. ✉ *8619 Rte. 6* ☎ *902/963–7874* ⊕ *www.pc.gc.ca/lhn-nhs/pe/greengables/index.aspx* 💲 *C$7.80 July–Labor Day; C$6.30 May, June, and day after Labor Day–Oct. 31; C$3.90 Nov. and Apr. 15–30* ⏲ *May–Oct., daily 9–5; Apr. 15–30 and Nov. by appointment.*

Lucy Maud Montgomery Birthplace. The cottage-y white house with green trim overlooking New London Harbour, 11 km (7 miles) southwest of Cavendish, is where the *Anne* author was born in 1874, and the interior has been furnished with antiques to conjure up that era. Among memorabilia on display are a replica of Montgomery's wedding gown and personal scrapbooks filled with many of her poems and stories. ✉ *Junction of Rtes. 6 and 20* ☎ *902/886–2099* ⊕ *www.lmmontgomerybirthplace.ca* 💲 *C$4* ⏲ *Mid-May–mid-Oct., daily 9–5.*

FAMILY **Sandspit.** The largest amusement park on PEI kicks things up a notch with midway rides and go-cart tracks that appeal to tots and tweens alike. Single-ride coupons and park passes are available. ✉ *8986 Rte. 6* ☎ *877/963–3939, 902/963–3939* ⊕ *www.sandspit.com* 💲 *Day pass C$25; single coupons C$1.50 (individual rides require 2–7 coupons* *each)* ⏲ *Mid-June–early Sept., daily 9:30–3 on school days, otherwise 10–10 or 11 (occasionally closes at 6 pm).*

Site of Lucy Maud Montgomery's Cavendish Home. The Site of Lucy Maud Montgomery's Cavendish Home is where the writer lived with her maternal grandparents after the untimely death of her mother. Though the foundation of the house where Montgomery wrote *Anne of Green Gables* is all that remains, the homestead's fields and old apple-tree gardens are lovely. A bookstore and small museum are also on the property, which is operated by descendants of the family and is a National Historic Site of Canada. ✉ *8521 Rte. 6* ☎ *902/963–2231* 🌐 *www.peisland.com/lmm* 💲 *C$5* ⏲ *Mid-May–mid-Oct., daily 10–5.*

WHERE TO EAT

$$ CANADIAN ✕ **Café on the Clyde at Prince Edward Island Preserve Company.** One of the best spots on the Island to stop for a bite, this café has wonderful desserts and an extensive tea list. The dining room has a soaring ceiling and two walls of windows looking over the Clyde River, and everything served is noted for freshness—even the ice cream is homemade. Particularly praiseworthy items include the savory potato pie with maple-bacon cream, available at lunch and dinner; other entrées include pan-seared haddock with lobster velouté and barbecue-style ribs, which you could follow with a not-too-sweet raspberry cream cheese pie. $ *Average main: C$17* ✉ *2841 New Glasgow Rd., New Glasgow* ✣ *Off Rte. 13* ☎ *902/964–4300, 800/565–5267* 🌐 *preservecompany.com* ⏲ *Closed mid-Oct.–late May.*

$$$ SEAFOOD FAMILY Fodor's Choice ★ ✕ **New Glasgow Lobster Suppers.** Established in 1958, New Glasgow Lobster Suppers brings fresh lobster direct from a pound on the premises to your plate. Scallops, roast beef, salmon, chicken, haddock, ham, even a vegetarian dish are other choices if you've already had your fill of crustaceans. All come with fresh rolls, steamed mussels, seafood chowder, salads, homemade desserts, and beverages. Whew. Bar service is available, as is a separate children's menu. The bustling dining area can seat up to 500 guests, and it often fills up. Because turnover is fast, there isn't usually a long wait. $ *Average main: C$27* ✉ *604 Rte. 258, off Rte. 13, New Glasgow* ☎ *902/964–2870* 🌐 *peilobstersuppers.com* ⏲ *Closed mid-Oct.–late May. No lunch.*

WHERE TO STAY

Accommodations in the Cavendish area are often booked a year in advance for July and most of August. If you're late in planning, don't despair—hotels in Charlottetown and elsewhere in the central region are still within easy driving distance of "Anne's Land."

$ HOTEL FAMILY **Bay Vista Motel and Cottage.** This straightforward, spotlessly clean motel has real family appeal. **Pros:** friendly staff; picnic area with shared-use barbecues; free Wi-Fi; laundry facilities. **Cons:** looks like a motel inside and out. $ *Rooms from: C$119* ✉ *9517 Rte. 6* ☎ *902/963–2225, 800/846–0601* 🌐 *www.bayvista.ca* ⏲ *Closed late Sept.–early June* 🛏 *31 rooms, 2 suites, 1 cottage* 🍴 *Breakfast.*

$$ B&B/INN FAMILY **Cavendish Country Inn and Cottages.** The family atmosphere of this 9-acre cottage complex is a big draw for some folks; there are several playgrounds on-site, as well as a pair of pools, fire pits, and outdoor

games (complimentary movies help on rainy days). **Pros:** choice of accommodations for the budget-conscious; free Wi-Fi; laundry facilities. **Cons:** no air-conditioning; dated decor; if you want a quieter holiday, this isn't the place. $ *Rooms from: C$150* ✉ *8405 Cavendish Rd., Rte. 6* ☎ *902/963–2181, 800/454–4853* 🌐 *www.cavendishpei.com* ⏲ *Closed late Oct.–mid-May* 🛏 *11 rooms, 35 cottages* 🍽 *No meals.*

$ B&B/INN FAMILY **Kindred Spirits Country Inn and Cottages.** Named in a nod to Anne, this lovely 6-acre property is just a short walk from Green Gables. **Pros:** helpful staff; National Park passes provided; free Wi-Fi; laundry facilities. **Cons:** style is a bit twee for some tastes; breakfast not included in cottage rates. $ *Rooms from: C$115* ✉ *Memory La., off Rte. 6* ☎ *902/963–2434, 800/461–1755* 🌐 *www.kindredspirits.ca* ⏲ *Closed late Oct.–mid-May* 🛏 *25 rooms, 20 cottages* 🍽 *Breakfast.*

SPORTS AND THE OUTDOORS

GOLF

Andersons Creek Golf Club. Designed by Graham Cooke, this rolling parkland course features some tricky terrain and water hazards on nine holes. The third hole is one to watch out for, with a steep downward slope to the green. Proud of the game's Scottish roots, the championship course employs its own bagpiper. ✉ *68 Rte. 240, Stanley Bridge* ☎ *902/886–2222, 866/886–4422* 🌐 *www.andersonscreek.com* 💲 *C$49.50–C$85 daily rate* ⛳ *18 holes, 6651 yards, par 72* ⏲ *Closed mid-Oct–mid-May.*

Eagles Glenn Golf Course. Graham Cooke was the designer behind this course, reminiscent of a Scottish links course, with 18 walkable holes in a stunning setting. This championship course is a testing one, but five sets of tees allow for various skill levels. ✉ *374 Eagles Glenn Blvd., Rte. 6* ☎ *902/963–3600, 866/963–3600* 🌐 *www.eaglesglenn.com* 💲 *C$49.50–C$85* ⛳ *18 holes, 6785 yards, par 72* ⏲ *Closed Nov.–Apr.*

Glasgow Hills Resort and Golf Club. About five minutes southeast of Cavendish, this course wins high praise for its challenging Les Furber–designed layout and killer clubhouse views. Kept in superior condition, it utilizes the natural, undulating landscape, with views of the River Clyde and the Gulf of St. Lawrence. It's popular with many top players, although every hole has multiple tee boxes to suit all levels of play. ✉ *98 Glasgow Hills Dr., New Glasgow* ☎ *866/621–2200* 🌐 *www.glasgowhills.com* 💲 *C$50–C$85* ⛳ *18 holes, 6915 yards, par 72* ⏲ *Closed mid-Oct–mid-May.*

Green Gables Golf Course. This classic Stanley Thompson–designed course was restored by Thomas McBroom in 2007. The result reflects many of Thompson's original features. With great views and ocean breezes tickling your shot, it's a good choice for both aspiring and avid golfers. The clubhouse lounge serves refreshments and light meals. The 18-hole, par-72 course opens for play May through October. ✉ *8727 Rte. 6* ☎ *902/963–4653, 888/870–5454* 🌐 *www.greengablesgolf.com* 💲 *C$45–C$100* ⛳ *18 holes, 6874 yards, par 72* ⏲ *Closed Nov.–Apr.*

THE CONFEDERATION TRAIL

In the 1980s, new life was given to the ground once covered by the Prince Edward Island Railway, when the abandoned track was converted into a recreational route dubbed the Confederation Trail. Gorgeous, well groomed, and generally flat, its 410 km (255 miles) are ideal for hiking and, above all, biking. Serious cyclists can race through it in 17 hours. But most pedal pushers opt for a more leisurely pace that allows them to stop and smell the lupines. If you're short on time, rent a bike from any cycle shop and just do a single section. Plum-color access gates are near roadways at many points, and food and lodging are available at villages along the way. Tourism PEI (🌐 *www.tourismpei.com*) provides details on rental locations and touring tips, and the website has interactive and downloadable maps. You can also pick up the "Confederation Trail Cycling Guide" that includes maps, itinerary highlights, and accommodations that are part of the Cyclists Welcome Program. Just a heads-up: helmets are compulsory in PEI for drivers and passengers, regardless of age.

WATER SPORTS

FAMILY **Inn at the Pier.** You can splash out in rented kayaks or Jet Skis, and parasailing rides and deep-sea fishing trips can also be arranged. ✉ *9796 Cavendish Rd., Rte. 6* ☎ *902/886-3126, 877/886-7437* 🌐 *www.innatthepier.com/watersports.*

MALPEQUE

Malpeque is 32 km (20 miles) west of Cavendish.

There are two good reasons why motorists make the drive to Malpeque. Some do it to cram in one last Anne shrine—specifically Silver Bush at Park Corner. Others continue westward to stuff themselves full of oysters. Named for the bay from which many are drawn, the Malpeque variety has had a huge cachet since earning the "best in show" title at the 1900 Paris World's Fair. Eating them is a time-honored tradition. The same goes for harvesting them: traditional methods are still employed (tongs are used, not dredgers) despite the fact that Prince Edward Island sells about 300,000 tons of oysters annually.

GETTING HERE AND AROUND

Malpeque is best accessed—and appreciated—by car. To reach it, veer off Route 6 at New London onto Route 20.

EXPLORING

FAMILY **Anne of Green Gables Museum at Silver Bush.** This was once home to Lucy Maud Montgomery's aunt and uncle. The writer also lived here for a time and was married in the parlor in 1911—in fact, that room serves as a wedding venue for modern-day couples. Inside the house, which is still owned by Montgomery descendants, are mementos such as photographs and a quilt Montgomery worked on. The site includes a gift shop jam-packed with licensed Anne of Green Gables goodies, and there is a Matthew Cuthbert look-alike on hand to take visitors on buggy rides around the pastoral 110-acre property. Trip lengths vary with rates starting at C$5.50. ✉ *4542 Rte. 20, Park Corner* ☎ *902/886–2884, 800/665–2663* 🌐 *www.annemuseum.com* 💲 *C$5.50* ⏲ *May and Oct., daily 11–4; June and Sept., daily 10–4; July and Aug., daily 9–7; off-season by appointment.*

St. Mary's Church. Built in 1902 by Island architect W. H. Harris, this church hosts performances by visiting artists from mid-June to mid-September as part of the Indian River Festival of Music. The church has very good acoustics plus a beautiful pastoral setting, and the concerts here are often broadcast nationally by the Canadian Broadcasting Corporation. ✉ *1374 Hamilton Rd., Rte. 104, Indian River* ✣ *6 km (3½ miles) south of Malpeque* ☎ *902/836–4933, 866/856–3733* 🌐 *www.indianriverfestival.com* 💲 *C$10–C$45.*

BEACHES

FAMILY **Cabot Beach Provincial Park.** In addition to a popular campground, 360-acre Cabot Beach Provincial Park has fine day-use facilities—particularly for families. In summer, the sandy beach is supervised, plus there's a playground and children's programming. Naturalist-led walks are also available. Surf conditions can sometimes deter swimmers, and alerts are issued if it becomes dangerous, but when it's calm, it's very calm. **Amenities:** lifeguards; parking (free); showers; toilets. **Best for:** sunset; surfing; swimming; walking. ✉ *449 King St., Rte. 20* ☎ *902/836–8945, 877/445–4938* 💲 *Free* ⏲ *Early June–mid Sept., daily dawn–dusk.*

FAMILY **Darnley Beach.** Just north of Darnley (on Route 20, about halfway between Park Corner and Malpeque), this long beach has a number of sandstone caves at the end. There are no developed facilities here, other than a campground, and the beach is often almost entirely deserted except for the seabirds—so it's perfect for those seeking a "castaway" experience. **Amenities:** none. **Best for:** solitude; sunset; walking. ✉ *Off Lower Darnley Rd.*

WHERE TO EAT AND STAY

$$ SEAFOOD ✕ **Malpeque Oyster Barn.** If it's oysters you're after, here's where to get 'em! You'll be hard-pressed to find fresher bivalves; after all, you can see their beds right outside the window of this casual wharf-side eatery. Nor will you find plumper, sweeter ones. Oysters can be prepared several ways, but purists should just order a dozen unadorned (with a cold beer as an accompaniment), then slurp away. Chowder, steamed mussels, lobster rolls, and similar fare appear on the menu as well, and there is a retail outlet in case you want to take some seafood home. 💲 *Average main: C$18* ✉ *Malpeque Wharf Rd., Rte. 20* ☎ *902/836–3999* 💳 *No credit cards* ⏲ *Closed Sept.–June.*

$$ B&B/INN **Noble House.** Staying at this cheery yellow heritage farmhouse with its welcoming front porch and gingerbread trim, you might feel like you have stepped into a Norman Rockwell painting—save for the fact that, back in the day, guests wouldn't have been able to book into well-equipped rooms that pair period charm with contemporary amenities like Jacuzzi tubs, cable TV, and high-speed Internet. **Pros:** close to Cabot Beach and Indian River Festival concerts; off-season rates available mid-September to mid-June. **Cons:** no air-conditioning; resident pets

CLOSE UP

A Bridge Too Far?

Gephyrophobiacs (people with an extreme fear of bridges) had best avoid the Confederation Bridge. Linking Borden-Carleton to Cape Jourimain, New Brunswick, it is the longest in the world spanning ice-covered water. But for anyone else intent on driving to or from PEI, the so-called fixed link is the way to go. Even if you're merely passing by while doing the Central Coastal circuit, this 13-km (8-mile) engineering marvel is worth a look. To construct it, massive concrete pillars—each 65 feet across and 180 feet high—were sunk into waters more than 110 feet deep. The cost? A cool billion.

First-time traversers invariably want to stop on the bridge itself to take a picture. Don't—it's illegal. You must maintain a speed of 80 kph (50 mph). The best angles are from the Prince Edward Island side anyway. For an up-close perspective, pull into Gateway Village at the foot of the bridge. In addition to a 3-acre park where you can take in the bridge view, it has a plethora of souvenir shops where you can buy postcards of said view.

may not appeal to those with allergies. $ *Rooms from: C$160* ✉ *187 Taylor Rd., RR No. 1* ☎ *902/836–4380* 🌐 *www.bbcanada.com/5051.html* 🛏 *3 rooms* 🍴 *Breakfast.*

SPORTS AND THE OUTDOORS

Dale's Deep Sea Adventures. Daily fishing trips leave from Malpeque Harbour (beside Cabot Beach Provincial Park) at 8 am, 1:15 pm, and 6 pm. The C$45 price (cash or travelers check only) includes all equipment, and Dale will clean what you catch. ✉ *Rte. 20* ☎ *902/836–3393, 902/439–3693 cell phone* 🌐 *www.kata.pe.ca/attract/dalesdeepsea* ⏲ *Closed early Sept.–early July.*

FAMILY **Malpeque Bay Kayak Tours.** Malpeque is a French corruption of the Mi'Kmaq word for "big water." You can go out and explore it in summer with these informative, half-day interpretive trips. The company also rents kayaks, stand-up paddleboards, and—for on-shore adventures—bicycles. And if you overdo the activities, there's an infrared sauna on-site. ✉ *Rte. 20* ☎ *902/836–3784, 866/582–3383* 🌐 *www.peikayak.ca* $ *Tours C$55; kayak rentals from C$30, bicycle rentals from C$15.*

VICTORIA

22 km (14 miles) east of Borden-Carleton.

Cross-country from the Green Gables Shore is the Red Sands Shore where charming, understated villages await. The jewel in this coastal crown is Victoria, known locally as Victoria-by-the-Sea. It's peaceful, lovingly preserved, and popular with artsy types who come to escape the hectic pace of modern life. Browse the shops; admire the architecture; then kick back on a nearby beach that's washed by the warm waters of Northumberland Strait.

GETTING HERE AND AROUND

Victoria—sitting just off the Trans-Canada Highway, 22 km (14 miles) east of the Confederation Bridge—is most easily reached by car. When you arrive in the village, park by the wharf and set out on foot. It's only two blocks wide and two blocks long, so you won't get lost.

WHERE TO EAT AND STAY

$$ FUSION **Landmark Café.** In spite of the name, this quirky, memorabilia-filled eatery is a full restaurant. And while the soups, salads, sandwiches, and a killer daily quiche are great lunchtime fuel, it's the fresh seafood that really stands out. Try Eugene's Cajun-style jumbo shrimp and scallop stir-fry, or go back to basics with what may be the Island's best seafood chowder. You can count on friendly service, too. Like so many places on PEI, this one is family owned and operated—and it shows. The caveat is that the little Landmark fills up quickly, so having reservations (or patience) helps. *Average main: C$15 12 Main St. 902/658–2286 www.landmarkcafe.ca Closed Oct.–May.*

$ B&B/INN **Orient Hotel Bed and Breakfast.** Cozy guest rooms and suites that are individually decorated lend this vintage B&B a comforting grandma's-house vibe. **Pros:** some rooms have water views; lovely hosts; free Wi-Fi and bicycle storage. **Cons:** some rooms are small; no air-conditioning. *Rooms from: C$100 34 Main St. 902/658–2503, 800/565–6743 www.theorienthotel.com Closed Oct.–May 4 rooms, 3 suites Breakfast.*

$ B&B/INN **Victoria Village Inn and Restaurant.** Guest rooms in this three-story Victorian—built for a sea captain in the 1880s—are basic in terms of interior design, but they have lovely "bones" (note the original plank floors and tall sash windows). **Pros:** common living room with TV and board games; free Wi-Fi; open year-round. **Cons:** some rooms are small; no TVs in rooms and no air-conditioning. *Rooms from: C$100 22 Howard St. 902/658–2483, 866/658–2483 www.victoriavillageinn.com 3 rooms, 1 suite Breakfast.*

NIGHTLIFE AND PERFORMING ARTS

Victoria Playhouse. Offering a renowned professional program that celebrates Canadian theater and music, this place may only have 150 seats but it has big talent and a huge heart. Between late June and mid-September, the circa-1914 venue mounts three different plays plus assorted concerts. *Howard and Main Sts. 902/658–2025, 800/925–2025 www.victoriaplayhouse.com C$32.*

SPORTS AND THE OUTDOORS

By-the-Sea Kayaking. June through September, you can join kayaking tours, including sunrise, sunset, full-moon, and full-day tours, with the opportunity to do some clam digging on the beach. Kayaks, stand-up paddleboards, and bicycles are also available for rent. *Victoria Wharf 902/658–2572, 877/879–2572 www.bytheseakayaking.ca Tours from C$80; rentals from C$15 for 1 hr to C$80 per 4 to 8 hrs.*

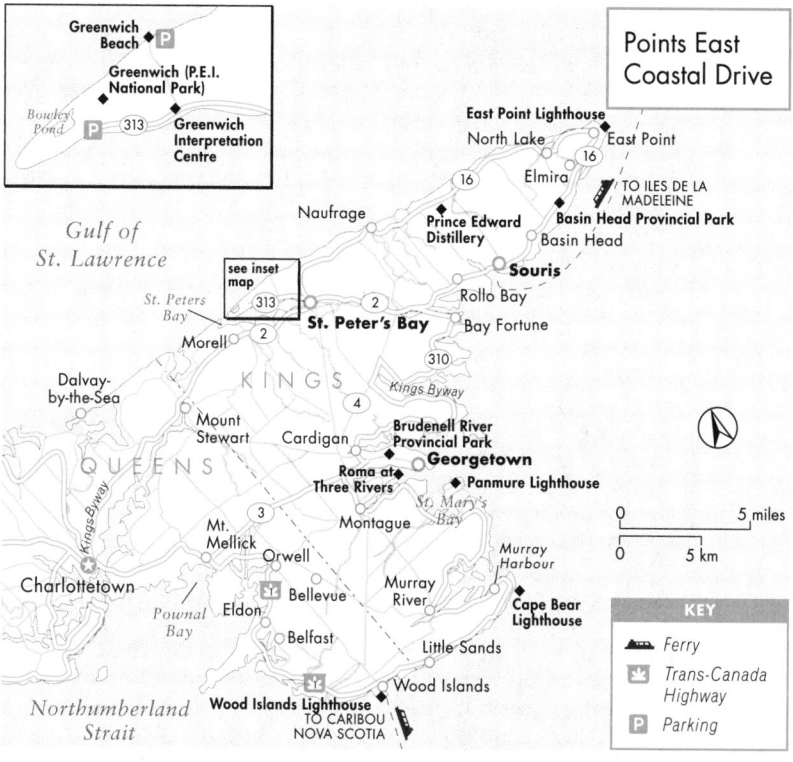

SHOPPING

Island Chocolates. A family-run chocolate factory in a 19th-century store, Island Chocolates sells sweets handmade with Belgian chocolate, fresh fruit, nuts, and liqueurs. Espresso, teas, and decadent desserts are also available, and there is a nice deck to sit on while you munch. Willy Wonka wannabes will enjoy the chocolate-making workshops (C$45) held on Wednesday and Sunday. ✉ *7 Main St.* ☎ *902/658–2320* ⏲ *Closed mid-Sept.–mid-June.*

POINTS EAST COASTAL DRIVE

For 375 km (233 miles), the Points East Coastal Drive traces the shoreline of tranquil Kings County on the east end of PEI. The route passes forests, farms, fishing villages, and (in early summer, at least) fields of blue, white, pink, and purple lupines that slope down to red cliffs and blue sea. Championship golf courses are also in abundant supply. Ditto for lighthouses and long beaches; among these, Basin Head and the Greenwich section of Prince Edward Island National Park stand out. Accessible by car from other parts of the province, the Points East Coastal Drive can also be reached via ferry from Nova Scotia.

GEORGETOWN

52 km (32 miles) northeast of Charlottetown.

The pint-sized capital of Kings County, at the tip of a peninsula jutting into Cardigan Bay, was a major shipbuilding center in the 19th century. Thanks to its location—and early settlers' vocation—the town has both wraparound sea views and a collection of charming, Victorian-era buildings. Georgetown is also a mere five minutes from Brudenell River Provincial Park (the county's largest such facility).

GETTING HERE AND AROUND

Georgetown is a drive-to destination. To get here from Charlottetown or the Wood Islands Ferry, follow the signs for the well-marked Points East Coastal Drive. Alternately, you can save time by cutting cross-country from Charlottetown on Route 3.

EXPLORING

Brudenell River Provincial Park. From late June to late August, the park promises interpretative programs, plus a wealth of outdoor opportunities—including boating, hiking, and supervised swimming. Two championship golf courses (Brudenell River and Dundarave) are the icing on its proverbial cake. ✉ *283 Brudenell Island Blvd., Rte. 3* ☎ *902/652–8966, 877/445–4938.*

FAMILY **Roma at Three Rivers.** This National Historic Site, about 2 km (1 mile) outside Georgetown, commemorates the trading post that French merchant Jean Pierre Roma established here in 1732. Costumed staffers offer interpretive programs and guided tours daily (there are trails with informational panels if you'd prefer to explore independently). Heritage lunches with sustaining soup and brick-oven-baked bread are also served on-site. ✉ *505 Roma Point Rd., Brudenell Pt.* ✣ *Off Rte. 319* ☎ *902/838–3413* ⊕ *www.roma3rivers.com* 🎟 *C$5* ⏲ *Late June–late Sept., daily 11–5.*

WHERE TO EAT AND STAY

$$$ SEAFOOD ✕ **Clamdiggers Beach House and Restaurant.** In theory you could come here and just gorge on the waterfront restaurant's namesake bivalves (the generous platter of whole, hand-breaded fried clams served with PEI fries and house-made coleslaw is always a hit). But if you did, you'd miss out on the fresh crab cakes . . . and the seafood stew . . . and the seared halibut. There are lots of options for meat lovers, too. All of the above can be enjoyed either inside the bright, beach house–style dining room or outside on a deck that sits a mere 26 feet from Cardigan Bay. [$] *Average main: C$26* ✉ *7 West St.* ☎ *902/652–2466* ⊕ *www.clamdiggers.ca* ⏲ *Closed Oct.–May.*

$$ RESORT FAMILY **Rodd Brudenell River.** If you've come to eastern PEI to golf, this resort is *the* place to stay because the provincial park that shares its name is home to two 18-hole championship courses. **Pros:** many rooms and all cottages have private decks or balconies; cottages have fireplaces and full kitchens. **Cons:** tired decor; fine dining available late June to mid-September only. [$] *Rooms from: C$126* ✉ *Brudenell River Provincial Park, 86 Dewars La.* ☎ *902/652–2332, 800/565–7633* ⊕ *www.roddvacations.com* ⏲ *Closed Nov.–Apr.* 🛏 *67 rooms, 32 suites, 16 cottages.*

NIGHTLIFE AND PERFORMING ARTS

Kings Playhouse. In summer months, the Kings Playhouse stages lighthearted comedies on Sunday and Wednesday evenings. On Tuesdays, the venue is turned over to fiddlers and dancers during the weekly ceilidh, and other productions include dinner theater, comedy shows, and concerts. ✉ *65 Grafton St.* ☎ *902/652–2053, 888/346–5666* 🌐 *www.kingsplayhouse.com.*

SPORTS AND THE OUTDOORS

GOLF

Brudenell River Golf Course. One of the best in the country and arguably the most popular on the Island, the Brudenell course hosts professional matches and numerous Canadian Tour events. Broad fairways and manicured greens are dotted with lakes, ponds, and gardens, adding to the pleasure of playing a round here. Blind shots and doglegs present a good challenge. Four sets of tees vary the distances. ✉ *Brudenell River Provincial Park, 82 Dewars La.* ☎ *800/235–8909* 🌐 *peisfinestgolf.com/brudenell/* 💲 *C$40–C$80* ⛳ *18 holes, 1541yards, par 72* ⏲ *Closed Oct.–late June (may vary).*

Dundarave Golf Course. With its striking red-sandstone bunkers, set out in equally striking patterns, the Dundarave Golf Course is Brundenell River's beautiful younger sister. Its wide fairways are lined by pine trees and the Brudenell River winds through, making for a stunning landscape. Watch out for the thick rough, though, and be prepared for some challenging moments. ✉ *Brudenell River Provincial Park, 82 Dewars La.* ☎ *800/235–8909* 🌐 *peisfinestgolf.com/dundarave/* 💲 *C$40–C$80* ⛳ *18 holes, 7089 yards, par 72* ⏲ *Closed Oct.–late June (may vary).*

WATER SPORTS

Outside Expeditions. Kayak rentals and kayak tours are offered here, in more sheltered waters than those at sea. The tours include everything from easy 90-minute paddles appropriate for any level of expertise to six-hour seal-watching excursions to St. Andrew's Point. Rental bikes and stand-up paddleboards are also available. They also have a location at North Rustico. ✉ *Brudenell River Provincial Park, 283 Brudenell Island Blvd., Rte. 3* ☎ *902/652–2434 Canada Day–Labor Day, 800/207–3899* 🌐 *getoutside.com* 💲 *C$45–C$125 for tours; from C$25 for rentals* ⏲ *Closed early Sept.–June.*

FAMILY **Tranquility Cove Adventures.** One way to experience PEI like a native is to sign up for a half-day of clam digging on an offshore island, complete with cooking up your finds. Another option is to set out for two hours of starfish hunting or deep-sea fishing. The experiences are both fun and informative. ✉ *1 Kent St., Georgetown Wharf* ☎ *902/969–7184* 🌐 *www.tcapei.com* 💲 *Clam digging C$98; starfish hunting and deep-sea fishing C$55* ⏲ *Closed Oct.–mid-June.*

SOURIS

Souris is 46 km (29 miles) northeast of Georgetown.

A pretty town perched on the water, Souris (pronounced "Surrey") gives easy access to PEI's essential sights and sounds. The seascape includes harbors, lighthouses, and bountiful beaches. There's music in the salt air, too, thanks to the seasonal ceilidhs and outdoor concerts Souris hosts (the events calendar at *www.sourispei.com* has full details), including performances at the town's new theater and concert venue, The Centre Stage (formerly St. James United Church). You'll hear more five minutes away in Rollo Bay, which holds the PEI Bluegrass and Old Time Music Festival (*902/566–2641* *peibluegrass.tripod.com*) in early July and the Rollo Bay Fiddle Festival midmonth (*902/687–2584,* *www.rollobayfiddlefest.ca*).

GETTING HERE AND AROUND

The East Connection Shuttle (*902/892–6760*) carries passengers on request from Charlottetown to Souris and other Kings County communities. The fare is approximately C$85 one-way. You'll want your own vehicle, however, to properly see outlying areas. To drive yours here from Georgetown, follow signs for the Points East Coastal Drive or veer a little inland to Route 4, which merges with Route 2 near Fortune.

EXPLORING

FAMILY **Basin Head Provincial Park.** This park, 13 km (8 miles) east of Souris, is noted for an expanse of exquisite silvery sand that's backed by grassy dunes. The beach (accessible via a boardwalk and supervised in peak months) is well worth visiting, and not only because it's one of the Island's most beautiful. If you scuff your feet in the sand here, you can hear it squeak and squawk. The so-called "singing sand" is a rare phenomenon produced by the sand's high silica content.

On a beach-top bluff inside the park, you'll also find the small **Basin Head Fisheries Museum** (*902/357–7233,* *www.peimuseum.com,* *$4,* *early June–Oct., daily 9–5*), which depicts the ever-changing nature of PEI's inshore fishing industry through artifacts, exhibits, and dioramas. *336 Basin Head Rd.* *Off Rte. 16* *902/357–7230, 877/445–4938* *www.tourismpei.com/provincial-park/basin-head* *Park free; museum C$4.*

Myriad View Artisan Distillery. In Rollo Bay, just west of Souris, handcrafted spirited spirits—like Strait Vodka and Dandelion "Shine" are produced. Complimentary tours and tastings are offered May through September and products can be purchased on-site. *1336 Rte. 2, Rollo Bay* *902/687–1281* *www.straitshine.com* *Free* *May, weekdays 11–5, June, Mon.–Sat. 11–6; July–mid-Sept., Mon.–Sat. 11–6, Sun. 1–5; mid-Sept.–Sept. 30, Mon.–Sat. 11–5; off-season by chance or appointment.*

Prince Edward Distillery. A must-see for tippling tourists is the Prince Edward Distillery, north of Souris. Its premium vodka proves that more than french fries and chips can be made from those famous PEI potatoes. Take a 25-minute tour that's followed by a tasting; then buy some liquid souvenirs to take home. *9984 Rte. 16, Hermanville* *902/687–2586, 877/510–9669* *www.princeedwarddistillery.com* *C$10* *Call ahead.*

WHERE TO EAT AND STAY

$$ CANADIAN **Sheltered Harbour Café & Pub.** Frequented mostly by locals, this café offers basic fare—think clams, scallops, and other seafood, plus burger platters and down-home roast turkey dinners—served in large portions at reasonable prices. Gluten-free options are always available and beer from the Gahan House Brewery is on tap. If you're gearing up for a long day at the shore, fill up here first with a hearty breakfast. *Average main: C$13 41 Breakwater St. 902/687–1997 www.shelteredharbour.com Closed Mon. Jan.–June.*

$$ SEAFOOD **21 Breakwater Restaurant.** A welcome find in a town where dining options are thin, this eatery overlooking Colville Bay stays true to its rural roots yet presents a menu with some international élan (witness the mussels in lime butter or the herby fish-and-chips that are baked Portuguese-style). The pretty deck offers diners the option to eat *plein air*, and there's a separate children's menu. *Average main: C$18 21 Breakwater St. 902/687–2556 Closed Sun.*

$$$ B&B/INN **Inn at Spry Point.** Hugging the end of a 110-acre peninsula a few kilometers east, this inn benefits from both an attractive shoreline and a 1-km (½-mile) sandy beach. **Pros:** ocean sounds lull you to sleep; comfy beds; free Wi-Fi. **Cons:** relatively remote; no TV; Continental breakfast is complimentary, but lunch and dinner aren't served on-site. *Rooms from: C$179 222 Ark La., Little Pond Off Spry Point Rd. 902/583–2400, 888/687–3745 www.innatsprypoint.com Closed early Oct.–mid-June 15 rooms Breakfast.*

ST. PETER'S BAY

28 km (17 miles) northwest of Souris.

St. Peter's Bay won the location lottery—at least that's what folks who love quiet, outdoorsy destinations think. The nearby Greenwich portion of Prince Edward Island National Park has dunes that draw beachgoers, hikers, and bird-watchers (so many avian species flock here that the park runs themed programs). If you'd rather pursue a different kind of birdie, the Links at Crowbush Cove are a short drive west. St. Peter's Bay, meanwhile, provides a sublime backdrop for cycling. On the waterside leg of the Confederation Trail between the village and Morell, you pedal past idyllic coves dotted with boats and buoys.

GETTING HERE AND AROUND

Driving independently is the best way to get here. From Souris continue along the Points East Coastal Drive or take a cross-country shortcut on Route 2. Alternately, the East Connection Shuttle (*902/892–6760*) will bring you here from Charlottetown; expect to pay about C$70 one-way.

EXPLORING

The Points East Coastal area is rich for lighthouse lovers. PEI has more than 50 of the navigational aids, but many of the highlights (literally) are right here. For further details, grab a copy of the themed brochure produced by the PEI Lighthouse Society.

OFF THE BEATEN PATH

East Point Lighthouse. Ships from many nations have been wrecked on the reef running northeast from here, necessitating the installation of the East Point Lighthouse in 1867. Guided tours of the towering edifice are offered mid-June through Labor Day. Books about life at sea, as well as local crafts, are available at the on-site gift shop. Because of the erosion, caution should be used when approaching the high cliffs overlooking the ocean here. ✉ *Lighthouse Rd., East Point* ✣ *Off Rte. 16* ☎ *902/357–2106* 🌐 *www.eastpointlighthouse.com* 💲 *C$5* ⏲ *June–Sept., daily 9–6 (craft shop open late May–early Oct.).*

Fodor's Choice ★

Greenwich (P.E.I. National Park). The west end of the Greenwich Peninsula, known for its superior beach and shifting sand dunes, was federally protected in 1998 when a 6-km (3½-mile) section was incorporated into Prince Edward Island National Park. Because the dunes are still moving, gradually burying the nearby woods, here and there bleached tree bits thrust up through the sand like wooden skeletons. The road in ends at an interpretive center (open early June to mid-September) where displays, hands-on activities, and themed programs teach visitors about the ecology of this unique land formation. Walking trails let you follow the progression from forest to dune to beach, and include a photogenic boardwalk over Bowley Pond. Due to the delicate nature of the dune system, you're required to stay on designated paths and refrain from touching flora. Changing facilities and a picnic area can be found at the beach, which is supervised from late July to late August. Beaches in the national park are pet-free areas from April to mid-October every year. ✉ *Rte. 313, Greenwich* ✣ *6 km (4 miles) west of St. Peters Bay* ☎ *902/672–6350* 🌐 *www.pc.gc.ca* 💲 *C$7.80 July and Aug.; C$3.90 other times* ⏲ *Mid-May–mid-Oct., daily dawn–dusk; full services July and Aug. only.*

Panmure Head Lighthouse. Marking the entrance to Georgetown Harbour, it stands more than 60 feet tall. You can ascend to the top; then catch your breath browsing the on-site gift shop. ✉ *62 Lighthouse Rd., Rte. 347, Panmure Island* ☎ *902/838–7082* 💲 *C$5* ⏲ *July and Aug., daily; June and Sept. by chance or by appointment.*

Wood Islands Lighthouse Museum and Interpretive Centre. This lighthouse by the ferry terminal contains exhibits on local history and marine lore—like the Phantom Ship of Northumberland Strait—along with period room settings, a gift shop, and an interpretive center. ✉ *173 Lighthouse Rd., Rte. 1, Wood Islands* ☎ *902/962–3110* 🌐 *www.woodislandslighthouse.com* 💲 *C$6* ⏲ *June–late Sept., daily 9:30–6 (last admission 5:30).*

WHERE TO EAT AND STAY

$ SEAFOOD FAMILY

✕ **Rick's Fish 'n' Chips and Seafood House.** Rick's french fries are fresh-cut, his haddock fresh-caught—and together they make one of the Island's top fish-and-chip platters. Also on the long menu at this spartan spot: deep-fried clams, scallop burgers, marinated mussels, and oysters on the half shell. The standard burger and wings selection is available for those who aren't seafood fans, and there are homemade pizzas, too. Service is friendly, but you might have to wait a bit during peak hours for a seat inside or a picnic table outside. 💲 *Average main: C$10* ✉ *5544 Rte.*

2, St. Peters ☎ 902/961–3438 ⊕ www.ricksfishnchips.com ⊙ Closed Oct.–Apr. ✍ Reservations not accepted.

$$$ B&B/INN Fodor's Choice ★ **The Inn at St. Peters.** One of the province's best-positioned inns occupies 13 idyllic acres minutes from the Greenwich segment of the national park. **Pros:** attentive service; free Wi-Fi; room perks include sofa, fireplace, DVD player, and mini-refrigerator. **Cons:** relatively pricey for PEI; two-night minimum stay in July and August. $ *Rooms from: C$235 ✉ 1668 Greenwich Rd., St. Peters Bay ✣ Off Rte. 313 ☎ 902/961–2135, 800/818–0925 ⊕ www.innatstpeters.com ⊙ Closed early Oct.–late May ⇨ 16 suites* |⊙| *Breakfast.*

NIGHTLIFE AND PERFORMING ARTS

St. Peters Courthouse Theatre. In summer, local musical acts perform and amateur actors mount plays several times a week at the St. Peters Courthouse Theatre. It's also the venue for the three-day Frank Ledwell Storytelling and Comedy Festival each July, and shows old-release movies. Logically enough, the venue is a restored courthouse that dates back to 1874. ✉ *5697 Rte. 2, St. Peters ☎ 902/961–3636, 902/961–3004 Oct.–May ⊕ www.courthousetheatre.ca* 💵 *C$12–C$20.*

SPORTS AND THE OUTDOORS

Confederation Trail Bike Rentals. This outfitter has cycles and accessories, including tag-along kid carriers. It's open daily in peak season, weekdays only in shoulder season. ✉ *15465 Northside Rd., St. Peters ✣ Junction of Rte. 2 and Rte. 16 ☎ 902/367–7900* 💵 *From C$25 per half day ⊙ Closed mid-Oct.–mid-May.*

The Links at Crowbush Cove. Designed by Thomas McBroom, the Links at Crowbush Cove is a Scottish-style course with dune views. With a pleasing combination of nature and design, it features undulating fairways, challenging greens, pot bunkers, and water hazards hardly affected by prevailing winds. ✉ *710 Canavoy Rd., Rte. 350, Lakeside ✣ Between West St. Peter's and Morell ☎ 800/235–8909 ⊕ peisfinestgolf.com* 💵 *C$60–C$100* ⛳ *18 holes, 6903 yards, par 72.*

NORTH CAPE COASTAL DRIVE

Prince County's 350-km (217-mile) North Cape Coastal Drive winds along the west coast of the Island, through very old, very small villages that still adhere to a traditional way of life. Fishermen plowing boats through choppy seas and farmers driving tractors through fields of rich, red soil are common sights. (The potatoes the latter grow prove Anne and oysters aren't the Island's only major exports!) You may be tempted to stay on the straight, flat Route 2 most of the way. But to see all that "Up West" has to offer take Route 14 to West Point and continue north along Northumberland Strait, returning along the Gulf of St. Lawrence via Route 12.

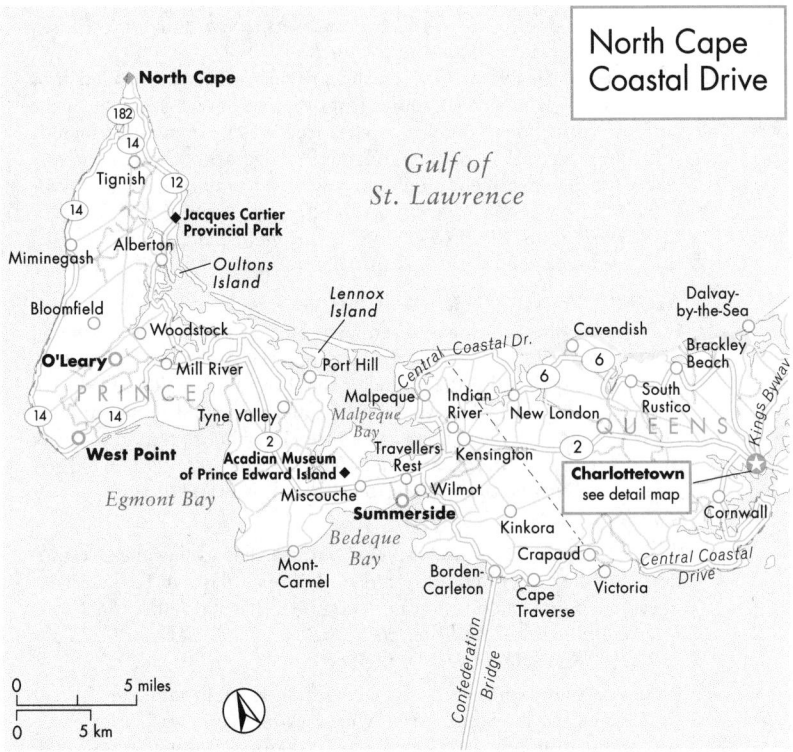

SUMMERSIDE

71 km (44 miles) west of Charlottetown.

Summerside, the second-largest city on PEI, has an attractive waterfront with a beach and boardwalk in the west end. It has a fine collection of heritage homes, too, many of them erected around the turn of the 20th century when Summerside was the headquarters of a virtual gold rush based on silver-fox ranching (a small municipal museum tells that tale). Today fishing and potato processing are more profitable enterprises—though good fish-and-chips spots are curiously in short supply. Happily, lobster is plentiful in early July during the 10-day **Summerside Lobster Festival.**

GETTING HERE AND AROUND

Summerside can be accessed by car, bus, or shuttle. Maritime Bus can get you here from Charlottetown or from the mainland via Confederation Bridge. Once here, you're best off exploring on foot. Biking is another option: the Confederation Trail passes through the city, and the former train station makes an excellent starting point for cycling excursions.

TOURS

PEI Segway Tours. These tours put a different spin on two-wheeling fun. One- and two-hour tours depart daily from the Spinnakers' Landing Lighthouse. If you are uncertain, you can have a 10-minute demo for C$10, which goes toward the price of the tour if you then decide to take it. ✉ *150 Heather Moyse Dr.* ☎ *902/436–8184* ⊕ *www.peisegway.com* ₵ *$39 for 1 hr, $69 for 2 hrs.*

EXPLORING

TOP ATTRACTIONS

Spinnakers' Landing. The cornerstone of Summerside's waterfront revitalization project is this collection of cheery little structures that are linked by a boardwalk and designed to evoke a seaside fishing village. The development offers a good blend of shopping, history, and entertainment; plus you can climb a lighthouse lookout for panoramic views of Bedeque Bay and the city. In summer, weather permitting, there's often free weekend entertainment (usually starting at 6 pm) on the outdoor stage over the water. ✉ *150 Heather Moyse Dr.* ☎ *902/432–6531* ⊕ *www.spinnakerslanding.com* ⏲ *Mid-June–mid-Sept.; shops daily 9:30–5:30 (9:30–9 in July and Aug.).*

Wyatt House Museum. Built in 1867 (the year Canada was "born"), the restored, heirloom-filled home of a prominent local family feels like a Summerside time capsule. Guided interpretive tours last about 50 minutes. The entry fee also admits you to another of the Wyatt Heritage Properties: the Lefurgey Cultural Centre at 205 Prince Street. ✉ *85 Spring St.* ☎ *902/432–1327* ⊕ *www.culturesummerside.com/wyatt-historic-house-museum* ₵ *C$10* ⏲ *July and Aug., Mon.–Sat. 10–5; June and Sept., weekdays 10–5; off-season tours by appointment.*

WORTH NOTING

Acadian Museum of Prince Edward Island (*Musée Acadien*). Many descendants of PEI's first French settlers still live in the Miscouche area, 10 km (6 miles) northwest of Summerside, and the Acadian Museum commemorates their history. This National Historic Site includes a permanent exhibition on Acadian life, including six large paintings by Claude Picard that portray Acadian national symbols, as well as an audiovisual presentation outlining the story of Island Acadians from the early 1700s onward. A genealogical center, heritage walking trail, and themed gift shop are also on-site. ✉ *23 Main Dr. E, Rte. 2, Miscouche* ☎ *902/432–2880* ⊕ *www.museeacadien.org* ₵ *C$4.50* ⏲ *July and Aug., daily 9:30–7; Sept.–June, weekdays 9:30–5, Sun. 1–4.*

Bishop's Machine Shop. Once part of a foundry complex, this old-fashioned machine shop houses an interesting collection of tools and gadgets. ✉ *101 Water St.* ☎ *902/432–1296* ₵ *By donation* ⏲ *July and Aug., Mon.–Sat., 10–4; June and Sept. by appointment.*

Eptek Art and Culture Centre. On the waterfront, this center has rotating exhibits of PEI history and fine arts on display in the main gallery: the variety of the exhibitions is one of the center's hallmarks. ✉ *130 Heather Moyse Dr.* ☎ *902/888–8373* ⊕ *www.peimuseum.com* ₵ *By donation* ⏲ *June and Sept., weekdays 9–4, Sun. noon–4; July and Aug., Mon.–Sat. 9–5, Sun. noon–5; Oct.–May, Tues.–Fri. 10–4, Sun. noon–4.*

International Fox Museum and Armoury. Housed in a 1911 armory used by local militia until 1992, the museum recounts the days when fox fur was the height of fashion—and fox "farming" was a thriving Summerside industry. ✉ *33 Summer St.* ☎ *902/432–1296* 🌐 *culturesummerside.com/international-fox-museum/* 💲 *By donation* ⏲ *July and Aug., Mon.–Sat. 10–4; June and Sept. by appointment.*

WHERE TO EAT AND STAY

$$ CANADIAN ✕ **The Deckhouse Pub & Eatery.** Summerside hardly qualifies as a foodie haven, so your best picks are places that keep it simple. The Deckhouse delivers on that front; generous portions of traditional pub grub are supplemented by a range of tasty seafood dishes (try the chowder). Its location at Spinnakers' Landing means that water views are an added bonus. Live music on Friday and Saturday evenings is another. The downside is that it's only open in summer. $ *Average main: C$15* ✉ *150 Heather Moyse Dr.* ☎ *902/436–0660* ⏲ *Closed early Sept.–mid-June.*

$ CAFÉ ✕ **Samuel's Coffeehouse.** Along with the requisite lattes and cappuccinos, Samuel's Coffeehouse serves homemade soups, bagel sandwiches, paninis, and such inside a handsome 1895 building. Tempting baked goods are also available. There's another location in Cavendish at the Avonlea Village complex. $ *Average main: C$7* ✉ *4 Queen St.* ☎ *902/724–2300* 🌐 *samuelscoffeehouse.ca.*

$ RESORT **Clark's Sunny Isle Motel.** PEI may be one of the last places in Canada where motels are plentiful and worth recommending, and Clark's Sunny Isle is a case in point, since it has managed to stay in business for more than 50 years by providing affordable, whistle-clean rooms and unwaveringly pleasant service. **Pros:** well-tended 20-acre property includes a gazebo and a walking trail to the water; each room has a mini-refrigerator, HD LCD TV, and free Wi-Fi. **Cons:** free Continental breakfast only served in May and October; basic interior design. $ *Rooms from: C$66* ✉ *720 Water St. E* ☎ *902/436–5665, 877/682–6824* 🌐 *www.sunnyislemotel.com* ⏲ *Closed Dec.–late Apr.* 🛏 *21 rooms* 🍽 *Breakfast.*

PERFORMING ARTS

College of Piping and Celtic Performing Arts of Canada. An energetic revue—featuring more than 30 bagpipers, Highland dancers, step dancers, and fiddlers—is hosted here three nights a week in July and August. During the same months, mini-concerts also run three times daily, and the C$5 tab can be credited towards the price of evening show tickets. Other events include piping contests and a Robbie Burns Dinner on the Scottish bard's birthday in January ✉ *619 Water St. E* ☎ *902/436–5377, 877/224–7473* 🌐 *www.collegeofpiping.com* 🎟 *C$5–C$39.*

Feast Dinner Theatre. A musical comedy is served up with a buffet meal Tuesday through Saturday. ✉ *Brothers 2 Restaurant, 618 Water St.* ☎ *902/436–7674* 🌐 *www.brothers2.ca* 🎟 *From C$36.99* ⏲ *Closed Sept.–mid-June.*

Harbourfront Theatre. Sharing space with the Eptek Art and Culture Centre (but accessed through a different entrance), this 527-seat theater stages dramatic and musical productions year-round. Touring musicians routinely drop by, too. ✉ *124 Heather Moyse Dr.* ☎ *902/888–2500, 800/708–6505* 🌐 *www.harbourfronttheatre.com.*

SPORTS AND THE OUTDOORS

Two Fish Bike Co. If you are interested in cycling the Summerside section of the Confederation Trail, this place has all the rental equipment you'll need. ✉ *368 Water St.* ☎ *902/303–4362* 🌐 *www.peibikerentals.ca* 💲 *C$35 per day.*

O'LEARY

37 km (23 miles) northwest of Summerside.

Central Prince County is composed of a loose network of small communities set amid green fields. In the tradition of their forebears, most residents are farmers, and those in O'Leary are no exception. In terms of preferred crops, the potato is big here—literally. A giant fiberglass one that looms outside the PEI Potato Museum is the town's distinguishing feature. After eating potatoes prepared every possible way, you can work off the calories in nearby Mill River Provincial Park with golfing and other outdoor activities.

GETTING HERE AND AROUND

You'll need a car to explore O'Leary and the surrounding area. To get here from Summerside, follow Route 2 west; then transfer onto Route 142.

EXPLORING

Canadian Potato Museum. The potato is one terrific tuber: that's the message delivered by this museum. Earnest and intriguing, it has exhibits devoted to "The Amazing Potato," displays of antique potato-farming equipment, a Potato Hall of Fame, even a gift shop selling potato-themed goods. The museum also runs fun add-on tours, which include a guided spin through the facility, plus a trip out to a potato farm, a potato fudge-making lesson, and a lunch of (you guessed it) potato-based dishes. ✉ *1 Dewar La.* ☎ *902/859–2039 mid-May–mid-Oct., 902/853–2312 mid-Oct.–mid-May* 🌐 *www.peipotatomuseum.com* 💲 *C$8.25; farm tours C$79 (reduced to C$65 if 3 or more adults take the tour)* ⏲ *Mid-May–mid-Oct., Mon.–Sat. 9–5, Sun. 1–5.*

WHERE TO STAY

$$ RESORT **Rodd Mill River.** Since full-blown resorts are so rare in this portion of the province, this hotel provides a welcome change of pace, with amenities that range from spa facilities and tennis courts to an indoor pool with a curling 90-foot waterslide. **Pros:** good base for exploring western PEI; golf packages are frequently available. **Cons:** dated decor, some public areas could be refreshed. 💲 *Rooms from: C$156* ✉ *180 Mill River Resort Rd., Woodstock* ✣ *Off Rte. 136, 5 km (3 miles) east of O'Leary* ☎ *902/859–3555, 800/565–7633* 🌐 *www.roddvacations.com* ⏲ *Closed Nov.–Jan. and Apr.* 🛏 *80 rooms, 10 suites* 🍴 *Some meals.*

SPORTS AND THE OUTDOORS

Mill River Golf Course. This is among the most scenic and challenging courses in Eastern Canada, with mature woodland, many lakes and streams, well-placed bunkers, and doglegs that call for accurate shots. It has been the site of several championship tournaments, and a season of the golf reality show *The Big Break* was filmed here. Book in advance.

CLOSE UP

Club Hopping—Island Style

Great golf clubs are par for the course on PEI, where green gables and green fields are complemented by challenging golf greens. There are more than 30 courses, both 9- and 18-hole, open to the public from May through October, with top choices including—from west to east—Mill River, Andersons Creek, Eagles Glenn, Green Gables, Glasgow Hills, Stanhope, Fox Meadow, Links at Crowbush Cove, Brudenell River, and Dundarave. All are within a 45-minute drive of one another, which means ambitious golfers can play 27 or 36 holes a day. Contact Golf PEI (☎ *866/465-3734* ⊕ *www.golfpei.ca*) for details on courses, events, and play-and-stay packages, or to book tee times.

✉ *Mill River Provincial Park, 180 Mill River Resort Rd., Woodstock* ✣ *Off Rte. 2* ☎ *800/235-8909* ⊕ *peisfinestgolf.com* ₵ *C$35–C$65* ⛳ *18 holes, 6840 yards, par 72* ⏲ *Closed late Oct.–early May.*

SHOPPING

MacAusland's Woollen Mills. The mills, 5 km (3 miles) west of O'Leary, have been producing their famous MacAusland 100% pure virgin wool blankets since 1932. ✉ *38317 Hwy. 2, Bloomfield* ☎ *902/859-3005, 877/859-3005* ⊕ *www.macauslandswoollenmills.com* ⏲ *Closed weekends.*

WEST POINT

24 km (15 miles) south of O'Leary.

West Point, on the southern tip of the western shore, may be tiny (there are only about 700 residents), but it is home to PEI's tallest functioning lighthouse. After admiring the handsome structure, you can stroll the 4,921-foot beachfront boardwalk; then cool off with a swim at Cedar Dunes Provincial Park.

GETTING HERE AND AROUND

Easily accessible by car from O'Leary via Route 14, West Point is usually viewed as a day trip. The presence of the West Point Lighthouse Inn, however, gives lighthouse-loving motorists an incentive to stay overnight.

EXPLORING

FAMILY
Fodor's Choice
★

West Point Lighthouse Museum. Built in 1875, lit in 1876, manned until 1963, and still operating today, the West Point Lighthouse is a certifiable PEI icon. A gracefully tapered shape and eye-popping black-and-white stripes make the 69-foot structure very photogenic. Inside, displays and assorted artifacts relating to lighthouses provincewide make it educational, too. Be sure to climb the 72 steps to the top for panoramic views. Beautiful any time of day, they are especially glorious at sunset because the lighthouse faces west. ✉ *364 Cedar Dunes Park Rd., Rte. 14* ☎ *902/859-3605, 800/764-6854* ⊕ *www.westpointlighthouse.com* ₵ *C$3.50* ⏲ *Mid-June–mid-Dec., daily 9–9.*

WHERE TO STAY

$$ B&B/INN **West Point Lighthouse Inn.** Few people can say they've spent the night in a lighthouse—or at least in a guest room adjacent to one—so take the opportunity when you're here. **Pros:** unique lodgings; original rooms full of character; some pets allowed. **Cons:** dearth of area dining options; books quickly; lighthouse equals bright flashing light. *Rooms from: C$155 364 Cedar Dunes Park Rd., Rte. 14 902/859–3605, 800/764–6854 www.westpointlighthouse.com Closed mid-Sept.–mid-June 13 rooms Breakfast.*

SPORTS AND THE OUTDOORS

Cedar Dunes Provincial Park. Encompassing the lighthouse site, this park boasts blissful beaches and supervised swimming in summer. Recreational programs—including guided walks of the park's nature trails—are also available seasonally. *265 Cedar Dunes Park Rd., Rte. 14 902/859–8785, 877/445–4938 Free.*

NORTH CAPE

47 km (29 miles) north of O'Leary.

Mother Nature meets modern technology at PEI's northwest tip. The Gulf of St. Lawrence and Northumberland Strait converge at North Cape's reef (the longest rock reef in North America) creating a popular hangout for seals, seabirds, and other forms of marine life. But it's the wind sweeping over the water that makes this place really stand out. Scores of windmills—some of them 262 feet high—dot the site. Part of the Atlantic Wind Test Site and Wind Farm, they were built to make the "Gentle Island" even greener.

GETTING HERE AND AROUND

North Cape is another drive-to destination. To reach it, take Route 14 along the strait or Route 12 along the gulf.

EXPLORING

North Cape Wind Energy Interpretive Centre. Exhibits here explain how turbine technology channels wind power to produce "clean" electricity for Islanders. It also includes a few displays pertaining to local history and a touch tank with lobster, crabs, and starfish that kids will enjoy. (A staff member will lift one out so you can get a real feel for these aquatic creatures.) *21817 Rte. 12 902/882–2991 www.northcape.ca C$5.70 July and Aug., daily 9–8; May, June, Sept., and Oct., daily 10–6.*

WHERE TO EAT AND STAY

$$ SEAFOOD **The Boat Shop Steak & Seafood Restaurant.** There's a harbor view from every table in this converted boatbuilder's workshop—which explains not only its waterfront location but its oversized windows and soaring ceiling. Fine, fresh seafood, not surprisingly, dominates the menu. (Time your visit right and you may be able to see fishermen unloading the catch of the day or graceful blue herons angling for their own dinner.) Traditional homemade desserts like blueberry bread pudding and sticky date cake are another highlight. Patio seating is available on fine days. *Average main: C$18 296 Rte. 152, Northport 33 km (21*

miles) south of North Cape ☎ 902/853–4905 🌐 www.northportpier.ca ⏲ Closed mid-Sept.–early June.

$$ SEAFOOD ✕ **Wind & Reef Restaurant.** Dining options are few and far between in this remote corner of PEI, so it's a blessing that the airy eatery above the North Cape Wind Energy Interpretative Centre offers more than mere sustenance. The Island seafood—including oysters, mussels, and lobster—is fresh and well prepared. Service is unfailingly friendly. The restaurant's panoramic windows, providing views of the water and (at low tide) the reef, are an added bonus. $ *Average main: C$20 ✉ 21817 Rte. 12 ☎ 902/882–3535 ⏲ Closed Oct.–May.*

$ B&B/INN **La Petite France B&B.** Built in the 1890s, this heritage home with its plentiful gables and pretty bay windows has a classic Island look. **Pros:** attentive hosts; near a popular biking trailhead; free Wi-Fi. **Cons:** two rooms share a bathroom; the largest room is in a new addition. $ *Rooms from: C$70 ✉ 441 Church St., Alberton ☎ 902/853–3975 🌐 www.lapetitefrance-pei.com ⏲ Closed Nov.–Apr. 🛏 4 rooms 🍽 Breakfast.*

$$ B&B/INN **Northport Pier Inn.** Conveniences like air-conditioning and Wi-Fi set this spot a notch above many rural inns, but it's the view that guests really rave about. **Pros:** restaurant and marina next door; roomy kitchenette suites work well for families. **Cons:** interior style is basic; during lobster season (May and June) early morning harbor traffic might disturb light sleepers. $ *Rooms from: C$125 ✉ 298 Rte. 152, Northport ✢ 33 km (21 miles) south of North Cape ☎ 902/853–4900, 855/887–4520 🌐 www.northportpier.ca ⏲ Closed Oct.–May 🛏 12 rooms, 2 suites 🍽 Breakfast.*

SPORTS AND THE OUTDOORS

Black Marsh Nature Trail. One of the best ways to see North Cape's natural and man-made assets is by hiking this trail. The 5½-km (3½-mile) out-and-back path extends past tidal pools, whirring windmills, and the cape's 1908 lighthouse to a pretty bog crossed via a boardwalk. ✉ *21817 Rte. 12.*

FAMILY **Jacques Cartier Provincial Park.** South of North Cape, this park was named for the famed French explorer who came ashore nearby in 1534, an event that's celebrated each July. In July and August, you can take naturalist-led hikes on park trails or swim on the supervised Gulf of St. Lawrence beach. ✉ *16448 Rte. 12, Kildare Capes ☎ 902/853–8632, 877/445–4938 $ Free.*

Matthews Deep Sea Fishing & Ocean Adventures. Fishing trips (sometimes with bird- and whale-watching on the side) sail out of Northport. The price includes tackle and bait, wet gear, bottled water, fish cleaning, and a serving of Island mussels, cooked on board. Bay cruises and beach picnics are other options. ✉ *265 Rte. 152, Northport ☎ 902/853–7943 🌐 www.matthewsdeepseafishing.ca $ C$40 ⏲ July–mid-Sept.*

NEWFOUNDLAND

WELCOME TO NEWFOUNDLAND

TOP REASONS TO GO

★ **Gros Morne National Park:** Magnificent mountains, fine hiking, sweeping vistas, quaint lighthouses, hidden fjords, and the deep blue sea are just some of the reasons people flock to this park.

★ **Meet the people:** You'll never get lost here because the people go out of their way to help visitors. These are some of the friendliest folks you're likely to meet.

★ **See the wildlife:** Watch pods of humpbacks dive and breach alongside your boat tour, and see puffins, caribou, moose, and more in bird sanctuaries and ecological reserves.

★ **Spot icebergs:** Newfoundland is one of the easiest places to see these 10,000-year-old beauties of the ocean. See them from St. Anthony to St. John's.

★ **Enjoy the arts:** From traditional accordion concerts to art-house cinema and award-winning plays, the local and touring talent should not be missed.

★ **Eat amazing food:** Cod, mussels, scallops, lobster, whelk, and crab straight from the sea complemented by locally sourced savory, moose charcuterie, spruce-tip oil, and every other wild flavor found on the island.

1 St. John's. The capital of Newfoundland is usually the starting point for visits to the province. At the heart of the city is a working harbor full of fog and music. You'll find buskers, boat horns, cranes loading large vessels at the docks, seagulls, and wind. Beyong the harbor, St. John's has beautiful houses and lots of soul.

2 Avalon Peninsula. This picturesque region is home to about half of Newfoundland's population. Cape Spear National Historic Site, consisting of wild cliffs, walking paths, historic bunkers, barrens, and a lighthouse, is the easternmost point in North America.

3 Eastern Newfoundland. The Bonavista Peninsula has history, archaeological artifacts, and a burgeoning arts scene; the Burin Peninsula is more about stark landscapes.

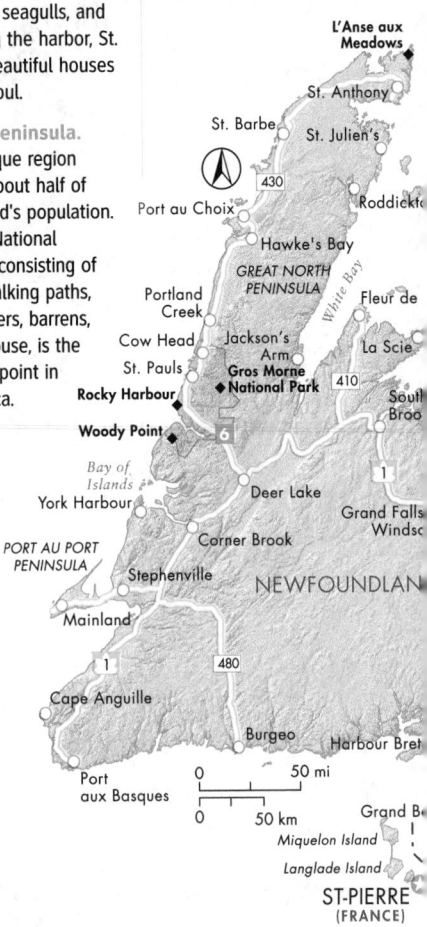

Clarenville, halfway between the two, is a good base for exploring, though not much of a destination in itself. Terra Nova was Newfoundland's first national park.

4 Central Newfoundland and Notre Dame Bay. The central town of Gander is known for its airport and aviation history; it's mostly a good base for exploring fishing villages like Twillingate with its famous "Iceberg Alley" views.

5 Fogo and Change Islands. These are remote islands off an already out-of-the-way island. Known for modern artists' studios and luxury accommodations, Fogo and Change islands have not lost their timelessness or air of solitude. This is truly the end of the earth.

6 Western Newfoundland. The wild and rugged Great North Peninsula is home to two UNESCO World Heritage Sites (Gros Morne National Park and L'Anse aux Meadows), and the west coast is famed for its Atlantic salmon fishing, Long Range Mountains, winter sports, and the hub of the west coast, Corner Brook.

GETTING ORIENTED

Newfoundland is part of the Newfoundland and Labrador province; the latter is on the mainland, bordering Québec. Most airlines fly in to the provincial capital of St. John's (not to be confused with the city of Saint John, in New Brunswick), on the Avalon Peninsula, making it the logical starting point for visitors to Newfoundland. Farther west is the Burin Peninsula, and to the north are the Bonavista Peninsula and Notre Dame Bay. On the west side of Newfoundland, the Northern Peninsula stretches up toward Labrador; Corner Brook is a good starting point for exploring the mountains. In Newfoundland, you'll do much of your driving on Route 1, the Trans-Canada Highway, which goes east–west from St. John's to Port aux Basques.

Updated by Emily Deming

Magnificent mountains, sweeping vistas, colorful wooden houses perched on rocky sea cliffs, hidden fjords, and the deep blue sea define Newfoundland. "The Rock" as the island is sometimes affectionately called, lures visitors with the promise of dramatic landscapes, incredible hiking and outdoor experiences, and the warmth of the people. Canada starts here, from the east, on the island of Newfoundland in the North Atlantic. Labrador, to the northwest, is on the mainland bordering Québec. Along the province's nearly 17,699 km (11,000 miles) of coastline, humpback whales feed near shore, millions of seabirds nest, and 10,000-year-old icebergs drift by fishing villages.

Off the east coast of Canada, the province of Newfoundland and Labrador, as it is officially called, is a bit of a contradiction in terms: it's the youngest province—it joined the Confederation in 1949—but its European timeline stretches back to AD 1000, when Vikings made first landfall on the Great Northern Peninsula. They assembled a sod-hut village at what is now L'Anse aux Meadows National Historic Site, calling their new home Vinland. They stayed less than 10 years and then disappeared into the mists of history. Preceding the Vikings were the Maritime Archaic people who lived in the region as long ago as 6,000 years. L'Anse Amour, a 7,500-year-old burial ground in southern Labrador, is the oldest-known cemetery in North America.

When explorer John Cabot arrived at Bonavista from England in 1497, he reported an ocean so full of fish they could be caught in a basket lowered over the side of a boat. Within a decade, St. John's had become a crowded harbor. Soon, fishing boats from France, England, Spain, and Portugal vied for a chance to catch Newfoundland's lucrative cod, which would shape the province's history.

At one time, 700 outports dotted Newfoundland's coast, devoted to the world's most plentiful fish. Today, only about 400 of these settlements survive. By 1992, cod had become scarce from overfishing and the federal government called a moratorium, throwing thousands of citizens out of work. The moratorium is still in place, forcing generations of people to retrain for other industries or leave, and the fishing industry has since diversified into other species, mainly shrimp and crab. The development of one of the world's richest and largest nickel deposits at Voisey's Bay in northern Labrador, near Nain, holds hope for new prosperity, as does tourism and the growing offshore oil and gas industry.

Despite Newfoundland and Labrador's more than 50 years as a Canadian province, its people remain resolutely independent and maintain a unique language and lifestyle. E. Annie Proulx's Pulitzer Prize–winning novel *The Shipping News* (1993) brought the province to the world's attention, and Newfoundland writers such as Wayne Johnston (*The Colony of Unrequited Dreams, The Navigator of New York*), Michael Crummey (*River Thieves* and *Galore*), and Lisa Moore (*February* and *Caught*) continue to introduce international audiences to the province.

Visitors to Newfoundland find themselves straddling the centuries. Old Irish, French, and English accents and customs still exist in small towns and outports despite television and the Internet, but the cities of St. John's in the east and Corner Brook to the west are very much part of the 21st century. Wherever you travel in the province, you're sure to meet some of the warmest, wittiest people in North America. No matter how remote the spot, no one is ever bored in Newfoundland.

PLANNING

WHEN TO GO

Seasons vary dramatically in Newfoundland and Labrador. Most tourists visit between June and September, when the bogs and meadows turn into a colorful riot of wildflowers and greenery and the province is alive with festivals, fairs, and concerts. Daytime temperatures may hover between 20°C (68°F) and 25°C (77°F) in July and August, but June can be quite cool and foggy. In spring, icebergs float down from the north, and in late spring, whales arrive to hunt for food along the coast, staying until August. Fall is also popular: the weather is usually fine, hills and meadows are loaded with berries, and the woods are alive with moose, caribou, partridge, and rabbits. In winter, ski hills attract downhillers and snowboarders, forest trails hum with snowmobiles, and cross-country ski trails in various communities and provincial and national parks are oases of quiet.

This rocky island perched on the edge of the cold North Atlantic Ocean might be the only place in the world where you can have four seasons blow through in one day and where the saying "If you don't like the weather out your front door, go look out the back door" rings true. St. John's is a weather champion in Canada. It holds the distinctions of being the foggiest, snowiest, wettest, windiest, and cloudiest of all major Canadian cities.

When packing for the trip, remember it's all about layers in Newfoundland. You'll need shorts and short-sleeve shirts for when it's warm and sunny. Pack a fleece jacket or a hoodie in case the temperature drops. A windbreaker might be the most important piece of clothing; you'll need it to keep the chill out when the winds are up. To top off your ensemble, you'll need rain gear, like a slicker. Throw in a pair of gloves, hat and scarf, too. May the sun shine on your holidays, but if it doesn't, you'll be dressed for it.

FESTIVALS

Newfoundlanders love a party, and from the cities to the smallest towns, they celebrate their history and unique culture with festivals and events throughout the summer. "Soirées" and "times"—big parties and small parties—offer a combination of traditional music, recitation, comedy, and local food.

Festival of New Dance. Fall in St. John's brings energy into the arts scene. Boundary-pushing and beautiful dance performances, curated for an audience of both aficionados and the newly dance-curious, arrive from around the world every October. ✉ *St. John's* ☎ *709/722–3663.*

Fish, Fun & Folk Festival. During the last full week in July, the town of Twillingate hosts this festival where you can enjoy fish cooked every possible way while listening to folk musicians perform. If you are looking for the town at its liveliest, this is it. ✉ *Twillingate* ⊕ *www.fishfunfolkfestival.com.*

George Street Festival. George Street in St. John's is famous for its live-music pubs, and for six days at the beginning of August the entire street becomes an open-air party, with big-name bands taking the main stage. ✉ *St. John's* ⊕ *www.georgestreetlive.ca.*

Fodor's Choice ★ **Newfoundland and Labrador Folk Festival.** The province's biggest traditional-music festival takes place in St. John's in early August. ✉ *St. John's* ☎ *709/576–8508, 866/576–8508* ⊕ *nlfolk.com.*

Fodor's Choice ★ **Roots, Rants and Roars.** Two days of food, music, and ocean air. The signature event is a food hike with Canada's top chefs cooking in the elements right in front of you along the coastal cliffs of Elliston, which are dotted with historic root cellars. ⊕ *www.rootsrantsandroars.ca.*

St. John's Women's International Film Festival. Mid-October brings film to the capital city. Local and international documentaries, features, and short films are a perfect way to get a feel for the culture in town while getting away from the wind and fog. ✉ *St. John's* ☎ *709/754–3141* ⊕ *www.womensfilmfestival.com.*

Trails, Tales & Tunes. In mid-May picturesque Norris Point, in the Gros Morne National Park, hosts events that include concerts, art exhibits, storytelling, culinary events, guided walks and hikes, and trail riding on bicycles. ✉ *Norris Point* ☎ *709/458–3604* ⊕ *www.trailstalestunes.ca.*

PLANNING YOUR TIME

Many visitors to Newfoundland and Labrador arrive in St. John's, the provincial capital and a great place to get a sense of the region's history. Spend a few days touring downtown, including Water Street, the oldest street in North America, or hike part of the East Coast Trail right from town. Less than an hour's drive south of St. John's, you can see whales, icebergs, and huge seabird colonies at Bay Bulls. You can also take a side trip to Cape St. Mary's, one of the best places in the world to see gannets up close—you can walk to within 10 yards of their nests!

Those with more time often drive across the island. Twillingate, 444 km (276 miles) from St. John's (a five-hour journey), is an especially scenic destination, and Fogo Island is gaining acclaim for its unique artists' studios, artists-in-residence programs, and the architecturally groundbreaking Fogo Island Inn. The ferry to Fogo Island takes about an hour each way. You could enjoy a marvelous three-day interlude touring the Bonavista Peninsula in eastern Newfoundland with its visually stunning coastline and settlements such as picturesque Trinity.

Allow at least three days to appreciate western Newfoundland's dramatic mountains and rugged shoreline. One fly-and-drive option is through Deer Lake Regional Airport. An alternative would be to take the car ferry from Nova Scotia, which arrives in Port aux Basques, on the southern coast. Corner Brook, this region's main city, makes a fine base for exploring the picturesque Bay of Islands. You won't want to miss the glacier-carved fjords and magnificent mountains at Gros Morne National Park, a UNESCO World Heritage Site. Take a boat tour, go hiking or sea kayaking, and visit an interpretation center to learn more about what you've seen. Many people spend at least a couple of days here—if you're a hiker, you could easily spend a week exploring the multitude of trails. Farther up the peninsula, at L'Anse aux Meadows National Historic Park, another UNESCO World Heritage Site, you can visit the only authenticated Viking settlement in North America.

TIME ZONES

Newfoundland has its own time zone—Newfoundland standard time—a half hour ahead of the rest of Labrador and the other Atlantic provinces. When time zones were established, the Dominion of Newfoundland was an independent country with its own time zone. The government tried to make the province conform to Atlantic standard time in 1963, 14 years after it became part of Canada, but the measure was quashed by public outcry, so Newfoundlanders remain the first people in Canada to welcome the new year.

GETTING HERE AND AROUND

AIR TRAVEL

The province's main airport is St. John's International Airport, and another international airport is at Gander, farther west. Domestic airports are at Stephenville, Deer Lake, and St. Anthony. ■ TIP→ **If you plan to fly in and rent a car, book as far in advance as possible; rental vehicles are in limited supply, and in peak season they go quickly.**

BOAT AND FERRY TRAVEL

Marine Atlantic operates a car ferry from North Sydney, Nova Scotia, to Port aux Basques, Newfoundland (crossing time is 6 hours), and, from June through September, from North Sydney to Argentia (crossing time is from 12 to 14 hours).

Contacts **Marine Atlantic.** ☎ *902/794-5254, 800/341-7981* ⊕ *www.marineatlantic.ca.*

CAR TRAVEL

Newfoundland has an excellent highway system, and most secondary roads are paved, but some are winding, and most suffer seasonal damage and potholes from the frequent freeze-thaw cycles through the winter, which will require you to moderate your speed. Bear this in mind when deciding how far to travel in a day. Also remember that summer is road-mending season and speed limits are reduced to 50 kph (31 mph) in construction areas. With time out for a meal, it takes about 11 hours to drive along the Trans-Canada Highway (Route 1) from Port aux Basques to St. John's. The trip from Corner Brook to St. Anthony, at the northernmost tip of the island, takes about five hours. Driving from St. John's to Grand Bank, on the Burin Peninsula, takes about four hours. If you're heading for the southern coast of the Avalon Peninsula, pick up Route 10 just south of St. John's and follow it toward Trepassey.

TIP→ More than 110,000 moose live in Newfoundland, and most highways run through their habitats. If possible, avoid night driving, as most moose-related vehicle accidents (about 700 a year) happen between dusk and dawn. Watch for vehicles that slow down or stop on the side of the road; the driver may have spotted a moose. Pay attention to the caution signs indicating where moose cross frequently.

In winter, some highways close during and after severe snowstorms. Year-round, the Department of Transportation's website has up-to-date information on road conditions and closures. The website of the province's tourism board has a handy Scenic Touring Routes page listing itineraries—categorized by region and then by areas of interest—all over Newfoundland.

Contacts Department of Transportation & Works. ☎ *709/635-4127 Western Region, 709/292-4300 in Grand Falls-Windsor and Central Newfoundland, 709/466-4120 Eastern Region, 709/729-2382 Avalon Region* ⊕ *www.roads.gov.nl.ca.* **Scenic Touring Routes.** ⊕ *www.newfoundlandlabrador.com/placestogo/scenictouringroutes.*

OUTDOOR ACTIVITIES

Fishing the unpolluted waters of Newfoundland is an angler's dream, and many outfitters are available to make the dream come true. The website of the Newfoundland & Labrador Outfitters Association contains a list of members, with contact details and online links.

Many provincial parks and both of the national parks have hiking and nature trails, and coastal and forest trails radiate out from most small communities. The East Coast Trail, on the Avalon Peninsula, covers 540 km (336 miles) of coastline, passes through two dozen communities and along cliff tops that provide ideal lookouts for icebergs and seabirds, and is a beautifully maintained international destination for hikers. The East Coast Trail Association has details. Gros Morne Adventures runs guided day and multiday hikes in Gros Morne National Park.

Fodor's Choice ★ **East Coast Trail Association.** This organization is a very-well-put-together resource for those who like to hike in groups or on their own. Volunteers lead free scheduled day hikes along all sections of the breathtaking East Coast Trail. If you would rather hike without a guide, you can purchase their printed trail maps, which are detailed, easy to navigate, and list interesting information about each leg to make sure you know "what to look for" so you get the most out of a hike even if you are new to the area. Their website lists, and links to, community resources for food, supplies, overnight camping, or other accommodations for any extended hiking trips. ☎ *709/738-4453* ⊕ *www.eastcoasttrail.ca.*

Contacts Gros Morne Adventures. ☎ *709/458-2722, 800/685-4624* ⊕ *grosmorneadventures.com.* **Newfoundland & Labrador Outfitters Association.** ☎ *709/639-5926, 866/470-6562* ⊕ *www.nloa.ca.*

RESTAURANTS

Until recently, eating out in Newfoundland was all about cod. Today, Newfoundland cuisine fuses tradition, a fierce locavore movement focused on taking full advantage of the diverse bounty of ocean, bluff, bog, and pasture, and serious talent. The culinary scene in St. John's is a bounty and a treat. Towns outside St. John's might lack its concentration of excellent dining options, but talented chefs live and work beyond the capital, many of them committed to using fresh, local, and organic ingredients. Some unique dining experiences unfold as well, like the Great Viking Feast, staged by Lightkeepers Seafood Restaurant in St. Anthony, at which diners tuck into moose stew in a sod hut.

You'll find plenty of seafood, including cod, cold-water shrimp, snow crab, lobster, steelhead trout, salmon, mussels, and sea scallops.

Unlike elsewhere in Atlantic Canada, you'll find moose meat on restaurant menus here. It's very lean, very tasty, somewhat similar to beef, and certainly worth ordering if you get the chance.

In July and August, Newfoundland's wild berries ripen. Bakeapples, blueberries, and partridge berries (also called mountain cranberries, cowberries, and lingonberries) are used for pies, jams, cakes, pancakes, and in sauces for meat.

You won't find much in the way of local wines, with just two or three small-scale operations making artisanal wines from grapes and wild berries. You can, however, find good craft beers and spirits, including varieties made using water from icebergs.

HOTELS

Most hotels in Newfoundland are casual, friendly, and with the kind of amenities, standards, and room styles you'd expect elsewhere in North America. Wi-Fi is widespread, and you won't have to search hard to find a room with a view. Recognizable brands, Sheraton, Marriott, Ramada, and Holiday Inn among them, do business in St. John's, in historic buildings or standard modern structures. Lodgings outside the city are more varied. You'll find motels, bed-and-breakfasts, timber-frame lodges, inns comprised of one or more heritage houses, and all kinds of rental properties. There's also the unique Fogo Island Inn, a cutting-edge architectural marvel atop a rugged cliff on a remote offshore island.

Hotel reviews have been shortened. For full information, visit Fodors.com.

WHAT IT COSTS IN CANADIAN DOLLARS				
	$	$$	$$$	$$$$
Restaurants	under C$12	C$12–C$20	C$21–C$30	over C$30
Hotels	under C$125	C$125–C$174	C$175–C$250	over C$250

Restaurant prices are per person for a main course at dinner. Hotel prices are for two people in a standard double room in high season, excluding 13% harmonized sales tax (HST).

TOURS

Local operators offer sea kayaking, ocean diving, canoeing, wildlife viewing, mountain biking, white-water rafting, hiking, and interpretive walks in summer. In winter, snowmobiling expeditions are popular. In spring and early summer, a favored activity is iceberg watching. Maxxim Vacations in St. John's organizes packaged adventure and cultural tours. McCarthy's Party in St. John's arranges guided bus tours, learning vacations, and charter services. The luxurious Tuckamore Lodge, in Main Brook, on the Great Northern Peninsula, is a base for winter snowmobile excursions and for viewing caribou, seabird colonies, whales, and icebergs. Wildland Tours in St. John's operates weeklong guided tours to view wildlife and visit historically and culturally significant sites.

Maxxim Vacations. Offering a range of tours, they are notable for their "self-drive" options where they plan your trip and book the rental car and accommodations for you but you enjoy the trip unescorted. ☎ *709/754–6666, 800/567–6666* ⊕ *www.maxximvacations.com* ✉ *Self-drive weeklong tours start at C$1,019; escorted tours from C$1,800.*

McCarthy's Party. Specializing in bus tours, the guides are never a letdown; they show intimate knowledge of the area and with plenty of humor. Offering everything from three-hour tours of St. John's to 12-day tours of the entire province, they will handle all aspects of your trip including luggage handling. ☎ *709/579–4444, 888/660–6060* ⊕ *www.mccarthysparty.com* ✉ *Half-day tours start at C$55; weeklong tours start at C$2,090.*

Tuckamore Lodge. Activity packages specialize in fishing, and the outdoor experience with whale- and iceberg-watching, wilderness adventures, snowmobiling, kayaking, and hiking. ☎ *709/865–6361, 888/865–6361* ⊕ *www.tuckamorelodge.com/tour-packages-cat.htm* ✉ *Weeklong hiking tours start at C$1,550; fishing tours C$700/day.*

Wildland Tours. These are full-week packages focusing on various parts of Newfoundland or Labrador. They include all accommodations but not airfare. ☎ *709/722–3123, 888/615–8279* ⊕ *www.wildlands.com* ✉ *Tours in summer start at C$2,950.*

VISITOR INFORMATION

Newfoundland and Labrador Tourism distributes brochures from its offices. The province maintains a 24-hour tourist-information line year-round that can help with accommodations and reservations.

A network of visitor information centers, open daily 9 to 9 from June to Labor Day, dots the province. These centers have information on events, accommodations, shopping, and crafts stores in their areas. The airports in Gander and St. John's operate in-season visitor-information booths. The city of St. John's operates an information center at 348 Water Street. Ask for its excellent series of free brochures, "A Step Back in Time," which enable you to take informed walking tours on your own in various parts of town.

Contacts **Newfoundland and Labrador Tourism.** ☎ *709/729–2830, 800/563–6353* ⊕ *www.newfoundlandlabrador.com.*

ST. JOHN'S, NEWFOUNDLAND

Old meets new in the province's capital (metro-area population a little more than 200,000), with modern office buildings surrounded by heritage shops and colorful row houses. St. John's mixes English and Irish influences, Victorian architecture and modern convenience, and traditional music and rock and roll into a heady brew. The arts scene is lively, but overall the city moves at a relaxed pace.

For centuries, Newfoundland was the largest supplier of salt cod in the world, and St. John's Harbour was the center of the trade. As early as 1627, the merchants of Water Street—then known as the Lower Path—were doing a thriving business buying fish, selling goods, and supplying alcohol to soldiers and sailors.

The city of St. John's encircles St. John's Harbour, expanding past the hilly, narrow streets of old St. John's. Downtown has the most history and character. The city was destroyed by fire many times, and much of its row housing was erected following the last major blaze, known as the Great Fire, in 1892. Heritage houses on Waterford Bridge Road, winding west from the harbor along the Waterford River, and on Rennies Mill Road and Circular Road to the east (backing onto Bannerman Park) were originally the homes of sea captains and merchants. Duckworth Street and Water Street, which run parallel to the harbor, are where to find the shops and restaurants, but take a trip down the narrow lanes and paths as you get farther from the harbor to get the best sense of the city's history.

Signal Hill in the east end, with its distinctive Cabot Tower, is the city's most prominent landmark. The hill rises up from the Narrows, the appropriately named entrance to St. John's Harbour. Standing at Cape Spear and looking back towards St. John's, you will see Cabot Tower (and Signal Hill) but you'll scarcely believe there's a city there, because the entrance to the port is narrow and almost hidden.

GETTING HERE AND AROUND

The only direct way to get to St. John's is to fly in or arrive by cruise ship. The nearest ferry route from the mainland docks at Argentia, about an hour's drive from the city. From the airport, it's a 15-minute taxi ride to downtown. There are no public transit routes or private shuttle buses between the downtown and the airport. Cabs are exclusively operated by City Wide Taxi, with fixed rates to certain hotels, ranging from C$12.50 to C$30 plus C$3 for every extra passenger. For other destinations, fares are metered, with a C$3.50 basic charge.

Metrobus Transit operates more than 20 bus routes (C$2.25 per ride) in St. John's. The transit company also operates a "step-on, step-off" trolley (seasonal) serving downtown, major hotels, and visitor attractions for a flat fee of C$5 per day for individuals or C$20 for a family. You can also purchase a single trolley trip for C$2.25. For rides within the city, taxis carry a flag rate of C$3.50, with increments of C$0.25 for every 0.166 km (0.1 miles) and C$0.25 for each 30 seconds of stop time. Downtown is walkable, but you'll want a car to explore farther afield because public-transit options are few (or none).

NEWFOUNDLAND ITINERARIES

IF YOU HAVE 3 DAYS

Pick either the west or east coast of Newfoundland. On the west coast, after arriving by overnight ferry at **Port aux Basques,** detour off the Trans-Canada Highway (Route 1) through St. Andrews to explore the **Codroy Valley** and **Cape Anguille** before continuing north to **Gros Morne National Park.** Drive over the Tablelands to **Trout River,** then stay overnight in Woody Point. On Day 2, hike up **Gros Morne Mountain** or take the shorter, easier walk to **Western Brook Pond** for the boat trip. Spend the night at Rocky Harbour or Norris Point. On Day 3, drive to **Corner Brook** and explore the scenic **Bay of Islands,** then make your way back to Port aux Basques for the overnight ferry.

On the east coast, the ferry docks at Argentia. Explore the Avalon Peninsula, beginning in **St. John's,** where you should spend your first night. The next day visit **Cape Spear,** the most easterly point in North America, and the **Witless Bay Ecological Reserve,** where you can see whales, seabirds, and icebergs. Drive through **Placentia** and spend Day 3 at **Cape St. Mary's Ecological Reserve,** known for its gannets and dramatic coastal scenery. The drive from St. John's to Cape St. Mary's takes about 2½ hours each way. If you don't want to drive back to St. John's the same day, stay overnight at the Bird Island Resort in St. Brides.

IF YOU HAVE 6 DAYS

Spend your first day in **St. John's** and stay overnight there. The next day, visit **Cape Spear** and the **Witless Bay Ecological Reserve.** Spend the night in **Placentia,** and on Day 3 visit **Cape St. Mary's Ecological Reserve** before heading to picturesque **Trinity.** Explore the town and stay overnight there. On Day 4 take the Rugged Beauty Boat Tour, then drive up to **Cape Bonavista.** Stay there, and on Day 5 visit **Terra Nova National Park.** Spend the night at **Clarenville,** getting up on the sixth day to explore the picturesque villages on Conception Bay's north shore, including **Cupids** and **Harbour Grace,** before returning to St. John's.

IF YOU HAVE 9 DAYS

After spending your first day and night in **St. John's,** head for the Bonavista Peninsula and picturesque **Trinity** on Day 2. Spend the night in Trinity, then continue north to visit **Terra Nova National Park** and continue to **Twillingate,** renowned for icebergs and whale-watching. Next, head for **Gros Morne National Park** for Days 4 and 5, then return east on Day 6 to spend the night in **Clarenville.** On Day 7 drive down to **Cape St. Mary's Ecological Reserve.** Overnight in **Placentia,** then head for **Cape Spear** and the **Witless Bay Ecological Reserve,** before spending the final day back in St. John's.

Taxi and Bus Contacts **City Wide Taxi.** ☎ *709/722-7777* ⊕ *www.citywidetaxi.ca.* **Metrobus Transit.** ☎ *709/722-9400* ⊕ *www.metrobustransit.ca.*

FESTIVALS

Buskers Festival. For three days in early August, magicians, circus artists, comedians, and other street performers entertain on three stages in downtown St. John's. ✉ *St. John's* ☎ *709/726-8244* ⊕ *www.downtownstjohns.com.*

FAMILY **St. John's Storytelling Festival.** Stories and songs are performed in venues inside and out, all around town, for one week each October. With something for every age, it's a special way to exerience Newfoundlanders' famous humor, quick wit, and unique turns of phrase. ✉ *St. John's* ⊕ *storytellingstjohns.ca/wp/.*

TOURS

An alternative to driving yourself around is to take a sightseeing jaunt with a local guide, who can offer an insider's perspective. One specialized walking tour is the St. John's Haunted Hikes, in which the Reverend Thomas Wickam Jarvis, played by actor Dale Jarvis, leads several different and very popular walking tours of city sites linked to hauntings and urban legends; on summer evenings, the tours (C$10–C$15) begin at the west entrance of the Anglican Cathedral on Church Hill at 9:30 pm. Look for the crowd of people standing in the dark. The ToursByLocals website has links to accredited St. John's guides who lead walking and other tours for cruise-ship passengers and other visitors.

St. John's Haunted Hikes. When you are the oldest city in North America, you contain your fair share of ghoulish histories, both real and mythological. This walking tour explores them all as your guide spins tales of murder most foul and famous ghost sightings associated with the darkened alleys and streets you tread. ☎ *709/685-3444* ⊕ *www.hauntedhike.com* 💲 *C$10.*

ToursByLocals. These vary in content and length, as each tour is created and given by an individual guide. It is a great way to get a local to yourself! The itineraries range from a half-day tour of a park to multiday road trips. ✉ *St. John's* ☎ *866/844-6783* ⊕ *www.toursbylocals.com/St-Johns-Newfoundland-Tours* 💲 *Starting at C$154.*

ESSENTIALS

City of St. John's Visitor Information Centre. ✉ *348 Water St.* ☎ *709/576-8106* ⊕ *www.stjohns.ca.*

EXPLORING

TOP ATTRACTIONS

Basilica Cathedral of St. John the Baptist. Consecrated in 1855 after 14 years of construction, this Romanesque-style Roman Catholic cathedral holds a commanding position above Military Road, overlooking the older section of the city and the harbor. The Irish sculptor John Hogan carved the sanctuary's centerpiece, *The Dead Christ,* out of Carrara marble in the mid-19th century. Also note the many stained-glass windows, side altars, and statuary. A museum with vestments and religious objects is next door in the Episcopal Library of the Bishop's Palace.

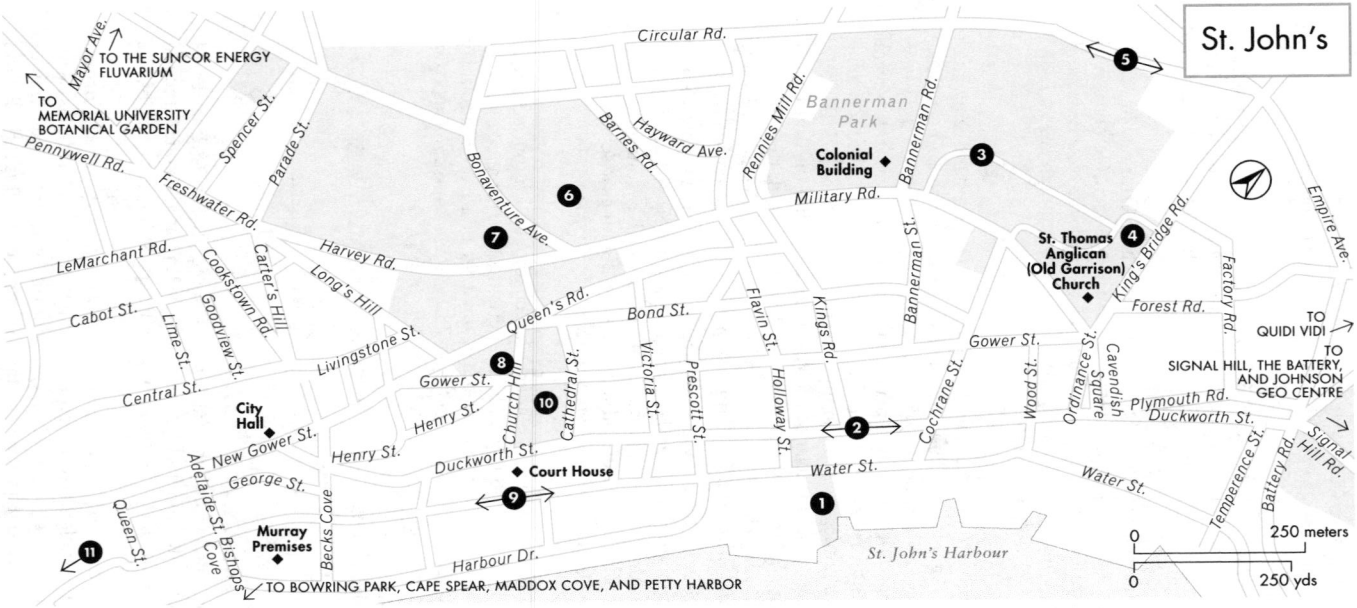

Anglican Cathedral of St. John the Baptist **10**

Basilica Cathedral of St. John the Baptist **6**

Circular Road **5**

Commissariat House **4**

Duckworth Street **2**

Government House **3**

Gower Street United Church **8**

Harbourside Park **1**

Newman Wine Vaults ... **11**

The Rooms **7**

Water Street **9**

CLOSE UP

A Good Walk

Begin at **Harbourside Park,** on Water Street, where Gilbert planted the staff of England and claimed Newfoundland. When you leave, turn left on Water Street, right on Holloway Street, and then right onto **Duckworth Street.** The east end of this street is full of crafts shops and other stores. After walking east for five blocks, turn left onto Ordnance Street, one of several streets that recall St. John's military past. Cross Military Road to **St. Thomas Anglican (Old Garrison) Church,** built in the 1830s as a place of worship for British soldiers.

Turn left as you leave St. Thomas and walk up King's Bridge Road. The first building on the left is **Commissariat House,** an officer's house restored to the style of the 1830s and one of the oldest buildings in the province. North of here, a shady lane on the left leads to the gardens of **Government House**. **Circular Road,** where the business elite moved after a fire destroyed much of the town in 1846, is north of Government House. Back on Military Road, cross Bannerman Road to the **Colonial Building,** the former seat of government. Walk west on Military Road. The Roman Catholic **Basilica Cathedral of St. John the Baptist** is on the right. Cross Bonaventure Avenue as you leave the Basilica to visit the **Rooms,** the province's one-stop shop for arts, culture, and heritage and the home of the provincial archives, museum, and art gallery. As you leave the Rooms, turn right down Garrison Hill, so named because it once led to Fort Townshend, now home to fire and police stations. Cross Queen's Road and walk down Cathedral Street to Gower Street and the Gothic Revival **Anglican Cathedral of St. John the Baptist.** The entrance is on the west side on Church Hill. **Gower Street United Church** is directly across from the cathedral on the west side of Church Hill. Continue to the bottom of Church Hill to see the Duckworth Street **Court House,** with its four different turrets. Exit the courthouse and turn right; then go down the long set of steps to **Water Street,** one of the oldest commercial streets in North America. Turn right to reach the **Murray Premises,** a restored mercantile complex with boutiques, a science center, offices, restaurants, a coffee bar, and a wine cellar. Exit Murray Premises, take a left on Water Street, and continue to the last stop, the historic **Newman Wine Vaults,** at 436 Water Street, just west of the corner of Water and Springdale streets, where for 200 years the legendary Newman's Port has been aged.

Downtown St. John's is compact but hilly. Expect to spend up to a full day visiting these sights, depending on how long you stay at each location. This walk is best undertaken from spring to fall.

5

✉ 200 Military Rd. ☎ 709/754–2170 🌐 www.thebasilica.ca 🎟 Museum C$2 ⏲ Museum mid-June–Aug., Mon.–Sat. 10–4, Sun. 1–4; Sept.–mid June, daily 8–3.

Duckworth Street. Once called the Upper Path, this has been the "second street" of St. John's for centuries, Water Street being the main street. Stretching from the bottom of Signal Hill in the east to near City Hall in the west, Duckworth Street has restaurants, bars, antiques and crafts shops, and lawyers' offices. A few blocks east of City Hall, the late-19th-century **Court House** has an eccentric appearance: each of its four turrets is in a different style. It's not possible to go inside, but the exterior is worth a look. Lanes and stairways from Duckworth Street lead down to Water Street and up to higher elevations. ✉ *St. John's.*

Government House. The lieutenant governor—the Queen's representative in Newfoundland—lives at Government House. Myth has it that the moat around the 1830s structure was designed to keep out snakes, though Newfoundland is among the few regions in the world (along with Ireland and New Zealand) where there are none. The house, so the story goes, was originally intended for the governor of a warmer colony where serpents might be a problem, but in fact the moat was designed to allow more light into the basement rooms. House tours (free), can be arranged by appointment; the marvelous garden you can explore on your own. ✉ *50 Military Rd.* ☎ *709/729–4494, 709/729–2669 tour reservations* ⊕ *www.govhouse.nl.ca* 💲 *Free* ⏲ *By appointment; garden open daily.*

Gower Street United Church. This 1896 church has a redbrick facade, green turrets, 50 stained-glass windows, and a massive pipe organ. The church itself is on a sort of concrete island, the lone occupant of a small tract of land surrounded by four streets. ✉ *99 Queen's Rd., at Gower St.* ☎ *709/753–7286* ⊕ *www.gowerunited.ca* 💲 *Free* ⏲ *Sept.–May, weekdays 9–4; July and Aug., weekdays 9–noon; closed Wed. Tours available year-round during office hrs or by appointment.*

FAMILY **Harbourside Park.** This is the spot where Sir Humphrey Gilbert claimed Newfoundland for Britain in 1583, much to the amusement of the French, Spanish, and Portuguese fishermen in port at the time. They thought him a fool, a judgment borne out a few days later when he ran his ship aground and drowned. The small park is a good vantage point to watch the boats come and go and a nice spot to stop for a rest. Kids love the bronze Newfoundland and Labrador dog statues you can sit on, and there are family-friendly concerts every Friday at 12:30 through July and August. The area down here where the harbor pilot boat is docked is known as the Queen's Wharf. The park and wharf are wheelchair accessible. ✉ *Water St. E* ⊕ *stjohns.ca/events/music-harbourside.*

FAMILY Fodor's Choice ★ **The Rooms.** An eye-catching feature of the cityscape since 2005, this lively space celebrating the arts and cultures of Newfoundland and Labrador has a design inspired by traditional "fishing rooms," shacks by the waterside where fishing families would process their catch. Exhibits in the Connections Gallery, the Husky Energy Gallery, and the Elinor Gill Ratcliffe Gallery explore the region's cultural heritage, while the Provincial Art Gallery presents contemporary and older works from the permanent art collection and mounts temporary art exhibitions. Displays at the Provincial Archives include historical photos and documents. The Rooms hosts many family-oriented activities—summer events for children include arts and crafts, Inuit games, nature projects, and creative workshops. The facility's observation deck has awe-inspiring views over St. John's, even in the worst weather. The fourth-floor Rooms Café serves tasty seafood dishes and has special kids' and organic menus; on Wednesday nights it's open for dinner and is a great place to watch the sun set or the fog creep in over the city. ✉ *9 Bonaventure Ave.* ☎ *709/757-8000* 🌐 *www.therooms.ca* 💲 *C$10; free Wed. 6–9 pm and first Sat. of each month (Nov.–May); special exhibits extra* ⏲ *June–mid-Oct., Mon.–Sat. 10–5 (to 9 Wed.), Sun. noon–5; mid-Oct.–May, Tues.–Sat. 10–5 (to 9 Wed.), Sun. noon–5. Archives closed Sun. year-round. Orientation tours 10:30 and guided tours for some exhibits July and Aug.*

Water Street. Originally called the Lower Path, Water Street has been the site of businesses since at least the 1620s. The older architecture resembles that of seaports in southwest England and Ireland. If you do nothing else in St. John's, take a walk down Water Street. This is the center of the downtown universe, and on a sunny day it will be packed with smiling locals. ✉ *St. John's.*

WORTH NOTING

Anglican Cathedral of St. John the Baptist. Designed by Sir George Gilbert Scott, this fine example of Gothic Revival architecture was erected in the mid-1800s, with major additions in the 1880s, but it had to be rebuilt after the 1892 fire. Free lunchtime organ recitals take place on Wednesday afternoons at 1:15. From mid-July through August, you can slip into the crypt for a cup of tea and homemade scones, tea biscuits, and cookies (C$8). Tea service, run by the women of the parish, operates from 2:30 to 4:30 pm on weekdays except Wednesdays, when it starts at 2. ✉ *16 Church Hill* ☎ *709/726-5677* 🌐 *www.stjohnsanglicancathedral.org* 💲 *Free* ⏲ *Tours: July and Aug., weekdays 10–noon and 2–4; Sat. 10–noon; Sun. after 11 am service.*

Circular Road. After the devastating fire of 1846, the business elite of St. John's moved to Circular Road. The street contains some very fine Victorian houses and shade trees. ✉ *St. John's.*

Commissariat House. The residence and office of the British garrison's supply officer in the 1830s has been restored to reflect that era. Interpreters sometimes dress in period costume, and the videos and labels are engaging and informative. ✉ *King's Bridge Rd. and Military Rd.* ☎ *709/729-6730* 🌐 *www.seethesites.ca* 💲 *C$6 also gets you into the Newman Wine Vaults* ⏲ *May, June, Sept., and Oct., Wed.–Sun. 9:30–5; July and Aug., daily 9:30–5:30, Tues. 9:30–9.*

Newman Wine Vaults. This 200-year-old building with stone barrel vaults is where the renowned Newman's Port was aged. According to legend, a Newman and Company vessel loaded with port wine was driven off course by pirates in 1679 and forced to winter in St. John's. Upon its return to London, the cargo was found to have improved in flavor, and after that the company continued to send port to be matured in these wine cellars. The vaults are now a historic site, with guides who interpret the province's long and unique association with port. ✉ *436 Water St.* ☎ *709/739-7870* 🌐 *www.seethesights.ca* 💲 *C$6 includes admission to Commissariat House* ⏲ *May, June, Sept., and Oct., Wed.–Sun. 9:30–5; July and Aug., daily 9:30–5, Thurs. 9:30–9.*

GREATER ST. JOHN'S

A number of must-see attractions can be found a short drive from the downtown core of St. John's. When you stand with your back to the ocean at Cape Spear National Historic Site—the easternmost point of North America—the entire population of the continent is to your west. Cape Spear and the historic property with Hill National Historic Site are excellent places to see icebergs and whales in spring and early summer. Plan to spend a full day exploring Greater St. John's to give yourself some time at each spot.

EXPLORING

TOP ATTRACTIONS

The Battery. This tiny fishing village perches precariously at the base of steep cliffs between Signal Hill and St. John's Harbour. Narrow lanes snake around the houses, so it's a good place to get out of the car and walk. ✉ *St. John's.*

Fodor's Choice ★ **Cape Spear National Historic Site.** At the easternmost point of land on the continent, songbirds begin chirping in the dim light of dawn, and whales (in early summer) feed directly below the cliffs, providing an unforgettable start to the day. From April through July, you might see icebergs floating by. **Cape Spear Lighthouse,** Newfoundland's oldest such beacon, has been restored to its original form and furnishings. There's a small, well-stocked souvenir kiosk in the parking lot for those who don't want to or are unable to climb the path to the main gift shop. ✉ *Cape Spear Dr., Rte. 11* ☎ *709/772–5367* ⊕ *www.pc.gc.ca* 💲 *Site free; lighthouse C$3.90, C$6.30 for same-day access with Signal Hill* ⏲ *Site: daily dawn–dusk. Lighthouse: mid-May–mid-June, Wed.–Sun. 10–6; mid-June–Sept., daily 10–6; Sept.–mid-Oct., Sat.–Wed. 10–6. Visitor Interpretation Centre and Heritage Gift Shop: mid-May–mid-Oct., weekdays 10–5:30.*

FAMILY **Johnson GEO CENTRE.** Built deep into the earth with only the entryway protruding aboveground, this geological shrine is literally embedded in Signal Hill, itself made up of 550-million-year-old rocks. (The province's oldest rocks date back 3.87 billion years.) There are exhibits about how Earth was made and on the solar system. *The Titanic Story,* a multimedia exhibition, includes fascinating artifacts and video footage from the wreck site. Step on an oil platform in the ExxonMobil Oil & Gas Gallery, and learn about how oil and gas are formed. Kids five and up love the 3-D Earth and Space Theatre. There is also a playroom for babies and small children. ✉ *175 Signal Hill Rd.* ☎ *709/737–7880, 866/868–7625* ⊕ *www.geocentre.ca* 💲 *C$12* ⏲ *Daily 9:30–5.*

Fodor's Choice ★ **The Leyton Gallery of Fine Art.** In a cozy space tucked between the industry of the harbor and the commercial buzz of Water Street, this gallery invites an intimacy and comfort with art, with a range of work from affordable new artists to museum pieces. For first-time buyers or serious collectors, you can invest in a souvenir that will garner interest, not gather dust. ✉ *6 Clift's-Baird's Cove* ✣ *Off Water St.* ☎ *709/722–7177* ⊕ *theleytongallery.com* ⏲ *Closed Mon.*

FAMILY Fodor's Choice ★

Maddox Cove and Petty Harbour. These neighboring fishing villages lie along the coast between Cape Spear and Route 10. Petty Harbour has become the best day trip for a family near the city. It has something for every age and inclination all around one scenic harbor. The wharves and sturdy seaside sheds hearken back to a time not long ago when the fishery was paramount in the economy and lives of the residents. Throughout the summer, you can enjoy boating, zip-lining, a mini-aquarium, two great restaurants, and two of the prettiest segments of the East Coast Trail starting from either end of town. Island Rooms of Petty Harbour is dedicated to keeping the fishing and boating heritage of the town alive and will arrange walking, fishing, and traditional boating excursions (☎ *709/740–3474;* ⊕ *www.islandrooms.org*). North Atlantic Ziplines boasts the longest zip line in North America, with views over the hills and ocean and plenty of adrenaline (☎ *709/368–8681;* ⊕ *www.zipthenorthatlantic.com*). The Petty Harbour Mini Aquarium (June–October) has a touch tank and daily family programming (☎ *709/330–3474;* ⊕ *www.miniaqua.org*). When you get hungry, head to The Watershed Coffee Shop for a hot drink and a fresh bite with a harbor view (☎ *709/747–0500*), or get the best seafood and moose sausages in the Greater St. John's area at Chafe's Landing (☎ *709/747–0802;* ⊕ *www.chafeslanding.com*). ✉ *St. John's* ⊕ *www.pettyharbourmaddoxcove.ca.*

5

NEED A BREAK?

The Garden Café. On the grounds of the Memorial University Botanical Garden, this café has many teas to choose from, along with fresh-baked scones, soups, salads, and sandwiches. The menu changes daily and includes vegetarian and vegan choices. The restaurant will pack a picnic lunch for you. ✉ ***306 Mt. Scio Rd.*** ☎ ***709/753–0173*** ⏲ ***May–Oct., daily 11–4.***

Quidi Vidi. No one knows the origin of the name of this fishing village, one of the oldest parts of St. John's. The town is best explored on foot, as the roads are narrow and make driving difficult. The inlet, known as the Gut, is a traditional outport in the middle of a modern city, though a recent slew of new building permits means it is changing rapidly. It's also a good place to catch sea-run brown trout in the spring. Down on the waterfront is the Quidi Vidi Village Plantation, an open arts-and-crafts studio where you can meet the artists and buy textiles, prints, handmade clothing, and more. It has parking and is a good place to start your walk around the village. The Inn of Olde, Quidi Vidi Brewery, and Mallard Cottage are great stops for food and shelter and, of course, beer and spirits to keep you warm as you explore. ✉ *St. John's* ✣ *Take the first right off Kings Bridge Rd. (at the Sheraton Hotel Newfoundland) onto Forest Rd., which heads into the village* ⊕ *qvvplantation.com* ⏲ *Plantation: Jan.–Apr., Tues.–Sat. 10–4; May–mid-Oct., Tues.–Sat. 10–5, Sun. noon–5; mid-Oct.–late Dec., Tues.–Sat. 10–4, Sun. noon–4.*

FAMILY Fodor's Choice ★

Signal Hill National Historic Site. In spite of its height, Signal Hill was difficult to defend; throughout the 1600s and 1700s it changed hands with every attacking French, English, and Dutch force. In 1762, this was the site of the final battle between the French and British in the Seven Years' War (usually called the French and Indian War in the United States). A wooden palisade encircles the summit of the hill, indicating the boundaries of the old fortifications. In July and August, cadets in 19th-century-British uniforms perform military tattoos. En route to the hill is the **Visitor Center,** with exhibits describing the history of St. John's. There's also a café for hunger emergencies (open from 8 to 9 daily).

Cabot Tower, at the top of Signal Hill, was constructed in 1897 to commemorate the 400th anniversary of explorer John Cabot's landing in Newfoundland. In 1901 Guglielmo Marconi received the first transatlantic-wire transmission near here, and today you can visit the Marconi exhibit on the top floor. The drive to the tower along Signal Hill Road affords fine harbor, ocean, and city views, as does the tower itself. Walking trails take you to the base of the hill and closer to the ocean. Dress warmly; it's always windy. ✉ *Signal Hill Rd.* ☎ *709/772–5367* 🌐 *www.pc.gc.ca* 💲 *Site and tower free; visitor center C$3.90, C$6.30 to include same-day visit to Cape Spear* ⏲ *Site: daily dawn–dusk. Cabot Tower: mid-May–Aug., daily 10–8; Sept.–Nov., daily 10–6. Visitor center: mid-May–mid-Oct., daily 10–6.*

WORTH NOTING

FAMILY **Bowring Park.** An expansive Victorian park west of downtown, Bowring resembles famous city parks of London, after which it was modeled. Dotting the grounds are ponds and rustic bridges; the statue of Peter Pan just inside the east gate was cast from the same mold as the one in Kensington Park in London. The wealthy Bowring family, which made its money in trade and shipping, donated the park, which in 2014 celebrates its 100th anniversary. There is a swimming pool, a splash pad (both open July and August), and a large playground. ✉ *305 Waterford Bridge Rd.* 🌐 *www.bowringpark.com* 💲 *Free* ⏲ *Daily dawn–dusk.*

Christina Parker Gallery. The gallery specializes in works by local artists—paintings, sculptures, drawings, prints, and other media. ✉ *50 Water St.* ☎ *709/753–0580* 🌐 *www.christinaparkergallery.com.*

Eastern Edge Gallery. Artists that run this center present everything from paintings and drawings to performance and video art from emerging talents. In August each year, this artists' collective puts on "Hold Fast," a contemporary arts festival with events and installations throughout the city. ✉ *72 Harbour Dr.* ✢ *Between Clift's-Baird's Cove and Prescott St.* ☎ *709/739–1882* 🌐 *easternedge.ca* ⏲ *Closed Sun. and Mon.*

Emma Butler Gallery. Some of the province's more prominent and established artists show their works here. The gallery is closed on Sundays and Mondays, except by appointment. ✉ *111 George St. W* ☎ *709/739–7111* 🌐 *www.emmabutler.com.*

Memorial University Botanical Garden. The gardens at this 110-acre natural area include rock gardens, a Newfoundland historic-plants bed, peat and woodland beds, an alpine house, a medicinal garden, a native plant collection, a vegetable garden, a crevice garden, a shade garden, a dried-flower garden, and a compost demonstration garden. There are also five pleasant walking trails. You can see scores of rhododendron varieties here, as well as many kinds of butterflies and the rare hummingbird hawkmoth. Guided walks are available with advance notice for groups of 10 or more. The nature trails and gardens are closed to the public from November through April, but the gift shop remains open. ✉ *C.A. Pippy Park, 306 Mt. Scio Rd.* ☎ *709/864–8590* 🌐 *www.mun.ca/botgarden* 💲 *C$8, C$6 off-season* ⏲ *May–Aug., daily 10–5; Sept.–Nov., daily 10–4.*

FAMILY **The Suncor Energy Fluvarium.** A tributary of a nearby river was diverted here so visitors could see the life that inhabits it from underwater. See into the river through nine large windows at the only public facility of its kind in North America. In season you can observe spawning brown and brook trout in their natural habitat. There are also tanks housing other fish and amphibians and exhibits relating to the aquatic environment. Feeding time for the fish, frogs, and eels is at 4 pm daily. ✉ *C.A. Pippy Park, 5 Nagle's Pl.* ☎ *709/754–3474* 🌐 *fluvarium.ca* 💲 *C$7* ⏲ *July and Aug., weekdays 9–5, weekends 10–5; Sept.–June, weekdays 9–4:30, weekends noon–4:30.*

DAY AT THE RACES

If you're in St. John's on the first Wednesday of August, head down to Quidi Vidi Lake and experience the Royal St. John's Regatta (🌐 *www.stjohnsregatta.org*), the oldest continuous sporting event in North America. The fixed-seat rowing shells hold a crew of six and the coxswain. The town shuts down for this lowbrow but big-fun party/reunion/sporting event that is packed with food vendors and carnival games and draws more than 30,000 people. If the winds are high, the holiday's off, shops open, and the regatta moves to Thursday, Friday, or whenever the weather clears.

WHERE TO EAT

$$$$ CANADIAN ✕ **Bacalao.** The four rooms of this old house in St. John's have been converted into cozy dining rooms, all with fireplaces. Bacalao, pronounced "back-allow," is salt cod, a staple for Newfoundlanders and the Mediterraneans who came to fish here, and a variation of it is featured every night. Other nouvelle-Newfoundland options include moose and caribou dishes, and mussels in Quidi Vidi Iceberg beer. Everything, including desserts, is prepared from scratch, using local ingredients wherever possible. Even the washroom soap is locally made. In addition to global wines, you can also sample local vintages here, among them the distinctive Lady of the Woods, made from birch sap. Off-street parking keeps this spot attractive to its more suburban customer base. [$] *Average main: C$33* ✉ *65 LeMerchant Rd.* ☎ *709/579–6565* 🌐 *www.bacalaocuisine.ca* ⏲ *Closed Mon.* ✍ *Reservations essential.*

$$ SEAFOOD FAMILY ✕ **Ches's.** Since the 1950s, this restaurant has been serving fish-and-chips to a steady stream of customers from noon until after midnight. They come from all walks of life to sample the flaky fish fried in a batter whose recipe the owner keeps under lock and key (literally). Ches's decor is strictly laminated tabletops and plastic chairs, but the fish is hot, fresh, and delicious. From the sea you can also order shrimp, scallops, and salmon with chips, and there are wings, fried chicken, and burgers for those seeking a meal with origins on terra firma. Additional

locations do business in St. John's and beyond. $ *Average main: C$13* ✉ *9 Freshwater Rd.* ☎ *709/722–4083* 🌐 *www.chessfishandchips.ca.*

$$$ BISTRO ✕ **Chinched Bistro.** House-made infused spirits and handcrafted charcuterie are the two best reasons to visit this culinary diamond. With so much perfect meat and seafood tucked into one tiny building, this is more than a hidden gem. If the pork theme seems heavy, be assured the handling of flavors is light and responsive. With a small enough group, you can sit at the bar downstairs and enjoy your tapas. $ *Average main: C$30* ✉ *7 Queen St.* ☎ *709/722–3100* 🌐 *chinchedbistro.com* ⏲ *Closed Sun. No lunch* ✍ *Reservations essential.*

Fodor's Choice ★

$$ BISTRO ✕ **Hungry Heart Café.** This café makes the perfect spot to take a break from touring and try shrimp pad thai, chanterelle bacon tagliatelle, roast cauliflower soup or any number of daily changing specials crafted by one of the most versatile chefs in Newfoundland. $ *Average main: C$15* ✉ *142 Military Rd.* ✣ *At Rawlins Cross* ☎ *709/738–6164* 🌐 *hungryheartcafe.ca* ⏲ *No dinner.*

$$ INDIAN ✕ **India Gate.** Consistency and quality in service and food make this one of the busiest restaurants in St. John's for evening dining, takeout, or the popular weekday lunch buffet. Lunch turnover is high, and the buffet steamers are continuously replenished with steaming "rice pillow," mulligatawny soup, lamb, and vegetable korma. In the evening, you can choose a five-course dinner for two (C$50–C$60) or share options such as butter chicken or the exceptional prawns *nilgiri* (prawns in a rich sauce of spices and cashews). The presence of the owner on-site and the (recorded) sitar music add to the inviting atmosphere. $ *Average main: C$20* ✉ *286 Duckworth St., Downtown* ☎ *709/753–6006* 🌐 *www.indiagatenl.ca* ⏲ *No lunch weekends. No buffet weekends.*

$$ PAKISTANI ✕ **International Flavours.** This restaurant at the foot of Signal Hill may not look like much, but the home-style curry is delicious and a good value. The menu has kept its reliable simplicity for years with one dish served with vegetables, chicken, or lamb, plus samosas, naan, baklava, and mango lassi. It's easy to miss, as there's almost no storefront, but worth persevering to find. There's only street parking, so the best idea is to combine your visit with a stroll through the Battery or reward yourself after a hike up to Cabot Tower. $ *Average main: C$12* ✉ *4 Quidi Vidi Rd.* ☎ *709/738–4636* ⏲ *Closed Sun. and Mon.*

$$$$ INTERNATIONAL ✕ **Magnum & Steins.** Exposed stone walls, original paintings, and chic furnishings make for a serene (if dark) dining atmosphere in this restored heritage building right downtown. The short but classic dinner menu features steak, seafood, lamb, and poultry, with interesting accompaniments such as garlic-fried spinach and organic radish sprouts. The lunch and bar menus display some international influences (Asian duck-confit nachos and crispy coconut prawns, for example), and there's a lengthy international wine list with a decent selection available by the glass in addition to many cocktail specials. $ *Average main: C$36* ✉ *329 Duckworth St.* ☎ *709/576–6500* 🌐 *www.magnumandsteins.ca* ⏲ *No lunch weekends.*

$$$ MODERN CANADIAN Fodor's Choice ★ **Mallard Cottage.** Roaring fires, an open kitchen, and jars of homemade pickles lining the rafters create a beautiful setting in this renovated historic building in Quidi Vidi Village. The menu changes daily based on the best ingredients available from local sources and might include spit-roasted pork shoulder or tuna tartare, always accompanied by novel and succulent vegetable dishes like carrot purée, crispy shallots, or some simple and perfect take on greens. With an on-site sommelier, the wines and cocktails keep up with the food. Sundays the restaurant has live music and no reservations. [$] *Average main: C$29* ✉ *8 Barrows Rd.* ☎ *709/237–7314* 🌐 *mallardcottage.ca* ⏲ *Closed Mon. No lunch Tues., no dinner Sun.* ✍ *Reservations essential.*

$$ PIZZA **Pi Pizzeria.** This gourmet-pizza shop has been winning international competitions for years with their innovative thin-crust creations. The ingredients on their signature "Pi" pizza (pesto tomato base topped with shaved steak, roasted red pepper, mushrooms, avocado slices, and leeks) or on the "Fibonacci" (roasted garlic and olive oil base, topped with compote of caramelized pear and red onion braised in port, baby greens, toasted walnuts, and Gouda cheese) may sound random, but the chef has all the golden ratios down and the taste is perfect. [$] *Average main: C$18* ✉ *10 Kings Rd.* ☎ *709/726–2000* 🌐 *www.gourmetpi.com* ⏲ *No lunch Sun.*

$$$$ MODERN CANADIAN Fodor's Choice ★ **Raymonds.** This is arguably the best restaurant in Canada today and one of the best in the world. Prepare yourself for a night here and pace yourself with the excellent wine list; this will be a meal worth remembering. The menu covers basic Continental cuisine (beef tenderloin, seared trout, roast cod, duck breast, salad niçoise, charcuterie, etc.) but takes these familiar dishes to the acme of perfection. A tasting menu is also available. The atmosphere in the dining room is elegant and grand, with chandeliers overhead and the city lights off the harbor surrounding you through massive plate windows. For a more intimate evening, book into the bar where you can eat off the same menu but in a softer, almost vintage, setting. [$] *Average main: C$47* ✉ *95 Water St.* ☎ *709/579–5800* 🌐 *raymondsrestaurant.com* ⏲ *Closed Sun. and Mon. No lunch* ✍ *Reservations essential.*

$$$$ MODERN CANADIAN **The Reluctant Chef.** With five courses and full wine pairings, dinner may take all evening, but it will be an evening well spent. The staff's enthusiasm is as palpable as the plates are palatable. The house sommelier can find the perfect wine to go with whelk drizzled with locally tapped maple syrup and spruce oil, ultracreamy pâté, or hearty falafel. [$] *Average main: C$60* ✉ *290 Duckworth St.* ☎ *709/754–6011* 🌐 *thereluctantchef.ca* ⏲ *Closed Mon. No lunch* ✍ *Reservations essential.*

$$ VEGETARIAN FAMILY **The Sprout.** Local artists and craftspeople display their creations on the walls here, but works of vegetarian art also arrive at your table in the form of salads, soups (including the Me-So Hungry Miso Soup), sandwiches (a house favorite being the Bravocado—cheese, avocado, and sprouts on homemade whole-grain bread), tapas, and mains. Even meat eaters relish the hearty chili and burgers of tofu, lentil, or chickpea ("Give Peas a Chance") variety. The vegan desserts are decadent, and there are plenty of gluten-free options in addition to beer, wine, and a house-made sangria. This is a warm and friendly place, comfortable for both children and adults who don't want to compromise on grown-up food and fun. [$] *Average main: C$14* ✉ *364 Duckworth St.* ☎ *709/579–5485* 🌐 *thesproutrestaurant.com* ⏲ *Closed Sun. No lunch Sat. No brunch weekdays* ✍ *Reservations not accepted.*

WHERE TO STAY

$$$ HOTEL **Blue on Water.** A modern boutique hotel with stylish contemporary interiors, Blue on Water is the essence of its name—a calm, comfortable lodging with a whiff of the Atlantic when the windows are open if you have a room facing the harbor. **Pros:** spacious bathrooms; great restaurant and bar downstairs. **Cons:** street noise can sometimes be heard in rooms. [$] *Rooms from: C$189* ✉ *319 Water St.* ☎ *709/754–2583* 🌐 *www.blueonwater.com* 🛏 *4 rooms, 7 suites* 🍽 *No meals.*

$$$ HOTEL **Courtyard St. John's Newfoundland.** Business travelers in particular like this attractive Marriott property at the east end of Duckworth Street. **Pros:** business center; workout room; open laundry facilities; in-house restaurant/bar has high-quality food and exceptional views; complimentary valet parking. **Cons:** working harbor can be noisy. [$] *Rooms from: C$179* ✉ *131 Duckworth St.* ☎ *709/722–6636, 866/727–6636* 🌐 *www.marriott.com* 🛏 *61 rooms, 25 suites* 🍽 *No meals.*

$$$ HOTEL **Delta St. John's.** Half the rooms in this popular downtown convention hotel overlook the harbor; the others look out on the city but tend to be quieter (rooms facing New Gower Street have the best views). **Pros:** floor-to-ceiling windows in guest rooms; fitness center includes squash courts; next door to the Mile One entertainment complex; connects to convention center with covered walkways. **Cons:** not in the prettiest part of downtown. [$] *Rooms from: C$229* ✉ *120 New Gower St.* ☎ *709/739–6404, 888/793–3582* 🌐 *www.deltahotels.com* 🛏 *373 rooms, 30 suites* 🍽 *Breakfast.*

$$$ HOTEL **JAG.** With triple-paned windows, this new boutique hotel has brought the option of a good night's sleep into the more industrial end of downtown with stylish rooms and modern furnishings. **Pros:** nice bathrooms; quiet rooms; fully wheelchair-accessible amenities; convenient to convention center, downtown core. **Cons:** harsh LED lighting in rooms; windows do not open. [$] *Rooms from: C$250* ✉ *115 George St.* ☎ *844/564–1524* 🌐 *www.steelehotels.com/our-hotels/jag/* 🛏 *65 rooms, 19 suites.*

$$$ HOTEL **Murray Premises Hotel.** Part of the Murray Premises National Historic Site near St. John's harbor front, this delightful boutique hotel pairs original architectural features with luxurious contemporary furnishings and amenities. **Pros:** historic character; short (though uphill) walk to downtown attractions. **Cons:** soundproofing could be better. [$] *Rooms from: C$239* ✉ *5 Beck's Cove* ☎ *709/738–7773, 866/738–7773* 🌐 *murraypremiseshotel.com* 💳 *No credit cards* 🛏 *69 rooms* 🍽 *Breakfast.*

$$ HOTEL **Quality Hotel Harbourview.** In the core of downtown, directly overlooking the harbor, this hotel has friendly staffers who immediately flash welcoming smiles when you enter the tiled, sand-colored lobby. **Pros:** connecting rooms available; refrigerators available on request. **Cons:** harbor can be noisy; you have to hike a hill if you're walking from Water

CLOSE UP

Newfoundland English

Listen for Newfoundland expressions for everything, from food terms like *scoff* (a big meal), *touton* (fried bread dough), and *duff* (a pudding), to words to describe the fickle weather, such as *leeward* (a threatening storm), *airsome* (bracing cold), and *mauzy* (foggy and damp). "The sun is splitting the rocks!" is something you might hear on a fine day.

A plethora of terms relate to the fishing industry: a *flake* is where you dry fish, perhaps after having caught them in your *dory*, a small rowboat. A *bedlamer* is a young seal. And, of course, there are plenty of words to describe all manner of people: a *gatcher* is a show-off and a *cuffer* tells tall tales.

A *drung* is a narrow road, a *scuff* is a dance, to *coopy* means to crouch down, and if you're going for a *twack*, you're window-shopping. If you're from *Upalong*, that means you're not from here.

Street. $ *Rooms from: C$149* ✉ *2 Hill O'Chips* ☎ *709/754–7788, 800/424–6423* 🌐 *www.choicehotels.ca* 🛏 *160 rooms* 🍽 *No meals.*

$$$$ HOTEL **Sheraton Hotel Newfoundland.** With charming rooms and no bad views, this hotel overlooks the harbor. **Pros:** heritage neighborhood; walking distance to Signal Hill and the Battery; spa and hair salon on-site; excellent restaurant. **Cons:** no indoor parking. $ *Rooms from: C$263* ✉ *115 Cavendish Sq.* ☎ *709/726–4980* 🌐 *www.starwoodhotels.com/sheraton* 🛏 *282 rooms, 19 suites* 🍽 *Breakfast.*

NIGHTLIFE AND PERFORMING ARTS

St. John's has tremendous variety and vitality considering its small population. Celtic-inspired traditional music and folk rock are the city's best-known music genres, although there's also a vibrant blues and alternative-rock scene. For theater, venues include traditional spaces, courtyards, and parks. A growing film and TV industry have added to the artistic and technical talent in recent years.

NIGHTLIFE

The well-deserved reputation of St. John's as a party town has been several hundred years in the making. To become an "honorary Newfoundlander," visitors can take part in the screech-in ceremony, which involves reciting the "Screecher's Creed," kissing a cod, and knocking back a shot of Screech Rum.

George Street. The city's most famous street may be short and cobblestoned, but it is said to have more bars per capita than any other street in North America—25 total, as it happens. Trapper John's, to name one, has been named the fourth-greatest drinking establishment in the world by *Readers' Digest*. (It's also a great place to undertake the screech-in ceremony.) Seasonal open-air festivals, which close off the street, include the George Street Festival in August, with big-name headliners. ✉ *St. John's* 🌐 *www.georgestreetlive.ca.*

O'Reilly's Pub. When Russell Crowe comes to town, he jams at O'Reilly's Pub, famous for its nightly live Irish and Newfoundland music. Starting times vary, but shows typically begin late. O'Reilly's also has a full pub-grub menu; the fish-and-chips is excellent. ✉ *13 George St.* ☎ *709/722–3735, 866/307–3735* ⊕ *www.oreillyspub.com.*

Ship Pub. Traditionally this pub has served as the local arts watering hole and attracts a hip crowd of all ages. There's live music from Wednesday through Saturday year-round, with Wednesday a folk-music night. Good pub food is served between noon and 4 Wednesday through Friday, and until 8 pm Saturday and Sunday. ✉ *265 Duckworth St.* ☎ *709/753–3870* ⊕ *www.stjohnsnightout.com/bars.*

PERFORMING ARTS

Arts and Culture Centre. A 1,000-seat main theater is the focal point of this center, which also houses the St. John's Public Library. It's the site of musical and theatrical events from September through June. ✉ *95 Allandale Rd.* ☎ *709/729–3650, 709/729–3900 box office* ⊕ *artsandculturecentre.com.*

Resource Centre for the Arts. An innovative theater with professional mainstage and experimental second-space productions year-round, the center has been the launching pad for the province's most successful theatrical exports. ✉ *LSPU Hall, 3 Victoria St.* ☎ *709/753–4531* ⊕ *rca.nf.ca.*

SPORTS AND THE OUTDOORS

HIKING

Fodor's Choice ★ **The East Coast Trail.** A world-class destination for hikers, some segments of the East Coast Trail start in St. John's. The Sugarloaf Trail from Quidi Vidi Village to Logy Bay will give you a great work out, spectacular views, and, depending on the season, sightings of whales and icebergs, and buckets of blueberries. ✉ *St. John's* ☎ *709/ 738–4453* ⊕ *eastcoasttrail.ca.*

Grand Concourse. A well-developed and marked trail system, the Grand Concourse, crosses St. John's, Mount Pearl, and Paradise, covering more than 120 km (75 miles). Some trails traverse river valleys, parks, and other open areas; others are sidewalk routes. Well-maintained trails encircle several lakes, including Long Pond and Quidi Vidi Lake, both of which are great for bird-watching. Detailed maps are available at tourist information centers and many hotels. Some segments are maintained through the winter. ✉ *St. John's* ☎ *709/737–1077* ⊕ *www.grandconcourse.ca.*

SCUBA DIVING

The ocean around Newfoundland and Labrador rivals the Caribbean in clarity, though certainly not in temperature. There are thousands of known shipwreck sites. One, a sunken whaling ship, is only several feet from the shore of the Conception Bay community of Conception Harbour. The wrecked ship and a wealth of sea life can be explored with a snorkel and a wet suit.

Ocean Quest. This outfitter leads "Close Encounter Adventures," giving you opportunities to not only see icebergs and whales but to snorkel with the whales and dive to shipwrecks aboard either Zodiacs or a 38-foot custom boat. Tours depart out of the Sunset Marina in Long Pond and also operate out of Twillingate. ✉ *Head office and dive shop, 17 Stanley's Rd., Conception Bay South* ☎ *709/834–7234, 866/623–2664* ⊕ *www.oceanquestadventures.com.*

SEA KAYAKING

One of the best ways to explore the coastline is by kayak, which lets you visit sea caves and otherwise inaccessible beaches. There's also a very good chance you'll see whales, icebergs, and seabirds.

Stan Cook Sea Kayak Adventures. The guides at Stan Cook lead kayaking tours to world-famous sanctuaries, through waterfalls and into caves; in season you can paddle near whales and around icebergs. To provide the most time at the main destinations, participants on the two-hour (C$99) and 3½-hour (C$149) "Go and Tow" tours, which depart from Cape Broyle, kayak out to the ocean, and return by motorized towboat. You can also combine kayaking with a hiking tour along the East Coast Trail (C$339), or just hike (C$69 half day, C$109 full day). Lunch is included on all tours. ✉ *67 Circular Rd.* ☎ *709/579–6353, 888/747–6353* ⊕ *www.stancook.ca.*

WHALE-WATCHING

The east coast of Newfoundland, including the area around St. John's, provides spectacular whale-watching opportunities. Twenty-two species of dolphins and whales are visible along the coast—huge humpback whales weighing up to 30 tons come close to shore to feed in late spring and early summer. You may be able to spot icebergs and large flocks of nesting seabirds in addition to whales on many boat tours.

Iceberg Quest Ocean Tours. Expect to see whales, icebergs, and intensely beautiful scenery on two-hour fully narrated boat tours (C$60) to the most easterly points in North America. As the vessel heads out through the harbor narrows between Signal Hill and Fort Amherst on its way to Cape Spear, you'll be entertained with traditional and local music. From May through August, departures take place daily at 9:30, 1, 4, and 7. ✉ *Pier 6, 135 Harbour Dr.* ☎ *709/722–1888, 866/720–1888* ⊕ *icebergquest.com.*

SHOPPING

ARTS AND CRAFTS

Devon House Craft Centre. Serving as headquarters of the Craft Council of Newfoundland and Labrador, the center displays local works and showcases innovative designs. Check out the exhibits upstairs. ✉ *59 Duckworth St.* ☎ *709/753–2749* ⊕ *www.craftcouncil.nl.ca.*

Downhome Shoppe and Gallery. With thousands of books, music, crafts, artwork, and souvenirs created by Newfoundlanders and Labradorians, this shop occupying two late-1850s buildings is a great place to pick up a homegrown memento. ✉ *303 Water St.* ☎ *709/722–2970, 888/588–6353* ⊕ *shopdownhome.com.*

Newfoundland Weavery. You'll find throws, prints, lamps, books, crafts, and other gift items here. ✉ *177 Water St.* ☎ *709/753–0496.*

Quidi Vidi Village Plantation. Local artists and artisans have their studios here, making this a perfect place to pick up original art and craft works, including textiles, prints, pottery, stained glass, and jewelry. It's closed on Monday. ✉ *10 Maple View Pl., Quidi Vidi* ☎ *709/570–2038* 🌐 *qvvplantation.com.*

PINK, WHITE, AND GREEN

You won't be in St. John's long before you'll ask what's with the pink, white, and green? The tricolor flag flies from houses and buildings, and in souvenir shops the cheerful bands of color show up on rings, earrings, fleece, windbreakers, mittens, and aprons. To quote the song "The Flag of Newfoundland": "The pink the rose of England shows, the green St. Patrick's emblem bright, while in between a spotless sheen of Andrew's cross displays the white." The 19th-century flag has gained popularity in recent years as an affectionate symbol of the "secret nation."

MUSIC

Fred's Records. The best selection of local recordings—about 1,000 individual titles—can be found at this independent store, along with other music. ✉ *198 Duckworth St.* ☎ *709/753–9191* 🌐 *www.fredsrecords.com.*

O'Brien's Music Store. This shop bills itself as the oldest store on the oldest street in the oldest city in North America. It's worth a visit just to see the accordions, tin whistles, fiddles, ukuleles, and ugly sticks (traditional Newfoundland instruments made from discarded tools and household items) on display. The shop also stocks recorded music, and you are sure to see your favorite local musicians popping in for a purchase or a chat. ✉ *278 Water St.* ☎ *709/753–8135* 🌐 *obriens.ca.*

CLOTHING AND GIFTS

Broken Books. This is St. John's only independent bookstore. The well-curated selection ranges from the Penguin Classics to locally produced, hand-printed, small-press poetry and art books and magazines. ✉ *183a Duckworth St.* ✣ *Down the steps from Fixed Coffee and Baking by the side of the War Memorial* ☎ *709/754–2442* ⏲ *Closed Mon.*

Johnny Ruth and Living Planet. A merger of two beloved retail establishments, this large, eclectic space now houses a fashionable clothing store, specialty gifts, gags, and gadgets, and the signature Living Planet eco-friendly T-shirts, dresses, and baby onesies designed by local artists. This is the place to buy your family at home something they will actually wear. ✉ *181 Water St.* ☎ *709/722–7477* 🌐 *www.johnnyruth.com.*

NONIA (*Newfoundland Outport Nursing and Industrial Association*). This nonprofit shop was founded in 1920 to raise money for public health services, with the proceeds from the sale of the homespun, hand-knit clothes used to hire nurses. Today it sells a variety of knits for all ages including the classic and much-coveted full-suit onesies for babies and toddlers. ✉ *286 Water St.* ☎ *709/753–8062, 877/753–8062.*

Rosemill Antiques. Rosemill Antiques specializes in Newfoundland formal furniture, silver, glass, and china. Open Wednesday–Saturday 11–5. ✉ *556 Water St. W* ☎ *709/754–8224.*

AVALON PENINSULA

On the southern half of the Avalon Peninsula, small Irish hamlets are separated by large tracts of wilderness. You can travel part of the peninsula's southern coast in one or two days, depending on how much time you have. Quaint towns line Route 10, and the natural sights are beautiful. La Manche and Chance Cove, both abandoned communities–turned–provincial parks, attest to the region's bounty of natural resources. At the intersection of Routes 90 and 91 in Salmonier, you can head west and then south to Route 100 to Cape St. Mary's Ecological Reserve, or north toward Salmonier Nature Park and on to the towns on Conception Bay. Each of these routes takes about three hours. On the latter, Harbour Grace is a good place to stop; if you plan to travel on to Bay de Verde, at the northern tip of the peninsula, and down the other side of the peninsula on Route 80 along Trinity Bay, consider overnighting in the Harbour Grace–Carbonear area. Otherwise turn around and retrace your steps to Route 1.

WITLESS BAY ECOLOGICAL RESERVE

29 km (18 miles) south of St. John's.

Four small islands and the water surrounding them make up the reserve, the summer home of millions of seabirds—puffins, murres, kittiwakes, razorbills, and guillemots. The birds and the humpback and minke whales that linger here before moving north to their summer grounds in the Arctic feed on capelin (a fish that belongs to the smelt family) that swarm inshore to spawn.

GETTING HERE AND AROUND

The departure point for boat trips around the reserve is Bay Bulls, about 32 km (20 miles) south of St. John's via Route 10. Gatherall's *(See below)* provides shuttle-bus service from St. John's if you're taking one of the company's tours.

EXPLORING

Witless Bay Ecological Reserve. Besides the colonies of seabirds and pods of whales, in late spring and early summer, this is an excellent place to see icebergs, which can remain in Newfoundland's waters into June and sometimes July. The loud crack as an iceberg breaks apart can be heard from shore, but a boat gets you a closer look at these natural ice sculptures. Icebergs have spawned a lucrative business in Newfoundland beyond tourism. Iceberg water and iceberg vodka are now on the market, made from ice chipped from the 10,000-year-old bergs as they float by.

The best views of birds and icebergs are from the tour boats that operate here and are the only way to visit the reserve. There is no public access to the islands themselves—only management staff and scientific researchers (with a permit) are allowed to land. If you're driving down from St. John's, allow about four hours: between 30 and 45 minutes each way for the drive, about 90 minutes for the boat trip, and a bit of time to spare. ✣ *Take Pitts Memorial Dr. (Rte. 2) from downtown St. John's and turn right onto Goulds off-ramp, then left onto Rte. 10.*

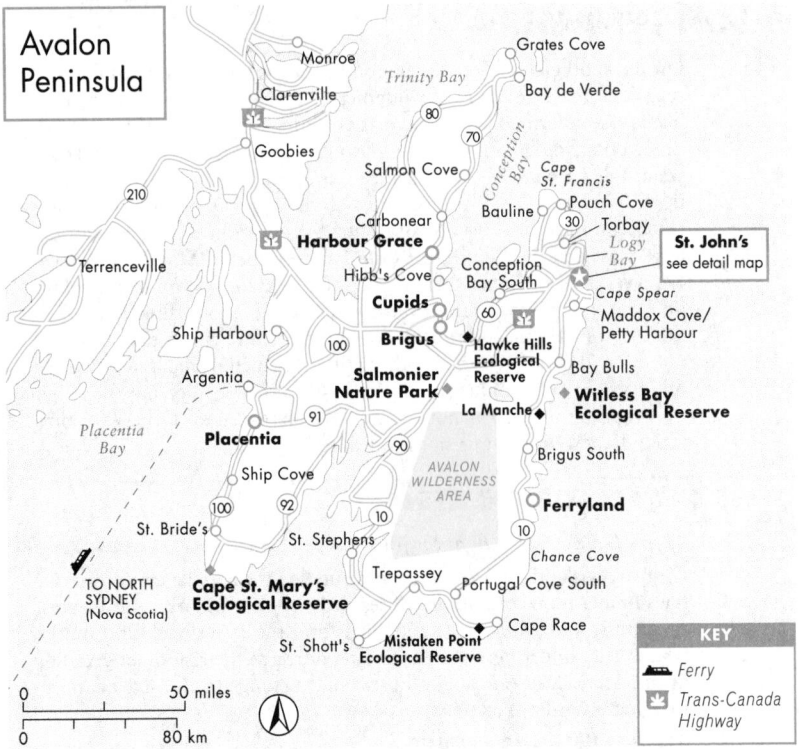

WHERE TO EAT

$ DINER ✕ **Irish Loop Coffee House.** Seeing whales and puffins in their element may feed the soul, but the brisk sea air makes a body awfully hungry. This restaurant, just a few minutes' drive from the boat-tour docks in Bay Bulls, is affectionately know as "Judy's" to locals. Lamb sandwiches, gluten-free and vegetarian options, and diner classics like tuna melts and BLTs are served with tea, excellent coffee, or beer to sate the hikers and tourists who have gratefully come upon this friendly beacon. $ *Average main: C$8* ✉ *409 Southern Shore Hwy., Witless Bay* ☎ *709/334–1085, 709/682–0472* ⊕ *www.irishloopcoffeehouse.com.*

SPORTS AND THE OUTDOORS

Gatherall's Puffin and Whale Watch. From early May to late September, Gatherall's conducts six 90-minute trips (C$56) per day into the waters of Witless Bay Reserve on a high-speed catamaran. The catamaran is stable even in rough seas, so if you're the queasy type, this one might be right for you. Shuttle service (C$25 additional, round-trip) is available from hotels in St. John's. ✉ *90 Northside Rd., Bay Bulls* ☎ *709/334–2887, 800/419–4253* ⊕ *gatheralls.com.*

O'Brien's Whale and Bird Tours. This company offers two-hour excursions (C$55) in a 100-passenger boat to view whales, icebergs, and seabirds. You can also board a 12-passenger boat for a 90-minute tour (C$85). ✉ *22 Lower Rd., off Southside Rd., Bay Bulls* ☎ *709/753–4850, 877/639–4253* 🌐 *www.obriensboattours.com.*

EN ROUTE

Although there are many pretty hamlets along the way from Witless Bay to Ferryland on Route 10, **La Manche,** accessible only on foot, and **Brigus South** have especially attractive settings. La Manche is an abandoned fishing community between Tors Cove and Cape Broyle. The former residents moved to other towns after a storm destroyed part of the community in 1966; a suspension bridge washed away by the storm's tides has since been rebuilt and is worth a visit. Brigus South is a fishing village with a strong traditional flavor whose name is derived from an old French word for "intrigue."

THE IRISH LOOP

The Irish Loop (Route 10) goes around the southern shore of the Avalon Peninsula below St. John's. The highway hugs the coastline and takes you into the heart of Irish Newfoundland—to Bay Bulls, Witless Bay, Ferryland, Aquaforte, Fermeuse, Portugal Cove South, Trepassey, and Salmonier. It's a world filled with whales, caribou, and seabirds. If you keep following the loop around, you'll end up back in St. John's.

FERRYLAND

43½ km (27 miles) south of Witless Bay Ecological Reserve.

The main road into Ferryland hugs the coastline, where tiny bay houses dot the steep hills. Ferryland is one of the oldest European settlements in North America; the Englishman Sir George Calvert, later Lord Baltimore, settled it in 1620. Calvert didn't stay long on this cold windswept shore—he left for a warmer destination and is more commonly credited with founding Maryland. In the summer this is a great spot to whale-watch.

GETTING HERE AND AROUND

There is no public transportation to Ferryland, which is south of St. John's on Route 2 and then Route 10, a total of about 76 km (47 miles).

EXPLORING

FAMILY **Colony of Avalon.** A major ongoing archaeological dig at Ferryland has uncovered this early-17th-century colony founded by George Calvert, later Lord Baltimore. The highlights of a visit here include six dig sites, exhibits of artifacts uncovered at them, two period gardens, and a reconstructed 17th-century kitchen. You can watch the conservationists at work in their laboratory, examining and restoring newly discovered artifacts, and take in living-history demonstrations that provide a feel for colonial times. Absorbing guided tours often take place. ✉ *Rte. 10* ☎ *709/432–3200, 877/326–5669* 🌐 *www.colonyofavalon.ca* 💲 *C$9.50 includes tour* ⏲ *Early June–early Oct., daily 10–6.*

Fodor's Choice ★ **Ferryland Lighthouse.** This historic lighthouse, built in 1871, now signals the spot for breathtaking views, worry-free picnics, and great food such as smoked salmon and ice-shrimp sandwiches, green salads, and gooseberry fools. You bring the appetite, and the lighthouse staff packs everything else—even the blanket. Bread is baked daily here; in fact everything is made on-site down to the desserts and freshly squeezed lemonade. Check the website for menus. Picnics start at C$25 per person (C$12 for children) and reservations are required. There must be romance in the shadow of the lighthouse, because it has become a popular destination for engagement proposals. ✉ *Rte. 10* ☎ *709/363–7456* 🌐 *www.lighthousepicnics.ca* ⏲ *Late May–late Sept., Wed.–Sun. 11:30–4:30.*

OFF THE BEATEN PATH

Mistaken Point Ecological Reserve. At 575 million years old, this is one of the most significant fossil sites in the world. Fossils of more than 20 species of ancient organisms are found in the mudstones here, and almost all of them represent extinct groups unknown in our modern world. Mistaken Point is 145 km (90 miles) south of St. John's via Route 10. Access to the fossils is by guided hike only. Tours are offered daily at 1 pm and begin at the Edge of Avalon Interpretive Centre in Portugal Cove South. Tours generally take from 3½ to 4 hours and include a 3-km (1.8-mile) one-way hike across the barrens towards the ocean to the fossil site. Call ahead to ensure availability and to check weather conditions.

While you're here, travel 8 km (5 miles) farther along the road to **Cape Race Lighthouse,** famous for receiving one of the first SOS messages from the *Titanic.* ✉ *Portugal Cove South* ✣ *Off Rte. 10, about 16 km (10 miles) southeast of Portugal Cove South on minor roads* ☎ *709/438–1012 reservations, 709/438–1100 lighthouse* 🌐 *www.env.gov.nl.ca* 💵 *Free* ⏲ *May–mid-Oct.*

SALMONIER NATURE PARK

88 km (55 miles) northwest of Ferryland; 11 km (7 miles) south of the Trans-Canada Highway.

GETTING HERE AND AROUND

There is no public transportation to the park. By road, it's off the Trans-Canada Highway (Route 1). Take Exit 35 and drive south on Route 90.

EXPLORING

Salmonier Nature Park. Many indigenous animal species—including caribou, lynx, and otters—along with moose, which were introduced from New Brunswick a little more than a century ago, can be seen at this 3,460-acre wilderness area. An enclosed 100-acre exhibit allows up-close viewing. ✉ *Salmonier Line (Rte. 90), Ferryland* ✣ *19 km (12 miles) south of Trans-Canada Hwy. (Hwy. 1)* ☎ *709/229–7888* 🌐 *www.env.gov.nl.ca/env/snp/index.html* 💵 *Free* ⏲ *Early June–early Sept., daily 10–6; early Sept.–mid-Oct., weekdays 10–4.*

EN ROUTE

Hawke Hills. From Salmonier Nature Park to Brigus, take Route 90, which passes through the scenic Hawke Hills before meeting up with the Trans-Canada Highway (Route 1). This reserve is the best representative of alpine barrens in Canada east of the Rockies. Turn off at Holyrood Junction (Route 62) and follow Route 70, which skirts Conception Bay, to get there. ✉ *Ferryland.*

BRIGUS

19 km (12 miles) north of the intersection of Routes 1 and 70.

This compact historic village on Conception Bay is wonderfully walkable, with a public garden, winding lanes, and a teahouse. Brigus is best known as the birthplace of Captain Bob Bartlett, the famed Arctic explorer who accompanied Admiral Robert Peary on polar expeditions during the first decade of the 20th century.

GETTING HERE AND AROUND

There is no public transportation to Brigus. By road, leave the Trans-Canada Highway (Route 1) at Exit 31, drive north on Route 70 toward Conception Bay, and turn right onto the Conception Bay Highway (Route 60) for the last few kilometers. From St. John's, head southwest on Route 2 and pick up Route 60 heading west around the coast, a total of about 74 km (46 miles).

EXPLORING

Hawthorne Cottage. The home of the Arctic explorer Robert Bartlett is one of the few surviving examples of picturesque cottage style, with a veranda decorated with ornamental wooden fretwork. It dates from 1830 and is a National Historic Site. During July and August a local troupe performs several vignettes about the town of Brigus and Bartlett's adventures. Look for postings for Live! On the Lawn Theatre (the performances take place outdoors). ✉ *South St. and Irishtown Rd.* ☎ *709/528–4004 May–Oct., 877/753–9262 off-season appointments* 🌐 *www.historicsites.ca* 💲 *C$5 (theater and house tour)* ⏲ *May–Oct., daily 10–6, or by appointment.*

WHERE TO STAY

$ B&B/INN **Brittoner Bed & Breakfast.** This restored home dating to 1842 is in the heart of Brigus, near Hawthorne Cottage and hiking trails. **Pros:** on a pond; harbor view from some rooms; full hot breakfast. **Cons:** no credit cards accepted. 💲 *Rooms from: C$90* ✉ *12 Water St.* ☎ *709/528–3412, 709/579–5995 Nov.–Apr.* 💳 *No credit cards* ⏲ *Closed Nov.–Apr.* 🛏 *3 rooms* 🍽 *Breakfast.*

CUPIDS

5 km (3 miles) northwest of Brigus.

Cupids is the oldest English colony in Canada, founded in 1610 by John Guy, to whom the town erected a monument in 1910. Nearby is a reproduction of the enormous Union Jack that flew during that 300th-anniversary celebration. When the wind snaps the flag, you can hear it half a mile away. Cupids recently celebrated its 400th anniversary, and the new Cupids Legacy Centre was built to house the many artifacts that have been found related to the archaeology of John Guy's settlement.

GETTING HERE AND AROUND

To get to Cupids, drive west from Brigus on Route 60 and turn right on Keatings Road.

EXPLORING

Cupids Legacy Centre & Museum. With interactive displays, interpretive tours, a shop, and an archaeological lab, this is a good place to get a glimpse of the English settlement founded here in 1610. The bright and modern museum traces 400 years of settlement in the area through interactive exhibits and a selection of the 153,000 artifacts recovered to date at the archaeological site. These include trade beads and the oldest coin found in Canada. You can visit the plantation site dig nearby and see (and talk to) technicians at work in the laboratory. ✉ *368 Seaforest Dr.* ☎ *709/528–1610* 🌐 *www.cupidslegacycentre.ca* 💲 *C$8.50 for Legacy Centre only, C$6 for plantation site only, C$14.50 for both* ⏲ *June–Oct., daily 10–5; off-season by appointment.*

WHERE TO STAY

$ B&B/INN **Skipper Ben's.** This restored 1891 heritage home has wood ceilings and antique furnishings, and its three rooms are spacious. **Pros:** ocean views from deck and rooms; excellent meals; the sound of the sea will lull you to sleep at night. **Cons:** no private bathrooms; no air-conditioning; road runs between B&B and water. 💲 *Rooms from: C$79* ✉ *408 Seaforest Dr.* ☎ *877/528–4436, 709/528–4436* 🌐 *www.skipperbens.ca* 🛏 *3 rooms with shared bath* 🍽 *Breakfast.*

HARBOUR GRACE

21 km (13 miles) north of Cupids.

Harbour Grace, once the headquarters of 17th-century pirate Peter Easton, was a major commercial town in the 18th and 19th centuries. Beginning in 1919, the town was the departure point for many attempts to fly the Atlantic. Amelia Earhart left Harbour Grace in 1932 to become the first woman to fly solo across the Atlantic. The town has two fine churches and several registered historic houses.

GETTING HERE AND AROUND

Harbour Grace is off Route 75, which leaves the Trans-Canada Highway (Route 1) at Exit 31.

WHERE TO STAY

$ B&B/INN **Rothesay House Inn Bed & Breakfast.** The front of this charming provincial heritage building has a lovely harbor-view porch. **Pros:** local seasonal produce and seafood; engaging and helpful hosts; pretty garden. **Cons:** no air-conditioning; two resident dogs (could be a plus for animal lovers). 💲 *Rooms from: C$120* ✉ *34 Water St.* ☎ *709/596–2268, 877/596–2268* 🌐 *www.rothesay.com* 🛏 *4 rooms* 🍽 *Breakfast.*

OFF THE BEATEN PATH

Grates Cove. Grates Cove community is 73 km (45 miles) north of Harbour Grace on Route 70. Here is a photographer's dream, with vistas of both Bonavista and Conception bays from the flat rocks by the harbor. In Iceberg Season you cannot find a wider field of view for the startling magnificence. The fields are covered with the remains of dry stone walls built by the original Irish settlers. Maintained and well-marked walking paths wind through the hills, the community, and along the cliffs. A community-built museum is always open to the public. For food and a place to stay, there is the most excellent Grates Cove Studios with vacation homes and a café that has become a community gathering place. The restaurant combines Newfoundland home cooking with Cajun and Korean cuisine, including burgers, gumbo, and Korean barbecue. Contact them to find out about upcoming live music events. ✉ *Grates Cove* ☎ *709/587–3880* 🌐 *www.gratescovestudios.com.*

PLACENTIA

48 km (30 miles) south of the Trans-Canada Highway.

Placentia was first settled by 16th-century Basque fishermen and was Newfoundland's French capital in the 1600s. The remains of an old fort built on a hill look out over Placentia and beyond, to the placid waters and wooded, steep hillsides of the inlet.

GETTING HERE AND AROUND

The Nova Scotia–Argentia ferry docks 7 km (4½ miles) north of Placentia. From the port, head south to Route 100 and continue south to reach Placentia. From the Trans-Canada Highway (Route 1), take Route 100 south.

> **ROUTE 100: THE CAPE SHORE**
>
> The Cape Shore area, which includes Cape St. Mary's north to Argentia, is culturally and historically rich; the French settlers had their capital here in Placentia, and Irish influence is also strong in music and manner. Birders come to view the fabulous seabird colony at Cape St. Mary's. You can reach the Cape Shore, on the western side of the Avalon Peninsula, from Route 1 at its intersection with Route 100. The ferry from Nova Scotia docks in Argentia, near Placentia.

EXPLORING

Castle Hill National Historic Site. Just north of Placentia, Castle Hill is what remains of the French fortifications. The visitor center has a "Life at Plaisance" exhibit that shows the hardships endured by early English and French settlers. Performances of *Faces of Fort Royal,* a play about the French era, take place from mid-July to mid-August (call for times). There are hiking trails from the forts and many lookouts on-site. ✉ *Castle Hill Rd.* ✣ *Off Rte. 100* ☎ *709/227–2401* 🌐 *www.historicplaces.ca* 💵 *Site C$3.90; play by donation* ⏲ *June–early Oct., daily 10–6.*

WHERE TO STAY

$ HOTEL **Harold Hotel.** Convenient to the Argentia–Nova Scotia Ferry, just 5 km (3 miles) away, this hotel is in the heart of Placentia and a two-minute walk from the boardwalk and the ocean. **Pros:** smoke-free; minutes to ferry terminal; dining room is air-conditioned. **Cons:** no air-conditioning in guest rooms. 💲 *Rooms from: C$89* ✉ *Main St.* ✣ *Off Rte. 100* ☎ *709/227–7700, 709/227–2107* 🛏 *18 rooms* 🍽 *No meals.*

$ B&B/INN Fodor's Choice ★ **Rosedale Manor Bed & Breakfast.** Gorgeous rooms at this 1893 waterfront heritage home far exceed what you'd expect for the low price, and tall guests will be happy with the Blueberry Room, with its extra-long bed. **Pros:** 1 km (½ mile) from Argentia Ferry; cordless phones available with free long distance. **Cons:** no elevator. 💲 *Rooms from: C$99* ✉ *40 Orcan Dr.* ☎ *709/227–3613, 877/999–3613* 🌐 *www.rosedalemanor.ca* 🛏 *6 rooms* 🍽 *Breakfast.*

CAPE ST. MARY'S ECOLOGICAL RESERVE

65 km (40 miles) south of Placentia.

The third-largest nesting colony of gannets in North America resides here, at the most accessible seabird colony on the continent. A paved road takes you within a mile of the colony.

GETTING HERE AND AROUND

Public transit doesn't serve the cape. By road, it's about an hour from Placentia, south and then briefly east on Route 100 to Route 90 south. Alternatively, from Route 91 you can head south on Route 92 and then west on Route 100 to Route 90 south. A 1-km (½-mile) cliff-top path leads from the reserve's parking lot to an observation point. The path is not suitable for wheelchairs or strollers.

EXPLORING

Fodor's Choice ★ **Cape St. Mary's Ecological Reserve.** The reserve has some of the most dramatic coastal scenery in Newfoundland and is a good place to spot whales. Most birds visit from March through August. You can visit the interpretation center—guides are on-site in summer—and then walk to within 100 feet of nesting gannets, murres, black-billed kittiwakes, and razorbills. At busy times you may have to wait your turn at the observation point. Call the weather line to check on conditions before heading out. In July, August, and September the interpretation center presents local artists performing traditional music. ✉ *Cape St. Mary's ✣ Off Rte. 100* ☎ *709/277–1666 cell phone, 709/337–2473* ⊕ *www.env.gov.nl.ca* ₹ *Free* ⏲ *Mid-May–June and Sept.–mid-Oct., daily 9–5; July and Aug., daily 8–7.*

WHERE TO STAY

$ HOTEL **Bird Island Resort.** The landscape around this lodging a half-hour drive from Cape St. Mary's has the dramatic touches one expects of Newfoundland, but the facility itself feels more motel than resort. **Pros:** basic but clean rooms; suites have decks and kitchenettes. **Cons:** no restaurant; no air-conditioning. $ *Rooms from: C$89* ✉ *Off Rte. 100, St. Bride's* ☎ *709/337–2450, 888/337–2450 NL only* ⊕ *www.birdislandresort.com* ⇨ *15 rooms, 5 suites* ⊞ *No meals.*

$ HOTEL **Capeway Motel & Efficiency Units.** This former convent, built in 1968, is about a 15-minute drive from the seabird sanctuary at Cape St. Mary's. **Pros:** complimentary breakfast; well-equipped one- and two-bedroom suites with kitchenettes; guest rooms have in-room tea/coffee. **Cons:** plain decor. $ *Rooms from: C$89* ✉ *11 Main St. (Rte. 100), St. Bride's* ☎ *709/337–2163, 866/337–2163* ⊕ *www.thecapeway.ca* ⇨ *2 rooms, 5 suites* ⊞ *Breakfast.*

EASTERN NEWFOUNDLAND

Eastern Newfoundland packs in plenty of history and fabulous natural landscapes. The Bonavista Peninsula has archaeological artifacts; the Burin Peninsula is more about stark landscapes. Clarenville, halfway between the two, is a good base for exploring. Terra Nova was Newfoundland's first National Park.

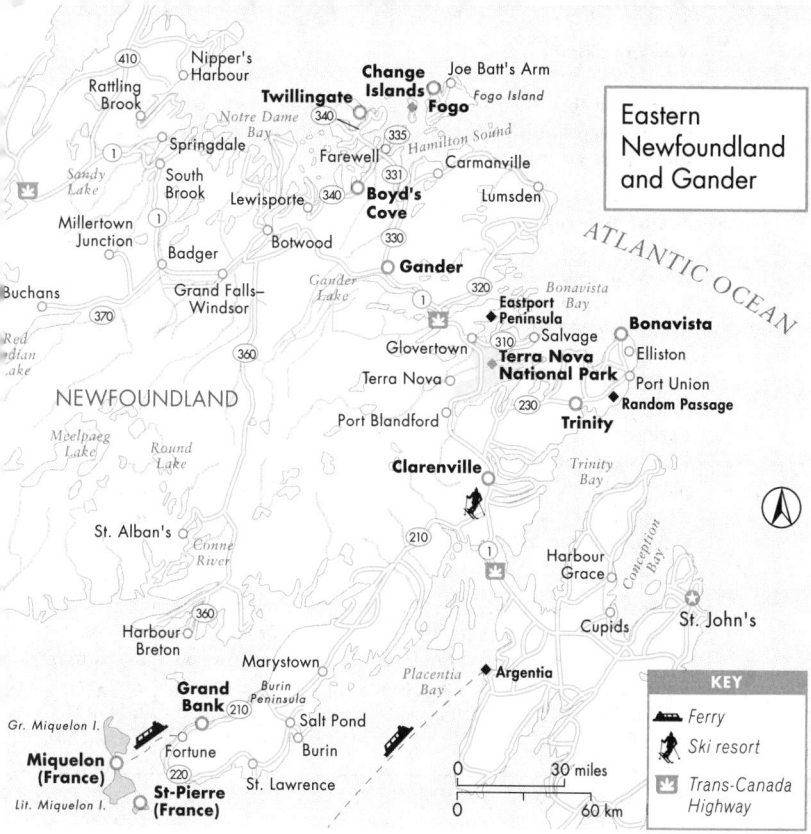

CLARENVILLE

189 km (117 miles) northwest of St. John's.

Pleasant little Clarenville has a marina, a small bird sanctuary, and a monument commemorating the landing of the first transatlantic telephone cable. The town makes a convenient base for several excursions: the Bonavista Peninsula, with its Discovery Trail and the twin communities of Trinity and Bonavista; Terra Nova National Park; and the Burin Peninsula.

GETTING HERE AND AROUND

No useful public transit serves Clarenville. To drive here from St. John's by car, a two-hour trip, take the Trans-Canada Highway (Route 1) west.

ESSENTIALS

Visitor Information **Clarenville Visitor Information Centre.** ✉ *379 Trans-Canada Hwy.* ☎ *709/466-3100.*

EXPLORING

Discovery Trail. If history and quaint towns appeal to you, follow this trail, which begins in the east in Clarenville, on Route 230A, or from the west at Port Blandford, on Route 233. It includes two gems: the old town of Trinity, famed for its architecture and theater festival, and Bonavista, one of John Cabot's reputed landing spots. The provincial tourism website (www.newfoundlandlabrador.com) has a more detailed description. Clarenville itself is largely a departure point for these more attractive destinations. ✉ *Clarenville.*

WHERE TO STAY

$$ HOTEL **Clarenville Inn.** This hotel on the Trans-Canada Highway has comfortable rooms, and the ones in the back have a view of Clarenville and Random Sound. **Pros:** heated outdoor pool in summer; lounge with a patio. **Cons:** right on the highway. $ *Rooms from: C$145* ✉ *134 Trans-Canada Hwy. (Rte. 1)* ☎ *709/466–7911, 877/466–7911* www.clarenvilleinn.com *63 rooms, 1 suite* No meals.

$$ HOTEL **St. Jude Hotel.** Situated on the highway, this hotel is conveniently placed for touring the Bonavista Peninsula and Terra Nova National Park, or skiing at the White Hills Mountain. **Pros:** friendly staff; restaurant has an outdoor patio; elevator. **Cons:** construction-company parking lot near hotel; right on the highway. $ *Rooms from: C$129* ✉ *247 Trans-Canada Hwy. (Rte. 1)* ☎ *709/466–1717, 800/563–7800* www.stjudehotel.com *60 rooms, 3 suites* No meals.

SHOPPING

Mercer's Marine. Family-run Mercer's stocks marine gear and clothing, rainwear, outdoor apparel, rubber boots, warm clothing, in case you didn't pack enough, and knitting materials, in case you want to make your own. The shop, which also sells just about everything else, including kitchenware, is worth a stop if you're in the neighborhood. ✉ *210 Marine Dr.* ☎ *709/466–7430* www.mercersmarine.com *Closed Sun.*

TERRA NOVA NATIONAL PARK

24 km (15 miles) north of Clarenville.

Fodor's Choice ★ Newfoundland's first national park, established in 1957, offers natural beauty, dramatic Bonavista Bay coastline, rugged woods, and many outdoor activities. Moose, black bear, and other wildlife roam freely in the forests and marshy bogs, pods of whales play in the waters within view, and many species of birds inhabit the cliffs and shores.

GETTING HERE AND AROUND

The park straddles the Trans-Canada Highway (Route 1). The southern entrance is near Port Blandford, the northern one near Glovertown.

EXPLORING

FAMILY **Terra Nova National Park.** Golfing, sea kayaking, fishing, camping, and canoeing are among the activities the 400-square-km (154-square-mile) park supports. You can arrange guided walks at the visitor center, which has exhibits, a small shop, and a decent snack bar–cafeteria. ■ TIP→ **The visitor center can also provide connections to a local tour company for boat tours and kayaking activities while in the park.** ✉ *Trans-Canada Hwy., Glovertown* ☎ *709/533–2801 National Parks Service, 709/533–2942 Terra Nova National Park* www.pc.gc.ca *C$5.80* *Daily dawn–dusk. Visitor center: mid-June and Aug., daily 10–6; mid-May–mid-June and Sept.–mid-Oct., Thurs.–Mon. 10–4.*

WHERE TO STAY

$$ B&B/INN **Freshwater Inn.** On a quiet cove on Freshwater Bay, this little inn has large, well-equipped rooms and is a decent base for visiting Terra Nova National Park, 25 km (15 miles) south. **Pros:** no stairs; owner is a licensed fishing guide for local salmon rivers and sea angling; owner can provide personalized walking tours. **Cons:** no choice at breakfast; no good restaurants nearby; nothing within walking distance. *Rooms from: C$135 Rte. 320, Gambo 10 km (6 miles) northeast of Trans-Canada Hwy., Exit 24 709/674–5577, 877/674–5577 www.freshwaterinn.com Closed Nov.–Apr. 4 rooms Breakfast.*

$$ RESORT FAMILY **Terra Nova Resort and Golf Community.** This 220-acre oceanfront resort near Terra Nova National Park combines big-city hotel luxuries with the charm of a country inn—and it has two of the most beautiful golf courses in Canada. **Pros:** heated indoor/outdoor pool year-round; dining room overlooks Clode Sound; several dining options. **Cons:** some rooms could use some renovations. *Rooms from: C$135 Port Blandford Off Trans-Canada Hwy. 709/543–2525, 877/546–2525 terranovagolf.com 73 rooms, 7 suites, 7 chalets No meals.*

OFF THE BEATEN PATH

The Eastport Peninsula. A short, pretty drive from Terra Nova National Park, part of it on a thin strip of road between two bodies of water, will take you to the Eastport Peninsula; take Route 310, at the northern boundary of the national park. There are two beautiful, sandy beaches—at Eastport and at Sandy Cove—and either is perfect to laze away an afternoon, or you can sightsee. The very old outport of Salvage and the small port of Happy Adventure are charming. B&Bs and cabins dot this agricultural peninsula, and the schedule of musical and literary festivals (*www.beachesheritagecentre.ca*) might convince you to stay a night or two. At Burnside, you can visit an archaeology center with Beothuk artifacts or take a boat ride to the Beaches, once the largest Beothuk settlement in Bonavista Bay (*www.burnsideheritage.ca*). The Inn at Happy Adventure is a good choice for travelers. An all-in-one vacation stop with a restaurant, comfortable accommodations, views, boat and kayak tours, and the perfect location from which to enjoy Eastport's sandy beaches and Terra Nova National Park. Rental kits of camping supplies are also available through their tour company, NL Coastal Cruising (*www.innathappyadventure.com*).

TRINITY

71 km (44 miles) northeast of Clarenville.

Fodor's Choice ★ Trinity is one of the jewels of Newfoundland. The village's ocean views, winding lanes, and snug houses are the main attractions, and several homes have been turned into museums and inns. In the 1700s, Trinity competed with St. John's as a center of culture and wealth. Its more contemporary claim to fame, however, is that its intricate harbor was a favorite anchorage for the British navy. The smallpox vaccine was introduced to North America here by a local rector. On West Street an information center with costumed interpreters is open daily mid-June through October. Please keep in mind there is no grocery store, and restaurants are not open late at night. Plan ahead when traveling to small communities so you do not end up waiting until morning for a meal.

GETTING HERE AND AROUND

To get here from Clarenville, take Route 230 to Route 239.

EXPLORING

Mercantile Premises. At this provincial historic site you can slip back in time more than a century to the era when mercantile families ruled tiny communities. Next door the counting house has been restored to the 1820s and the retail store to the 1900s. An interpretation center traces the history of the Trinity, once a hub of commerce. ✉ *West St.* ☎ *709/464–2042* ⊕ *www.seethesites.ca* 💳 *C$6* ⏲ *Mid-May–mid-Oct., daily 9:30–5* ☞ *Ticket price gets you in to all Trinity Provincial Historic Sites (Mercantile Premises, Hiscock House and the Vistors' Centre) and all Trinity Historical Society sites (Trinity Museum, Green Family Forge, Cooperage, Lester Garland House).*

Skerwink Trail. About 9,000 people a year come to hike this historic footpath, a cliff walk with panoramic vistas of Trinity and the ocean. On the trail you'll see sandy beaches, sea stacks (giant protruding rocks that have slowly eroded over time), seabirds and, in season, whales, icebergs, and bald eagles. The 5.3-km (3¼-mile) walk, which begins across the harbor in Port Rexton–Trinity East, is not for the faint of heart—it takes about two hours and can be steep in places. There are benches along the way, though. Trail maps are available at the visitor center in Southern Bay. Trinity Bay Tours, operating out of the Skerwink Hostel in Port Rexton, can provide transportation to and from the trailhead and guided hikes (☎ *709/468–4597,* ⊕ *www.trinitybaytours.com).* ✉ *Port Rexton* ✣ *Off Rte. 230* ☎ *709/464–2006* ⊕ *www.theskerwinktrail.com.*

WHERE TO EAT AND STAY

$ CAFÉ FAMILY ✕ **Trinity Mercantile.** This café knows where to put its energies, with consistently well-brewed coffee roasted in-house, good service, and a small menu focusing on healthful and comforting foods like house-smoked salmon on bagels, fresh sandwiches, and homemade soups. All are served in an open room with long wooden tables and just enough books, crafts, and local art for sale to give you an excuse to stay inside a little longer and enjoy the welcoming atmosphere. 💲 *Average main: C$8* ✉ *24 West St.* ☎ *709/464–3040* ⊕ *www.trinitycoffeecompany.ca* ⏲ *Closed mid-Oct.–mid-May. No dinner May, June, Sept., Oct.*

$$ B&B/INN **Artisan Inn.** Six houses in the heart of Trinity make up this inn, two of which—the Campbell and Gover houses—are from the mid-1800s and are Registered Heritage Structures. **Pros:** owners are very friendly; all accommodations are in historic Trinity; several choices within the set menus at on-site restaurant. **Cons:** no à la carte dining; no elevators; only a Continental breakfast included, and not for the vacation-home rentals. 💲 *Rooms from: C$139* ✉ *57 High St.* ☎ *709/464–3377, 877/464–7700* ⊕ *www.trinityvacations.com* ⏲ *Closed Nov.–Apr.* 🛏 *5 rooms, 1 suite, 4 vacation homes* 🍽 *Breakfast.*

$ B&B/INN **Eriksen Premises.** One of Trinity's heritage structures, this two-story mansard-style building with ocean views has been restored to its original elegance, but with modern comforts added. **Pros:** good location with multiple properties; large sitting room has cable TV, mini-refrigerator, and tea and coffee; eclectic gift shop on premises. **Cons:** no elevator; no air-conditioning; dining room very busy before theater shows. $ *Rooms from: C$110* ✉ *8 West St., Trinity Bay* ☎ *709/464–3698, 877/464–3698* 🌐 *www.mytrinityexperience.com* ⏲ *Closed mid-Oct.–Apr.* 🛏 *6 rooms, 1 suite* 🍴 *Breakfast* ☞ *Breakfast included for all properties except Trinity Suites.*

$$ B&B/INN **Fishers' Loft Inn.** These are without a doubt the best accommodations on the Bonavista Peninsula, with beautiful gardens and stunning views. Fodor's Choice ★ **Pros:** colorful kitchen gardens enrich the dining experience; main-floor wheelchair-accessible rooms; parking at each building. **Cons:** no air-conditioning in some rooms; only one dining option; some hillside walking between buildings. $ *Rooms from: C$140* ✉ *Mill Rd., Port Rexton* ✣ *15 km (9 miles) northeast of Trinity* ☎ *877/464–3240* 🌐 *www.fishersloft.com* ⏲ *Closed Nov.–Apr.* 🛏 *26 rooms, 7 suites* 🍴 *No meals.*

$$ B&B/INN **Maidment House.** This restored three-bedroom house just a short block from the theater, harbor, and historic center of Trinity has elegant antique and local furnishings and comfortable bedding that create a refined yet colorful and cozy atmosphere for a good night's sleep—and one of the best gourmet breakfasts on the peninsula. **Pros:** high-quality breakfast; a stone's throw to the historic sites of Trinity; one of the few places available year-round. **Cons:** no air-conditioning; small sitting room. $ *Rooms from: C$150* ✉ *4 Dandy La.* ☎ *709/464–2220* 🌐 *maidmenthouse.wordpress.com* 🛏 *3 rooms* 🍴 *Breakfast.*

$ RENTAL FAMILY **Sherwood Suites.** These affordable self-service efficiency suites are spacious and have living rooms and private patios from which to enjoy tranquil views. **Pros:** beautiful 20-acre property near Skerwink Trail; on-site laundry facilities; free Wi-Fi in all rooms. **Cons:** no restaurant; no air-conditioning. $ *Rooms from: C$89* ✉ *32–34 Rocky Hill Rd., Port Rexton* ☎ *709/464–2130, 877/464–2133* 🌐 *www.sherwoodsuites.com* ⏲ *Closed Oct.–late May* 🛏 *4 rooms, 12 suites* 🍴 *No meals.*

NIGHTLIFE AND PERFORMING ARTS

Rising Tide Theatre. Dinner theater, local dramas, comedies, and newly commissioned plays are performed from mid-June to mid-October as part of the Bight Festival at the Rising Tide Theatre. The theater company also presents the New-Founde-Land Trinity Pageant and conducts walking tours of lanes, roads, and historical sites. More theater than tour, with actors in period costume, the strolls take place on Wednesdays and Saturdays at 2. ✉ *40 West St.* ☎ *709/464–3232, 888/464–3377* 🌐 *www.risingtidetheatre.com* 🎟 *From C$18.*

SPORTS AND THE OUTDOORS

Fodor's Choice ★ **Rugged Beauty Boat Tours.** Experience much more than the rugged beauty of the glorious coastline on this excellent three-hour open-boat trip (C$90) with a knowledgeable skipper whose family has lived here for generations. You'll be moved by true stories about the lives of the fisherfolk, and enjoy some local humor, too. And you'll disembark for an informal cup of tea at the skipper's vacation cabin on a beautiful bay before heading back. This could be the best half day of your entire Newfoundland trip. Tours on the skipper's 27-foot boat, which can accommodate 12 guests, take place from May to October. ✉ *Rte. 239 at New Bonaventure* ✣ *Off Rte. 230* ☎ *709/464–3856* ⊕ *www.ruggedbeautyboattours.net* ₤ *C$90.*

Sea of Whales Adventures. Sea of Whales guides have a true passion for the ocean and the life it contains. Their knowledge of the area makes each trip out in their 25-foot Zodiac a trip to remember. They keep the guest number between 4 and 11 people for each three-hour tour (C$80). If there are whales in the area, you will find them with this outfit. With guides fully versed in both boating and science, you will be thrilled and educated before returning to dry land. A break for coffee and cookies is included. ✉ *1 Ash's La.* ☎ *709/464–2200* ⊕ *www.seaofwhales.com* ₤ *$80.*

OFF THE BEATEN PATH

Random Passage. Sometimes referred to locally as "Little Hollywood," the community of New Bonaventure is about 14 km (8½ miles) down Route 239 from Trinity and has been the backdrop for two movies (*The Shipping News* and *The Grand Seduction*) and an internationally televised miniseries based on Bernice Morgan's *Random Passage*. At the end of the road, walk a short ways, and you'll reach the breathtaking cove now known as Random Passage where the set of the miniseries was constructed and eventually donated to the community as an early-19th-century outpost. You can roam the church, schoolroom, houses, and a fishing stage and flakes (where the fish is dried), or sit near the vegetable garden and enjoy the quiet beauty of the cove's meadows and pastures. There are guided one-hour site tours which include "Joan's place," which was the bar featured in *The Grand Seduction*. The website is updated seasonally with frequent programming and events. The Old Schoolhouse tearoom (open from 9:30 to 4:30) serves homemade fish cakes, pea soup, and light lunches. ✉ *Rte. 239, New Bonaventure* ✣ *Off Rte. 230* ☎ *709/464–2233* ⊕ *www.randompassagesite.com* ₤ *C$8* ⏲ *June–Sept., daily 9:30–5:30 (last tour at 4:30).*

BONAVISTA

28 km (17 miles) north of Trinity.

No one knows exactly where explorer John Cabot landed when he came to Atlantic Canada in 1497, but many believe, based on his descriptions of the newfound land, it was at Bonavista.

GETTING HERE AND AROUND

Public transit doesn't serve Bonavista. From Trinity, drive north on Route 239 and continue north (turn right) on Route 230; from the Trans-Canada Highway, take the exit for Route 230A and join Route 230 north of George's Brook.

EXPLORING

Cape Bonavista Lighthouse. A provincial historic site on the point, about 1 km (½ mile) outside town, the lighthouse was built in 1843 and has been restored to the way it looked in 1870. ✉ *Bonavista* ☎ *709/468–7444* ⊕ *www.seethesites.ca* ₤ *C$6, includes entry to Mockbeggar Plantation* ⏲ *Mid-May–early Oct., daily 9:30–5.*

FAMILY **Mockbeggar Plantation.** The home of F. Gordon Bradley, a proponent of Confederation, has been restored to its 1939 appearance, the better to chronicle the days leading up to Newfoundland becoming a province of Canada a decade later. The site's history goes back to the 1700s, when it was a fishery plantation. Interpreters lead tours of the plantation house known as the Bradley House. A café, Neil's Yard, operates on-site but under private ownership and serves a modern range of espressos, coffees, fine teas, crepes, and soups that includes gluten-free and vegan options. ✉ *Roper St.* ✣ *Off Rte. 230* ☎ *709/468–7300* ⊕ *www.seethesites.ca, www.neilsyard.org* ₵ *C$6, includes entry to Cape Bonavista Lighthouse* ⏲ *Mid-May–early Oct., daily 9:30–5:00.*

Ryan Premises National Historic Site. On the waterfront, this restored fish merchant's property depicts the history of the commercial cod fishery that prospered here between 1869 and the 1950s. ✉ *Rte. 235* ✣ *Off Rte. 230* ☎ *709/468–1600* ⊕ *www.pc.gc.ca* ₵ *C$3.90* ⏲ *June–Sept., daily 10–6.*

5

WHERE TO EAT AND STAY

$$ PIZZA Fodor's Choice ★ ✕ **Bonavista Social Club.** The name implies more than just a restaurant and it is: a view, a respite, a community. On the deck, the views of the sea and gardens and farms surrounding the restaurant are unimpeded. From a table inside, you can watch pizzas cook in a wood-fired oven while sitting on handcrafted wooden furniture. This has fast become a locals' and travelers' favorite, and you are likely to bump into a friend here, even on your first visit. Located in Upper Amherst Cove just off Route 235, it is a short drive out from Bonavista. $ *Average main: C$12* ✉ *Bonavista* ✣ *Follow Rte. 235 to just south of Bonavista. Turn at the sign for Upper Amherst Cove. Follow the road into Amherst Cove around to the right.* ☎ *709/445–5556* ⊕ *bonavistasocialclub.com* ⏲ *Closed Oct.–Apr.*

$$ B&B/INN **The Harbour Quarters.** Overlooking Bonavista Harbour, just a few steps from the Ryan Premises, this heritage property is a great place to drop anchor for the night. **Pros:** easy walk to everything; sunset view from restaurant and deck; smoke-free; elevator. **Cons:** on the main road; no lunch at restaurant during the off-season. $ *Rooms from: C$155* ✉ *42 Campbell St.* ☎ *709/468–7982, 866/468–7982* ⊕ *www.harbourquarters.com* ⇨ *10 rooms, 1 suite* ⊠ *No meals.*

GRAND BANK

62 km (38 miles) west of Burin.

One of the loveliest communities in Newfoundland, Grand Bank has a fascinating history as an important fishing center. Because of trading patterns, the architecture here was influenced more by Halifax, Boston, and Bar Harbor, Maine, than by the rest of Newfoundland.

GETTING HERE AND AROUND

Grand Bank is on the Burin Peninsula Highway (Route 210), which winds south and then west down the Burin Peninsula.

EXPLORING

Provincial Seamen's Museum. An outpost of The Rooms in St. John's, this sail-shaped building contains a bright and lively museum celebrating the province's connection with both land and sea. Exhibits include boats, ship models, and artifacts from the 1800s to the present. ✉ *54 Marine Dr.* ☎ *709/832–1484* 🌐 *www.therooms.ca* 💲 *C$2.50* ⏲ *Mid-Apr.–early Oct., Mon.–Sat. 9–4:45, Sun. noon–4:45.*

WHERE TO STAY

$$ B&B/INN Fodor's Choice ★ **Thorndyke Bed & Breakfast.** This 1917 Queen Anne–style mansion, a former sea captain's house, is a designated historic structure with great views. **Pros:** fresh nongreasy food and alcohol served; comfortable beds; pretty neighborhood and oceanfront for walks. **Cons:** no air-conditioning. 💲 *Rooms from: C$130* ✉ *33 Water St.* ☎ *709/832–0820, 877/882–0820* 🌐 *www.thethorndyke.ca* 🛏 *4 rooms* 🍽 *Breakfast.*

ST-PIERRE AND MIQUELON

70-minute ferry ride from Fortune.

The islands of St-Pierre and Miquelon, France's only territory in North America, are but a ferry ride away from Newfoundland. Shopping and dining on French cuisine are both popular pastimes here. The bakeries open early, so there's always piping-hot fresh bread for breakfast, and bargain hunters can find reasonably priced wines from all over France. An interesting side trip via boat takes you to see seals, seabirds, and other wildlife, plus the huge sandbar (formed on the bones of shipwrecks) that now connects formerly separate Great and Little Miquelon.

GETTING HERE AND AROUND

You can fly to St-Pierre from St. John's, Halifax, Sydney, or Montréal with Air Saint-Pierre, or you can take a ferry from Fortune, which is 10 km (6 miles) from Grand Bank. Visitors to the islands must carry proof of citizenship—all non-Canadians must have a passport, and Canadians should have a passport or a government-issued photo ID. Because of the ferry schedule, a trip to St-Pierre means an overnight stay in a hotel or a *pension*, the French equivalent of a B&B. If you're flying, you'll need to stay longer—from St. John's flights (C$217 one-way, C$353 round-trip) are on Wednesday, Friday, and Sunday, and schedules don't allow for a one-day round-trip; the other departure points are seasonal. St-Pierre is on French time, a half hour ahead of Newfoundland, so make sure you adjust your watch for the ferry schedule. Once you arrive in St-Pierre, everything is within a short taxi ride or walking distance.

Air Saint-Pierre. International flight service is provided between St. John's and the French island of St-Pierre, as well as domestic service between the islands of Miquelon and St-Pierre. ☎ *877/277–7765* 🌐 *www.airsaintpierre.com.*

ESSENTIALS

If you plan to stay here for any length of time, be aware that the electrical supply is the same as in France—220v, 50 Hz. Check for compatibility with your electronic equipment, and carry adapters if necessary.

For other information about traveling to and within the islands, check with their tourist board.

Contacts **St-Pierre and Miquelon Tourist Board.** ✉ *Saint-Pierre and Miquelon* ☎ *011-508/410-200* ⊕ *www.tourisme-saint-pierre-et-miquelon.com.*

EXPLORING

Le Cabestan (Ferry from Fortune to St-Pierre). A passenger ferry operated by this company leaves Fortune (south of Grand Bank) from April through October. Through July and August there is close to daily service (with twice-daily service some days) but the schedule thins out rapidly in the shoulder season so check the schedule for the current year and plan ahead. The crossing takes roughly an hour; one-way is C$63, round-trip is C$93. ✉ *14 Bayview St., Fortune* ☎ *709/832-3455, 855/ 832-3455* ⊕ *www.saintpierreferry.ca.*

WHERE TO EAT AND STAY

$$$ FRENCH ✕ **L'Atelier Gourmand.** This small restaurant is popular for its well-made standard French fare specializing in fresh seafood from the surrounding waters. Meat and pasta dishes range from simple peppered steak to upbeat flavor pairings such as lime and apples with poultry. As might be expected, the wine list favors France. In fine weather you can dine on the outdoor patio. Cash payments must be in euros or U.S. dollars. [$] *Average main: C$26* ✉ *12 rue du 11 Novembre, St-Pierre* ☎ *011-508/415-300* ⊕ *www.lateliergourmandspm.com.*

$$ HOTEL **Hôtel Robert.** Convenient to the ferry, this waterfront hotel used to accommodate Al Capone when he ran rum through St-Pierre during Prohibition—you can see his hat in the mini Prohibition-era museum on-site. **Pros:** on the waterfront, a five-minute walk from ferry; rental car available; ocean views from breakfast room. **Cons:** no elevator; no room service. [$] *Rooms from: C$127* ✉ *2 rue du 11 Novembre, St-Pierre* ☎ *011-508/412-419* ⊕ *www.hotelrobert.com* ⇨ *40 rooms, 3 suites* ⊞ *Breakfast.*

CENTRAL NEWFOUNDLAND AND NOTRE DAME BAY

Though called "Central," the most visited destinations in this area lie to the north between the Trans-Canada Highway and the shoreline. The true center of the island is mostly uninhabited, and many of the communities along the south coast are accessible only by boat. Gander, in east-central Newfoundland, is known for its airport and its aviation history. North of it is Notre Dame Bay, an area of rugged coastline and equally rugged islands that was once the domain of the now extinct Beothuk tribe. Only the larger islands are currently inhabited. Before English settlers moved into the area in the late-18th and early-19th centuries, it was seasonally occupied by French fisherfolk. Local dialects preserve centuries-old words that have vanished elsewhere. The bay is swept by the cool Labrador Current, which carries icebergs south through Iceberg Alley; the coast is also a good whale-watching area.

GANDER

367 km (228 miles) north of Grand Bank; 331 km (207 miles) west of St. John's; 149 km (93 miles) west of Clarenville.

Gander, a busy town of 11,000 people, is notable for its aviation history. During World War II, the airport here, now called Gander International, was a major strategic air base because of its favorable weather and secure location. After the war, the airport became a hub for civilian travel. It gained some renown when planes destined for the United States were diverted here following the September 11, 2001, terrorist attacks. The movie *Diverted* told the heartwarming story. Today the airport is a major air-traffic-control center.

With its varied lodging options, Gander is a good base for travel in this part of the province, including to Twillingate, the town of Change Islands, and Fogo Island.

GETTING HERE AND AROUND

Gander is on the Trans-Canada Highway (Route 1). To get to Twillingate, take Route 330 north to Route 331 north, eventually connecting to Route 340 to Twillingate. To visit Change Islands and Fogo Island, depart Route 331 at Route 335 and head northeast. You can drive on causeways to Twillingate but will need to catch the ferry in Farewell to get to Change Islands and Fogo Island. If you fly into Gander's airport, book a rental car in advance, as supplies are limited.

Gander International Airport. This is a nice stop if you are interested in the more recent history of Newfoundland, regardless of whether you fly in or out from here. The International Departures Lounge was opened in 1959 by Queen Elizabeth II and has remained a stylish, though now underused, time capsule of modernist design and the jet-setting '60s. If no flights are arriving, the Commissionaires may make time for a quick tour. However, the original furniture (some of which was designed by Arne Jacobsen), geometric terrazzo floors, and Kenneth Lochhead's singular and timeless mural can all be viewed at your leisure from a glass observation corridor. ✉ *1000 James Blvd.* ☎ *709/256–6666* 🌐 *www.ganderairport.com.*

EXPLORING

FAMILY **North Atlantic Aviation Museum.** Just down the highway from the visitor information center, this museum provides an expansive view of Gander's and Newfoundland's roles in aviation. In addition to viewing the aircraft collection (including a World War II–era Lockheed Hudson and a Voodoo fighter jet) and some photographs, you can climb into the cockpit of a real DC-3. There's also a unique aviation gift shop. ✉ *135 Trans-Canada Hwy.* ☎ *709/256–2923* 🌐 *www.northatlanticaviationmuseum.com* 💲 *C$6* ⏲ *June–mid-Sept., daily 9–7; mid-Sept.–May, weekdays 9–5.*

Silent Witness Memorial. The memorial marks the spot where, on December 12, 1985, an Arrow Air DC-8 carrying the 101st Airborne Division home for Christmas crashed, killing 256 American soldiers and civilian flight crew. The site lies off the highway a short distance on a rough gravel road, but it's a must-see. The setting, a clearing in the woods overlooking the grandeur of Gander Lake, is peaceful and moving, and the memorial sculpture, of a boy and girl holding the hands of a peacekeeper, is poignantly rendered. ✉ *Eastern side of Trans-Canada Hwy.* ✣ *4 km (2½ miles) from Gander.*

WHERE TO EAT AND STAY

$$$ BISTRO ✕ **Bistro on Roe.** Enjoy the creative cuisine, reasonable prices, and a friendly atmosphere at this bistro. The combination of crisp brown paper place mats and often whimsical local art mirrors the simple-yet-rich fare like Black Angus filet mignon in a bourbon-and-brown-sugar sauce or handmade ravioli stuffed with butternut squash in a butter-and-pecan sauce. A decent wine list and classic, soundly made cocktails make this a well-placed mid-island stop to experience a last bite of the "city" before moving on to more remote areas in the morning. $ *Average main: C$26* ✉ *110 Roe Ave.* ☎ *709/651–4763* 🌐 *www.bistroonroe.com* ▭ *No credit cards* ⏲ *Closed Sun. No lunch.*

$$ HOTEL FAMILY **Hotel Gander.** Past its heyday but not yet "vintage" in style, the excellent service, comfortable beds, and convenient location nonetheless make this a a good stopover if you're traveling from coast to coast. **Pros:** vehicles with boat trailers can park easily; bright, cheerful dining room; bar has outside patio; children under 12 stay and eat for free; exceptionally helpful and competent staff. **Cons:** living room in suites not air-conditioned; highway traffic makes front rooms noisy. $ *Rooms from: C$144* ✉ *100 Trans-Canada Hwy.* ☎ *709/256–3931, 800/563–2988* 🌐 *www.hotelgander.com* 🛏 *147 rooms, 4 suites, 2 cottages* 🍴 *No meals.*

5

FOGO AND CHANGE ISLANDS

90 km (56 miles) north of Gander.

Tales of the famous Fogo Island Inn have revived interest in this area for travelers from around the world. While Fogo Island has begun to reinvent itself with modern artist studios, arts-residency projects, and home-built economic engines, neighboring Change Islands has remained almost frozen in time. The barren landscape and remote location of these communities are both a draw and a barrier to tourism. Once ensconced, there seems to be no end to what you can experience. The natural landscape is continually stunning, and the people are warm, creative, and entrepreneurial. See the islands from the sea with Ketanja Boat Tours or come during the annual Great Fogo Island Punt Race for a more raucous and participatory boating experience. You can lose yourself in quiet and beauty in every cove and spit and feel like you're at the end of the earth.

GETTING HERE AND AROUND

From Gander, head north on Route 340. At Gander Bay turn left towards Twillingate on Route 331. Keep a lookout for signs to the Fogo and Change Islands Ferry and turn right onto Route 335 heading North to Farewell. The ferry crossing to Fogo takes 45 minutes; the crossing to Change Islands is 20 minutes. Pay attention to which lane you should be in for Fogo versus Change Islands (or Change Islands versus Farewell when returning from Fogo, as there is limited to no signage, and the ferries wait for no man's mistakes!) Provincial Ferry Service charges C$18.50 for a vehicle and driver from Farewell to Fogo (return); C$7.15 for vehicle and driver to Change Islands; additional fees for other passengers. Space is limited. Plan to arrive at least one hour prior to departure. Check the website prior to travel for schedule updates (🌐 *www.tw.gov.nl.ca/ferryservices*). There are clean public restrooms at each ferry terminal.

Evasair Charter planes, seating up to 12 people, fly right into Fogo from St. John's, Deerlake, Gander, and Halifax (🌐 *www.evasair.com*). A planned upgrade to the airstrip will soon have it able to accommodate private jets seating 20 to 25 passengers.

TOURS

FAMILY **Great Fogo Island Punt Race.** Watch or participate in this recently updated version of an ages-old tradition. Now open to participants "from away," this is a challenging race in small wooden boats powered by oars over 11 km (7 miles) of open ocean. Activities for the whole family onshore keep everyone entertained throughout the day. ✉ *Government Wharf in Joe Batt's Arm, Fogo Island* ☎ *709/266–7192* 🌐 *www.tothereandback.com.*

Ketanja Boat Tours. With two daily scheduled departures for regular three-hour sightseeing trips and options for more personalized chartered tours, you can experience Fogo Island and its coastlines, architecture, whales, icebergs, and seabirds from the sea itself. This fully equipped boat has you covered for any whim (and most weather) with bathrooms and options of indoor seating. ✉ *Government Wharf in Joe Batt's Arm, Fogo Island* ☎ *709/658–3452* 🌐 *www.fogoislandboattours.com* 💲 *C$85.*

EXPLORING

FOGO ISLAND

Herring Cove Art Gallery and Studio. Traditional paintings and stunning quilts along with sweet souvenirs of wooden houses and homemade pickles and preserves can all be purchased and appreciated in this homey store and gallery. The quilts display stunning originality and beauty. Bring an empty suitcase! ✉ *27 Herring Cove Rd., Shoal Bay, Fogo Island* ☎ *709/658–3418.*

Hiking Trails. The landscape is the main attraction here, and finding windswept wildflower patches, carpets of bakeapples, crashing waves or brilliant pack ice (depending on the season) is as simple as walking a path. Many footpaths along the coasts of Fogo lead to small surprises (a bronze sculpture of the giant auk on a remote rock), the modern architectural silhouettes of Shorefast's artist-in-residence studios (🌐 *www.shorefast.org*), or even one of the four corners of the world (at Brimstone Head according to the Flat Earth Society). See the visitor center in Seldom for more information. ✉ *Fogo Island.*

Tilting National Historic Site. The community of Tilting, on Fogo's far end, is famous for how well they have preserved their "vernacular" architecture—small boxy wooden houses right on the water's edge with a simple and practical center-hall design broken into four small bedrooms upstairs to maximize on privacy and minimize on heating costs. The

Dwyer Fishing Premises won an award for preservation of the architectural heritage of Newfoundland and Labrador, and along with the Old Irish Cemetery, the Lane House Museum, and Sandy Cove Park, make for a complete afternoon outing. If the weather is nice, a picnic or camping on Sandy Cove beach is a treat. ✉ *Tilting, Fogo Island* ⊕ *www.communityoftilting.com.*

CHANGE ISLANDS

FAMILY **Newfoundland Pony Sanctuary.** Newfoundland ponies are a part of the Island's cultural heritage and history. Sanctuary founder Netta LeDrew will tell you of the work this breed did hauling capelin in from the stages and plowing the fields. But the ponies under her care know no such rigors; these sturdy little beauties are a part of a rescue and breeding program. You can come and meet them and appreciate their picturesque lives with their devoted caretaker, a brand new barn, and plenty of space to graze and roam. ✉ *Change Islands* ☎ *709/621–6381* ⊕ *www.nlponysanctuary.com* ✉ *Suggested donation of C$5.*

Olde Shoppe Museum at Change Islands. Finding a one-room museum built and maintained by a local character is a given on most trips through small towns. Finding one that holds any interest or is meticulously well organized, with each artifact researched through painstaking tracking of oral histories, is usually akin to a snipe hunt. But Peter Porter is a curator by deep instinct if not training. His stories and anecdotes may be oft repeated and almost pat in their singsong cadence, but his respect for the history he is preserving is contagious. His accordion playing isn't shabby either. ✉ *Change Islands* ☎ *709/621–4541* ✉ *fancyporter@gmail.com.*

Squid Jiggers Trail. There are more than a few nice hikes on Change Islands, but this one is the most notable. It is a moderate hike of 6.3 km (about 4 miles) with some steep sections. Following along the northeastern coast, it provides an alternate view of Brimstone Head on Fogo and is a peaceful vantage for whale-watching and iceberg sightings. ✉ *Change Islands* ✣ *At the northern end of Change Islands. Trail head at "Tall Boy" lookout hill just behind the Olde Shoppe Museum.*

WHERE TO EAT

$ CAFÉ ✕ **Flat Earth Coffee Company.** Being on a small, rural island off another island in the North Atlantic is no reason to be without good coffee. With the in-house roaster going full tilt and the proprietor's singular commitment to distilling his business into the simple act of making great coffee (and providing a few sandwiches and treats as accompaniment), this roadside pit stop would keep any big-city coffee connoisseur happily caffeinated. $ *Average main: C$2* ✉ *652 Main Rd., Fogo Island* ☎ *709/571–9271* ⊕ *flatearthcoffee.com.*

$$ CANADIAN ✕ **Nicole's Café and Growlers Ice Cream.** This is exactly the restaurant that has been missing from Newfoundland outports: a place to eat traditional and regional dishes prepared up to global traveler standards. The fried squid is the perfect example, as it is fresh, barely battered, and served with a spicy sauce that has kick enough for folks used to eating international cuisine. Growlers Ice Cream, Nicole's sister establishment just down the road, has the same homemade magic. $ *Average main: C$18* ✉ *159 Main Rd., Joe Batt's Arm, Fogo Island* ☎ *709/658–3663* ⊕ *nicolescafe.ca* ⏲ *Closed Sun.*

WHERE TO STAY

$$$$ RESORT Fodor's Choice ★ **Fogo Island Inn.** Everything about this place, perched on the very edge of the continent, invites superlatives—stunning modern architecture and interior design, breathtaking ocean views, exquisite cuisine, advanced technology, and renowned hospitality. **Pros:** matched with a "community host" from Fogo to show you around the island; all meals, snacks, and gratuities included in price; in-house cinema, art gallery, library, lectures, outdoor activities, and special events. **Cons:** expensive and a two-night minimum; access sometimes affected by weather. *$ Rooms from: C$875 ✉ Joe Batt's Arm, Fogo Island ☎ 709/658–3444 🌐 fogoislandinn.ca 🛏 29 rooms 🍽 All-inclusive.*

$$ RENTAL **Old Salt Box Company.** These traditional houses have been reinvigorated into luxurious and comfortable rentals with all the original charm and scale but with a modern design palette that includes floor-to-ceiling windows facing the ocean. **Pros:** great views; full kitchen; washer and dryer. **Cons:** must provide your own meals and groceries; no pets; interior design more "modern Scandinavian" than "local flavor". *$ Rooms from: C$155 ✉ Fogo Island ☎ 709/658–7392, 844/280–1558 🌐 theoldsaltboxco.com 🛏 3 rental houses on Fogo Island.*

$ B&B/INN **Peg's.** Clean and bright with large rooms, this B&B has an upscale-hostel vibe with a large deck to sit and meet the other visitors and a front hall chock-full of useful information and brochures on what to see and do during your visit. **Pros:** easy walk to area attractions; shared common spaces for interaction with fellow guests. **Cons:** on the main road with no "grounds"; no air-conditioning; no unifying interior design. *$ Rooms from: C$90 ✉ 60 Main St., Fogo Island ☎ 709/266–2392 🌐 pegsbb.com 🛏 6 rooms 🍽 Breakfast.*

$$ B&B/INN Fodor's Choice ★ **Quintal House.** Restored to full beauty, the workmanship of this 160-year-old house speaks for itself, with the original floorboards and white walls and moldings throughout to set off the dark beams, while keeping the feeling bright and uncrowded. **Pros:** next to restaurants and walking distance from shops and galleries; great interior design highlighting "local flavor"; beautiful surrounding property. **Cons:** no air-conditioning; no full-serve breakfast; less communal interaction with strangers. *$ Rooms from: C$130 ✉ 153 Main Rd., Joe Batt's Arm, Fogo Island ☎ 709/658–7829 🌐 quintalhouse.ca 🛏 3 rooms 🍽 Breakfast 💳 No credit cards.*

$ B&B/INN **Seven Oakes Inn and Cottages at Change Islands.** This all-frills B&B is spotlessly clean with old-school charm and grand rooms adorned with lace and doilies wherever possible. **Pros:** comfortable beds; multiple common rooms for whiling away bad weather; large wraparound decks with exceptional views of sea and houses. **Cons:** meals cost extra; "social" tables only option for meals; no alcohol available to purchase. *$ Rooms from: C$95 ✉ Change Islands ✣ Take the ferry from Farewell or Fogo to Change Islands. Drive down the main road and cross the bridge to the north island ☎ 709/621–3256 🌐 www.sevenoakesislandinn.com ⏲ Closed Oct.–May 🛏 7 rooms, 3 cottages 🍽 No meals 💳 No credit cards.*

BOYD'S COVE

71 km (44 miles) north of Gander.

Between 1650 and 1720, the Beothuk (an indigenous culture know as the "Red Indians" to settlers due to the use of red ocher body paint) main summer camp on the northeast coast was at the site of what is now Boyd's Cove. The coastline in and near Boyd's Cove is somewhat sheltered by Twillingate Island and New World Island, linked to the shore by short causeways.

GETTING HERE AND AROUND

From Gander, head north on Route 330 to Gander Bay South and Harris Point. Here, turn left onto Route 331 toward Twillingate, crossing the causeway over Gander Bay, then swing right and continue north.

EXPLORING

Beothuk Interpretation Centre. Explore the lives of the Beothuk, a First Nations people who succumbed in the early 19th century to a combination of disease and battle with European settlers. A 1½-km (1-mile) trail leads to the archaeological site that was inhabited from about 1650 to 1720, when the Beothuk departed this stretch of coast as settlers moved in. Walk softly to feel *"The Spirit of the Beothuk,"* represented by a commanding bronze statue by Gerald Squires that stands almost hidden in the woods. Just in back of the center is a Spirit Garden, opened in consultation with First Nations in Newfoundland, which is the site of an annual "Voices on the Wind" ceremony in September. ✉ *Rte. 340* ☎ *709/656–3114 seasonal contact, 800/729–0592 Kim Ship (off-season contact)* 🌐 *www.seethesites.ca* 💲 *C$6* ⏲ *Mid-May–mid-Oct., daily 9:30–5.*

TWILLINGATE

41 km (25 miles) north of Boyd's Cove.

The inhabitants of this scenic old fishing village make their living from the sea and have been doing so for nearly two centuries. Colorful houses, rocky waterfront cliffs, local museums, and a nearby lighthouse add to the town's appeal. One of the best places on the island to see icebergs, Twillingate is known to the locals as Iceberg Alley. These majestic and dangerous mountains of ice are awe inspiring to see when they're grounded in early summer. With its range of lodging options, and live local entertainment through the summer season at the Orange Lodge on the main strip (aka the "Touton House"), Twillingate makes a good base for exploring the surrounding region.

GETTING HERE AND AROUND

From Boyd's Cove, continue north on Route 340.

EXPLORING

Long Point Lighthouse. Among the few Newfoundland lighthouses you can climb (55 steps), this 1876 structure on a 300-foot cliff inspires gasps with its panoramic view, which includes whales and icebergs at the right times of year. Groomed hiking trails begin at the base, and the nearby Long Point Centre has a fascinating collection of local artifacts. ✉ *Main St., Long Point, Crow Head* ☎ *709/884–1467* 💵 *C$7 for museum exhibit plus C$3 for tower tour; C$5 for just tower tour* ⏲ *June–Sept., daily noon–5.*

Prime Berth Twillingate Fishery & Heritage Centre. A *prime berth* was the term for the best fishing grounds in this area. Berths were allocated by annual lottery to local fishermen, whose livelihoods depended quite literally on the luck of the draw. This museum pays tribute to those fishermen and portrays their lifestyle. There's also a blacksmith shop, an aquarium, an observation tower, and a crafts studio. The facility's owner, David Boyd, aka Captain Dave, conducts boat trips to fish for lobster and cod or to watch whales and icebergs. ✉ *118 Main St.* ☎ *709/884–5925* 🌐 *www.primeberth.com* 💵 *C$5; C$10 for guided tour* ⏲ *June–Sept., daily 10–5.*

WHERE TO EAT AND STAY

$ CAFÉ ✕ **Crow's Nest Café.** On the way to the Long Point Lighthouse, this friendly little café has a great ocean view and a deck from which to enjoy it—you might even see a passing whale or two if you're here in July or August. Light meals, including homemade soups, wraps, and chili, are served until 5 pm, or you can drop in for high-quality coffee and a delicious cinnamon bun. This is a good place to pick up a bagged lunch before you hike or to replenish your energy upon your return. $ *Average main: C$8* ✉ *127 Main St., Crow Head* ☎ *709/893–2029* ⏲ *Closed Mon. in July and Aug., Mon. and Tues. in June and Sept. Off-season: Closed Mon., Tues., Thurs.*

$$ HOTEL **Anchor Inn Hotel and Suites.** Overlooking "iceberg alley," this hotel has a pleasant, welcoming atmosphere and large, comfortable rooms, with at least a queen-size bed or two doubles. **Pros:** great views; spacious rooms; friendly staff. **Cons:** breakfast is only included off-season. $ *Rooms from: C$135* ✉ *3 Path's End* ☎ *709/884–2777, 800/450–3950* 🌐 *www.anchorinntwillingate.com* ⏲ *Closed Jan.* 🛏 *14 rooms, 8 suites* 🍽 *No meals.*

$ B&B/INN **Paradise Bed & Breakfast.** Watch icebergs and whales from the deck of this modern, one-story ranch home overlooking Twillingate Harbour. **Pros:** all rooms have private bathrooms; Continental breakfast includes a hot item; host is a knowledgeable and avid trail guide. **Cons:** no air-conditioning; two rooms have showers, not tubs; house doesn't reflect Twillingate history and heritage. $ *Rooms from: C$110* ✉ *192 Main St.* ☎ *709/884–5683, 877/882–1999* 🌐 *www.capturegaia.com/paradiseb&b.html* 💳 *No credit cards* ⏲ *Closed Oct.–mid-May* 🛏 *3 rooms* 🍽 *Breakfast.*

$ B&B/INN **Toulinguet Inn Bed & Breakfast.** In this 1920s-era home on the harbor front, rooms are old-fashioned, bright, and airy, and a common area balcony looks out over the Atlantic Ocean. **Pros:** sunroom and balcony overlook the harbor; all rooms have private bath/shower; away from the highway. **Cons:** smoking permitted on balcony; no air-conditioning in rooms. $ *Rooms from: C$107* ✉ *56 Main St.* ☎ *709/884–2080* ⏲ *Closed Oct.–mid-May* 🛏 *4 rooms* 🍽 *Breakfast.*

SPORTS AND THE OUTDOORS

Iceberg Man Tours. Owner Cecil Stockley's local nickname is "Iceberg Man," and he's been leading tours for more than 30 years. Two-hour cruises (C$50) take you out to see not only icebergs, but also whales and birds. Iceberg photography is the company's specialty, helping amateur photographers to get that perfect shot. Tours depart at 9:30, 1, and 4, and sunset charters are available. The Iceberg Shop craft emporium on the harbor is under the same ownership. ✉ *Twillingate* ☎ *709/884–2242, 800/611–2374* ⊕ *www.icebergtours.ca.*

Twillingate Adventure Tours. Headquartered at the docks next to its sister business, Addy's (a friendly restaurant serving classic pea soup and other standard outport fare), these two-hour guided cruises (C$50) on the MV *Daybreak* take you to see icebergs, whales, and seabirds. ✉ *128 Main St.* ☎ *709/884–5999, 888/447–8687* ⊕ *twillingateadventuretours.com.*

WESTERN NEWFOUNDLAND

The Great Northern Peninsula is the northernmost visible extension of the Appalachian Mountains. Its eastern side is rugged and sparsely populated. The Viking Trail—Route 430 and its side roads—snakes along its western coast through Gros Morne National Park, fjords, sand dunes, and communities that have relied on lobster fishing for generations. At the tip of the peninsula, the Vikings established the first European settlement in North America a thousand years ago, but for thousands of years before their arrival, the area was home to native peoples who hunted, fished, and gathered berries and herbs.

Corner Brook boasts a fabulous natural setting on the Gulf of St. Lawrence, ringed by mountains, and with plenty of green spaces within its boundaries. It has good shopping and a lively arts scene, and the nearby Humber River is world renowned for its salmon fishing. To the south, the Port au Port Peninsula, west of Stephenville, shows the French influence in Newfoundland, distinct from the farming valleys of the southwest, which were settled by Scots. A ferry from Nova Scotia docks at Port aux Basques in the far southwest corner.

DEER LAKE

208 km (129 miles) west of Grand Falls–Windsor.

Deer Lake was once just another small town on the Trans-Canada Highway, but the opening of Gros Morne National Park in the early 1970s and the construction of Route 430, a first-class paved highway passing right through to St. Anthony, changed all that.

GETTING HERE AND AROUND

Today, with an airport and car rentals available, Deer Lake is a good starting point for a fly–drive vacation, and it's open all year. There are connections from eastern and central Canada, and from St. John's. From the airport, there is a shuttle bus into Deer Lake (and Corner

Brook), as well as major car-rental outlets, but make early reservations because stocks are limited.

ESSENTIALS

Visitor Information **Deer Lake Visitor Information Centre.** ✉ *60A Trans-Canada Hwy.* ☎ *709/635-2202* ⊕ *www.town.deerlake.nf.ca.*

EXPLORING

Long Range Mountains. Stretching all the way from the southwest coast to the Northern Peninsula, a distance of about 400 km (250 miles), the Long Range Mountains form the northernmost extent of the Appalachian Mountains. Their highest point, southwest of Corner Brook, is 2,670 feet, and the range encompasses the Gros Morne National Park and several provincial parks. Jacques Cartier, who saw them in 1534 as he was exploring the area on behalf of France, noted that their shape reminded him of the long, rectangular-shaped farm buildings of his home village in France. Among the mountains, small villages are interspersed with rivers teeming with salmon and trout.

FAMILY **Newfoundland Insectarium.** An intriguing collection of live and preserved insects, spiders, and scorpions from six temperate zones is housed here, and there's a glass beehive with 10,000 honeybees. The greenhouse is home to hundreds of live tropical butterflies. A walking trail leads through woodland to the Humber River and Rocky Brook—you have a good chance of spotting beavers and muskrats from the viewing deck. Check out the gift shop, which sometimes stocks lollipops with edible dried scorpions inside. The insectarium is a one-minute drive off the Trans-Canada Highway at Deer Lake; turn north onto Route 430, also signed here as Bonne Bay Road. ✉ *2 Bonne Bay Rd., Reidville* ☎ *709/635-4545, 866/635-5454* ⊕ *nlinsectarium.com* 🎟 *C$12* ⏲ *July and Aug., daily 9–6; mid-May–June and Sept.–mid-Oct., weekdays 9–5, weekends 10–5.*

WHERE TO EAT AND STAY

$$ AMERICAN ✕ **Deer Lake Irving Big Stop.** Good home-cooked meals, burgers and fries, and healthy options like salads and salmon make this franchise eatery a welcome pit stop, as do the reassuringly clean washrooms. The adjacent convenience store sells gifts, souvenirs, some outdoor apparel, magazines, and basic motoring supplies. $ *Average main: C$12* ✉ *Trans-Canada Hwy. (Rte. 1), Exit 16* ☎ *709/635-2129.*

$$ HOTEL **Deer Lake Motel.** Recent renovations have perked up what was already a clean and comfortable motel, the nearest lodging to Gros Morne National Park. **Pros:** easy to find, at the junction of the Trans-Canada Highway and the Viking Trail (Highway 430); fitness room. **Cons:** restaurant more like a coffee shop; highway traffic noisy; no elevator. $ *Rooms from: C$139* ✉ *15 Trans-Canada Hwy.* ☎ *709/635-2108, 800/563-2144* ⊕ *www.deerlakemotel.com* 🛏 *53 rooms, 2 suites* 🍽 *Breakfast.*

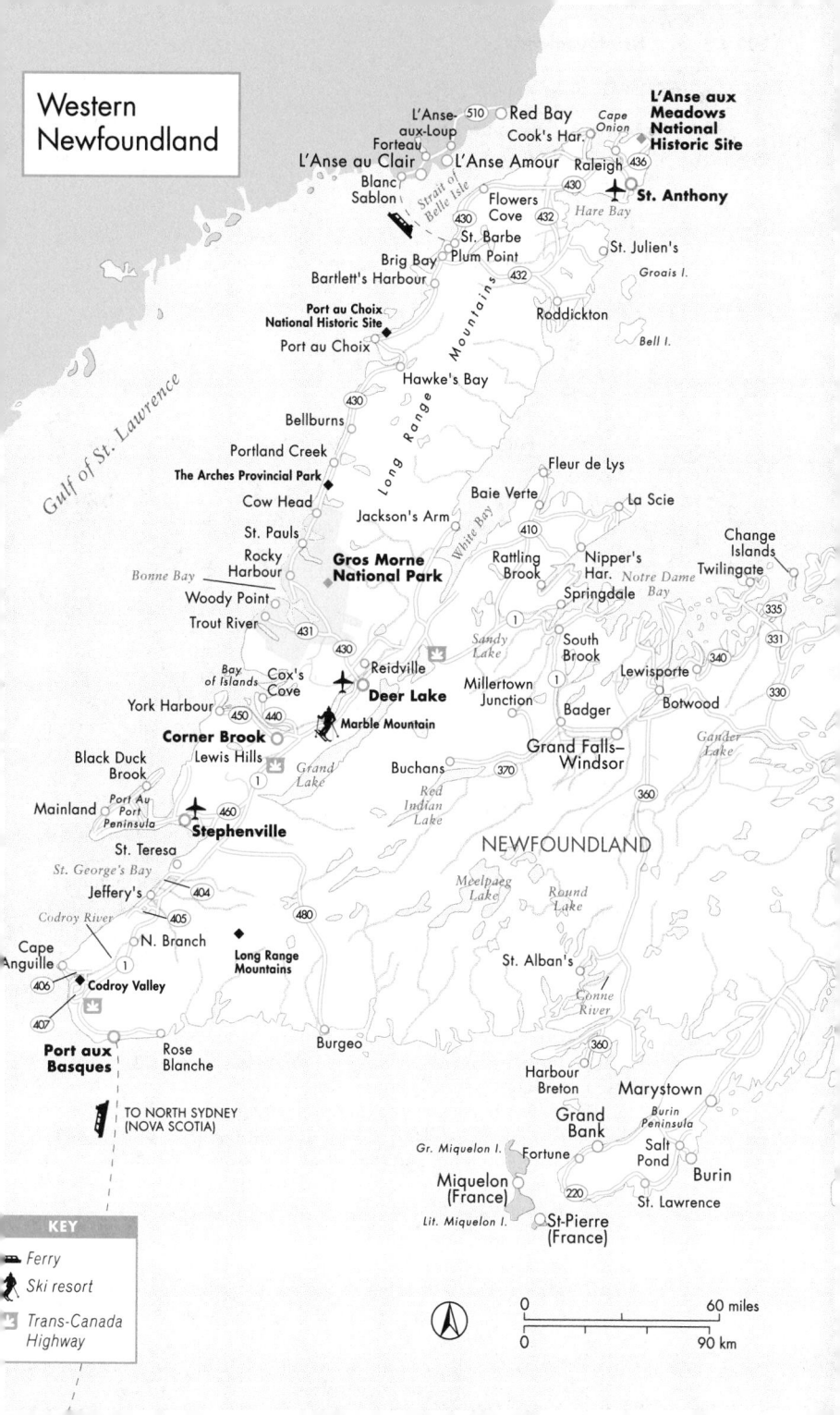
Western Newfoundland
L'Anse-aux-Loup
510
Red Bay
Cape Onion
L'Anse aux Meadows National Historic Site
Forteau
Cook's Har.
L'Anse au Clair
L'Anse Amour
Raleigh
436
Blanc Sablon
Strait of Belle Isle
430
St. Anthony
Flowers Cove
432
Hare Bay
430
St. Barbe
St. Julien's
Brig Bay
Plum Point
Groais I.
Bartlett's Harbour
432
Port au Choix National Historic Site
Roddickton
Port au Choix
Bell I.
Mountains
Hawke's Bay
Long Range
430
Bellburns
Gulf of St. Lawrence
Portland Creek
The Arches Provincial Park
Fleur de Lys
Cow Head
Baie Verte
La Scie
Jackson's Arm
White Bay
410
St. Pauls
Change Islands
Rocky Harbour
Gros Morne National Park
Rattling Brook
Nipper's Har.
Twilingate
Bonne Bay
Notre Dame Bay
Springdale
Woody Point
335
Trout River
431
1
Sandy Lake
South Brook
331
430
340
Bay of Islands
Cox's Cove
Reidville
Lewisporte
Deer Lake
Millertown Junction
1
330
York Harbour
450
440
Marble Mountain
Badger
Botwood
Corner Brook
Grand Falls–Windsor
Gander Lake
Black Duck Brook
Lewis Hills
Grand Lake
Buchans
370
1
Red Indian Lake
360
Mainland
Port Au Port Peninsula
460
Stephenville
St. Teresa
NEWFOUNDLAND
St. George's Bay
Jeffery's
404
Meelpaeg Lake
Round Lake
Codroy River
405
480
N. Branch
Cape Anguille
Long Range Mountains
St. Alban's
1
406
Codroy Valley
Conne River
407
Port aux Basques
Rose Blanche
Burgeo
360
Harbour Breton
Marystown
TO NORTH SYDNEY (NOVA SCOTIA)
Grand Bank
Burin Peninsula
Gr. Miquelon I.
Fortune
Salt Pond
Burin
Miquelon (France)
St. Lawrence
220
Lit. Miquelon I.
St-Pierre (France)
KEY
Ferry
Ski resort
Trans-Canada Highway
0
60 miles
0
90 km

GROS MORNE NATIONAL PARK

46 km (29 miles) north of Deer Lake.

Fodor's Choice ★ Because of its geological uniqueness and immense splendor, this park has been named a UNESCO World Heritage Site. Camping and hiking are popular activities, and boat tours are available.

To see Gros Morne properly, you should allow yourself at least two days, but once they're here, most people would appreciate having a few more. Scenic **Bonne Bay,** a deep fjord, divides the park into distinct northern and southern sections.

GETTING HERE AND AROUND

Traveling north from Deer Lake, the park's main entry point is just before the community of Wiltondale. Continue on Route 430 to Rocky Harbour for the main visitor center and Cow Head, at the northern end of the park. For the southern part of the park, turn left on Route 431.

FESTIVALS

Gros Morne Summer Music. Live music is presented from mid-July to late August at venues that include locations in Corner Brook, Woody Point, and Norris Point. The main focus is classical, but you might also hear jazz or traditional sounds by international artists. ☎ *709/639–7293* ⊕ *gmsm.ca.*

Gros Morne Theatre Festival. Enjoy a mixed bag of quality contemporary plays with first-rate actors, musical perfomances based on local stories and songs, and some dinner theater, from May through mid-September at this festival in Cow Head, by the northern end of Gros Morne National Park. ✉ *Cow Head* ☎ *877/243–2899 box office* ⊕ *www.theatrenewfoundland.com.*

EXPLORING

FAMILY **Bonne Bay Marine Station.** A visit here is a must, especially for kids, who often find themselves enthralled by the touch tank, the centerpiece of the 45-minute guided aquarium tours. In addition to experiencing sea stars, crabs, algae, and other marine life firsthand, participants also learn about the station's past and current research projects. Tours begin every 30 minutes. ✉ *1 Clarke's Rd., Norris Point* ☎ *709/458–2874, 709/458–2550* ⊕ *www.bonnebay.ca* 💵 *C$6.25* ⏲ *Mid-May–mid-Oct., daily 9–5.*

Discovery Centre. On the outskirts of Woody Point, a charming community of old houses and imported Lombardy poplars, this is the main center for interpreting the geology of Gros Morne National Park. Educational programs about natural history are conducted, and there's a craft shop. At the back of the center's parking lot is the fine Lookout Hills trail, a 5-km (3-mile) trek with outstanding views of Bonne Bay, Gros Morne Mountain, and the Tablelands. ✉ *Rte. 431* ✣ *Head west toward Trout River* ☎ *709/458–2417* ⏲ *Mid-May–mid-Oct., daily 9–5 (to 6, mid-June–early Sept.).*

Green Gardens Trail. As depicted beautifully in the movie *Hold Fast* (2014), this spectacular 9-km (5½-mile) round-trip hike starts at Long Pond, on Route 431, 3 km (2 miles) east of Trout River, passes through the Tablelands barrens, and descends sharply to a coastline of eroded cliffs and green meadows. Be prepared to do a bit of climbing on your return journey. A longer version of the trail includes a loop around Wallace Brook. Some parts of the cliff edges are undercut, so stick to the trail. ✉ *Rte. 431* ☎ *709/458–2417* ⊕ *www.pc.gc.ca.*

Gros Morne National Park. Head to the northern side of the park, along coastal Route 430, to visit **Rocky Harbour,** with its range of restaurants and lodgings, plus a luxurious indoor public pool and large hot tub—the perfect place to soothe tired limbs after a strenuous day; it's open from late June to early September. The most popular attraction in the northern portion of Gros Morne is the boat tour of **Western Brook Pond.** You park at a lot on Route 430 and take a 45-minute walk to the boat dock through an interesting mix of bog and woods. Cliffs rise 2,000 feet on both sides of the gorge, and high waterfalls tumble over ancient rocks. Those in good shape can tackle the 16-km (10-mile) hike up **Gros Morne Mountain,** at 2,644 feet the second-highest peak in Newfoundland. Weather permitting, the reward for your effort is a unique Arctic landscape and spectacular views. The park's **northern coast** has an unusual mix of sand beaches, rock pools, and trails through tangled dwarf forests (called tuckamore forests locally). Sunsets seen from **Lobster Head Cove Lighthouse** are spectacular. In season you might spot whales here, and a visit to the lighthouse museum, devoted to the history of the area, is rewarding. At the very north end of the park is the community of Cow Head, home to the Gros Morne Theatre Festival's popular summer program of theater and music. Also nearby, Shallow Bay Beach has a 3-km (2-mile) stretch of soft sand ready-made for beachcombing. Woody Point, a community of old houses and imported Lombardy poplars, is in the southern part of the park, on Route 431. Rising behind it are the **Tablelands,** a unique rock massif that was raised from the earth's mantle through tectonic upheaval. Its rocks are toxic to most plant life and have weathered to a rusty brown color. The Tablelands provide a remarkable exposure of mantle rock, rarely seen at the earth's surface; it's the main reason Gros Morne National Park has received UNESCO World Heritage status. The small community of **Trout River** is at the western end of Route 431 on the Gulf of St. Lawrence. You pass the scenic Trout River pond on the way there. ⊕ *www.pc.gc.ca* 🎟 *C$9.80.*

Gros Morne Visitor's Centre. The thoughtful displays and videos about the park make this a good place to familiarize yourself with the park and what it has to offer. ✉ *Rte. 430, Rocky Harbour* ☎ *709/458–2417, 709/458–2066* ⊕ *www.pc.gc.ca* ⏲ *Mid-May–late Oct., daily 9–5 (to 8 late June–early Sept.).*

WHERE TO EAT

$$$$ MODERN CANADIAN

✕**Black Spruce.** The short but enticing menu here reflects the kitchen team's expert touch and dedication to the concepts of sustainable farming and incorporating local ingredients. You could start with the particularly tasty seafood chowder with smoked bacon and crème fraîche, then move on to perfectly cooked beef tenderloin with champ, Stilton crust, and seasonal vegetables. For a fish dish, you'll have to wait and see what the local fishermen have just brought in. Desserts range from beautifully light to naughtily rich choices, the latter well represented by the figgy duff (a local pudding) served with molasses and Sea Buckthorn ice cream. Arrive before the sun goes down to enjoy the stunning view over Bonne Bay. $ *Average main: C$31* ✉ *Neddies Harbour Inn, 7 Beach Rd., Neddies Harbour* ☎ *709/458–3089* 🌐 *theblackspruce.ca* ⏲ *Closed Mon. and mid-Oct.–mid-May.*

LEAVE THE CAR BEHIND

You can drive to the pretty town of Woody Point, but why not leave the car behind and take a boat? Leave your wheels at Norris Point and take the water taxi (Bon Tours). The journey takes 15 minutes, and you'll probably see whales and kayakers out on the water. In Woody Point, you can have lunch and spend the day strolling, or stay overnight. The water taxi leaves Norris Point at 9 am, 12:30 pm, and 5 pm daily and leaves Woody Point roughly half an hour later, mid-June through August (C$14 return). 🌐 *www.bontours.ca* ☎ *888/458–2016.*

$$$ SEAFOOD ✕ **Fisherman's Landing.** The wide-ranging menu at Fisherman's Landing includes plenty of seafood as well as other options like pizza. Both the food and the service here are reliable, which means that the place can get busy, but you can always browse the crafts shop upstairs until your table's ready. The restaurant is open from 6 am to 11 pm. $ *Average main: C$25* ✉ *44 Main St., Rocky Harbour* ☎ *709/458–2060* 🌐 *www.fishermanslandinginn.com.*

$$$ CANADIAN Fodor's Choice ★ ✕ **Java Jack's Restaurant and Gallery.** The pleasures of this lively restaurant begin with a stroll past the meticulously kept organic garden, where you can see the herbs, peas, and other vegetables you'll enjoy inside. The dinner menu has many seafood options—the pan-seared scallops in mild mango curry are especially good—as well as meat dishes and vegan and vegetarian selections. The wines are well chosen and reasonably priced. The restaurant doubles as a gallery; works by Atlantic Canadian artists (all for sale) decorate the walls. Stop in for a take-away bag lunch—perhaps a shredded-pork sandwich slathered with partridgeberry-honey mustard—for the boat trip to Western Brook Pond, or dine here and enjoy the splendid harbor views. $ *Average main: C$27* ✉ *88 Main St. N, Rocky Harbour* ☎ *709/458–3004* 🌐 *javajacks.ca* ⏲ *Closed Fri. (and Thurs. in Sept.) and Oct.– mid-May* ✍ *Reservations not accepted.*

$$$ SEAFOOD ✕ **Seaside Restaurant.** The chefs at this two-story restaurant overlooking the ocean prepare fresh seafood in traditional, innovative, Newfoundland style. A perfect meal might start with northern scallops served on greens brightened with deep burgundy partridgeberries, followed by grilled shark. Cod tongues—a secret recipe—are popular and offered throughout the season, and the ocean catfish is also highly recommended. The boardwalk is delightful for a stroll before or after you eat, and you can watch the sunset from the upper deck. $ *Average main: C$22* ✉ *Main St., Trout River* ☎ *709/451–3461* 🌐 *www.grosmorneescapes.com* ⏲ *Closed Oct.–late May.*

WHERE TO STAY

$ B&B/INN 🏨 **Blanchard House.** Well located for visits to the southern section of Gros Morne National Park, this spotlessly clean 1904 heritage home has been renovated but retains its period character. **Pros:** some rooms have gorgeous bay windows; all rooms have private baths; one hot item daily with Continental breakfast. **Cons:** no Internet access; three rooms have shower but no tub; beds are all standard double size. $ *Rooms from: C$69* ✉ *12 Blanchard La., Woody Point* ☎ *709/451–3236, 877/951–3236* 🌐 *www.crockercabins.com* ⏲ *Closed early Oct.–late May* 🛏 *4 rooms* 🍽 *Breakfast.*

$$ HOTEL **Fisherman's Landing Inn.** Although it's not on the water as the name implies, this is a spacious, bright, and well-maintained property. **Pros:** smoke-free; crafts shop off lobby; cross-country-skiing and snowshoeing winter packages. **Cons:** a bit overpriced; limited food and wine menu; 2-km (1¼-mile) walk from most other eateries; away from the waterfront. $ *Rooms from: C$139* ✉ *2129 W. Link Rd., Rocky Harbour* ☎ *709/458–2711, 866/458–2711* 🌐 *www.fishermanslandinginn.com* 🛏 *37 rooms, 3 suites* 🍽 *No meals.*

$$$ B&B/INN Fodor's Choice ★ **Neddies Harbour Inn.** In a picture-perfect location overlooking beautiful Bonne Bay, this boutique-style inn has spacious rooms and a fine restaurant. **Pros:** perfect location; excellent breakfasts included in the price; hot tub, sauna, and fitness room. **Cons:** breakfast service stops at 9 am. $ *Rooms from: C$185* ✉ *7 Beach Rd., Neddies Harbour* ☎ *709/458–3089, 877/458–2929* 🌐 *theinn.ca* 💳 *No credit cards* ⏲ *Closed Nov.–Apr.* 🛏 *14 rooms, 1 suite, 4 cottages* 🍽 *Breakfast.*

$$ HOTEL **Ocean View Hotel.** Right on the water, this two-story hotel has good-size modern rooms and nightly entertainment in summer. **Pros:** near crafts stores and dining options; there's a small strand of beach across the street. **Cons:** open windows bring loud music from pub; pub accessible only with cover charge. $ *Rooms from: C$149* ✉ *38–42 Main St., Rocky Harbour* ☎ *709/458–2730, 800/563–9887* 🌐 *www.theoceanview.ca* 🛏 *38 rooms, 5 suites* 🍽 *No meals.*

$$ B&B/INN **Sugar Hill Inn.** The inn is quiet and relaxing; large windows throughout the building let in lots of light, and the warm color schemes and natural wood on floors and ceilings add character to the spacious, uncluttered guest rooms, most of which have a private deck. **Pros:** cedar-lined hot tub and sauna; water comes from a spring on the property. **Cons:** exterior doesn't suggest the quality inside. $ *Rooms from: C$170* ✉ *115–129 Main St., Norris Point* ☎ *709/458–2147, 888/299–2147* 🌐 *www.sugarhillinn.ca* ⏲ *Closed Nov.–mid-May (except for group bookings)* 🛏 *3 rooms, 7 suites, 1 cottage* 🍽 *Breakfast.*

$ B&B/INN **Wildflowers Country Inn.** Set back from the main road on a property full of trees, this grand 80-year-old clapboard house overlooks the ocean. **Pros:** common room with a refrigerator; guided tours include back-country snowmobile tours in season. **Cons:** no air-conditioning; some rooms have shower, not bath. $ *Rooms from: C$99* ✉ *108 Main St. N, Rocky Harbour* ☎ *709/458–3000, 888/811–7378* 🌐 *www.wildflowerscountryinn.ca* 🛏 *4 rooms, 1 cottage* 🍽 *Breakfast.*

NIGHTLIFE AND PERFORMING ARTS

Two major festivals, Gros Morne Summer Music and the Gros Morne Theatre Festival *(See Festivals in Planner)* make for a lively arts scene during high season.

SPORTS AND THE OUTDOORS

BonTours. BonTours runs sightseeing boat tours of Western Brook Pond (C$56–C$60, depending on time of day) in Gros Morne National Park and on Bonne Bay (C$40) as well as a water-taxi service (C$8 one-way or C$14 round-trip) between Norris Point and Woody Point. ✉ *42 Main St., Rocky Harbour* ☎ *709/458–2016, 888/458–2016* 🌐 *www.bontours.ca.*

Gros Morne Adventures. Sea kayaking on Bonne Bay in Gros Morne National Park is offered by this outfitter, as well as guided coastal and mountain hiking (C$125 for a full day) in the area. Guided sea-kayaking tours start at C$55 for two hours, rising to C$125 for a half-day outing. Kayak rentals start at C$35 (single) and C$45 (double). ✉ *Clarkes Rd., Norris Point* ☎ *709/458–2722, 800/685–4624* 🌐 *grosmorneadventures.com.*

EN ROUTE

The Arches Provincial Park and Port au Choix National Historic Site. The Arches are a geological curiosity; the park contains rock formations made millions of years ago by wave action and undersea currents. The succession of caves through a bed of dolomite was later raised above sea level by tectonic upheaval. This is a good place to stop for a picnic.

The Port au Choix National Historic Site is 94 km (58 miles) farther north. The remains of Maritime Archaic and Dorset people have been found along this coast between the Arches Provincial Park and L'Anse aux Meadows, and this site has an interesting interpretation center with exhibits about what's been uncovered to date. Archaeologists digging in the area uncovered an ancient village. Ask at the center for directions to it. ✉ *Rte. 430, Portland Creek* ✣ *For Port au Choix continue 94 km (58 miles) north of the Arches on Rte. 430. It is on Point Riche Rd. west of Rte. 430 off Fisher Rd.* ☎ *709/635–4520 Arches Provinical Park off-season, 709/861–3522 Port au Choix National Historic Site* 🌐 *www.explorenewfoundlandandlabrador.com/provincial-parks/the-arches; www.pc.gc.ca* 💲 *C$3.90 for historic site* ⏲ *Mid-June–mid-Oct.*

L'ANSE AUX MEADOWS NATIONAL HISTORIC SITE

295 km (183 miles) northeast of Arches Provincial Park.

Around the year 1000, Vikings from Greenland and Iceland founded the first European settlement in North America, near the northern tip of Newfoundland. They arrived in the New World 500 years before Columbus but stayed only a few years and were forgotten for centuries. Since the settlement's rediscovery in the last century, the archaeological site has brought tourism to the area. Viking themes abound but so do views, whales, icebergs, fun dining experiences, and outdoor activities.

GETTING HERE AND AROUND

Follow Route 430 north to Route 436 and continue north for 30 km (18½ miles) more.

EXPLORING

L'Anse aux Meadows National Historic Site. It was only in 1960 that the Norwegian team of Helge and Anne Stine Ingstad discovered the remains of the Viking settlement's long sod huts. Today L'Anse aux

Meadows is a UNESCO World Heritage Site. Parks Canada has a fine visitor center and has reconstructed some of the huts to give you a sense of centuries past. An interpretation program introduces you to the food, clothing, and way of life of that time. Bilingual guides are available. ✉ *Rte. 436, St. Anthony* ☎ *709/623–2608* 🌐 *www.pc.gc.ca* 💲 *C$11.70* ⏲ *June–early Oct., daily 9–6 (closes at 5 near beginning and end of season).*

FAMILY **Norstead.** Two kilometers (1 mile) east of L'Anse aux Meadows is Norstead, a reconstruction of an 11th-century Viking port, with a chieftain's hall, church, and ax-throwing arena. Interpreters in period dress answer questions as they go about their Viking business. ✉ *Rte. 436, St. Anthony* ✣ *Off Rte. 430, 40 km (25 miles) north of St. Anthony* ☎ *709/623–2828, 877/620–2828* 🌐 *www.norstead.com* 💲 *C$10* ⏲ *June–mid-Sept., daily 9–6.*

WHERE TO EAT

$$$ SEAFOOD Fodor's Choice ★ ✕ **Norseman Restaurant.** One of the attractions of this restaurant on the harbor front is that you can pick your own lobster from a crate. Other seafood on the menu includes fresh mussels, crab, and shrimp from the area; from the land there's sometimes caribou. The wine list and spirits list is extensive and smartly selected. The paintings, jewelry, and carvings on display are for sale, and in July and August there's live traditional music on Tuesday and Friday. 💲 *Average main: C$25* ✉ *L'Anse aux Meadows* ✣ *Turn right at end of Rte. 436* ☎ *709/623–2370, 877/623–2018* 🌐 *www.valhalla-lodge.com/restaurant* ⏲ *Closed late Sept.–mid-May.*

WHERE TO STAY

$$$$ B&B/INN **Quirpon Lighthouse Inn B&B.** This restored 1920s lighthouse is on a small—7 km (4 miles) by 1½ km (1 mile)—island off Quirpon (pronounced kar-poon), on the northern tip of Newfoundland, and getting here is half the fun. **Pros:** indoor whale-watching station; package includes return boat trip and all meals; visit L'Anse aux Meadows by boat. **Cons:** the only option is the full package. 💲 *Rooms from: C$350* ✉ *Rte. 436, Quirpon Island* ✣ *Off Rte. 430, about a 3½-hr drive north of Cow Head* ☎ *709/634–2285, 877/254–6586* 🌐 *www.linkumtours.com* ⏲ *Closed Oct.–Apr.* 🛏 *9 rooms, 1 suite* 🍽 *All meals.*

$ B&B/INN **Tickle Inn at Cape Onion.** This refurbished, century-old fisherman's house on the beach is probably the northernmost residence on the island of Newfoundland. **Pros:** close to Burnt Cape ecological reserve; optional four-course dinner reasonably priced (C$25). **Cons:** meals served at one table with the owner hosting; small bedrooms; no rooms with private bath. 💲 *Rooms from: C$85* ✉ *Cape Onion* ☎ *709/452–4321 June–Sept., 866/814–8567, 709/739–5503 Oct.–May* 🌐 *www.tickleinn.net* ⏲ *Closed Oct.–May* 🛏 *4 rooms with shared bath* 🍽 *Breakfast.*

$ B&B/INN Fodor's Choice ★ **Valhalla Lodge Bed & Breakfast.** On a hill overlooking "Iceberg Alley" 8 km (5 miles) from L'Anse aux Meadows, the Valhalla has quiet and brightly painted rooms with large windows, pine Scandinavian furniture, and handmade quilts. **Pros:** view of whales and icebergs (and occasionally the aurora borealis) from the lodge; sauna; sitting room with fireplace and patio. **Cons:** few services or restaurants within walking distance; some bathrooms small. [$] *Rooms from: C$95* ✉ *Rte. 436, Gunner's Cove* ☎ *709/623–2018, 877/623–2018, 709/754–3105 off-season* 🌐 *www.valhalla-lodge.com* ⏲ *Closed Oct.–Apr.* 🛏 *5 rooms* 🍽 *Breakfast.*

$ B&B/INN **Viking Nest/Viking Village Bed & Breakfast.** These two B&Bs on the same property are convenient for visits to the Viking settlement at L'Anse aux Meadows. **Pros:** proximity to L'Anse aux Meadows; bathrooms en suite in the Viking Village; full hot breakfast included. **Cons:** no elevator; two rooms at Nest share a bathroom; no air-conditioning. [$] *Rooms from: C$65* ✉ *Rte. 436, Hay Cove, L'Anse aux Meadows* ☎ *877/858–2238* 🌐 *www.vikingvillage.ca* ⏲ *Viking Village closed Oct. 15–May 1* 🛏 *9 rooms, 7 with bath* 🍽 *Breakfast.*

ST. ANTHONY

16 km (10 miles) south of L'Anse aux Meadows.

The northern part of the Great Northern Peninsula served as the setting for *The Shipping News,* E. Annie Proulx's 1993 Pulitzer Prize–winning novel. St. Anthony is built around a natural harbor on the eastern side of the Great Northern Peninsula, near its tip. If you take a trip out to the lighthouse, you may see an iceberg or two float by, and it's a good spot for whale-watching.

GETTING HERE AND AROUND

St. Anthony is the terminus of Route 430, and most travelers arrive via this highway. For variety, some return to St. John's or other destinations by heading south from St. Anthony on Route 432, which rejoins Route 430 near Plum Point, a drive of about 140 km (87 miles).

EXPLORING

Grenfell Historic Properties. A museum and a nearby interpretation center document the life and inspirational work of the English-born doctor Wilfred Grenfell (later Sir Wilfred), who in the early 20th century provided much-needed medical services and transformed the lives of the people of this remote land. ✉ *4 Maraval Rd.* ☎ *709/454–4010* 🌐 *www.grenfell-properties.com* 🎟 *C$10* ⏲ *May–Sept., daily 9–8.*

WHERE TO EAT AND STAY

$$$ SEAFOOD ✕ **Lightkeepers Seafood Restaurant.** Good seafood and solid Canadian fare are served in this former lighthouse-keeper's home on a parkland site overlooking the ocean. Halibut, shrimp, crab, and cod are usually good bets, as is the seafood chowder. Watch whales and bergs (when they oblige) as you feast on bakeapple cheesecake for dessert. The owners also operate the raucous Great Viking Feast dinner theater, housed in a turf-roof building. [$] *Average main: C$22* ✉ *21 Fishing Point Rd.* ☎ *709/454–4900, 877/454–4900* 🌐 *www.lightkeepersvikingfeast.com* ⏲ *Closed Oct.–late May.*

$ HOTEL **Hotel North.** The centrally located Hotel North might not be the most scenic spot in town, but it contains pleasant and comfortable rooms (also two self-contained cottages), all with Sealy Posturepedic mattresses. **Pros:** all rooms have mini-refrigerators and coffeemakers. **Cons:** parking for registration is congested; no landscaping. [$] *Rooms* *from: C$119 ✉ 19 West St. ☎ 709/454–3300 🌐 www.hotelnorth.ca/three ▭ No credit cards ☙ 46 rooms, 2 cabins 🍴 No meals.*

$$ B&B/INN **Tuckamore Lodge & Country Inn.** About an hour from St. Anthony, this Scandinavian-style cedar lodge with a lofty ceiling is a luxurious base from which to explore the natural bounty of the area. **Pros:** outdoor wooden sauna; many on-site activities; canoes available; billiards table. **Cons:** meals served at communal tables; few dining options nearby. *$ Rooms from: C$150 ✉ 1 Southwest Pond Rd., Main Brook ☎ 709/865–6361, 888/865–6361 🌐 www.tuckamorelodge.com ☙ 9 rooms, 3 suites 🍴 Breakfast.*

SPORTS AND THE OUTDOORS

Northland Discovery Boat Tours. Specialized 2½-hour trips (C$59) aboard a custom-built vessel will take you to see whales, dolphins, icebergs, seabirds, and sea caves. A local naturalist always accompanies the tours, which take place from mid-May through mid-September. *✉ St. Anthony ✣ Off West St., behind the Grenfell Interpretation Centre ☎ 709/454–3092, 877/632–3747 🌐 www.discovernorthland.com.*

SHOPPING

Grenfell Handicrafts. Training villagers to become self-sufficient in a harsh environment was one of the British missionary Wilfred Grenfell's aims, and a windproof cloth that they turned into well-made parkas came to be known as Grenfell cloth. Here you can purchase it in the form of mittens, coats, and tablecloths embroidered with motifs such as polar bears and dog teams. The shop also stocks other handicrafts, most of them locally made. *✉ 4 Maraval Rd. ☎ 709/454–3576 🌐 www.grenfell-properties.com.*

CORNER BROOK

50 km (31 miles) southwest of Deer Lake.

Newfoundland's fourth-largest city, Corner Brook is the hub of the island's west coast. Hills fringe three sides of the city, which has dramatic views of the harbor and the Bay of Islands. The town is also home to a large paper mill and a branch of Memorial University. Captain James Cook, the British explorer, charted the coast in the 1760s, and a memorial to him overlooks the bay.

The town enjoys more clearly defined seasons than most of the rest of the island, and in summer it has many pretty gardens. The nearby Humber River is the best-known salmon river in the province, and there are many kilometers of well-maintained walking trails in the community.

GETTING HERE AND AROUND

Corner Brook is a convenient hub and point of departure for exploring the west coast. It's about a three-hour drive (allowing for traffic) from the Port aux Basques ferry. The north and south shores of the Bay of Islands have fine paved roads—Route 440 on the north shore and Route 450 on the south—and both are a scenic half-day drive from Corner Brook. Route 450 is especially lovely, and there are many well-developed hiking trails near the end of the road at Bottle Cove and Little Port. The town has two public bus routes. Bus fare is C$2.50 for one ride, C$11 for five.

EXPLORING

Newfoundland Emporium. This store is crammed from wall to wall with Newfoundland-related stuff—reputedly more than 16,000 items. The main three-level store is full of books (including ones by Newfoundlanders and about Newfoundland, as well as volumes about ships and sailing), art, crafts, music, antique furniture, collectibles, and art. ✉ *11 Broadway* ☎ *709/634–9376.*

WHERE TO STAY

$$ HOTEL **Glynmill Inn.** Tucked away on a treed property with a pond and a walking trail, this well-built Tudor-style inn once housed the senior staff and visiting top brass of the local paper mill. **Pros:** quiet, pleasant setting; art gallery; Deer Lake airport shuttle service (C$22). **Cons:** hard to find from the highway; small windows in many rooms; older rooms not as nice as ones in newer wing. $ *Rooms from: C$141* ✉ *1B Cobb La.* ☎ *709/634–5181, 800/563–4400 in Canada* 🌐 *www.steelehotels.com* 🛏 *55 rooms, 23 suites* 🍴 *No meals.*

$$$ RENTAL **Marble Villa.** These spotless condo-style units are meant for skiers, but they're perfect for a quiet summertime break and as a base from which to make Bay of Islands and Gros Morne day trips. **Pros:** beautiful property with pond and walking trails; kitchens with dishwashers and fireplaces in most units; spacious, comfortable rooms; packages include zip-lining and ATV tours. **Cons:** cafeteria-style restaurant closed except during ski season; few eating options in area. $ *Rooms from: C$189* ✉ *Dogwood Dr.* ✣ *Off Rte. 1, Exit 8* ☎ *709/637–7666, 800/636–2725* 🌐 *www.skimarble.com* 🛏 *29 condos* 🍴 *No meals.*

SPORTS AND THE OUTDOORS

FAMILY **Blow Me Down Cross-country Ski Club.** This place is as warm and welcoming as a cold weather sport club can be. Show up with any skill level and the regulars here will help you find the right trails for you. Skis and snowshoes available to rent for reasonable prices. If you make it to the very top of the mountain on a weekend, you may be rewarded with a full hot breakfast cooked by volunteers over a woodstove in a cozy hut for just a few dollars, and drop of hot chocolate, too, before you head out into the soft, silent forest and trails. ✉ *Lundrigan Dr.* ✣ *Off Lewin Pkwy.* ☎ *709/639–2754* 🎟 *C$20 day pass.*

Crystal Waters Boat Tours. From May to early October, Crystal Waters conducts Bay of Islands cruises (C$40) at 10 am, 2 pm, and 6 pm, depending on demand. ✉ *Bay of Islands Yacht Club, Pikes Ave.* ✣ *Off Griffin Dr.* ☎ *866/344–9808, 709/632–1094* 🌐 *www.crystalwatersboattours.com.*

Marble Mountain Ski Resort. Here you'll find the best skiing and snowboarding in the province. With the piles of snow on the west coast every winter, this is your best bet for winter fun anywhere on the island. In the summer, zip-lining and other seasonal events are available. ✉ *Corner Brook* ☎ *709/637–7601, 888/462–7253* 🌐 *www.skimarble.com* 🎟 *C$59 lift tickets.*

STEPHENVILLE

82 km (51 miles) south of Corner Brook.

The former Harmon Air Force Base is in Stephenville, a town best known for its summer theater festival. To the west of town is the Port au Port Peninsula, which was largely settled by the French, who brought their way of life and language to this small corner of Newfoundland.

GETTING HERE AND AROUND

Stephenville is off the Trans-Canada Highway (Route 1). Take Exit 3, then drive southwest on Route 460 most of the way. After briefly heading southwest on Route 490, follow Minnesota Drive to get downtown.

EXPLORING

Port au Port Peninsula. A slender isthmus tethers this peninsula to the west coast. About 20 tiny communities retain a French and First Nations heritage, but other than that it's largely undeveloped, with a wilderness interior and a rocky coastline. There are superb ocean views from Cape St. George, and some rewarding hiking trails. ✣ *Drive west on Rte. 460 from Stephenville to Cape St. George, at the southwestern extremity; continue north up the peninsula's west side (Rte. 460 becomes Rte. 463 after about 15 km [9 miles]) and loop east back to Rte. 460. Turn left (east) to return to Stephenville.*

EN ROUTE

Codroy Valley. As you travel down the Trans-Canada Highway toward Port aux Basques, Routes 404, 405, 406, and 407 bring you into the small Scottish communities of the Codroy Valley. Some of the most productive farms in the province are nestled in the valley against the backdrop of the Long Range Mountains, from which gales strong enough to stop traffic hurtle down to the coast. Locally known as Wreckhouse winds, they have overturned tractor trailers. The Codroy Valley is great for bird-watching, and the Grand Codroy River is ideal for kayaking. Walking trails, a golf course, and mountain hikes make the area an appealing stop for nature lovers. ⊕ *www.codroyvalley.com.*

PORT AUX BASQUES

166 km (103 miles) south of Stephenville.

In the 1500s and early 1600s, there were seven Basque ports along Newfoundland's west coast and in southern Labrador; Port aux Basques was one of them and was given its name by the town's French successors. It's now the main ferry port connecting the island to Nova Scotia.

GETTING HERE AND AROUND

The ferry from Sydney, Nova Scotia, docks at Port aux Basques. By road, the town is at the western end of the Trans-Canada Highway (Route 1).

ESSENTIALS

Visitor Information **Port aux Basques Visitor Information Centre.** ✉ *Trans-Canada Hwy.* ☎ *709/695-2262* ⊕ *www.portauxbasques.ca.*

EXPLORING

J. T. Cheeseman Provincial Park. If you are using the Port aux Basques ferry, this park 10 km (6 miles) from the port makes a good first or last stop, particularly if you're on a camping trip. Rich in natural flora, this is a nesting site for the piping plover. One of the hiking trails leads to waterfalls on Little Barachois River; another, with views of Table Mountain, includes fitness stations. The long, sandy Cape Ray Beach is good for swimming and sunbathing—its day-use area has picnic tables and fireplaces, and there are about a hundred campsites. ✉ *Trans-Canada Hwy. (Rte. 1)* ☎ *709/695–7222, 709/695–4520* 🌐 *www.nlcamping.ca* ⏲ *Mid-May–mid-Sept., daily.*

WHERE TO STAY

$ HOTEL **St. Christopher's Hotel.** A comfortable two-story hotel near the Nova Scotia ferry, St. Christopher's serves good food at reasonable prices. **Pros:** business center; local fare, such as moose stew, served in the restaurant; waterfront boardwalk close by. **Cons:** limited, overpriced wine list; noise from conventions, weddings, and visiting sports teams; air conditioners sometimes loud. $ *Rooms from: C$120* ✉ *146 Caribou Rd.* ☎ *709/695–7034, 800/563–4779* 🌐 *www.stchrishotel.com* 🛏 *76 rooms, 7 suites* 🍽 *No meals.*

UNDERSTANDING NOVA SCOTIA AND ATLANTIC CANADA

BOOKS, MOVIES, AND MINISERIES

FRENCH VOCABULARY

BOOKS, MOVIES, AND MINISERIES

Books

New Brunswick. David Adams Richards' novels *Mercy Among the Children* and *Bay of Love and Sorrows,* both set in northern New Brunswick, explore decidedly bleak themes. Beth Powning offers a more pastoral perspective in her memoir *Home: Chronicle of a North Country Life.* For a witty primer on Acadian culture, read the original French or translated English version of Antonine Maillet's *La Sangouine.* The title character is popular enough to have inspired a mini–theme park near Bouctouche.

Newfoundland. For contemporary fiction, pick up *The Shipping News,* the Pulitzer Prize–winning novel by American author E. Annie Proulx. It's an atmospheric and moving tale of fishing and family, set in Newfoundland (the book is much better than the movie). *The Colony of Unrequited Dreams* and *February,* written respectively by native Newfoundlanders Wayne Johnston and Lisa Moore, have an added ring of realism. The former is a comic epic about provincial political icon Joey Smallwood, while the latter focuses on the impact the 1982 sinking of the oil rig *Ocean Ranger* had on one fictional woman. Fans of historical novels can try Bernice Morgan's *Random Passage,* a bestseller about early settlers. Prefer nonfiction? *The Day the World Came to Town: 9/11 in Gander,* by Jim DeFede, tells the story of the passengers on the 39 flights that were diverted and the townsfolk who pulled out all the stops to accommodate and feed them.

The Lure of the Labrador Wild, Dillon Wallace's account of his 1903 trek across Labrador, is a classic. Wallace's companion, Leonidas Hubbard, died on the trip, but his wife, Mina, wrote her own book: *A Woman's Way Through Unknown Labrador.*

Nova Scotia. In recent decades this province has become a literary powerhouse. Cape Breton, in particular, has provided a backdrop for award-winning authors like Lynn Coady (*Strange Heaven*), Linden MacIntyre (*The Bishop's Man*), Joyce Barkhouse (*Pit Pony*), and Anne-Marie MacDonald (*Fall on Your Knees*). But if you only have room for one novel in your suitcase, make it *No Great Mischief,* Alistair MacLeod's poignant exploration of familial bonds. History buffs can read Longfellow's 1841 epic poem *Evangeline,* about lovers separated during the Acadian deportation. Lawrence Hill's *The Book of Negroes* (published in the United States as *Someone Knows My Name*) is Canada's answer to *Roots*, and Hugh MacLennan's *Barometer Rising* is a classic novel that recounts the devastating 1917 Halifax Explosion.

Prince Edward Island. It goes without saying that L.M. Montgomery's *Anne of Green Gables* is a must-read. Contemporary novelist Hilary McLeod's punnily named Shores Mysteries—think *Bodies and Sole*—provide a different kind of guilty pleasure.

Movies and Miniseries

Rain, Drizzle, and Fog (1998) is a documentary about Newfoundland seen through the eyes of a "townie," or resident of St. John's. *The Shipping News* (2001), set in Newfoundland, was filmed primarily in Corner Brook, New Bonaventure, and Trinity. Evidence of the miniseries *Random Passage* (2002), based on the book of the same name, lingers on in New Bonaventure, where the set was left in place and has become a tourist attraction. Trinity Bay was again used as a location for the English-language remake of the Québec comedy, *The Grand Seduction* (2013).

A popular filming locale, Nova Scotia often doubles for New England. But sometimes it plays itself. One example is *The Book of Negroes.* Based on Lawrence Hill's novel, the miniseries premiered on CBC and BET in 2015. For a much less edifying look at modern life, catch one of the Trailer Park Boys' big-screen adventures.

FRENCH VOCABULARY

ENGLISH	FRENCH	PRONUNCIATION
BASICS		
Yes/no	Oui/non	wee/nohn
Please	S'il vous plaît	seel voo **play**
Thank you	Merci	mair- **see**
You're welcome	De rien	deh ree- **ehn**
Excuse me, sorry	Pardon	pahr- **don**
Good morning/ afternoon	Bonjour	bohn- **zhoor**
Good evening	Bonsoir	bohn- **swahr**
Good-bye	Au revoir	o ruh- **vwahr**
Mr. (Sir)	Monsieur	muh- **syuh**
Mrs. (Ma'am)	Madame	ma- **dam**
Miss	Mademoiselle	mad-mwa- **zel**
Pleased to meet you	Enchanté(e)	ohn-shahn- **tay**
How are you?	Comment allez-vous?	kuh-mahn- tahl-ay **voo**
Very well, thanks	Très bien, merci	tray bee-ehn, mair- **see**
And you?	Et vous?	ay **voo**?
USEFUL PHRASES		
Do you speak English?	Parlez-vous anglais?	par-lay **voo ahn**-glay
I don't speak . . .	Je ne parle pas . . .	zhuh nuh parl pah
French	français	frahn- **say**
I don't understand	Je ne comprends pas	zhuh nuh kohm- **prahn** pah
I understand	Je comprends	zhuh kohm- **prahn**
I don't know	Je ne sais pas	zhuh nuh say **pah**
What's your name?	Comment vous appelez-vous?	ko-mahn voo za-pell-ay- **voo**
My name is . . .	Je m'appelle . . .	zhuh ma- **pell** . . .
What time is it?	Quelle heure est-il?	kel air eh- **teel**
How?	Comment?	ko- **mahn**
When?	Quand?	kahn

ENGLISH	FRENCH	PRONUNCIATION
Yesterday	Hier	ee-air
Today	Aujourd'hui	o-zhoor- **dwee**
Tomorrow	Demain	duh- **mehn**
Tonight	Ce soir	suh **swahr**
What is it?	Qu'est-ce que c'est?	kess-kuh- **say**
Why?	Pourquoi?	**poor**-kwa
Who?	Qui?	kee
Where is . . .	Où est . . .	oo ay
the train station?	la gare?	la gar
the subway station?	la station de métro?	la sta- **syon** duh may- **tro**
the bus stop?	l'arrêt de bus?	la- **ray** duh **booss**
the bank?	la banque?	la bahnk
the . . . hotel?	l'hôtel . . .?	lo- **tel**
the store?	le magasin?	luh ma-ga- **zehn**
the . . . museum?	le musée . . .?	luh mew- **zay**
the elevator?	l'ascenseur?	la-sahn- **seuhr**
the telephone?	le téléphone?	luh tay-lay- **phone**
Where are the restrooms?	Où sont les toilettes?	oo sohn lay twah- **let**
(men/women)	(hommes/femmes)	(**oh**-mm/ **fah**-mm)
Here/there	Ici/là	ee- **see** /la
Left/right	À gauche/à droite	a goash/a dwaht
Straight ahead	Tout droit	too dwah
Is it near/far?	C'est près/loin?	say pray/lwehn
I'd like . . .	Je voudrais . . .	zhuh voo- **dray**
A room	une chambre	ewn **shahm**-bruh
I'd like to buy . . .	Je voudrais acheter . . .	zhuh voo- **dray** **ahsh**-tay
How much is it?	C'est combien?	say comb-bee- **ehn**
A little/a lot	Un peu/beaucoup	uhn peuh/bo- **koo**

ENGLISH	FRENCH	PRONUNCIATION
More/less	Plus/moins	plu/mwehn
Enough/too (much)	Assez/trop	a-say/tro

DINING OUT

A bottle of . . .	une bouteille de . . .	ewn boo- **tay** duh
A cup of . . .	une tasse de . . .	ewn tass duh
A glass of . . .	un verre de . . .	uhn vair duh
Bill/check	l'addition	la-dee-see- **ohn**
Bread	du pain	dew pan
Breakfast	le petit-déjeuner	luh puh- **tee** day-zhuh- **nay**
Butter	du beurre	dew burr
Cocktail/aperitif	un apéritif	uhn ah-pay-ree- **teef**
Dinner	le dîner	luh dee- **nay**
Dish of the day	le plat du jour	luh plah dew **zhoor**
Enjoy!	Bon appétit!	bohn a-pay- **tee**
Fixed-price menu	le menu	luh may- **new**
Fork	une fourchette	ewn four- **shet**
I am diabetic	Je suis diabétique	zhuh swee dee-ah-bay- **teek**
I am vegetarian	Je suis végétarien(ne)	zhuh swee vay-zhay-ta-ree- **en**
I cannot eat . . .	Je ne peux pas manger de . . .	zhuh nuh **puh** pah mahn- **jay** deh
I'd like to order	Je voudrais commander	zhuh voo- **dray** ko-mahn- **day**
Is service/the tip included?	Est-ce que le service est compris?	ess kuh luh sair- **veess** ay comb- **pree**
It's good/bad	C'est bon/mauvais	say bohn/mo- **vay**
It's hot/cold	C'est chaud/froid	Say sho/frwah
Knife	un couteau	uhn koo- **toe**
Lunch	le déjeuner	luh day-zhuh- **nay**
Menu	la carte	la cart
Napkin	une serviette	ewn sair-vee- **et**

ENGLISH	FRENCH	PRONUNCIATION
Pepper	du poivre	dew **pwah**-vruh
Plate	une assiette	ewn a-see- **et**
Please give me . . .	Donnez-moi . . .	doe-nay- **mwah**
Salt	du sel	dew sell
Spoon	une cuillère	ewn kwee-air
Sugar	du sucre	dew **sook**-ruh
Wine list	la carte des vins	la **cart** day vehn

MENU GUIDE

FRENCH	ENGLISH
POISSONS/FRUITS DE MER (FISH/SEAFOOD)	
Anchois	Anchovies
Bar	Bass
Brandade de morue	Creamed salt cod
Brochet	Pike
Cabillaud/Morue	Fresh cod
Calmar	Squid
Coquilles St-Jacques	Scallops
Crevettes	Shrimp
Daurade	Sea bream
Harengs	Herring
Homard	Lobster
Huîtres	Oysters
Langoustine	Prawn
Lotte	Monkfish
Moules	Mussels
Palourdes	Clams
Saumon	Salmon
Thon	Tuna
Truite	Trout

FRENCH	ENGLISH
VIANDE (MEAT)	
Agneau	Lamb
Boeuf	Beef
Boudin	Sausage
Boulettes de viande	Meatballs
Brochettes	Kebabs
Cassoulet	Casserole of white beans, meat
Châteaubriand	Double fillet steak
Choucroute garnie	Sausages with sauerkraut
Côtelettes	Chops
Côte/Côte de boeuf	Rib/T-bone steak
Entrecôte	Rib or rib-eye steak
Épaule	Shoulder
Escalope	Cutlet
Foie	Liver
Gigot	Leg
Porc	Pork
Ris de veau	Veal sweetbreads
Saucisses	Sausages
Selle	Saddle
Tournedos	Tenderloin of T-bone steak
Veau	Veal
METHODS OF PREPARATION	
Au four	Baked
Ballotine	Boned, stuffed, and rolled
Bien cuit	Well-done
Bleu	Very rare
Frit	Fried
Grillé	Grilled

FRENCH	ENGLISH
Rôti	Roast
Saignant	Rare

VOLAILLES/GIBIER (POULTRY/GAME)

Blanc de volaille	Chicken breast
Canard/Caneton	Duck/Duckling
Cerf/Chevreuil	Venison (red/roe)
Coq au vin	Chicken stewed in red wine
Dinde/Dindonneau	Turkey/Young turkey
Faisan	Pheasant
Lapin/Lièvre	Rabbit/Wild hare
Oie	Goose
Pintade/Pintadeau	Guinea fowl/Young guinea fowl
Poulet/Poussin	Chicken/Spring chicken

LÉGUMES (VEGETABLES)

Artichaut	Artichoke
Asperge	Asparagus
Aubergine	Eggplant
Champignons	Mushrooms
Chou-fleur	Cauliflower
Chou (rouge)	Cabbage (red)
Laitue	Lettuce
Oignons	Onions
Petits pois	Peas
Pomme de terre	Potato
Tomates	Tomatoes

TRAVEL SMART NOVA SCOTIA AND ATLANTIC CANADA

Visit Fodors.com for advice, updates, and bookings

GETTING HERE AND AROUND

AIR TRAVEL

Flying time to Halifax is 1½ hours from Montréal, 2 hours from Boston, 2½ hours from New York, and 6 hours from London. The flying time from Toronto to both Charlottetown and St. John's is about 3 hours; a flight from Montréal to St. John's takes 2 hours. Visitors from New York can expect a 4-hour flight to St. John's, while Bostonians can expect a 3-hour trip to Newfoundland and Labrador's capital. Inside the Atlantic provinces, a jump from Halifax to Charlottetown or Moncton takes only about 30 minutes, while a trip from Halifax to St. John's takes about 90 minutes.

Departing passengers at all major airports must pay an airport-improvement fee (typically C$20–C$25) plus a security fee before boarding (up to C$14.25 for round-trip flights within Canada and C$24.25 for international ones), though these are usually rolled into the ticket price. All major, regional, and charter airlines that serve Atlantic Canada prohibit smoking, as do all Canadian airports.

Airlines and Airports **Airline and Airport Links.com.** *www.airlineandairportlinks.com.*

Airline-Security Issues **Canadian Air Transport Security Authority.** *www.catsa-acsta.gc.ca.* **Transportation Security Administration.** *www.tsa.gov.*

AIRPORTS

The largest airport in the area is Halifax Stanfield International Airport (YHZ). *For information about smaller airports, see the individual chapters.*

Information **Halifax Stanfield International Airport.** *Halifax 902/873-4422 hiaa.ca.*

FLIGHTS

Air Canada and its partners (Air Canada Express and Air Canada Rouge) dominate the national airline industry, serving every major city in the region as well as many smaller centers. WestJet, the main competitor, serves select cities both within Atlantic Canada and elsewhere on the continent, while Porter Airlines, a comparative upstart, flies direct to Halifax from Ottawa, Montréal, and St. John's with connections to other locales. As for U.S.–based carriers, American Airlines, Delta, and United provide service to Halifax. European budget airlines, including Condor, Europe Airpost, and Icelandair, also have service to Atlantic Canada on a seasonal basis.

Regional carriers like Provincial Airlines and Air Labrador connect Newfoundland and Labrador with destinations in Québec and other Atlantic Canadian provinces. Contact regional travel agencies for charter companies. Halifax's airport is 40 km (25 miles) northeast of downtown, and ground transportation takes 30 to 40 minutes, depending on traffic. If you're flying nonstop to the States at the end of your trip, remember that in addition to leaving time for the drive back to the airport you must also leave yourself sufficient time *in* the airport because air travelers are required to preclear U.S. Customs before departing.

Information **Air Canada.** *888/247-2262 www.aircanada.ca.* **Air Labrador.** *800/563-3042 www.airlabrador.com.* **American Airlines.** *800/433-7300 www.aa.com.* **Condor Airlines.** *866/960-7915 www.condor.com.* **Delta Airlines.** *800/221-1212 for U.S. reservations, 800/241-4141 for international reservations www.delta.com.* **Europe Airpost.** *www.europeairpost.com.* **Icelandair.** *800/223-5500 www.icelandair.com.* **Porter Airlines.** *888/619-8622*

WORD OF MOUTH

After your trip, be sure to rate the places you visited and share your experiences and travel tips with other Fodorites in "Forums" on *www.fodors.com.*

www.flyporter.com. **Provincial Airlines.** 800/563-2800 www.provincialairlines.com. **United Airlines.** 800/864-8331 www.united.com. **WestJet.** 888/937-8538 www.westjet.com.

BOAT TRAVEL

Car ferries provide essential transportation on the east coast of Canada, connecting Nova Scotia New Brunswick, PEI, and Newfoundland.

Bay Ferries Ltd. sails the *Fundy Rose* between Saint John, New Brunswick, and Digby year-round. There is at least one round-trip per day—typically two from mid-May to mid-October—and the crossing takes approximately two hours and 15 minutes.

Weather permitting, from May through late December, Northumberland Ferries operates between Caribou, Nova Scotia, and Wood Islands, Prince Edward Island, making the 75-minute trip several times each day.

Marine Atlantic operates daily year-round between North Sydney and Port aux Basques, on the west coast of Newfoundland. Thrice-weekly service between North Sydney and Argentia, on Newfoundland's east coast, is offered from late June through mid-September. Reservations are required. *For additional information about regional ferry service, see individual chapters.*

Information **Bay Ferries, Ltd.** 877/762-7245 www.ferries.ca. **Marine Atlantic.** 800/341-7981 www.marine-atlantic.ca. **Northumberland Ferries.** 877/762-7245, www.ferries.ca.

BUS TRAVEL

If you don't have a car, you'll likely have to rely on bus travel in Atlantic Canada, especially when visiting the many out-of-the-way communities that don't have airports or rail lines. Buses usually depart and arrive only once a day from any given destination. Maritime Bus provides regional service throughout Nova Scotia, New Brunswick, and PEI, while DRL serves Newfoundland.

Bus terminals in major centers and even in many minor ones are usually efficient operations with service all week and agents on hand to handle ticket sales. In some less-trafficked spots, however, the bus station is simply a counter in a local convenience store, gas station, or snack bar. If you ask, the bus driver will usually stop anywhere on the route to let you off, even if it's not a designated terminal. There are a number of small, regional bus services, but connections are not always convenient.

Tickets may be purchased in advance, but—capacity-wise—it isn't usually necessary to do so.

Information **DRL.** 888/263-1854 www.drl-lr.com. **Maritime Bus.** 800/575-1807 www.maritimebus.com.

WORD OF MOUTH

Was the service stellar or not up to snuff? Did the food give you shivers of delight or leave you cold? Were the prices fabulous or infuriating? Rate restaurants and write your own reviews or start a discussion about your favorite places in "Forums" on www.fodors.com. Your comments might even appear in our books. Yes, you, too, can be a correspondent!

CAR TRAVEL

Your own driver's license is acceptable in Atlantic Canada for up to three months, and the national highway system is excellent. It includes the Trans-Canada Highway, the longest in the world—running about 8,000 km (5,000 miles) from Victoria, British Columbia, to St. John's, Newfoundland, with ferries bridging coastal waters at each end.

FROM THE UNITED STATES

Drivers must carry owner registration and proof of insurance coverage, which is compulsory in Canada. The Canadian Non-Resident Inter-Provincial Motor Vehicle Liability Insurance Card, available from any U.S. insurance company, is accepted as evidence of financial responsibility within the country. The minimum liability coverage in New Brunswick, Newfoundland and Labrador, and Prince Edward Island is C$200,000; in Nova Scotia, it's C$500,000. If you're driving a car that is not registered in your name, carry a letter from the owner that authorizes your use of the vehicle.

The U.S. Interstate Highway System leads directly into Canada along Interstate 95 from Maine to New Brunswick, and there are many smaller highway crossings between the two countries as well.

TIP→ Motorists crossing into Atlantic Canada from the United States can check border-wait times online; they're updated hourly. Click on "Border wait times" at *www.cbsa-asfc.gc.ca.*

Information Insurance Bureau of Canada. *902/429-2730, 800/565-7189 within Atlantic Canada www.ibc.ca.*

GASOLINE

Because Canada uses metric measurements, gasoline is always sold in liters with one gallon equaling about 3.8 liters. The cost is regulated by provincial governments and can change weekly, often by zone. (You can expect to pay C$1.18—or C$4.46 per gallon—in Halifax for mid-grade unleaded gas.) For up-to-date per-liter prices, check the individual governmental websites.

Contacts New Brunswick Energy and Utilities Board. *www.nbeub.ca.* **Newfoundland and Labrador Public Utilities Board.** *www.pub.nf.ca.* **Nova Scotia Utility and Review Board.** *nsuarb.novascotia.ca.* **Prince Edward Island Regulatory and Appeals Commission.** *www.irac.pe.ca.*

ROADSIDE EMERGENCIES

In case of an accident or emergency, call 911. If you're a member of the American Automobile Association, you're automatically covered by the Canadian Automobile Association while traveling in Canada.

Emergency Services Canadian Automobile Association. *800/222-4357 roadside assistance, 800/561-8807 other member services www.caa.ca.*

TIP→ Motorists should bear in mind that many roads in rural areas require attentive driving, as they are often narrow and don't always have a paved shoulder (sharply curving ones warrant special attention). That said, they're generally well surfaced and offer exquisite scenery.

RULES OF THE ROAD

Speed limits, always given in kilometers, vary from province to province, but are usually within the 90- to 110-kph range outside cities. (As a mile equals 1.6 km, that translates into 50 to 68 mph.) Radar-detection devices are illegal, and speed limits are strictly enforced. Depending on where you are and how far over the limit you go, speeding tickets can start in the C$200 range and rise quickly.

By law, you are required to wear a seat belt. Children must also be properly restrained regardless of where they're seated. Those under 40 pounds must be strapped into approved child-safety seats. Even children over 40 pounds are legally required to use child seats if they are less than 57 inches tall or under a set age (8 in Newfoundland and Labrador, 9 in New Brunswick and Nova Scotia, 10 in PEI). This rule does not apply, however, if you're visiting from outside Atlantic Canada and driving your own vehicle, provided it complies with the child-restraint safety laws of the province or country where the car is registered.

Drinking and driving (anything over 0.08 blood-alcohol level) is a criminal offense. In the Atlantic provinces, however, there are also serious penalties—including license suspension and vehicle confiscation—if you're found to have a 0.05 blood-alcohol level. Road-block checks are not unusual, especially on holiday weekends.

Another no-no is using a handheld cell phone while driving. All four provinces have banned the practice. Other regulations, such as those concerning headlight use and parking, differ from province to province. Some have a statutory requirement to drive with your headlights on for extended periods after dawn and before sunset. Parking rules are set by individual municipalities. In Halifax, tickets for violators are common and start at C$20.

CRUISE SHIP TRAVEL

Every season, from mid-April to early November, cruise ships sailing up from New England, and in some cases across the ocean from Europe, arrive in Atlantic Canadian waters. In terms of traffic, Halifax is hands down the most popular port of call, annually receiving more than 130 ships representing major lines such as Royal Caribbean, Holland America, Princess, Silversea, Carnival, Crystal, and Cunard.

Saint John (New Brunswick), Charlottetown (PEI), and Sydney (Nova Scotia) each receive about 75 cruise ship calls annually. Cruise ships are also an emerging element of the Newfoundland and Labrador tourism sector. Right now, the province plays host to a relatively small number of major lines, and they must first dock at either Corner Brook or St. John's; however, there are another 30-odd outports all over the province that attract smaller, more intrepid operators like Adventure Canada or Lindblad Expeditions (a National Geographic Society partner).

Contacts **Adventure Canada.** ☎ *800/363-7566* ⊕ *www.adventurecanada.com.* **Atlantic Canada Cruise Association.** ⊕ *www.atlanticcanadacruise.com.* **Cruise Halifax.** ☎ *902/426-8222* ⊕ *www.cruisehalifax.ca.* **Cruise Newfoundland and Labrador.** ☎ *709/738-7530* ⊕ *www.cruisenewfoundland.com.* **Cruise Saint John.** ⊕ *www.cruisesaintjohn.com.* **Historic Charlottetown Seaport.com.** ⊕ *www.historiccharlottetownseaport.com.* **Lindblad Expeditions.** ☎ *800/397-3348* ⊕ *www.expeditions.com.* **Port of Sydney.** ☎ *902/564-0800* ⊕ *portofsydney.ca.*

TRAIN TRAVEL

VIA Rail, Canada's Amtrak counterpart, provides rail service to Atlantic Canada, but it's limited to an overnight Montréal-to-Halifax trip, called The Ocean, which runs three times per week. The train stops in a dozen Nova Scotian and New Brunswick communities along the way, among them Truro, Amherst, Moncton, and Miramichi. There are three service classes: Economy Class, featuring an upright seat with foot- and head-rest, is the least expensive; Sleeper Class, with a bedroom cabin, is the middle-of-the-road option; and Sleeper Plus is an upgraded version of the latter that includes preboarding privileges, cabin accommodations, meals, year-round access to the panoramic Park Car, and complimentary educational activities in peak season (mid-June to mid-October). You can expect to pay more than double for accommodations in Sleeper Plus over seats in Economy Class.

Information **VIA Rail Canada.** ☎ *888/842-7245* ⊕ *www.viarail.ca.*

ESSENTIALS

ACCOMMODATIONS

In Atlantic Canadian cities, you may choose between luxury hotels (whether business-class or boutique-y), moderately priced modern properties, and older ones with fewer conveniences but more charm. Options in smaller towns and in the countryside include large full-service resorts, small privately owned inns, bed-and-breakfasts, and a diminishing number of roadside motels.

Accommodations will generally cost more in summer than at other times (except in places, such as ski resorts, where winter is high season) and should be booked well in advance for peak periods. A special event or festival that coincides with your visit might fill every room for miles around. Inquire about special deals and packages when making reservations. Big-city hotels that cater to business travelers often offer weekend packages. Discounts are common when you book for a week or longer, and many urban hotels offer rooms at up to 40% off in winter.

The lodgings we list are the cream of the crop in each price range. Properties are assigned a price category based on the lowest nightly rack rate for a standard double room in high season (excluding holidays). When budgeting, be sure to check which hotel facilities or amenities are included in the rate and which qualify as add-ons.

It's worth noting that most hotels allow children under a certain age to stay in their parents' room at no additional cost, yet some charge for them as extra adults; also ask about the cut-off age for discounts if you're traveling as a family.

Most hotels and other lodgings require your credit-card details before they will confirm your reservation. Whether you provide these online or over the phone, get confirmation in writing and have a copy of it handy when you check in.

Be sure you understand the hotel's cancellation policy. Some places allow you to cancel without any kind of penalty—even if you prepaid to secure a discounted rate—if you cancel at least 24 hours in advance. Others require you to cancel a week in advance or penalize you the cost of one night. Small inns and B&Bs are most likely to require you to cancel far in advance.

APARTMENT AND HOUSE RENTALS

Rental cottages are common in the Atlantic provinces, especially Nova Scotia and Prince Edward Island. Many of them are privately owned but only used by the family for a few weeks each summer. That leaves week after week available for rental potential, with most owners leaving the booking to an online agency or enterprising neighbor. Start your house hunting by visiting reliable commercial websites or search under "Where to Stay" at the official provincial tourism websites *(See individual chapters)*.

Information **Atlantic Canada Vacation Rentals.** *www.atlanticcanada.worldweb.com.* **HomeAway.** *www.homeaway.com.*

BED-AND-BREAKFASTS AND INNS

Staying in smaller, more intimate spots is a wonderful way to meet people who are passionate about their communities and well versed in local events and history. Inns and B&Bs are both prevalent in Nova Scotia, particularly in the Annapolis Valley and the South Shore, where you can stay in the magnificent homes once occupied by shipbuilders, politicians, and other esteemed citizens. Prince Edward Island and New Brunswick also have a number of stately lodgings.

Information **B&B Canada.** *www.bbcanada.com.* **The Inns of Distinction of Prince Edward Island.** *www.innsofpei.com.* **Nova Scotia Bed & Breakfast Guide.** *www.*

nsbedandbreakfast.com. **Select Inns of Atlantic Canada.** ⊕ *www.selectinns.ca.* **Unique Country Inns.** ⊕ *www.uniquecountryinns.com.*

HOTELS

Although Canada doesn't have a national government-run system for rating hotels, many have joined the voluntary Canada Select program, which assigns member properties one to five stars based on strict criteria. Most hotel rooms have air-conditioning, private baths with tubs and showers, and two double beds; *all those we list have air-conditioning and private bath unless otherwise noted.*

Information Canada Select. ☎ *506/458-1995 in New Brunswick, 709/722-3133 in Newfoundland and Labrador, 902/406-4747 in Nova Scotia, 902/566-3501 in PEI* ⊕ *www.canadaselect.com.*

COMMUNICATIONS

INTERNET

Getting online in Atlantic Canada isn't a problem. Most hotels—as well as many inns and B&Bs—provide either a public computer, in-room broadband connections, or wireless capabilities to guests, although some only offer the last of these in the lobby or other common areas. It's also increasingly easy to find a coffee shop where you can surf while you sip, especially now that the ubiquitous Tim Hortons chain has introduced free Wi-Fi at countless outlets (to locate the closest one, click ⊕ *www.timhortons.com/ca/en/tools/wifi.html*). Airports and ferry terminals have also jumped on the wireless bandwagon, offering travelers an option for computer time while they wait for their next flight or boat ride.

PHONES

Phone numbers in Atlantic Canada have a three-digit area code followed by a seven-digit local number. The area codes are: 506 in New Brunswick, 709 in Newfoundland and Labrador, and, as of 2014, 902 and 782 in Prince Edward Island and Nova Scotia. Note that in the PEI and Nova Scotia, 10-digit dialing is now required: in other words, you must include the area code even when calling within the same community. Note that if you are placing a long-distance call—whether within a province, to another province, or to the United States—you must dial 1 first. If you're phoning another country, ⊕ *www.howtocallabroad.com* can guide you through the process.

LAND LINES

Calling from a hotel phone is almost always the most expensive option as lodgings usually add huge surcharges to all calls, particularly international ones. Calling cards help keep costs down but only if you purchase them locally. (They're readily available at grocery and drug stores as well as some convenience stores and gas stations.) Pay phones, which cost C50¢ per call, are still quite common in airports, bus depots, and other such venues. They can be used to make long-distance calls either by phoning the operator ("0") to reverse the charges, by depositing coins to pay for the first minute of talk, or by using credit or phone cards (some pay phones, especially in airports, are equipped to handle cards directly).

MOBILE PHONES

If you have a multiband phone (some countries use different frequencies from what's used in the United States) and your service provider uses the world-standard GSM network (as do AT&T and Verizon), you can probably use your phone abroad. Long-distance charges, however, can be steep—ditto for roaming fees (C$1 a minute is considered reasonable).

The good news is that there are several strategies for minimizing costs. If you're on a short trip, expect to call home frequently, or just want the convenience of keeping your usual cell number, simply request that your service provider temporarily add Canadian access to your existing plan before you cross the border. If you're mainly interested in making calls inside the region, save one of your old mobile phones (or buy a cheap one online), ask your provider to unlock it, and take it with you as a travel phone, buying a new SIM card with pay-as-you-go service in each destination. This way you'll have a local number and will be able to take advantage of low local rates when making local calls. Renting a travel phone before you go through Cellular Abroad or Mobal and then installing a Canadian SIM card will achieve the same end.

However you proceed, bear in mind that it's typically cheaper to send a text message than to make a phone call, as text messages have a very low set fee (often less than C5¢).

TIP→ If you are carrying a laptop, tablet, or smartphone, downloading Skype software (*www.skype.com*) will enable you to make no- or low-cost calls anywhere in the world via the Internet.

Contacts Cellular Abroad. *800/287-5072 www.cellularabroad.com.* **Mobal.** *888/888-9162 www.mobal.com.*

CUSTOMS AND DUTIES

You're always allowed to bring goods of a certain value back home without having to pay any duty or import tax, but there's a limit on the amount of duty-free tobacco and liquor you can return with, and some countries have separate limits for perfumes. For exact figures, check with your customs department. The values of so-called duty-free goods are included in these amounts. When you shop abroad, save all your receipts, as customs inspectors may ask to see them as well as the items you purchased. If the total value of your goods is more than the duty-free limit, you'll have to pay a tax (most often a flat percentage) on the value of everything beyond that limit.

U.S. Customs and Immigration has preclearance services at international airports in Halifax, as well as Montréal, Toronto, Ottawa, Winnipeg, Calgary, Edmonton, Vancouver, and Victoria.

American and British visitors may bring the following items into Canada duty-free: 200 cigarettes, 50 cigars, and 200 grams (7 ounces) of tobacco; 1.14 liters (40 imperial ounces) of liquor, 1.5 liters (53 imperial ounces) of wine, or 24 355-milliliter (12-ounce) bottles or cans of beer for personal consumption. Any alcohol and tobacco products in excess of these amounts are subject to duty, provincial fees, and taxes. You can also bring in gifts valued at C$60 or less without paying duty. Neither alcohol nor tobacco products qualify as gifts, and all gifts—regardless of their value—must be declared.

Cats and dogs must have a certificate issued by a licensed veterinarian that clearly identifies the animal and certifies that it has been vaccinated against rabies during the preceding 36 months. Guide dogs are allowed into Canada without restriction. Plant material must be declared and inspected, as there may be restrictions on some live plants, bulbs, and seeds. Although there are certain restrictions or prohibitions on some fruits and vegetables, visitors may bring food with them for their own use, providing the quantity is consistent with the duration of the visit.

Canada's firearms laws are significantly stricter than those in the United States. Only sporting rifles and shotguns may be imported, provided they are to be used for sporting, hunting, or competition while in the country. All firearms must be declared to Canadian Customs at the first point of entry. Failure to declare firearms will result in their seizure, and criminal charges may be laid. Regulations require visitors to have a confirmed "Non-Resident Firearms Declaration" to bring any guns into Canada; a fee of C$25 applies, and the declaration (which acts like a temporary license) is valid for 60 days. For more information, contact the Canadian Firearms Program.

Information in Canada Canada Border Services Agency. *800/461-9999 within Canada, 506/636-5064 outside Canada www.*

cbsa.gc.ca. **Canadian Firearms Program.** *800/731-4000 www.rcmp-grc.gc.ca.*

Information in the United States
U.S. Customs and Border Protection. *877/227-5511 within the U.S., 202/325-8000 outside the U.S. www.cbp.gov.*

EATING OUT

The Atlantic provinces are a preferred destination for seafood lovers. Excellent fish and shellfish are available in all types of dining establishments. *The restaurants we list are the top picks in each price category.*

MEALS AND MEALTIMES

Unless otherwise noted, the restaurants listed are open daily for lunch and dinner. Pubs generally serve food all day and into the wee hours of the night. The dinner meal at restaurants usually begins around 5 pm with seating through 9 or 10 pm.

RESERVATIONS AND DRESS

Regardless of where you are, it's a good idea to make a reservation if you can. We only mention them specifically when reservations are essential (in short, when there's no other way you'll ever get a table) or when they are not accepted. We mention dress only when men are required to wear a jacket or a jacket and tie.

SMOKING

Smoking in *all* indoor public places is prohibited in Atlantic Canada. Smoking in private vehicles is also banned when children are present (the age limit is 16 in New Brunswick and in Newfoundland and Labrador, 19 in Nova Scotia and PEI).

WINES, BEER, AND SPIRITS

Locally produced wines, ranging from young table wines to excellent vintages, are offered in most licensed restaurants and are well worth trying. Provincially owned liquor stores, as well as private outlets, are operated in Atlantic Canada. Stores selling alcohol are permitted to be open on Sundays (typically from noon or 1 until 5 pm). But provinces like Prince Edward Island allow certain outlets to open on that day in peak months only. Sundays aside, most liquor stores open at 10 am and close at 9 or 10 pm. For a list of government-operated stores (including private "agents" who sell beer through convenience stores in Newfoundland and Labrador), check out the website for each province.

ELECTRICITY

Canada uses the same voltage as the United States, so all your electronics should make the transition without any fuss at all. There's no need for adapters.

EMERGENCIES

The U.S. embassy—like all other foreign embassies—is in Ottawa, Ontario (the nation's capital). There are also seven U.S. consulates in Canada, including one in Halifax.

Foreign Consulates **U.S. Consulate.** *Purdy's Wharf Tower II, 1969 Upper Water St., Suite 904, Halifax 902/429-2480 halifax.usconsulate.gov.* **U.S. Embassy.** *490 Sussex Dr., Ottawa 613/688-5335 canada.usembassy.gov.*

HOURS OF OPERATION

Most banks are open Monday through Friday from 10 am to 5 or 6 pm and have automatic teller machines (ATMs) that are accessible around the clock. All banks are closed on national holidays.

Hours at museums vary, but most open at 10 or 11 and close in the evening. Many are closed on Monday; some stay open late one day a week, and admission is sometimes waived during that period. Stores are usually open Monday through Saturday from 10 to 6, and Sunday from noon to 5; many extend their hours on Thursday and Friday, remaining open until 9. In major cities supermarkets are generally open from 7:30 am to 11 pm, although some operate 24 hours a day. Drugstores in major cities are often open until midnight, and convenience stores tend to be open until at least that time every day.

Canadian national holidays are as follows: New Year's Day (January 1), Good Friday (late March or early April), Easter Monday (the Monday after Good Friday), Victoria Day (the first Monday preceding May 25), Canada Day (July 1), Labour Day (the first Monday in September), Thanksgiving (the second Monday in October), Remembrance Day (November 11), Christmas Day (December 25), and Boxing Day (December 26).

New Brunswick, much of Nova Scotia, and parts of PEI recognize the first Monday in August as a holiday, while Newfoundlanders and Labradorians, who love any excuse to party, also celebrate St. Patrick's Day (March 17), St. George's Day (April 23), Discovery Day (the Monday nearest to June 24), and Orangemen's Day (July 12).

MONEY

ATMS AND BANKS

Your own bank will probably charge a fee for using ATMs abroad; the foreign bank you use may also charge a fee. Nevertheless, you'll usually get a better rate of exchange at an ATM than you will at a currency-exchange office or even when changing money in a bank. And extracting funds as you need them is a safer option than carrying around a large amount of cash. The easiest way to minimize transaction fees is by making withdrawals from ATMs affiliated with your home bank. Users of Cirrus or PLUS networks can locate them at *www.mastercard.com/atmlocator* and *www.visa.com/atms* respectively.

TIP→ PIN numbers with more than four digits are not recognized at ATMs in many countries. If yours has five or more, remember to change it before you leave.

Most banks, gas stations, malls, and convenience stores have ATMs that are accessible round the clock.

CREDIT CARDS

American visitors should note that in Canada, as in Europe, chip-and-pin cards are now widely used; however, most venues that accept credit cards are still equipped to process transactions by the traditional swipe-and-sign method as well. It's a good idea to inform your credit-card company before you leave home. Otherwise, it might put a hold on your card owing to unusual activity—not a good thing halfway through your trip. Record all your credit-card numbers—along with the phone numbers to call if your cards are lost or stolen—in a safe place, so you're prepared should something go wrong. Both MasterCard and Visa have general numbers you can call if your card is lost, but you're better off phoning the number of your issuing bank, as MasterCard and Visa usually just transfer you to your bank anyway.

If you plan to use your credit card for cash advances, you'll need to apply for a PIN at least two weeks before your trip. Although it's usually cheaper (and safer) to use a credit card abroad for large purchases (so you can cancel payments or be reimbursed if there's a problem), note that some credit-card companies *and* the banks that issue them add substantial percentages to all foreign transactions, whether they're in a foreign currency or not. Check on these fees before leaving home, so there won't be any surprises when you get the bill.

TIP→ Before you charge something, ask the merchant whether or not he or she plans to do a dynamic currency conversion (DCC). In such a transaction the credit-card processor (shop, restaurant, or hotel, not Visa or MasterCard) converts the purchase price, charging you in your home currency rather than the local one. In most cases you'll pay the merchant a 3% fee for this service in addition to any credit-card company and issuing-bank foreign-transaction surcharges.

Reporting Lost Cards American Express. *800/528-4800 within the U.S. or Canada* *www.americanexpress.com.* **MasterCard.** *800/627-8372 within the U.S. or Canada www.mastercard.com.* **Visa.** *800/847-2911 within the U.S. or Canada www.visa.com.*

CURRENCY AND EXCHANGE

Unless otherwise stated, all prices are given in Canadian dollars.

U.S. dollars are accepted in much of Canada (especially in communities near the border), though you should expect to receive any change in Canadian currency. To get the most favorable exchange rate, convert at least some of your money into Canadian funds. Major U.S. credit cards are also accepted in most areas.

The units of currency in Canada are the Canadian dollar (C$) and the cent, in almost the same denominations as U.S. currency ($5, $10, $20, 5¢, 10¢, 25¢, etc.). Note that C$1 and C$2 coins are used in Canada instead of bills (these are known as a "loonie," because of the loon that appears on the coin, and a "toonie," respectively). The Royal Canadian Mint stopped distributing pennies in 2013; however, you will still find some in circulation. When prices include pennies (i.e., $9.99), the amount is rounded up or down at the cash register.

Prices are given for adults. Substantially reduced fees are almost always available for children, students, and senior citizens.

PASSPORTS AND VISAS

Citizens of the United States need a passport or other WHTI-compliant document to reenter their country when returning by air from Canada. Passports, passport cards, or other WHTI-compliant documents are also required for adults crossing the border by land or sea, though children under age 16 may continue to do so using only a U.S. birth certificate. Check with U.S Customs and Border Protection (*www.cbp.gov*) for full details.

Anyone under 18 who is either traveling alone or with only one parent should carry a signed and dated letter from both parents or from all legal guardians authorizing the trip. It's also a good idea to include a copy of the child's birth certificate, custody documents (if applicable), and death certificates of one or both parents (if applicable). Be aware that most airlines do not allow children under age five to travel independently. Air Canada is particularly strict: children must be at least eight years of age to fly unaccompanied and can only travel on nonstop flights. Citizens of the United States, United Kingdom, Australia, and New Zealand do not need visas to enter Canada for a period of six months or fewer. Visitors from numerous other countries are also exempt: see Citizenship and Immigration Canada's website (*www.cic.gc.ca*) for a complete list.

TAXES

A goods and services tax (GST) of 5% applies on virtually every transaction in Canada except for the purchase of basic groceries. Newfoundland and Labrador and New Brunswick have a 13% single harmonized sales tax (HST), which combines the GST and the provincial sales tax. In PEI it is 14%, and in Nova Scotia it is 15%.

Information Canada Customs and Revenue Agency. *800/267-6999 within Canada and the U.S. www.ccra-adrc.gc.ca.*

TIME

New Brunswick, Nova Scotia, and Prince Edward Island are on Atlantic time, which is (during daylight saving time) three hours earlier than Greenwich mean time (GMT) and one hour later than eastern daylight time (EDT). Newfoundland and Labrador are on Newfoundland time, which is -2:30 GMT and +1:30 EDT.

TIPPING

Tips and service charges are not usually added to a bill in Canada. In general, tip 15% of the total bill (before tax). This goes for waiters and waitresses, barbers and hairdressers, and taxi drivers. Porters and doormen should get about C$2 a bag. For maid service, leave at least C$2 per person a day (C$3 in luxury hotels).

TOURS

SPECIAL-INTEREST TOURS

The companies listed offer multiday tours. *Additional operators that run different-length trips are listed in each chapter either in the Planner or with the specific community.*

ACTIVE ADVENTURES

Atlantic Canada Cycling. Bike junkets in all four Atlantic provinces are organized by Atlantic Canada Cycling. ☎ *888/800–2498* ⊕ *www.atlanticcanadacycling.com* ✉ *From C$804.*

Backroads. Backroads offers two-wheel trips all over the globe, including Nova Scotia's Lighthouse Route and the Bay of Fundy area. ☎ *510/527–1555, 800/462–2848* ⊕ *www.backroads.com* ✉ *From C$3,356.*

Coastal Adventures. This company has sea-kayaking options in Nova Scotia and Newfoundland based around themes such as icebergs and buried treasure. ☎ *902/772–2774, 877/404–2774* ⊕ *www.coastaladventures.com* ✉ *From C$595.*

Eastwind Cycle. Bespoke bike adventures are a specialty here. Personalized trips in Nova Scotia, New Brunswick, and PEI are available. ☎ *866/447–7468* ⊕ *www.eastwindcycle.com* ✉ *From C$1,500.*

Freewheeling Adventures. This outfit arranges Atlantic Canadian holidays for bikers, hikers, paddlers, and yoga enthusiasts; multisport offerings for families are organized, too. ☎ *902/857–3600, 800/672–0775* ⊕ *www.freewheeling.ca* ✉ *From C$980.*

Fresh Air Adventure. Fresh Air Adventure focuses on sea-kayaking trips in New Brunswick's fabled Bay of Fundy biosphere. ☎ *506/887–2249, 800/545–0020* ⊕ *www.freshairadventure.com* ✉ *From C$398.*

Pedal & Sea Adventures. Pedal & Sea specializes in guided and self-guided bike tours in Eastern Canada. ☎ *877/777–5699* ⊕ *www.pedalandseaadventures.com* ✉ *From C$1,249.*

CULTURAL AND CULINARY TOURS

Atlantic Tours. A broad selection of escorted bus tours and independent driving itineraries are available from this Grayline affiliate. ☎ *902/423–7172, 800/565–7173* ⊕ *www.atlantictours.com* ✉ *From C$206.*

Maxxim Vacations. The guided and self-guided trips that Maxxim Vacations runs throughout the region typically serve up a hefty dose of history and culture. ☎ *709/754–6666, 800/567–6666* ⊕ *www.maxximvacations.com* ✉ *From C$1,019.*

Nova Scotia Seafood Cooking School. Trout Point Lodge offers highly regarded culinary vacations for visitors who want to learn how to prepare local delicacies themselves. ☎ *902/761–2142* ⊕ *www.troutpoint.com* ✉ *From C$899.*

Vision Atlantic Vacations. This company offers standard tours along with more specialized options: including a 16-night itinerary that showcases Newfoundland's lighthouses and legends. Gourmets will also appreciate the multiday food-focused trips, which might include visits to wineries, lobster pounds, apple orchards, and maple sugar farms. ☎ *877/847–4660* ⊕ *www.visionatlanticvacations.com* ✉ *From C$839.*

FISHING

Big Intervale Fishing Lodge. Packages put together by the Big Intervale Fishing Lodge lure anglers to Cape Breton's Margaree, a Canadian Heritage River. ☎ *902/248–2275* ⊕ *bigintervalelodge.com* ✉ *From C$780 for 2 guests.*

Tuckamore Lodge. Newfoundland's Tuckamore Lodge schedules fresh- and saltwater fly-fishing trips, including ones for women only. ☎ *888/865–6361* ⊕ *www.flyfishing-tuckamore.com* ✉ *From $C2,299.*

GOLF

Golf Coastal Canada. Golf is a popular pastime here, and Golf Coastal Canada's umbrella website connects you to provincial associations regionwide. Follow the links for information on 300-plus courses as well as stay-and-play packages ⊕ *golfcoastalcanada.ca* ✉ *From $159.*

VISITOR INFORMATION

Provincial tourism offices are an invaluable source of information. Parks Canada (⊕ *www.pc.gc.ca*)—which oversees the country's National Parks, National Marine Conservation Areas, and National Historic sites—is another helpful resource.

INDEX

A

Aberdeen Cultural Centre, *162*
Acadia University Art Gallery, *79*
Acadian Coast (New Brunswick), *167–180*
Acadian culture, *52, 173*
Acadian Festival, *178–179*
Acadian Historical Village, *179*
Acadian Interpretive Centre and Museum, *71*
Acadian Museum, *163*
Acadian Museum of Prince Edward Island, *241*
Admiral Digby Museum, *73*
Adventure tours, *332*
New Brunswick, 150
Newfoundland and Labrador, 256, 299
Novia Scotia, 65, 73, 99
Prince Edward Island, 235
Advocate Harbour, *93*
Age of Sail Heritage Museum, *93*
Air travel, *322–323*
New Brunswick, 128
Newfoundland and Labrador, 253
Nova Scotia, 29
Prince Edward Island, 204
Alexander Graham Bell National Historic Site, *114*
Alexander Keith's Nova Scotia Brewery, *39*
Algonquin Resort, The ⊡, *147*
Alma, *155*
Amherst, *92–93*
Amusement parks
New Brunswick, 160–161
Nova Scotia, 76
Prince Edward Island, 226–227
Andrew and Laura McCain Gallery, *183*
Anglican Cathedral of St. John the Baptist, *263*
Anna Leonowens Gallery, *39*
Anna Swan Museum, *90*
Annapolis Royal, *74–78*
Annapolis Royal Farmers' and Traders' Market, *76*
Annapolis Royal Historic Gardens, *76*
Annapolis Valley, *51–82*
Anne Murray Centre, *91*
Anne of Green Gables, *225–226, 227, 229–230*
Anne of Green Gables Museum at Silver Bush, *226, 229–230*
Antigonish, *86–87*
Apartment and house rentals, *326*
Aquarium and Marine Centre (Shippagan), *178*
Aquariums, *145, 178, 302*
Archelaus Smith Museum, *68*
Arches Provincial Park, *306*
Arichat, *121–122*
Art Gallery of Nova Scotia, *35*
Art Gallery of Nova Scotia (Western Branch), *69*
ATMs, *330*
Avalon Peninsula (Newfoundland and Labrador), *275–282*

B

Baddeck, *113–116*
Bailey House, The ⊡, *77*
Balmoral Grist Mill, *89*
Banks, *330*
Barrington and Cape Sable Island, *67–68*
Barrington museums, *68*
Basilica Cathedral of St. John the Baptist, *259, 261*
Basin Head Provincial Park, *236*
Basin Head Fisheries Museum, *236*
Battery, The (St. John's), *264*
Bauer Theatre, *86*
Beaches, *18*
New Brunswick, 143, 170, 172
Nova Scotia, 42, 64, 83, 85, 88, 97–98, 102, 109
Prince Edward Island, 221–222, 223–234, 230, 236, 245
Beaconsfield Historic House, *210–211*
Beothuk Interpretation Centre, *297*
Beaubears Island, *176*
Beaverbrook Art Gallery, *189*
Bed and breakfasts, *326–327*
Bicycling, *332*
New Brunswick, 132, 148
Nova Scotia, 58, 61, 88, 110
Prince Edward Island, 207, 223, 224, 229, 239, 243
Big and Little Tancook Islands, *55*
Big Pond, *121*
Bird-watching
New Brunswick, 131, 151, 170–171
Newfoundland and Labrador, 275, 276–277
Nova Scotia, 74, 79–80, 88, 92–93, 113
Prince Edward Island, 246
Bishop's Machine Shop, *241*
Bistro 22 ✕, *99*
Black Loyalist Heritage Site, *66*
Boardwalk (Charlottetown), *211*
Boat and ferry travel, *323*
New Brunswick, 128, 189
Newfoundland and Labrador, 253, 291, 304
Nova Scotia, 30
Prince Edward Island, 205
Boating and sailing
New Brunswick, 183
Newfoundland and Labrador, 287–288, 294, 299, 309, 310
Nova Scotia, 54, 58, 62, 67, 74, 88, 99, 107, 109, 110, 113–114
Prince Edward Island, 210, 218
Bonavista, *288–289*
Bonavista Social Club ✕, *289*
Bonne Bay Marine Station, *302*
Books about Nova Scotia, *314*
Bouctouche, *174–175*
Bowring Park, *266*
Boyd's Cove, *297*
Brackley Beach, *221, 223–234*
Brier Island, *73–74*
Brier Island Whale and Seabird Cruises, *74*
Brigus, *279*
Brigus South, *277*
Brudenell River Provincial Park, *234*
Brule Fossil Centre, *90*
Bus travel, *323*
New Brunswick, 130
Nova Scotia, 29–30
Prince Edward Island, 204
Business hours, *329–330*

C

Cabot Beach Provincial Park, *230*
Cabot Links, *104*
Cabot Tower, *266*
Cabot Trail, *18*
Cabot's Landing Provincial Park, *109*

Campobello Island, *152–153*
Canadian Museum of Immigration at Pier 21, *35–36*
Canadian Potato Museum, *243*
Canoeing, *47, 142, 194, 224*
Cape Bonavista Lighthouse, *288*
Cape Breton Centre for Craft and Design, The, *119*
Cape Breton Highlands National Park, *107–108*
Cape Breton Island (Nova Scotia), *100–122*
Cape Breton Miners' Museum, *117*
Cape Chignecto, *93–95*
Cape Chignecto Provincial Park, *94*
Cape d'Or, *93–95*
Cape Enrage, *157–159*
Cape Forchu Lighthouse, *69*
Cape Jourimain Nature Centre, *171*
Cape North, *109–110*
Cape Race Lighthouse, *278*
Cape Sable Island, *67–68*
Cape St. Mary's Ecological Reserve, *282*
Cape Shore, *281*
Cape Smokey Provincial Park, *110*
Cape Spear Lighthouse, *264*
Cape Spear National Historic Site, *264*
Car travel, *18, 323–325*
New Brunswick, 130
Newfoundland and Labrador, 253–254
Nova Scotia, 30
Prince Edward Island, 204
Caraquet, *178–180*
Carleton Martello Tower, *137–138*
Carriage House Inn ⊡, *193*
Casinos
New Brunswick, 165
Nova Scotia, 47, 118
Prince Edward Island, 212
Castle Hill National Historic Site, *281*
Cavendish, *225–229*
Cavendish Beach, *222*
Central Coastal Drive (Prince Edward Island), *18, 220–233*
Celtic Colours International Festival, *28*
Celtic Music Interpretive Centre, *101*
Central Newfoundland, *291–299*
CFB Gagetown Military Museum, *196*
Change Islands, *293–296*
Charlotte County Courthouse and Old Gaol, *146*
Charlotte Lane Café ✕, *67*
Charlottetown (Prince Edward Island), *207–219*
Cherry Brook Zoo, *134*
Chester, *55–56*
Chéticamp, *105–107*
Children, attractions for, *22*
Chinched Bistro ✕, *268*
Chocolate Museum, *145*
Christ Church Cathedral, *190*
Christina Parker Gallery, *266*
Church Point (Point de l'Eglise), *70–72*
Churches
New Brunswick, 138, 146, 178, 190
Newfoundland and Labrador, 259, 261, 262, 263
Nova Scotia, 41, 71, 72
Prince Edward Island, 212, 230
Circular Road (St. John's), *263*
Clam digging, *235*
Clarenville, *283–284*
Climate, *14*
Cobequid Interpretation Centre, *97*
Codroy Valley, *311*
Colony of Avalon (archaeological dig), *277*
Commissariat House, *263*
Confederation Bridge, *231*
Confederation Centre of the Arts, *211*
Confederation Landing Park, *212*
Confederation Trail, *229*
Connell House, *186*
Corner Brook, *309–310*
Cossit House, *117*
Costs, *10*
Covered bridges, *184–185*
Crafts, *50*
Creamery Museum, *90*
Credit cards, *10, 330–331*
Cruise travel, *325*
Cuisine, *20*
New Brunswick, 141
Nova Scotia, 43
Prince Edward Island, 215
Cultural and culinary tours, *332*
Cupids, *279–280*
Cupids Legacy Centre & Museum, *280*
Currency and exchange, *331*
Customs and duties, *328–329*

D

Darnley Beach, *230*
Deadman's Island, *39*
Deer Island, *151–152*
Deer Lake, *299–300*
Deer Point, *151*
DeGarthe Memorial, *54*
Delta Beauséjour ⊡, *165*
Delta Fredericton Hotel ⊡, *193*
DesBrisay Museum, *62*
Dieppe, *159–167*
Digby, *72–73*
Dining, *10, 329.* ⇨*See also* under cities and provinces
Discounts and deals, *30*
Discovery Centre (Gros Morne National Park), *302*
Discovery Centre (Halifax), *39–40*
Discovery Trail, *283–284*
Domaine de Grand Pré (winery), *78*
Dominion Park, *137*
Dorchester, *167–170*
Downtown Fredericton Culture Crawl, *191*
Drives, *18*
Duckworth Street (St. John's), *261–262*
Duties, *328–329*

E

East Coast Bistro ✕, *139*
East Coast Trail, *272*
East Coast Trail Association, *254*
East Point Lighthouse, *238*
Eastern Edge Gallery, *266*
Eastern Newfoundland, *282–291*
Eastern Shore (Nova Scotia), *82–100*
Eastport Peninsula, *285*
Edmundston, *180–181*
Église Ste-Marie (St. Mary's Church; Nova Scotia), *71*
Electricity, *329*
Emergencies, *329*
and car travel, 324
Emma Butler Gallery, *266*
Eptek Arts and Culture Centre, *241*

F

Fairholm National Historic Inn and Carriage House 🏨, *216*
Fairview Lawn Cemetery, *40*
Ferry service. ⇨ *See* Boat and ferry travel
Ferryland, *277–278*
Ferryland Lighthouse, *277–278*
Festivals and seasonal events
New Brunswick, 127, 178–179
Newfoundland and Labrador, 251–252, 259, 267, 302, 305
Nova Scotia, 27–29, 55, 72, 88, 95–96, 103
Prince Edward Island, 203–204, 212, 239, 240
Fisheries Museum of the Atlantic, *59–60*
Fishers' Loft Inn 🏨, *287*
Fishing, *18, 332–333*
Nova Scotia, 61, 105
Prince Edward Island, 218, 223, 231, 235, 246
Five Islands, *97–98*
Five Islands Provincial Park, *97–98*
Fleur de Sel ✕, *60*
Florenceville-Bristol, *183–184*
Fodor, Eugene, *10*
Fogo Island, *293–296*
Fogo Island Inn 🏨, *296*
Foire Brayonne, *127*
Fort Anne National Historic Site, *76*
Fort Beauséjour National Historic Site, *170*
Fort Point Lighthouse Park, *63*
Fortress of Louisbourg National Historic Site, *19, 119–120*
Founders' Hall-Canada's Birthplace Pavilion, *211*
Fredericton (New Brunswick), *188–197*
Fredericton Boyce Farmers' Market, *190–191*
Fredericton Region Museum, *191*
French vocabulary, *315–320*
Fresh Fine Dining ✕, *184*
Fundy Coast (New Brunswick), *143–167*
Fundy Geological Museum, *95*
Fundy National Park, *154–156*
Fundy Trail Parkway, *154*

G

Gaelic College of Celtic Arts and Crafts, *111–112*
Gagetown, *196*
Gallery 78, *191*
Gampo Abbey, *108–109*
Gander, *292–293*
Gardens
New Brunswick, 131, 145, 181
Newfoundland and Labrador, 266–267
Nova Scotia, 40, 76, 79
Prince Edward Island, 225
Gardens of Hope, *225*
Georgetown, *234–235*
Golf, *333*
New Brunswick, 132, 148, 156, 166, 194
Nova Scotia, 49, 104, 107, 111, 115
Prince Edward Island, 218, 223, 228, 235, 239, 243–244
Gorge Walk, *182*
Government House (Fredericton), *191*
Government House (St. John's), *262*
Gower Street United Church, *262*
Grand Bank, *289–290*
Grand Falls (New Brunswick), *182–183*
Grand Falls Museum, *182*
Grand Manan Island, *149–151*
Grand Pré National Historic Site, *78–79*
Grates Cove, *280–281*
Great George, The 🏨, *216*
Greater St. John's, *264–274*
Green Gables, *225–226*
Green Gardens Trail, *302–303*
Greenock Church, *146*
Greenwich (P.E.I. National Park), *238*
Greenwich Beach, *222*
Grenfell Historic Properties, *308*
Gros Morne Mountain, *303*
Gros Morne National Park, *19, 302–306*
Gros Morne Visitor's Centre, *303*

H

Haliburton House Museum, *81*
Halifax (Nova Scotia), *33–51*
Halifax Citadel National Historic Site, *36–38*
Halifax International Busker Festival, *28*
Halifax Seaport Farmers' Market, *40, 51*
Halifax Waterfront Boardwalk, *38*
Hall's Harbour, *79*
Hall's Harbour Lobster Pound & Restaurant, *79*
Handworks Gallery, *138*
Harbour Grace, *280–281*
Harbourside Park, *262*
Harriet Irving Botanical Gardens, *79*
Hartland, *184–185*
Harvest Jazz and Blues Festival, *127*
Hawke Hills, *278*
Hawthorne Cottage, *279*
Hector Heritage Quay, *88*
Herring Cove Art Gallery and Studio, *294*
Herring Cove Provincial Park, *152*
Highland Village Museum, *19, 116*
Hiking and walking
New Brunswick, 135, 142, 195
Newfoundland and Labrador, 254, 259, 271, 286, 294, 295, 302–303
Nova Scotia, 36, 49, 81, 87, 88, 91, 97, 104, 116, 119, 121
Prince Edward Island, 209, 246
Hilton Saint John 🏨, *140*
Historic Garrison District (Fredericton), *189*
Historic Properties (Halifax), *38*
Historical Association of Annapolis Royal, *75*
Hopewell Cape, *157–159*
Horse racing, *212*
Horseback riding, *49, 97, 158*
Hotel Paulin 🏨, *179*
Hotels, *10, 327.* ⇨ *See also* under cities and provinces
prices, 33, 131, 206, 255
House rentals, *326*
Houses and buildings, historic
New Brunswick, 138, 168, 186–187, 189–190, 191
Newfoundland and Labrador, 263, 279, 286, 289, 294–295
Nova Scotia, 66–67, 68, 81, 82, 96, 117, 121
Prince Edward Island, 210–211, 225–226, 227, 229–230, 241
Huntsman Fundy Discovery Aquarium, *145*

I

Icebergs, *275, 299*
Île Miscou, *178*
Imperial Theatre, *141*
Ingonish, *110–111*
Inn at St. Peters, The ⊡, *239*
Inns, *326–327*
International Fox Museum and Hall of Fame, *242*
Internet, *327*
Irish Loop, *277*
Ironworks Distillery, *62*
Irving Eco-Centre: La Dune de Bouctouche (coastal ecosystem), *174*
Irving Nature Park, *134, 136, 137*
Isaac's Way ✕, *192*

J

J.T. Cheeseman Provincial Park, *312*
Java Jack's Restaurant and Gallery ✕, *304*
Jeremiah's ✕, *185*
Joggins Fossil Center, *92*
Johnson GEO Centre, *264*
Jost Vineyards, *89–90*
Judique, *101*

K

Kayaking, *332*
New Brunswick, 131, 132, 142, 148, 150, 152, 156, 158, 194
Newfoundland and Labrador, 273, 306
Nova Scotia, 49–50, 73, 95, 110, 112, 114
Prince Edward Island, 207, 224, 229, 231, 232, 235
Keillor House Museum, *168*
Kejimkujik National Park and Historic Site, *19, 64–65*
Kejimkujik National Park-Seaside, *63*
King Street (Saint John), *138*
Kings Landing Historical Settlement, *19, 186–187*
King's Square (Saint John), *138*
Kingsbrae Arms ⊡, *147*
Kingsbrae Garden, *145*
Kouchibouguac National Park, *19, 175–176*

L

La Cuisine Robicheau ✕, *71–72*
La Fine Grobe Sure Mer ✕, *179*
La Manche, *277*
Labrador. ⇨ *See* Newfoundland and Labrador
Language, *21, 271, 315–320*
L'Anse aux Meadows National Historic Site, *19, 306–308*
Le Caberstan (ferry), *291*
Le Pays de la Sagouine, *174–175*
LeNoir Forge Museum, *122*
Lepreau Falls Provincial Park, *142–143*
Les Trois Pignons Cultural Center, *106*
Lexicon Books, *62*
Leyton Gallery of Fine Art, The, *264*
Lighthouses, *20*
Newfoundland and Labrador, 264, 277–278, 288, 297–298, 303
Nova Scotia, 63, 68, 69
Prince Edward Island, 238, 244–245
Little Louis' ✕, *163–164*
Liverpool, *62–64*
Lobster Head Cove Lighthouse, *303*
Lodging, *10, 326–327.* ⇨ *See also* under cities and provinces
Long Island, *73–74*
Long Point Lighthouse, *297–298*
Long Range Mountains, *300*
Longest Covered Bridge, *184–185*
Louisbourg, *119–121*
Loyalist Burial Ground, *136*
Loyalist House, *138*
Lucy Maud Montgomery Birthplace, *226*
Lunenburg, *59–62*
Lutz Mountain Heritage Museum, *163*

M

Mabou, *101–104*
Mabou Highlands, *104*
Mactaquac Provincial Park, *187–188*
Maddox Cove and Petty Harbour, *265*
Magic Mountain Water Park, *160–161*
Magnetic Hill, *161*
Magnetic Hill Zoo, *161*
Mahone Bay, *56–58*
Mahone Bay Museum, *57*
Mallard Cottage ✕, *269*
Malpeque, *229–231*
Marconi National Historic Site, *117*
Margaree Harbour, *104–105*
Margaree Salmon Museum, *105*
Margaret Fawcett Norrie Heritage Centre, *90*
Maritime Museum of the Atlantic, *38–39*
Market Square (Saint John), *136*
Marshlands Inn ⊡, *171*
Mary Celeste (ship), *95*
Mary E. Black Gallery, *40–41*
Marysville, *191*
Memorial University Botanical Garden, *266–267*
Memramcock, *167–170*
Menu guide, *318–320*
Mercantile Premises, *286*
Mermaid Theatre of Nova Scotia, *81–82*
Metepenagiag Heritage Park, *176*
Minas Basin, *95*
Ministers Island, *146*
Miquelon, *290–291*
Miramichi, *176–177*
Miscou Island, *178*
Mistaken Point Ecological Reserve, *278*
Mockbeggar Plantation, *289*
Moncton, *159–167*
Money matters, *10, 330–331*
Montgomery, Lucy Maud, *225–226, 227, 229–230*
Monument Lefebvre National Historic Site, *168*
Motorcycle travel, *205*
Mount Carleton Provincial Park, *182*
Movies about Nova Scotia, *314*
Museums and galleries, *19*
New Brunswick, 136, 137, 138, 145, 161, 162, 163, 168, 170, 182, 183–184, 186–187, 189, 191, 196, 197
Newfoundland and Labrador, 262–263, 264, 266, 279, 280, 286, 289, 290, 292, 294, 295, 298, 302, 303, 308
Nova Scotia, 35–41, 55, 57, 59–60, 62, 63, 66–67, 68, 69, 71, 73, 79, 81, 82, 86, 90, 91, 92, 93, 95, 96, 97, 101, 105, 106, 114, 116, 117, 122

Prince Edward Island, 210–211, 225–226, 227, 229–230, 234, 236, 238, 241–242, 243, 244, 245
Music
New Brunswick, 127, 193–194
Newfoundland and Labrador, 302, 305
Nova Scotia, 47, 88, 101, 103, 104, 115, 118–119
Prince Edward Island, 217–218, 232, 239, 242
Musique Saint-Bernard, *72*
Myriad View Artisan Distillery, *236*

N

Neddis Harbour Inn ☰, *305*
New Brunswick, *12, 124–197*
Acadian Coast, 167–180
children, attractions for, 22
cuisine, 141
dining and lodging, 131, 139–140, 146–148, 150, 151–152, 153, 154, 155, 158, 163–165, 168, 170, 172–174, 175, 177, 179, 181, 192–193, 197
festivals and seasonal events, 127, 178–179
Fredericton, 188–197
Fundy Coast, 143–167
itinerary recommendations, 129
nightlife and the arts, 141–142, 165–166, 191, 193–194
outdoor activities and sports, 142, 148–149, 151, 152, 156, 158–159, 166, 169, 170, 172, 179–180, 183, 184, 185, 186, 194–195
prices, 131
Saint John, 132–143
St. John River Valley, 180–188
shopping, 142–143, 149, 159, 166–167, 195–196, 197
timing the visit, 126–128
tours, 131–132, 135, 150, 152, 160, 189, 191
transportation, 128, 130
visitor information, 131–132
New Brunswick Botanical Garden, *181*
New Brunswick Museum, *136, 137*
New Glasgow Lobster Suppers ✕, *227*
New River Beach, *143*
Newfoundland and Labrador, *12, 248–312*
Avalon Peninsula, 275–282
Central Newfoundland and Notre Dame Bay, 291–299
children, attractions for, 22
dining and lodging, 255, 265, 267–271, 276, 279, 280, 281, 282, 284, 285, 286–287, 289, 290, 291, 293, 295–296, 298, 300, 303–305, 307–309, 310
Eastern Newfoundland, 282–291
festivals and seasonal events, 251–252, 259, 267, 302, 305
itinerary recommendations, 258, 261
language, 271
nightlife and the arts, 271–272, 287, 305
outdoor activities and sports, 254, 267, 272–273, 276–277, 287–288, 294, 295, 299, 302–303, 306, 309, 310, 312
prices, 255
St. John's, 257–274
shopping, 273–274, 284, 309, 310
time zone, 253
timing the visit, 251–243
tours, 256, 259, 261, 276–277, 294, 306, 309
transportation, 253–254
visitor information, 256
Western Newfoundland, 299–312
Newfoundland and Labrador Folk Festival, *252*
Newfoundland Emporium, *310*
Newfoundland Insectarium, *300*
Newfoundland Pony Sanctuary, *295*
Newman Wine Vaults, *263*
Nightlife and the arts. ⇨ *See* under cities and provinces
Norseman Restaurant ✕, *307*
Norstead, *307*
North Atlantic Aviation Museum, *292*
North Cape, *245–246*
North Cape Coastal Drive (Prince Edward Island), *239–246*
North Cape Wind Energy Interpretive Centre, *245*
Northern Nova Scotia, *82–100*
Notre Dame Bay, *291–299*
Nova Scotia, *12, 24–122*
Cape Breton Island, 100–122
children, attractions for, 22
cuisine, 43
dining and lodging, 32–33, 42–47, 54, 55–56, 57–58, 60–61, 64, 65, 67, 69–70, 71–72, 73, 74, 77, 80, 82, 85–87, 88, 90, 93, 94–95, 96, 99, 102–104, 105, 106–107, 107–111, 112, 114–115, 117–118, 120
discounts and deals, 30
Eastern Shore and Northern Nova Scotia, 82–100
festivals and seasonal events, 27–29, 55, 72, 88, 95–96, 103
Halifax, 33–51
itinerary recommendations, 31
nightlife and the arts, 47–48, 56, 77, 88, 97, 103, 104, 115, 118–119, 121
outdoor activities and sports, 30, 32, 48–50, 54, 58, 61–62, 64, 65, 67, 73, 74, 81, 85, 87, 88, 91, 95, 97, 99, 104, 105, 107, 110, 111, 112, 115, 119, 121
prices, 33
shopping, 50–51, 54, 56, 58, 62, 70, 77–78, 87, 89, 91, 99–100, 107, 112–113, 119
South Shore and Annapolis Valley, 51–82
timing the visit, 27–29
tours, 33, 34, 36, 58, 59, 65, 67, 74, 75, 88, 113–114, 116
transportation, 29–30
visitor information, 33
Nova Scotia Gem and Mineral Show, *95–96*
Nova Scotia Museum of Natural History, *41*

O

Old County Court House, *186*
Old Gaol (St. Andrews by-the-Sea), *146*
Old Home Week, *212*
Old Meeting House, *68*
Old Sow (whirlpool), *151*
Olde Shoppe Museum at Change Islands, *295*
O'Leary, *243–244*
Olivier Soapery, The, *175*
Ottawa House-by-the-Sea Museum, *96*

Outdoor activities and sports. ⇨ *See* under cities and provinces
Owens Art Gallery, *170*

P

P.E.I. National Park (Greenwich), *238*
Panmure Head Lighthouse, *238*
Parks, *19*
New Brunswick, 134, 136, 137, 142–143, 152–153, 154–156, 157–158, 162, 170–171, 172, 175–177, 179–180, 182, 187–188
Newfoundland and Labrador, 262, 266, 275–277, 278, 282, 284–285, 302–308, 312
Nova Scotia, 41, 63–65, 79–80, 82, 83, 85, 88, 94, 97–98, 102, 107–108, 109, 110, 114, 119
Prince Edward Island, 212–213, 221–223, 230, 234, 236, 238, 245, 246
Parlee Beach Provincial Park, *172*
Parrsboro, *95–97*
Parrsboro Rock and Mineral Shop and Museum, *96*
Partridge Island, *96*
Passports and visas, *331*
Peggy's Cove, *51, 54*
Peter Buckland Gallery, *138*
Petty Harbour, *265*
Pictou, *87–89*
Placentia, *281*
Plane travel. ⇨ *See* Air travel
Playhouse (theater), *194*
Pleasant Bay, *108–109*
Point de l'Eglise (Church Point), *70–72*
Point Pleasant Park, *41*
Points East Coastal Drive (Prince Edward Island), *233–239*
Port au Choix National Historic Site, *306*
Port au Port Peninsula, *311*
Port aux Basques, *311–312*
Port Bickerton Lighthouse Beach Park, *83, 85*
Port Royal National Historic Site, *75–76*
Potato World, *183–184*
Press Gang, The ✕, *45*
Prices
dining and lodging, 33, 131, 206, 255
New Brunswick, 131
Newfoundland and Labrador, 255
Nova Scotia, 33
Prince Edward Island, 206
Prime Berth Twillingate Fishery & Heritage Centre, *298*
Prince Edward Distillery, *236*
Prince Edward Island, *12, 200–246*
Central Coastal Drive, 18, 220–233
Charlottetown, 207–219
children, attractions for, 22
cuisine, 215
dining and lodging, 205–206, 213–217, 222–224, 227–228, 230–231, 232, 234, 237, 238–239, 242, 243, 245–246
festivals and seasonal events, 203–204, 212, 239, 240
itinerary recommendations, 208, 209
nightlife and the arts, 217–218, 224, 232, 235, 239, 242
North Cape Coastal Drive, 239–246
outdoor activities and sports, 218, 221–222, 223, 224, 228–229, 230, 231, 232, 235, 239, 243–244, 245, 246
Points East Coastal Drive, 233–239
prices, 206
shopping, 219, 224, 233
timing the visit, 203–204
tours, 206–207, 209–210, 218, 225, 241
transportation, 204–205
visitor information, 207
Prince Edward Island National Park, *19, 221–223*
Prince William Street (Saint John), *138*
Province House, *41*
Provinces, *15*
Provincial Legislature, *189–190*
Provincial Seamen's Museum, *290*

Q

Queens County Museum, *197*
Quidi Vidi, *265*
Quintal House 🏨, *296*

R

Random Passage, *288*
Raymonds ✕, *269*
Red Shoe ✕, *103*
Red Shores Racetrack and Casino, *212*
Rendez-vous de la Baie, *71*
Restaurants, *10, 329.* ⇨ *See also* under cities and provinces
prices, 33, 131, 206, 255
Resurgo Place, *161*
Reversing Rapids, *136, 137*
Richard's Fresh Seafood ✕, *222*
Rita's Tea Room, *121*
Ritchie Wharf Park, *177*
River Breeze Farm, *98*
River Valley Scenic Drive, *18*
Road to the Isles (Newfoundland), *18*
Robie Tufts Nature Center, *79–80*
Rockwood Park, *137*
Roma at Three Rivers, *234*
Rooms, The, *262–263*
Roosevelt Campobello International Park, *152–153*
Roots, Rants and Roars (festival), *252*
Rosedale Manor Bed & Breakfast 🏨, *281*
Ross Farm Living Museum of Agriculture, *55*
Rossignol Cultural Centre, *63*
Ross-Thomson House and Store, *66–67*
Route 100, *281*
Rowing, *267*
Royal St. John's Regatta, *267*
Rugged Beauty Boat Tours, *287–288*
Ryan Premises National Historic Site, *289*

S

Sackville, *170–171*
Sackville Waterfowl Park, *170–171*
Sailing. ⇨ *See* Boating and sailing
St. Andrews by-the-Sea, *143–149*
St. Ann's Bay, *111–113*
St. Anthony, *308–309*
St. Bernard Church, *72*
St. Dunstan's Basilica, *212*
Saint John (New Brunswick), *132–143*
Saint John Ale House ✕, *139*
Saint John City Market, *137*
St. John River Valley (New Brunswick), *180–188*

St. John's (Newfoundland), *257–274*
St. Martins, *153–154*
St. Mary's Church (Église Ste-Marie; Nova Scotia), *71*
St. Mary's Church (Prince Edward Island), *230*
St. Paul's Anglican Church (Halifax), *41*
St. Peter's Bay, *237–239*
St-Pierre, *290–291*
Sainte Famille Winery, *82*
Ste-Cécile Church, *178*
Salmonier Nature Park, *278*
Sandspit (amusement park), *226–227*
Savour in the Garden ✕, *147*
Scuba diving, *18*
New Brunswick, 131, 148
Newfoundland and Labrador, 272–273
Nova Scotia, 61
Seafood, *20*
Seal Island Light Museum, *68*
Seal watching, *62, 235*
Segway tours, *241*
Shediac, *172–174*
Shelburne, *66–67*
Shelburne Museum Complex, *66–67*
Shepody National Wildlife Area, *157–158*
Sherbrooke and Sherbrooke Village, *83, 85–86*
Shippagan, *177–178*
Shopping. ⇨ *See* under cities and provinces
Shubenacadie River Runners, *99*
Signal Hill National Historic Site, *265–266*
Silent Witness Memorial, *292–293*
Site of Lucy Maud Montgomery's Cavendish Home, *226, 227*
Skerwink Trail, *286*
Skiing, *179–180, 194–195, 310*
Souris, *235–237*
South Shore (Nova Scotia), *51–82*
Spinnakers' Landing (Summerside), *241*
Sports and outdoor activities. ⇨ *See* under cities and provinces
Springhill, *91*
Springhill Miners Museum, *91*
Squid Jiggers Trail, *295*
Stephenville, *311*
StFX Art Gallery, *86*
Stone Church, *138*
Stories ✕, *45*
Sugar Moon Farm Maple Products & Pancake House, *99–100*
Summerside, *240–243*
Summerside Lobster Festival, *240*
Sunrise Trail Museum, *90*
Surfing, *18, 64*
Sutherland Steam Mill Museum, *90*
Swan, Anna, *90*
Swimming, *50*
Swissair Memorial, *54*
Sydney, *116–1119*
Sydney Mines Heritage Museum and Cape Breton Fossil Centre, *117*
Symbols, *10*

T

Tablelands, *303*
Tait House 🏨, *174*
Tantramar Marsh, *92–93*
Tatamagouche, *89–91*
Taxes, *331*
Telephones, *327–328*
Television shows about Nova Scotia, *314*
Terra Nova National Park, *284–285*
Theater
New Brunswick, 141, 166, 189, 194
Newfoundland and Labrador, 271, 287, 302, 305
Nova Scotia, 47, 55, 77, 81–82, 86, 97, 104, 118–119, 121
Prince Edward Island, 217–218, 224, 232, 235, 239, 242
Thomas Raddall Provincial Park, *63–64*
Thorndyke Bed & Breakfast 🏨, *290*
Tidal Bore and Riverfront Park, *162*
Tilting National Historic Site, *294–295*
Time zones, *253, 331*
Timing the visit, *14*
Tipping, *332*
Titanic, *38*
Toose's Bijoux (shop), *149*
Tours and packages, *332–333*
Train travel, *325*
New Brunswick, 130
Nova Scotia, 30
Trinity, *285–288*
Trout Paint Lodge 🏨, *70*
Truro, *98–100*
Twillingate, *297–299*

U

Uniacke Estate Museum Park, *82*
Upper Clements Park (amusement park), *76*
Usige Bàn Falls Provincial Park, *114*

V

Valhalla Lodge Bed & Breakfast 🏨, *307–308*
Victoria, *231–233*
Victoria Park (Charlottetown), *212–213*
Victoria Park (Truro), *98*
Victoria Row (Charlottetown), *212*
Vikings, *307*
Village of Gagetown, *196–197*
Visas, *331*
Visitor information; *333*
Vocabulary, *315–320*

W

Wagmatcook Culture & Heritage Centre, *114*
Walking tours
New Brunswick, 135, 189
Nova Scotia, 59, 75, 97, 116
Prince Edward Island, 209
Water sports, *218, 229, 235*
Water Street (St. John's), *263*
Waterfalls, *142–143, 182*
Weather, *14*
West Mabou Beach Provincial Park, *102*
West Point, *244–245*
West Point Lighthouse Museum, *244*
Western Brook Pond, *303*
Western Counties Military Museum, *68*
Western Newfoundland, *299–312*
Whale Interpretive Centre, *109*
Whale watching
New Brunswick, 131, 148–149, 151
Newfoundland and Labrador, 273, 276–277, 288

Nova Scotia, *61–62*, *74*, *107*, *109*, *110*
Prince Edward Island, *246*
Windjammer ✕, *164*
Windsor (Nova Scotia), *81–82*
Windsor Hockey Heritage Centre, *81*
Wineries, *78*, *82*, *89–90*, *132*
Witless Bay Ecological Reserve, *275–277*
Wolfville, *78–81*
Wood Islands Lighthouse Museum and Interpretive Centre, *238*
Woodstock, *185–186*
Woolen Mill Museum, *68*
Wyatt House Museum, *241*

Y

Yarmouth, *68–70*
Yarmouth County Museum & Archives, *69*

Z

Zip-lining, *158–159*, *166*, *183*
Zoos, *134*, *161*

PHOTO CREDITS

Front cover: Jacques Laurent/Design Pics/Corbis [Description: Nova Scotia, Canada]. Back cover, from left to right: Elena Elisseeva / Shutterstock; ggw1962 / Shutterstock; Mighty Sequoia Studio / Shutterstock. Spine: Matthew Jacques / Shutterstock. 1, Willy Matheisl / age fotostock. 2, Barrett & MacKay / age fotostock. 4, Helen Filatova/Shutterstock. 5 (top), David P. Lewis/Shutterstock. 5 (bottom), Josef Hanus/Shutterstock. 6 (top left and top right), Tourism PEI / John Sylvester. 6 (bottom left), cworthy/iStockphoto. 6 (bottom right), Tourism PEI. 7 (top), Miles Ertman / age fotostock. 7 (bottom), Tourism PEI. 8 (top left), ImagineGolf/iStockphoto. 8 (top right), Tom Eagan | Dreamstime.com. 8 (bottom), Thomas Kitchin & Vict / age fotostock. Chapter 1: Experience Nova Scotia and Atlantic Canada: 11, ImagineGolf/iStock. 20, Nova Scotia Tourism, Culture and Heritage. 21, Walter Bibikow/viestiphoto.com. Chapter 2: Nova Scotia: 23, Rubens Abboud/age fotostock. Chapter 3: New Brunswick: 123, xela / Alamy. Chapter 4: Prince Edward Island: 199, Tourism Prince Edward Island. Chapter 5: Newfoundland and Labrador: 247, ARCO/R. Hicker/age fotostock. About our Writers: All images courtesy of the writers.

Fodor's NOVA SCOTIA & ATLANTIC CANADA

Publisher: Amanda D'Acierno, *Senior Vice President*

Editorial: Arabella Bowen, *Editor in Chief*; Linda Cabasin, *Editorial Director*

Design: Tina Malaney, *Associate Art Director*; Chie Ushio, *Senior Designer*; Erica Cuoco, *Production Designer*

Photography: Jennifer Arnow, *Senior Photo Editor*; Mary Robnett, *Photo Researcher*

Production: Linda Schmidt, *Managing Editor*; Evangelos Vasilakis, *Associate Managing Editor*; Angela L. McLean, *Senior Production Manager*

Maps: Rebecca Baer, *Senior Map Editor*; David Lindroth, Mark Stroud (Moon Street Cartography), *Cartographers*

Sales: Jacqueline Lebow, *Sales Director*

Marketing & Publicity: Heather Dalton, *Marketing Director*; Katherine Punia, *Publicity Director*

Business & Operations: Susan Livingston, *Vice President, Strategic Business Planning*; Sue Daulton, *Vice President, Operations*

Fodors.com: Megan Bell, *Executive Director, Revenue & Business Development*; Yasmin Marinaro, *Senior Director, Marketing & Partnerships*

Copyright © 2016 by Fodor's Travel, a division of Penguin Random House LLC

Writers: Emily Deming, Susan MacCallum-Whitcomb, Penny Phenix

Editors: Teddy Minford (lead project editor), Róisín Cameron

Production Editor: Elyse Rozelle

Fodor's is a registered trademark of Penguin Random House LLC. All rights reserved. Published in the United States by Fodor's Travel, a division of Penguin Random House LLC, New York, and in Canada by Random House of Canada, a division of Penguin Random House Limited, Toronto. No maps, illustrations, or other portions of this book may be reproduced in any form without written permission from the publisher.

14th Edition

ISBN 978-1-101-87980-1

ISSN 1558-8173

All details in this book are based on information supplied to us at press time. Always confirm information when it matters, especially if you're making a detour to visit a specific place. Fodor's expressly disclaims any liability, loss, or risk, personal or otherwise, that is incurred as a consequence of the use of any of the contents of this book.

SPECIAL SALES

This book is available at special discounts for bulk purchases for sales promotions or premiums. For more information, e-mail specialmarkets@penguinrandomhouse.com.

PRINTED IN THE UNITED STATES OF AMERICA

10 9 8 7 6 5 4 3 2 1

ABOUT OUR WRITERS

Emily Deming is a St. John's-based freelance writer. With a background in the sciences, she now writes primarily about food, travel, and the arts. Her work appears regularly in *The Overcast*. For this edition, she updated the Newfoundland chapter.

Having visited countless countries on six continents, frequent Fodor's contributor **Susan MacCallum-Whitcomb** can say with some certainty that Atlantic Canada is her favorite place on Earth. Born and bred in New Brunswick, Susan has strong family ties to Prince Edward Island, and currently resides with her husband and two children in Nova Scotia—so she pretty much has the region covered. She updated the Experience, Prince Edward Island, Travel Smart, and Understanding Nova Scotia and Atlantic Canada chapters for this edition.

Penny Phenix moved to New Brunswick in 2009, after a long association with the province through travel writing commissions and marriage to a New Brunswicker. She has written or contributed to many guidebooks, including *Spiral Guide Canada, Key Guide Canada, Essential Canada East,* and *Explorer Canada*. For this edition, she updated the Nova Scotia and New Brunswick chapters.